PRAISE FOR
Paid to **THINK**

"*Paid to Think* is an invaluable source of step-by-step methodologies and best practice processes illustrated by plenty of stories to make you think or rethink how to better and faster achieve your goals. It certainly has been one of the most precious gifts given to me."
—MELANIE ALBARIC, Marketing Manager, Rail Europe, Inc.

"If you're tired of leading at 65 mph in a 200 mph world, *Paid to Think* will give you the Ferrari toolset and mindset to accelerate results and think differently. Its tools are both contrarian and powerfully simple. This is the one book you must read—right now!"
—DAVID NEWMAN, Author, *Do It! Marketing*

"Thanks to David and the tools in *Paid to Think*, we now prioritize our major projects, think them out more thoroughly in advance, and get most of them done on time and on budget, which has had a huge impact on our business."
—JAMES F. VAUDREUIL, CEO, Huebsch Services

"Using the tools in *Paid to Think* has resulted in a complete overhaul of our strategic planning process and a dramatically improved approach to strategy and leadership development. David's easy-to-use frameworks and models bring pragmatic solutions that drive progress. As a strategist, I anticipate that his book, *Paid to Think*, will be my go-to guide for years to come."
—ELLA CHAN, Director, Strategy Walmart Asia,
Former Head of Group Strategy, City Super Group

"*Paid to Think* shows leaders how to think more and think better to meet their challenges. David Goldsmith brings structure and rigor to how leaders can think more effectively with easy-to-understand principles and practices."
—MARK SANBORN, President, Sanborn and Associates, Inc.,
Bestselling Author, *The Fred Factor* and *You Don't Need a Title to Be a Leader*

"*Paid to Think* shows leaders how to think and how to lead. This is the book that should be at the top of your reading list."
—ERIC CHESTER, President, Reviving Work Ethic, Inc.

"*Paid to Think* enables you to find the root of your challenges, implement solutions, and quickly take your organization to the next level."
—JENNIFER SCHRODER, VP Marketing,
Special Market Sales, Galison Publishing LLC

"David Goldsmith is unique in that he can see a 50,000-view of business and management and can also deliver the hand-to-hand tools to win."
—JEFFREY GITOMER, Author, *The Little Red Book of Selling*

"*Paid to Think* provides straightforward tools to help you strategically position your organization forward."
—JANINE McBEE, CUDE, Southwest CUNA Management School

"I thought that *Paid to Think* was about work. It's not. It's about life, and it has changed my life in many ways. This book is a must-read for anyone who is daring enough to change!"
—SHEILA FRANCIS JEYATHURAI, Director of Business Development, Rouse

"David's mind works in the most incredibly unique fashion I have ever seen. Read *Paid to Think* as if your entire strategic life depends on it, because it does!"
—ADAM BROITMAN
Global VP Digital Marketing, Mastercard, Former Chief Creative Strategist, Something Massive

"*Paid to Think* will help you make higher-quality decisions and better outcomes. Don't miss this read!"
—DON HUTSON, #1 *New York Times* Bestselling Coauthor,
The One Minute Entrepreneur; CEO, U.S. Learning

"In an age when so much management flimflam masquerades as new knowledge, David Goldsmith's *Paid to Think* provides a refreshingly detailed study in the proven mechanics of sound business thinking. Read and re-read this book!"
—JAMES H. GILMORE, Coauthor, *The Experience Economy:
Updated Edition* and *Authenticity: What Consumers Really Want*

"*Paid to Think* bridges the gaps left by management techniques one learns in business schools."
—ARUCHA PROMYANON, Former Channel Manager,
Fuji Xerox (Thailand) Co., Ltd.

"This book does more than provoke thought—it creates results!"
—JOE CALLOWAY, Author of *Becoming A Category of One*

"*Paid to Think* gives you all the tools you need to focus your organization, be innovative, and achieve targeted results. No guiding guru needed."
—SANTIAGO JOHNSON, Branding Director, Leonisa S.A., Colombia

Paid to THINK

A Leader's Toolkit for Redefining Your Future

ACHIEVE MORE, EARN MORE, LIVE MORE

BY DAVID GOLDSMITH

WITH LORRIE GOLDSMITH

BenBella Books, Inc.
Dallas, Texas

BenBella Books, Inc.
10300 N. Central Expressway, Suite 400
Dallas, TX 75231

Printed in Hong Kong
10 9 8 7 6 5 4 3 2

Library of Congress Cataloging-in-Publication Data is available for this title.
978-1-936661-70-1

Indexing by Barbara Holloway, WordCo Indexing Services, Inc.
Cover design by Jelena Mirkovic
Text design and composition by Maria E. Mendez, Neuwirth & Associates, Inc.

Distributed by Perseus Distribution
www.perseusdistribution.com

To place orders through Perseus Distribution:
Tel: 800-343-4499
Fax: 800-351-5073
E-mail: orderentry@perseusbooks.com

Significant discounts for bulk sales are available. Please contact David Goldsmith at books@paidtothink.com or 315-682-3157.

To my wife, Lorrie, my love of 26 years,
thank you for everything. There are no words to describe
what you mean to me.

∽DAVID

To my sons, Adam and Jake,
I wish for you love, happiness, and experiences
that will enrich your lives as much as you have mine.

∽DAD

PAID TO **THINK**

CONTENTS

FOREWORD

The Entire Concept of Management Thought (and Action) Just Got Shaken to Its Roots

OKAY, SO WE'VE COME A long way, you say, in the field of managing people, leading teams, collaborating productively. We've figured out everything from how to be great to how to work a four-hour week. Oh yes, and in between, we've had corporate love affairs with disruptive thinking, top-grade thinking, good-to-great thinking. You name it, our management leaders have surely had their "fling" with it. Well, what I'm about to say won't sit well with a lot—maybe, most of you. Certainly I will shake many if not every one of your beliefs and perceptions to their very roots.

But facts are facts. Results speak for themselves and everyone from the CEO of Wipro to the founders of Infosys to the executives and leadership of organizations all over the world agrees: there's a new sheriff in "Management Town," and he's cleaning up all the displaced, underperforming, and limited-yielding thinking and actions that drive the majority of corporations and enterprises run by entrepreneurs in the business world today.

That sheriff is David Goldsmith, and his brand of law enforcement is to introduce a stratospherically higher set of leadership "laws" within his model called Enterprise Thinking, the concept of rethinking the role and value of leadership within organizations. David's approach is an entirely new slant on what leaders should be doing every day. Plus he provides practical, easily applicable tools and instruction so that leaders know how to think optimally and turn their ideas into results. While every other management guru you've heard of, read about, or studied may teach on how to do more, David teaches you how to get everyone, including yourself, to *be* more: More of a thinker. More of a strategist. More of a leader. More of a collaborator. More of an entrepreneurial thinker. More of a creative thinker. More of a transformational thinker.

When people ask me to explain, define, qualify, or categorize David, the man, let alone David, the book, I truly can't. Not because I don't have a diverse and vivid vocabulary. Rather, it's because both the man and the message are uncategorizable. On the one hand, he's the one, true voice of awareness, knowledge, and learning that can propel you and your management to truly decisive performance enhancement. But on the other hand, he's a management scientist who has just uncovered, discovered, and perfected the "cure for the common corporation."

Let me repeat that statement: David, through his mammoth work and even more mammoth mind, has redefined the entire concept of what a healthy, higher performance organization or entrepreneur needs to look like, think like, *be* like. He's finally figured out how to take an organization—any organization, whether large, small, complex, simple, worldwide, or localized—and get it, and every key team member within it, thinking and leading (and managing) in a highly improved way.

How does he do it? A clear-cut understanding will evolve as you progress through David's breakthrough work. I call it a work because referring to it as a book would demean its importance and impact on the future of your business life.

I struggled for days trying to come up with the proper definition, description, and denomination of precisely what *Paid to Think* really is. Think about it this way:

What the Egyptians did for planning and the Hebrews did for organization, scalar principles and exception-based thinking; what the Sun Tzu did for planning and directing; what Plato did for specialization; what both Al-Farabi and Ghazali did (separately) for distinguishing the traits of a leader; what the Venetians did for cost accounting; what Adam Smith did for the concept of ROI; what Eli Whitney did for scientific management; what W. Edwards Deming did for the concept of quality process; what Marshall Laughlin did for the function of management; and what Henry Gantt did for humanistic thinking; on up to what Peter Drucker did for current management theory and practice—that is what David Goldsmith has done for modern-day leadership with Enterprise Thinking, a "rethinking" of *all* of those factors and forces and functions. And so very much more.

David's monumental work raises, then fully answers so many thought-provoking questions. It challenges many, if not most, of our current precepts on everything from our basic operating/management assumptions to the very economics of thinking versus doing. It looks at strategy through an entirely fresh, new prism that breaks open the facets into laser-like beams of newfound possibility.

I don't think anyone can read the section on creating new products and services without gasping, then releasing a thunderous "AHA!" David's take on ideation and eliminations are, well, let's just say they are paradigm-shifting.

Probably my personal favorite part of this work—although not necessarily the only vein of enrichment you'll read here—is the chapter on establishing alliances. David's six forms of alliances and two key alliance-building tools bring disciplined, performance-based thinking to the concept of establishing alliances for probably the first time ever. Certainly he views the topic in a much more rarified light of understanding than I've seen professed before.

He also shows you how to correctly leverage and harness technology, first redefining exactly what technology is and the role it must hold in any organization. Perhaps the finest, single service David's enormous work achieves is taking you back to the title: he teaches you how to get far more lavishly paid for thinking—differently, masterfully, preemptively, preeminently. I could go on for pages about exploring awareness, since David delves deeper into its meaning and implications than any of the hundreds of other management books I've ever read dare pursue. And his section in innovating will rock your reality in ways innovation should.

This work is anything but abstract: it's the polar opposite of theoretical. It's an all-encompassing new vision and playbook for managers that applies brilliantly and immediately to just about every managerial, operational, strategic, competitive, or organizational issue your organization currently faces and will unquestionably face in the world, today. The more deeply you probe this work, the more certain you'll be of its priceless importance to the very lifeblood of your enterprise.

My only words of warning are these: Take the time required to grasp all the interconnected meanings of these cutting-edge principles. I doubt that you can possibly absorb everything contained in this powerhouse work on first read. It took David twelve years to evolve and refine it, two full years to write it, and nearly a year to final-edit it. I urge you to read each chapter again (and again) to embrace the full scope of what this man has revealed here. Your organization and your life will unquestionably become the beneficiaries.

JAY ABRAHAM
International Marketing Strategist, founder
and CEO of Abraham Group
March, 2012

INTRODUCTION

You're Paid to Think

THINK BACK TO A TIME you made a run for leadership. Perhaps you applied for a managerial opening in an already-established company or nonprofit, ran for class president in school, or ventured out on your own to start a new business. Whichever path you took, you had to put yourself out there to be judged by someone who held the key to your success, be it an HR person for an interview or a loan officer for start-up capital. Surely your clothing, speech, and credentials could have played a role in securing your achievement, but more than likely, the person or people who were considering your abilities were looking for more than whether you could mulch a garden, design a bridge, or mount a tire on a car; they were assessing you most on one particular quality, one not discussed much in management circles: how you think.

I doubt you'll find many supervisors or HR managers who will articulate their decision-making thoughts in those words, but that's what is really going on in their minds. They consider whether a prospective leader or manager has the *thinking skills* to create new opportunities, solve challenges, and redirect the energies of others in order to achieve success. Looking at yourself from this perspective, you can see that your thinking skills set you and your organization apart from the crowd when you want to get ahead, and they keep you in your leadership position. As Warren Buffett[1] has said, companies "occasionally . . . excel because of luck. But usually they excel because of brains." The rewards you've earned and those you have yet to seek—a new job, a better quality of life, higher income, or more respect—come down to your thinking skills. In other words, you are paid to think.

So the big question is, what should you be thinking about? I promise that by the time you reach the end of this book, you'll have a definitive (and possibly surprising) answer to that question, and you'll also possess an abundance of tools that will enable you to convert your thoughts to realities. *Paid to Think* has been written so that you will know more precisely where to focus your energies and how to put your newfound knowledge to immediate and practical use.

You won't end up like the pharmaceutical company manager who told me how disappointed she was with many of the books she'd read on leadership and business. She explained that although these books contain good ideas, she was never able to duplicate the types of improvements they recommended, because they told her *to* be great but didn't teach her *how* to be great. She is not alone. Countless other leaders and managers have expressed that same sentiment to me, and I'm guessing you've had a taste of this disappointment at one time or another, too. It doesn't have to be that way, which is why this book is structured in a manner that will empower you with the information, instruction, and tools you need to turn your ideas into realities.

Years ago, as a business owner and entrepreneur, I found myself frustrated with the disconnect between how I was learning to lead and manage, and the realistic demands of everyday life and work. The educational gap seemed to exist not only in *my* businesses, but also in the nonprofits where I volunteered my time and in the various organizations led by my colleagues. It didn't seem to matter what type or size of organization I looked at, nor did the location of the organization suggest that certain parts of the world were better at minimizing the discrepancies between what leaders needed to know and what they'd been taught about leading. If you've found yourself coming to a similar realization over the course of your career, be assured that the problem hasn't been you.

Even then, I knew something needed to change, and I was determined to find better answers. As my career transitioned into consultative work, where I've had opportunities to work with thousands of decision makers worldwide, I have found that methodologies such as on-the-job training (OJT) techniques, while better than nothing, can miss the mark, because oftentimes they perpetuate misconceptions and mistakes. Many training programs consist of little more than a series of rote actions built upon the trying and testing of ideas to see what works. As a result, they risk multiplying flaws, errors, or misperceptions unknowingly. They also leave out a key component to leadership success: thinking. When you watch others perform and then imitate what they do, you are learning to do what they *do*, but you are not learning how they *think*—the mental conclusions behind their actions. This is why most processes are not easily transferrable from one leader, department, or organization to another, and in a world where leadership prospects are in short supply, transferability is extremely important.

Maybe you didn't go to business school, so you've been quietly insecure about what you've been missing. I can assure you that throughout my experiences consulting and advising leaders like you, the lack of good thinking tools is as prevalent among MBAers as it is high-school dropouts. Most leaders and managers never went to business school.[2] According to Chad Moutray, chief economist for the Small Business Administration's Office of Advocacy, there are 27 million American businesses and only eight million U.S. business-degree graduates,[3] and that includes retirees and those who pursue careers outside the United States. (We have to consider, also, the large number of business-degree graduates who are non-management-level employees, many working for large corporations who hire thousands of new MBA grads each year.) Moutray and I did the math and found that less than one business in five has a business-degree holder calling the shots. If you were to include government, not-for-profit, military, and education, the ratio may be as great as one organization out of twenty. Furthermore, on a global scale, the number could be less than one in fifty!

But even organizational leaders who did go to business school aren't necessarily fully equipped to make the best decisions and manage as effectively as they are capable of doing. The reason is that most business schools teach subjects separately—finance, accounting, marketing, and so on—rather than integrating them to mimic the realities of day-to-day leadership and management.[4] For instance, you can take an accounting course and learn the single subject of accounting, but you won't be taught how to use accounting to lead others, nor will you learn how your accounting decisions will affect other aspects of your organization. I believe this silo approach is why many of my clients with MBAs will readily admit behind closed doors that although they knew how to play the game to earn good grades in college, they are uncertain, even lost at times, about what to do on the job.

If you're tired of hunting and pecking for answers and still not getting them from books, conferences, training programs, or other types of courses, rest assured that the problem lies more in that educational gap than it does with you. For too long, you and leaders like you have navigated through your careers without the benefit of a comprehensive guide and a universally applicable kit of tools to solve your everyday challenges. Certainly, your journeys could have been made simpler and could have generated more reliable outcomes with better resources.

For example, have you ever considered how people working in the trades are better equipped with tools than you are? The plumber who comes to fix your sink has a van filled with wrenches, torches, pipes, snaking devices, and more to solve the majority of challenges he faces in a day. He or she has been taught how to use those tools to get the best outcomes. What tools are in your toolkit? A computer? A desk? Spreadsheets of data? A SWOT analysis? Though they are types of tools for the person who is paid to think, the need for the types of tools that are not so visible, like intellectual or *thinking* tools is critical. Yet these assets are in short supply for most leaders. It is this lack of reliable thinking tools that causes you to constantly ask, "What do I do now?" without a flood of viable answers coming to mind. This is a scary situation to be in, and it happens to experienced leaders and new managers alike. Wouldn't it be nice to experience this dilemma less often?

Don't get me wrong. You may have some great tools that have helped you to get where you are today. Furthermore, I don't believe that you are "broken" or in need of fixing; instead, I believe you've come to this book looking to improve upon the successes you have already achieved to date, and it's my aim to guide you with tools that will accelerate your growth and give you more opportunities both at work and in life.

The decision to transition my career from that of business and organizational leader to consultant and advisor presented me with the opportunity to work with outstanding leaders and managers worldwide, learning about their challenges and the thinking and activities they used to overcome them. As you will learn in Chapter 1, my work with decision makers in large to small firms and in nonprofits nested in both the private and public sectors has given birth to an approach to leadership and management that I call Enterprise Thinking, the heart of this book and the guide and toolkit that will help you achieve noteworthy successes as you face the challenges that assuredly come your way on a daily basis.

I've not only shared Enterprise Thinking with my consulting clients and speaking-engagement audiences, but I've also taught it to bodies of students at New York University for the past twelve years. Tens of thousands of people, your "leadership colleagues," have used the Enterprise Thinking approach to leading and managing as a means to transform their careers, organizations, and lives in ways they never could have imagined and in ways that I never could have anticipated when I embarked on this journey.

The Value of Thinking

You can never underestimate the value of thinking before taking action, especially when you're about to invest labor, capital, time, and your reputation on an initiative. Unlike some of the resources you've turned to in the past, *Paid to Think* will give you the tools you need to make better, faster, and more accurate decisions that will ultimately lead to improved outcomes with less risk, waste, and mistakes.

I often see how easily people can forget the power that a single decision has to make hugely positive transformations within organizations and lives. Keep in mind that this power is not limited to traditional businesses, either. Say that you work within a school system; one better decision could lead to thousands of more students graduating from high school with a diploma. If you're a decision maker in a military organization, your one better decision could save millions of dollars and countless lives. In for-profit organizations, one better decision made by several staff members could mean the difference between enjoying thriving profitability versus partaking in the agonizing process of filing bankruptcy.

Consider how advancements in technology and communications are speeding up an already fast-paced marketplace. You have less time to make decisions now than leaders did in years past, and in many instances, the decisions carry more weight, promise higher rewards, and threaten greater consequences. Unfortunately, most decision makers are still trying to drive their organizations at 200 mph using only the skills, knowledge, and tools of a 65-mph driver. If you plan to keep pace at 200 mph, you'll want to arm yourself with tools like the ones you'll learn here.

Ultimately, you are responsible for making the kinds of decisions that will affect your organization and your life both in the present and the future. Your decisions are rooted in your ability to think, which is not as simple as it seems. As Henry Ford once said, "Thinking is the hardest work there is, which is probably the reason why so few engage in it." That's why it's important to have the Enterprise Thinking resources you need to make your best decisions from one day to the next.

Organizationally, you will be able to use the tools in this book to get your entire management staff—from the senior level to the front line—up to speed in less time and with better returns than you do now. If you have a small organization where there are no distinct groups like senior managers or frontline staffers, these tools will just as effectively enable you to transform your ideas to realities. Individually, you can use them to drive your career regardless of where you are today and where you end up years from now.

From this point forward, consider any improvement to be one that will in some way sharpen all your thinking skills, because all the activities (and their tools) are interconnected; improve one group and overall potential increases. The advantages you will enjoy by improving your thinking skills are limitless. Through Enterprise Thinking, you can gain higher returns on your investments of time, money, labor, and resources, which is particularly beneficial when you're trying to do more with less. Enterprise Thinking also accelerates the rate of personal and organizational achievement, allowing you to make proactive decisions rather than reactive ones in our increasingly fast-paced world. If you've ever felt less than confident about how to lead and manage others, you'll find that many of the gaps left by traditional means of education will be filled by the time you become an Enterprise Thinker.

Furthermore, the universality of the activities and tools empower you to tear down silos and barriers that would have previously prevented individuals, departments, organizations, cultures, and even countries from working synchronously, thus effectually, on reaching shared or complementary goals. And if these plusses weren't enough, here's one more: your "aerial perspective" of your organization will expand to a virtual 50,000-foot view, allowing you to improve upon the systems, structures, and processes that drive performance and attract the rewards that come along with it.

Even before you finish reading the book, you can expect to see drastic improvements in your ability to know what to do and how to do it. Yet I caution you to be patient, too, because as you learn how to perform Enterprise Thinking's twelve core leadership activities, there will be times when your beliefs and accepted ways of performing will be challenged. Rather than discount the unknown or immediately inexplicable as wrong, false, or unbelievable, I urge you to see these moments as great opportunities for learning and growth. Simply put, if something doesn't make sense initially, give it some time to marinate in your mind, because it most likely will by the end of the book. For the most part, however, you will find yourself quickly applying what you learn here to transform your outcomes and convert your ideas to more certain realities.

We'll begin with an overview of Enterprise Thinking in Chapter 1 to lay the foundation for learning the activities and tools throughout the rest of the book. Then, in Chapter 2, we will begin to expand your scope of opportunities by rethinking many of the common perspectives and beliefs that could be preventing you from optimizing your full potential. Chapters 3 through 14 will provide you with the activities and thinking tools you need to make improved transformative advances in your career and organization. In Chapter 15, you will learn how to take your new thinking tools with you to forge the type of future you envision for yourself and your organization.

Congratulations on taking the time to improve as a leader and manager. I guarantee that by the book's end, you will not see your role, your organization, or your ability to capture opportunities the same way ever again.

1

ENTERPRISE THINKING

EXECUTIVES AND SALES PERSONNEL AT an American company worked for years negotiating a deal to sell $2.4 million of laser equipment to a prospective buyer in Japan. After numerous correspondences, it appeared that the Americans had finally made some progress. They were to ship one of the lasers to Japan, where it would undergo a thorough inspection. If it could meet the Japanese buyer's strict quality standards, standards that were higher than those of the U.S. domestic market, then the Americans could close their sale.

The equipment arrived on time as promised. It was immediately tested and inspected. Then the laser was dismantled so that each component could be examined meticulously. At every step of the process, the laser passed inspection with flying colors. The sale seemed inevitable until one of the buyer's managers passed by the laser's packaging and caught a glimpse of something that didn't look quite right.

Peering into the shipping carton to get a closer look, he found a shoe print left behind by one of the packagers at the American facility. The buyer could surmise no reasonable explanation for the footprint besides sloppiness, because the inside of a box is never exposed from the time it is die-cut to when it is folded by machine into its boxy shape. He directed his team to repackage the laser into its box along with the following message: "If you can manage to get a footprint in the box, I can't imagine what you might have done to the product." Another two years passed before the Americans were able to close that sale. Imagine the increased time, money, and resources that were expended within that span of time, because the seller lost an opportunity through its back door.

Situations like this occur all the time within organizations throughout the world. The timeliness of a contractor's bid submission, the politeness of a company's receptionist, the cleanliness of a restroom . . . every component of an organization contributes to its success or failure. And it's up to leaders like you to make sure that you're continually focused on the right matters at the right time—systems, structure, processes, personnel, capital, and more—to keep all of those components working harmoniously and optimally. Compound this awesome responsibility with the impact that an increasingly rapid pace of technological change is having on our organizations and you can quickly see how important it is to make great decisions fast. The Enterprise Thinking approach, which I'll explain shortly, will improve upon your current decision-making processes.

Your Challenges Are Universal

For more than a decade, I've worked with decision makers worldwide as a consultant, speaker, and New York University instructor. These experiences have afforded me the opportunity to talk in depth with a wide range of leaders. Prior to developing Enterprise Thinking, I had conducted more than 1,800 one-on-one interviews with top leaders, midlevel decision makers, and frontline managers across countless industries in diverse specialties like nanotechnology, aerospace, water and sewage, construction, and so on. To be clear, my role as an interviewer has never been that of a researcher, per se, but as someone who is hired to help organizations grow and prosper. Therefore, my aim is always to get to know my clients, their needs and challenges, and their strengths and weaknesses, *not* to uncover their thoughts on leadership traits, an exercise that typically leads to ethereal answers like "charisma" and "steadfastness."

By approaching each interchange wanting to know how I can assist leaders to better solve their present challenges, I glean the types of information I need to empower them to better address future challenges independently, long after my association with them has ended. Accordingly, I begin each interview with one specific question: *What are some of the challenges you're facing today?*

Because my interviews were consultative in nature, this question opened the door to more than just a list of challenges, however. I was also able to uncover the thinking behind leaders' attempts to solve their challenges, giving me an insight that I'm not sure I would have gained had my mission been simply to research these individuals. From thousands of hours of confidential interviews, lasting on average forty-seven minutes, I uncovered more than 7,000 specific challenges, tens of thousands of tangential challenges, and insight into the minds of leaders in businesses, nonprofits, government, military, and education around the globe.

You would think that such a diverse group of interviewees would present similarly diverse responses, but as it turns out, the opposite is true. Even though their products and services differ, the leadership challenges are universal across industries and sectors. They ignore boundaries or silos that separate departments, business units, and management levels. For instance, a public-utility vice president told me that he has to recover and control cost increases. A medical-office manager needs to keep up with the increasing onslaught of information. An Air Force lieutenant colonel must create new products, and a school-district superintendent, reacting to a recent tax-base erosion, is forced to do more with less. Surely you've faced similar issues at one time or another, too.

As I studied these collective challenges as well as their solutions, patterns emerged, revealing a significant conclusion—*there exist twelve universal activities that all leaders perform on a daily basis*—regardless of organization type, and these activities are not taught in business schools or OJT programs!

Just as a biologist uses taxonomy to categorize life species, I categorized the activities into four groups—Strategizing, Learning, Performing, and Forecasting—and these are the cornerstones of Enterprise Thinking, a comprehensive and holistic approach to leadership and management. Know Enterprise Thinking and you will clearly know what you are paid to think about.

What Enterprise Thinking Means to You and Your Organization

The word "enterprise" seems apropos for a leadership model that makes holistic, unsiloed organizations a reality. Just as enterprise integration and enterprise architecture are used by IT professionals to technologically integrate all the tentacles of organizations for greater efficiencies and better outcomes, think of Enterprise Thinking as the leader's mental arsenal to accomplish the same. Because all of Enterprise Thinking—the twelve activities and their companion tools, such as processes, concepts, methodologies, charts, forms, and principles—is universal, scalable, and transferrable, you and others within your organization will achieve desired outcomes more reliably and more often. An added bonus is that everyone in your organization will be equipped with a common vocabulary that will accelerate the rates of individual and organizational achievement. Consider Enterprise Thinking as a rapid means of getting your organization up to speed and on the same page, fast. Military leaders learned long ago that they didn't have a limitless reserve of time to build their troops, so they devised basic-training programs to teach a core set of tactical skills that would ready their teams for the job ahead. By selecting and teaching twelve hand-to-hand combat skills, leaders could arm their troops with a basic foundation of essential skills in six weeks and focus on expanding upon those skills later. Enterprise Thinking will serve a similar purpose within your organization both now and in years to come.

As you progressively make Enterprise Thinking a part of who you are, your current thinking and decision-making skills will improve. As you will see, you don't have to function at any particular management level, operate an organization in any specific industry or sector, or be familiar with any single culture to become an Enterprise Thinker. All you need is a desire to improve and the willingness to learn and use the tools you'll find in this book. The rest will unfold for you.

Perhaps you believe you already have all the tools you need. It wouldn't be the first time I've heard that sentiment, but all I ask is that you keep an open mind and give this a try. If you're not yet convinced that you want to move forward here, consider the process you currently use to strategically think. Can you outline the steps? Have you ever outlined the steps? If I were to ask your staff what strategic-thinking process your organization uses, would their model mirror yours?

Of the tens of thousands of decision makers who have been asked these questions, only a handful can answer yes. As you read through the chapters in this book, many of the questions and uncertainties you've most likely had about strategizing and decision making will dissolve, and in their place will be a newfound sense of clarity, direction, and confidence. Like the decision makers who have already learned these tools, you may begin to wonder how you ever got by without them.

Enterprise Thinking provides you with the ability to think through the numerous solutions available, gives you the right tools to make a solid decision rapidly, and shows you how to set your best solution in motion immediately so you can enjoy peace of mind knowing that everything will work out as intended.

An Overview of the Enterprise Thinking Categories and Corresponding Activities

Before you and I get into the specifics of Enterprise Thinking (ET), let's begin with an overview of the approach, its four categories, and their accompanying activities. In the pie-shaped diagram, Figure 1.1, each consumes an exact quarter of the figure, indicating each category's equal value to you. If we had the benefit of 3D, the figure would constantly be in motion, since none of the categories and activities fall in any chronological order, nor does any single category take precedence over another. They work as an interconnected web, where you are constantly drawing from the contents of all four categories; therefore, as you get stronger in one category, you automatically get better in all others, as well. The concept is similar to the athlete who improves one muscle group and ultimately bolsters overall potential.

The cyclone in the center of the figure represents your mind's natural tendency to rapidly gather and swirl thoughts. Every day, you constantly pull from all four categories as you search for ways to lead others and improve your organization. But, as noted above, you don't just travel into one category, back out, then go to the next. Instead, your mind darts from one category to another, blending thoughts and activities together. That's why the lines separating each category are left open near the cyclone; the open gaps signify the free, haphazard flow of ideas that eventually give birth to new solutions.

Enterprise Thinking®

Strategizing
Developing Plans
Creating New Products & Services
Establishing Alliances
Leveraging Technology

Learning
Acquiring New Knowledge
Enhancing Global Awareness
Watching Competition

Performing
Leading the Charge
Empowering Others
Innovating Everywhere
Selling Continuously

Forecasting
Forecasting the Future

Figure 1.1—Enterprise Thinking

We will go over each activity in its entirety in later chapters. For now, here is an overview of the four categories:

- **Strategizing:** Due to the fact that your mind is typically abuzz with thoughts of how you can improve your organization and strengthen its ability to function, you are strategizing all the time. Yet, if you were to attempt to break down your strategizing into a stepped thought process, you'd probably struggle to pin down just *how* you do it. In the Strategizing category, you will learn the processes and tools you need to effectively develop targeted strategies that drive your organization forward, and at the same time, direct every project, initiative, group member, and resource toward common goals to maximize their collective strengths. This category encompasses the activities of developing strategically superior plans, creating new products and services, establishing alliances, and leveraging technology to accelerate organizational and individual achievement.

- **Learning:** As a leader, you are continually in one of two states of learning. You're either gaining awareness about a topic or you are developing in-depth knowledge. When it comes to learning, most leaders don't realize that they spend most of their time becoming *aware* of topics and not enough time building actual knowledge. As a result, they may know they *should* make changes, but they lack the information and depth of knowledge needed to actually effect transformation. This is often what happens when you attend a conference or read a book. You get excited about the material, decide you want to make changes, but then never can seem to take what you've "learned" a step further to create change. Within the Learning category, you will gain an understanding of how to acquire new knowledge (more than simply awareness), enhance your global awareness, and watch your competition in ways that give your organization the edge it needs to survive and thrive now and well into the future. You will also discover how these three activities play upon each other, and how they will improve your decision-making skills.

- **Performing:** The role of leadership demands that you put into action steps from the other ET categories. Whether you're leading directly or indirectly, you must perform specific action-related activities to be an effective decision maker. While the other three categories of Enterprise Thinking focus on *thinking*-related activities to ensure that you make good decisions before acting upon them, the Performing category addresses action itself: how you take action, how you engage in internal dialog to determine your next best steps, and how you reach organizational goals through other people. The activities, tools, and knowledge you will acquire in this category are universal and easily adaptable to any leadership style, so you can still be yourself while becoming a more effective leader and manager than you are today. In the Performing category, the activities you will learn about are leading the charge, empowering others, innovating everywhere, and effectively selling your ideas and objectives, all of which will enhance your ability to better achieve desired outcomes.

■ **Forecasting:** Leadership is about looking far enough ahead to envision and build a promising future for one's organization, so in essence you are always forecasting. There are specific activities and tools you can use to gain a more comprehensive perspective and, therefore, be more on target with the decisions you make. The better you are at forecasting opportunities and challenges within and outside your organization—economic and political evolutions, industry cycles and changes, and global trends and patterns—the better you'll be at making decisions today that have lasting power well into the future. The Forecasting category shows you how to gain a future-oriented mindset necessary to forecast tomorrow's trends, opportunities, and challenges to better ensure a strong and healthy future for your organization, your career, and your life.

The interconnectivity of all four categories mirror the realities of leadership thought processes in any given day. For example, say that you discover through a trade journal article that your primary supplier of raw materials is facing serious financial problems (Learning). You immediately begin searching alternate options in the event that this supplier is unable to deliver product and thinking through the ramifications of broaching the subject with the supplier immediately (Strategizing). You need to apprise your team of the impending development, and you contemplate assigning the search for a new supplier to one of your staff members (Performing). Maybe the time has come to add new technology, reducing the need for this or any other supplier, because it seems that trends on the horizon are impacting business earlier than expected (Forecasting).

Perhaps already you can see how much easier it is going to be to develop leadership within yourself and others by learning about concrete activities and tools versus trying to emulate personality traits like "persevering," "intelligent," "charismatic," "driven," "focused," or "organized." Enterprise Thinking provides you with a practical, proven, step-by-step guide that empowers leaders of all abilities and degrees of experience to realize their greatest potential.

The Universality of Enterprise Thinking

Any decision maker can use Enterprise Thinking to solve daily challenges because of its universality. People at all management levels, geographic locations, industries, and even your other stakeholders, including suppliers, lenders, and strategic allies, can equally benefit from Enterprise Thinking. By sharing a set of universal tools, you can all work more effectively to achieve common desired outcomes. Acting in unison helps break the silos that foster a "we versus them" mentality that can impede progress.

The 7Crosses™ of ET

Cross Functional (HR, Engineering, Logistics, etc.)
Cross Level (CEO, VP, Manager, Director, Superintendent, Colonel)
Cross Industry (Nano Technology, Garbage Removal, Retail)
Cross Sector (Profit, Not for Profit, Military, Education, Government)
Cross Culture (Irish, Australian, Chilean - Asian, European, American - Latino)
Cross Time (Caesar, Napoleon, Ghengis Kahn, Gandhi)
Cross Life (ET works at work, home, and play)
ET is universal and therefore, can be used anywhere, for any reason.

Figure 1.2—The 7Crosses™ of ET

The approach's universality is summed up in the 7Crosses of ET:

1. **Cross functional.** ET is cross functional, because people in all disciplines, including finance, HR, engineering, logistics, and marketing, daily engage in the same activities. With ET, you can interconnect and communicate better among your peers and with colleagues in other disciplines.

2. **Cross level.** From senior level down to the front line, and from the small business owner to the regional manager, everyone engages in the same activities, so it makes sense to share ET to multiply achievement throughout your organization.

3. **Cross industry.** Leaders and managers from nanotechnology to supply chain, and from trash removal to retail can use ET,

because the activities are exactly the same for every industry. This is a huge plus when you want to transition your career from one industry to another.

4. **Cross sector.** Wherever possible, I have used the words "organization" or "group" to describe your workplace or any other leadership environment, since ET is for leaders and managers in private and public sectors alike. Whether your expertise lies in the military, government, or education, or you work in a nonprofit or association, ET enables you to work capably with colleagues outside your sector, too.

5. **Cross culture.** ET's universality means your geographic location will not prevent you from becoming an Enterprise Thinker. Use ET to bridge cultural boundaries, dissolve cultural divisions, and make visible solutions and opportunities that you may have previously overlooked.

6. **Cross time.** Whether you're comparing the similarity of challenges between historical and present-day leaders or the similarity of leadership activities you performed early on in your career versus today, you'll see that the challenges and activities of leading and managing haven't changed. The specific tools have changed, yet the premise of creating new products and services, establishing alliances, and empowering others, has not. As a result, you can acquire and use ET as readily in the early stages of your career as you can in the latter stages, building skill upon skill over the span of your work life.

7. **Cross life.** ET can be used outside your organizational environment: at home and anywhere else that requires you to make good decisions. For example, an ET tool used to develop a standard procedure in your office can also be used to outline an emergency fire drill procedure in your home.

ET will not only help you build the next generation of leaders, but it will expand your pool of prospective leaders across geographies, cultures, industries, sectors, and management levels. Between 50% and 75% of U.S. senior managers became eligible for retirement in 2010,[5] nearly a third of employers worldwide report suffering from a shortage of qualified leaders to fill the shoes of retiring senior managers,[6] and 44% of Chinese executives view lack of leadership talent as their biggest barrier to achieving their global ambitions.[7] In this day and age, you need a reliable instrument to build tomorrow's leaders.

ET is universal enough that you can work it compatibly into other leadership and management processes, also. If you already have a leadership-performance program in progress—Six Sigma, Balanced Scorecard, etc.—ET will accelerate and enhance its effectiveness by increasing performance, driving internal business processes, promoting future-oriented strategizing, heightening learning, distributing knowledge and skills, and improving decision-making capabilities throughout your organization. In essence, ET surrounds your leadership and management with a framework that fosters and supports success.

The 50,000-Foot Perspective

My first flying lesson took place in a two-seat Piper with an instructor named Beth. Little did I know as the two of us taxied the plane down the runway and took off into the sky that I was about to get more than a lesson in aircraft navigation. Looking down, I saw the airport drop away and the landscape below take on an unfamiliar appearance. Boundaries that separated farms, villages, and counties seemingly disappeared, and my perspective of Central New York instantly expanded. Even though I had flown in commercial airplanes many times before, I realized after landing the plane that my mind's eye would never picture the region around my home as it had before.

As a decision maker, you're a pilot, too. You have to know your organization's "landscape," and you need certain tools to help you navigate it. In essence, your job is to keep your organization on course to arrive at its desired destinations.

The higher you rise in your organization, or the more you wish to have an impact, the broader your perspective needs to become. You have to see that departments, teams, organizational units, competitors, vendors, customers, and markets are separated only by artificial boundaries; from your figurative 50,000-foot aerial view, you work with a single interlinked landscape. And it's that view that you need to maintain when you're performing your daily activities, because a decision made in one area has an effect on the whole.

Not everyone in your organization needs to have the same 50,000-foot perspective that you maintain, especially when you build the systems and structures that integrate all the components into one holistically functioning unit. Of course, having managers who share your similar perspective will strengthen your organization. That's where a blending of ET activities, from empowering others to leveraging technology, will ensure that your entire organization is operating optimally. ET's tools support those activities, preventing you from becoming the gourmet restaurant that loses patrons because of your dirty restroom and showing you how to be the fastest-growing tech company because your departmental collaborations bring product to market faster than your competition can. An elevated mental perspective is essential to winning in today's world.

An Underlying Precept That Improves Decision Making

We've become quick to reward people for *doing* rather than *thinking*, mistaking busyness for progress and assuming that inactivity equals regression. As a person who is paid to think, however, your best contribution to your organization is most often not physical busyness but rather the activity that takes place in your mind beforehand. To avoid impeding yourself and your organization, you must not leap to action before truly understanding a situation or knowing your best options prior to making decisions.

Every day, you face a wide range of challenges at your job, such as deciding how to handle an underachieving staffer, knowing whether to improve upon a product or scratch it altogether in favor of a new one, and determining what it will take to keep a key client from the clutches of an aggressive competitor. If you were to watch yourself addressing daily challenges from the vantage point of an outside observer, what would you see? A person thinking at a desk? A leader heading up a meeting asking others for input? A "go-getter" putting the wheels in immediate motion?

What I've found in my work with decision makers is that it's common for them to jump to action too quickly—the downside of heralding "execution" too fervently—before they've adequately gathered and thought through their most advantageous options.

Obviously, time is money and what got you to where you are is your ability to act and achieve results. However, there's an excellent chance that you've rushed to action on numerous occasions without having made (or even entertained) the best decision you could have. Even a seemingly benign press of a "send" key can set off a domino effect of costly missteps, forcing you to unnecessarily overspend resources without achieving your intended outcomes. In other words, there are costs of not thinking and there are rewards for great decision making.

However, with the right tools and know-how, you can deliver exceptional value to your organization through efficient and purposeful thinking. I call one such tool the Economics of Thinking. Simply put: *The better able a leader is to think through an idea before committing to action, the greater the chances an organization has to achieve higher returns, all while mitigating risk and reducing expense.*

Your job is to think through ideas well enough so that when they are put into action, they achieve the results you want. The diagram of the Economics of Thinking (Figure 1.3) illustrates the correlation between thinking and costs, showing that it's far cheaper to think than to launch any initiative. In the diagram, time is represented on the x-axis and capital/resources expenditures on the y-axis. As a leader progresses his or her idea along the timeline, costs rise. In brief, thinking better, faster, and more accurately before you act improves the chances that the idea or initiative is a winning one and worth the expenditures that will be made in later stages of development and launch.

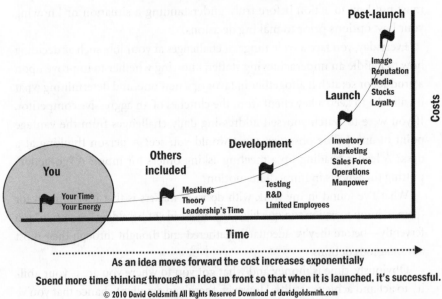

Figure 1.3—Economics of Thinking™

When you first contemplate choosing and launching any new initiative, you begin to ask yourself many questions. Maybe you're wondering if you have the time or resources or which technologies and tactics are the best for the situation. Right now, your initiative is just an idea you are mulling over in your mind. In the diagram above, this stage of the process is represented by the shaded circle. Your objective here is to expend your own time and energy thinking through your idea. Compared to the action you'll be taking later, your thinking at this juncture is relatively inexpensive.

As your idea progresses forward, you reach beyond your own thoughts to gather new information, insight, and input from other people such as designers, architects, staffers, specialists, and vendors. You are still expending your own time, but now, because you are also involving others and pulling them away from their current responsibilities, you're spending more money. However, the costs are still not as high as they will be later when you develop and launch your idea. Already you can see that if you do the necessary thinking-related activities, you can make a better determination to either develop your idea or make changes before proceeding.

If you decide to proceed with your idea or initiative, it is at this development stage where you begin to add staff, use organizational resources, and spend capital. Now, the pace of investment costs accelerates well beyond what you had spent in the first two stages. All of the pre-thinking that occurred before this point will improve the chances that you have a winning idea versus one that could be unnecessarily costly to your organization and possibly to your career.

When you finally launch the initiative, your costs peak (with the post-launch effects). If you hadn't thought the initiative through well enough at the beginning (or should have stopped but didn't), then you now suffer the losses associated with a bad launch. No one enjoys losing money, watching great staff members leave, dealing with poor media exposure, attempting to redeem a tarnished reputation, regaining lost lines of credit or dropped bond ratings, and struggling to earn back investors' trust.

The costs of any idea's development and launch, large or small, are enormous compared to those early days spent thinking. This reality impacts nonprofits and government-funded entities just the same as it does businesses and corporations. The Economics of Thinking works for any leader at any time.

Take Ron Righter, a college basketball coach for twenty-seven years, who engaged the Economics of Thinking to improve Clarion University's athletic recruiting process. Like many coaches, prior to revamping the university's recruiting process, Righter would spend a full season going through the process of recruiting basketball players, each year finding himself working throughout the summers and pushing deadlines. With the old process, he just couldn't land all of the talent he needed as efficiently as he wanted, and often, not unlike all his coaching colleagues, he was still scrambling to recruit players into August or even into September.

A few years ago, Righter and five coaches of other sports teams at the university took some time to change their approach. I collaborated with them to come up with a powerful one-page strategic and tactical plan for their recruiting program. Two months into the season, Righter stopped me during a meeting to express how happy he was with the outcome. "Typically, at this two-month mark, I'm still reviewing candidates and praying that I secure the talent I need," he said. "For the first time ever, I went five-for-five, signing every student athlete I wanted. I even landed the number-one athlete in Pittsburgh, which would never have happened if I hadn't been thinking bigger and following the plan. In all my years coaching, this will be the first time I'll have a full summer to start getting ready for next year's schedule."

The Economics of Thinking enabled the coaches to come up with a better process that freed up their time, gave them peace of mind, and captured high-caliber student athletes for their sports teams. And on the financial side, Clarion's athletic director, Bob Carlson calculated that in two tested sports, the new strategy generated more than $144,000 in freed-up cash with less effort expended by the coaches.

The Benefits of Interplaying Concepts and Tools

As you read through *Paid to Think*, you will come to realize more and more that Enterprise Thinking's activities, concepts, and tools can be combined in limitless ways to create opportunities and solve challenges. For instance, you just learned about three overarching precepts: the universality of ET, the 50,000-foot perspective, and the Economics of Thinking. See how they played out for an Enterprise Thinker named Shelley Zapp.

UNIT4 (formerly Agresso North America), a Victoria, British Columbia, subsidiary of the $500-million Enterprise Resource Planning (ERP) company (headquartered in the Netherlands), had a significant hurdle to overcome. The company was bursting at the seams, and UNIT4's software-installation team needed to hire thirty additional employees in its professional services department to keep up with demand. The issue at hand: this staff increase would double the installation team's size, which had just doubled the previous year, posing a challenge to managers.

Since being promoted to president of UNIT4, Shelley Zapp had broken revenue numbers. She worked efficiently and had pulled together a stellar team. Now the subsidiary's rapid growth was in danger of slowing down, because the installation team couldn't keep pace with sales. The sales staff didn't want to close a software system deal only to have to tell their client that installation wouldn't begin for another six months. But the company's sales cycle operated on a six- to twenty-four-month sales cycle with hundred-thousand- and multimillion-dollar deals, so any letup in sales would deliver a big blow to the company's long-term revenues.

Zapp and her management team thought through their challenges in a two-day strategy session. They stepped back to understand where their biggest challenges existed, which skill sets each manager brought to the table, and where those skills could best be used, forgetting titles and current roles.

Their strategy was to keep UNIT4 operating at full speed and on target for explosive growth during a major staffing ramp-up. After two days of strategic and tactical thinking, Zapp's team had arrived at a two-part solution.

First, they eliminated silos by temporarily reallocating some management responsibilities of the VP of program management to the director of operations and the VP of sales and marketing; the latter two not only had the time to assist, but they also had the skills and leadership tools to work successfully outside their positions. This gave the VP of program management more time to hire the right thirty people, and Zapp stepped in to assist in the hiring process, thereby shortening the time it took to get new hires productive.

Second, they leveraged technology to allow clients to enter their own data into UNIT4's system during the pre-installation stage. This freed up time for Zapp's people to focus on internal changes aimed at growing the installation team without compromising its ability to install new products. Sales doubled again!

Taking the time to think through their best options before making a decision focused Zapp's team on addressing its highest priorities first. In addition, the universality of ET meant that all leaders were equally empowered with the right mental "equipment" to utilize their talents where the organization needed them most. And finally, the 50,000-foot approach to thinking ignored silos and allowed those decision makers to bypass the traditional boundaries that compartmentalize thinking-related resources so that each leader could make their highest contribution to the organization.

What's Ahead

Paid to Think is divided into four sections, each corresponding to one of the four categories of ET activities. You've most likely concluded by now that you will learn the specifics of each category and will be provided with instructions on how to perform the activities and use the tools. You may start to believe that in order to be a great Enterprise Thinker, you must master every activity to improve your performance, *but nothing could be further from the truth*. Instead, I want you to think of ET as a group of activities that are so enmeshed with each other that even a slight improvement in one will improve the performance of others.

Strategizing is the topic of the first section, yet its chronological positioning in no way means that you must (or should) perform Strategizing activities first. In fact, none of the categories have to be performed sequentially; they are not linear, and they do not fall within any hierarchy of importance. For educational purposes, Strategizing appears first only because many of its tools and language form the basis for the other three categories' activities and tools.

In the introduction to this book, I touched on the frustrations of leaders who read great books but find themselves unable to duplicate the books' suggestions. I assure you that you won't experience this issue here, because I will provide you with instructions on how to perform each activity and how to use each tool.

Before you get into these four categories of activities, we need to lay the foundation for learning by expanding your mind. In Chapter 2, some of your existing beliefs about leading and managing will be challenged. Although many of your beliefs may already be true, surely there are times when you've said, "I have to rethink this," and come up with better solutions. By expanding your perspectives, more opportunities will become visible to you. Take the time to consider some of the new perspectives presented in the next chapter, for they are important foundational concepts that you will use throughout subsequent chapters to perform ET activities and to build your tool kit.

Finally, I doubt you'll complete this book and ask, "What should I do now?" Instead, your mind will be abuzz with all the possibilities that you can now see before you, and I expect that you'll be excited to start applying what you've learned. As an added bonus, you'll progressively see blocks of time opening up in your schedule, giving you more time to think, plan, and create a better future for your organization . . . to do what you're paid to do.

2

RETHINKING

EVEN THE BEST LEADERS CAN benefit from adopting a new perspective or expanding upon an old one. Take, for instance, Sheila, an attorney who works as the head of marketing for a multinational legal firm specializing in intellectual property. Intelligent and progressive, this perpetual learner would be an asset to any organization. Yet, even she admits that it wasn't until after rethinking some of her perceptions about managing a team of global subordinates that she was able to identify opportunities and solutions as readily as she does today.

Sheila explains an incident during which she received an e-mail from a subordinate who blamed his late assignments on the constant crashing of his computer. She had become instantly annoyed, because the computer issue had been ongoing for months, and Sheila was being pressured by upper management to turn around work for their clients faster and on time.

"Why can't this guy handle even the simplest of tasks on his own?" she thought. "After all, I oversee this entire department, I've got reports due this afternoon, the meeting on Friday to prepare for, and now this? I don't have time to hold Marty's hand today." The more she thought about it, the more Sheila couldn't understand why he couldn't just solve his own challenge.

All the managers in Sheila's division had been under a lot of pressure to do more with less lately, and this incident was just adding to the pressure. Looking back, she couldn't identify where the problem originated, since the firm provided seemingly adequate training, positive reinforcement, and incentive programs.

Moments later, her boss walked into her office and closed the door. "Sheila, I want you to take a look at this. It's some information about a new software program that can consolidate data from accounting and sales. The rep I just spoke with estimates that you could shave between seven and twelve hours a week off your number-crunching time. Take this file home with you tonight, and let me know what you think about it in the morning."

Instantly, she was excited at the prospect of saving that much time in a single week. "What I could do with that kind of time! This thing could really take some of the pressure off."

In that moment, Sheila had a sudden epiphany that gripped her with guilt. Her boss was presenting her with a tool to make her work life easier. How many times had she overlooked opportunities to do the same for *her* subordinates? She would have to rethink her approach to solving Marty's challenge.

A simple upgrade to Marty's computer—an action that she, not Marty, had the authorization to approve—would result in more projects being completed on time. Sheila picked up the phone and called Marty. "Let's talk about this problem you're having with your computer."

Within days, Sheila had solved an ongoing challenge by rethinking. In this instance, by focusing her attention on systems and structures rather than on employee performance alone, which is more often than not a leadership reaction, Sheila could see more and better options for solving her challenge. Every leader can open more doors of opportunity by rethinking their beliefs. Rethinking expands your scope of mental options, jars your habitual thought processes out of their ruts, and awakens your mind to new possibilities.

Challenging Your Current Viewpoints

Let's explore and challenge a few concepts that you may have accepted as conventional wisdom but that aren't necessarily working in your favor. As you engage in rethinking, you will make immediate sense of some of these new perspectives while others will require you to take longer to digest and assimilate, simply because they may run counterintuitive to beliefs you've held about leadership and management. Taking the time to accept and integrate new ideas is always one of the challenges of learning something new, but as long as you're present and open, you will complete this book changed, improved, and empowered as a better leader and manager.

It's time to prep your mind and open pathways for new ways of thinking. These rethinking concepts will come back into play in upcoming chapters, some of them playing a critical part in key Enterprise Thinking tools and activities.

Rethink Your Assumptions about Leadership and Management

Do you think of yourself as a leader or manager? Typically, people associate themselves more strongly with one or the other because of the specific characteristics they apply to each title. Yet if you were to closely consider the responsibilities of each—managing people, selecting projects, weighing in on budgets, prioritizing, developing strategy, working relationships, innovating, and so on—you'd see that in reality, if you hold a decision-making position, you're both a leader and a manager.

Former AARP CEO Bill Novelli once told me that he had 120 managers on his leadership team. His use of the integrated terminology—calling managers leaders and vice versa—was a display of Novelli's understanding that there's an interconnectivity between how leaders manage and how managers lead. Without understanding the functions of both roles, no one could do their job well. Try to manage a group of people without leading them, and you'll get nowhere fast.

Over the years I've seen how even the best and brightest decision makers unconsciously allow their stereotypes and assumptions about leadership and management to hinder their ability to achieve. This belief that the two disciplines are different developed over the course of several generations, almost by default. But if you were to see how we arrived at the point in which we work today, we would better understand how to reverse our success-blocking thoughts and how to incorporate the best features of both roles into our day-to-day lives.

Both leadership and management have very different roots in history. In Western civilization's early history, leadership played a role in large organizations, which primarily consisted of religious groups and militaries. Prior to the 1870s, when 26,000 workers built the U.S. transcontinental railroad, very few large private commercial organizations even existed. Educated people typically had military experience, so they were versed in the intricacies of leadership, not management, where leaders were expected to play a hands-on role, accompanying their troops onto the battlefield and guiding their forces through missions.

Circumstances forged the leader's methodologies. Mobilizing large forces with limited means of communication and travel meant that leaders had to plan strategies and tactics well in advance since unexpected needs weren't likely to be met in real time. If the leader and his group traveled by horseback for a couple of days to reach a battle site, they couldn't radio home base for reinforcements or to complain about sexual harassment within a particular unit. Everyone had to be battle ready. Planning tools—like Julius Caesar's battlefield simulations played out in a sandbox—prepared the leader and his troops. So, historically, leaders were actively engaged in developing strategy and guiding others through tactics.

Then management entered the picture. Although evidence exists that management techniques were employed by the Egyptians[8] as far back as 4000 BC, we consider modern-day management to be little more than a hundred years young, coinciding with the emergence of industrialization.

Modern management principals and technological advancements have their purpose, and they have improved leadership in many ways, but they have had a negative effect on leadership, too. For one, management has often clouded the role of the leader and weakened it. When managers entered the scene, leaders moved from their on-the-field command positions to the seclusion of the executive office, rendering many (though certainly not all) decision makers out of touch with the realities that challenged their organizations. This is still the case today.

For example, one director of operations (DO) for a national association explained that she is overwhelmed by the barrage of demands placed on her by the president to whom she reports. The president reminds the DO and her colleagues regularly that it's his job to come up with ideas, and it's their job to make them happen. However, he doesn't follow through on creating winning strategies, and he is never present to assist and guide others as they execute on tactics. Because of his perceptions about leadership and management, he gets in the way of his organization's ability to succeed.

The pendulum has swung too far in any one direction; the mindset of leaders being in ivory towers and managers working the front lines needs to change if we want to make our organizations stronger and more effective. Regardless of their titles, decision makers need the skills of both disciplines, and I use both terms interchangeably throughout the book to refer to anyone in a decision-making role. Enterprise Thinking integrates these skills and gives you the tools and instruction to act on them.

Rethink Your True Value to Your Organization

Have you thought about what your greatest value is to your organization? There may be times when you have to do some hands-on or labor-intensive tasks, especially if you're part of a small business or volunteer organization, but if you are a decision maker, your greatest value comes not from your hands but from your mind. You weren't hired to put out fires, to jump into the trenches and work alongside your employees, to make your team feel loved, or even to charm the board of directors. You have no doubt found yourself participating in these activities from time to time, but your true value comes from your ability to develop successful strategies and to ensure that all organizational resources—internal and external, human, tangible and intangible—are orchestrated to reach desired outcomes. Whether you're establishing alliances, leveraging technology, or empowering others, your job is to continually improve how you make decisions from the 50,000-foot perspective. Part of your job is also to develop thinking skills in others, as this is key to building leaders who can take the organization into the future.

Likewise, in looking at where your value lies as a leader, you also should consider what doesn't provide value. In your role as a decision maker, you don't want to confuse busyness with providing value. Often we can feel that if we're not physically busy, then we must not be making progress. However, busy for the decision maker is different than it is for the front-line worker such as a production line employee or a volunteer working at a blood drive. You might perform some tactical duties, but your busyness is focused on thinking activities like strategizing, planning and overseeing projects, and building alliances that support your strategies.

During an August 2009 airing of the public television program *CEO Exchange*, Symantec Corporation's chairman and CEO John W. Thompson showed that he recognized his true role as leader of the company. An interviewer asked Thompson if he saw technological advances as being a threat. "I view all of them as an opportunity," he responded. "It may force us to reconfigure the way we think about our business, but that's what I get paid to do as a CEO."[9]

The leadership team at New York's Paulson and Co., a leading hedge fund, knows the value of thinking, and the firm's track record, which includes the successful leveraging of the 2008 financial meltdown, illustrates how well thinking can pay off. Senior Vice President Michael Waldorf ensures that operations at Paulson and Co. are running smoothly so that the firm's leader, John Paulson, has time to develop effective strategies—like the one he created to short subprime lenders and generate $17 billion in profits for clients in 2007 and again in 2008. Although your organization will have its ups and downs from one year to the next, having decision makers who understand the value of thinking will bring more ups to the table.

Peter Blake, the CEO of Ritchie Brothers, a world leader in the auctioning of heavy-duty construction equipment, understands that his job is to think, and his days are filled with the types of "busyness" that feed his thinking and improve his decision making. Responsible for managing a firm that grosses $3.2 billion in sales, Blake still takes time to host regular "Eat-with-Pete" luncheons, where employees throughout the company can share their problems, issues, and ideas with their CEO. These discussions trigger Blake's own thinking, as he and his team develop strategies for the firm's future. While Blake doesn't hesitate to pick up garbage as he walks in through the parking lot, help set up for auctions and meetings, or sit in on important sales calls, he knows that thinking is how he provides value to Ritchie Brothers and maintains its success as a market leader.

Knowing your value—and how it's tied in with thinking and developing thinking skills in others and not with physical busyness—helps you determine where best to expend your time and energy.

Rethink What Constitutes "Winning": The Benefits of Winning by a Nose

Many decision makers put a lot of pressure on themselves to come up with the next killer idea, believing that they have to wow customers, prospective employees, or other stakeholders in order to win sales, key talent, or other advantages for their organizations. But you don't always have to reel in the "big fish" to enjoy great rewards. In fact, more often than people realize, great rewards don't necessarily come from earth-shattering factors. Instead, they are oftentimes the result of minor factors that cause us to win or lose "by a nose."

In case you are not familiar with the terminology of winning or losing by a nose, let me explain its origin. Have you ever seen a horse race in which one horse won by the narrow margin of inching his nose over the finish line before the second-place horse? This horse achieves a win by a nose (WBAN)—and his stakeholders go home with a huge pile of cash—while horse number two loses out on the big win by a nose.

Organizations can win and lose by a nose, too. And whether it's losing by a nose or by a long shot, you've still lost the prize. When you go out on a sales call and you lose by a nose, you lose the whole sale as well as everything you invested in pursuing it. These by-a-nose defeats can pack a major punch to your organization or career. Take for instance Common Councilor Michael Heagerty of Syracuse, New York. He needed 335 valid signatures on his petition to run for reelection on the Democratic Party line, a generally routine task for any incumbent. He was mortified to find that he ended up one signature short . . . and that *he* forgot to sign his own petition.[10] The spot on ballots where Heagerty's name was supposed to appear remained blank for the election.

WBANs are powerful, whether you're talking signatures or votes in politics, artillery strikes in military battles, sales in businesses, public perception or funding in nonprofits, or countless other circumstances related to every other type of organization. They are, in fact, so powerful that they can mean the difference between life and death for people, careers, organizations, movements, cultures, and countries.

In your organization, you need to look at all areas and all factors that could potentially make or break a success. Also remember these two principles:

1. *A micro adjustment can determine a by-a-nose win or loss.* A micro adjustment can determine a by-a-nose win or loss. Space Exploration Technologies (SpaceX), founded by native South African Elon Musk who also founded PayPal and Tesla Motors, exists for "space exploration and the extension of life to multiple planets,"[11] putting satellites in space at a fraction of competitors' costs. Its first two $6-million rockets failed on launch, and the third suffered a loss-by-a-nose at an altitude of 217km when a single line of code did not allow enough time for "commanding main engine shut down and stage separation."[12] In other words, the fate of a multi-million-dollar project rested on a single line of code within a rocket's millions of lines of code, a simple loss by a nose.

2. *A by-a-nose win or loss can dramatically change your outcomes.* Russell, a manager from Bayer Healthcare Pharmaceuticals, was responsible for a team of eight sales executives covering the eastern part of the United States. On the West Coast, another Bayer sales manager headed a team of nine. Russell told me how each year Bayer gives a bonus to the team that best meets or exceeds budgeted revenue goals. One year, Russell's East Coast team was excited about coming in at 108.3% of a budget running in the hundreds of millions of dollars in revenues. Then, the numbers came in from the West Coast. At 108.7% of budget, the West Coast team had eked out a win by a mere 0.4%. The narrow loss robbed each member of Russell's high-achieving group of a $25,000 bonus: a big hit for a job with an annual average salary of about $80,000.

Consider if you were able to land a few more of your lost wins. If you had just one more sale per day in a retail shop, one more home sold per month in real estate, 1% more of your customers saying "Yes!" These small improvements can snowball into huge results.

Take, for example, a bid by your organization on one hundred jobs a year. If your staff wins half of them, you might be able to accept twenty-five of the lost bids as bad matches for your firm—too small or big, unrealistic delivery dates, not profitable enough, etc.—but what about the other twenty-five losses? Perhaps you lost them by a nose: a botched detail perhaps, or a deadline missed by an hour. In one true incident, a client of mine named Rich said he lost a sale, because a competitor put the prospective buyer's logo on a proposal, and Rich didn't. Imagine getting the phone call saying that the only advantage your competitor had over you was that his placement of a logo showed that he "cared more."

Do the math. If you had won just 10% more of the contracts you had lost, what would your world be like today? Remember you've already done all the traveling, mock-ups, research, and proposal work. If you're going to invest the time, energy, and money into an endeavor, you might as well walk away a winner, even if the win is only by a nose, because micro wins can result in huge changes. One client mentioned that if he won 10% more of his contracts, he would not have enough project managers to handle capacity nor would he be able to manage the cash flow of his $3 billion organization.

Here's another example. Suppose you put measures in place to make it possible for your production department to ship just 20% of goods a single day sooner than you do now, and the time compression grew your bottom line by 4%. With that success, you might now be in a position to fund a project that could grow the bottom line by an additional 20% next year. The big-picture solution is to continually rethink current beliefs to bring new opportunities for growth and rewards into view.

Rethink Your Belief That People Hate Change

Why do we constantly hear that people hate change, when there's evidence to the contrary? After all, people love receiving pay raises, moving into their dream home, welcoming the arrival of a new baby, and finding a fun, new restaurant to frequent. And no one from Oprah's audience[13] complained when she gave them a car, even though that was a "change." In actuality, people don't repel *all* change, only change that is negative—and in some instances when change is perceived as negative because it simply wasn't expected.

Though it seems obvious that you need to manage the changes that take place within your organization so that they produce favorable outcomes, this feat can be easier said than done. That's because the changes people hate and resist—negative and unexpected changes—are the ones that are most common in organizations: modifications to a benefits program that make paychecks come up twenty dollars short, a new computer system that requires overtime hours to work out the kinks, an additional weekly meeting added to the schedule that takes away time from other tasks, and so on.

Years ago, a state-run environmental conservation organization replaced its manual process of administering hunting and fishing licenses with a computerized system. The new system cost $15 million and initially extended patrons' wait time from twenty minutes to five hours and fourteen minutes. Imagine dealing with those customers. If you worked at this organization, how receptive would you be to the next initiative? Change is necessary in organizations—without it, organizations stagnate and die. So despite resistant workers, as a decision maker you have to forge ahead with making the upgrades and improvements that sustain and grow your organization. Understanding why people resist change and which types of changes they actually hate will help you do the job your organization needs and achieve targeted results. However, the first step is properly rolling out the change.

When you know how to introduce change and how to follow it through so your group achieves more gains with fewer pains, change can become a welcomed friend within your organization. Picture this: Kyle is a midlevel manager who picks up some ideas at a conference and decides to use them to develop a new initiative that he thinks may improve his organization. He pulls his team together to tell them the details of his plan. His team is not receptive to the change, because Kyle has a history of poor follow-through and for not thinking through projects well, and his staff is already overloaded with projects and will not receive extra pay for the late nights they'll have to work to complete this new initiative on time.

Let's change the story. After Kyle attends the inspiring conference, he doesn't rush ahead to tell his staff, but he lets them do their jobs while he takes time to think and to select one best idea from the many he came away with from the conference. Kyle gains input and ideas from a few coworkers as he develops a realistic plan.

After a week of refining the details, Kyle invites one coworker, Mary, to manage the project. He has calculated the ROI as $200,000 for the next three years and he explains that if Mary's project comes in on time and on budget, he will reward her with a salary increase of $2,000. Mary manages the project, and because Kyle has given her the supplies she needs and the right balance of freedom and direction to succeed, she finishes it a few weeks early, bringing additional benefits to their organization. In this scenario, Kyle, with Mary's help, has a Wildly Successful Project (WSP), and if this is Mary's first experience with Kyle and his projects—versus an experience of him lacking follow-through and failure with projects—she's going to be more receptive to changes initiated by him in the future.

Let me define what I mean by a Wildly Successful Project. A WSP is a completed project that demonstrates a manager's ability to deliver results that extend beyond normal expectations and causes others to take notice. Typically, WSPs come from projects that others consider to be undesirable or challenging to pull off, not necessarily projects that are fun and easy to perform. For example, say that you're on the board of an association whose president is looking for someone to tackle membership recruitment. You volunteer for the project at a time when no one else is willing to take on this huge challenge. Although you accept the responsibility of increasing membership by 10%, you actually achieve a 230% increase by improving your association's product offerings, rolling out more attractive membership packages, and redirecting publicity to active members. By proving yourself as a person who delivers on challenging projects, you have added a WSP to your track record. Opportunities for completing WSPs are boundless; completing projects that enable your organization to gain a foothold in an emerging market or that turn around a money-bleeding social program would be considered WSPs, in contrast to average projects that are easy to do or that don't present outstanding outcomes.

Like Kyle, you want to establish a track record of WSPs, because projects of this caliber do more than earn profits or funding. They also earn the confidence and trust of all organizational stakeholders, from the boardroom to the front line and from the managers on staff to the allies and colleagues external to your organization.

When you are known for your WSPs, you can more easily gain buy-in on future projects from the stakeholders who play a role in your success. If Kyle were your manager and he helped you succeed on past projects where the rewards involved promotions, awards, projects for your resume, or cash raises, how likely would you be to approach Kyle and *request* to manage more projects in the future? Is *your* group excited to take on more work? Do they come to you and ask for more work?

The kind of change that managers and leaders like Kyle introduce is both expected and positive. And people love this kind of change.

Rethink Your Concerns about Doing More with Less

If you feel you're being expected to do more with less, you're certainly not alone. "Employers are looking for ways to accelerate their business strategy with fewer people," says Jeffrey Joerres, chairman and CEO of employment giant Manpower.[14] While the concept of doing more with less is true, it's not new. Nor should you perceive it as a negative challenge. Throughout history, leaders have always needed to do more with less, and they have developed innumerable measures to improve speed, accuracy, and quality, all while decreasing costs. In 1792, Eli Whitney invented the cotton gin to do more with less. The invention increased productivity and improved quality at a lower cost and in less time than humans could. Two years later, horses were displaced by the first working steam locomotive that transported people and products faster and with greater storage capacities. In the 1900s, Henry Ford implemented the Persian assembly line to transform production and quicken the rate at which products came to market. In the 1950s, mainframe computers in the back room were a revolutionary step toward work efficiencies of the present.

With the emergence of computers, efficiencies have moved from the back room, where human labor was needed for manual activities such as production, farming, and construction, to the front office. The front office similarly transformed as leaders responded to doing more with less. Functions that were once performed manually—think manual accounting ledgers—became manually automated in the 1980s with personal desktop computers. Today, more functions are automated through local networks, intranets, and extranets. Imagine losing computers or e-mail for a day; how many other functions and people would you need to perform the same tasks? An accounting department might need a hundred people to do the job that twenty can do with the help of computers.

The next logical progression in our quest to do more with less will be to increase the speed and accuracy with which decision makers think. As far-fetched as it may sound, scientists already have technology in the works that is capable of merging human thought with automation to compensate for the unchanging rate of thinking. For now, there are numerous ways in which leaders and managers can do more with less to move their organizations forward no matter where they fall on history's timeline. Leveraging technology and building systems and structures are among the ways to successfully accomplish this.

For example, e-file tax returns, online banking, self check-out lines, and self-serve movie ticket kiosks were all born from the enterprising desire to do more with less—and they've not only helped businesses, they've made consumers' lives more convenient. In 2008, when e-commerce was down for the first time ever, online shoe retailer Zappos actually grew its gross merchandise sales to more than $1 billion, because it successfully used technology to provide excellent customer-service procedures such as ease of online ordering and returns, clear product displays, and rapid delivery times as well as to manage the databases of shoe suppliers, the coordination of shipping requirements, and the coordination of vendor warehouses. The online shoe company's COO/CFP Alfred Lin attributed the firm's ability to do more with less as the reason Zappos had cash flow in the black and even turned a profit.

Though the pressure appears to mount with the passage of time, rethink your beliefs that doing more with less is some new (and negative) challenge; it is a natural progression of potential opportunity, and it will always be. As you've been asked to do more with less, so, too, will those working in the year 2038 or 2078. Embrace the concept, because if you know what to do with that opportunity by using the tools you already have and the ones you will be learning in this book, you can generate limitless rewards.

Rethink Your Methods of Teaching and Learning about Leadership

With each passing year, the number of job candidates who are qualified for leadership positions decreases. That means eventually you'll have to educate the leaders of the future, if you're not doing so already.

Countless numbers of leaders gain much of their education from on-the-job training, where they watch and mimic the behaviors of others. This has its merits, but the serious downside is that the leaders in the making aren't necessarily learning how their mentoring leader thinks. You could watch a master gardener plant a rose bush and duplicate the behavior but still not understand the gardener's reasoning for selecting where that bush was planted, how it will be affected by other plants around it, and how to care for the plant in different seasons. This example shows how on the surface, actions can seem simple to duplicate, but when you try to act on your own without the rationale behind the actions, you can easily find yourself at a loss. The necessity of transferring thinking skills to new recruits is a big part of what makes being the teacher so challenging.

When you teach leadership, talking about what you do isn't always as important as teaching people how you think. Therefore, it may be more important to explain the series of thoughts that have led to a decision rather than the series of actions that have resulted in an outcome when you're grooming decision makers. From my work around the globe, I consistently see a vast majority of decision makers who miss this distinction between teaching thought versus teaching action. Consider this "teaching moment." Imagine that you have to fire an employee. Members of your management team watch him enter your office, emerge a few minutes later, clean out his desk, and leave. Everyone knows he missed an important deadline, but he's only weeks away from his wedding, and this is a lousy time to lose his job. To some members of your leadership team, you look like an ogre. To others, this situation is interpreted as a normal occurrence when employees don't work out. However, you know that there is an entire back story to this situation that your management staff doesn't know.

So what do you do next? If your true desire is to build leaders, your next move is to explain to your team the thinking behind your actions. If you share your thoughts, others learn that this layoff wasn't your angry response to one missed deadline. Instead, they understand how your decision came about after months of careful consideration and planning. You can divulge the following: "You may have seen that he rarely shows up for work on time. But there is more you might not know. For the last year, we've had two complaints about him regarding serious misconduct, and this is the third time he's missed an important deadline. His performance numbers have fallen off, and though I've worked in direct contact with him for months now to improve his performance, it's been to no avail. Considering the new objectives for the company, I realized that he has not and will not work out. So I have let him go, but I have come up with a plan for picking up the slack until we replace him."

If you don't explain how you think, the next generation of leaders could mistakenly believe that leadership is about making snap decisions rather than about the mental preparedness to recognize opportunities when they come along. By taking the time to explain your rationale and strategy, you strengthen the leadership of your organization and your up-and-coming leaders see that seemingly quick decisions actually can take days, months, or years to generate. As you learn Enterprise Thinking, you will acquire tools and instruction on how to develop a structured thinking process for yourself to use and that you can teach to others with success.

Invaluable to the growth and development of any organization is leadership's ability to transfer to other decision makers how and what they think. General Electric's Jack Welch has been a prime example of this strategy. During his tenure at GE, Welch regularly used his firm's Crotonville facility on the Hudson River[15] to educate his team of leaders about how they can think better as leaders and managers. In moments like these, leaders are developed. They need to see inside all the windows of thought, not just the one you remember to reveal to them on rare occasions. When you teach people how to think, you empower them to make better decisions than they would have otherwise.

Rethink the Time Needed to Make Good Decisions

Earlier in this book I introduced the concept of the Economics of Thinking—the better able a leader is to think through an idea before committing to action, the greater the chances an organization has to achieve higher returns, all while mitigating risk, expense, and negative consequences. Certainly, the decisions you make carry immense weight, but also be aware that the *timing* of your decision making—when you arrive at a decision and when you decide to act upon it—is just as important as the decision itself! So, how much time should you spend thinking? Spending too little time (or too much) making a decision leads to negative outcomes instead of desired results.

The amount of time necessary to make a decision is going to be different for each person and for each project. A CEO who is addressing a large-scale expansion project may need two years to decide what action to take, whereas a frontline manager who is determining the location of the staff holiday party may wrap up his decision in less than an hour. Certain factors, such as your position within your organization and the industry or sector of your organization, will influence thinking time. Every decision has its optimal trigger point, and it's your job to determine to the best of your ability where that point is for you at any given time.

One of my NYU students, Javier Suarez, likens the relationship of thinking time and outcomes to boiling time and the perfectly poached egg. One minute under-poaches the egg, five minutes over-poaches it; but three to four minutes yield just the right results. He calls this the Economics of Timing, a supplement to the concept of the Economics of Thinking you learned about in Chapter 1. To determine how much time is right for each decision, Suarez created an Economics of Timing diagram (Figure 2.1). It not only addresses your position and your situation (industry, sector, etc.), but it also illustrates the correlation between these factors and the issue of acting too quickly, too slowly, or possibly not at all.

In the Economics of Timing diagram, the vertical line represents benefits (at the top of the line) and costs (at the bottom), which are associated with the Economics of Thinking. This line is intersected by a horizontal line indicating the amount of time one takes to make a decision: too fast is on the left (Fast Shooter), and too slow is on the right (Paralysis Due to Analysis).

The wave indicates a leader's decision-making time; your optimal decision-making time is where the decision-making time wave touches the Timeline.

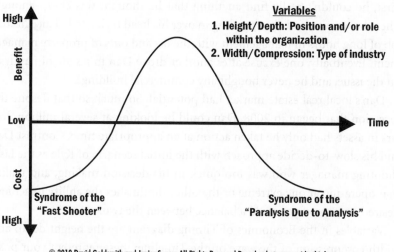

© 2010 David Goldsmith and Javier Suarez All Rights Reserved Download at www.paidtothink.com

Figure 2.1—Economics of Timing

Rushing to action before doing the homework or laying a solid foundation can result in costly mistakes, as is the case with the Fast Shooter. Fast Shooters want everything done "yesterday." They're quick to act and prone to snap decisions and impulses.

At the opposite extreme is the sluggish decision maker who suffers Paralysis Due to Analysis. These decision makers are so slow to make decisions that they are often guilty of making no decision at all. They seem almost paralyzed by their own over-thinking, and as a result, they allow opportunities to slip away and problems to fester to potentially destructive levels. Make sure that you don't slide too far on the scale one way or another.

In addition, you may want to ask people who know you well to weigh in on where they see you falling on this spectrum. I have worked with students and clients who have, on occasion, assumed they were Fast Shooters, when in fact, they were very slow to act—and vice versa.

Paralysis Due to Analysis

Dan is an acquaintance who has enjoyed a successful career in manufacturing. Prior to the U.S. real estate boom, his wife recommended that they look into purchasing a couple of reasonably priced commercial properties and leasing them to local businesses. Dan's response was that he would think it over, do some research, crunch the numbers, and let the missus know his conclusion.

The process didn't work out quite as neatly as Dan had initially anticipated. First, he couldn't really find anything that he thought was cheap enough. Then, he was worried about getting in over his head trying to balance his day job of long hours in management with the ins and outs of property management. Eventually, one excuse after another drove Dan to a state of paralysis on the issue, and he never bought any commercial buildings.

Dan's local real estate market had potential. So much so that despite the recession that began in 2008, Dan could be looking at several million dollars in assets had only he taken action at an appropriate time. Contrast Dan and his slow-to-decide approach with the initial scenario of Kyle as the fast-shooting manager who was too quick in his decision making, and realize that operating at one extreme or the other diminishes the ability to achieve desired outcomes; you need a balance between the two.

Variables in the Economics of Timing diagram are the height/depth and width/compression of the wave on the Timeline; these represent your position within your organization and your organization's industry (or sector), respectively. Let's look at the height/depth of the wave first. The higher your position within your organization rests, the more likely your decisions are to carry greater weight, incur greater costs, meet greater risks, and yield greater benefits or consequences. In terms of this diagram, the wave of any high-ranking decision maker, such as a business owner or a C-level executive, will reach higher on the Cost scale and drop deeper on the Benefit scale than will the wave of a midlevel or frontline manager. Picture a COO who can authorize the purchase of a million-dollar piece of equipment in contrast to a frontline manager who is limited to a budget cap of $5,000 for a single equipment purchase.

The width/compression of the wave is typically determined by your situation, which could refer to your organization's industry or sector, market demands, competition, obsolescence, risks and rewards, regulations and laws, etc. This concept is universally applicable and is effective for people facing decisions in fast-paced and slow-paced industries alike. Simply adjust your wave's length to a shorter bend if your industry is fast paced (such as high tech), and lengthen the wave's bend to accommodate a slow-paced industry (like real estate).

What about you? Do you relate more to the Fast Shooter or the person who suffers Paralysis Due to Analysis? This is not an easy answer, because we often see ourselves differently than others see us. Understanding your own tendencies can help you identify whether you need to decide more quickly or if you need to slow down and take your time.

Also keep in mind that sometimes what looks like a hasty decision might not really be one. Take the real estate developer who walks onto a piece of land and decides, "This is it." That snap decision actually could be the result of months, years, or even decades of careful thought about the development site's requirements. All that preparation enables the developer to quickly assess how well the parcel matches those requirements.

Striking the Right Balance

Jeff Gaspin, the 2009 choice to head NBC's television network, had achieved a twenty-five-year track record of success in the media industry by knowing when to think and when to act. He oversaw the turnaround of non-news cable networks such as USA and Bravo, where he provided the backing for the show *Queer Eye for the Straight Guy* and other successful reality programs.

John Sykes, former chief of VH1, the network where Gaspin developed the musical biography series *Behind the Music,* described Gaspin's careful approach to innovation and decision making: "He would have hundreds and hundreds of ideas before he had a show," Sykes noted. "It wasn't his whim, or throwing something against the wall." In an interview with the *Wall Street Journal,* Gaspin alluded to this when he noted that it was "going to take some time" for him to help NBC develop its brand.[16]

Gaspin's early successes came from taking the right time to make the right decisions so that his organization could capture opportunities and turn them into successes.

Rethink Your View that Employees Are the Most Important Part of Your Organization

Over the years, I've heard many decision makers say that people are the most important part of their organization. While I agree that good organizations are made up of great people doing great work and that employees play an extremely important role in the success of any organization, the idea that people are the *most* important part of an organization is a wrong assumption that can actually hinder the people it intends to credit. We've all seen first-hand how even the most talented people turn in substandard performance if they don't have the systems and structures they need to excel in their work.

Therefore, if you make this assumption and are willing to rethink it, you can more readily capture opportunities to empower your people to achieve more successes within your organization!

Imagine that you're a rookie race car driver sitting behind the wheel of a minivan. On the racetrack next to you is Mario Andretti, revving the engine of his high-performance race car. You're thinking there's no way for you—a rookie driver, and in a minivan, no less—to win against one of the world's all-time Formula One winning race car drivers. But what if Andretti's car has no tires? Without the complete vehicle—the necessary structure—then all of Andretti's skill and experience goes unrealized.

In order to gain the successes that come from talent and skill, your systems and structures must be in place. The systems and structures include everything from computers, tools, and equipment to the rules, regulations, laws, procedures, and policies that govern how your staff works within your organization. These systems don't always have to be elaborate; they just have to be appropriate. For example, in 2011, Boeing relocated passengers' flight attendant call buttons in their new 737 aircrafts away from reading-light buttons.[17] The seemingly small change is anticipated to reduce the number of unnecessary trips that flight attendants will have to make down the aisles of planes in response to typically apologetic customers who mistakenly press their call buttons rather than their reading-light buttons. Similarly, replace a hairstylist's dull scissors with sharp ones and the stylist can produce better haircuts in less time. Conversely, take away the cameras from a film crew, and you're going to shut down production quickly.

Having the appropriate systems and structures in place is one of the most effective ways of bringing out the best talents and highest productivity of your people. Yet it's one of the most ignored factors in organizations today. When leaders see dipping productivity levels and low morale, they often want to address personnel and personality issues, an attempted solution known as "hugging and kissing" your people. The hugging-and-kissing approach typically yields only temporary relief, if it solves anything at all. Then conditions return to the same or get worse. Instead of fixing the real challenges, these leaders have missed the mark altogether (and they've wasted time, money, and resources in the process).

Think back to the lead-in example at the beginning of this chapter; as was the case with Sheila (the manager of a global workforce who improved productivity when she shifted her focus away from her employee and onto the task of upgrading his computer), when you encounter problems with employee performance or morale issues, a good rule of thumb is to check *your systems and structures first,* before you assume that issues stem from your people. If you don't, you might just be spinning your wheels. I encountered one such instance years ago, when a prominent U.S. government agency hired me, along with many other speakers, to give a series of speeches as part of leadership's plan to motivate their employees.

During a pre-event phone call with a woman who would be in my audience, I discovered a major problem. She grumbled in frustration that her computer was down again and complained how all the computers would go down for two to three hours every day. Once the computers, referred to as "ticking time bombs," were up and running, employees could return to work, but they were still expected by supervisors to get all their work done in the shorter amount of time. This complaint was reiterated by employees in one interview after another. Decision makers had good intentions when they invested in motivational programs, but like so many leaders, they hadn't considered how their people were in need of better systems and structures. Perhaps you can look back on situations in your past where a fix to a computer system or other structural issue could have done more to improve morale than a direct attempt to "fix" people. If, after the systems and structures are remedied, leaders still have issues, then leadership would be wise to address morale, but not before.

Another example is one I read about in an article in the *Wall Street Journal,* about the struggles that meteorologists in India experienced when they were trying to forecast weather conditions with outdated equipment. H.R. Hatwar, the head of India's meteorological department, was responsible for delivering accurate forecasts for every sort of weather condition, including droughts, monsoons, and typhoons. The country's 600 million farmers (18% of the nation's GDP) were relying on him. Yet it was not uncommon to see Hatwar using tools from 1950, such as paper charts and graphs, to predict the weather in the twenty-first century. Errors were of national concern, because Hatwar and his staff's inaccuracies had the potential to shave 2% of annual growth from the GDP and impact the fate of the farmers and the billions of people they fed.[18]

In this case, however, the powers that be recognized the system error. To improve forecasting, India's government planned to invest $620 million to establish a thousand automated weather stations and two thousand precipitation stations nationwide, measures that empowered Hatwar and his team to be able to make new and better forecasts.

Systems really can make the difference. In fact, the presence of a supportive system is one reason why decision makers who leave major corporations don't always succeed when they start their own businesses. Many have been so accustomed to a support system that gave them what they needed to be successful, that they either flounder or must invent new systems and structures to maximize their skills once again.

The Goldsmith Productivity Principle

Italian economist Vilfredo Pareto put forth the notion of the vital few in 1906,[19] when he observed that 20% of the population owned 80% of the wealth. Ninety-two years later, investor and entrepreneur Richard Koch authored *The 80/20 Principle*,[20] a book based on an adaptation of Pareto's concept, whereby Koch stated that "80% of output comes from 20% of inputs, not only in the business world, but also in virtually every aspect of life."

I've taken Koch's idea one step further to form the Goldsmith Productivity Principle (GPP), which states that *80% of an organization's ability to compete and perform is driven by its systems and structures, and only 20% is by its people.* Doubt the percentages here? Accepting the exact numbers doesn't matter as much as understanding the concept right now, because in time, you'll probably see that the 80% is actually higher in most instances. Certainly, people are essential, but if yours got locked out of your building tomorrow, even the highest performers would struggle to achieve.

In the visual representation of the GPP, shown in Figure 2.2, the largest boxed area represents this 80% that influences your productivity. Once you have determined that you have given your people the necessary tools they need to achieve success, you can directly address any personnel issues, shown as the larger inset box in the diagram. This 20% should be assessed and assisted only after running a check on their systems.

I want you to pause for a moment and consider what you have just read, because while many decision makers quickly "get it" and start seeing the GPP everywhere—at work, at home, during civic and religious services, at social events—others still hold on to the belief that the 80% is too high a figure to assign to systems and structures *or* they think they already have the best systems in place and don't need to improve in this area. Moreover, leaders often blame others for mediocre output, when in reality, the blame lies with the leader's mediocre systems and structures that cap the potential of individuals and organizations.

To become a catalyst for progress and achievement, you may need to rethink some of your current beliefs and be willing to trade your opinions for new ways of thinking. Eventually, even the initial resisters come on board once they learn about ET and its activities; they realize that 80% may even be a conservative figure, and they also recognize that great opportunities can be mined from improving systems and structures.

All people need the tools to succeed, even you. Imagine losing your computer and access to any data for a month. What would your productivity levels become? Often I hear from leaders that they'd accomplish nothing. That little box is a part of the systems and structures you need to be productive and successful.

Goldsmith Productivity Principle
"The GPP"

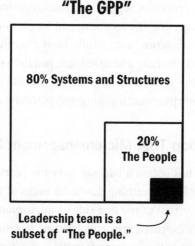

80% Systems and Structures

**20%
The People**

**Leadership team is a
subset of "The People."**

Figure 2.2—Goldsmith Productivity Principle

That said, I'm not proposing that more structure versus less structure will automatically produce your desired returns; this isn't a more-versus-less issue. What you need is the *right* structure—that you or you and your management build—to secure the best talent and keep it continually performing optimally.

Here's an important part of the GPP to note. Take a look at the smallest inset box in the diagram. This is a subgroup of decision makers—you and other decision makers—who create the GPP's 80%, the systems and structures. (The diagram's separation of you from other people in your organization does not mean that you are more important than your engineers, designers, or customer service representatives; it just indicates that you play a different role.)

You are building the systems and structures from the 50,000-foot view. The larger the picture you see, the better your systems are likely to be, because you have a better understanding of how a decision applied to one area of the organization affects another area. However, not all leaders fulfill this responsibility and follow the GPP. In fact, in instances where leadership fails to create the systems and structures, someone who is not in leadership is apt to build the systems and structures simply out of necessity to succeed. But without this staff member having the big picture, his or her well-intentioned systems and structures are unlikely to be as effective as they could be.

As you address challenges that arise throughout your organization, keep the GPP in mind and remember that you are responsible for delivering and managing the tools, processes, reporting structure, infrastructure, technologies, physical space, geographic location, and so on to enable the organization and its people to function successfully. Only after this 80%—the systems and structures—has been fully addressed, can you then plug your people into the GPP, optimize the returns of your staff's collective effort, and redirect your attention to your purpose: thinking and planning for the future.

Rethink the Notion That Micromanagement Is Bad

Micromanagement has gotten a bad rap over the years, because it conjures up images of the big boss breathing down the necks of hard-working subordinates. But in reality, that's only one side of micromanagement and is only the case when it isn't executed properly. It's time to rethink the opinion that all micromanagement is this in-your-face type of suffocation that smothers people and decreases their abilities to perform optimally.

In reality, micromanagement can be one of the most effective ways to increase performance. In addition, there are some environments where micromanagement through systems and structures are necessary to ensure specific outcomes and safety.

In the stereotypical, negative view, the word "micromanagement" makes us think of leaders who are so engrossed in the daily doings of their subordinates that they get in everyone's way and don't get their own work done. By filling their days with tasks that belong in someone else's daily planner, these micromanagers fail to give ample time to their own responsibilities like thinking, strategizing, and moving their organizations forward. In this scenario, micromanaging efforts ultimately hurt the organization on multiple levels, not the least of which may be employees, volunteers, or other group members reacting negatively to feelings of frustration and needless pressure resulting from the constant monitoring. This means that neither the micromanaging boss nor the subordinates are performing as optimally as they could.

By contrast, when leaders have the right mental tools to be effective micromanagers, they are able to direct their organization's people and resources in the direction of shared goals. Effective micromanagement through setting structure, developing strategy and plans, creating reliable systems for others, and teaching people how to be independent thinkers can actually empower others to do their jobs with little involvement from you at all. Yet truthfully, they *are* being micromanaged; they just don't feel it, because you're not in their faces.

Micromanagement isn't always a choice. You may be entrenched in an industry or sector that *requires* a certain degree of micromanagement, so the question isn't whether or not you micromanage; it is how to do it correctly. Leadership in toxic waste or medical waste-management facilities must follow strict procedures to ensure the safety of their staffers, customers, and the general public.

For decision makers, striking the right balance between being involved and letting others work independently can be a challenge. Regardless of your organization's circumstances, following the GPP is how you effectively micromanage your organization's people and resources to achieve desired outcomes. Build an environment of systems, structures, tools, equipment, etc. to support the talents and skills of your people, and you will earn their trust, gain their cooperation, and increase their productivity levels. When micromanagement is done right, you are able to achieve the results your organization needs to grow and survive.

Here's an example of micromanagement done right according to the GPP. Think about when you drive on the highway; do you feel micromanaged? Most likely you feel pretty independent. You select your destination and the vehicle you'll use to get there. You also determine the vehicle's air temperature, whether you'll listen to music, who your passengers are, and what type of car you'll drive. But if you look closer, you are actually very micromanaged. You must drive on predetermined roads, streets, and ramps. You must maintain certain speeds. You must pass only in predesignated passing zones. In some areas, you must pay a toll for using the road. However, you don't resent being micromanaged, and you don't feel that you're constantly running into roadblocks due to the micromanagement, because the road system enables you to reach your targeted destinations, much like systems help your staffers to reach their targeted goals.

Systems and structures also direct your organization toward innovative solutions both internally, as organizational improvements, and externally, as product and service improvements. Consider how a restaurateur might opt to "micromanage" his establishment's reservation process by using a proven software system—one that employees manage internally or one that patrons can access externally through the Internet—to achieve reliable outcomes. Micromanaging systemically removes the crises that erupt from inefficiencies and replaces problems with opportunities. Additionally, micromanagement done right prevents waste, so your organization has more resources to dedicate to these improvements.

■ ■ ■

Untying the Gordian Knot

As the Greek myth goes, in the center of the Middle Asian city of Gordium, King Midas had tied a chariot to a post with an intricate knot. A great oracle predicted that the man who could untie the knot would become Asia's next king. Hundreds of men tried and failed at the endeavor. A man approached, studied the knot, and with one sword strike, sliced the knot in two thus claiming his title as king.[21] This man was Alexander the Great.

Alexander's strength and his army's might did not grant him the position of leader. His ability to think and rethink about a current challenge was the key to his rise. In essence, that's what every leader who is paid to think does, too.

As you move through the upcoming chapters of this book, you will revisit some of these concepts and you will learn more. Though some of the new information you receive will likely be common sense, some of it may seem counterintuitive, but a mind that is willing to rethink will enjoy the greatest opportunities for positive change and growth. And now that you've had an opportunity to jumpstart the rethinking process, you're mentally better positioned to learn about Enterprise Thinking in more depth.

CATEGORY 1:
[STRATEGIZING]

Strategizing
Developing Plans
Creating New Products & Services
Establishing Alliances
Leveraging Technology

Learning
Acquiring New Knowledge
Enhancing Global Awareness
Watching Competition

Performing
Leading the Charge
Empowering Others
Innovating Everywhere
Selling Continuously

Forecasting
Forecasting the Future

YOU FIND YOURSELF STANDING ON a mountainside overlooking the small town of which you're the mayor. In your peripheral vision, you glimpse the hand gestures of your lifelong friend who is standing next to you, drinking in his experience of a beautiful autumn day. You find yourself somewhat envious of his free spiritedness, wishing that you could stop the rush of thoughts flooding into your mind.

"Gorgeous day! Not a cloud in the sky. If only they could all be like this . . . " His comments fade into the background as your eyes dart from one area of town to another, at each visual stop vacuuming more tidbits of information into your brain for further processing.

As the leader of the bubbling community below, you can't seem to arrest this cyclonic swirl of questions and possibilities. When you glimpse the winding streets, you think of the annual salary budget for the road maintenance workers, the new snowplows on order for the public works department, last week's town meeting where townspeople presented a petition to install a traffic light at the increasingly busy intersection, and the potential to merge ambulatory services across the region.

"Yeah, it's a great day," you respond. "Guess it's time to head back into town." Your buddy, who hasn't a clue about your mental wrestling match, nods, hops into his pickup truck, and starts the engine.

The mind of any leader is a busy place, jam-packed with potential. Yet to harness the potential of your ideas and ultimately convert your thoughts to realities, you need the right tools to develop strategies and plans and mobilize the resources available to you to arrive at predictable, reliable results.

In the next four chapters, you are going to learn the ET tools of Strategizing, how to use them at the 50,000-foot level, and how to share them with the people who help you produce results. As you will soon conclude, these chapters are integrated and build upon each other. In addition, all of the tools of the Strategizing category are processes, concepts, methodologies, and principles that you will use in other ET categories, too.

Again, I urge you to approach these chapters with an open mind. Much of their contents will make immediate sense to you, while other areas may initially seem counterintuitive or require a bit of cultivation time. Either way, you are likely to emerge from this section with new perspectives and proven tools to harness your brainpower and create countless new opportunities for yourself, those around you, your organization, and perhaps even your community, your country, or the world at large.

DEVELOPING PLANS

TWENTY-THREE YEARS AGO, AN ENTERPRISING man by the name of Hee Bong Park departed his native country of Korea for a trip around the Asia Pacific region in search of a place to set up manufacturing facilities for his growing tent manufacturing firm, HKD International. After stopping in several countries on his fact-finding mission, Park elected to look into the possibility of Bangladesh as one of his site locations.

While he traveled the countryside of this impoverished area, two thoughts repeatedly ran through his head. The first was that if he were to build a manufacturing facility in Bangladesh, the development of infrastructure and personnel would be more challenging than in any other country he had visited thus far. Yet he knew that if he drew up a solid plan and addressed these issues, he could establish his facilities in Bangladesh and reap significant rewards both economically and personally. He knew in his heart that if he were to make this decision, he could help to create jobs, offer new opportunities, and provide improved futures for many of the citizens of Chittagong, the city he was contemplating as the place of operations. Second, Park believed Bangladesh would be a good location for a successful and long-term business, even though most of the people in the industry thought building a manufacturing plant in Bangladesh was impossible at that time. On this visit, he made up his mind that this was to be his future. His next call was to his two sons to tell them the news.

Today, HKD International has grown far beyond Park's imagination. His firm now produces more than 60% of the tents manufactured worldwide and has recently entered into the outdoor furniture business, already with great success. He's also working on constructing a new 500,000-square-foot facility that will improve working conditions and quality and increase capacity.

As Park recounted his firm's beginnings to me while we took a ride in his car, I vividly remember his body language as he moved forward in his seat so that he could address me face to face. "I did the right thing, right?" My heart went out to this man whose focused plans have enabled him to provide good jobs for 7,000 employees, whose products have touched so many people, and who has transformed tens of thousands (if not hundreds of thousands) of Bangladeshi lives over the decades. Choked up, I could say nothing but, "Yes, yes you did."

A decision has the power to transform entire lives. Sometimes we can forget that fact. I'm betting that you can look back on a single moment in your own life where you made a decision that affects how you live today.

Think about all the decisions that your stakeholders make in a day on behalf of your organization. Frontline workers, vendors, allies, board members, volunteer workers, decision makers, bankers, and other individuals are making decisions every day that, collectively, will impact your organization's future. What if each one of them made just one better decision per day?

Consider the positive outcome arising from a manager's decision to fight her temptation to close up shop five minutes early. She keeps your doors open until closing time and ends up securing a new loyal customer who refers her friends to your boutique.

Picture a machinist who decides to speak up about a tiny rattling noise he notices in a piece of equipment, even though no one else hears it. By catching a minor precursor to an otherwise costly imminent breakdown, this decision keeps your equipment operational throughout your busy season.

Imagine the president of a robotics company who decides to expand on a technology that he has used for multiple consumer products—including a robotic home vacuum cleaner—and apply it to military situations. As a result, military decision makers eventually purchase radio-controlled surveillance devices using this technology for the purpose of entering dangerous areas ahead of foot soldiers, ultimately replacing human risk with robotics.

If ten people in your organization each make one smarter decision each day, that's 2,500 better decisions over the course of a 250-day work year. If your organization consists of 50, 200, 5,000, or 30,000 people, the numbers of better decisions per year rise to 12,500, 50,000, 1,250,000, and 7,500,000 respectively. Think of how much better your organization could be a year from now!

The types of decisions that best solve challenges and usher in new opportunities are decisions that are in sync with strategy and desired outcomes. Just as you wouldn't want to determine the location of your home by throwing a dart at a world map, you don't want random decision making within your organization. Therefore, it is essential that you develop great strategic and tactical plans that *both clarify desired outcomes and guide others to achieve them.*

There are three components to Developing Plans, which is why this chapter is divided into three corresponding parts:

1. **Part I: Creating Strategy.** Strategy determines the direction of your entire organization. The plans you develop to support strategy determine whether your organization reaches its targeted outcomes. That's why you will learn a proven process tool that will empower you to create winning plans and to lead others to success. You will also take away several other new tools and instructions on how to use them so that you can keep your entire organization on track, no matter how many responsibilities and challenges arise along the way.

2. **Part II: Transforming with Projects.** Once you know your strategy, you will search for the tactics that allow your organization to play out that strategy. A project, unlike a task, advances your organization by keeping it current, competitive, and strong. In essence, projects are the building blocks of organizations. In this chapter you will learn immediately applicable tools that will (1) ensure that you select, organize, and implement the best and right projects for your organization at any given time, and (2) allow you to guide others to the successful completion of projects.

3. **Part III: Managing Your Priorities.** Setting direction, implementing projects, and guiding others can become overwhelming even for the most experienced leaders, which is why you need tools to keep yourself focused and on track on a daily basis. Surely you've heard of time management, but this section offers a better alternative in the form of priority management tools. Research indicates that very few leaders use a daily planning tool or are even aware that they need one. FYI: You *definitely need* one. Better than a time-management planner, the priority-management system that you will learn here will help you to diminish "fires" and interruptions, accelerate desired outcomes, enable you to sleep better, and reward you with a higher quality of life.

All three chapter parts are important components of Developing Plans. In addition to learning how to create winning strategies, select and implement high-impact projects, and focus yourself each day on your priorities, the tools you will pick up in this chapter can be used to enhance your performance in all other ET categories' activities. Therefore, absorb what you can from this, the longest chapter, and trust that it will all come together as you progress through this book.

■ ■ ■

[PART I]
CREATING STRATEGY

BILL AND DON are brothers who like to do everything together. Last year, the two decided to take their wives on a joint six-night Mediterranean cruise, beginning in Italy and snaking its way through the waters near France, the UK, and Spain. Since Bill's time is usually limited due to the demands of his job, Don typically plans these annual vacation trips for the group on his own. He scanned the Web for several nights and eventually settled on four reasonably priced airline tickets to fly the couples from Boston to Rome, the departure point for their cruise. Don also secured the cruise tickets and ground transportation from the airport to Civitavecchia, the ship's port of call.

When the day of the big trip arrived, the excited foursome boarded the plane, chattering on about all the great spots they would see and the amazing food they would eat. Then they settled in for their long flight, caught some zzz's en route, and a half a day later found themselves in the customs line at Leonardo da Vinci–Fiumicino Airport. As they waited, Bill's wife, Eileen, opened the paper folder containing her tickets and glanced quickly from her watch to the cruise ticket's departure time and date. "Oh no, Bill, look at this," she said frantically while displaying her ticket for Bill to see. Eileen could hear her heart pounding in her ears, and when she saw the look of shock come over Bill's face, she knew this trip was over.

"Don, you're not going to believe this," Bill reluctantly said to his brother. "The cruise took off hours ago."

Don pulled the nonrefundable cruise ticket from Bill's hand and gave it a once-over. Suddenly his memory flashed back to one of those late nights when he sat at his computer deciding among several different travel options, his head spinning with confusion over the time-zone differences. He realized now that he must have made a miscalculation.

Here the four of them stood, stranded an ocean's distance from home because of a plan that was doomed before they'd ever left the ground.

Even the smallest error in planning can derail an entire initiative, which is why developing a solid strategy up front is so important. Your new tool, the Cyclonic Strategic Thinking (CST) Model, will help you create plans that are right, complete, and on target from the start. The CST Model is a universal Strategizing tool, meaning you can use it regardless of your industry or sector and teach it to others, no matter their management levels. Besides its ability to drive better decision making, the CST Model enables all staffers to communicate more easily and accurately with each other about where everyone stands in terms of progress.

You will see as you read through this book that you can use this model to do much more than build strategic plans. Throughout your career, you can use the CST Model for a variety of purposes—when you want to create new products and services; when you want to build alliances; when you consider, select, and use technology; when you lead and empower others or help them to succeed; when you seek to innovate and beat out your competition; when you're supporting community and cultural causes; when you're directing a nonprofit or business unit; when you're organizing a party or planning a personal vacation; and more.

It's time for a change in the way we create and evolve strategic plans. The method of the once-a-year strategic planning retreat—where management teams set goals and benchmarks for the upcoming year and then may or may not revisit that plan at some time during the year to see where the organization stands—will not work in today's fast-evolving world. This is true whether you run a small organization or a large one and whether you consider your organization local or global or somewhere in between the two, because in reality no one is immune from rapid changes occurring geopolitically, economically, and especially technologically. Certainly, worldwide economic upheaval isn't the norm, but to illustrate my point, take a moment to consider the economic woes from 2008 through 2012 when the global recession, residential real estate collapse, and banking and stock market declines drastically affected organizations worldwide. A strategic plan accommodating an organization's needs in January of that year wouldn't necessarily work by December.

Simply put, the old ways of plan development typically leave decision makers and their staff members with plans that aren't as clear as they need to be, don't accommodate today's rapidly changing world, and fail to account for innovation, communication speeds, compression in price, and more. In most instances, factors requiring you to make changes in the way you do your planning don't have to be drastic at all. Even subtle shifts and changes can greatly impact your organization, which is why you need to be able to quickly create great strategies, know where their progress stands on a daily basis, and be equipped to rapidly adapt to the evolving needs of your organization, whether the adaptation is required a few times a year or every day.

The Process of Strategic Thinking

Great strategic plans are born just as much from *how* leaders think as they are from *what* they think. The typical Basic Strategizing process tends to occur as an informal and unstructured two-phase process: phase one is strategy and phase two is tactics. If you were to view it in diagram form, it would look something like Figure 3.1:

Basic Strategizing

Figure 3.1—Basic Strategizing

Though I like simplicity, this model is too simplistic to adequately direct and guide organizations to desired outcomes with certainty. Several pitfalls accompany this overly simplistic method of strategizing. First, the vocabulary points people in different directions, because both words carry different meanings to different people. I've heard strategy defined in as many as fifty different ways: as vision, outline, complete plan, or things to be done, for example. The definition of tactics is equally unclear: a plan, things to do, or blocking and tackling. Some people even use the words interchangeably. For instance, some people use "road map" to define both strategy and tactics.

How can anyone win at strategizing if leaders and their people don't even speak the same language?

The two-part model of Basic Strategizing (strategy and tactics) often fails to address all components of the strategic-thinking process. As a result, you could have some great ideas, but they may never materialize into the results that you want to achieve. By contrast, the Cyclonic Strategic Thinking (CST) Model is an advanced version of the strategizing process described above. This new model has five clearly defined phases that force you to address each component of strategizing before moving onto the next. As a result, you don't overlook important elements. Additionally, this model:

- helps you make decisions with your entire organization in view rather than from a silo mindset—your organization's overall Desired Outcomes are the starting point for Strategy.
- is versatile enough to use for any type of strategic thinking, not just for creating strategic plans.
- gives you a broader range of strategic and tactical options to consider before you commit to any final selections, and superior selections increase the likelihood that your organization stays on target and that Desired Outcomes are reached.
- is universal, giving you and your staff a common language for improved communications and enabling you to track your team's progress, both of which minimize errors.

So universal is this strategizing tool that whether you're a TV producer, a public works commissioner, or a medical office manager, as soon as you learn how to use the CST Model, not only will *you* be able to use it, but it's simple enough that you can teach it to other members of your executive team as a standard procedure for creating Strategy and for making better organization-wide decisions. Furthermore, as you use the CST Model at work, at home, and in areas of your everyday life, you will see how reliably it converts your thoughts to reality.

From Thought to Reality: How Do You Create a Successful Strategy?

Take a look at Figure 3.2. Even at first glance, you can see how the CST Model takes you through five phases of good strategizing rather than simply strategy and tactics like the less-detailed traditional model. You start with determining your Desired Outcome, then you develop a Strategy, next you identify Macro Tactics, then you finalize Tactics, and lastly, you address Execution.

Advanced Strategizing
Cyclonic Strategic Thinking Model (CST)

Note: Whenever you see these terms capped throughout the text, it refers to the CST Model or to your use of the CST Model as an Enterprise Thinker. This is why you will see "strategy" in some mentions and "Strategy" in others.

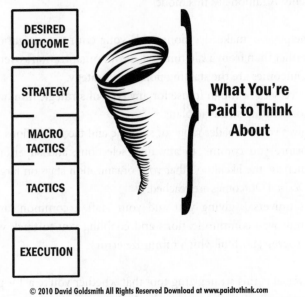

Figure 3.2—Advanced Strategizing (CST Model)

When you look at the CST Model, you see that the strategy and tactics from the earlier Basic Strategizing Model are present, but that they are now a part of a larger and more comprehensive process. Notice, too, the lines separating the three phases of Strategy, Macro Tactics, and Tactics have gaps in them. These gaps reflect a realistic representation of the way that we naturally shift our attention from one phase to another, mentally darting from Strategy to overarching tactics (Macro Tactics), then to details of Tactics, and so on in order to consider all the options we have before ultimately choosing the best.

See, too, how the final phase, Execution, has been separated out from the tactical phases. Execution is a key factor in converting thoughts to reality, yet it is often blended into Tactics when people do their strategizing. You rarely hear people talk about Strategy, Tactics, *and Execution.* The vast number of decision makers who believe that Execution is a mere subset of Tactics boggles my mind, because this single incorrect assumption is often the wrench that screeches all strategic-planning cogs to a halt without anyone being aware of the problem. If leaders assume that Execution is going to be addressed, but the people they work with don't make the same assumption, Execution might occur haphazardly or not at all.

The cyclone to the right of the phases represents the way people naturally think when they're searching for answers. Like a spinning cyclone that gathers up objects and swirls them around, your mind picks up ideas and tosses them around, assessing each for its viability. The term I use to describe this fast whirling of options is Cyclonic Thinking.

Detailed View of Cyclonic Thinking

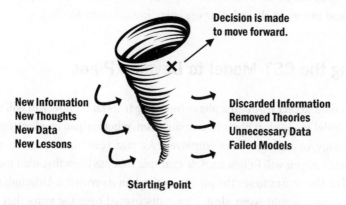

Decision is made to move forward.

New Information
New Thoughts
New Data
New Lessons

Discarded Information
Removed Theories
Unnecessary Data
Failed Models

Starting Point

Figure 3.3—Detailed View of Cyclonic Thinking

When you're engaged in Cyclonic Thinking, your mind does more than swirl ideas around, however. It rapidly pulls in many ideas, draws fast connections and comparisons among them, and thrusts out the least-usable material. Your mind gathers ideas for Cyclonic Thinking from numerous places, like your past experiences and current knowledge banks or from the collection of new data, research, statistics, financials, and information from other people. This cyclonic action of vacuuming in and sifting out ideas happens all the time, whether you're strategizing for your organization's next new initiative or figuring out the best contractor to use for your home's renovation project.

And although Cyclonic Thinking occurs naturally, every decision maker still needs focused Cyclonic Thinking Time to generate ideas and options. Instead of waiting until Cyclonic Thinking Time just happens, you can initiate intentional Cyclonic Thinking at any time, like during strategic-planning sessions or between meetings. You've probably noticed that some of your best thoughts and greatest moments of clarity happen when you've stepped out of the fray and have let yourself relax, like when you're driving in your car or taking a shower.

As you use the CST Model to strategize, you will continually engage in Cyclonic Thinking throughout all of its five phases. If at any time you come to a dead end in one phase, perhaps because a selection made in a previous phase doesn't play out as expected, you will find yourself naturally going back to the previous stage to rework the ideas.

Rushing to action too soon is a common saboteur of creating Strategy. But just by becoming aware of the cyclone and the CST Model, you are now likely to gather more options than you would have before and to spend more time thinking about them. This ultimately will lead you to make improved decisions and put yourself and your organization on surer footing.

Using the CST Model to Develop Plans

Let's walk together through a phase-by-phase tutorial on how you will use the CST Model to develop plans in any situation, whether you're adopting a new technology or hiring a new employee. As you read through each phase's instructions, you will follow a single example that has been threaded throughout all of the phases to see the process at work in its entirety. Although a business example would seem ideal, I have discovered over the years that at this point in the learning process, most people relate best to the simple and common scenario of planning a week off from one's work.

PHASE I: DETERMINE DESIRED OUTCOME

 Your Desired Outcome is the end objective you want to achieve; some people call it their mission, credo, vision, goals, or objectives. However, you and I are going to avoid using these types of words for two reasons. First, because many leaders of groups who need to develop plans don't necessarily have a "vision" or "mission," nor do they need them to perform these phases. (You don't create a mission statement to plan a training program any more than you do to plan a wedding.) And second, the words have become so bastardized that it would be difficult for us to settle on any one definition. Instead, let's use the

more universal term "desired outcome." Your Desired Outcome is the starting reference point for all Strategy.

So what constitutes a Desired Outcome? The answer varies depending on the situation and your role in it. For a school district's superintendant, the Desired Outcome might be to turn out a high percentage of high school graduates who are adequately prepared for their next stages of life. For an executive of a single business unit, the Desired Outcome might be to hit a gross sales mark or to drop a particular product line to hit profitability targets. The director of a government-funded organization might want to provide specific services to the elderly that allow them to live more years independently.

You'll find that by starting with the Desired Outcome, you'll immediately begin to infuse your planning process with a clarity that is typically lacking in the basic model. Give some thought to your Desired Outcome before developing the Strategy to support it.

Example thread

Imagine that you have just learned that you will have a week off from work in July. If I were to ask you what you would call that week, like many other people, you might say "vacation" or "holiday." Without realizing it, your mind has already begun to think of what you will be *doing* during that week. What I want you to do is to start to ask yourself, What is my Desired Outcome from this week off from work? By asking the question, you control your mind to focus on thinking versus acting. Furthermore, you are preventing yourself from developing a Strategy that may not be in alignment with your true Desired Outcome.

Uncovering your Desired Outcome can require some serious thinking. Do you want to connect with your family? Do you want to catch up on paperwork? Must you get certain affairs in order which precludes the lounging-around options? If you realize your family is your priority, then your Strategy might be to go away where your teens are free from distractions or to stay home and invite extended family to come visit your new baby. You can see why the first step in this process is to determine your Desired Outcome (and *not* to confuse it with Strategy or Tactics) to ensure that you don't head in the wrong direction before you even get started.

PHASE II: DEVELOP STRATEGY

A Strategy is where you want to go and possibly where you want to lead your group, organization, or yourself. This is where you set the direction for your people and your organizational resources. When you develop a Strategy, you're engaged in Cyclonic Thinking, pulling together thoughts from everywhere—from forecasting activities, competitive intelligence, other leaders and colleagues, etc.—to come up with the best path for reaching your Desired Outcome.

However, there are many paths—Strategies—that will take you to your Desired Outcome, and your challenge is to select the best one. For instance, say that you're the school superintendent whose Desired Outcome is to graduate a high percentage of students who are adequately prepared for life beyond high school. You have strategic options. Do you create a Strategy that prepares more students for college beginning as early as preschool, or do you go with a Strategy to develop a learning environment that promotes blue-collar skills, both because you foresee long-term growth in this area and because blue-collar jobs are plentiful in your district's geographic location?

The Strategy that you select will set people, money, and other resources on a potentially time-consuming and costly path. Therefore, you must create a Strategy that points everyone in the right direction at this early phase. Whenever you're developing a Strategy, remind yourself of this:

An excellent Strategy executed poorly is still better than a poor Strategy executed well.

The importance of having an on-target Strategy can be likened to having the right aim when you point a laser at the moon; if your aim is off by an inch, you'll miss your target altogether. In business and in life, you can deploy the most talented people and give them the finest state-of-the-art equipment, but if your Strategy points them in the wrong direction from the get-go, they are still going to miss their mark.

That's why you have to resist the urge to jump to action too soon. Think through your options to avoid the risk of pointing everyone toward an off-target goal from the beginning. Take your time. If you get to a subsequent phase and discover that the original Strategy isn't the best way of reaching your Desired Outcome, you're better off returning to this phase early on and making modifications rather than continuing down a losing path that will ultimately waste time and money and de-motivate your people. In essence, this is the Economics of Thinking explained in Chapter 1.

Additionally, as you'll see later in the book, forecasting plays an important role in developing Strategy. As in a game of checkers or chess, you need to play out your Strategy combined with the next phases, a few steps ahead, considering how its direction will impact your organization; each Strategy has long-term upsides and downsides.

A few years ago, the National Transportation and Safety Board (NTSB) announced a major shift in strategy. Rather than directing its actions and resources toward the strategy of reducing vehicular deaths and injuries, the NTSB's new strategy would be to prevent accidents from happening altogether. The NTSB had based its previous strategy on the premise that accidents were inevitable. Imagine if they'd aimed their strategy at preventing accidents forty years ago. Engineers, designers, politicians, and construction firms would have generated very different solutions: safer roads, skid-resistant substrates, or side-collision prevention systems rather than side-collision airbags. The board could have taken numerous other directions; even changing its name to something alluding to the elimination or prevention of accidents would have changed its purpose.

The point here is that you have to determine the best course for your organization given your unique circumstances. For example, Amazon.com's president and[22] CEO Jeff Bezos has a strategy with three components: obsess over customers, invent on behalf of the customers, and think long term, where projects may take between five and seven years before they pay off for his company. Notice how cleanly this strategy is stated: no details, no projects, no steps, only a strategy to support his desired outcome.

Example thread

As you contemplate your options for the week off from work in July—a prime opportunity to enjoy life more—you might ask, Where do I want to go on vacation? Your "innocent" question has already pointed you in some direction; either you've already chosen your Strategy without realizing it, or you've chosen it without having thought it through. By stating that you want to go on vacation, you've opted to go away instead of stay at home to paint your kitchen, visit your parents, volunteer with your local religious group, or stay in town so that you're available to help your closest friends move into their new home. In the flash of a second, you discarded the stay-at-home options without fully thinking them through.

Jumping ahead to next phases before thoroughly thinking through a Strategy tends to be a natural inclination for decision makers. Slow down, and don't let the "if-you're-not-busy-you're-not-doing-anything" mentality push you forward too rapidly. At this point, you haven't yet entertained enough strategic options to determine the best one, so if you don't know where you're going, you're certainly not ready to decide how you will get there or what it will cost. Moving too quickly now is likely to produce mistakes that could steer you away from your Desired Outcome.

Expand your vision and give yourself some Cyclonic Thinking Time. As you search for your best Strategy, consider the big picture of your Desired Outcome, not just the micro-view of a single week. In this example, if you're drowning in credit-card debt but know that you'll have to charge travel expenses to your credit cards, will the weight of more debt bring enjoyment to your life? Through Cyclonic Thinking, you might decide that a combination of short day trips and home activities is a more suitable fit for you at this time. Cyclonic Thinking also helps you weigh the obligations and desires of your travel partner and family as well as what will be happening at your organization that might require your occasional attention. The extra few moments spent thinking can drastically improve your outcomes.

Once you've given ample consideration to your options, you can determine your Strategy. In this example thread, we'll say that your Strategy is *I am going away on vacation.*

Developing the right Strategy doesn't happen overnight or on a weekend retreat. Strategy takes time, requires continual attention, and shouldn't be mistaken for idleness or down time. Resist the temptation to rush forward too soon, like the CFO of a $300-million German-based equipment manufacturing firm did during a monthly strategic-planning session with fourteen of his peers, also top executives. At a critical decision-making juncture, this CFO stood up and barked, "I hate sitting around and talking. When are we actually going to do something?" (I think he'd been reading too many books about how leadership's primary role is execution.) He didn't understand the importance of his role as a thinker, nor did he understand that by strategizing, the group was already "doing something" very valuable.

Once you've established your Strategy, you are ready to select Macro Tactics and detail its Tactics.

PHASE III: SELECT MACRO TACTICS

 As noted earlier, unlike the Basic Strategizing Model, which has just one tactical phase, the CST Model has two: Macro Tactics and Tactics. The CST Model's two tactical phases ensure that you're selecting your overarching Macro Tactics in the first phase and then adding the appropriate details to them in the second phase before moving ahead. By getting the Macro Tactics and Tactics right, you build better plans that are easier for other people to execute, your Strategy plays out as intended, and you reach your Desired Outcome.

In the Macro Tactics phase, you gather, assess, and select your overarching Macro Tactics, but you don't finalize their details just yet. By nature, you already select Macro Tactics before you formulate their details. For instance, when you determine that you need a partner to help you enter a new market, you're establishing a Macro Tactic. Obviously, you must determine the Macro

Tactic—"I need a partner"—before you decide its details—the name of the partner and type of partnership, for example.

If you're like most decision makers, you may be anxious to get everyone in your group busy, but this tendency towards "busyness" could prevent you from gathering enough options to include your best alternatives before making a final decision. During the strategizing process, any time you feel the urgency to push forward quickly, slow down and harness those urges instead.

One simple way to slow yourself down is remember how the lines separating the blocks of Strategy, Macro Tactics, and Tactics are broken and not solid in the diagram of the CST Model. Remind yourself that these broken lines represent the fluidity of thought that runs through these three phases. Be conscious of how your thinking naturally flows up to the Strategy phase and down to the Tactics phase, and allow yourself the time to bring in knowledge, costs, feasibility, and so on, as you rapidly accept or reject pursuing various options. The key is that you don't want to close out a phase before you've made your best selections. This type of free-flow thinking is not only an alternative to making fast choices and racing through phases; it also helps you generate more Macro Tactics and better assess their viability.

Example thread

You're now thinking, For my vacation, where will I go, how will I get there, and how much will I pay? Some of the Macro Tactics that you bring into your Cyclonic Thinking are Buenos Aires, Paris, and London. You also question how much money you are willing to spend, what types of hotels you want to stay in, and whether you want to take a tour or find your own way around. With all of these Macro Tactics in mind, you might make a list of the resources you have at your disposal. You might decide to check with a travel agent, search online, review your frequent-flyer mileage, and talk to friends. As this phase progresses, you consider the possible implications of these tactical options, but you do not finalize their details just yet.

At this time, engage in simple research techniques that you can perform from your desk: review similar projects, talk with industry experts, run cost analyses, consider financial data, research the marketplace, etc., to uncover your optimal opportunities.

Push yourself to come up with better Macro Tactics than you might have previously considered by asking, What would it take . . .

- to do this in half (a third, a tenth) of the time?
- to achieve our objective with little or no human involvement?

- to reach our objectives with the resources we already have?
- to double our returns in the same amount of time?
- to eliminate our competitors from the equation altogether?
- to triple our benefits (profits, return on investment)?

Notice how the new questions force you to think differently, because they are asking significantly different questions than, What would it take to grow 10%? The hard push forces radical thinking and new Macro Tactic options. If I asked you to open a new market for your company in one year, you'd have to have different solutions than if I asked you to open the same market in three months.

Decision makers find that asking what-would-it-take questions gives them more, better, and different Macro Tactics from which to choose. As a result, they put themselves and their organizations in stronger positions to achieve their Desired Outcome and they avoid costly and preventable mistakes. Decision makers at a bank in Texas wanted to increase market penetration by specifically targeting consumers who were twenty-five to thirty-four years old. Decision makers immediately jumped to Tactics and decided to build a new brick-and-mortar branch, geographically locating it where 15,000 new houses were being built. Although that Tactic would have worked fifteen or twenty years ago when the Internet wasn't a part of life, in the age of online banking, it was a flop.

Had leaders spent more Cyclonic Thinking Time asking different questions, studied market-research data and behavioral shifts, and waited until they had identified better Macro Tactics, they would have discovered that their target demographic prefers to do their banking online and only visits banks when they absolutely have to.

Quite often people confuse Macro Tactics with Tactics. They believe when they identify Macro Tactics, they are done. Macro Tactics do not form a plan; they create the foundation for selecting the right Tactics.

PHASE IV: FINALIZE TACTICS

You've now reached a point where you can finalize the details of your Macro Tactics into a type of road map that can be handed off to the people who will ultimately execute those Tactics. In this phase, you collect and assemble "things that need to be done" to transform your Macro Tactics into actionable steps that will deliver you to your Desired Outcome once they are completed.

As you create your plan, you will constantly try to achieve a careful balance between providing enough direction and guidance for others to do the job and overdoing the plan to the point of overkill. Tactics should be prepared well enough that others can perform Execution independently, with only little guidance from you.

The Tactics are the how-to part of your plan. One consideration as you develop the detailed Tactics should be the Goldsmith Productivity Principle (where 80% of an organization's outcomes are based on the systems and structures and 20% on its people). I am making this recommendation, because you can certainly give a list of Tactics to people, but you also have to make sure that they have the systems and structures set in place to round out the "tools" they may need to execute your plan successfully. Keep in mind that you may have two sets of Tactics: one for leaders who do the planning and another for the people who will execute the plan. What kinds of software, equipment, or space will your people need? How will the executors access you or your fellow managers when they have questions, and who are their contacts? Although these factors will vary depending on your circumstances, it's always up to leadership to figure out the systemic and structural details of their Tactics.

Example thread

This phase is where you would detail plane and rental car reservations, chart your driving route and note the places where you want to make stops, make a list of restaurants where you want to dine, decide on travel insurance, record emergency phone numbers, etc. The amount and types of detail you incorporate into your final plans will depend on your experience level as a traveler (are you a world traveler or is this your first time out of your country?), the type of trip you have planned (are you planning each detail yourself or are you buying a prepackaged trip where the details are left to its organizers?), and so on.

Tactics can be presented to others as a one-sheet list of items or a complete tactical plan. The assembled Tactics go by many names: plan, map, road map, architectural blueprints, project plan, strategic plan, and shopping list to name a few. Your tactical details can include charts, like the Critical Path Method (CPM) chart that you will learn about later in this chapter; modeling software; and various other types of planning tools to keep everyone on target. Your Strategy, work culture, and particular circumstances determine how you assemble your Tactics.

As you finalize details, consider the knowledge and experience levels of the people who will execute the Tactics so that your Tactics fit their levels of knowledge and skills. This is why it's important to really get to know the other people who will be involved in your endeavors. For instance, if you were running a charity cooking event, and I were one of your volunteer cooks, you would want to know that I have had no professional training. The recipes and instructions that you would give to me would be more basic—"these are the steps to sautéing onions and mushrooms"—than those you would give to another volunteer who is a professional chef. By knowing your people and resources, you are better able to tailor the complexity of the plan to match their abilities, skills, and knowledge.

Ultimately, you want tactical details that are realistic and doable. If others can't follow your plan, the fault lies with you, not them. Walk through the plans mentally or follow some of the directions to see how they will work. Fill out a form before passing it off to others to catch any flaws, or try the first run of activities yourself before leaving your executors on their own. You can also observe activities from time to time to see if the details are working or if they need some adjustments. This testing measure helps you to catch missing steps or vague directives early on, thus preventing the types of problems that cause organizations to lose by a nose.

The television program *Undercover Boss*[23] highlights the gap that often exists between leaders' assumptions and frontline workers' realities when it comes to strategies, and tactics. With their identities disguised, CEOs and executives of very large companies enter frontline positions within their firms and work alongside unsuspecting employees. In this rare opportunity, leaders get to experience firsthand the working environments that their decision making has created, most often learning that their tactics do not align staffers as well as the leaders had assumed with objectives and strategy. They not only hear their workers complain about unrealistic expectations given the working environment, but the leaders experience the disconnection and frustrations on a personal level, granting them new insight into the changes they will need to make in order to synchronize strategy with tactics in the real world.

At times, you may decide that your circumstances call for a tactical plan that offers less detail. Different organizations and situations require varying levels of leadership involvement. For example, I know of one small company that takes a day to share the leadership team's strategy with the employees and field their questions, and then the executive team gets back to business, leaving the executors of the strategy to figure out the details on their own. The decision to not develop a tactical plan is still a tactic. Since you have the

50,000-foot view, the responsibility to determine the type and amount of detail is yours.

The seemingly simple decision of determining tactical details has a huge impact on outcomes. Take, for instance, the results achieved by television contestants during *Oprah's Big Give*,[24] a 2008 Harpo Productions special reality series, where seven contestants were given $100,000 each and instructed to give as much of the money away as they could within twenty-four hours. The contestants were given identical tools—cash, car, cell phone, and rules—yet their outcomes varied drastically. Why? Because Oprah's only "tactics"—in addition to the lump sum of money and the time frame—were limited to caps on the amount that could be dispensed to a single recipient, $500, or at a single location, $10,000. Left to their own devices, the contestants generated widely varied outcomes: one contestant gave away $8,000 at an autobody repair shop while another dispensed $30,000 worth of appliances and electronics to people living in poverty. One contestant was eliminated after getting lost driving, which hindered her ability to give away money to those in need. Overall, *Oprah's Big Give* was a success in bringing awareness to the countless people who live in need, yet the overall message to you in terms of Tactics is, if you want to control the predictability and reliability of your outcomes, you must address the details of Tactics in ways that are appropriate for each situation.

Tactics must fulfill five requirements. Use this checklist as you finalize the details of Tactics as a way of keeping your tactical plan on track:

- *Tactics must be detailed and specific.* Specify person(s), group(s), department(s), or outsider(s) who will perform each action, and whether they will need to act as a cross-functional group. When people know what their roles and responsibilities are, morale tends to be higher, plans move forward more smoothly and in the right direction, and you become trusted as someone who can lead others to predictable, reliable outcomes. Plus, you avoid negative issues such as product recalls, bad publicity, injuries, and legal action.
- *Tactics should highlight interdependencies and chronology.* Explain what activities within the process must be completed before other activities can begin. Reveal where some actions rely on others interdependently so that resources like working capital, equipment and supplies, and labor are available when needed. Because tactical plans often involve cross-functional activities and responsibilities, bring in vendors, customers, consultants, and others to gain valuable input.

- *Keep your tactical details reasonably flexible.* Tactics' details must be flexible enough to accommodate new ideas or changing circumstances that might arise unexpectedly, and at the same time be rigid enough to achieve the Desired Outcome depending on the environment. You'd want the Tactics provided to a nuclear reactor operator to be very specific, whereas you might have a looser list of Tactics for your floor sales staff to sell baby furniture. Later in the chapter you'll learn more new tools to enable you to build flexibility into your Tactics.

- *Tactics must be appropriately matched to the skill levels of the executors.* The details must be outlined with the executors in mind—managers versus front-liners, skilled versus unskilled—to ensure that they are realistic and appropriate for the job at hand and that they match the skill levels and knowledge of the executors.

- *Tactics must adhere to the 51% Rule.* Tactics must be *perceived* as achievable by the people who will execute them. Otherwise, executors are unlikely to act or to give a project their all. The 51% Rule says that *executors must believe that they have at least a 51% chance of achieving success with your Tactics in order for the plan to work.* If they can't buy in because the success of the plan *seems* unrealistic, then the quest to fulfill the Strategy is doomed from the start.

When you've completed this phase, review your Tactics to be sure that they will still point your organization in the direction of your Desired Outcome. The time, effort, and money you've spent so far and that you will continue to spend as more people become involved should support the Strategy and Desired Outcome.

PHASE V: ADDRESS EXECUTION

The Execution phase is another important difference between Basic Strategizing and the CST Model that will assuredly help improve your outcomes. My research has shown that in Basic Strategizing, execution is usually lumped into the tactical phase and is either referred to as "execution" or "tactics," with little to no distinction made between the two when planning.

Pause for a moment and let that last sentence sink in; Tactics and Execution are two different and separate phases of planning. Yet when I tell this to decision makers, many of them tell me that they never have considered them to be so, and they find that this slight shift in vocabulary has immediately opened their eyes to reasons why some of their past plans failed to yield the results they had expected.

Before you write off this distinction as one of semantics only, be aware that I'm not just talking about words here. I'm going to be making some very clear points about the role that you must fulfill at each phase of the planning process in order to make better plans than you have in the past. So, whether you're a leader who takes an out-of-sight, out-of-mind approach to execution or one who has previously revered execution as the champion of greatness, *the Execution-related activities you engage in at the 50,000-foot level are different than those of your tactical people, meaning you are responsible for two sets of Execution-related actions: one for you as a leader/planner and another for people who are executing plans.* For now, our focus will be on ensuring that you build into your plans the most appropriate tools, structures, systems, knowledge, and authority so that whoever ends up executing them will be able to do so optimally. (Later, I will go into the second and separate role of Execution that every planner must fulfill.)

The achievement of a Desired Outcome is dependent on how well leadership performs the previous phases in the strategizing process. One of the beauties of the CST Model is that it slows you down and ensures that you don't jump to Execution before you've adequately completed the phases that give Execution the proper foundation that it needs.

> *Execution is an essential and distinct step in the strategic-planning process. When Execution isn't addressed properly, the entire strategizing process is compromised.*

Another important aspect of Execution is determining who will execute Tactics. Obviously, the structure and circumstances of your organization dictate your selection of executors. If you're part of a large organization, you may be accustomed to seeing top decision makers assigning others to act as executors. If your organization is a smaller establishment, you might find yourself executing Tactics or you may select other people to execute Tactics, depending on the staffing available to you. In either situation, you are still ultimately responsible for tracking Execution and guiding its progress.

Furthermore, there is another type of Execution that occurs in the CST Model, and it has *nothing to do with executing the Tactics*. This second type of Execution is called "Execution of strategizing," and it is performed strictly by the leader. Execution of strategizing does not occur in the Execution phase;

instead, it occurs in the previous four thinking-related phases—Desired Outcome, Strategy, Macro Tactics, and Tactics—as you perform, or execute, these phases. Let's take a look at the two types of Execution, and discuss your role within each of them.

- EXECUTION OF TACTICS: Occurs in the Execution phase and is performed by the executors. The people involved in the Execution of Tactics are those who carry out the Tactics. These people may be frontline personnel or members of your management team. Depending on the size and needs of your organization, you may or may not be involved in the actual Execution of the Tactics. In most cases, you will not execute the Tactics, but you must guide the people who do.
- EXECUTION OF STRATEGIZING: Occurs in the first four phases of the CST Model (Desired Outcome, Strategy, Macro Tactics, Tactics) and is performed by the decision maker. In Enterprise Thinking, you—the decision maker who is paid to think—perform a specific type of leadership Execution when you carry out the first four phases of the CST Model.

Example thread

Here's how the two types of Execution play out in our going-on-vacation example.

- *EXECUTION OF TACTICS:* When you purchase your airline ticket, pack your suitcase, drive to the airport, board your plane, check into your hotel, and follow your itinerary, you (and your fellow travelers) are executing the Tactics of your vacation.
- *EXECUTION OF STRATEGIZING:* When you were planning your vacation— from Desired Outcome to Strategy to Macro Tactics, and then finally Tactics—you were executing the strategizing. And if you had decided to buy into a guided-tour vacation, the Execution of strategizing would have also become a shared endeavor between you and the organizers of the tour company. You would decide how to get to the airport, what to pack, etc. But the other details of the trip, those you experience once you reach the tour group—where you sleep, when and where you stop to eat, the schedule of sightseeing, etc.—would have been handled by the tour company.

At this point, what you need to be thinking about is how you have a choice to be tactical or strategic. Because you're paid to think, you understand that your greatest value to your organization is to be strategic, which occurs by

Execution of strategizing. This is how you continually make decisions that move your organization forward in the direction of its Desired Outcome. If you're involved in an organization where you must be tactical—Execution of Tactics—that's okay, as long as you realize that your primary role is to be strategic, *and that you don't let tactical activities consume your days to the point where the strategic responsibilities suffer.* If you've ever felt like you're just keeping up and have little time to think, you've already experienced this condition.

Okay, so let's say that you've handed off the Tactics to those who are executing them. What should you be looking for, and what should you be doing? First, look for the sign that your Tactics are solid and realistic. The sign is when you see that everyone, from top leadership all the way down to the front line, can place the "road map" of Tactics in front of them and follow it daily rather than putting it on a shelf to collect dust. Tactics that are out of sight are no more useful than a grocery list that's been left on your kitchen counter. Then, be careful not to do what many leaders do, especially those in senior management, and assume that since Execution is someone else's job, then following the plan is someone else's responsibility, too. Open the plan, place it on *your* desk, and follow it daily, because the outcome still rests on your shoulders. You will learn how to follow the Tactics and monitor progress in Part III of this chapter, Managing Your Priorities.

The benefit of using a structured strategic-thinking process like the CST Model is that you keep your organization focused on activities that matter most. That's because from the very beginning, every decision and activity is connected to your Desired Outcome. Then, every subsequent phase is performed to reach that Desired Outcome.

Solving the Right Challenges by Asking the Right Questions: Redefining

Before you set out on any endeavor, you have to be sure that you're headed in the right direction and have your eye on the right target. Simply doing all the right things without first addressing the right challenges and opportunities dooms your success before you ever get started. Unfortunately, decision makers everywhere are taking the path to futility, because they don't have an actual *process* that improves their ability to think, so they're taking a chance on asking the wrong questions rather than assuredly asking the right ones.

Years ago, when a U.S. retailer, its decision makers were perplexed when the retailing giant's sales of popular laundry detergents didn't take off. The detergents were hot sellers in other markets, but they were being ignored in this new locale. As executives faced the challenge of nearly nonexistent detergent sales, they began to ask questions. However, they had to be careful what they asked, because the types of questions they asked and the assumptions they made would ultimately steer the future of detergent sales in different directions.

For instance, "What would it take to sell these brands of detergents to this market?" is different than, "What would it take to offer products that consumers want?" Further research into the culture and consumer behavior revealed that most Chinese citizens did not own automatic washers and driers, thus eliminating the need for the glut of detergents sitting idle on store shelves. Had decision makers asked only how to push the type of product they were accustomed to selling, they would have ended up with disappointing and costly results. But because they asked a better question that focused on what the consumer wanted, they were able to adjust their product offerings to be in alignment with the needs of the consumer.

Asking better questions—whether you're addressing personnel, systems, operations, vendors, products, or other challenges related to different aspects of your organization—will lead to better decisions and solutions. One way to ensure that you're asking better questions is to use a process like the one you're about to learn here.

Have you personally ever examined how you think? On occasion I'll meet someone who says they have a thinking process, but when they describe it, it's usually not a formal or structured process, nor is it something that is shared with the rest of his or her staff as an overall standard for creating Strategy.

If you wanted to solve your biggest challenge right now, what would you do? Do you currently have a process or sequential technique for solving your challenges? Most leaders have never even considered the possibility that such a process even exists, so I'd like us to try something together. Ask yourself, What is the biggest challenge I face today?

Write this challenge in one sentence on a sheet of paper, and do so clearly enough that if someone else were to look at it, they would understand what your challenge is. Now stop for a moment and think about how you would typically go about solving this challenge. If you've never followed a stepped process for addressing your challenges, this may be the first time you're aware that such a process even exists. The one that you are about to learn is called Redefining.

Redefining is a tool leaders and managers use to always find a better way to discover new competitive mega-advantages by identifying true challenges, problems, and opportunities.

Each day, you're constantly asking a whirlwind of questions about your work: How do I expand my business into new markets? How do I motivate Jane and her group of volunteers to work more independently? Is there a way to sell my idea to my VP so that my project will be approved? Asking questions is both a natural and essential first step to improving your organization.

But asking is not enough. You must be sure that you're asking the *right* questions and addressing your *real* challenges, which are challenges in and of themselves. Ironically, however, there are very few tools in the world that help individuals identify the right questions. In fact, most tools you'd consider to be tools to help you think are only data-gathering devices—the thinking process is still up to you. An example would be the SWOT analysis.

Redefining is a tool that will always help you come up with a better solution than the one you might have developed otherwise, because when you ask the right questions (which are *better* questions), you make better decisions that lead to improved outcomes. Even a slight improvement, like a 1% increase in sales for a company like Turner, GE, or Hyundai could create massive returns.

Asking better questions increases your chances of creating better outcomes.

Redefining came to be a decision-making tool after examining 1) my methodologies for distinguishing true challenges from their imposters (assumptions, symptoms, solutions, etc.) and 2) the process of steps for solving those challenges. My consulting clients who have learned Redefining have been able to use it reliably and to teach it to others in their organizations and their lives. In essence, Redefining is a nine-step thinking process of sequential questions and micro jumps in thought so that people can duplicate it and share it with others to address actual challenges rather than symptoms of them. Earlier I suggested that you imagine how much improvement you would see in your organization if everyone made just a single better decision each day. Just picture the momentum you can generate if everyone is asking the *right* questions before they decide.

Redefining can be an involved process, so I am presenting it to you here in three steps as a way of enabling you to make rapid sense of it and be able to apply it immediately. These three steps are (1) develop your Challenge Statement, (2) reframe your Challenge Statement to a Should Statement, and (3) convert your Should Statement into a What Would It Take . . . challenge to solve.

Before we address the particulars of Redefining, here are three points (which are different than the three steps of Redefining) to consider as you work through the process.

One: Always begin by addressing a *present challenge* and not a goal, because goals are future-oriented targets that originate from challenges. Google's founders saw a challenge in accessing data online and sought to solve it with the goal of developing a search engine. If you want to provide clean water to an African community, that goal is rooted in the challenge that villagers are getting sick from impure water. For some, the goal to become wealthy is rooted in the challenge of wanting a better lifestyle or needing to erase a past hurt of feeling unaccepted by others.

Two: Follow the steps precisely, without shortcuts, so that you come up with your actual challenge rather than imposters like assumptions, solutions, or symptoms that will derail you. Precision during Redefining is important, as Joe Geizeman of Searcy, Arkansas, will attest. He likens the right question you discover (by adhering to the Redefining steps) to uncovering the actual question you had to answer in a tricky math problem when you were back in school. The teacher would often hint, "Make sure you answer the right question." If you read through the details in the math problem too quickly, you decreased the likelihood that you would be answering the right question. Life and life's challenges are typically not cut and dry, and what seems real and right on the surface is often anything but.

Three: Be sure to use the word "challenge" rather than a negative word like "problem" to remove subjectivity and any emotional obstacles that can distract you. Both a problem and an opportunity can be a challenge, and if you're having an issue with an opportunity, then you want to be able to include it in Redefining.

The Redefining Process in Action

The majority of leaders and managers that I have worked with are bright and hardworking. But few of them—including those who think they have a challenge-solving process—actually have a concrete methodology for approaching and solving their challenges. Redefining is unlike any tool you've ever used, and you'll love how you can expend less energy and take fewer risks than you have in the past. With Redefining, you will find that the time spent up front thinking through what you're really trying to accomplish ensures that you're focusing your organization on solving the most appropriate real challenge at the time, which will ultimately deliver back to you unimaginable rewards.

So let's get started. Take a look at Figure 3.4, which outlines the steps of the Redefining process. The steps are essential to converting your challenge into a forward-focused directive called your What Would It Take . . .® (WWIT) question. Notice, too, that once again you have a cyclone. Taking the time to think about your options within each step plays an important role in Redefining, just as it did in the Cyclonic Strategic Thinking (CST) Model.

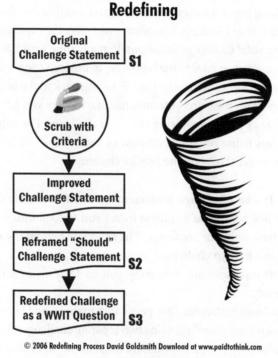

Redefining

© 2006 Redefining Process David Goldsmith Download at www.paidtothink.com

Figure 3.4—Redefining

Step 1: Develop Your Challenge Statement

In this step, your objective is to develop a single statement that explains your true challenge: your Challenge Statement (CS). Coming up with a Challenge Statement might sound simple at first, but in reality we're often unaware that our true challenges are hidden in underlying challenges, perceptions, assumptions, or solutions. Often, we assume we're focusing on our challenges, when we're unknowingly spinning our wheels on a host of misdirected statements. Step 1 contains a process in and of itself where you will write your CS, then scrub it against specific criteria to ensure that it is your actual challenge. When you emerge from this step, you will have a clear and valid Challenge Statement.

Begin by writing down your biggest challenge as a one-sentence statement. This single sentence forces you to be clear about your real challenge. Take out a piece of paper and try it right now. Notice that your mind will immediately and cyclonically race to find the right words. Once you are satisfied with your Challenge Statement (CS), scrub it against the following six criteria to determine if the challenge you think you should be addressing is an actual challenge and that it is the right one to address at this time.

The scrubbing process forces you to ask questions that you may not otherwise have asked. *Your Challenge Statement must meet the requirements of each criterion to be a valid Challenge Statement.* If at any time your CS fails to meet a criterion, you must *go back to the beginning of this step* (don't just return to the previous criterion), and rewrite the CS. Going back to the beginning is an extremely important measure; you can't just start where you left off or you'll steer yourself away from uncovering your true challenge. I've witnessed challenge statements being rewritten upward of twenty-four different times as someone tries to get clarity on the precise challenge.

Criterion 1: The Challenge Statement must address only one challenge. The first scrub you'll address forces you to look into your CS to see if you have only one challenge. The rationale behind the criteria is that you can't fix two challenges simultaneously, since each challenge demands its own solution, requiring you to solve them individually and differently.

The Challenge Statement, "My pants are too short, *and* I need to be in San Francisco tomorrow," contains two separate challenges that require separate solutions. The pants will have to go to the tailor, and the travel plans will have to be discussed with your travel agent. If, however, you mean that you need your pants tailored in time to bring them to San Francisco with you, then you need to refine the CS to say just that.

Catch yourself making dual challenge statements like, "Our sales are down *and* our engineers are not creating new products fast enough." One way to flag a CS that contains more than one challenge is to be on the lookout for diverters; these are words or symbols that veer you away from meeting the criteria.

Diverters for Criterion 1 include words like "and," "but," and "or" and symbols like commas, semicolons, or periods. These indicate that you have more than one challenge in your CS and that you must modify the CS before proceeding.

Criterion 2: The Challenge Statement must be in the present tense. Let your mind rest on the fact that you can't fix yesterday, you can only create tomorrow. And since you can't go back in time, your present actions and decisions must be put to their best use now. Translated in terms of Redefining, this means that you must be sure you're addressing a current challenge and not a past challenge. If you're familiar with basic accounting and financial statements, think of this criterion as a snapshot of your condition as it is happening in real time right now.

Say that you own a furniture store, and your customer calls you complaining that the couch your firm delivered to her has a broken armrest. You're likely to offer a set of options to remedy a manufacturer's defect, like free repair or replacement. But if while reviewing her delivery slip you learn that your customer received her couch three years ago instead of eight hours ago, you are likely to approach the challenge differently, since the disrepair could have been caused from excessive abuse or neglect by the customer.

Diverters for Criterion 2 include words that focus on the past or future, such as "was," "didn't," "won't," "hadn't" as well as words that hint at a past disappointment—"always" and "never"—or a future desire—"wish" and "want."

Criterion 3: The Challenge Statement must be a problem or opportunity rather than a solution. As obvious as this criterion sounds, you can't solve a solution. People often think they have identified a challenge when in fact they're focused on a solution. Already they're headed off in a wrong direction that will ultimately deliver disappointing (maybe even devastating) outcomes.

For example, what would you do if you saw that your sales were down by 14%? Many decision makers fall into that "get busy" trap and jump immediately to stating their challenge as, "My sales people need more sales training." However, that statement could be inaccurate, because it contains a *solution* for building sales volume through your sales force, when in fact, you don't know that the sales force is the actual challenge. What if the true reason for dipping sales has nothing to do with your sales personnel? Maybe your products are out of date and customers are buying new-and-improved products from competitors or most orders come in through your website, and it hasn't functioned properly recently? More sales training won't fix these causes, so be sure the statement is not a solution.

Diverters for Criterion 3 are words or phrases that could be perfectly okay in a CS as long as they're not used in the context of offering solutions, such as when you say you need more and better "quality," "service," "money/capital," or "staff/manpower." These are all solutions. If you focus on solutions, you're limiting your options for Strategy and Macro Tactics.

Criterion 4: The Challenge Statement should contain facts that are verifiable. You can't solve a challenge that doesn't exist, and trying to do so will just create a new list of challenges.

If you state that shrinkage (theft) in your warehouse is at 14%, verify that figure before proceeding, because if you find the number to be 33% or 1%, the solutions are drastically different for each situation. At 33%, you may call the police to investigate, but if numbers are off by 1%, you may assert that you don't have a shrinkage challenge and address another more pressing issue.

Diverters for Criterion 4 tend to be words that indicate an extreme condition, such as "everyone," "no one," "always," "never," and so on. If you find yourself using these types of words, see if you're speaking from emotion that has caused you to draw nonfactual conclusions.

Criterion 5: The Challenge Statement's assumptions must be valid. You can't fix a true challenge while you're focused on non-challenges. Assumptions can be invalid, and invalid assumptions will distract you and eat up resources, steering your organization away from solutions and into more challenges and crises.

Let's consider for a moment that you want to address the challenge of obesity. You come up with a CS that "Fast-food restaurants make people obese." This CS is an assumption. Yes, fast-food restaurants offer menu items that are high in fat and sugar, but they also give consumers healthful choices like bottled water, scrambled eggs, and salads with grilled chicken. By assuming that the fault lies with the restaurant, you're already heading off course, because the choices that people make about the food they consume is what makes them obese.

Furthermore, who you are makes a difference in how you address this obesity challenge. If you're a community health commissioner, your focus might be on reducing obesity, which requires you to expand your scope of options beyond only fast-food restaurants to other possible factors and conditions: Are healthy alternatives available? Are people making poor menu choices? Is this a challenge for restaurants or for mothers of young children? If you're a fast-food executive, your focus might be on your stock value and the market, which requires you to address public perception and find out what consumers want so that you can give it to them: Is the media portraying fast foods negatively? Are all consumers of fast-food restaurants obese? Are sales or public image actually at risk?

A military hospital's administrator originally stated, "Our patients in the emergency room area aren't being treated quickly enough." My first question to him was, "*All* of your patients?" After scrubbing several revisions of his Challenge Statement, he realized that his statement was inaccurate—the inadequate treatment time did not apply to all patients throughout the entire emergency room—and that only *one area*, a triage area for extreme emergency services, was failing to treat patients quickly enough. The administrator went back to the beginning of the Redefining process and rewrote his CS: "Patients in triage are taking more than twenty-two minutes to service." Notice the clarity of the CS. Knowing that the entire emergency room was operating well and that only the triage patients needed faster attention, he now had a more manageable challenge to solve. That's the power of the scrubbing process.

Diverters for Criterion 5 are not always as easy to flag, but you can start by challenging your own views about people, any stereotypes you have, and any problems that you've had in the past that might lead you to jump to unfair or untrue conclusions. Look for words like "always," "never," "need," "lack," and so on to see if you're making exaggerated assumptions, too.

Criterion 6: The Challenge Statement must be essential to your Desired Outcome. Don't waste your time, money, and other resources on endeavors that don't support your Desired Outcome; focus instead on where they can produce the best returns.

How would you typically solve the challenge, My office manager is grouchy? Perhaps you would allow for more time off, put another person on the phone to handle complaints, or take a number of other measures to either cheer this manager up or keep her from having direct contact with customers. But now look at the Challenge Statement in terms of your organization's Desired Outcome. When you observe the challenge from a big-picture perspective, you might realize that the manager's mood isn't really your challenge. (I bet you can think of a few grouchy people who are fantastic at what they do.)

From the 50,000-foot view, you see that your Desired Outcome is to retain your current customer base while growing that base by 30% this year. Now look back at the CS about the office manager within this larger context and consider your Goldsmith Productivity Principle (GPP). Before addressing the human factor, assess the systems and structures in place to see how they factor into the situation. Perhaps you lost two longtime customers in one week due to conflicts they had with your office manager, but upon further observation, you realize that your current order-entry system has been dropping orders. The ailing system had a negative impact on the office manager, overloading her and disrupting her ability to service customers properly. Your revised CS becomes: "Our order-entry system drops two out of every 1,000 orders." This CS is current, accurate, and pertains to one issue. In reality, now even your office manager can contribute to finding a solution.

If you had not scrubbed your challenge against this criterion, you may have addressed the human factor in your GPP and fired the office manager or reassigned her duties to keep her away from customers. You would never have uncovered the faulty order-entry system, which was your true challenge, and may not have realized your error until months later, at which time you might have been kicking yourself for firing a valuable employee.

Diverters for Criterion 6 are statements about annoyances, assumptions, petty matters, or nonessential issues that have little or nothing to do with fulfilling your Desired Outcome. Every so often, remind yourself to elevate your perspective to 50,000 feet before you attempt to identify your challenge.

One final diverter that you need to watch for in all six scrubbing steps is that of blame. It is very easy to quickly point a finger at individuals, departments, business units, colleagues, and others and jump to a rapid conclusion that they're to blame for the challenge you're facing. Typically, blame will divert you in the opposite direction of solutions, so when you find yourself pointing the finger of blame, take a moment to ask, What can I do to transform this situation? The simple shift in focus back onto yourself is often enough to pull the CS back into alignment, because you are the impetus behind the GPP's systems and structures that drive events to occur.

These six scrubbing criteria refine your Challenge Statement into a more on-target baseline for use in the next two steps of Redefining. Fine-tuning your statement may seem laborious at times, especially if you continually have to go back to the beginning of this step and find that you're having to come up with a half a dozen Challenge Statements or taking days or weeks to arrive at your true challenge, but scrubbing is worth the effort. The more on-target you are at this point, the more on-target your final question will be, leading to better decisions and outcomes.

Step 2: Reframe the Refined Challenge Statement into a Should Statement

Now that you've developed an improved and more precise Challenge Statement, you will morph the CS into a Should Statement (SS). The SS is your way of moving beyond the challenge and toward an ideal solution. For instance, if your CS was, "We are losing five volunteers per month," your SS might be, "We should be gaining fifteen volunteers per month."

Here's how it works. Begin the reframing process by determining your optimum condition, called the Positive Opposite Ultimate End (+OUE). (Yes, it's a mouthful.) This is a wordsmithing exercise that adds clarity to your Challenge Statement by shifting your focus away from a past challenge and into the future.

POSITIVE OPPOSITE ULTIMATE END (+OUE) SAMPLES

Use the following list as a guide in determining your +OUE. These opposing and ultimate conditions will help you come up with your Should Statement.

POSITIVE OPPOSITE	ULTIMATE END
Low-High	ultimate customer
Slow-Fast	ultimate vendor
Weak-Strong	ultimate economy
Fat-Thin	ultimate footprint
Down-Up	ultimate industry
Don't-Do	ultimate power
Can't-Do	ultimate duration
Lose-Win	ultimate shape
Losing-Keeping	ultimate capacity

Playing the role of wordsmith here marks a crucial turning point between sitting with a challenge and establishing your best WWIT question. It pulls your focus away from the challenge and directs it toward a solution. So if your challenge begins with, "We are losing _____," then selecting words to focus your thoughts on its solution will likely produce a sentence beginning with, "We *should be* winning _____." A Challenge Statement that talks about prices declining would convert to a Should Statement that says prices *should be* rising. This is what is meant by positive opposite (+O).

At the same time, you're looking for your optimum condition, which is the ultimate end (UE). Who is your ultimate customer or ultimate vendor? What would be the ultimate footprint for your organization, the ultimate power demands, the ultimate size, weight, direction, and efficiency? While the answers to these types of questions can seem obvious at first glance, I can't tell you how often I've experienced smart decision makers struggling to clearly define their ultimate customer when I've asked them to do so. You might need to give your UE some thought, and while you do, try to broaden your scope, because in a case like defining the ultimate customer, custom- ers are not always external buyers, but may be different types of groups altogether.

For instance, Wilma Grant, the publications and telecommunications manager within the document-management office of the United States Supreme Court delivers her services to internal "customers" working in the legislative arm of government and to those involved in legal cases. Once you've considered the various ultimate factors that are pertinent to your situation, then you reword the sentence to include what you believe to be a combination of them. Figuring out your UE may take a lot of Cyclonic Time.

In the scrubbing criterion about assumptions, you read about the hos- pital administrator who wanted to reduce the average twenty-two-minute wait time for emergency triage patients. In this second step of Redefining, he determined that his +OUE was to treat patients within a fourteen-minute window of time. From this +OUE, his SS became, "We should treat all tri- age patients in fourteen or fewer minutes." Depending on your Challenge Statement, your UE might be the ultimate power supply, the ultimate cus- tomer, the ultimate duration, the ultimate profitability, or the ultimate size.

Step 3: Convert the Should Statement into a Redefined What Would It Take . . . ® (WWIT) Question

In this final step, you will convert your Should Statement into a future- oriented question that prepares your mind to find solutions. This end ques- tion is called What Would It Take . . .® (WWIT), and its purpose is to move your focus from rearview thinking—where you can unknowingly hold yourself back and clutter your mind with negativity such as blame, regret, and other emotions that surface from asking "why"—and place your focus where it can do the most good, which is onto the road of possible solutions and opportunities that stretches out ahead of you.

You can ask WWIT to find the best Strategy for reaching your Desired Outcome, to gather and assess your best options for Macro Tactics, to finalize the details of your Tactics, and to select the people who will execute Tactics. But asking "What would it take . . . ?" is not a question restricted to strategizing activities. You can ask WWIT to solve *any* challenge you face, and in this section, you will learn how to come up with your best WWIT question.

One note before we proceed: If you ask WWIT, and you find that you or your people are asking more questions rather than offering answers, then you've missed something during this or a previous step of Redefining, and you have to go back and rework your statements. A WWIT question should energize and mobilize individuals and groups, pushing them forward by generating the right mental activity within them. You'll know when you have a great WWIT question, because it causes a myriad of potential Strategies, Macro Tactics, and Tactics to begin to flood your mind, making you want to solve it right then and there.

Shifting Your Focus from the PAST and TODAY to the FUTURE

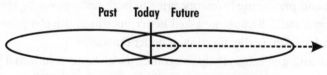

© 2010 David Goldsmith All Rights Reserved Download at www.paidtothink.com

Figure 3.5—Shifting Your Focus from the Past and Today to the Future

Notice that you're asking "What would it take . . . ?" instead of following the natural tendency to ask why this condition exists. It's important to begin your search for solutions by asking *what*, rather than *why*, because *why* doesn't matter. At this point in the Redefining process, asking *why* is like trying to drive your car forward by staring into the rearview mirror.

Say that you crash your car and your car is towed to a repair shop. Does the mechanic need to know who was driving the car, where you were driving, the conditions on the road, or why you did what you did? Not really. Besides pure curiosity, a mechanic's questions are typically not about the past; they need to be about the future solution. Therefore, he might ask, "What would it take to restore this car to perfect, working, showroom condition?" Notice how the WWIT statement now directs his focus onto a Positive Opposite Ultimate End question.

Redefining enabled the president of a farm-equipment manufacturing facility and his company to gain this forward-moving perspective and solve their true challenge. For years he wrestled with how to stop his firm from receiving complaints and canceled orders, especially during his busy season. When he tried Redefining, the president initially thought his challenge was, "We can't find the right staff." But if you remember our scrubbing criteria, you know that "finding the right staff"—like finding money or capital—is a solution, not a challenge. After scrubbing the challenge again and again and again against the criteria, the president came up with, "We missed 14% of our order ship dates." Now he was addressing a specific condition that was happening in the present. Upon further scrubbing, he found that the CS was still not clear enough, because his bigger challenge actually was his larger orders.

Finally, he ended up with the Redefined question, What would it take to ship all orders totaling more than $25,000 within four business days? (This was not a goal, however. His question was derived from Redefining and thinking with solid research behind his thinking.) This Redefined question became a rallying call for the entire organization. He and his staff solved the challenge by installing a new computerized inventory-software system to balance inventory, outsourcing production at peak production-overflow times, and preloading inventory prior to peak seasons, *not* by searching for the "right staff." Because he asked better questions, the company president pointed his firm in the direction of better outcomes.

Redefining will always help you come up with better solutions if you follow the steps precisely, take the time to develop a refined Challenge Statement, reframe it into a specific Should Statement based on your optimal +OUE, and shift your thinking onto future-focused answers using a solid WWIT question.

Redefining is valuable in numerous ways. It strengthens your decision making by giving you a uniform approach to thinking and step-by-step activities to ensure your focus is where it needs to be at any given time. A uniform approach to thinking with step-by-step activities allows for (1) easy transferability from you to others, multiplying the effects of better decision making by more people, and (2) increased collaboration and cohesiveness through more streamlined thinking and a shared vocabulary. Think of the impact on your organization when stakeholders like managers, front-liners, allies, and board members improve their decision making at all levels. In addition, realize that you can enjoy the value of Redefining outside the realm of professional use; this tool works at home and in social and community venues to solve challenges everywhere.

Using Redefining to Determine Desired Outcomes and Innovative Solutions

Redefining can be used to establish one's Desired Outcome as well as it can to uncover solutions to challenges. Once the mind begins to ask, "What do I really want," the many uses of Redefining become instantly available, ranging from strategic direction to Tactics and beyond the scope of strategizing altogether.

Here's an example: The college bookstore industry,[25] composed of university-owned bookstores and outsourced vendors that gross between $2 million and $50 million annually, attributes declining profitability in recent years to three factors: (1) loss of market share to online competitors, (2) erosion of sales due to students sharing and gaining access to book content via technology, and (3) fast-rising operating costs, including inventory and personnel.

Decision makers considered their challenge to be, "Our profits are declining." Without understanding Redefining, they have focused on, "What would it take to increase profits?"

An approach to increasing bookstore sales has been to expand product lines to include novelties, garments, school supplies, nonacademic books, computer software, food, and more. But although this Tactic increased gross sales, it also increased operating expenses of infrastructure and personnel to manage the additional products and services, so profit margins remained compressed.

Let's go to 50,000 feet to look for the real challenge. Consider how a bookstore is just one element of a larger educational picture of students and researchers, professors and their departments, and college/university administrators.

By examining the value of each bookstore within this larger context, a bookstore manager and university-wide management (deans, directors, and the president) can now think beyond product sales and profitability margins. In fact, the original purpose of bookstores was to support academic activities through textbooks and learning materials, not to serve as revenue centers. Like college libraries and maintenance departments, bookstores were not originated to generate profits; student tuition, alumni donations, and research grants provided revenue.

What if management were to consider the outcome of the bookstore resuming its original strategic role within the scope of the entire university, which had nothing at all to do with generating a profit center, and instead had its focus on education? The WWIT of the past would have been stated as, "What would it take to assist the university in delivering the highest educational experience it can for students?" This different question focuses the bookstore on different solutions.

[continues on page 86]

[continued from previous page]

If the bookstore manager were to work in conjunction with the biology department's dean and professors to provide the most up-to-date technologies for studying biology, and their efforts raised the university's national ranking from thirty-sixth to seventh, the outcomes might include: better professors want to teach at their school, the university receives more money in grants and endowments, and more students enroll in their programs. Multiply fifty additional students by an annual tuition of $30,000, and already the bookstore has contributed $1.5 million per year or $6 million over the course of four years.

Now apply the same alliance throughout an entire university's many departments, and the contribution could add up to hundreds of millions of dollars in revenue over several years.

Redefining can be used to define your Desired Outcome to help you uncover the answer to "What do I really want?" As you use the tool of Redefining in your own life, you will realize that you are progressively asking different and stronger questions than you have asked in the past, and as a result, you can do anything from aligning yourself with more appropriate Desired Outcome to generating better and more innovative opportunities for yourself and those around you.

The Critical Path Method (CPM) Chart: A Tool for Building Superior Tactical Plans

The ways in which you assemble, describe, and organize Tactics ultimately impacts how successfully they are executed. Your new tool, the Critical Path Method (CPM) chart, helps you achieve your Desired Outcome by ensuring that Tactics are detailed, specific, and flexible and that they highlight interdependencies and chronology.

Imagine that you and two other decision makers, Yuri and Louisa, are making arrangements to move a business unit into a new office building. Yuri is responsible for packing and moving furniture, files, and equipment. Louisa is working with a contractor and zoning administrators to prepare the new space. You are coordinating operations to keep the business unit functional throughout the moving process. How successful will this move be if you, Yuri, and Louisa work in silos rather than together? How operational will your business unit remain if Yuri moves furniture before Louisa's contractor builds out the workspace?

Use a CPM chart to coordinate the elements of any project, initiative, new product launch, purchase, etc., so that all parties involved in its success work harmoniously together and perform chronological or functionally interdependent activities in their most efficient orders.

Traditionally, the CPM chart has come from the marketing and project-management disciplines. If you've never worked in those areas, you were probably never exposed to this valuable tool. The CPM chart you will learn here is an abbreviated version of its original form—I have modified it for you to use as a universal leadership tool.

How to Build and Use a CPM Chart

The CPM chart is a project-planning tool[26] that DuPont, the U.S. Navy, General Dynamics, and Britain's Central Electricity Generating Board, all developed almost simultaneously in the 1950s to analyze and manage task sequences in large projects and manufacturing processes over time. Its developers believed that a visual and mathematical tool would enable leaders to plan, schedule, and evaluate their projects, increasing the chances that projects would be completed on time and on budget. Today, the tool's uses have evolved and expanded to include research, marketing, software development, new-product development, and more.

CPM charts can be quite in-depth and involved. The basic model consists of four steps: (1) determine your project, (2) complete the Activity-Planning Chart, (3) transfer activities to the Critical Path, and (4) share the completed CPM chart with others.

Step 1: Determine Your Project

You will learn more about selecting and developing the right projects for your organization in the next section of this chapter. For now, let's say that you've decided to create a new website.

Step 2: Complete the Activity-Planning Chart

Using an Activity-Planning Chart like the one shown in Figure 3.6, list all the activities that will need to be completed during the course of your project. In the Designation column, designate a letter to each activity. In the far right column, Time (Weeks), record the estimated time needed to complete each activity.

CPM Activity-Planning Chart

Activity	Designation	Immediate Predecessor	Time (Weeks)
Assess your needs	A	None	1
Search for Web developer	B	A	2
Outline site	C	B	1
Write and submit copy	D	C	2
Create and submit images	E	C	1
Test prototype	F	D, E	2
Launch	G	F	1

Figure 3.6—CPM Activity-Planning Chart

Now you will place the activities in chronological order by first determining each activity's immediate predecessor and placing that predecessor's corresponding letter in the Immediate Predecessor column. For example, "Search for Web developer (B)" must occur immediately prior to "Outline site (C)." Therefore, in the Immediate Predecessor column, add the letter B for "Outline site (C)." Activities that are independent may still have an immediate predecessor, such as "Write and submit copy (D)" and "Create and submit images (E)." In addition, independent activities can be done simultaneously, which tightens up your timeline, as you will see in the next step.

Although the big picture is usually clear to the leader, now others in the group can begin to see a snapshot-like overview, too.

Step 3: Transfer Activities to a Critical Path

Based on data from your Activity-Planning Chart, transfer each activity into a visual time diagram, called a Critical Path, to see how long the project will take to complete.

Begin by making a circle for each activity. Within each circle, write an activity's letter and its time in weeks. Position the circles in chronological order. The visual representation serves as a road map of activities and gives you four pieces of valuable information.

CPM Generic Path

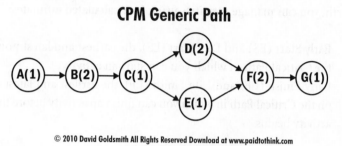

Figure 3.7—CPM Generic Path

First, you see that the entire project will take nine weeks to accomplish. Calculate completion time by adding up the activities with the longest path, or what's called the Critical Path.

Look at activities D and E in Figure 3.8. D takes one week more to complete than does E, so account for the longest-time activity in your overall calculation. D and E appear on the Critical Path as they do, because they are independent activities and don't rely on one another to be completed. Remember that you can perform these activities simultaneously to complete the project sooner.

CPM with Critical Path

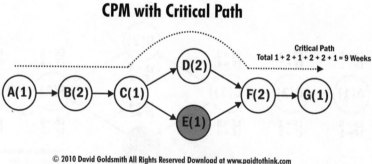

Figure 3.8—CPM with Critical Path

Second, you can view the entire plan to catch whether you have missed any activities. One missing activity can throw off the people who are executing a project and can extend the project's timeline.

Third, the visual helps you to calculate where you can best allocate your resources. If someone suggests that they can complete activity E faster by paying $200 more to a designer, you can immediately see that there's no benefit in assigning $200 to activity E, because activity D is still two weeks long. On the other hand, if someone says that you can pay $200 to complete activity D a week earlier, you may determine that the results of this expenditure are worthwhile.

Fourth, you can manage activities using four calculated estimates:

- Early Start (ES) and Late Start (LS), the earliest and latest points on the Critical Path in which you can start an activity;
- Early Finish (EF) and Late Finish (LF), the earliest and latest points on the Critical Path in which you can finish an activity before the next activity begins.

People make these types of calculations mentally all the time. You estimate the latest you can leave for an appointment and still get there on time. If you're planning to paint your house, you need to know the latest you can start in order to complete the project before the weather gets too cold. If you're hosting an outdoor wedding in May and need to order a tent in January, you can place the order in September (ES) or December (LS) and still get it on the date you need it. The beauty of the CPM chart is that as your projects become more detailed and more people become involved in them, you can plan, monitor, and execute with more accuracy.

CPM with Early Start Late Start

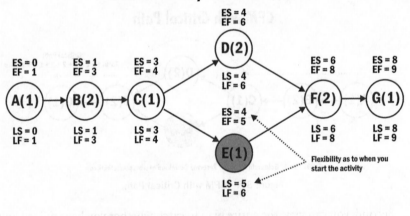

Figure 3.9—CPM with Early Start Late Start

The number next to ES, EF, LS, and LF indicates the week number of the *project.*

- You can start activity A on day zero (right now) and the earliest you can finish the activity is in one week.

- The earliest you can start B is in one week, because you have to wait one week for the previous activity to be accomplished. The earliest you can finish is two weeks later. The person thinking through the project knows it will take two weeks.
- The earliest you can start C is at week three, and the earliest you can finish is week four.
- D and E are a little complicated. The earliest you can start D is week four and finish two weeks later at week six. E can be started at week four, but it will only take one week and be completed at week five. This is called slack time.
- F's Early Start is week six, and its Early Finish is week eight.
- G's Early Start is week eight, and its Early Finish is week nine.

Let's do the same for LS and LF, since it reflects what is happening whenever you work with others, whether you realize it or not. You and those you work with are making these calculations, but everyone needs to be accurate and to understand the numbers. One mistake could cause the whole project to be late or to be much more costly to complete on time.

Think about the time someone forgot to purchase supplies and as a result you had to place an emergency order and incur a large overnight freight bill. Perhaps you paid more per unit, because your preferred vendor couldn't fill the order quickly enough. The person who didn't purchase the supplies on time may not have understood your timeline math, although you may have assumed they did.

In the diagram, the latest you can start the project is day zero, and the latest you can finish the project is at the end of week one. Do this and you're on target to complete the project in nine weeks.

- B's LS is week one, and LF is week three (given the two weeks necessary to complete the project.)
- C's LS is week three and LF is week four.
- Here's where the diagram becomes a little more complex. You must start D at its LS time of four weeks to finish at the LF time at six weeks if you are to keep the project moving.
- E, on the other hand, has some slack time. The latest you can start E is week five, so you have a week to slack off. However, you must start E no later than week five, because you must finish it by week six.
- F and G then follow the same pattern.

When changes occur, a CPM chart helps you to make better time and resource allocation adjustments. If the nine-week website-design schedule needed to be shortened to seven weeks, a look at the critical path could help you consider assigning two people to activity F (test prototype) to shave a week off this activity and shorten the project's overall completion time.

Step 4: Share the Completed CPM Chart with Others

Share the CPM chart with others and discuss their responsibilities. Some organizations create subcharts, but the main CPM chart puts everyone on the same page about the project.

When members of a chapter of the American Society for Training and Development used a CPM chart to plan their local conference, they needed only three committee members instead of their usual ten to complete the process. They ended up with more time to market the event, tripling the number of attendees and selling out booth space—setting up was completed two days prior to the conference, and unlike past years, no one was running around at the last minute tying up loose ends, picking up banners, or creating badges. All items were ordered well in advance, projects were bid out to gain better pricing, and merchandise was shipped directly to the conference venue, saving time and money.

Some people post their CPM chart online and update it regularly as activities are completed. This activity keeps participants in the know and puts the Escalator Theory in motion—just as riders on an escalator tend to walk the last few steps to the top, as teams near the end of their projects, they tend to work faster and harder to complete them.

Now that you have some new planning tools and concepts to add to your Enterprise Thinking toolkit, let's take a look at how you can propel your organization to make positive transformations through the selection, allocation, and completion of projects.

■ ■ ■

[PART II]
TRANSFORMING WITH PROJECTS

IN THE MID-1980s, our company was a vendor to many retail stores in the central region of New York State. Most of the time, our customers came to our shop to place their orders, but occasionally, I would go on sales calls at customers' places of business. I remember one such call in particular, a half-hour drive to meet with the elderly owner of a Woolworth's five-and-dime store. Upon arrival, I told him that I hadn't been able to locate his phone number in our files or in the phone book to confirm the meeting time in advance. It was then that I learned why; he didn't have a phone. You see, my customer wasn't too happy one afternoon back in the 1950s when his "salesgirls" got too chatty on the phone with their girlfriends while they were supposed to be minding the store. So he removed the phone and never replaced it. If I needed to reach him, he said, then I could call his daughter's house, and if I caught her at home, she could track him down and deliver my message to him. That's when I gave him a tip that earned a little chuckle:

"The phone is not a fad."

Imagine trying to do business today without e-mail capabilities, bar-code packaging, integrated logistics systems, or computers and software programs. How effectively would your organization function using thirty-year-old methodologies and equipment against competitors who had the benefits of state-of-the-art tools? This brings us to an important point about the role of leadership, which is that leaders must continually select and implement projects that keep their organizations upgraded, updated, and poised to compete and win.

Staying competitive isn't a concept restricted to businesses looking for profits; all organizations compete for something. Nonprofits must win grants and funding, military organizations must win recruits and battles, universities must win good professors and new students, and the list goes on. Regardless of your industry or sector, you need projects to advance your organization and keep it strong.

Projects are the essential building blocks of all organizations. If you were to continue to do what you're doing today, your organization would be the same tomorrow, and everyone knows that a static entity will eventually be consumed by the changeable world around it. So what does this mean to you in terms of developing plans? It means that as you are strategizing, it is essential that you select (as some of your Macro Tactics) the types of projects that will best improve your products, services, and operations to keep your organization—at the very least—on par with its competitors and, ideally, positioned to survive, grow, and succeed in the months and years ahead.

The types of projects you must select and stay on top of in order to improve operational efficiencies run a wide gamut of possibilities. Some projects improve hiring processes so that they suitably match job candidates to an organization's needs and culture. Other projects can result in superior employee-benefits packages that retain talented and skilled employees. You may also implement projects to maintain and improve your office or production space, or to install and utilize new technologies and equipment. Projects are how you maintain a functionally healthy organization.

Then there are the types of projects that develop and improve products and services, too. They also help organizations to market and "sell" to their current and prospective patrons, move into new markets, secure funding, attract staffing, and remain strong.

Without projects, organizations don't evolve, and everything stays pretty much the same, which is not a good thing in an ever-changing world. So the logical question every decision maker should be asking is, How do I determine which projects to work on?

By the end of Part II of this chapter, you will have a better answer to that question. I will show you how projects factor into the development of plans, and more specifically, at which stage in the CST Model you select projects to reach Desired Outcome. In addition, you will pick up new tools for selecting your best projects and overseeing them to their successive completions.

How Projects Fit into the CST Model

To begin, let's take a look at how projects fit into Strategizing and the CST Model. You have established your Desired Outcome, created your Strategy, and now you must select the best Macro Tactics—which can be projects—to support your Desired Outcome.

Your responsibilities are twofold, here: (1) you must select the project(s) that will best support your Strategy, and (2) you must ensure that those projects come to a successful conclusion, whatever that may mean to your organization and your particular circumstances.

First and foremost, realize that your relationship to projects is different than that of the professional project manager who actually manages projects. While your responsibility is to select and oversee projects, a project manager is in the trenches managing the day-to-day work of moving the project forward. That means if your organization has sixteen projects in progress at one time, you maintain a 50,000-foot view of all of them while a project manager applies specialized skills to manage one or two or a multitude of those projects to completion. This chapter section will provide you with several new tools to effectively handle project selection and implementation.

The Tools Leaders Use to Fulfill Their Project-Related Roles

The first tool, the Project Evaluation Chart, enables you to select the best and right projects to move your organization forward. This tool gives you an opportunity to list all your prospective projects on one chart, assign a rating score to each project based on specific criteria, and through a side-by-side comparison, select the project that creates best transformative improvement for your organization at a given time. Once you give this tool a try, you may likely find that you're one of the many leaders who have never compared your projects to each other in such a comprehensive way.

When the creative director of TBWA/Colombia, Santiago Johnson, used this tool, he (like many other decision makers) experienced an eye-opening realization. "I always thought that I selected the right projects, but after learning this approach, I realized I was wrong. This simple approach slowed down my decision making and forced me to spend a little more time thinking. The surprise to me was that what I thought needed to be accomplished were not the best decisions to implement." In Johnson's situation, the two projects that he ultimately selected were completely different than the two he had originally thought were best.

The second tool helps you to better oversee and guide projects. It is a modified version of the Critical Path Method (CPM) chart that will keep the projects you have selected on target with Strategy and in alignment with Desired Outcome. This tool ensures that all involved parties—from the executive office where Strategy is created to the frontline office where Tactics are executed—know how to fulfill their responsibilities and meet deadlines, and can communicate effectively to ensure the success of projects. The CPM chart is a big-picture tool that enables you to coordinate many resources successfully at once.

In addition to these two major tools, you will also learn about proven methods you can use to avoid overloading your staff, overspending your resources, and fizzling out your projects before they reach their targeted conclusions.

Doing the Right Projects: Differentiate or Die

How can you determine that one project is better than another? How do you choose between developing a new product to gain market share and upgrading your phone system so that it doesn't drop important calls with your customers? The foundation underlying the answers to these questions must always relate to how your organization distinguishes itself from others around it.

This section will give you an effective way of making these determinations by showing you how to continually differentiate your organization from others like it. Understanding how three factors—Order Qualifiers, Order Winners, and Forecasted Winners—influence your organization's health today is the starting point for making decisions and selecting projects that will affect your organization's growth and survival tomorrow.

ORDER QUALIFIERS AND ORDER WINNERS

Nearly thirty years ago, manufacturing strategist and London Business School professor Terry Hill[27] introduced the terms Order Qualifiers and Order Winners to manufacturers.Whether you're in manufacturing or not, you can use these concepts as universal tools to determine the right projects for your organization.

Hill defined Order Qualifiers as the basic characteristics that a company, product, or service need in order to compete in the marketplace. Order Qualifiers are typically no more than entry-level requirements you must meet in order to play in your arena and keep on par with your competitors—requirements that enable you to start up a new organization, launch a new project, or maintain status quo within an existing group or organization. However, Order Qualifiers are not stand-out features that motivate people—such as buyers, investors, volunteers, allies, etc.—to choose your organization or its offerings over the competition.

Hill's Order Winners, on the other hand, are unique and distinguishing attributes that give organizations an edge over their competitors. They are specific characteristics that earn sales, memberships, grants, and other desired returns. Order Winners—typically determined by an industry or sector—can be patents, certifications, education, locations, compositions, designs, equipment, apps, or licenses, or they can be attributes like advanced-tread tires that prevent skidding better than traditional tires, employee-benefits plans that attract higher-caliber managers to an organization's leadership team, or six-hour brochure-printing services as compared to competitors' three-day turnaround times.

Every leader, from those in government to those in small business, must be sure they understand whether their offerings are Order Qualifiers or Order Winners. Take, for instance, how government and economic development officials in two separate cities—Effingham,[27] Illinois, and Fort Wayne, Indiana—handled the same opportunity. Years ago, executives at the paint company Sherwin Williams entertained the option of either staying in Effingham or moving operations to Fort Wayne. Both cities provided Order Qualifiers, but officials in Effingham offered a $2.5 million economic incentives package and a $3 million break from the company's landlord to tip the scales in their favor and win Sherwin Williams away from Fort Wayne. An important truth about Order Winners is that they are organic and ever changing, so you want to be a proactive game changer like Effingham.

But having Order Winners today doesn't mean your work is done.

HOW ORDER WINNERS REGRESS AND BECOME ORDER QUALIFIERS

Even when your organization is functioning optimally, you should be asking, What would it take to specifically differentiate ourselves? and, How are we losing by a nose? That's because Order Winners regress and become Order Qualifiers as competitors catch up. When this regression happens, organizations and products lose, sometimes merely by a nose, especially when leaders assume they're offering Order Winners when in fact, they are nothing more than Order Qualifiers. At one time, not long ago, offering an app on a phone was an Order Winner, but now there's not a smartphone without apps. Apps have become Order Qualifiers. When a pharmaceutical patent runs out, generics can slide in and capture market share. Rethink the attributes that you assume are Order Winners; perhaps they've become Order Qualifiers.

One way to play the game is to create new Order Winners by working on projects that develop new products and services in your market—these might be entirely new products, new efficiencies that improve services, or improved iterations of both. That's just what Thomas Mathes, former general manager of the Muse Hotel in Manhattan did when he wanted to elevate his hotel's three-star status to four stars. Mathes knew that the change would require him and his staff to adopt the Order Qualifiers of other four-star establishments and then determine the Order Winners unique to the Muse, a Kimpton Hotel. Mathes spearheaded the spectacular makeover in Times Square, New York City, with upgraded furniture, décor, and linens, a new bar, and a grand facelift to the hotel's lobby and lounge to craft a boutique "personality" and a differentiated image from competitors, as well as completely redesigned guest rooms.

These Order Winners, which also included upgraded systems (Goldsmith Productivity Principle [GPP]) within Kimpton's regional offices throughout the United States, made the job easier for Kimpton's northeast regional director of revenue Steven Rubin, boosting his unit's ability to book the hotel to capacity and at full-price rates during 2009 while competitors were slashing prices, shutting off floors, and suffering with 30%–50% vacancy rates. Order Winners don't just come from improvements to the actual products and services you offer to customers. They also arise from internal improvements that empower your staffers to do their jobs better. And the positive effects of improvements can be long-lasting Order Winners, too.

In 2010, Rubin reported that market growth for hotels in general was at 15%, but the Muse was blowing those numbers away at an impressive growth rate of 24.2%—and the American economy still wasn't in recovery at the time.

To keep ahead of other players in your space, you must be proactive, and that means being on the lookout for regressing Order Winners while simultaneously developing tomorrow's Order Winners with some degree of certainty. That's why I've taken Hill's two concepts a step further, developing spinoff that will give you the power of pro-activity called Forecasted Winners.

FORECASTED WINNERS

Your greatest advantage comes from being prepared for the future. To do so, you need ways in which you can identify and create tomorrow's Order Winners by monitoring trends, patterns, and cycles. Forecasted Winners are projected Order Winners that you anticipate will edge out competitors in the future. What you're trying to do is extend your thinking and planning forward to become better prepared for the future and to give your organization advantages over the competition. Although the activities of the Learning and Forecasting categories of Enterprise Thinking will help you do this, there are some simple ways in which you can develop Forecasted Winners.

You want to continually keep pace with the evolution of your own industry, and the resources and methodologies that you have today are bound to be different in tomorrow's world. However, right now you can read journals and industry-specific blogs, magazines, and newsletters, or watch videos about significant breakthroughs. Stay conscious of the fact that your competitors may not be who you think they are, meaning that they aren't just entities that offer the same products and services that you offer. They could be any source that detracts buyers, members, or patrons from your organization, pulls key talent and recruits from your payroll, displaces your offerings, or makes what you do or offer no longer desirable.

That said, you need to stay abreast of technologies and innovations outside your industry that threaten your position in the marketplace. If you stay focused on only industry-specific happenings, you won't gain the advantages of seeing other evolutions on the horizon that can affect your organization or even displace it and its offerings altogether. To open your mental blinders and extend the scope and depth of potential threats and opportunities, subscribe to intelligent content that focus on all areas of life, including business, science, arts, society, nature, politics, etc.

Also learn about global business markets that increasingly present new and unexpected competitors or indicators of future change. You can do this by reading books that offer a perspective on global change, like Tom Friedman's[29] book *The World Is Flat*, by scanning major newsfeeds and international newspapers, and by travelling globally. Try to always be on the lookout for today's landscape changers.

Gather competitive intelligence. In Chapter 9, you will learn a proven technique to collect, assemble, interpret, and distribute information about your customers, competitors, products, threats, and opportunities to extrapolate tomorrow's Order Winners.

Many smart leaders understand the priceless value that comes from tapping great minds and surrounding themselves with intelligent people with whom they can bounce around ideas and create new knowledge. Look to surround yourself with progressive thinkers from inside and outside your organization. These people might be members of your current management team, respected colleagues, mentors, or others who have come across your life's path who can offer a mutually beneficial exchange of ideas.

The key to developing Forecasted Winners with staying power is to pull your thinking out of the present and project it into the future. One recommendation that I've made to clients is they pull together a group of future-oriented thinkers that are not tied to the constraints of the business. Consider conducting "future meetings," perhaps once a month, where you meet with these innovative thinkers to discuss the "what ifs," connect the dots from data that has been collected by your organization or group members, and to ideate. This group should be made up of individuals who think differently, from any discipline and any role. Members should not be selected by their title (since title often doesn't necessarily equate with talent), only by their ability to innovatively project their thinking forward and offer potential solutions and ideas that will help your organization. You may have to go out and find thinkers, since groups like the board of directors, who serve their existing purpose well, aren't necessarily wired for "what-if"–type thinking.

Using these tips, you are now ready to come up with differentiated reasons why people buy from your organization. I suggest that you come up with five reasons using the following exercise, aptly named the Five Reasons Why exercise.

Five Reasons Why: Standing Out from the Crowd in a World of Vanilla

One way to identify whether you've established differentiating Order Winners and Forecasted Winners is to try the Five Reasons Why exercise, where you list five reasons why someone would buy from or fund your organization over competing entities who are vying for those same dollars.

If you had to list the five reasons why people buy from (or join) your organization, would your reasons be much different than your competitors'? Superior quality, exceptional service, and competitive pricing might keep you in the game, but because they are mere Order Qualifiers, they will never differentiate you enough to guarantee the win.

During some of my past speaking engagements, I've asked audience members to try the Five Reasons Why exercise with the person sitting next to them. I ask one person to tell their partner five reasons why anyone would buy from them (join them, work for them, etc.). The second person writes these reasons on paper. After two minutes—a time frame that seems reasonable enough considering people should already know five Order Winners—the partners switch roles and repeat the exercise. When both partners have expressed their Order Winners, I select a volunteer from the audience to read his or her list to the entire group. The lessons learned from this activity typically surprise participants, who expect to hear very different answers from one another but instead hear strikingly similar responses regardless of the industries, sectors, geographies, and organizational sizes being represented in the room.

The usual Order Winners recited by the volunteer are nothing more than common Order Qualifiers such as "excellent service" and "high quality." Participants quickly realize that they could swap lists with just about anyone in the audience and the so-called Order Winners would work for their own organization, too. The takeaway here is that most leaders think they are taking action to differentiate their organizations from others in the marketplace, but in reality, they're not. Realize that this exercise doesn't need to be restricted to customers' reasons for buying from an organization; it can be used for different market segments, different talent, different locations, and for media, banks, stockholders, and more.

Finding that you don't have five differentiated reasons why people should choose your organization over another shouldn't discourage you. In fact, you should be motivated to take action. Here are four suggestions:

1. Say that you realize that you probably have at least five reasons but that you've never actually identified them clearly; take a little time to think about what they are and how to best articulate them to others.

2. On the other hand, you may have a clear understanding of your five reasons, but you may need to expand on them—enhance product features, speed up your service time, extend your office hours—to improve their strength.

3. Often people need to wordsmith their five reasons. "We have great scientists," is very different from, "Our scientists have secured 492 patents in the past 10 years." Who would you work with if you had to make a choice right now?

4. Or you may need to come up with new reasons altogether, taking one or both of the following routes. First, you can thoroughly examine your Order Winners, and if they truly differentiate your organization, put them on your list. Or, if you don't have clearly identifiable Order Winners, start selecting projects that will improve your organization's products and services or its internal operations so that you now have five solid reasons.

Knowing the five reasons and being able to express them well are how organizations win in all areas. And when you have five distinguishing reasons, you can also use them in your everyday conversations with others to sell yourself, your ideas, and your organization to all types of current and prospective stakeholders who play a role in the growth, development, and survival of the organization. For example, when vendors buy into your five reasons, they may have more confidence in your ability to succeed and be more willing to extend better credit terms and priority delivery times to your organization. When community government officials believe in your financial stability, they may offer hiring incentives, enabling you to hire the help you need and offer jobs to more citizens. And if you can offer five great reasons why a highly talented manager should join your organization instead of competing organizations, you can have more leverage in securing and retaining quality personnel.

It's your turn. List five reasons why anyone would want to conduct business with your organization, work in your department, attend your university, vote for you, etc. Does your list contain items such as great service, high quality, exceptional returns, "our people," and so on? Welcome to the club of "vanilla," where everything emits the same bland flavor. If you find that you have no unique Order Winners to differentiate your organization from the pack, go back to your list and rethink your advantages.

To gain a competitive edge, you must define your Order Winners with *specificity*. Stakeholders tend to react more positively to specific Order Winners: award-winning designs, deliveries made in four hours, 12% more revenue for clients, awards, ROI, 30% less energy, or 90% graduation rate. Play the role of wordsmith and carefully craft your pitch with specificity, such as, "We own seventeen unique patents for chemical processing that increase product strength by 22%." That's a statement you can call an Order Winner.

Once identified, Order Winners become your sales-force mantra, advertising edge, new-product-development rallying cry, hiring advantage, contract winners, and any other win-by-a-nose advantages over competitors. When you find the five Order Winners that separate your organization, group, or products from the pack, you're taking a step in the right direction. At the same time, realize that you constantly need to make improvements and be on the lookout for ways to develop new and better Order Winners, because once an Order Winner is not always an Order Winner, considering how they regress and eventually become Order Qualifiers.

You can perform this Five Reasons Why exercise on an organization-wide level, for a particular business unit, in a single department, or in venues internal and external to your organization, such as when you are applying for funding or trying to negotiate a deal with a vendor, ally, or customer.

Doing Projects Right: Directing Everyone toward the Desired Outcome

As a leader and manager, you have a great deal of influence over the people, systems, and resources of your organization, perhaps at times not fully understanding how you may be positively or negatively impacting outcomes. Before we get into the selection of projects, it's important to highlight some of the important nuances of projects that can have a large impact on the outcomes of your organization's efforts.

The Number of Projects One Person Can Work on Effectively

Your aim should be to assign projects to other managers on your team in a way that gains maximum productivity levels but doesn't overwhelm your people and outspend your resources. Overwhelming managers with too many projects jeopardizes the success of all their projects. This is a timeless challenge that is as true today as it was a hundred years ago. In their book *Revolutionizing Product Development*,[30] authors Steven Wheelwright and Kim Clark describe their quest to find the optimal number of simultaneous projects a person can handle well, using a study they performed on a precision equipment company they referred to PreQuip, Inc.

In 1989, PreQuip's management reviewed their product-development projects after a number of projects came in late, increased in budget, or weren't completed. The review confirmed management's suspicions that the firm had more projects in process than their resources could sustain. Calculations proved that PreQuip would need 300% more staff than it currently had on hand to complete the firm's thirty active projects and to do these projects right. And "right" is the crucial word.

The engineers should have been completing projects within a reasonable period of time, but they had more projects in house than they could realistically handle. The overload forced engineers into a type of juggling act where they would jump from one project to another just to keep them all alive. Thus, they weren't able to complete the projects in a timely fashion. The company's staff was already overwhelmed, and resources were stretched so thin that when a project needed extra resources, staff lacked the slack they needed to be able to pull from other projects.

Wheelwright and Clark referenced John Bennion's (Bain and Company) "canary cage approach"[31] to project planning that likened the consequences of thrusting too many projects onto the labor and resources of a company to stuffing too many canaries into the same cage. Once the optimal number of canaries that can thrive within the cage is exceeded, each new addition threatens the survival of not just one other canary but of *all* the other canaries, because all the canaries have less space and less food.

PreQuip's management team analyzed productivity of its engineers by isolating one engineer at a time and observing his or her performance. While you might assume that one engineer working on only one project and one project only would be very productive because the engineer is free from becoming distracted or overwhelmed, quite the opposite happens. Projects are not done in isolation, nor are they always linear. An engineer who needs a special part before proceeding on with a project may have to wait a full week for that part to arrive. Or, without a second project to work on, an engineer might get brain freeze or be so bored that they lose focus and produce nothing during that week. If other engineers are involved, and they also sit idle, the standstill in productivity multiplies.

Management then decided to test productivity levels by adding a second project to each engineer's workload and observed what engineers did during slack time. Management found that engineers could shift attention to their second projects. The mental shift from one project to another stimulated focus, enhancing and accelerating productivity.

Number of Projects Assigned Concurrently to a Single Engineer

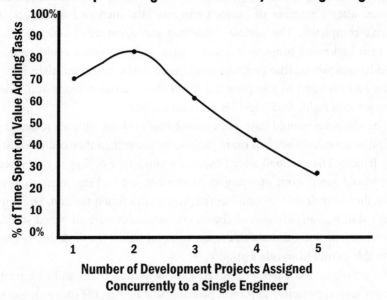

Number of Development Projects Assigned Concurrently to a Single Engineer

Value added tasks - transforming development, ideation, improvements
Non-value added tasks - coordinating, remembering, waiting, tracking down information, reworking, transporting, etc.

Reprinted with permission from Revolutionizing Product Development - Stevens C. Wheelwright and Kim B Clark

Figure 3.10—Number of Projects Assigned Concurrently to a Single Engineer

When management added a third project to engineers' workloads, all three projects' productivity levels suffered. Juggling the schedules, activities, and mental attention of three projects was deemed overload. And if you put yourself in the shoes of the engineers, the overload makes sense. It would be easy to pull out a project that you're personally working on, find that you don't have the supplies or the involvement of others at the time to move forward, jump to a second project, then to a third, and lose track of where you stood on the first project's progress.

Too many projects overload people with too many thoughts, details, and activities, which ultimately leads to decreased performance levels, like in an instance where an individual is working on a spreadsheet, becomes interrupted, loses his or her train of thought, and makes a small error in calculation that could snowball into disastrous results later.

The PreQuip managers concluded:

> *Two projects is the optimum number of projects that one person can work on effectively at a single time.*

I've coined this conclusion the Two-Project Rule, and it is an important one to heed, because people can burn out just like machines do. Just as you wouldn't run a piece of equipment at full bore for fear of potentially burning out its engine, you also wouldn't want to ruin a good worker by overburdening them with more work than they can handle.

Note: A project is not to be confused with a task. Rather, it is a series of grouped activities that change the face of the organization. When the project is done, the organization is different than it was before. Be sure that everyone on board understands that this is what you mean when you use the word "project," because many people refer to projects as any type of activity they perform. This misuse of the word leads to confusion and oftentimes the wasteful allocation of resources on activities that will not move the organization forward.

Two Roles of Leadership in Managing Projects

Before we get into this next section, I want to address a few issues regarding the Two-Project Rule. The first is a reiteration that every decision maker within an organization should be working on two projects at any given time that move the organization forward. Taking ownership of only two projects at one time should not be considered an ideal, either; it should be considered standard practice. Having said that, you may still be tempted to occasionally discount the Two-Project Rule. But understand that I'm not saying your entire organization should have only two projects in progress at any given time, only that an *individual* should be responsible for no more than two projects at once; nor am I telling you that a leader can't supervise many more projects than two.

Furthermore, you may need to remind yourself or others on your leadership team to distinguish between projects and the daily tasks of one's job. So if you're a manager and also play the role of an editor, the editing is not a project; it's your job. The restructuring of how you process projects internally would be a project.

Lastly, notice I say "managing projects," but I do not say "project management." The first term is a function of your role as a leader, and the second is a specific discipline where people often gain certification; we are not discussing the expert-level project manager in this chapter.

If you hold a leadership or managerial position, your first role in managing projects involves being personally responsible for managing (or sharing the management of) two projects and bringing them to a successful completion. All subordinate managers should be responsible for two projects at any given time as well.

If you are a senior manager who manages other leaders in your organization, then your second role takes place at the 50,000-foot perspective; you must perform three other project-related functions that will advance your organization: (1) select the right projects (in alignment with organizational Desired Outcomes), (2) assign the right leadership to manage those projects, and (3) guide managers as they bring those projects to completion. In addition, you must be conscious of the fact that you can overwhelm a manager if you violate the Two-Project Rule.

I realize that the Two-Project Rule may be a new concept for you, and that you may need a period of adaptation in order to pare down or complete a number of projects currently on your plate before you can strictly adhere to this rule.

One of the first steps to whittling down your number of projects to two is to list all the projects you currently have. Take a few days to ensure your list is complete. At this first stage, your list should contain only *your* projects, not those of your management team. Here's an account of an experience that a previous client had, which may help you as you make your transition.

I asked my client, Jim, the CEO of a 140-person service company, for a list of his projects—projects that were separate from those of his 18-person executive team. He alone had sixty-eight projects on his list. (Imagine the number of projects his firm's VPs, management team, and assistants had in totality!) Just making the list was an eye-opening experience for Jim, who immediately said, "No wonder nothing is getting done!"

Together, we assessed his list using a form called the Project Evaluation

Chart, a project-selection tool that you will learn about later in this chapter. We refined his list by eliminating items that weren't projects, such as daily tasks and activities associated with larger projects. With more than thirty projects still listed, we pared down the list again by removing any items that did not fit Jim's Strategy for his organization or where he could no longer see any value in continuing the project for a variety of reasons, and when we were finished, I then asked him, "If you could work on only one project and one project only, what would it be?" The question moved Jim to have to choose the one project that he determined would provide the greatest impact and highest value to his organization.

Jim wanted to focus on his organization-wide, custom software installation project that had stalled out. Already a year behind schedule, it hindered his firm's ability to initiate services to customers. Employees were frustrated knowing that they had to work with a system that didn't offer the upgrades and features that would help them do their jobs better and keep their organization ahead of its competition. However, I cautioned Jim not to work off hunches and guesses; he would need to fill out the Project Evaluation Chart to compare this project against others and to add objectivity to his decision.

After assessing ROI and impact, Jim concluded that this software project would indeed become Project #1. We assessed other projects, choosing his second "one and only project," and we identified it as Jim's Project #2. Now Jim had two valuable and realistically achievable projects that were *his own* to work on to completion.

The computer-system-installation project was back on track within weeks. Jim used his IT background to take charge, working personally with a tech expert in the Netherlands to knock off items on their punch list and prevent the project from dragging on for another estimated two years. He also created new project-planning maps tied to his history in the IT industry, addressed key concerns and obstacles between the firm and the vendor, secured concessions, and conducted their first test by month three. Within six months, the software was operational and its rewards were enormous, yet without having taken the time to think, he would have never selected this project.

Let's shift gears a bit. In addition to Jim's two projects, he was also responsible for assisting each member of his sixteen-person management team to list, evaluate, and select their two personally managed projects. If your role is like Jim's in that you are leading a group of leaders and managers, then you must oversee and guide your managers to success by allocating the right number of projects, assigning the right leaders to each project, and ensuring that all managers have adequate resources to do their jobs successfully.

Organizations have limits just like equipment does, but management seldom reviews them to prevent overload. Without limit indicators, you can pile too many projects onto yourself and others, so set the number of projects at two per person.

The Number of Projects a Group of People Can Work on Effectively

Your organizational resources are like the canaries in Bennion's canaries-in-the-cage concept. You must strike the right balance among assets like human labor, time, and capital to ensure that you're not taxing resources beyond their capabilities. With that in mind, let's look at how you can coordinate entire groups, which can become overwhelmed with projects, too, to make their best contributions to your organization.

Before we go into the details of this topic, I need you to be clear that we are *not* discussing the types of projects sold to customers, such as building-design projects developed by architects for sale to prospective home builders or advertising campaigns designed by ad agencies' creative departments to service their clients.

Our focus here is on the types of projects that leaders work on to specifically improve and transform their own organizations (or their products and services). For example, when a group of engineers work on installing a new intra-network, they are working on a project that improves their organization. Or, when a CEO develops a training program, she is working on a project that transforms her company.

How many of these types of projects are adequate for your team? Exactly how does the Two-Project Rule translate from individual leaders to an entire management group? The answer varies depending on your circumstances. So let's look at three project-limitation capacities—(1) Full Capacity, (2) Full Capacity with Shared Projects, and (3) Extended Capacity with Outsourced Projects—and do some simple math.

1. Full Capacity

Full Capacity is just a multiplication of the Two-Project Rule. Therefore, a six-person management group—five managers and you—has a Full Capacity limit of twelve projects. Simple enough.

FULL CAPACITY: (No shared projects)
6 people x 2 individual projects each = 12 projects

Full Capacity with No Shared Projects

- Every decision maker, including you, has the responsibility of two of their own projects.
- In this diagram, you can supervise, oversee, direct the projects of 5 other decision makers.
- This group's maximum amount of projects is 12. Each decision maker, including you, has 2 projects for a total of 12.

Figure 3.11—Full Capacity with No Shared Projects

If you head the group, Figure 3.11 is a visual illustration of how you play a dual role in ensuring that all twelve projects are completed properly. On one hand, you are overseeing the other managers and monitoring their progress on their ten of the projects. However, you do not play a hands-on role in these projects. You may meet with your five managers, answer their questions, offer guidance and direction, but they are responsible for the day-to-day management of their own two projects.

Keep in mind that *the two projects that belong to you typically have a wider-scoped impact on your managers or organization just because of your role.* For instance, your projects might include a monitoring program for a whole business unit or building an alliance that exponentially benefits the leadership team or the organization as a whole.

2. Full Capacity with Shared Projects

At one time or another, you are likely to face a situation where a single project requires the attention of more than one manager. For instance, Bob from IT will have to work with Lois in marketing to create and launch a new service on your website. In Figure 3.12, Full Capacity with Shared Projects, you and two of your managers each have your own two projects, but the three other managers each have a single project to man on their own (solo) as well as a single project that the three of them are sharing (shared). The shared project is equivalent to three separate projects joined into one. The shared project is defined as one project in name only but not in size and scope. In this variation, the maximum number of projects for the group is ten.

FULL CAPACITY WITH SHARED PROJECTS:

3 managers x 2 projects each	=	6 projects
3 managers x 1 solo project each	=	3 projects
3 managers sharing a single project	=	1 project
Total number of projects	=	*10 projects*

Full Capacity with Shared Projects

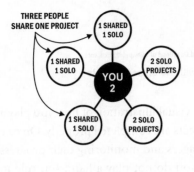

THREE PEOPLE SHARE ONE PROJECT

1 SHARED 1 SOLO

1 SHARED 1 SOLO

2 SOLO PROJECTS

YOU 2

1 SHARED 1 SOLO

2 SOLO PROJECTS

- Three team members have the same shared project to manage. The reasons may include the size and complexity, resources, etc. Your strategizing concludes the need for multiple individuals.
- In this diagram YOU can supervise, oversee, direct the projects as in the FULL CAPACITY illustration.
- The group has 10 projects in progress. Two individuals have 2 projects, three have a shared project and a solo project, and you have 2 projects.
- There are many variations of the shared projects illustration.

Figure 3.12—Full Capacity with Shared Projects

3. Extended Capacity with Outsourced Projects

Sometimes you recognize that an additional project, such as adding a new warehouse in Zurich, is so promising that it needs to be accomplished immediately, but all of your managers are already busy working on two projects. At other times, you may realize that doing certain projects in house will outstrip the capacities of your current managers' skills, knowledge bases, free time, or budgets. Do not break the Two-Project Rule. Instead, outsource the project to someone externally or to a temporary internal staffer who is not part of the management team.

Let's say that you determine that an outsourced facility-management company is a more appropriate match to handle a maintenance issue or that a private shipping company can come in to handle shipping needs so that current projects stay on track for their targeted completion dates. When you outsource, the underlying rationale is that you are (in theory) hiring other management to take care of your projects. You need energy supplied to your office, so you hire the electric company. You need a brochure printed, so you hire another team of managers to take care of the details. The expectation is that they are managing their organizations well.

Take a look at the diagram Full Capacity with Outsourcing (Figure 3.13). In this diagram, you have outsourced three additional projects to external project managers.

EXTENDED CAPACITY WITH OUTSOURCED PROJECTS:

6 internal managers x 2 projects each	=	12	projects
3 external managers x 1 project each	=	3	projects
Total number of projects	=	*15*	*projects*

Full Capacity with Outsourcing

- You can outsource as many projects as you feel you can allocate time to oversee. Leaders often forget that outsourcing requires reviews, meetings, negotiations, and tracking, to keep vendors on target or to integrate the vendor's and supplier's projects with your internal operations.
- This group's maximum amount of projects is unlimited. Each decision maker, including you, has 2 projects for a total of 12, however, you may have as many outsourced vendors as you can support or need.

Figure 3.13—Full Capacity with Outsourcing

Keep in mind that not all projects are worthy of this last option. Take some time to consider the costs (of all your resources) in soliciting the help of an outsourced manager, because if you can't justify the added expense, then the project might not be all that promising. You will soon learn how to use the Project Evaluation Chart to make determinations like this one.

Although you are already better positioned to prevent overwhelming your team, make better use of your organization's resources, and increase the odds that the projects you select will come to completion, you will gain even more tools here.

Tools for Transforming with Projects

Now that you have some important project-related concepts under your belt, let's get into the details of four new tools that will help you select the right projects, assign the best leaders to those projects, and keep everyone focused on their projects to completion:

- **Project Evaluation Chart.** We'll begin with the Project Evaluation Chart. This tool is a means of laying out all your project options in front of you in a format that allows you to compare projects and select them based on factors such as priority and impact rather than on what you think or guess is important.
- **Project Assignment Worksheet.** Then you will learn the Project Assignment Worksheet. Once you have determined what projects your organization is going to work on, the chart helps you to determine who will take on those projects as their own.
- **Parallel Project Tracks.** Another tool, the Parallel Project Tracks, keeps you (and anyone else who is responsible for handling two projects) focused on their projects until completion. The Parallel Project Tracks ensure that no one takes on additional projects until they have completed their two prioritized projects.
- **Critical Path Method (CPM) Chart.** Finally, you will learn how to use the Critical Path Method (CPM) chart, a modified tool that will help you and your managers organize projects and plans, keep those who need to be in the know on the same page, and ensure that interdependent activities within a project or plan stay on track in terms of time and budget.

How to Select the Best Projects: The Project Evaluation Chart

On the surface, it can seem quite simple, but figuring out the next best project to tackle can be a challenge. For many decision makers, this process is more intuitive than analytical, which can be a risky way to make important determinations. You can probably recall a project (your own or someone else's) that was originally touted as great, but then it never got off the ground or didn't pan out right in the end. One of the probable reasons for fizzles like these is that leadership doesn't have a tool like the Project Evaluation Chart, which enables them to line up their projects in one place and compare them to each other using apples-to-apples criteria. As a result, projects are selected based on assumptions but not concrete data. Once you learn about the Project Evaluation Chart, you are likely to see how tempted you can be to move forward too quickly, before spending enough time thinking about the choices you have and all the factors that affect those choices.

The Project Evaluation Chart enables you to evaluate opportunities of various projects in order to increase the accuracy of selecting the right project. By weighing the impact of each project, you are more likely to select the project that delivers the highest value. This is another tool that slows you down enough to Cyclonically Think through your options fully up front, making it possible for you to move faster later on, because you avoid wasted time and resources and lessen the risk that a project will fail, which is all part of the Economics of Thinking.

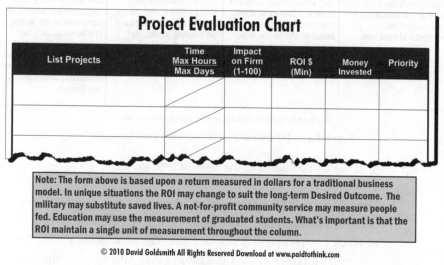

Project Evaluation Chart

List Projects	Time Max Hours Max Days	Impact on Firm (1-100)	ROI $ (Min)	Money Invested	Priority

Note: The form above is based upon a return measured in dollars for a traditional business model. In unique situations the ROI may change to suit the long-term Desired Outcome. The military may substitute saved lives. A not-for-profit community service may measure people fed. Education may use the measurement of graduated students. What's important is that the ROI maintain a single unit of measurement throughout the column.

Figure 3.14—Project Evaluation Chart

Here's how the Project Evaluation Chart works:

Step 1: Start by listing all of the projects you currently have in house and any projects that you've been thinking about that might move your organization forward. Don't feel bad if you find that you have a high number of projects; it's a common situation and one that you're correcting with this exercise.

Step 2: Eliminate nonprojects and "imposters" like obvious tasks (closing a sale, filling out an employee-evaluation form, or calling a vendor) that masquerade as projects, and subactivities of a project you've already listed. Removing this clutter will help you think more clearly. While you clear items off your list, you may also notice that some large projects will have subprojects that stand on their own as true projects, and that's fine, too.

Here's a handy chart to help you eliminate nonprojects from your list:

Differentiating Projects from Their Imposters

How to discern a project from a task and identify tasks masquerading as projects

Project	Imposter Type 1 Everyday Tasks & Tactics	Imposter Type 2 Large Tasks & Tactics	Imposter Type 3 Organizational Tasks
A true project is any set of related activities that, upon completion, will transform the face of an organization. Think of projects as organizational building blocks, much like those that make up the foundation and framework of an architectural structure.	While tasks and Tactics are essential to the growth and sustenance of an organization, neither will single-handedly transform the organization the way that a project will. Consider tasks and Tactics as either activities that are needed to maintain status quo or as supporting elements within the larger context of a project.	Often misperceived as projects due to their large size or potentially high consumption of resources, large tasks and Tactics will no more transform the face of an organization than their smaller counterparts. If the tasks and Tactics are not building blocks that transform the organization, they are not projects.	Origin and labeling are not criteria for determining whether a group of activities are projects or not. A high-level decision maker in a corporate office can request that a set of tasks labeled "project" be performed by the manager of a business unit, but unless those tasks fit the true definition of a project, they remain imposters and should be handled as tasks and Tactics.

Figure 3.15—Differentiating Projects from Their Imposters

Step 3: Fill in the four columns to the right of each project.

■ **Time Required (Max Hours/Max Days):** The first number represents the estimated maximum number of hours the project requires to reach completion if it's *done right*. The second number is the maximum number of days the project may take to be completed, which doesn't always correspond easily with the number of hours, because a project that appears to take twelve hours to complete, for example, may require three hours of attention this month and nine hours next month, so the total could be thirty-nine days. You have to allow for down time, such as ordering a software package, waiting for a machine to be available, or waiting for participants to return from a business trip.

■ **Impact:** Rate the project's potential effect on organizational performance; one means no effect, and one hundred represents a complete organization-wide transformation. *No two projects can have the same rating*, so you can't have two projects with an impact rating of 91. One project is always more impactful, even if by a nose, so do not assign the same impact number twice. This forces you to mentally weigh your options. Consider the big picture—finances, staffing, competitiveness, new products and services, strategies, organizational culture, marketplaces, etc.—when determining a project's impact.

- **ROI:** Estimate each project's *minimum* payoff or return on investment (ROI). This column is often the most difficult to fill in for a number of reasons. One reason is that individuals don't often think this way. Yet, all projects must have an ROI in one way or another, otherwise, why do them? Realize that this column can be challenging to complete for people who don't have access to certain information—quite often financial data—that is only available to certain leaders.

  ROI on the sample chart is based on financial returns, but depending on your organization, your ROI might be the number of students educated or the number of lives saved. What's important here is that the same ROI measure or unit of measure must be used for all projects. If your ROI is the number of hungry people you feed, then this ROI must be calculated for every other project on your list.

- **Money Invested:** This figure should include more than cash estimates: fixed overhead expenses, salaries, supplies, and so on. Say that you are responsible for creating a sales video, and you budget $12,000 to pay the videographer. Be sure that you also include the additional costs like the salaries of your staff members who have to set up all the props and write the script, and the CEO who has to fly from Toronto to Houston to be on set for the actual shooting. With all costs factored in, your final investment could climb to $40,000.

As you fill in your Project Evaluation Chart, *do not change the system by adding extra columns!* Too many columns overcomplicate the chart, threaten the accurate transferability of the tool, and present the risk that the columns will not give the necessary data. I have encountered too many intelligent leaders who thought they could change the columns, and every time they have added confusion and disrupted the chart's ability to serve them. The beauty of the four columns is that they are simple enough to work with, but underlying them is a complexity that will ultimately guide you to your best outcomes.

Most people can't fill in this chart without taking additional measures like researching, calling vendors, gathering data, making calculations, and redoing numbers upon further evaluation. Take your time and do this right. The creative director mentioned earlier in this chapter, Santiago Johnson, spent five weeks refining his Project Evaluation Chart to arrive at the two projects he originally hadn't assumed would be his best selections. But when you and your colleagues take the time to do this right, the outcomes are much better.

I foresee that in the future, leaders will have the advantage of using automated Project Evaluation Charts to ensure that data is more inclusive. These automated charts might be able to pull data from your financials, insert costing off the Web, compare organizational lists of projects, or have the intelligence to consider new products, patents, services, or other information that humans alone would not be able to collect as efficiently.

Finally, beware of overestimating outcomes, especially in the ROI column. The owner of a chain of restaurants in Manila thought that her ROI would be $600,000 on a particular project that costs $30,000. However, the research she performed to fill in the Project Evaluation Chart revealed that the actual ROI would be closer to $50,000. There were too many assumptions and not enough data, so her numbers were inflated. This is what can happen when you fall in love with your own ideas.

Once all the columns are completely filled in, you are prepared to move on to the next step. Watch out for the Fast Shooter mentality that may tempt you to believe that a Project Evaluation Chart with incomplete columns and missing numbers is good enough. Moving forward in such an instance tends to lead to errors in judgment that can snowball into costly mistakes later.

Step 4: Take an overall comparative view of your options and prioritize each project based on its data by numbering each project beginning with #1, then #2, #3, and so on. Do not get creative with your numbering system, as I have seen many people attempt to do over the years. In other words, if you've listed eight projects to compare, then simply rank them one through eight rather than playing games like, "I will prioritize my top three options as #1, #2, #3 on my 'High' list, then I will number these next three options as #1, #2, #3 on my 'Medium' list, and then I will rank these last two options as #1 and #2 on my 'Low' list." Keep it simple. The best way to get started is to ask yourself, If I could do only one project, which one would I choose? This is your highest priority item. Then go on to the next and so on until all of your projects have been prioritized.

In the past, you may have had to rely on your intuition to come up with the answer, but now you have better data and a side-by-side comparison of your options with which to work.

In the Project Evaluation Chart Example (Figure 3.16), Improve Workflow jumps out as the highest-ranking project, requiring up to sixty hours to complete and a maximum of $25,000 to implement. With its 98 impact rating, it will almost completely transform the organization and deliver an estimated ROI of $1 million. Although the New Software project costs slightly less and offers nearly the same ROI, its impact rating is lower.

Project Evaluation Chart Example

List Projects	Time Max Hours Max Days	Impact on Firm (1-100)	ROI $ (Min)	Money Invested	Priority
Move Office	300 / 30	72	$750K	$300K	3
Improve Workflow	60 / 54	98	$1M	$25K	1
Floor Redesign	100 / 21	68	$300K	$200K	4
New Software	50 / 8	75	$1M	$22K	2

Figure 3.16—Project Evaluation Chart Example

Even though, through use of the Project Evaluation Chart, we're trying to add objectivity to the selection process, a certain degree of subjectivity will always be present. That's because currently, no formula exists for calculating projects' priority, since every organization has unique factors that require subjective analysis. A military group may have a Desired Outcome where assigning a higher value to the impact of saving lives is more important. A small business may put more weight on money invested due to cash flow. And since subjectivity is present to some degree, be sure that you don't under think your options and their criteria. Give yourself enough Cyclonic Thinking Time to consider the depth of your options prior to mobilizing your people and other resources.

Looking back at our sample chart (Figure 3.16), you might need to initiate the project Move Office, but if the required investment of $300,000 exceeds your cash-flow capacity, you must be respectful of your limited amount of resources and capital and move it to a lower priority position. So in spite of there being no perfect formula for calculating priority, this chart will still help you do a better job than you would do without it, because it initiates the Economics of Thinking and highlights plusses and minuses that may have otherwise been overlooked. And that brings us to an important conclusion that you must always keep in mind when you're engaged in the selection process:

Sometimes, what appears to be your best move is not your best move.

Vlasios Lapatas, a partner at Maltezana Beach Hotel in Greece, had his own kind of aha moment while evaluating his list of projects (see Figure 3.17) in search of his next best move. For five weeks, Lapatas worked through the Project Evaluation Chart to prioritize his projects. (This is not a one-night tool.) His list contained seven projects until week five, when he added a POS System project.

Lapatas reviewed the rankings and determined that the Pool Bar placed first, and to his surprise, the POS System became his number-two priority based on its relatively low investment requirement and its 85 impact rating. For the first time, Lapatas was able to compare project options by their values, changing his entire way of thinking.

Project Evaluation Chart

List Projects	Time Max Hours Max Days	Impact on Firm (1-100)	ROI $ (Min)	Money	Priority
Pool Bar	100 / 40	80	48K	23K	1
POS System	24 / 20	87	7.2K	4.5K	2
Wellness Center	80 / 70	90	13K	25K	4
Restaurant Pergola	40 / 4	75	36K	14K	3
Hotel's Bus	16 / 14	50	18.8K	90K	6
Wireless Internet	24 / 10	70	1.2K	1.6K	5
Diving/Sea Center	180 / 150	85	38.6K	75K	7
Solar Panels	96 / 60	90	12.6K	110K	8

Figure 3.17—Project Evaluation Chart Extended

This exercise is eye opening for most leaders, not because it's rocket science, but because few leaders that I've worked with have ever listed their projects in one place for review and comparison, and many have a limited understanding of ROI or total investments, especially as they pertain to the entire organization. The Project Evaluation Chart prevents you from overloading other managers, ensures that staff is tied back to the Two-Project Rule, and that the projects your team works on accelerate the achievement of the Desired Outcome.

Long-Range Planning

The Project Evaluation Chart can be used for long-range planning as well as for selecting current day projects, and the process itself remains relatively similar in both situations. The main difference is that instead of listing the projects you would like to do presently, you list the projects you foresee doing in the future. Once you've read about ET Forecasting in Chapter 14, you'll have some new tools to help you jump mentally into the future and make projections about technologies, industries, policies, and so forth that might warrant the need for certain types of projects within your organization. Then you list the projects on your chart and proceed as you have done with the current-day project options.

By now, I'm sure you've already concluded that the Project Evaluation Chart and other tools of Enterprise Thinking can be used in limitless combinations to fulfill your role as a person who is paid to think. Consider the positive outcomes you can achieve by combining the Project Evaluation Chart with various Forecasting activities that you will learn about in Chapter 14. Once you have completed *Paid to Think,* you can return to portions of the book, like this one, and combine Forecasting with Strategizing by mentally mapping one project to another as if you were traveling on train tracks and had to link the completion of one track to the commencement of another.

Selecting the Right People for the Right Project: The Project Assignment Worksheet

Once you have selected the projects that will deliver the greatest impact to your organization, you must determine who has the best skills to manage each of those projects. On the Project Assignment Worksheet, you list each project that you have selected and then under each project's title, record the name of each leader who is responsible for that particular project. Not only does this give you a visual reference for tracking projects, but it also helps you to avoid assigning too many projects to each manager.

In the Project Assignment Worksheet shown in Figure 3.18, you'll see that there are spaces for recording the projects that you have selected. Then under each project, notice that there are four spaces labeled "Leadership:_____ Project # ___ of 2," allowing you to assign up to four managers to manage each project. You can adapt the sample chart to accommodate more or fewer managers per project depending on your organization's needs.

Simply fill in the projects in order of priority on this chart. Then, assign the leader or leaders to each project, including any outsourced managers who are not part of your regular management group. Be sure to assign no more than two projects per leader—as indicated by "Project # (1 or 2) of 2"—keeping in mind that you may be assigning more than one leader to any particular project. Depending on the project, you may have to assign three or more leaders to a single project, although in most instances, the number tends not to exceed two leaders.

Project Assignment Worksheet

Priority	Prioritized Project		
# 1	**Website with Shopping Cart**		
Leadership: Lois	Project # 1 of 2	Leadership:	Project # of 2
Leadership: Bob	Project # 1 of 2	Leadership:	Project # of 2
# 2	**Campaign #4 Developed**		
Leadership: Bob	Project # 2 of 2	Leadership: Hazel	Project # 1 of 2
Leadership: Camilo	Project # 1 of 2	Leadership:	Project # of 2
# 3	**Warehouse Expansion**		
Leadership: Barbara	Project # 1 of 2	Leadership:	Project # of 2
Leadership:	Project # of 2	Leadership:	Project # of 2
# 4	**Acquisition of Altban Chemicals**		
Leadership: Mohammed	Project # 1 of 2	Leadership:	Project # of 2
Leadership: Yann	Project # 1 of 2	Leadership:	Project # of 2

Figure 3.18—Project Assignment Worksheet

In addition to helping you adhere to the Two-Project Rule, another great benefit of the Project Assignment Worksheet is that it can help you keep a big-picture view of your organization so that you don't overextend its resources. As you assign leaders, you will continue to fill in the blank spaces until you have run out of leaders, money, or time to do certain projects right.

There may be times when you will have to skip a project for the time being and go to the next ranking project, because the most appropriate leader for the job already has two projects in progress. For example, you know that one of your managers, Rick, would be the best person to oversee your sixth project, but Rick won't be available for another two weeks, so you skip to project number seven where you place the best-matched leader on the project.

Used correctly, this tool breaks silos that can stunt organizational growth by creating and working off a master Project Evaluation Chart so that title and role are no longer as valuable as the ability to complete the project. Remember the UNIT4 (Agresso) example in Chapter 1 where the firm's president reassigned her sales and operational managers to fill in some of the daily responsibilities of one vice president so that another VP could work on a high-impact hiring project? Don't limit yourself by thinking in silos. Instead, think about results and consider pairing people to projects based on skills and talents rather than titles, departments, or other mentally siloed compartments. *The holistic perspective is how you get everyone on the bus and in the right seats!*

Staying Focused: Parallel Project Tracks

Since every decision maker needs to stay focused on two prioritized projects, wouldn't it be great to have a tool that prevents them and you from straying onto third, fourth, and fifth projects? Adhering to the canaries-in-the-cage concept and the Two-Project Rule, you can safeguard yourself and your organization's resources from becoming overextended by setting your projects on Parallel Project Tracks.

Managing Projects

Parallel Project Tracks

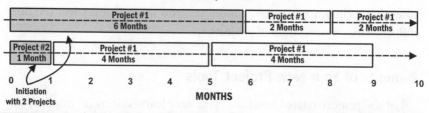

Note: The first two blocks in the diagram above, Project #1 and Project #2, represent the best two projects you wish to use to initiate the Parallel Project Tracks. Each new project identified as your next best move would be labeled Project #1 because this project is selected out of a newly generated list of potential projects at a time in the future. Using the example above you would complete Project #2 in a month, generate a new project list and select the best option. A project that is your number-one choice and will last for 4 months. In 5 months from the initiation you'd create another list and select your Project #1, another 4-month project. At 6 months you'd repeat the process and then again at 8 months. All the while never expanding past the two-project guideline.

Figure 3.19—Managing Projects

Picture two railroad tracks running parallel to each other. Now see a single train on each track, both heading east. The trains represent your projects and the tracks represent a timeline. Each track can support only one project at a time. When you begin using the Parallel Project Tracks, you will transfer your top-priority project from your Project Evaluation Chart onto the first track and your second-place project on the second track. Since you've already selected two projects with the highest priority, don't jump to lesser-valued projects. You leave these two projects on your Parallel Project Tracks until you complete one of them, after which you will remove the completed project and place in its position your next top-priority project. However—and this counterintuitive move is an extremely important key to successfully using the Parallel Project Tracks—*you do not select the next highest ranking project from your existing Project Evaluation Chart!*

Instead, consider your original Project Evaluation Chart dead and start a completely new one. That's because time has passed and any emerging factors that might influence your organization's well being must be taken into consideration since they will affect the prioritization of projects. Besides, you may have new ideas for projects you'd like to put onto the table. Taking the time to refresh your options with a new and updated list of projects ensures that you are truly taking on your absolute next best project.

When you or your managers complete your first project, *fill out a new and updated Project Evaluation Chart before determining your next top-ranking project to place onto the empty track.*

Another reason that it is extremely important not to just pull the next project off an old Project Evaluation Chart is because your organization may have experienced changes to its Desired Outcome and Strategy in response to evolving circumstances and conditions, and these changes will certainly influence the prioritization of projects.

Benefits of Your New Project Tools

All of the project-related tools that you have learned thus far improve the chances that your projects will become Wildly Successful Projects, not only because they deliver the greatest impact, but because you have the tools to ensure their success. WSPs boost morale, establish successful track records for management, and make the tasks of gaining buy-in and cooperation from others much easier on future projects.

Again, because the tools' methodologies are transferrable, traceable, and measurable, they are easy for leaders to teach to others. In addition, the tools facilitate more accurate communication among management and enable higher-level leaders to monitor the progress of those who report to him or her.

Furthermore, these tools break silos and maximize organizational resources. If you were to bring your entire management team together and

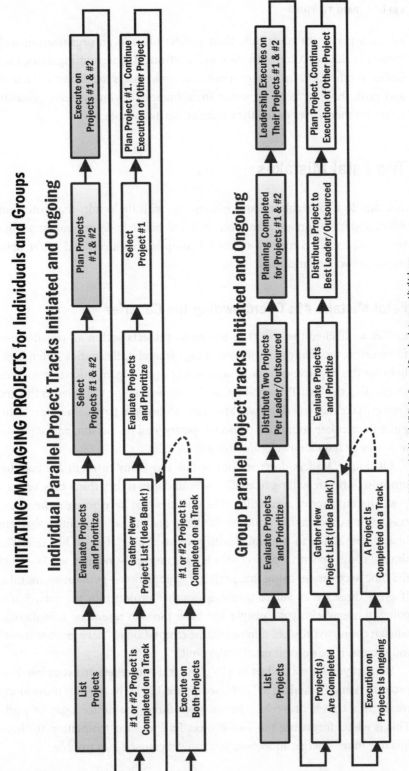

INITIATING MANAGING PROJECTS for Individuals and Groups

Individual Parallel Project Tracks Initiated and Ongoing

List Projects → Evaluate Projects and Prioritize → Select Projects #1 & #2 → Plan Projects #1 & #2 → Execute on Projects #1 & #2

#1 or #2 Project is Completed on a Track → Gather New Project List (Idea Bank!) → Evaluate Projects and Prioritize → Select Project #1 → Plan Project #1. Continue Execution of Other Project

Execute on Both Projects → #1 or #2 Project is Completed on a Track

Group Parallel Project Tracks Initiated and Ongoing

List Projects → Evaluate Projects and Prioritize → Distribute Two Projects Per Leader/Outsourced → Planning Completed for Projects #1 & #2 → Leadership Executes on Their Projects #1 & #2

Project(s) Are Completed → Gather New Project List (Idea Bank!) → Evaluate Projects and Prioritize → Distribute Project to Best Leader/Outsourced → Plan Project. Continue Execution of Other Project

Execution on Projects Is Ongoing → A Project Is Completed on a Track

Figure 3.20—Initiating Managing Projects for Individuals and Groups

ask each person to contribute their project ideas to an organization-wide Project Evaluation Chart, decision makers from HR, accounting, sales, marketing, production, customer service, etc. could assess the projects as a team and rank those projects in order from highest- to lowest-level priorities either for themselves or for the organization as a whole.

Two Fatal Mistakes

You can do a lot right and still not end up with the results that you want. Effort and intention are admirable qualities, but they do not guarantee that your projects will come to a successful completion, especially if you're making these two fatal mistakes.

Fatal Mistake #1: Overcrowding the Canaries

Earlier we likened the effects of too many projects within an organization to thrusting too many canaries into a cage whereby all canaries suffer, highlighting the negative effects of overtaxing one's organizational resources. Overriding the Two-Project Rule, or Overcrowding the Canaries, is the first fatal mistake that you don't want to make. Unless you have some super computer to calculate your exact project-capacity load per person, *do not take on any more or less than two projects at a time!*

Obviously, leaders don't set out to fail, but many of them are habitual optimists who are willing to challenge boundaries if they think they've got a pretty decent shot of succeeding. The qualities that have brought them success, such as risk taking and fast thinking, are the same qualities that can hijack their ability to transform with projects. Think about it like this: The time to come up with a project idea is a lot shorter—say three weeks—than the time necessary to bring that project to completion—perhaps six months. If every three weeks you're throwing another project into the mix, you're going to overwhelm your people and burn through resources. Like dieting, when it comes to projects, don't allow the temptation to "have just one more" foil success. Here's how it usually plays out:

Say that you have a budget of $100,000, and you've selected your two best projects, A and B, totaling $97,000 (see Figure 3.21). The projects move along nicely for a couple of weeks. Then in week three, you notice a gap in work. This is where forgetting the Two-Project Rule and the temptation to "have just one more" merge, and where you can get yourself into trouble.

Fatal Mistake #1—Overcrowding the Canaries

(Overall Budget is $100,000)

Project A $80,000   ❶ _The Canary Decision_ begins when the leader starts a small $3,000 project believing that it can be completed quickly because there is some free time and cash available to spend.

Project B $17,000   Impact: Additional project has unexpected challenge requiring an additional $2,000 to complete the project.

—————————

$97,000   ❷ Decision made to slow down and cut back Project B due to resources required for Project C including capital and manpower. Impact: Project timeline changes due to contractor commitments.

Add Project C $3,000   Delay also impacts opportunity cost. Project total now $21,000.

❸ Combined impacts create a juggling of cash environment with vendors. Group is now distracted by other work and projects. Project completed 2 months behind schedule.

❹ Employee confidence in leadership drops. A leader unexpectedly decides to take another job with competitor. Leader is constantly fire fighting due to delays and overruns. New project to hire leader becomes a #1 priority resulting in months of work. Target goals not reached. Sold to organization as, "This is just normal everyday business."

© 2010 David Goldsmith All Rights Reserved Download at www.paidtothink.com

Figure 3.21—Fatal Mistake #1—Overcrowding the Canaries

The time gap and the $3,000 budget surplus seem like the perfect chance to initiate a small project, shown in Figure 3.21 as Project C. Unfortunately, Project C doesn't progress as smoothly as you had anticipated. Due to a glitch in C, you pull $2,000 and your time away from Project B. Project B's $2,000 shortage forces you to select a less expensive vendor whose delivery time pushes B's timeline out by one week. Now, like dominoes, all three projects begin to fall.

The first consequence is that during the unproductive downtime, you must pay out $21,000 and "invisible" payroll expenditures. Second, you put A on hold while you deal with B and C. When the dust settles, Project A comes off two months later than scheduled. Project B still isn't finished, and because the less expensive vendor provided cheaper parts, your staffers can't get a piece of equipment to work reliably. But money isn't the only resource that suffers.

The frustration causes one of your best managers to quit. Now you have to take time away from the projects to find a replacement, which requires you or other manpower to pull attention away from projects and onto the hiring process. In the end, the costs of your small project have ratcheted up well above its $3,000 budget. By Overcrowding the Canaries, you've hurt the trust that others had in you, and you have made the task of gaining buy-in on future projects more difficult for yourself.

Avoid the temptation to bite into projects that seem quick and easy. If you can't wait to take on a third project, work harder and smarter to complete one or both projects sooner to gain the value earlier or find a competent external manager to handle it, but don't make Fatal Mistake #1.

Fatal Mistake #2: Jumping the Tracks

The Parallel Project Tracks are designed to keep you focused on your two highest priority projects until you have completed them successfully. However, your success with Parallel Project Tracks is dependent on your willingness to complete one project before taking on another. This leads us to Fatal Mistake #2, the cycle of jumping from one unfinished project to another that I call Jumping the Tracks. Don't allow yourself to become a "Jumper" who selects a project, rallies your team to work on it, then replaces that project before it's completed with another one.

Fatal Mistake #2—Jumping the Tracks

Figure 3.22—Fatal Mistake #2—Jumping the Tracks

Jumping the Tracks can result in burning through money too quickly and/or burning out people too fast with nothing to show for the expenditures. Note that the funding for projects comes from profits (in businesses), from special grants, fund-raising, or funds left over after covering operating expenses (in nonprofits), from taxes or fund-raising (in government, military, and education) but rarely, if ever, does the money needed for projects come out of operating budgets. So when you're Jumping the Tracks, you often spend faster than you earn profits or you can raise new capital, and you may be forced to dip into operating expenses. If you're not careful, you'll come up short to meet payroll or vendor obligations, pay your building lease, or produce products to sell. Many organizations never recover from this downward spiral.

When you begin to use your new tools, you may find that you still have more than two projects to complete, because you had started them before you knew about the Two-Project Rule. In those instances, do your best to stick to the Parallel Project Tracks to remain focused. *Some* improvement and *some* ROI are still better than Jumping the Tracks and ending up with nothing. In no time, you will have two manageable projects.

As you stay on the tracks and complete projects, you should start to see results immediately in profits, morale, and in other areas. Additionally, others will notice, too, and their confidence in you is likely to increase. Like Kyle, the manager from Chapter 2 with a track record of Wildly Successful Projects, when you have a history of successful projects, you have an easier time gaining the support of others—bankers who lend, board members who vote, managers who take on the extra work, and so on—which feeds your success.

As philosopher and writer Alfred Montapert commented, "Do not confuse motion and progress. A rocking horse keeps moving but does not make any progress."[32]

■ ■ ■

[PART III]
MANAGING YOUR PRIORITIES

I CAN'T TELL you how many leaders have asked me to show them how they can "get everything done." Most likely, you've asked yourself the same question (and not just once or twice). The truth of the matter is that it's not the job of leadership to get everything done. Realistically, if you listed everything that needed to get done in your organization, you would find it impossible to get it all done at once anyway. Therefore, you need to shift your focus away from this unrealistic quest to get everything done and place it on getting the right things done, a better alternative that is more about managing priorities. This requires you to extricate from your to-do list those activities that you *wish* you could do from those that you *need* to do, then keep yourself focused on completing those items to advance your organization, your career, and your life.

The value you will get from this section is that you will be able to focus yourself better on a daily basis. I can't teach you to be focused, but I can give you the tools you need to stay on target. Think of how many times you or someone on your staff stops at one point in a day and asks, Where was I going before I picked up the phone? or you thought to yourself, Where has the time gone? and then you noticed you had seven tabs open in your Internet browser that had nothing to do with what you needed to get done. With the tools in this section, you will stay focused more often and be able to pull yourself back in line when you veer off track.

In order to manage all aspects of your daily life, you need to understand the basic differences between time management and priority management. Whether you're a newbie to time management or have tried time management techniques in the past and found them underwhelming enough to discontinue, I expect you'll be quite happy with the invaluable impact these priority management techniques will have on your organization and on your life.

One of decision makers' chief complaints is not having enough time in a day to do their jobs as well as they would like. On top of daily demands is the flood of additional distractions such as e-mails, calls, meetings, and unexpected occurrences that pose challenges and swallow up time, threatening to pull you off course and potentially steer your organization in the opposite direction of a Desired Outcome. You need a daily priority-management system.

In addition to all that you can accomplish by using a priority-management system, you can actually create pockets of time, too. Did you realize that efficient management of priorities, even if it "creates" only ten minutes a day, could net you a full week's worth of open time in a single year?

Unfortunately, most leaders don't see value in traditional time-management systems (and perhaps rightly so), which is why so few actually use them. In 2009, I polled utility sector managers about their approaches to time management and found that most of them knew very little about advanced time-management tools, despite the plethora of time-management books, audios, articles, and courses that are available to them. Furthermore, nearly 61% had never taken a course in time management, and 2% didn't know what a time-management system was. Only 36% of respondents almost always scheduled their days, while 52% did so only on occasion, and 12% didn't plan their days at all. Most planning tools were variations of informal to-do lists that did not prioritize activities.

Surprised at the results, I contacted the undergraduate and MBA offices at *Business-Week*'s top American business schools—University of Virginia, University of Michigan, Notre Dame, The Wharton School of the University of Pennsylvania, Harvard University, Cornell University, Massachusetts Institute of Technology, and University of California–Berkeley—and I asked them if they offered either undergraduate or graduate courses in time management. *None* offered any course on the topic! That's astounding when you fathom the importance of establishing priorities and managing time.

By these two polls alone, it's my belief that many people don't see the value in priority management or the potential that any form of time management can have. If they saw the value, they'd be using the tools that are available. Looking back, I was once ignorant about the subject, too. Twenty-plus years ago, I sat in on a two-day program about the Priority Management System,[33] at that time called the Time Text System, and I became a believer in the benefits of priority management. When the program concluded, I returned to my office armed with the system and a new perspective. Instead of trying to "get everything done," I was determined to accomplish my highest priorities. Focusing on priorities netted me a $44,000 sale—within thirty days of taking the course—at 50% profit that I know I wouldn't have closed had I been bent on crossing off tasks on a traditional to-do list. Over the years, the single sale generated more than a quarter of a million dollars in reorders with no work on my part! I've been a believer ever since.

Priority management has immeasurably improved every organization I've owned, worked with, and advised throughout my career. Notice I didn't say *time* management, although time management is better than nothing. There's an important distinction between the two ways of thinking, and that distinction yields vastly different outcomes. In this section, you will go way beyond scheduling appointments and working off lists of tasks and activities. Instead, you will have exactly what you need to easily incorporate priorities into a single priority management planner each day that come directly from your tactical plans, CPM charts, to-do lists, and other tools to ensure that your energies are focused on items that deliver the greatest rewards back to your organization.

Managing Time

Just for a second, think about the concept of managing time. Move ten o'clock to the late afternoon and tuck Monday morning into Tuesday afternoon since no one likes Monday mornings anyway. Sounds ridiculous, right?

That's because even though we loosely throw around the terminology of "managing time," in reality, no one can manage time. Period. What you can manage is the completion of your tasks and activities within a specific window of time. So to get started on managing your day to day, we first need to briefly address the difference between traditional time management and priority management.

Most daily planners, digital systems, handheld calendars, and simple lists are nothing more than task-management tools that help people to remember appointments and activities. These tools don't prioritize items by importance, and they don't assign definite start and finish times to activities, which ultimately means that you don't have cushions of time to address interruptions, opportunities, or crises.

In addition, traditional time-management systems that place your focus on tasks rather than priorities chew up time reserves and reduce your ability to find those extra pockets of time that you sometimes need when you approach the completion of projects, such as those last few hours or days that require a push at the end. When you consider how important projects are to moving your organization forward, a good priority-management system is a must for all decision makers.

Take a look at how you currently manage your tasks and/or priorities. Even if you're working with a preprinted time-management system or digital pages in your handheld device, do you find yourself basically working from a daily to-do list? If you were to look at today's list, you might already identify some items that will likely make their way onto tomorrow's list, because already you know that you won't have the time to complete them. The carrying over of unfinished tasks from one day to another—and then oftentimes to yet another tomorrow until some of these items ultimately fall off the list altogether—is a distraction that leads to frustration and more time wasted.

Case in point: Karyn, the busy VP of a financial institution, created her own time-management system coined "catch as you can." Each morning, Karyn would enter her office, assemble a stack of papers on her desk representing matters she intended to address for the day, place them in a bin on her desk, and then attempt to burrow through this 3D to-do list to the best of her ability, barring the usual interruptions from coworkers and bank patrons. At various times, she or her staff members would add a paper here or there to the pile as new matters presented themselves, and Karyn would catch as many of these unprioritized issues as she could until the close of the business day.

Despite her best efforts and intentions, Karyn would emerge from her office each evening leaving behind a stack of carry-over papers—few, if any, that called for urgent attention—that she would have to face the following morning. In situations like these, carry-over lists not only come with a price tag of discouragement and stress to leaders, they hinder the organization from completing projects and reaching desired strategic outcomes, too.

What most people don't realize is that time-management techniques and systems are rarely (if ever) tied directly to strategizing activities, like those you read about in the first two sections of this chapter. So if you're not prioritizing your days, you may not be as focused on strategizing activities, CPM chart items, project follow-up matters, and so on, which robs you and your organization of opportunities to complete projects. That said, prioritization puts your most important activities on a timeline, thus creating the sense of urgency that we often need to help us achieve more.

Research has shown that when people near the accomplishment of goals, they naturally self-motivate and put forth an extra burst of effort to complete them. I learned about this particular research while earning my MBA, and I call it the Escalator Theory. (For years I've attempted to find its source, but the professor has passed away, and other attempts thus far have been unsuccessful.) In the study, researchers observed people riding on escalators and found that most riders stood still until they approached the last few stairs, at which time they would walk up the remaining few stairs to disembark faster. (This tends to be true even in cities and cultures where the agreed-upon way to ride an escalator is to move to the right to stand and leave the area to one's left open for those riders who like to walk up the escalator.) You've probably experienced the escalator theory many times before, like when you've been tired but you've come to the last few pages of a book, so you push through those last few pages just to finish up, or on a Friday afternoon prior to a weeklong vacation when you have put forth the extra effort to complete some activities or projects quickly so that they were done by the time you left the office at the end of your day.

The advantage of the Escalator Theory when it is applied to managing priorities is that the urge to wrap up tasks quickly at the end of a specified period of time—which is typically a single workday—prevents you from the unproductive cycle of the dreaded carry-over list, where completion of a task loses its importance as that task passes tiredly from one day's to-do list to the other.

Let's take a closer look at your next new tool, the priority-management system, and how you can use it to create new opportunities.

Managing Priorities

Since your job is to develop plans and select projects that will advance your organization, you need a way of keeping yourself focused on these activities so that you and your organization stay on target to your Desired Outcome. As a decision maker who once felt buried under mounds of paper (before the onslaught of digital clutter that can invade our lives today) and who has enjoyed countless opportunities and achievements through priority management for more than twenty years, I believe that *having a priority-management system that ties strategizing activities to your day to day is essential for every decision maker.*

If you've ever had big plans but were disappointed when they didn't go anywhere, chances are your daily planning system, or lack thereof, was a significant part of the failure, because it did not lead you through the progression from Strategy to Macro Tactics to Tactics, nor did it catch all the details you needed at each stage of your involvement in a project—say, from your CPM charts and other types of road maps—and place them in full view on a daily basis. Whether your organization needs you to follow its strategic plan on a daily basis and ensure that everyone is on track, or you need to guide others through a specific project in order for the plan or project to work, you must address plans and projects regularly, if not each day.

So let's think back to the Goldsmith Productivity Principle (GGP) for a moment and consider what options you can expand upon by improving your organization's systems and structures—that 80% of the results equation—and more specifically those areas that will most likely channel your attention, energies, and resources toward the achievement of your Desired Outcome. In this instance, your priority-management system is the 80% of the equation, because it serves as the structure that ensures that you address Strategy, Tactics, and projects. Balancing out the equation is *you*. You are the 20%, because you leverage the system by working it each day. Once you become accustomed to seeing priority management as an important piece of your organization's GPP, you'll probably want every decision maker on staff to use a priority-management system. After all, who doesn't want (and need) to achieve Desired Outcomes rapidly and accurately?

In this section, you will learn what your new tool is and how to use it, so that you can adapt it to fit your style and needs. You may want to add more structure or simplify depending on your situation. Regardless of whether you work with an assistant who keeps you on track each day or you work entirely alone, this priority-management system is easy enough for you to put to use immediately.

Some people prefer paper versions of a system, while others like digital systems. You can always adapt the general concepts of managing priorities to a style that is best for you. As technologies enabling users to have their daily planner always visible on a computer screen become increasingly available and costs of such technologies decline, I may even recommend digital forms over paper. But despite the prolificacy and usefulness of digital tools like smartphone and computer apps, I want you to have your daily planner open and in plain sight all day so that you can look at it periodically to keep yourself on track. You're less likely to do so with digital items, especially if they are on your computer, where the planner will have to compete with other screens for your attention. My past experience has been that digital planning systems, whether smartphone- or Web-based systems, have allowed priorities to slide out of sight, which is counterproductive when you need those priorities in front of you as reminders and guiders all day. But you shouldn't let that deter you from trying proven digital forms. People now tend to have multiple electronic devices in front of them continually—from computers and smartphones to tablets and netbooks—so many leaders can now keep a digital priority-management system visibly in front of them throughout their day.

From Conversion to Proficiency: Becoming a Priority Manager

Your journey to becoming a priority manager will occur in two multistep phases.

- **Phase I: Conversion:** You begin conversion by pulling together all your lists, piles, and random thoughts into a cohesive system to ensure that nothing falls through the cracks. You will schedule and prioritize important items for completion.
- **Phase II: Daily Routine:** You will learn how to effectively maintain a priority-management system that focuses your attention on strategizing and transforming and improving your organization.

If you think that you'd like other decision makers in your organization to convert to a priority-management system, too, make the conversion on your own first and work the system for a couple of weeks before introducing it to others. When you become an actual user of a system, you lead more authentically by example and your directives carry much more credibility.

PHASE I: CONVERSION

As you convert from an existing (or nonexistent) time-management system to your new priority-management system, you will be performing the three functions shown in Figure 3.23.

Priority Management Conversion

FUNCTION 1: ASSEMBLY	FUNCTION 2: INSERTION	FUNCTION 3: FILING & DISCARDING
The collection of all information related to your day-to-day activities: Post-It Notes, planners, messages, CPM/Gantt charts, schedules, notes, digital forms, e-mails, plans, idea lists, due from others, etc.	Assembled activities and responsibilities are recorded on calendar pages and daily planning pages in the new priority-management system	After the activity is scheduled, the related items are either filed (digitally, manually) or discarded.

Figure 3.23—Priority Management Conversion

In brief, you'll be gathering all the essential information that belongs in your priority-management system, beginning with the basics like appointments and meetings from your calendar and to-do list tasks from various areas. However, now you'll also be revisiting your strategic plan if you have one and any projects that are currently in progress to catch time-sensitive items that need your attention. This is the first step to gaining the benefits of priority management that most leaders and managers miss by using time-management systems alone. Once you have collected all the materials you need, I'll show you step by step how and where to insert them in the priority-management system. At this point, you'll really see how the pieces of the puzzle come together and how easily and assuredly you'll be able to track your responsibilities and be able to make smarter decisions.

And finally, we'll address what you should do with the items that you had previously assembled once you have inserted them into your planner. You'll get suggestions on filing certain items and discarding others.

Typically, you can expect to accomplish the conversion process over the course of a day or two, either amid your current daily responsibilities or at the end of the day or in the early evening when you've got some quiet time to yourself. Everyone who has converted to priority management agrees that they feel relief, confidence, and renewed motivation once they begin using their priority-management system on a daily basis.

Pre-Conversion: Your Planner

Before you begin the conversion process, you need to have a physical planner to use. You can search online for some of the companies that provide priority-management systems, but just be careful that you're not getting a simple time-management program. Another option is to visit us online at www.paidtothink.com and download free priority-management pages like those shown in the diagram below.

Your planner should contain the two components: a calendar and a daily-planning page (as shown below on Figure 3.24).

Calendar and Planner Example

Printed with permission of © Priority Management International Inc.

Figure 3.24—Calendar and Planner Example

Conversion Function 1: Assembly

Go around your office, your home, your vehicle, and your suitcases, computer bags, handbags, etc., and assemble all the activities, appointments, and tasks that require your attention. Nothing is too large or too small. Assemble in one location the following types of materials: lists of large projects, notes scratched on a napkin, your smartphone, current to-do lists, paperwork, time-management tools, strategic plan, CPM charts or other project-planning materials, sticky notes, paperwork, and so on.

Your goal here is to bring together as much material as possible at this first function of the conversion process. (Don't be surprised, however, if you find that in the days—and even weeks—ahead, you come across other items that had gotten away from you that need to be inserted in your system.) You want everything out on the table, so to speak, so that you can address it once and for all. Be sure that you don't leave anything out simply because you don't think you'll be addressing it for awhile, because there are even places for items that will be put off for doing until a later date.

At this time, you may already find that your workspace is cleaning up!

Conversion Function 2: Insertion

Place your planning pages—the calendar and the daily planning pages—in front of you. You will now begin the second function of conversion, Insertion. The insertion process has been streamlined for you. All you have to do is follow the five steps below.

Step 1: Transfer Time-Specific Activities onto Your New Calendar

Move your current calendar's activities—appointments, travel dates, or specific time-related activities—onto your new calendar. These items have specific start and end times. Do not record items such as "finish report" or "call printer for estimate," because they are not calendar-specific items like the November 15 meeting from 11 to noon with XYZ Transport and the 3-to-5 pm teleconference with your offices in Brazil and Japan. Be sure to record any relevant calendar-specific items you haven't written down yet; for example, if you want to build an addition on to your facility to expand production space, and you need to attend your town's next zoning board meeting, then this is the time to place that October 3 meeting on your calendar, if it is not already there. Don't forget important personal dates: your daughter's graduation on June 12 at 10 and your road race on July 7 at 7 am.

Step 2: Transfer Date-Specific Activities from Your CPM Chart onto Your New Calendar

Review all current projects for date-specific activities, and your CPM chart, if you are working from one. Then, transfer them to your calendar. In the example above, where you need approval from your zoning board to add on to your production space, perhaps you will need to present surveys and documentation at the meeting. Schedule specific meetings with others who make this a possibility: "architect final plans" on August 15 at 4 pm, "developer site plan" on September 20 at 8 am.

Step 3: Transfer Non-Date-Specific Project Activities into Your Daily Schedule

Review current projects and the activities that you must perform to complete them. Many activities don't have specific do-by dates, so look at your CPM chart for Early Start and Late Start times, estimate when you need to do these activities, and transfer them to corresponding daily-planning pages: "review documents" on May 12, "submit proposal" on May 21.

In this step, schedule quarterly or semi-annual activities (such as performance reviews and tax-planning sessions) and personal priorities (like home maintenance issues and dental exams).

Step 4: Transfer Priorities from Other Locations onto Your Calendar or into Your Daily Schedule

This is where you will clean up the last loose ends. If you have sticky notes attached to the dashboard of your car, scraps of paper on your desk meant as reminders, items on your phone or tablet or sitting in your e-mail's inbox, or any other pieces of data that require your attention, gather them up and transfer these priorities to dates on your calendar (if appropriate) or within your daily-view pages. These non-date-specific activities might include:

- schedule meeting with Rick on October 5
- purchase airline ticket for trip to Chicago
- request information from credit union

Place items like the ones listed above close in date to where the activity will need to be completed to meet your Desired Outcome.

Step 5: Enter Reoccurring Activities

Enter all reoccurring date-specific activities onto your calendar and non-date-specific activities on your daily-view pages. Monday's early morning meeting with your management team and Thursday afternoon's phone call to your mentor should be entered at this time. Realize that your new system is not only a tool that you use within your organization but one that you can use in all aspects of life, as well. Personal commitments are part of your daily life that should be factored into your priorities and your time. Therefore, you list a task such as "order new tires for the car" on the same page that you record "call the director of XYZ Corporation."

Conversion Function 3: Discard or File

At this point, you have organized yourself according to your priorities, you've caught the loose ends that can easily get away from a decision maker and tied them into your new system, and you have a tool that you will be able to use on a daily basis to move your organization rapidly toward the achievement of Desired Outcomes. You may still find that your desk and desktop are not thoroughly clear of clutter, because you need to either discard some of the items that you initially assembled or because you need a better method of filing them.

Besides some of the common-sense solutions of throwing out sticky notes and outdated to-do lists and time-management systems, there are no hard and fast answers here. However, every decision maker can make use of some fantastic, and most times inexpensive, methods of filing and discarding the visual clutter that can easily become mental clutter.

During this function, you have some flexibility in terms of the choices you make, as long as you remember that your true objective is to make order out of chaos. To complete your conversion process, employ the Four S's:

- **Scan:** If you haven't started using one already, a scanner can be a versatile tool for accomplishing numerous functions in your office. Scan the documents that you can't part with but that you don't want cluttering your workspace. The scanned items are still available for retrieval at a later date, but they're no longer in your face when your mind needs to stay focused on its priorities. Be sure that when you scan a document that at some time will require your attention, you have recorded it on the appropriate calendar or daily planning page.
- **Store:** For many organizations, gone are the huge file cabinets that house paper documents. You know whether manila file folders or digital files are best for your organization, but in terms of

the conversion process, you'll probably find that if you can scan in the items you personally might need for later, then the retrieval of digital files can be faster, easier, and more easily accessible to the right parties than the space hogs of yesteryear. With this tool, you can find any document that's been filed digitally as long as you file it by person or organization. I recommend that your labeling of documents be consistent across the board. For example, if you would typically file a document under the name of the vendor, customer, or other stakeholder, you can still use the same account name. However, the documents within that file would now take on a uniform format, beginning with (1) the date (year, month, and day in that order numerically), then (2) an ID or name of the account, and finally (3) some description, number, or type of the document. So, if you received repair estimate #126789 from Lou at Lou's Plumbing on December 1, 2012, the digital folder would be labeled Lou's Plumbing, and this particular document would carry the name 2012-12-01 Lou's Plumbing Estimate 126789. The reason for this type of filing is different data stored in your mind will jar your memory, so while you might not remember the name of a Microsoft Word document you filed for Vendor A, you might recall that you transacted business with this vendor sometime during June or July. A quick scan allows you to see the four documents that you filed during that time frame. Even if you had to open them, you'd see a pattern or recognize the file. The date-ordering system creates a chronological folder in which you can find most items very quickly.

- **Shred:** As you continue to clear your work area of clutter, get in the habit of shredding items that you no longer need in hard-copy form, and continue the habit into the future. Although you can usually toss a useless document into your recycle bin, you don't want to leave to chance the problems that can arise when sensitive materials end up in the wrong hands. In addition, shredding not only eliminates clutter from your visual space, it gives you the peace of mind that comes from knowing that that particular document has been put to rest once and for all.

- **Shift:** Take a look at the remaining items that you have. If they have not yet been addressed during this conversion, perhaps the reason why is because they don't actually belong to you. Now is the time to make that determination and shift those responsibilities off your shoulders and onto the appropriate party's.

Upon completion of these conversion functions, your desk and computer desktop should be clean, but more importantly, you should be able to see everything at a glance and know where you stand now and at any time in the future.

Knowing where you are on a daily basis, whether you're working for months at a stretch without a break or coming back from a vacation or sick day, means that you are able to perform better without lapses in progress. When leadership is on target, the entire organization performs better and others tend to excel more.

Five Principles of Priority-Management Planning

You will achieve the best results from your priority-management system by adhering to the following five principles:

PRINCIPLE 1: PLAN YOUR DAY THE NIGHT BEFORE

You will get much, much, much more value out of your priority-management system if you plan your days the nights before. I can't stress enough how important it is that you go to a quiet place free from interruptions to evaluate and schedule the next day's priorities. In the beginning, you can expect to take twenty minutes to complete this activity, and thereafter, probably no more than ten minutes . . . and every second is worth it. You'll sleep better. Your mind will have time to Cyclonically Think throughout the night. More and more, your 50,000-foot perspective will become sharper. You'll feel less pressure when you wake up in the morning, and you'll feel more in charge when entering your office each day. Over time, you'll find that your mind is clearer and more relaxed, and you'll probably be surprised to find that you have more time and initiative to set more targets. Have I sold you yet?

Daily Planning Cycle

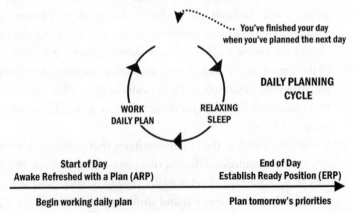

Figure 3.25—Daily Planning Cycle

Furthermore, by planning the night before, you begin each day completing priorities instead of trying to plan your schedule among distractions that could prevent you from scheduling your day at all: ringing phones, staffers who demand your time, crises, e-mails, texts, etc. You also sleep better knowing that you're covering all your bases and are prepared for the next day.

PRINCIPLE 2: SCHEDULE 60% OF YOUR DAY

A common mistake of planning occurs when people go to extremes and attempt to schedule every second of their day. Be realistic about what you can possibly do. Trying to lead 100% of the day doesn't give you enough of a cushion in your schedule to get priorities done. Unfinished items end up carrying over to the next day, setting off a potentially self-sabotaging cycle, because the impetus of the Escalator Theory is lost and people lose the drive to complete these tasks.

A good rule of thumb is to schedule no more than 60% of your day, because planning is not an exact science, and you never know what interruptions, unforeseen opportunities, problems, and other unexpected activities can encroach on your schedule. When you give yourself the extra cushion of 40%, you'll find that you'll accomplish your true priorities and still have time for the additional items that are bound to creep into your day. Besides, I've found that humans can become overly optimistic about what they can get done in a given time frame, so the 60% ensures you're not biting off more than you can accomplish.

Be sure to share this principle with other priority managers on staff, too.

PRINCIPLE 3: APPROACH EACH DAY WITH THE INTENT TO FINISH ALL ACTIVITIES

Have you ever seen those weight-loss programs on television where the trainers fill backpacks with rocks and bricks, then tell participants they have to wear the backpacks as they perform their daily workout? You can probably recall at least one such session where at the end of the training session, the trainers reveal to the participants that the weight they were carrying around that day is equivalent to the weight that the latter had lost to date. There's a moment where everyone "oohs" and "ahs" upon realizing how burdensome and tiring it was to have carried around all that unneeded weight. Unfinished activities that carry over from one day to the next have the same effect on your ability to perform mentally.

Intend to complete each day's priorities before the end of that day. You're less likely to develop carry-over items that lack a finite finish time, which can weigh you down. Your daily actions should move your organization forward, even if by a little, each day, so strive to keep projects and plans in direct focus by shooting for the achievable day.

[continues on page 142

[continued from previous page]

PRINCIPLE 4: WORK THE PLAN IF YOU WANT THE PLAN TO WORK FOR YOU

Your priority-management system is a personal navigation tool. In order for it to function as your daily road map, it must be visible and accessible throughout your days so that you can work from it as you travel from one hour to the next.

If you were to drive a long road trip or hike a complex mountain trail, think of how important it would be for you to keep your map in front of you throughout your journey. Simply having the map wouldn't be enough to get you where you want to go. Your daily planner is no different. Planning your priorities is a good first step, but it is not the end all. Make sure that you are using your planner to keep you on track as you address one priority after another over the course of your day.

Lauri is a hairdresser who took over ownership of the hair salon where she worked for years. One of her first projects as owner was to implement a computerized scheduling system—GPP. Now, employees receive a printout of their appointment schedules each day, saving them from having to mull through the old manual calendar that used to track appointments. If Lauri and her receptionist want this new planning tool to work for the salon, they will have to "work" the software by entering data as it occurs, and making sure that the data is entered into the appropriate places in the system.

PRINCIPLE 5: PLAN YOUR LIFE AS YOU DO YOUR WORK!

Chances are if you've been in a decision-making role for any length of time, you've encountered the age-old conflict of balancing life and work. Obviously, you must make the time for work because your organization, career, and livelihood are at stake. Yet when the scales tip too far in favor of work without the balance of life, you and those closest to you on the personal side can become pretty unhappy. The good news is you have more control over this balancing act than you may have otherwise thought. The answer comes from priority management.

Be sure that when you schedule your days that you are including priorities from your personal life. A quick look at the home calendar or a talk with your spouse are pretty much all it takes to incorporate important personal matters into your planner and to schedule them as you do work priorities. Let's face a reality here; there will be times when you'll still have to make the tough choices, but once you get in the routine of planning your priorities, you'll be less likely to find yourself between a rock and a hard place as often. That's because you'll be accomplishing more on the job, delegating responsibilities where they actually belong, and actually "finding" time in your schedule to strike the life-work balance.

PHASE II: DAILY ROUTINE

We are now making the shift from the big-picture view of your work and life priorities to the specific activities that will produce your daily schedules. You'll be performing the following steps each night in order to create the prioritized schedule that will guide you through the next day.

Go to a quiet place in your home or at work, away from the distractions and demands of your professional and personal life—a home office, your bedroom, or your desk at the office with the door closed. Let others know in advance that you will need ten to twenty minutes of uninterrupted time, and then keep the promise to yourself to use that time to organize yourself for the following day.

Get your daily priority planner and a pencil—*not* a pen, since you might need to make adjustments later—and let's get started!

Example Planner with Time Calculations

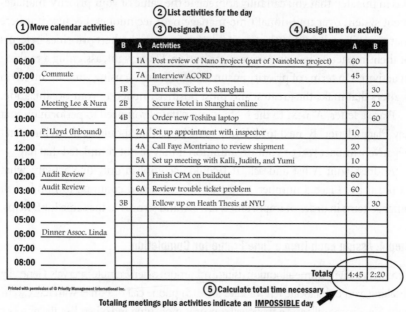

	B	A	Activities	A	B
05:00					
06:00		1A	Post review of Nano Project (part of Nanoblox project)	60	
07:00 Commute		7A	Interview ACORD	45	
08:00	1B		Purchase Ticket to Shanghai		30
09:00 Meeting Lee & Nura	2B		Secure Hotel in Shanghai online		20
10:00	4B		Order new Toshiba laptop		60
11:00 P: Lloyd (Inbound)		2A	Set up appointment with inspector	10	
12:00		4A	Call Faye Montriano to review shipment	20	
01:00		5A	Set up meeting with Kalli, Judith, and Yumi	10	
02:00 Audit Review		3A	Finish CPM on buildout	60	
03:00 Audit Review		6A	Review trouble ticket problem	60	
04:00	3B		Follow up on Heath Thesis at NYU		30
05:00					
06:00 Dinner Assoc. Linda					
07:00					
08:00					
			Totals	4:45	2:20

① Move calendar activities
② List activities for the day
③ Designate A or B
④ Assign time for activity
⑤ Calculate total time necessary

Totaling meetings plus activities indicate an **IMPOSSIBLE** day

Printed with permission of © Priority Management International Inc.

Printed with permission of © Priority Management International Inc.

Figure 3.26—Example Planner with Time Calculations

Step 1: Move Confirmed Meetings from Your Calendar onto Your Daily-View Page

Now that you've come to the end of your day or the near close of your day and are looking forward to the next day's responsibilities, it's time for you to transfer all confirmed meetings and time-specific events for tomorrow from your calendar to your daily-view page: staff meeting from 9 to 10, phone call from a vendor at 11, audit from 2 to 3, and dinner meeting at 6. Include any personal commitments, too, such as a dental appointment, soccer game, book club meeting, and so on.

Step 2: Transfer Tasks and Activities onto Your Daily-View Page

Looking at your daily-view page, you may find that you're working with a blank slate or that you have previously added one or more activities, some of which may have been added months earlier, as is the case with items like project activities from CPM charts or strategic plans. At this time, add any additional activities and priorities that you expect to accomplish tomorrow. Later you can edit this list, if you find that your time is better spent on higher-priority items, which is why using a pencil is important.

Step 3: Prioritize the List of Activities on Your Daily-View Page

It is in this step that you can fully appreciate the value of your priority-management system over traditional time-management techniques, because it is here that you will really put in the time to determine your highest priorities in terms of their impact on you and your organization. Done right, assigning a ranking of activities in terms of priority ensures that you are focusing your attention on matters that make the greatest and most positive impact on your organization.

Place a letter "A" next to the highest-value items you need to perform on that day. Place a letter "B" next to all lower-value items that should be done, but won't negatively impact you or your organization if they're not completed that day.

Address your A list and ask, If I could accomplish only one activity, what would it be? Place a number 1 next to this item, and continue to number all other A items in order of importance: 2A, 3A, and so on. Do the same for B items.

Step 4: Assign Each Item a Time Frame for Completion

Give every activity a time allocation using a minimum of ten-minute intervals. Generally speaking, you can allocate ten minutes for each phone call or e-mail with few exceptions. Since some calls and e-mails will consume more time and others less, the number of minutes usually averages out by day's end. (Look at the diagram, Figure 3.27, for an example of how minutes are listed in the right-hand columns labeled "A" and "B.")

Step 5: Balance Out the Big-Picture View of Your Daily Schedule

For our purposes here, we will use an eight-hour workday. However, I realize that for many people in management positions, *only* eight hours seems like a pipe dream. I've seen partners at a Madrid law firm who are expected to work from 8 am to 10 pm. A continent away in the United States, insurance company senior managers are arising by 4 am to get their prework tasks done before putting in twelve-hour work days. That leaves only eight hours for travel to and from work, for sleep, and for stolen moments with family. If you can relate to these situations, my hope is that your use of this tool over time will make the eight-hour workday more realistic.

Subtract from your eight hours of work time the amount of time you have already allocated for prescheduled meetings from your calendar, and for lunch and travel. Say that these activities total three hours. You may assume that you have five hours remaining for the activities on your daily-view page, but actually, if you follow Principle 2, you should only schedule 60% of those five hours, which amounts to approximately three hours.

Now tally up the minutes you've allocated for all of your daily activities. Write the total number of prescheduled minutes *in hours and minutes,* and subtract this number from the three hours you have left. If the sum of your activities exceeds three hours, then you must move your lowest-priority items (from your B list) to another day or week. By recording the activity in the future and eliminating it from your day, you know you won't forget it.

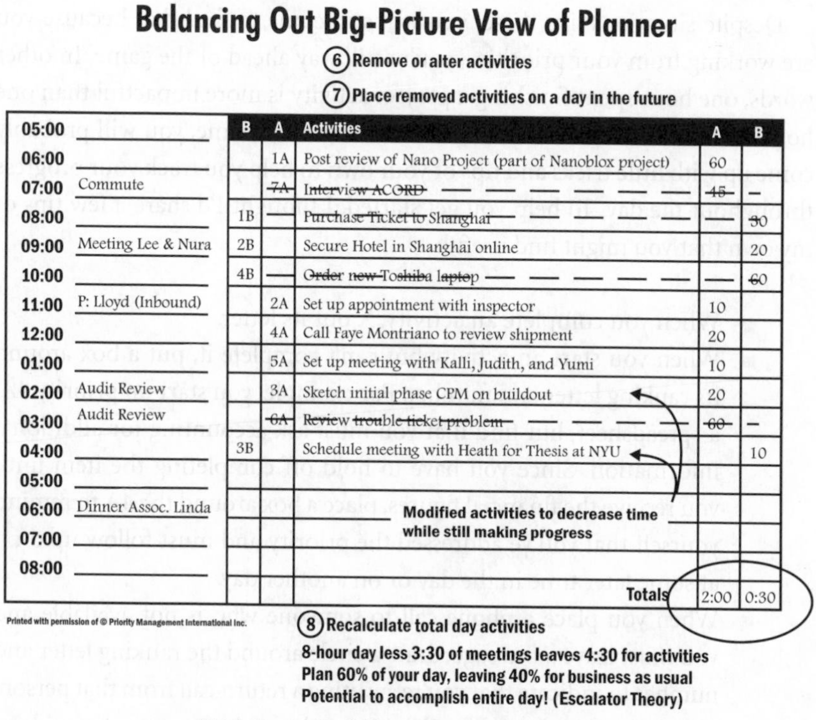

Balancing Out Big-Picture View of Planner

⑥ Remove or alter activities

⑦ Place removed activities on a day in the future

	B	A	Activities	A	B
05:00					
06:00		1A	Post review of Nano Project (part of Nanoblox project)	60	
07:00 Commute		~~7A~~	~~Interview ACORD~~ — — — — — —	~~45~~	—
08:00	1B		~~Purchase Ticket to Shanghai~~ — — — — —	—	~~30~~
09:00 Meeting Lee & Nura	2B		Secure Hotel in Shanghai online		20
10:00	4B		~~Order new Toshiba laptop~~ — — — — —	—	~~60~~
11:00 P: Lloyd (Inbound)		2A	Set up appointment with inspector	10	
12:00		4A	Call Faye Montriano to review shipment	20	
01:00		5A	Set up meeting with Kalli, Judith, and Yumi	10	
02:00 Audit Review		3A	Sketch initial phase CPM on buildout	20	
03:00 Audit Review		~~6A~~	~~Review trouble-ticket problem~~ — — — —	~~60~~	—
04:00	3B		Schedule meeting with Heath for Thesis at NYU		10
05:00					
06:00 Dinner Assoc. Linda			**Modified activities to decrease time**		
07:00			**while still making progress**		
08:00					
			Totals	2:00	0:30

Printed with permission of © Priority Management International Inc.

⑧ Recalculate total day activities

8-hour day less 3:30 of meetings leaves 4:30 for activities
Plan 60% of your day, leaving 40% for business as usual
Potential to accomplish entire day! (Escalator Theory)

Printed with permission of © Priority Management International Inc.

Figure 3.27—Balancing Out Big-Picture View of Planner

Here's where the Escalator Theory comes into play. If you plan a day that is achievable, you're more likely to feel a sense of urgency and to work a little faster to get the work done.

Step 5A: Put the planner aside and enjoy your evening knowing that you've planned your day and already directed tomorrow's focus on the right activities. You will most likely sleep better because your system removes the mental burden of uncertainty.

Step 6: Work from the Planner

When you begin your day, you start with item 1A, the most important item on your list. In an ideal situation, you try to complete one item before moving on to the next, which in this case would be item 2A, then 3A, and so on. As you move through the day, you may find that for any number of reasons, you're just not able to fully complete an activity before proceeding on to the next. Obviously, if you're waiting for a colleague to get back to you on a matter before you can perform an activity and cross the item off your list, you're not going to sit idle for very long. That's when you have to jump to the next priority on your list and expect to return to this preceding item when it's feasible to do so.

Despite situations like these, you will still come to find that because you are working from your priorities, you're still way ahead of the game. In other words, one hour spent finishing a project activity is more impactful than one hour spent on three trivial items. Over the course of time, you will probably come up with little tricks and tips of your own to help you track your progress throughout the day. To help you get started, I thought I'd share a few tips of my own that you might find useful:

- When you complete an activity, X out its letter.
- When you start an activity but can't complete it, put a box around its ranking letter and number. For example, you start on priority 4A, a spreadsheet, but find that you must ask accounting for additional information. Since you have to hold off completing the item until you receive the financial figures, place a box around the 4A to remind yourself that you've addressed the priority and must follow up on it at some later time in the day or on another day.
- When you place a phone call to someone who is not available and you must leave a message, draw a circle around the ranking letter and number to indicate that you're awaiting a return call from that person.
- If you discover that you no longer need to complete an activity, draw a horizontal line through its ranking letter and number.

- Say that you have already listed your daily activities and have assigned a priority ranking to each one. Then a new responsibility or activity arises that requires your attention on that day. You can easily incorporate this new item into your daily planner by listing it, assigning the letter C to it, and then ranking the item as a new priority. This way you will not forget to complete the activity during the day or in the future.

Planner Activity Example

Completed activity

Call initiated (left message/voicemail)

Started activity but not completed

Activity no longer necessary

Figure 3.28—Planner Activity Example

Step 7: At the End of Each Day, Reschedule Unfinished Activities

At the end of each day, you have to address any unfinished activities. It's at this point on many a day that you can look back on the planning you did the night before and feel grateful for having crafted a realistic and achievable schedule, because you'll have to make fewer decisions about the handling of unfinished items. Chances are, before you plan for the following day, you will move unfinished activities either to tomorrow's daily planner, to an appropriate future date, or to another person to ensure that they are addressed.

The Link between Priority Management and Thinking

Some decision makers want a lot of structure in a priority-management system, while some want a little. Where you fall on the spectrum depends as much on your leadership style and personality as it does on the structure and needs of your organization. The bottom line is this: Every decision maker needs to manage his or her priorities on a daily basis. Gone are the days of flying by the seat of one's pants or of simply attempting to "manage time." Ultimately, priority management boils down to one crucial benefit:

Priority management gives decision makers more time to think!

When you spend the right amount of time thinking and less time focused on the tactical or reacting, you make better decisions, avoid costly mistakes, identify and create opportunities faster and more accurately, earn WSPs (the building blocks of your organization), and move your organization, your career, and your personal life ahead by leaps and bounds. Thinking is your ultimate job, and priority management enables you to more effectively deliver good decisions back to your organization.

■ ■ ■

In this chapter, you learned about three interconnected elements that are essential to developing plans: Strategy, projects, and priority management. To the average leader, they may not appear as intrinsically symbiotic as they actually are, but through the eyes of the Enterprise Thinker equipped with the right tools, one element can't provide optimal benefits to an organization without the other two. The CST Model enables you to create a Strategy that is directly tied to an overall Desired Outcome so you set your organization's sail in the right direction at the start. Then, to reach that Strategy, you search for Macro Tactics, the best of which are often projects that can advance your organization not by inches, but by miles at a time.

Then every project needs to be carried out to its successful conclusion, made possible through proper planning, guidance, and attention on a daily basis, which is where the priority management system plays a vital role. Essentially, these three planning parts—Strategy, projects, and priority management—and their corresponding tools channel leadership thinking so that it provides the greatest value to the organization: the CST Model produces unsiloed strategic thinking at 50,000 feet, projects deploy assets to accelerate organizational transformation, and priority management ensures that day-to-day activities are focused on reaching Desired Outcomes.

You've learned some relevant concepts in this chapter that you will use throughout your career, and you've also gained some new leadership tools that you can put to immediate use to solve some of your most pressing challenges. As you read subsequent chapters, you will revisit some of these concepts and tools and continue to accumulate new ones that will empower you to perform the twelve leadership activities of Enterprise Thinking and ultimately boost your effectiveness as a leader and manager. In addition, these universal activities and tools are transferrable, meaning you can teach them to others—both internal and external people who play a role in the success of your organization—to communicate and work more effectively with each other and expand the benefits of Enterprise Thinking.

CREATING NEW PRODUCTS AND SERVICES

DAN WATSON SLID INTO THE chair behind his desk and smiled at his son, Peter, who was seated across from him. The two had come to look forward to the Tuesday morning meetings where Dan would impart nuggets of leadership wisdom to his one-day successor. For the last thirty-five years, Dan had built a multimillion-dollar die-casting business from the ground up, and he was grooming Peter to take the reins.

"What can you tell me about products? Give me some examples of products," Dan began.

Peter wasn't sure where his father was going with this, since both men knew that Peter understood what a product was, but he played along, anyway. "Things that go on store shelves like books and laundry detergent, as well as couches, wheel bearings, automobiles, and consumer goods."

"Anything else?"

"I'm not sure what you're asking," Peter responded.

"Okay, that's fine." Dan paused for a moment and asked, "Who in our company is responsible for creating new products?"

Peter's mind quickly scrolled through part of their employee roster, settling on the four staffers who pitch new product ideas to Dan. "Rick, Patricia, Larry, and Bill," he answered with a sense of satisfaction.

"Anyone else?" Dan asked.

This time, Peter just looked at his father. Dan pushed his chair away from his desk, stood up, and walked to the window.

"Tell me why companies create new products."

"So they can stay competitive."

"Right! But when you think about products, Pete, have you ever thought about *internal* products, like the new phone system we just got for the office? How about a new warehouse that improves operational efficiencies? Even the health insurance we offer to our employees so that they'll stay here and not go to work for a competitor across town is a product. These kinds of improvements keep us competitive too."

"I'll have to think about that," Peter said. "I've never thought of them as products."

"That's okay, Pete. Most people haven't. Let me put it this way. If we were to consider our internal products as well as our external products, can you think of any other people here outside of Rick, Patricia, Larry, and Bill who are responsible for product development?"

"I think I see where you're going with this. You're saying that everyone here is responsible for creating new products, not just the new product development team; that is, of course, if we expand the definition of what a product is."

Dan was pleased. Peter was getting it. "That's correct. Whether we're talking about phone systems in the office, health-care benefits in HR, direct-deposit payroll checks from accounting, or a standard procedure in production, everyone here is responsible for creating new products that keep us competitive."

Peter left the weekly meeting rethinking his outlook on products and how it might help him create opportunities for the organization. Instantly, he felt a renewed sense of excitement that he could provide greater value to the die-cast company, and he suspected that his coworkers would feel the same way once he shared this new perspective with them.

Like Peter, you may have previously thought of products as tangible items your organization offers to the outside world. And if your organization provides services, maybe you have considered those services to be your products. In both instances, you would be right. However, your definition wouldn't be as inclusive as it could be (or even should be) if you really want to propel your organization forward. As you read through this chapter, keep Peter's lesson at the forefront of your thinking. By expanding your definition of "products" to include internal offerings as well as external, you open the scope of opportunities available to your organization.

As a decision maker, you're regularly thinking about ways to strengthen your organization through its offerings: products you can create to capture market share, how you can improve upon existing products to retain customers, or services you must provide to gain funding and to keep your doors open. When you consider that the best organizations expect close to half of all sales to come from new products commercialized in the last three years, you quickly realize that developing your next winning product or service can't be left to chance.

Yet from my experience, most decision makers do just that. They approach new product development by the seat of their pants, assuming it's too creative a process to be systemized. But this "organic approach" is no approach at all. It's little more than guesswork that promises iffy outcomes at best. If this or a similar method has been your modus operandi, you'll know by chapter's end why a new approach is needed, because in this chapter you will learn new concepts along with a logical, step-by-step tool, the ET Development Funnel, which will empower you to achieve more targeted outcomes, mitigate risk, and optimize returns the next time you develop winning products or services.

Before we get to the tool, we need to lay some mental groundwork surrounding the concept of an expanded view of "products" and what this means to your organization today and in the future.

The Benefits of Expanding Your Perspective

Think about the products in your organization, starting with your accounting department. What would you say are the products and services that this department offers? To better answer that question, think about the 80% of your GPP equation: systems and structures. Within the context of the GPP, you may identify some of your accounting department's products as financial statements, invoices, and payroll checks. And while your accounting department isn't manufacturing consumer goods or selling retail, it does create products and services to do its work. Financial statements, for instance, are products of the accounting department, and if they're done wrong or they're late, it can wreak real havoc within an organization. I can't tell you how many companies that I've worked with—from small nonprofits to those doing billions in sales—whose management does not get weekly, monthly, or even yearly financial numbers until months after they're of any use at all! Mind you, the fault typically doesn't rest with the hardworking people in accounting offices, either. The true culprit tends to be the lack of appropriate systems that would enable staffers to properly address the functions of their job.

Take, for instance, a common scenario where a person who is working in accounts payable can't pay your bills, because he can never be sure how much cash is on hand to issue checks or electronic transfers to your vendors. The flawed system ties the hands of your staff member, causes a bill to be paid late, and could result in a vendor having to place a hold on your account. If someone in your production department is counting on a part to repair a piece of equipment from said vendor, he may not receive it, shutting down production for several days. The ripple effect such a shutdown creates is never good.

You can lose patrons when shipments are late, you can lose your credit and be forced to pay for items up front, and now you've tied up more cash and exacerbated your problems. In a $500 million company where I advised management, I discovered that employee turnover was incredibly high, but not because people didn't like working for the company. It was because payroll and especially commissionable sales checks were always wrong, and sometimes employees had to make multiple calls to the accounting department until the issues were corrected. Personally, I've switched vendors many times when I was happy with their products but too frustrated to deal with their accounting departments' errors.

So if people in your accounting department were to adopt this broadened view of products, they would be more likely to view the value to your organization within a broader context, perhaps becoming excited at the prospect of increasing their value, and in turn begin to increase the speed at which they pay vendors (a service) or produce more accurate sales commissions checks that retain your top sales earners (a product).

Keep in mind that not everyone on staff will share or understand your 50,000-foot perspective and how they fit within it in terms of products and services. It's okay that your frontline people or even midlevel managers might or might not see the bigger picture and understand how to improve their ability to create or deliver better products and services. Ultimately, you as a decision maker have the responsibility to assess how your staffers play an integral role in creating and/or delivering "products" that keep your entire organization strong, and it's up to you to provide them with updated and improved systems, knowledge, or tools they will need in order to provide internal and external products and services successfully.

As your mind becomes more accustomed to this expanded definition of organization-wide products and services, you almost can't help but see all the new ways that you can multiply improvements throughout your organization. For example, you and your human resource staffers can likely take on a renewed perspective of their value to your organization, prompting them to become more aggressive in their search to secure a superior benefits package that attracts key management-level talent and reduces frontline employee turnover, or they may introduce Enterprise Thinking as an educational "product" to all leaders in the organization to improve their productivity. Consider how your IT department, armed with the right product development process, might improve upon your systems and technologies in order to optimize the performance of their coworkers.

From here on out, whenever you think about "products" or read about them in this book, remind yourself of this expanded definition—that products are both internal and external products and services. Doing so will stretch your mind and your scope of opportunities. Perhaps you'll want to put your new way of thinking to use right away. The following is a list of some suggested areas where you can immediately begin identifying opportunities on your own:

DESIGN	online services, logos, prototypes, storyboarding
FINANCE	proposals, investment packages, credit card offerings
SALES	package deals, territory design, new videos, CRM implementation
MANUFACTURING	equipment purchases, staging systems, building purchase and design
OPERATIONS	24-hour tech support, site selection, logistics vendors, infrastructure, RFID
MARKETING	ad campaigns, surveys, new products or services, supporting literature, copy
ACCOUNTING	invoices and statements, reports, loans, internal software
IT	software, server, computers, partners, website for customer support, e-mail services
HUMAN RESOURCES	training, handbook, benefits, leasing, hiring new employees
MAINTENANCE	chemicals, tools, software, operational approaches, outsourcing
LOGISTICS	shippers, online tracking, rental storage, office space
ENGINEERING	new processes, forms, CAD system, tracking tools

By now, you're surely seeing how your expanded definition can drastically improve your organization. Let's make a slight shift in our thinking and apply this concept to your role as a decision maker: more specifically, how it will increase the *value you provide to your organization* by equipping you to increasingly make better decisions that will in turn skyrocket the potential of your organization. Yet, perception alone isn't enough to bring order out of new product and service development (NPSD) "chaos." You need to combine it with the right tools, which is where the universally applicable ET Development Funnel comes into play.

Whether you're a product developer in the traditional sense or a decision maker who works outside the realm of product development, you will now have the means to formalize your NPSD process and gain predictable and reliable results. You can be a business owner, CEO, film director, four-star general, school principal, company president, agency director, or prime minister and adapt the ET Development Funnel to make countless enhancements to your products, services, and operations.

Additionally, in upcoming chapters, you will learn how to further adapt the ET Development Funnel to bolster your performance of other ET activities, too, like leveraging technology or establishing alliances.

For now, we will look at how you're currently approaching NPSD and how you can easily transition to this advanced process.

Improving Your New Product Development Process

For a select group of leaders, new product and service development appears to come naturally. Take, for instance, Richard Branson, the creative founder behind the Virgin brand, who seems to easily recognize opportunities and convert them to winning results. Recalling a plane trip he once took, Branson said, "I wanted to talk to the pretty girl in the next aisle, but I was stuck in my seat the entire flight."[34] As a result of his feelings of being bogged down during that trip, he instituted stand-up bars in Virgin's cabins, an enhancement that enabled passengers to freely interact with one another. On another occasion, he took the advice of his wife's manicurist in introducing in-flight nail treatments and massages, skipping market research altogether and going directly to service development. "Sounds like a great idea. Screw it. Let's do it." The service exploded and Virgin's staff grew by 700 massage- and beauty-treatment therapists. Branson has a gift for successfully selecting winning products. What leader wouldn't love to have his talent? At the same time, he's not so married to his ideas that he isn't willing to let them go and evolve his offerings as the market dictates.

In reality, success for Branson and a handful of leaders like him comes from a natural internal process where the mind runs its own stepped NPSD process. Over time, the talent is honed, giving these "naturals" the ability to select the right idea at the right time and develop it into a winning product. But all is not lost if you're not naturally outfitted with this talent.

Fortunately, we nonnaturals can level the playing field by making use of tools that lead us through a structured NPSD process. The first step is to somehow transition away from the informal, organic approach where you can be easily tempted to act on what you consider a great idea with little or no research to back your assumptions, and to move toward a stepped process like the ET Development Funnel, where you are more assuredly empowered to create order from "chaos," identify your best opportunities, and similarly produce winning outcomes.

Figure 4.1 illustrates the typical informal ways in which many leaders select new products or services for development. At the top of the diagram, balls representing ideas fall into the mouth of a funnel. As you consider internal forces—manpower, resources, strengths and weaknesses, etc.—and external forces—vendor capabilities, deadlines, buying cycles, etc.—you conclude that some ideas won't achieve Desired Outcomes, and you eliminate them from contention. You allow other ideas, those that you label as good, to fall through the mouth of the funnel and remain viable. Using this model, you would select what you *think* is the best idea and develop it.

Funnel Diagram of Selection Process for New Products

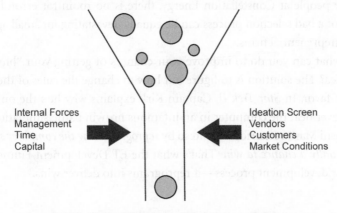

Internal Forces
Management
Time
Capital

Ideation Screen
Vendors
Customers
Market Conditions

Figure 4.1—Funnel Diagram of Selection Process for New Products

Sometimes, leaders don't even choose the idea that they believe is the best idea; they respond to internal politics and make their selections based on *who* presented the ideas rather than on the merits of ideas themselves. As bad as it is to make this error in judgment once or twice, organizations that continually determine projects based on personalities, positions of authority, or sales pitches increase risks, invest in projects that deliver lower returns, and over time, weaken their organizations to the point where their survival is at stake.

Working with an idea without some assurance that it is your best idea is a gamble that most leaders can't afford to take. You have to make the determination with more certainty, or you risk joining the ranks of the 25% to 45% of new product launches that fail.[35] Also, without an improved selection process, you are unlikely to choose your best idea on your first attempt. This is because the typical selection process is nearly as random as the way a gum ball machine dispenses gum balls.

Imagine yourself as a small child standing before a gum ball machine filled with red, green, blue, and yellow gum balls. You have two coins, and you want a blue gum ball, so you drop one coin into the slot and hope that your blue gum ball drops out of the machine. If you get a red gum ball instead, you can spend your last coin trying to get a blue gum ball, but you can only *hope* to get your Desired Outcome, because the machine is randomly selecting the gum ball for you. If you were to apply this analogy to your current situation, these gum balls represent ideas flowing through your organization, and the gum ball dispenser represents your current selection process.

The ramifications of leaving your selection process to chance can be huge. Obviously, if you're involved in building multibillion-dollar nuclear reactors like the people at Constellation Energy, there is no room for error, but the effects of a bad selection process can be equally devastating for small agencies and entrepreneurial firms.

So what can you do to improve your chances of getting your "blue gum ball" idea? The solution is to figure out how to change the rules of the game in your favor. In *Star Trek II*, Captain Kirk explains why he's the only person to ever beat the computer in an infamous no-win battle simulation (the Kobayashi Maru scenario). He did so by *reprogramming the computer so there was actually a chance to win*. That's what the ET Development Funnel does for your development process—it reprograms it to deliver wins.

A Better Way to Select Ideas for Development

In the organic NPSD process, too often leaders don't realize they're working with an idea that won't deliver the results they want until after they've invested resources like capital, time, and human labor into it. Yet, by installing mechanisms to filter out less-promising ideas from those that will deliver optimal outcomes, you can steer your selection and development in the right direction from the start.

For the purposes of carrying forth our analogy, let's empty the gum ball dispenser of its gum balls and replace them with one hundred toy balls, eighty made of aluminum, nineteen made of silver, and one encrusted with diamonds. The eighty aluminum balls are your product/service/improvement ideas that will generate modest returns, the nineteen silver balls promise better returns, and the single diamond ball is the superior idea that will generate the best returns for your organization.

Say that you had only two coins but absolutely had to have the diamond ball; you probably wouldn't risk both coins in the dispenser. Instead, you'd install a sorting mechanism to winnow out the diamond ball from the rest. Assuming that the diamond ball is heavier than all other balls, your mechanism could be programmed to prevent all lighter-weight balls from falling through the dispenser. The advantage of good selection mechanisms is that they increase the likelihood that only your "diamond ball" idea is dispensed for future development.

The funnel of your ET Development Funnel process works much like the ball dispenser. Once you have placed your ideas into the top of the funnel, the screens, composed of *predetermined criteria,* block the least viable options from passing through. Figure 4.2 highlights three types of screens that are essential to the product-development process:

- **Ideation Screen:** Filters out the highest volume of less-befitting ideas based on broad criteria.
- **Surface Evaluation Screen:** Filters out more of the weaker ideas based on specific criteria.
- **Detailed Evaluation Screen:** Filters out all but one best idea—your "diamond" idea—based on the most detailed criteria.

Funnel Diagram of Improved Process

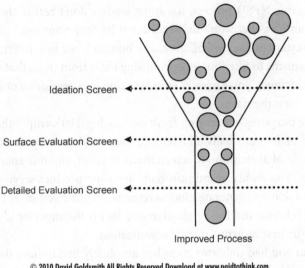

Ideation Screen

Surface Evaluation Screen

Detailed Evaluation Screen

Improved Process

Figure 4.2—Funnel Diagram of Improved Process

Already you can see how making (even micro) adjustments to your selection process can drastically improve outcomes, because even before you make the decision to spend resources on developing an idea, you've already ensured that it is a diamond idea that promises greater returns for your organization. That's the Economics of Thinking at work.

Gathering Better Ideas Up Front

Similarly, starting the entire process with an ample number of ideas can be just as important to final outcomes as your selection process itself. Too often, leaders select an idea from a collection of too few ideas, too few good ideas, or both. To gather more and better ideas up front, try using the Concept of $100 > 7 > 3 > 1$, where 100 represents the number of ideas you originally place into the funnel, 7 and 3 represent the number of ideas remaining after your first and second rounds of eliminations respectively, leading to 1 "diamond" idea that will go into development.

Why $100 > 7 > 3 > 1$? After years of working with clients and teaching leaders, I've found that most decision makers have a tendency to limit their options too quickly or to begin eliminating ideas before they've even accumulated their best options for consideration. So by starting with a hundred ideas, you have forced yourself and others to engage in some significant ideation, increasing your odds of finding the "diamond" idea. In addition, whittling the quantity of viable options to seven in the first round of elimi-nations has shown to give people a manageable number of ideas to evaluate while still keeping strong options alive. The same logic applies to the next round of elimination that leaves three ideas that you and your group must expand upon and give more involved consideration to before making a final determination. So, in essence, my experiences with decision makers (across all management levels, industries and sectors, and cultures and geographies) has shown that the formula of $100 > 7 > 3 > 1$ works.

Why *one* idea? You must focus energies and resources on developing one idea to its end "product" or risk suffering unfinished projects without any-thing to show for your investment.

One idea does not imply that an organization can't have several single ideas being developed simultaneously. It depends on the resources of the organization. IBM may roll out four different consulting services as part of a suite of offerings. Boeing may have several new product and service devel-opment groups working on several different market niches. Dubai's govern-ment, believing that oil revenues will one day decline, is investing billions in the construction of skyscrapers and other infrastructure as a means to attract tourism in the future. Each idea has to stand on its own, and the decisions behind these initiatives must all follow a similar process in order to ensure the Desired Outcomes. At this final stage of development, there will only be one product/service/improvement.

At this point, you now have two new concepts to help you gather more potentially successful ideas and to whittle them down to a single best idea. In the section below, you will see how you can use these concepts to cre-ate winning products, services, and improvements by examining the ET Development Funnel in its entirety.

The ET Development Funnel

The ET Development Funnel is a modified version of the Phase-Gate Process, a tool traditionally used within new product development circles for creating products that will be sold to customers. The modifications built into your new tool ensure that you and your staff members have a reliable universal process not only for developing winning products and services, but for creating inter-nal improvements, too. In addition, it is streamlined so that even beginners can learn and use it. If you have tried traditional new product development processes in the past, you will find this tool to be a simpler and easier version, because it graphically and visually represents what you do naturally.

The ET Development Funnel structures the creative and subjective aspects of the NPSD process into a series of logical steps that ensures that your selected idea is successfully developed into an end "product" that achieves your Desired Outcomes.

The ET Development Funnel process contains the three essential elements of successful product development:

- **Ideation (Activity I):** at the wide mouth of the funnel, which includes an Idea Bank for capturing many good ideas from the start.
- **Elimination (Activity II):** with its three screens for unveiling a single best idea worthy of placing into Development.
- **Development (Activity III):** the horizontal pipeline of phases and gates that coordinate the work of cross-functional groups responsible for converting your best idea into a winning end product.

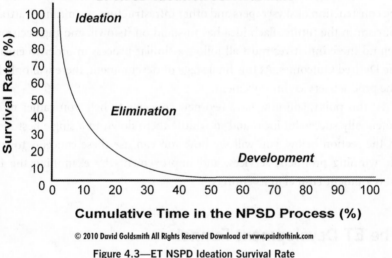

ET NPSD Ideation Survival Rate

Figure 4.3—ET NSPD Ideation Survival Rate

The chart (Figure 4.3) helps illustrate what you've just read. Let's assume you do everything right. The first thing you need to do is generate ideas (Ideation). In this case, there were 100 created. The next activity is Elimination. The screens help you to discern what has potential and what does not. Rapidly, your 100 ideas drop to only a few. The final activity is Development, where in the real world, organizations implement one idea for

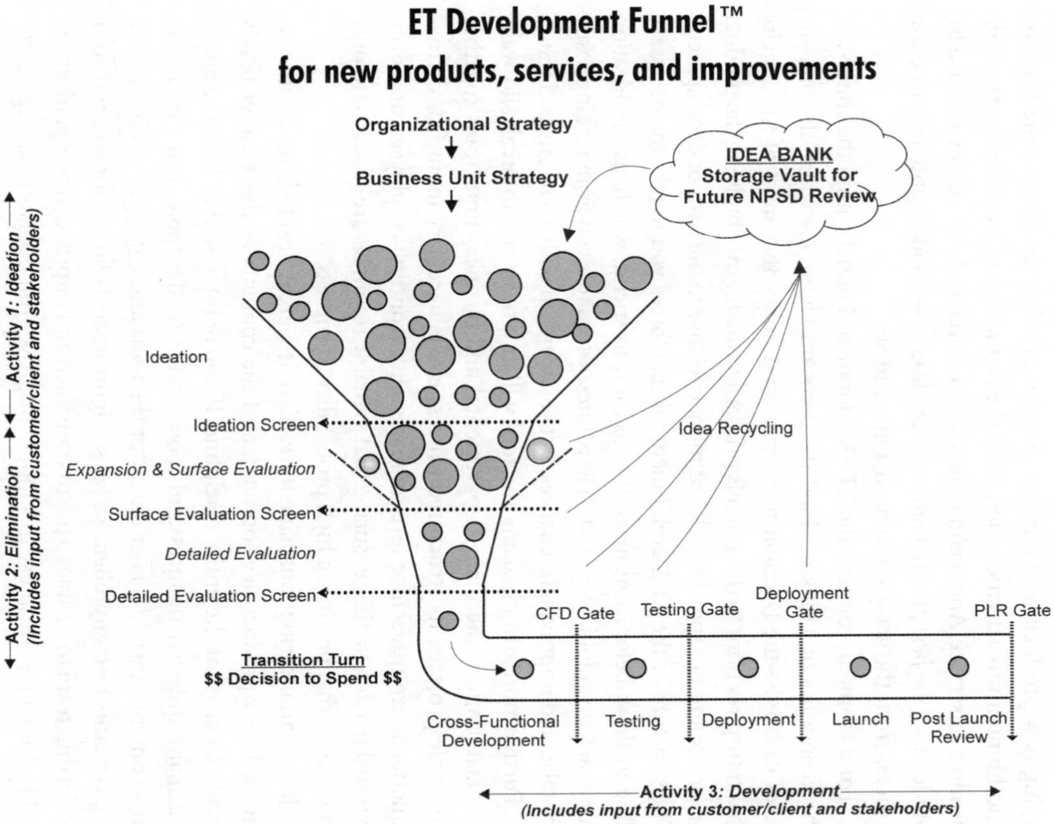

ET Development Funnel™
for new products, services, and improvements

Organizational Strategy

Business Unit Strategy

IDEA BANK
Storage Vault for
Future NPSD Review

Idea Recycling

Ideation

Ideation Screen

Expansion & Surface Evaluation

Surface Evaluation Screen

Detailed Evaluation

Detailed Evaluation Screen

Transition Turn
$$ Decision to Spend $$

CFD Gate

Testing Gate

Deployment Gate

PLR Gate

Cross-Functional Development

Testing

Deployment

Launch

Post Launch Review

Activity 3: Development
(Includes input from customer/client and stakeholders)

Activity 2: Elimination

Activity 1: Ideation
(Includes input from customer/client and stakeholders)

Figure 4.4—Enterprise Thinking Development Funnel™

one particular challenge. There would be no good reason, for example, to create two fresh produce sections in the same grocery store. The Development part of the NPSD process according to the timeline may require just as much time as the earlier activities. So we're really addressing two underlying points here. First, individuals and organizations that are the most successful at developing new products and services spend more time *up front* in the Ideation and Elimination activities, increasing the chances that they develop the *right* product or service. And second, the same research indicates that without a lot of ideation, the *best* product and service ideas never make it into the selection process from the get-go. You need a lot of ideas.

For a moment, consider the ET Development Funnel within the context of the Economics of Thinking. Find the point on Figure 4.4 where the pipeline takes its bend—the Decision to Spend—and notice that most of the activity that transpires prior to this point is primarily *thinking*, not building the product or service and not spending a lot of money relative to the costs of development. The structure of the ET Development Funnel forces you to take the necessary time to think before you make the decision to spend, which, as the Ideation Survival Rate graphic (Figure 4.3) illustrates, safeguards you from making costly mistakes and improves the chances that you wind up with a winning end result.

Furthermore, simply using the tool will empower you to break silo walls by default and bring many departmental and business-unit heads together on single projects. Its structured process elicits necessary input from cross-functional groups, senior-level management, frontline employees, and even external parties, further ensuring that valuable resources are allocated to only those ideas that promise a high probability of success.

Just as an informational side note, there is a great deal to learn about traditional new product development, and the contents of this chapter barely break the crust of the entire discipline. If you're interested in learning about the many different nuances and tools related to the topic, you can always do so on your own at a later date. But the tools and concepts you learn here will certainly be comprehensive yet straightforward enough for you and your leadership team to be able to use to transform and improve your organization.

Finally, you will also use this tool to improve your decision making. That's because data accumulated throughout the funnel and pipeline activities is fed back to leadership, where it can be used for current and future strategizing activities. When you see how all your ET concepts and tools feed into one another in this manner, you can't help but make the types of decisions that build a stronger future for your organization.

So let's walk through the ET Development Funnel process together.

Pre-Work to the Process

Any time that you set out to develop an idea, you must do some preparatory work so that all subsequent activities and expenditures take your organization where you want it to go. Before you begin the ET Development Funnel process, you will (1) predetermine screening and gatekeeping criteria that your ideas must meet in order to pass through the elimination screens, (2) choose your screeners, people who can objectively check ideas against criteria to ensure the right ideas are passing through each of the three elimination screens, (3) select your gatekeepers, an impartial group of people who make sure that all requirements have been met before your product/service/improvement is allowed to progress to the next phase of development, and (4) assemble your new product and service development group (NPSD group), the people with whom you will work throughout the process from Ideation to the final phases of Development.

1) PREDETERMINING SCREENING AND GATEKEEPING CRITERIA

Screens are the mechanisms within your process that filter out "aluminum" and "silver" ideas to eventually reveal your "diamond" idea. These screens and gates act as go/kill points, meaning that ideas meeting criteria are allowed to pass through to next phases, whereas ideas failing to meet criteria are "killed" at screening checkpoints. In the Development pipeline, where your "diamond" idea is developed, your go/kill points are called gates rather than screens, because the purpose of each type of checkpoint is different. Screens are meant to eliminate all but the best and most appropriate ideas so that you end up with a single best idea, whereas gates ensure that all persons have completed the necessary work to safely move your single best idea onto the next activity. From my years of working with clients, I have found it best if you can visualize screeners with sieves, sifting out better ideas from lesser ones, and gatekeepers as airport customs officers who make sure your idea has completed all the right paperwork and activities to gain entry to the next leg of your trip. For both screens/screeners and gates/gatekeepers, you must create the criteria in advance so that the process remains objective and you are prevented from allowing a lesser idea to slip through screens and gates simply because you fell in love with it.

When you build predetermined criteria into your screening and gatekeeping checkpoints, you are increasing the likelihood that the idea you eventually develop is the one that best aligns with Desired Outcome and supports

Strategy. For instance, if your organization places a strong focus on protecting the environment, one screening criterion could be to eliminate all product ideas that fail to make use of biodegradable materials.

There are three categories of criteria that respond to the three screens of the ET Development Funnel: (1) broad criteria of the Ideation Screen, (2) specific criteria of the Surface Evaluation Screen, and (3) detailed criteria of the Detailed Evaluation Screen.

Broad Criteria of the Ideation Screen

You will first establish the broad criteria that your ideas must meet in order to pass through the Ideation Screen. Depending on the product or service you want to develop, these criteria can cover a broad spectrum of options from utilizing an existing logistics system to being socially responsible. So if you were using the ET Development Funnel to accomplish the daunting task of hiring one "diamond" manager from a stack of a thousand resumes, you would establish a set of broad criteria—three years of experience in the industry, five references, and a degree in marketing—to eliminate the 900 people who definitely would not meet your needs.

To help you to determine the broad criteria of your product, you must first look to your Desired Outcome and Strategy, because what you select must be in alignment. When you're building your criteria list, here are some areas you may want to consider:

TECHNOLOGY	**RETURN ON INVESTMENT (ROI)**
DESIGN & PRODUCTION	**NET PRESENT VALUE (NPV)**
MARKETING	**ECONOMIC VALUE ADDED (EVA)**
DISTRIBUTION & SALES	**RISK-RETURN**
OPERATIONS	**CORE COMPETENCIES**

For example, you may say to your team, "We need a product that utilizes our existing distribution channel, can be designed for less than $4,000, can be sold for under $75, and will have a ROI of 37%." (**Note:** In case you needed to know, a simple ROI is calculated by dividing the amount of financial gain by total investment. However, be aware that not all organizations measure ROI in monetary terms.)

A toy manufacturer that wants to add a new product to its existing line might set broad criteria during the Ideation activity as:

- The toy must be a doll.
- The doll must appeal to the Latino market.
- The product must retail for less than $50.
- The product launch must occur within one year.
- Fifty percent of dolls must be manufactured in house.

Take time to meet with senior-level management at this early juncture to gain input from them. In this way, you protect yourself and your project from management interference at later points in the process where changes could potentially threaten development altogether. If you are a midlevel manager at this toy-manufacturing company, you might consult your CEO, the VP of sales, and the COO for input. Then use their responses to set broad and specific screening criteria. Taking this simple measure prevents leadership from becoming unhappy that their ideas are not being considered and possibly putting the kibosh on your project at a latter point in development, which can be very costly. Keeping them abreast of progress throughout the process typically ensures the likelihood that they can step back and allow the development process to move forward as it needs to proceed.

Specific Criteria of the Surface Evaluation Screen

Building the Surface Evaluation Screen involves similar work as that of the Ideation Screen, but your criteria become even more specific. You may find that consulting upper management and other personnel is helpful, since you may need additional information that only they are privy to, such as profit margins and raw materials' cost and availability. When determining the best go/kill criteria, you may want to consider some of the following factors:

MARKET ATTRACTIVENESS	**BUSINESS POSITION**
BARRIERS TO ENTRY	**STRATEGIC FIT**
BRAND LOYALTY	**CORE COMPETENCIES**
CUSTOMER BENEFITS	**INVESTMENT REQUIRED**
IMPROVED IMAGE	**RETURNS EXPECTED**
LOW VERSUS HIGH RISK	**LEGAL ISSUES**
MARKET POTENTIAL	**COMPETITIVE ADVANTAGE**
ENHANCED SERVICE	**ABILITY TO PRODUCE OR OFFER**
FORECASTED SHIFTS	**COMPATIBILITY WITH THE FIRM**

If we carry forward our doll-manufacturing example, we might consider appropriate specific screening criteria to look like this:

- The net profit margin must be no less than 14%.
- The doll must contain one unique characteristic that no other competitor offers.
- Forty percent of the product's raw materials must be made from recycled items.
- The line must have potential extension possibilities.

Detailed Criteria of the Detailed Evaluation Screen

The more detailed your criteria at the Detailed Evaluation Screen, the more likely your screeners are to eliminate lower return ideas and identify your "diamond" idea. Therefore, the criteria you use to build this final screen must be predetermined with great thought. Whether your idea will one day become a product, a service, or an improvement, it is at the building of this screen that you should definitely consult industry standards for legal restrictions, safety compliance, and so on. To be even more thorough, you could consult complementary or competing industries to gain the edge over others in your industry or sector to incorporate Order Winner features and characteristics that those within your industry don't yet offer.

Our doll manufacturer might require that all ideas pass criteria such as:

- The doll must meet strict government guidelines for age-appropriate safety features (e.g., no parts that pose a choking hazard to children between the ages of 3 and 8).
- The doll must fit within a 14" × 6" × 6" package weighing no more than 4 pounds.
- Paint and plastic used to create the doll and its accessories must be made of nontoxic materials.

Consider different cultures when you build screens, too. According to research conducted by Robert Cooper and Elko Kleinschmidt, products designed for an international market achieved an 85% success rate in the world market as opposed to 43% for domestically designed products aimed at a domestic market. As Cooper states in his book, *Winning at New Products,* "international new products aimed at foreign markets also do better in the home market—almost double the domestic market share versus domestic[ally-designed] products."[36]

A secret of many successful product developers is that they look around their markets for opportunities all while keeping a global mindset. If you're not thinking globally, you're missing opportunities. Now apply that concept to services and internal improvements as well. With our world becoming more of a melting pot where cultural diversity isn't just restricted to our major cities anymore, you're better off initially including criteria that appeals to a diverse market to prevent limiting your idea's potential by thinking too small.

Note: Although you may be tempted to get the project under way, be sure to build the criteria into your screens and gates *before* you move forward with the ET Development Funnel. As the leader, it's up to you to build the development process's Goldsmith Productivity Principle (GPP) before you plug people into it. If you fail to predetermine criteria, you and your NPSD group will find yourselves shooting for a moving target and eventually veering off course and away from your intended outcomes.

2) CHOOSING YOUR SCREENERS

Now that you have built criteria into your Ideation, Surface Evaluation, and Detailed Evaluation Screens, you must ensure that each and every idea meets screening criteria before it is allowed to pass through to the next phase. There have been occasions when leaders or members of the NPSD group have fallen in love with a particular idea to the point where they have been inclined to allow noncompliant ideas to pass through screens just the same. To be sure that your "diamond" idea is the one that eventually enters the Development pipeline, you need to safeguard against such biases. That is why at this step you choose an *impartial* "jury" of screeners outside your NPSD group to monitor ideas at screening checkpoints.

Have you ever been on your way out of a store and had to show your receipt to one of those attendants guarding the door? Their purpose is to make sure that you don't leave with an item without having paid for it. Your screeners perform a similar function at each screen. They must make sure that any idea passing through a screen has met the necessary requirements to pass on to the next phase. Just as the store's receipt checker is not there for the purpose of making recommendations on which products patrons should buy, your screeners do not evaluate, comment, or perform any function beyond the role of screening ideas against criteria.

Your particular situation will determine how your screeners will review the criteria that you have given them. Sometimes a simple checklist will suffice. Other times, the task of evaluating ideas against criteria is a bit more complex.

To accommodate the needs of some screeners, I have created a Product Matrix Chart as a sample of a methodology you can use. This is an optional measure, and you're free to modify the Product Matrix Chart you see in Figure 4.5 to meet your specific needs or not to use it at all. Basically, what you're doing is listing your ideas in the left-hand column, your criteria across the top, and then assigning points to each idea by category as a way of vetting your most viable ideas from the rest.

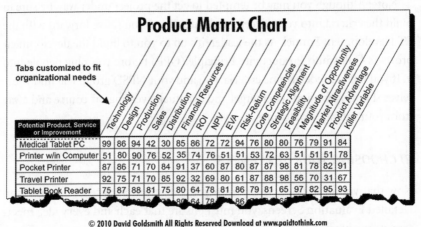

© 2010 David Goldsmith All Rights Reserved Download at www.paidtothink.com

Figure 4.5—Product Matrix Chart Sample

Rate ideas on a scale from 1 to 100, where 100 is the best possible score. Scores need to represent the relative importance of each criterion. A single legal criterion may be scored low enough to eliminate an idea from the running; a high score for a customer-benefit criterion could allow the idea to pass to the next step. Some of these ratings will be subjective, while others will come straight from statistical analysis. Either way, as long as screeners are clear about the criteria and adhere to their guidelines, you are assured that an idea isn't going to survive solely because someone fell in love with it.

3) SELECTING YOUR GATEKEEPERS

The function of gatekeepers is somewhat different than that of screeners. While screeners are active during the early activities of Ideation and Elimination to monitor the elimination of ideas at screens until a single best idea remains, gatekeepers work security at your gates within the Development activity—the pipeline process occurring after the bend in the pipe—to ensure that your "diamond" idea proceeds only when it is appropriate for it to do so. Gatekeepers keep your checkpoint gates closed, making sure that all participants have fully concluded their functions at each phase, before they open the gates and allow the idea to pass through to the next phase of Development. They're like sports referees who uphold the rules of a game but who do not play the game themselves—gatekeepers confirm that all parties have completed their roles and tasks, but they do not perform any of the work themselves. So if we were to look at this in terms of the legal side of our doll example, screeners would have to make sure that any idea passing through their screens incorporates all the necessary safety guidelines set forth in screening criteria, while gatekeepers would have to make sure that during Development, the legal department signs off on all legal documents at some gate prior to the launch of the product.

4) ASSEMBLING YOUR NPSD GROUP

You need a group of the best people from multiple disciplines and functional areas (throughout your organization and possibly from outside your organization) to help you plan, direct, and implement the development process from the commencement of Ideation to the completion of Development. This group will bring in others—cross-functional development teams, experts, customers, and others as deemed appropriate—to help at various points during the process and then release them when they've accomplished their purposes. Expect your core NPSD group to remain intact from start to finish.

The Benefits of Building the Infrastructure First

The Development Funnel works best when you build the entire process in advance of involving other participants. That's because other people might not understand how you need a new product, service, or internal improvement to tie to your Desired Outcome and Strategy, nor do these participants always need to. You must create the infrastructure, such as selecting criteria for screens and gates, as a tactical tool to guide others to success. When you build the infrastructure first, you will:

- **Ensure that all key steps are followed** to select and screen new ideas against broad and specific screening criteria and to perform surface and detailed evaluations of the final idea. These safeguards prevent skipping steps so that the process will work.
- **Help define areas that must be researched during the Surface Evaluation phase,** such as confirming that your product's name

doesn't infringe on existing trademarks or that a certain domain name is still available.

- **Make sure that your product—whether it is undifferentiated or a "me-too" product—is aligned with your Desired Outcome and Strategy.** Although there is a greater chance of failure with "me-too" products—you can go with either type of products as long as your eyes are open and that you have reason to believe that the product will enable you to reach Desired Outcome.

- **Ensure a smooth and synchronized Launch.** Cross-functional teams prevent situations where one silo develops an idea, notifies other silos too late or not at all, and then attempts to launch an end product while major components are missing. When the right people are brought onboard early, their cooperative efforts improve chances of a successful launch.

- **Be transferable.** Once the Development Funnel is ready and functional, everyone can get on the same page. When decision makers ask, "What are you doing with development," the reply can be as simple as, "We're pursuing three ideas, and we're now running a detailed evaluation." Everyone's in the know.

- **Kill off bad ideas before they become too costly.** Ideation is less expensive than Detailed Evaluation, which is less expensive than Launch. With each progression through the Development Funnel, expenditures increase, so use the process to stop if you identify a problem that jeopardizes the success of the project.

- **After senior leadership has built its criteria into the model, those leaders can get out of the way and let everyone do their jobs.** When senior managers build their criteria into the screens, they are less likely to halt a product or improvement's development because it fails to meet their ROI.

Once you have completed your "pre-work" of selecting your criteria, screeners, and gatekeepers, and given them the tools they need, you are ready to perform the first activity of the ET Development Funnel: Ideation.

Activity I: Ideation

The activity of Ideation includes a single phase, also called Ideation, that encompasses both the Idea Bank and the wide-mouthed funnel hopper illustrated in Figure 4.6.

Simply put, ideation is the gathering of ideas. It is based on the notion that your odds of selecting your best idea correlates to the number of good ideas you load into the funnel. Think $100 > 7 > 3 > 1$. Although loading ideas into the hopper seems like a simple enough task, most leaders do not ideate well—they either fail to capture ideas as ideas present themselves over time, or when pressed to come up with ideas on the fly, these leaders stop searching too soon—which diminishes the potential of their development process from the start.

Over a span of about five years, I worked as a facilitator for a group of noncompeting CEOs who met quarterly to review best business practices and share ideas. During one meeting, the group set out to replace one of its members who often missed meetings. They quickly generated a list of seventeen potential CEOs and wanted to get down to the task of selecting their best option. I encouraged them to hold off on proceeding with the screening process until they had given themselves another couple of days to add to the list of replacements. Twelve more names were added after a day of thought.

On the third day, they felt ready to proceed with their selection process, but again, we held off and continued ideating. The group conducted some research and added three contenders, bringing their list to a total of thirty-two names.

After screening their prospective members against broad and specific criteria, the CEOs were surprised to find that their final two contenders were actually the thirty-first and thirty-second names they had placed onto their original list. Had the group of CEOs rushed through Ideation, they never would have considered their best "idea."

Wider Funnel Mouth Diagram

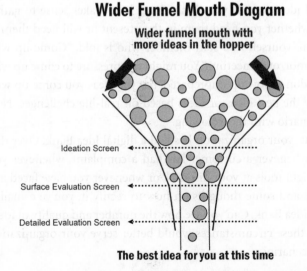

Wider funnel mouth with more ideas in the hopper

Ideation Screen

Surface Evaluation Screen

Detailed Evaluation Screen

The best idea for you at this time

Figure 4.6—Wider Funnel Mouth Diagram

The dark arrows in Figure 4.6 indicating the wider-than-usual funnel mouth are your reminder that Ideation shouldn't occur in one sitting or one meeting. It should be an ongoing activity that takes place throughout your organization for the purpose of capturing ideas as you and your people come up with them, since most people have plenty of ideas, but rarely do they capture their ideas well enough to put them to good use. That's why your next tool, the Idea Bank, is so important to have.

When Nolan Bushnell, one of the founders of the video game industry said, "Everyone who has ever taken a shower has had an idea. It's the person who gets out of the shower, dries off, and does something about it that makes a difference,"[37] he might as well have been pitching the concept of the Idea Bank. This "apparatus" is a place where you and members of your organization capture ideas for later use. You decide which form it takes in your environment; the Idea Bank can be an electronic file or folder stored on an intranet or extranet, a paper file, a suggestion box, or even a grouping of index cards or sticky notes. Besides adding to the Idea Bank yourself, encourage staffers to make deposits. David Annunziato[38] of Verizon once asked his team to use their smartphones to record improvement ideas throughout their day. Later, the ideas were captured in Verizon's Idea Bank when employees synched their phones. In the first week that the group participated in Annunziato's ideation activity, their volume of ideas went through the roof.

Leaders who use Idea Banks collect more ideas and often better-quality ideas than leaders who don't, and their teams often spur new ideas from the already-collected ideas, too. If you think about it, it makes sense to gather ideas over time whether you need them in the present or will need them in the future. Picture yourself as a staff member who is told, "Come up with three ideas for tomorrow's meeting." You might feel pressure to come up with anything so you don't show up unprepared, but the ideas you come up with aren't necessarily the best ideas or ideas based on real-life challenges. Now compare that scenario with the following.

For six months, your organization has had a digital Idea Bank. Over that course of time, whenever a customer has had a complaint, whenever you haven't had the right tools at your disposal, or whenever you have faced any type of challenge and some thoughts on how to rectify it, you've e-mailed your ideas to the Idea Bank. Can you see how the number and quality of ideas generated under these circumstances would better serve your organization than in the first scenario?

Although gathering ideas over the course of time is an easier way to stock your Idea Bank than to expect people to generate ideas in one sitting, if you haven't started an Idea Bank yet, the latter is a short-term alternative.

Note: Carefully consider who gets access to the Idea Bank once ideas are generated. It can be a tough decision, but one that can greatly impact some types of organizations, especially those pitted against rivals with strong intelligence services.

In this chapter and in Chapter 12, you will learn effective ideation techniques, such as reverse engineering, mind mapping, and storyboarding.

Activity II: Elimination

Once you've extracted 100 good ideas from your Idea Bank and have loaded them into your funnel, you need to engage a process that will ultimately eliminate all but a single best "diamond" idea. In the ET Development Funnel, this process occurs in Activity II, Elimination.

Elimination consists of three screens separated by two evaluation phases:

1. Ideation Screen
2. Expansion and Surface Evaluation
3. Surface Evaluation Screen
4. Detailed Evaluation
5. Detailed Evaluation Screen

Remember that screens are manned by screeners, an unbiased jury whose sole responsibility is to match ideas against the screens' predetermined criteria and to allow only those ideas that meet criteria to pass through screening checkpoints.

Mark Victor Hansen,[39] cofounder of the *Chicken Soup for the Soul* book series, insists that all manuscripts that are submitted must be evaluated *minus* the author's contact information. That way, each story earns its way into a book based on its own merits. Ironically, Hansen's staff has rejected all of his stories, because they don't know they're evaluating the boss's ideas. Members of your NPSD group are *not* involved in the screening process, because they may lack the impartiality needed to eliminate ideas. In order to prevent ideas that you or they have "fallen in love with" from passing through screens, restrict your screeners to the screening checkpoints and your NPSD group to the evaluation work that takes place between screenings.

1 – THE IDEATION SCREEN

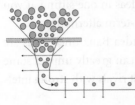

After all of your ideas have been loaded into the funnel, your NPSD group presents the ideas to the screeners, who match ideas against the screening criteria. At the Ideation Screen, screeners must eliminate ideas that don't match the criteria set. In this case, a good set of predetermined broad criteria would eliminate all but the seven best ideas that would fall through to the next level. (Ideas that are killed go back to the Idea Bank, as indicated by the Idea Recycling arrows in Figure 4.4.)

If you were to use the ET Development Funnel for the purpose of man-ufacturing the toy you read about earlier, your screeners would now be reviewing the seven ideas before them to make sure that each doll appealed to the Latino market and could retail for under $50. They would also be making sure that the product could launch within the span of a year and that 50% of production could be done in house.

During the economic slowdown in 2009, a job posting for a water-meter reader in Tacoma, Washington, drew more than 1,600 applicants, almost four times the typical number.[40] Broad criteria required that applicants pass a test administered by the utility company at the Tacoma Dome. Only 807 people showed up to take the test, quickly eliminating nearly half of the applicants. One of the broad criteria would be to have taken the test and passed.

More than 90% of Fortune 500 companies are using applicant tracking systems to achieve similar elimination returns. Their technology of choice is software that not only traces applicants within their pool of candidates—scanning documents and the Web for keywords, former employers, years of experience, schools attended, interests, social platforms and profiles, videos posted, and questionnaires returned during the submission process—but evaluates them as a way of prioritizing the best matches. What this means to job seekers is that honesty is probably the best policy, because putting incor-rect data on your submission can be easily detected, and the next thing you know, you're out. What this means to decision makers is that you have better tools to find your "diamond" applicants, but beware, because your competi-tors could be using the same technologies, though more optimally, to beat you to the punch.

If no ideas fit all of the screening criteria, return to Ideation and begin again. Don't fall prey to modifying your broad criteria to fit what's in your funnel. This defeats the purpose. Follow the structure of the process to ensure that you don't become too attached with ideas that don't meet criteria.

2 – EXPANSION AND SURFACE EVALUATION

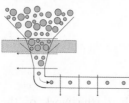

Once your screeners have reviewed the work from the Ideation phase and have agreed that they have followed all the criteria, the seven remaining ideas move back to the NPSD group for further evaluation. During Surface Evaluation, your NPSD group examines the remaining seven ideas in an attempt to explode any of them into better spin-off ideas that still fall within the parameters of the screening criteria. Oftentimes, expanding on an idea results in even the simplest of changes that can lead to significant improvements of a product, service, or operational innovaton. That's usually because the original idea has already met the criteria of the first screen, so any expanded offshoots of those ideas stand a better chance of meeting your criteria. The NPSD group can use existing studies, advice from experts, their existing knowledge and skills, or any other method to improve upon these ideas. (The explosion of ideas is illustrated on the diagram by the expanding walls of the Surface Evaluation phase on the snapshot diagram of your ET Development Funnel in Figure 4.4.)

Next, the NPSD group performs a gentle scan and conducts additional research to uncover potential reasons to eliminate more ideas so that they can present the best three ideas of this group of seven to the screeners. One of my students called this step "inexpensive desk research," because the research can often be conducted inexpensively from your desk using a phone and computer: searching on the Internet, calling a vendor, talking to a client, visiting a library, and using focus groups, concept tests, and user tests. Trying to secure a URL and finding that the Web address has already been taken is an example of a Surface Evaluation.

The NPSD group can also assess strategic alignment, feasibility, magnitude of opportunity, market attractiveness, product advantage, policy fit, and killer variables.

Think of these seven assessment factors as triggers for new ideas rather than as final products, services, or improvements. If you were developing a new external product, your team may review an idea and decide that it meets broad criteria but that it's not as strong as other ideas. Perhaps it lacks a feature, doesn't appeal to an international market, is too close to a product already on the market, or requires the use of raw materials that are too expensive.

Once the Surface Evaluation is complete, you and your NPSD group will objectively present all data to your screeners.

3 – SURFACE EVALUATION SCREEN

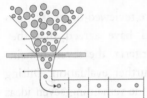

The screeners then evaluate the work of the NPSD group and scrub the three remaining ideas against the specific criteria of the Surface Evaluation Screen to make sure the remaining ideas are indeed the right ideas to survive and pass through to the next phase, Detailed Evaluation. Following the progress of the toy doll example, you would wrap up this elimination by asking your screeners to assess if your remaining three ideas could each bring in a 14% profit, contain a unique characteristic that your competitors' products don't offer, have potential extension possibilities, and could be manufactured to consist of at least 40% recyclable materials. If all ideas pass this test, screeners allow them to pass onto the next phase of elimination. (If no ideas pass through this go/kill checkpoint, the NPSD group stops and returns to Ideation.)

4 – DETAILED EVALUATION

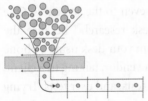

In the Detailed Evaluation phase, your NPSD group spends a larger amount of time performing an in-depth review of the three surviving options. Everyone knows that research performed in this phase will impact the rest of the process. Examples of what to do at this stage are competitive analyses, customer surveys, target-market studies, product-strategy analyses, product-benefits reviews, value propositions, features, attributes, specs, market studies, manufacturing-expense calculations, ROI, market investigation, manufacturability, and investment. (You may participate to a degree in these reviews, but remember that your job is to think and strategize for the future, so keep the tactical work in check.)

The type, size, complexity, and scope of the product/service/improvement determine the extent of the research and time you need to invest here. For smaller products, a one-page comparative summary may be adequate. For larger projects, a detailed analysis might be appropriate. The building of a 900-bed hospital in San Diego or installation of a research facility in Beijing will require much more research than is needed for the creation of a new video introduction for your website.

After completing their Detailed Evaluation, the NPSD group turns the three ideas over to the screeners for a final evaluation and verification. The NPSD group can recommend their top choice of a single, best idea and provide supporting material to the screeners.

5 – DETAILED EVALUATION SCREEN

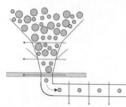

Because only the "diamond" idea passes through this last screen, the filtering process is more detailed than in previous screens. The size of the product, service, or improvement determines the amount of time that screeners spend on this screen. A nuclear reactor could consume a year of evaluation by the NPSD group while a new telephone might only take twenty minutes. Up to this point, very little money has been spent on the project.

Screeners must be objective and careful to ensure that the NPSD group eliminated the right items, because expenses rise exponentially in Development. Wrapping up our toy doll example, screeners must ask, Do the specs on this final selection show that the new product will fit into a 14" × 6" × 6" box, contain nontoxic paint and plastic, and pose no choking hazard to children between the ages of three and eight? No matter how much the NPSD group might like one of the three final ideas more, screeners still have the job of strictly monitoring the selection to ensure that a lesser idea is being passed through, simply, perhaps, because someone fell in love with it.

Screeners also need to consider that the organization will spend the bulk of this project's budget before the project produces any profit, so making the best selection is crucial to remaining in alignment with intended outcomes.

Once screeners have agreed that the NPSD group has eliminated all but your "diamond" idea, they dispense this best idea from the bottom of the funnel, allowing it to proceed into the Development pipeline.

Activity III: Development

Development is where the single best idea will develop into a final product, service, or improvement. The bend in the diagram represents the transition in activity, and the idea's path is now equipped with checkpoints that are gates instead of screens. Gatekeepers, not screeners, monitor gates. Some, all, or none of the gatekeepers might have been screeners at the screening checkpoints, depending on your needs and their expertise.

The five phases and four gates of the Development activity are:

1. Cross-Functional Development
2. Cross-Functional Development Gate
3. Testing
4. Testing Gate
5. Deployment
6. Deployment Gate
7. Launch
8. Post-Launch Review
9. Post-Launch Review Gate

Once you make the decision to spend, you will bring in more people—teams from individual departments, customers, and others—to help you develop the idea. Simply using the tool will empower you to break silo walls and bring many departmental and business-unit heads together on single projects. Its structured process elicits necessary input from cross-functional groups, senior-level management, frontline employees, and even external parties, ensuring that valuable resources are allocated to only those ideas that promise a high probability of success (rather than to ideas that an engineer or CEO falls in love with).

Note: At each step along the way, you can (and often should) involve customers and clients who can offer feedback on components of the product or service as these components are developed. You can engage in parallel processing, where customers are testing and providing feedback on one component, while another component is being developed, tested, and modified.

1 – CROSS-FUNCTIONAL DEVELOPMENT

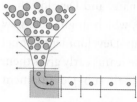

You will start this phase by triggering two activities to occur simultaneously. First, the idea enters Development and everyone performs the preliminary steps leading up to the launch of the product. This may mean drafting architectural plans for the new building, designing the automobile you're about to build, or writing code for the new software. If you were given the green light to make a movie, you wouldn't start filming yet, but you would start hiring staff, arranging shoot locations, and storyboarding scenes. (In this phase, you are not to produce the service, improvement, or product in volume.)

Secondly, smaller subset teams from other silos engage in their own parallel Development processes. From 50,000 feet, Development involves more than one single ET Development Funnel. It contains sub–Development Funnels used by other teams, such as departments, business units, outside vendors, etc., who are making their contributions to the launch. The benefit of these sub–Development Funnels (see Fig. 4.13) to the organization is that each cross-development team now has a tool to create their best contribution to the development process, too, which enhances the entire project's outcomes.

Enterprise Thinking Sub-Development Funnel™

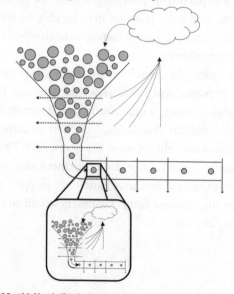

Figure 4.7—ET Sub-Development Funnel™

For example, the logistics team will develop their best logistic alternative for the new idea, and they will Ideate, Eliminate, and Develop their own contributions to you and your NPSD group, which might be a new process for freight handling. The concept of the sub–Development Funnel is highlighted in the diagram above. Involving these teams early gives them the time they need to perform the activities of their sub–Development Funnel.

Notice, too, that you are involving these teams at the beginning of Activity III, immediately after you've made the decision to spend. Until this activity, other areas, departments, and business units of the organization are likely to have been unfamiliar with or vague about your idea, so they have not yet participated. The earlier your teams get involved in Development, the easier it is for them to deliver their best "product"—each team's contribution to the whole—back to the project.

Engineering will have ample time to start idea generation for new ways to design the product. IT won't be rushed when looking to purchase the right operational software; instead, they will have time to issue a request for proposal and collect bids early enough to entertain multiple options (much like you were able to do when you loaded a 100 ideas into the mouth of the funnel). HR might have advanced information on a department that is closing and recommend staff that could be retrained for the new initiative before the staff members are assigned elsewhere. Operations may be able to reorganize a department, providing a "war room" to supervise the new product launch. And sales training may be able to start a month earlier, allowing the sales and marketing managers to develop a sales program that will return higher volume.

Eliminating silos by synchronizing cross-functional teams during Development prevents costly mistakes, like the one that happened to a high-end Japanese cosmetics manufacturer that targeted U.S. women for its $400-per-bottle products. Marketing launched its campaign before operations and production could get products to retailers. The result: the ad campaign lured would-be consumers to department stores where retailers had to tell them that the new products hadn't yet shipped from Japan. Instead of buying from the Japanese firm, consumers would go home with products from competing brands.

Detailed View of SUB–CROSS-FUNCTIONAL Development

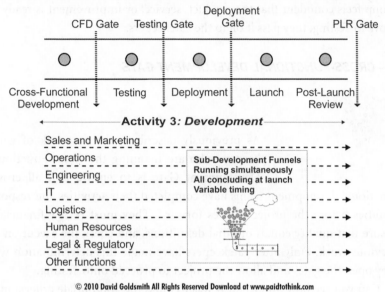

© 2010 David Goldsmith All Rights Reserved Download at www.paidtothink.com

Figure 4.8—Detailed View of Sub–Cross-Functional Development

The expanded view of the Cross-Functional Development portion at the beginning of the Development barrel (see Figure 4.8) contains a list of departments—IT, logistics, human resources, sales and marketing—that you may seek participation from at this time. The Development Funnel should be taught to every decision maker on staff, including but not restricted to those who contribute architectural plans, graphic designs, software code, parallel marketing and operations, rapid prototype, working model, first prototype, legal patents and trademarks, lab tests, in-house tests, alpha tests, updated financials, facilities requirements, market launch plans, customer feedback, and marketing analysis.

When all departments know how to use the ET Development Funnel, they can work together when needed in the development and testing of ideas. In one instance, an NPSD group designed a product without any help from logistics. When the first fully packaged skids of products were ready to ship, staff members noticed an expensive problem. Tractor trailers could hold only one level of pallets instead of the anticipated two levels, astronomically increasing shipping costs and decreasing efficiencies. A two-inch design modification to the packaging design could have eliminated this costly error.

When cross-functional teams have completed their work and your NPSD group feels confident that the product, service, or improvement is ready to move to Testing, they pass it on to the gatekeepers.

2 – CROSS-FUNCTIONAL DEVELOPMENT GATE

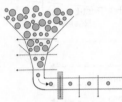

As previously described, the first task of gate-keepers who are manning the Cross-Functional Development Gate is to ensure that all cross-functional development teams have completed their activities and respon-sibilities before the project moves forward. They must review financials, ensure that quality equals original definitions, and check the execution of previous work. Only after gatekeepers have made this determination will they open the gates and allow the project to proceed onto Testing.

Can you see how important it was to build the appropriate criteria into this gate (way back, even before you began Ideation)? At that time, you had to consider the type of organization you had and the product/service or improvement so that your gatekeepers could do their best work at each checkpoint. And now, when gatekeepers are matching cross-functional teams' performance against criteria, you are assured that all the right require-ments have been met before your organization invests more time, money, and resources into the project.

3 – TESTING

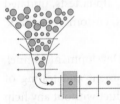

In traditional NPSD processes, leaders tend to over-look or just don't think about Testing. Yet proper testing ensures that built-in criteria are being met. There are many reasons why testing is so often ignored—some decision mak-ers believe their work is so good it needs no testing, others think that for security purposes, testing would allow too much time to pass and competi-tors to beat them to market, and still others fear running out of time to meet deadlines—but generally speaking, testing typically costs very little time and money relative to the consequences of *not* testing. You've got to test, as many firms say 'eat your own dog food.'"[41]

An executive at a worldwide firm decided to eliminate one of the company's best-selling brands of tomato sauce, believing that the company could fill the gap with other brands. No testing was performed to ensure that his assumptions would pan out as anticipated, and as a result, the company tossed away an $85-million brand. While the tomato sauce is now distributed in limited markets, it never bounced back.

Determine that the tests are accurate and complete before you run them; flawed tests lead to bad outcomes, but good testing directs your efforts safely forward.

A businessman came up with the idea to sell garage-organization systems, and, believing that big homes meant big profits, he targeted the wealthy. He built prototypes, created a channel to sell the product, and launched the product line, but his company did not take off. Most consumers who want garage organizers come from the middle class and below. They're do-it-yourselfers who like to work on small engines, do their own gardening, and spend time in their garages, whereas the wealthy often hire out landscaping and auto repair work, opting for home theaters instead of garage organizers. Today, Home Depot, Lowe's, and Sears carry relatively inexpensive versions of his product, ranging from hundreds to a few thousand dollars in price.

Meanwhile, Sherwin Williams did it right. When the paint company's leaders noticed that women were the primary purchasers of home painting products, they saw a unique opportunity to cater to that market. The final product wasn't paint, it was new packaging designed more like laundry detergent bottles, with a can sporting a plastic handle and a spill-proof lip. When the product was tested regionally in Syracuse, New York, results revealed that Sherwin Williams[42] had come up with a winner, and the company could proceed more assuredly.

The testing may analyze a physical product or customer feedback. Maybe the software you intend to install might be tested within a small division. Maybe you'll introduce a service in just one city to see how it's purchased. You'll want to test your new theme park ride to determine if it's safe or test a new football helmet to see if it really does reduce head injuries. Test a new ad campaign in a regional market to gauge the impact on sales, test a server to see that it can handle an anticipated load, allow a team of employees to try a new incentive program, and so on.

Testing options are available in a variety of forms. The cross-functional group might perform extensive validation, obtain customer acceptance, assemble an employee focus group, evaluate economics of the product, continue in-house testing and user trials, run a trial with limited production, and analyze financials.

Externally, testers can conduct consumer tests in various venues, such as homes, offices, gardens, and cars. They might perform regional tests to ensure that departments and business units perform at their expected levels of service. They also can scrutinize customer acceptance, the economics of the product, ROI, financials, or staffing. Movie studios do screenings. A software company may launch a beta test with a small group of users.

An additional form of testing is called process testing, whereby testers run an end-to-end test of a process to ensure it works. End-to-end testing could be as complex as watching a product's global rollout occur on a simulated model or as simple as a small delivery of data from one department to another. Say that you're developing an improved order-processing procedure in your organization. Maybe you would begin your process test by ordering a product online, then following the order through to accounting and order processing. After that, you monitor how the goods are picked, packed, and shipped by personnel. Finally, you track the shipment of goods to its destination and ensure that the invoice is sent in a timely fashion to its correct recipient.

Domino's Pizza[43] does an end-to-end test of its thirty-minute delivery guarantee when it wants to introduce a new product in its markets. The company knows that any new food item will have to pass a test where the phone call takes two minutes or less, the preparation of the food consumes no more than two minutes, baking time doesn't exceed eight minutes, and packaging and tagging with a promotional paper falls within another two minutes, finally allowing eight minutes for delivery. Sometimes, a standard procedure must be tweaked in different markets so that promised delivery times can be met. For instance, in Mexico, decision makers incorporated the use of motorcycles enabling drivers to beat traffic and stay within Domino's Pizza's eight-minute delivery time.

Keep in mind that not all testing involves a full test. When an organization puts on conferences, it can't do a complete test of the conference, but it can test individual components of the conference. For example, it can test a new registration system, create a scale model of the event to see the picture of traffic flow, model movement, and test the food. Within the conference arena, organizations that pay to participate in the conference can use a "whisper booth," a private, soundproof booth where key customers are invited to privately discuss a product or service so that their feedback can be used for future ideation. This is an idea that any organization can use for both ideation and testing.

There is always something to test in NPSD, so if you don't see an opportunity for testing, consider the possibility that you have become too attached to your idea and this is influencing your assumption that it will work without testing.

4 – TESTING GATE

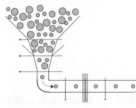

The Testing Gate is where the gatekeepers verify that testers performed the testing properly using accurate testing methodologies. It's called testing the Testing.

At this time, gatekeepers must ensure that the product, service, or improvement meets the original predetermined broad and specific criteria and that the product is once again aligned with its original intent. If you were to try developing your idea without an NPSD structure that required you to stop at a Testing Gate, your process could easily slide off track at this juncture. Although collaboration helps to catch flawed testing, you and gatekeepers have specific roles to fulfill. You make sure that Testing is performed. Gatekeepers make sure that tests are performed properly.

For instance, gatekeepers inspect whether testers asked the right questions of customers or prospects, if employees were put in situations where they felt unsafe expressing negative feedback, if questions were skewed, or whether Testing was skipped altogether. Quite often the design of a test is flawed in a way that produces false-positive results.

Say that you develop a line of camping gear and you decide to test your products on high-end mail-order catalog customers. The test results reveal rave reviews. However, your gatekeepers uncover a testing flaw. Your product's target market consists of budget-conscious suburban and rural families who shop for camping supplies at local retailers, and this group was not involved in the test. In this situation, you would need to modify the testing process and test anew so your target market is tested.

Unfortunately, without an NPSD process, leaders don't have the benefit of gatekeepers to catch testing flaws. In one situation, a product-development test was conducted on a group of users already familiar with the product, yet the product was supposed to open new markets. Testers realized the flaw in their methodology, but they remained silent and gave the product a green light. They blamed management for pressuring them, and in the absence of gatekeepers, the outcome of the product launch was disappointing.

At this point, as in any other, you can always stop. The benefit of using gates and of soliciting input from your gatekeepers is to continually check whether the investment is worth the risks. If gatekeepers uncover flawed tests, they should stop Development until the problem is resolved to prevent wasted resources down the line.

5 – DEPLOYMENT

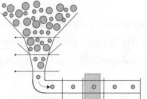

Deployment is not the same as Launch; it is the pre-work that leads up to and sets the conditions for the Launch. Mass production does not occur at this time.

Before the Launch, you and your NPSD group meet with all cross-functional development teams to determine the roles and activities that everyone must perform to make the actual Launch a success. When the military deploys troops and supplies, its leadership puts all resources into place prior to battle.

Organizationally, cross-functional teams prepare and arrange their resources and perform prelaunch activities. Production retools its machinery, HR hires new personnel, accounting and finance put the budget in place, and purchasing ensures that all necessary raw materials are on hand.

When an industrial power-tools manufacturer improved upon its line of drills, the firm needed to ready its development teams before launching the new product. Marketing and advertising teams produced website content and ordered promotional materials. Operations closed down part of a plant for retooling and positioning of new equipment. Purchasing bid out the components, and so on.

At no time during this deployment step did the manufacturer mass produce and distribute new drills on a large scale.

6 – DEPLOYMENT GATE

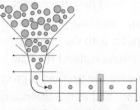

The Deployment Gate is the one last check that ensures everyone and everything is in position before the launch. Think of the Deployment Gate as NASA's countdown—ten, nine, eight, seven . . . until blastoff. This is a final safeguard where gatekeepers can still hit the kill switch if any component is off the mark and threatens your launch's success. It's worth the kill when you consider the time and energy needed to overcome a mistake and face its consequences in the media and with customers, vendors, bankers, the stock market, coworkers, regulators, and partners.

A national U.S. hotel chain known for its beautiful properties purchased an existing hotel with the intention of renovating it to match its other properties. Before renovations were completed, to meet the new owner's existing corporate standards, the property was marketed and rooms were booked. Guests who were loyal to the brand's exquisite locations and exemplary style arrived to find themselves in a dilapidated dive and newspaper reviewers gave the hotel poor ratings, which tarnished the entire brand.

Had management used a tool like the ET Development Funnel to guide their actions, gatekeepers would have blocked marketing and advertising to the public until renovations were completed. A structured NPSD approach would have saved the hotel chain from losing countless hours of handling customer complaints, prevented embarrassment to employees, eliminated the need for expensive charge backs and discounts, and contributed to the ease and success of future marketing efforts.

At Deployment, gatekeepers will make sure that all cross-functional teams have completed their work and that any other supporting parties are positioned and ready for launch. Once gatekeepers are assured that everyone and everything is ready for Launch, they open the gates and allow your project to proceed.

7 – LAUNCH

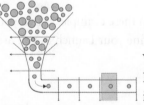

You are finally at Launch, where all systems are a go. Each team pulls the trigger and begins their activity for the Launch. External products are finally created, services are ready for delivery, and improvements (such as new computer networking systems) are installed and in the first stages of operations.

For more than sixty years and spanning three generations, family-operated Controlled Demolition, Inc. has been the premier demolition firm in the world. The National Geographic Channel's *Man-Made*[44] television series highlighted CDI's project to remove four nuclear-reactor cooling towers located within 40 meters of an active nuclear fuel processing plant in the United Kingdom.

President Mark Loizeaux stated that the project took two years of planning

(Ideation, Elimination, and Cross-Functional Development), ten days of on-site work (Deployment), and only seconds to topple the structures (Launch). Had CDI not done the two years of prep work, the towers may have destroyed the neighboring processing facility and released toxic materials and gasses into the air.

Different types of launches can take place. Your organization, your situation, and your particular product, service, or improvement will determine the type of launch that occurs. If you offer custom-made products or products that are made to order, your Launch involves placing people and components in the ready position so that when orders come in, activity takes place to fulfill the order.

On the other hand, if you produce products that are purchased in retail stores, your Launch is the point at which products are placed on store shelves and sit ready for consumers to purchase. This means that inventory and shipping activities have taken place at the Deployment phase of Development.

If your product offering involves a service component like that of an architectural firm, then your Deployment is the creation of the designs and blueprints, and your actual Launch happens when you deliver or present those designs and blueprints to your client.

Sometimes, however, your service might require a Launch that extends over a period of time. If you were responsible for putting on a concert at a park in the center of your town, your Launch may involve the distribution of fliers to local eateries as well as introducing the band the night of the concert. In addition, the selling of tickets, which takes place from May through July, could also be part of your Launch.

The important point for you to take away from these examples is that you must be as clear about the parameters which define your Launch as you are about executing the Launch itself.

8 – POST-LAUNCH REVIEW

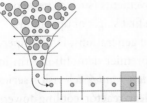 The Post-Launch Review is a measure of your Launch's effectiveness. It helps you determine improvements for subsequent projects, also. Everyone should conduct a Post-Launch Review, but in my work with many organizations—large and global and small and local—leaders seldom execute them. Anyone who expects to continually improve products and processes

should conduct the review to assess their costs, profits, and strengths and weaknesses after Launch.

Leaders' excuses for not performing the Post-Launch Review usually boil down to not having enough time or resources. But this review is too valuable to ignore. Lessons learned and data gleaned from your Post-Launch Review are fed back to management for better strategizing on this and future development projects.

Some of the questions to ask in this phase are:

- Were all tactics employed on time?
- Where were steps missed?
- Where were decisions not made accurately?
- Did the buyer of the service or the product use, repurchase, or return the product?
- Regarding internal products or services, did the new improvement deliver its projected returns?
- Did we miss opportunities? What were they?

When all phases, screens, and gates of the ET Development Funnel are completed, the Post-Launch Review should reveal few surprises if any, but that's not always the case. Furthermore, the review can offer new opportunities. Monitoring and critiquing the project, its ideas, and the ways in which decisions have been made can give you insight into how and where you can make improvements in the process, in your products and services, and in various areas of your organization in the future. These types of measures can strengthen the entire organization and in many ways, help it win by a nose or by a mile now and in the future.

If you're not sure where to begin, consider the following review options: costs, profits, team members, screen and checkpoint facilitators, strengths, weaknesses, and lessons learned.

9 – POST-LAUNCH REVIEW GATE

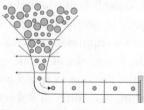

At the Post-Launch Review Gate, gatekeepers are either joined or replaced by members of management who will take the data and lessons from the Post-Launch Review and use it to determine how the organization will move forward.

Decision makers need to assess the viability of the finished product. Will the organization continue manufacturing its product without change, will members of the NPSD group need to make adjustments to the end service in order to continue to offer it, or should the new improvement be terminated altogether? If you're not convinced that this product/service/improvement is going to be a winner, it's still wise to stop, because you're better off stopping after three months instead of after a year.

You may be tempted to place this gate before your Post-Launch Review out of fear that you're not getting the information you need early enough to stop a failure. Rest assured that the earlier screens and gates have served their purpose in keeping your idea on track and that they have offered sufficient opportunity to stop the process in light of information available at each checkpoint. You want the Post-Launch Review Gate to remain in this position, because it offers you new data once again that you can use to determine next steps.

As a member of management, you will use what you learn in the Post-Launch Review Gate to establish future review intervals to make sure your product, service, or improvement is achieving the desired results or that it is changing, updating, or being terminated to suit the needs of your organization. The advantage here is that by watching progress, you prevent your organization from leaking profits and losing strength in the marketplace, problems that some organizations fail to identify until it's too late.

■ ■ ■

If you want your organization to stand the tests of time, you must continually take steps to improve, update, and innovate its products, services, and internal operations. The tools and methodologies for achieving all three are the same. By using these ET tools, you ensure that you are collecting an ample number of solid improvement-related ideas up front, filtering them down to your single best idea, and then developing that idea through an unsiloed approach into a successful improvement. Regardless of your industry or sector or whether your improvement is targeted to internal or external stakeholders, NPSD is the nutrition your organization requires for survival.

Earlier, we discussed the connection between the Economics of Thinking and the pre-work you perform before you make the decision to spend on developing a new product, service, or improvement. According to Robert Cooper in his book *Winning at New Products,* "overall, about 75% more 'person days' were devoted to pre-development of successful products than failures,"[45] proving that thinking first really does pay off (and that is true whether you're developing new products or performing any of the other activities of ET).

There may be times when you will want to rush to action, especially when you're excited about capturing a new opportunity or solving a challenge, but thinking up front first by using tools like the ET Development Funnel can actually expedite the progress you make by putting all of your assets and plans into order before taking action.

As you read through upcoming chapters, you will see the ET Development Funnel used in different ways, such as for selecting and establishing alliances or for choosing and implementing technologies that strengthen your organization. The takeaway here is that you can't become complacent with the status quo. Like every living cell that regenerates under optimal conditions, organizations renew themselves through NPSD.

ESTABLISHING ALLIANCES

AFTER SPEAKING AT A CONFERENCE for logistics firms, I was approached by
one of the audience members, the vice president of sales for a manufacturer
of large pieces of mail sorting and distribution equipment. During our conversation, he told me about a partnership his firm had with a trucking company. I was scheduled for an upcoming presentation before the American
Trucking Association (ATA), so I was particularly interested to learn more
about this arrangement. He labeled the relationship with the trucking firm a
partnership, because its driver waited three hours at the VP's shipping dock
while his staff packaged up a $300,000 piece of equipment that the driver
would transport to this conference. The VP used the equipment as a sample
at the conference, expecting to sell a dozen or so to gross $3.6 million in sales.

Considering how he used the term "partnership"—a word that I've found
to be interpreted differently by different people—I asked for more details of
his experience to be sure that I understood what he was trying to communicate to me. After a minute or two, I summarized, "You called your trucking
firm and asked for a price quote to ship the machine to Boston. After hearing
their price, you asked if they could do better." The vice president admitted
that he did ask for a better deal and got one.

I continued, "The driver arrived at your dock, but the equipment wasn't
ready for loading, so he waited for three hours until it was. He transported the
equipment here to the conference, where you will gross $3.6 million off it."

The VP agreed.

"Okay," I said. "So since the trucking firm is your partner, when you return,
you're going to send this partner a bonus check for helping you out. Right?"

He hesitated, then said, "I see what you mean; he's not really my partner."

Later, when I shared this story in my presentation to the ATA, some audience members laughed. Others, however, better understood how they had mistakenly assumed they were partners with their freight customers, when in fact, they were trucking vendors doing their jobs, sometimes eating the costs of down time but never sharing in the profits.

False Partners

These leaders aren't alone in their assumptions about what constitutes a real partnership. Misconceptions about partners are common, to say the least. Confusion stems from our lack of a shared vocabulary, leaving leaders with vague or diverse definitions for words, even those as seemingly simple as "partner." So let's start by defining a partnership. Partnerships are traditionally seen as relationships where all parties share in particular successes and failures together.

This isn't usually the case with vendors, customers, or others that you may call partners. In fact, assuming that the vendor-customer relationship is a partnership of sorts could really hurt your organization. You need to see the relationship for what it really is. We become accustomed to certain buying habits and patterns—for example, we use the dry cleaner near our home or office and we shop for groceries at neighboring stores, but wouldn't you say we do so more out of convenience than loyalty to a "partner"? How often have you heard salespeople and leaders talk about how they have built relationships where their customers, clients, and patrons are so loyal to them that they would never buy anywhere else? Now consider some of the purchases you make—your vehicle, your house, dinner out with friends, your shoes— and ask yourself if you feel so tied to any one vendor that you could buy those items from only him or her. If the customer and the vendor are not sharing in the profits or gaining any other mutual benefit beyond the exchange of money for products, they do not have a partnership.

To cut through the confusion, avoid making false assumptions, and eliminate some of the negative connotations that can plague the term "partnership" (expensive, time consuming, too binding for the long term), in this chapter and throughout the book, we use the words "alliance/s" and "ally/ allies" rather than partnerships.

Alliances are those people or organizations that can help you reach your Desired Outcomes faster and better than you or your organization can do on your/its own. Everyone establishes alliances all the time. On a personal level, think about the times you've given and gotten something from family members, friends, neighbors, and even doctors. Whether the terms of these agreements were written, spoken, or simply expected, you were involved in alliances with these people.

Now expand the circle to include the people in your professional life, like employees, coworkers, senior management, boards, departments, contractors, vendors, customers, competitors, media, service providers, foreign countries, industry experts, professional associations, lawyers, and lenders. Perhaps you've never thought of these people as your allies, but in essence, they are—or they could be. Even rivals can be allies when the purpose of the alliance brings a mutual benefit, such as putting a competitor out of business or buying rights to a technology that threatens to displace mutual rivals' products in a particular industry.

Allies are individuals, groups of people, or organizations who join with others, oftentimes combining resources, and abiding by certain guidelines that pertain to investments and draws as a way of leveraging their potential and expanding their opportunities. If your association with another person or group doesn't fulfill those criteria, you do not have an alliance with that other party.

For example, those pals you've become familiar with at your weekly networking meetings may be nice people who pass leads and opportunities on to you, and they may even be a type of alliance depending on the conditions of your affiliation, but if you were to break out of the mold of attending those weekly meetings, you would find that they would quickly replace you. These meetings serve a strategic purpose, that's all.

Business and personal connections are not always allies, either, although they could be. Sure, they can put you in touch with opportunities, but they are not necessarily tied to your success, nor are they guaranteed any compensation for helping you out. A longtime friend left the United States to work in a Middle Eastern country. When she couldn't find work in her field of expertise overseas, she returned to the American community where she had lived all her life, a community where she and her family knew the majority of business owners and organizational leaders. On a scale of 1 to 100 in the relationship category, her family is a 96. She would have been an asset to any organization fortunate enough to have her, but relying on her vast network of connections turned into a disappointing exercise when not a single one could offer her employment or put her in contact with someone else who could. Connections, not unlike social-networking "friends," can be valuable in your life, but they shouldn't necessarily be misinterpreted as allies.

Name Your Allies

While having breakfast one day with author Jeffrey Gitomer, the conversation turned to the topic of alliances, and Jeffrey suggested that I try an exercise with a group of executives that I would be meeting with in the upcoming week for the purpose of helping them become aware of who their allies were—and who they were not. I suggest you do the same.

Take out a sheet of paper and write down the names of your allies as instructed in the following list. You may realize that identifying your best current allies is tougher than you expect.

1. List your three closest family allies—the relatives you can count on to be there, no matter what, if you need their help.
2. List your three strongest coworker allies—colleagues who put your best interests on a par with their own, and who would never step over you to take a promotion.
3. List your three strongest organizational allies—other organizations that are working side by side with yours toward complementary goals and successes.

Now ask yourself some questions. Are these people and organizations really allies or people just doing their jobs because you pay them to do so? Do you have a metric for determining if these people are your allies or whether the alliances are actually producing the returns you want? Maybe some of these alliances have run their course and have become more work than they're worth.

Filling in the family list can be challenging enough for many people, but it can be especially unnerving for those who can't name a single family ally.

Many people realize that while their work-related allies appear to be on their side, the strength of the alliance when push comes to shove is not as strong as they originally thought it was. For instance, can you recall a time when you've left a job for another, and just as you were closing out your last day, a coworker promised to "keep in touch"? Months later, you think back to that promise and realize that neither of you have reached out for the other, nor do you have any intention of doing so in the future. Situations like this highlight what it means to assume you had a closer bond than what actually existed. Not always, but more often than not, once a coworker moves on to a new endeavor, the old life and the "partnerships" are left behind.

As for the list of organizational allies, most leaders list organizations that aren't allies at all; they're just individual entities who are out for themselves. That's realism, not cynicism talking. Ask someone who's retired from business, especially from the corporate world, to name an organizational ally, and the majority of them won't even consider their past place of employment. If you were to look at your organizational allies through this lens, you can see how scary your current (and possibly overly optimistic) assumptions are. On the bright side, people who have performed this exercise and then gone on to learn about how to establish alliances tend to reclassify some of the relationships they have listed in this lesson.

In this chapter, we're going to explore the different types of alliances available to you. Then we will tie alliance building to Strategy and show you how you can select the best types of alliances for your organization.

Expanding Opportunities with a Variety of Alliances

Leaders need allies for a multitude of reasons. You may need others to help launch a new division or open in a new market, or maybe something more simple, such as getting an interdepartmental project off the ground or getting press coverage for an event you're hosting. On a personal level, allies can help you advance in your career.

Like all activities in ET, establishing and cultivating alliances is an activity that leaders perform all day long. Yet, as important a role as alliances play in all our lives, most leaders have a limited understanding of what alliances are and of all the different ways they can be used. The more you know about alliances, the more you can win by a nose (or more) with them, because you now have tools to identify options and opportunities and to convert them to successes.

Among the common assumptions and misconceptions about alliances is the notion that organizational alliances are restricted to partnerships, mergers, or acquisitions. There are actually six different forms of alliances, each with varying levels of commitment and providing different benefits to their allies. Rarely in business schools or training programs will you find in-depth education about these six types of alliances, how to build them, how to maintain them, and how to assess, evolve, or terminate them properly. Not surprisingly, when leaders think they might need to establish alliances, they often frantically scan a book on the subject like a teenager "cramming" for a test last minute, hoping to grasp some nugget of wisdom before they embark on an important meeting, sometimes with millions of dollars on the line!

However, armed with the right terminology and some basic knowledge about establishing alliances—acquired by reading this chapter—you can be in the ready position whenever you want to use alliances as strategic and tactical tools.

Years ago one of my clients was contemplating working with another business owner on an upcoming project. I entered his office and saw that he was on the phone with his prospective "partner." He motioned for me to take a seat as he continued their conversation about the details of this potential new partnership. As I listened, it was not difficult to understand that their conversation was going in circles and leading nowhere. I quietly suggested that he hang up the phone, but to promise the other guy first that he would call him back in ten minutes.

In just ten minutes, I gave my client an overview of the six types of alliances, and then asked him, "What type of alliance do you want to create?" With no hesitation he stated that he wanted to form a project joint venture. He had known all along what he needed, but without the vocabulary and definition, he hadn't been able to articulate it clearly to the other person. When he called his colleague back, he explained that he wanted to establish a project joint venture that would give them two benefits: the outcomes of this particular project and the chance to see how well they could work together as a precursor to potential future projects. Within minutes, the two men agreed to the specific alliance, a challenge that they had struggled to work out for more than a month before.

Whether you want to eliminate crises, outpace competitors, overcome legal and governmental restrictions, expand into new territories, gain access to technologies, or handle countless other challenges, when you join together with an ally with whom you can pool your resources and produce greater outcomes as a combined unit than you would have otherwise produced individually, then you've got a good alliance on your hands.

As you read through this chapter, you might be surprised at some of the reasons why alliances are commonly formed, and you may become motivated to use alliances for the same purposes. In addition, you'll see how some alliances can improve your ability to perform other ET activities, too. For instance, the right allies can help you to develop, market, and distribute new products and services; select and implement better technologies than you could on your own; and alert you to competitive intelligence that will sharpen the accuracy of your forecasts.

Why Build Alliances?

An alliance is an engine for growth or progress. Two or more parties build an alliance when they realize that their combined resources and talents will produce better outcomes than if the parties were to act on their own. Together they can generate more profits, achieve greater results, better minimize risks, and decrease time to achieve Desired Outcomes.

Typically speaking, alliances are generally formed between and among parties who bring different assets to the union, namely the joining of a technology (or technologies) and one or more distribution channels. Say that you are an inventor—the *technology*—and you need an ally who can help you distribute your invention—the *distribution channel*—to bring your product to market. Both you and your ally agree to an alliance to reach outcomes that neither of you would have achieved on your own.

You see this formula everywhere, and it is customized in each alliance, from small to large organizations around the globe. For instance, Coca-Cola, who owns the "technology" of soft drinks, allies with not just one distributor but with a fleet of bottlers who are all responsible for the coordination of their designated distribution channels. In all instances, the parties involved must do more than select the right type of alliances; they must also coordinate the roles and tactical responsibilities of each party. In other words, whether the alliance has two allies or ten, the success of the alliance not only depends on the formation of the correct type of alliance from the start, but also on the planning, assignment, and execution of tactical activities.

Figure 5.1 is a graphic representation of this very common reason for alliances to be formed. As you see, the *technology*—product, service, (actual) technology, information, etc.—is joined with a *distribution channel*—across geographies, via digital means, and so on—to achieve greater outcomes than either ally could achieve alone.

Channel, Technology, and Greater Outcomes

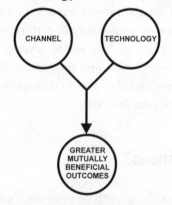

Figure 5.1—Channel, Technology, and Greater Outcomes

In his writings about the growth of alliances, attorney George Keeley noted that "alliances generally achieve a higher return on investment (17%) than U.S. industry in general (11%). The higher return is a direct result of leveraging partners' resources and assets, requiring lower investment to produce greater incremental returns."[46] Alliances enable individuals, departments, business units, organizations from multiple sectors, and even countries to open up new possibilities and extend their potential by leveraging the potential of people, processes, industries, trends, markets, cultures, and more.

This maximization of potential is illustrated in Figure 5.2. Three scenarios depicted here—the three common options that leaders have when facing the prospect of allying with another party—are shown in relation to three future conditions: Current Future, Resource Intensive Future, and New Improved Future.

In the first scenario, your organization—YOU—works alone without an alliance, carving out a single future by using resources exclusive to your organization: written in equation form, $1 + 0 = 1$.

Alliance Options

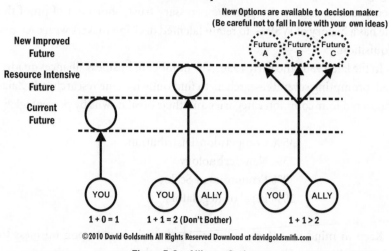

©2010 David Goldsmith All Rights Reserved Download at davidgoldsmith.com

Figure 5.2—Alliance Options

In the second scenario—YOU/ALLY/Don't Bother—your organization teams up with an ally, but the benefits of the alliance will not yield outcomes greater than what each party would have achieved if they worked alone: When $1 + 1 = 2$ or less, the benefits of forming the alliance are not great enough to enter into that alliance. There's too much work for the time with not enough return.

In the third scenario—YOU/ALLY/>2—illustrates a potentially viable alliance, where the combined efforts of both parties yield outcomes that are greater than the outcomes of each party individually: $1 + 1 = >2$ or more opportunities is a scenario for improved future conditions and is more likely worth pursuing.

When Kelly Winters of the Global Sales Planning and Enablemen of Symantec told me that her firm does approximately six major acquisitions per year that tend to result in some great talent leaving their rosters, I drew a similar diagram to outline the missing link that was responsible for these negative outcomes. I highlighted for her that the individuals engaged in the planning of this firm's acquisitions were only considering *a part* of each acquisition, the part affiliated with merging systems, organizational structure, financial reporting, etc. However, what they weren't doing, and what they needed to do in order to retain key talent, was to forecast each acquisition's future realities as a way of determining the future human resources needs of the new entity, even if they were not needed in the present. By considering the future, and creating strong, believable, workable plans, they could maintain their alliance with the new employees by showing them a new future where they could be engaged and useful. Granted, leadership would have to follow through on their promises in order to gain the necessary trust—born out of proof that one has a history of WSPs—to retain talented decision makers with each new acquisition.

In the late 1980s and early 1990s, the number of business alliances quadrupled, prompting several researchers to find out why. One researcher, E. Zajac, uncovered four common categories and their breakdowns by percentage:[47]

> 35% Competition/Distribution
> 25% New Technology
> 20% Economies of Scale
> 20% Legal or Regulatory

Keep in mind that these numbers were solely based upon business-to-business alliances. They do not account for the numerous other types of alliances that people form such as the manager-to–vice president alliance, the company-to-media alliance, or the marketing-department-to-IT-department alliance that might exist within a single organization. Additionally, some alliances are forced into existence, as is the case in China and India, where organizations from outside these countries that wish to do business within their borders are required by law to ally along very narrow specific guidelines. In an entirely different type of mandatory alliance, arranged marriages are not only acceptable in many cultures, they are the norm.

Two more researchers, Michael Hergert and Deigan Morris, set out on the same quest, and their research uncovered a surprise; nearly three-fourths of the alliances they studied were formed by rivals—individuals or organizations—that could mutually benefit by allying with their competitors.[48] More than a third of the time these alliances were formed to develop new products.

Rival alliances aren't restricted to manufacturers of products, however. You can find them in all industries and sectors. The joint promotion of the 2002 Mike Tyson/Lennox Lewis fight by HBO (aligned with Tyson) and Showtime (aligned with Lewis)[49] was a rival alliance. The fight generated $120 million in revenues, $60 million for each rival, and was the highest pay-per-view event ever broadcasted at that time.

Well-formed alliances compensate for individual allies' weaknesses and leverage their strengths, providing much stronger results than either ally could achieve individually. A group of attorneys might buy out another legal firm to gain a significant new case load or a new area of expertise, thereby increasing the value of their firm. Or one company might ally with another to gain access to a channel, a brand, cultural knowledge, or discounts. You might pull a team of people together to get a project done in three weeks that would have taken you a year to do on your own. In every case, the alliance's purpose is for both parties to produce improved returns that they would not have been able to do without the union.

External factors, such as economic changes or shifting technologies, can force organizations to establish alliances in order to survive. In the wake of the recession that originated in 2008, some credit unions merged with others, because combining resources allowed the allies to shave operating expenses and maintain services to their members. In October 2009, the governors of Alabama, Mississippi, and Louisiana[50] looked at creating an alliance to bring jobs and development to their states. They were the initial allies (who were later joined by Florida) in an alliance called the Aerospace Alliance, an aerospace and aviation corridor stretching from Louisiana to Panama City, Florida. The region, hard hit by Hurricane Katrina and the recession was expected to gain nearly 50,000 jobs from the pooling of economic development, government, and business resources. While decision makers did not move forward with the alliance in the end, this is an example of the types of options that are available to you.

Now that we've touched on the reasons why leaders establish alliances, let's take a closer look at the types of alliances that you can establish to strengthen your organization and create a better future for it.

Six Forms of Alliances

As I mentioned earlier, there are six forms of alliances. Let's take a look at the details of each form.

The six basic forms of alliances are:

1. Ad Hoc
2. Consortium
3. Project Joint Venture
4. Joint Venture
5. Merger
6. Acquisitions

The following chart lists the alliances, along with their typical lifespan and resource requirements. Some of what you learn here comes from the respected research teams of Peter Lorange and Dick Roos, as well as that of Fred Kuglin and Jeff Hook.

Six Forms of Alliances (internal & external)

Alliance Type	Duration	Resources
Ad Hoc	Short Term	Low Resources
Consortium	Long Term	Low Resources
Project Joint Venture	Short Term	Medium Resources
Joint Venture	Long Term	High Resources
Merger	Long Term	High Resources
Acquisition	Long Term	High Resources

Figure 5.3—Six Forms of Alliances (internal & external)

Take some time to review the chart, and then read the descriptions and examples that follow for each category. Although the categories may appear simple at first, they're not. There are nuances and in some comparisons, slight differences that distinguish one form from another. Once you understand the characteristics of each of alliance, you will be able to select the one that aligns most appropriately with your Strategy, Macro Tactics, and Tactics.

Ad Hoc

An ad hoc alliance is an impromptu committee or group that you pull together when you need to fulfill a specific purpose. As soon as your ad hoc alliance has completed what it has set out to do, it is disbanded. Ad hoc alliance members work together under their own authority. Most ad hoc alliances are short-lived and require minimum resources.

An ad hoc alliance would be a committee of educators that comes together to review the opening of a new tutoring center, and then disassembles once the group has served its purpose. A legal team aimed at researching court records for a short period of time would also be an ad hoc alliance. Consider, too, the county parks group and university that have banded together to explore options for landing a government grant, or a community development group united for determining local interest in a mall project.

Consortium

A consortium is a band of groups or individuals who pool a limited amount of their resources in the pursuit of some type of leverage and shared desired outcomes. When you join a consortium, you expect that your resources combined with the resources of others will produce greater value than your individual contributions. You also invest a smaller fee or contribution than you would if you were working on your own in order to gain access to some type of benefit, such as educational programs, social events, professional discounts, legal representation, news updates, client leads, lobbying, capital, technologies, and/or research, depending on the purpose of the consortium.

If you're a member of a consortium and your Desired Outcome changes, you are likely to leave the consortium. For instance, when a dues-paying member no longer needs the services of a professional association, they opt not to renew their members, or when a country encounters a conflict with other countries in a consortium, that country decides to pull out of a worldwide initiative.

Consortiums can be large or small. The Avaya Users Group, the Society of Thoracic Surgeons, the Association for Corporate Growth, the Wallcoverings Association, the United Nations, and chambers of commerce are all consortiums. A collaborative consortium based in Switzerland, the European Organization for Nuclear Research, or CERN, is a $9 billion, 20-year project involving 10,000 scientists from more than 100 countries, 38 participating countries, and 150 universities. CERN's purpose in creating the world's largest and highest-energy particle accelerator, the Large Hadron Collider (LHC),[51] is to test predictions of high-energy and particle physics. The value derived from these consortiums could never be produced by any one research group, firm, or university alone.

Perhaps you know of other organizations—noncompeting entities that are located outside your geographic area, earn a greater or lesser volume of gross annual sales, or service different customers or communities—who could benefit from joining forces with you to address a specific cause or challenge. For instance, if you're a Latin American cocoa producer whose crops are threatened by the fungal disease frosty pod rot, you could form a worldwide consortium with cocoa producers within your region as well as with Africa and Southeast Asia to combat a variety of fungal diseases in ways that you could never do on your own. Or say that you need a particular technology that costs $250,000, but you can't foot the investment on your own. Ally with other organizations that can each contribute $25,000 and share the technology with you.

The opportunities are there; you just have to reach out and make them happen.

Project Joint Venture

A project joint venture (PJV) is an alliance formed between two or more parties for the duration of a specific project. Although most PJVs are short-lived, some last longer than others depending on the project and the industry; one industry would consider "long" to be two months, while another would consider "short" to be two years. When you're involved in a PJV, both you and your ally maintain your own management structure and operation control throughout the PJV. Then, when you've completed the project, you part ways.

Regardless of your industry or sector, a PJV is advantageous when you need help on a project but don't want to be "married" to your ally. In 2009, a team of doctors allied in a PJV to help a patient regain her sight. The alliance, which was formed in Florida, brought doctors together from[52] the dental, ophthalmological, and general medical fields to perform different functions within the project. A dentist removed the woman's eyetooth and reshaped it, and then an ophthalmologist implanted the tooth into her eye as a structure to hold a new lens in place. Once the patient, who was blind for nine years, could see again, the doctors disbanded and went about work as usual in their individual practices just as they did before the PJV.

Earlier we talked about vendor-customer relationships, and I cautioned you not to mistake general transactions for alliances. However, there are times when the vendor-customer relationship—those where the customer is paying for a service—is typically a PJV type of alliance. When an advertising agency creates a campaign, an engineer creates a new product design, a videographer shoots a training film, or a landscaper spruces up a yard, the party that does the work and the one that does the paying are allied for the specified period of time. Think no further than your utility or phone companies, for they are PJVs. In a vendor-customer relationship where the terms of the PJV that are set beforehand have been fulfilled, the allies conclude the alliance and part ways.

PJVs exist for a period of time and utilize fixed resources to achieve a very specific purpose and a shared desired outcome, much like how the film industry approaches the making of numerous Hollywood movies, which I call the Hollywood Model.[53] An organization decides to make a film. It hires filmmakers, directors, casting agents, actors, makeup artists, composers, and computer-generated-imagery experts, who come together for the project. After the work has been completed, these people disband and part ways. These groups then reform within a new production. Most companies supporting the film industry are small firms of fewer than twenty people. That's why when you see the credits for a movie, you'll notice one company logo after another roll across the screen.

PJVs can be created internally among individuals, departments, and business units, too. If you were to host an open house at your company, and you decided to secure a purchase order with your food and beverage department for its catering services, you would, in essence, be establishing a PJV for the event. Once the event ends, the PJV ends as well. The next time you're selecting Macro Tactics and Tactics for a project or special event, strategize on how a PJV might expand your potential to do more with less, to capture new markets, to secure a new role within an organization, and so on.

Joint Venture

A joint venture (JV) is an alliance where two or more parties share resources and risks and invest some form of equity during a longer-term alliance than they would in a PJV. Although the allies in a JV tend to share management decisions (with legal parameters), they also retain their individual ownership and management structures. All parties are tied to the risks and responsibilities of the JV, and their investment tends to be significant.

Like local U.S. television stations who are allied with NBC, ABC, or CBS, affiliates are a type of JV. Affiliate is an old term that's taken on new meanings over the years. An organization that's owned by a much larger organization can be called an affiliate. Two organizations owned by a third organization also can be called affiliates. Affiliates tend to be looser alliances than mergers or acquisitions, and require fewer resources.

When Lockheed Martin and Boeing created the United Space Alliance[54] in 1996 with offices in Florida, Alabama, California, and D.C., its mission was to provide NASA with services related to the human space-travel industry: designing and planning flight operations, logistics, vehicle processing, payload integration, astronaut flight control and training, software development, launch and recovery, and so on. The JV was formed to leverage both parties' joint capabilities to handle a job that would be difficult for either party to take on alone. By pooling their resources, both organizations were able to take on this enormous task and still pursue other independent strategies.

Because the wording is similar between PJVs and JVs, some people are inclined to confuse them, so here's an example you can recall if you find yourself doing the same. Say you want to build a casino. You first form a JV by investing money in the building costs of the structure and the start-up costs of initial operations, while your ally contributes the expertise to develop and run the casino. The two of you are in this casino together for the long haul.

At the same time, you enter into a PJV with a developer who builds the casino. You hire the developer and work with him until the casino has been built. Once you cut the final check to him for his services, the building project is complete and your alliance terminates.

Mergers

Oftentimes, people talk about mergers and acquisitions as though they are the same, but when I ask them, "Would you rather be merged or acquired?" they express strong opinions for or against either, depending on their point of view. If you're being acquired, and you're the owner, you could be in for a windfall. If you're being merged, and you're the leader of a company, you have advantages. The point is mergers and acquisitions, while they can be similar, are separate and different.

A merger unites two or more groups into a single legal entity. The parties share ownership, leadership, and management structure, and they join their assets and resources. A merger is highly resources driven and considered to be long term. You might merge two development teams or two marketing departments or even two administrative pools. A marriage is a merger of sorts, and there would be some pretty upset spouses out there if they learned that their ally considered the alliance to be a PJV.

Governments may use internal mergers to leverage efficiencies, save manpower, and reduce costs. Around the world, you'll often hear about local government officials who are seemingly in continual talks about merging several districts' fire and police departments for these reasons. Washington State water district mergers[55] have reduced 800 districts to 171 over many years, enabling the state government to reduce head count, consolidate resources, improve services, and make more efficient use of the taxpayers' money.

Mergers carry a certain level of complexity to them, because parties must address legal issues such as conditions, representations, warranties, covenants, and operations and termination. In addition, if you're a decision maker who must manage the merger process and the ensuing daily responsibilities, you need to develop the new framework so that the merged alliance runs optimally. Determining the day to day responsibilities and functions of the merger will vary based on several different factors: the industry, the parties involved, and the size of the merger.

If you believe that a merger is the best alliance choice for you, it is important that you understand fully what you're getting into before you take action. This is a measure that many people fail to take, putting themselves and the merger at risk for failure.

Be careful that you don't let the popularity of mergers fool you into thinking that a merger is right for you until you have made certain that it actually is. Then choose your tactics carefully and detail them so that they are executed properly. One great decision can make everything work well, while one bad decision could impact your future for years to come. Seek expert legal representation when you enter into a merger to be sure that due diligence is performed and that all loose ends are tied up.

Acquisitions

Acquisitions, also known as takeovers or buyouts, occur when one entity takes complete control over another, either by purchasing it outright or by buying up more than 50% of its shares. Most acquisitions tend to be long-term alliances that demand a great deal of resources from those involved. When Chairman and CEO Michael Dell of Dell, Inc., the world's second-largest manufacturer of personal computers, shifted strategy to expand the firm's offerings, he acquired Perot Systems,[56] which provides computer services. The alliance was a logical one, because it afforded Dell the ability to add new services quicker and more cost effectively than if the computer giant had set out to build an entirely new company from scratch.

Like other forms of alliances, acquisitions occur for many reasons. Sometimes, decision makers need technologies and find that an acquisition allows them to accomplish the task easily, as was the case when Prime View International purchased E Ink,[57] the cutting-edge electronic paper technology used in the Kindle and other e-readers. Other acquisitions occur to gain personnel, with one organization headhunting to lure a talented employee away from a competitor. Still others take place to allow an organization to grow rapidly without expending the time to build a second organization from the ground up. Acquisitions involve the transfer of all kinds of assets.

Although acquisitions can be friendly, the types that make for juicy headlines are hostile takeovers, which occur when one firm loses control (possibly through a board vote to sell the organization), and an outside entity buys up a large number of shares of a public entity. However, most acquisitions, both public and private, are mutually agreed upon redistributions of equity.

Again, be sure that you work with legal representation and that due diligence is performed to avoid problems down the road.

Two Tools for Building Alliances

You are about to add two new tools to your ET toolkit. The first is the Alliance Pillars Checklist, a simple and informal tool that you can use as a guide when you want to build an alliance. The second is a version of the ET Development Funnel that has been modified for use as an alliance-building process. It gives you a structured approach to building alliances to ensure that you don't overlook important components. Both tools offer advantages, and having two tools means that you can select the one that best fits your needs at any given time.

TOOL #1: ALLIANCE PILLARS CHECKLIST

Just as buildings require a framework of timbers or steel beams to keep them standing, alliances need a framework of pillars shoring them up over a span of time. When you think about the Alliance Pillars Checklist, consider its pillars as the wooden-timber framework of your next alliance.

Alliance Pillars Checklist

☐ Form	Identify the form of alliance that best meets Desired Outcome and Strategy.
☐ Risk	Evaluate risk assessment thereby deciding if the alliance is worth the effort.
☐ Ally	Select the right ally by using the "Development Funnel."
☐ Objectives	Set clear objectives and commitment levels for all parties.
☐ Financials	Agree on financial contributions and draws for all parties.
☐ Budgets	Outline the budget and develop a financial management plan.
☐ Controls	Establish controls, metrics, and milestones along with how they will be developed.
☐ Human Resources	Determine human resources requirements including the who, what, and where.

* Establishing alliances requires Cyclonic Thinking and all the activities of Enterprise Thinking
* No one activity is more important than another: they all influence an alliance's ability to perform and succeed.

Figure 5.4—Alliance Pillars Checklist

Eight Alliance Pillars make up the Alliance Pillars Checklist (Figure 5.4). They are:

1. Form
2. Risk
3. Ally
4. Objectives
5. Financials
6. Budget
7. Controls
8. Human Resources

When you have the opportunity to advance your organization with an ally, you want to be sure that the alliance is of sound construction. There's a pretty good chance that at one time or another you've been involved in an alliance that encountered challenges. Sometimes a challenge occurs when one ally changes parameters after the alliance is in full swing; other times an ally is deceitful from the beginning, causing irreparable damage once people have invested resources into the alliance.

Let's take a closer look at the eight Alliance Pillars, because they not only help you have a solid framework for your alliances, but they also help you to avoid some of the common challenges that jeopardize alliances' successes.

Alliance Pillar #1: Form

Sometimes, the form of alliance is an obvious choice, while other times you may need to consult colleagues, experts, and members of your management team to decide if one form is more strategically or tactically advantageous than another. The form is one of the six types of alliances—ad hoc, consortium, project joint venture, joint venture, merger, and acquisition.

Alliance Pillar #2: Risk

Throughout the process of building an alliance—from deciding on the form, selecting the ally, and developing the alliance—you must continually assess risk. The purpose of an alliance should always be to advance you or your organization further, faster, and/or more cost effectively than it can do on its own, but it can only serve this purpose if risks are mitigated. Ask yourself what the risks are for both parties and whether the alliance is worth the risk. When you answer these questions, be sure that outcomes will produce greater results than only the sum of the two parts.

Alliance Pillar #3: Ally

Although it may seem obvious that you must build an alliance with the *right* ally, too often decision makers settle on an ally that only seems to fit the bill without any concrete reasons for selecting that particular ally. Ideally, you want to start out with a list of many potential allies so that you can narrow down your choices to the best one. Consult with people who know you and your circumstances well enough to judge when your choice of an ally is a bad one. If you find that selecting an ally is a challenging endeavor, you can use your next tool, the Modified ET Development Funnel, to select a best ally with structured Ideation and Elimination activities.

Alliance Pillar #4: Synchronization with Desired Outcome, Strategy, Macro Tactics, and Tactics

Your alliance must be aligned with your Desired Outcome for the project and be a Tactic that supports your Strategy. Realize, however, that you and your ally can have different tactical reasons for entering into the alliance as long as they are complementary. For example, you want to use their distribution channel to quickly enter a new market, and they want to ride the coattails of your brand name to grow their sales. As long as Desired Outcomes are discussed up front and everyone understands what they're getting into, you're on your way to establishing a solid alliance.

Two Desired Outcomes into Greater Outcomes

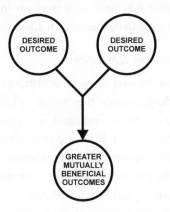

Figure 5.5—Two Desired Outcomes into Greater Outcomes

Alliance Pillar #5: Financials—Contributions and Draws

Determine contributions and draws early on, and make sure that all parties are in agreement before you invest money or resources into the alliance.

You may have to contribute your time, which is an additional expense, but considering the Economics of Thinking, the time spent righting your alliance in its early phases is relatively inexpensive compared to the costs of developing it later.

The type of alliance will determine the level of resources and degree of commitment required by everyone who is involved. A JV will require more clearly defined objectives and commitment levels than an ad hoc committee will.

Alliance Pillar #6: Budgets

Outline a budget and develop a financial management plan for your alliance. It's always better to know the financial parameters in the beginning so that there are no misunderstandings later. You can opt to increase the budget at a future point should new situations and conditions present themselves, but at least then you are making more informed and better controlled decisions to do so. It's the same advice you hear when you're about to visit an auction. Know how much you're willing to spend before the bidding begins. Otherwise, you may get carried away with emotion and end up investing more than you should.

Alliance Pillar #7: Controls

What are the metrics by which you will measure your alliance's success? Deciding on benchmarks, outcomes, and controls before you enter into a full-fledged alliance will help you control expenses, determine next best steps, and decide whether it is more advantageous to continue with the alliance, make changes to it, or to disassemble it altogether.

Alliance Pillar #8: Human Resources

While human resources are part of your contributions, they must stand out alone in alliance building, because they're not as one-dimensional as other resources, requiring them to be evaluated and allocated strategically. You need an accurate assessment of talents and skills so that you can allocate the best people to the right responsibilities. Furthermore, you want to be sure that you're not assuming you'll get high-caliber people from your ally only to be disappointed later when you end up with his or her "B team."

The CIO of a 5,000-employee medical-device manufacturing firm outsourced his IT activities to a firm that sold him on its top-tier IT experts for they considered themselves to be a large and valuable customer. The alliance was instantly put in jeopardy when the ally supplied B- and C-tier techs who couldn't do the job optimally and disappointed the CIO's staff. Within two years, the alliance was dead, leaving a trail of issues, such as a troubled infrastructure, wasted resources, and low morale due to numerous unresolved challenges, in its wake.

The Alliance Pillars Checklist can be a good way *to start* (and build) many forms of alliances. However, it is not the only tool you have at your disposal. Whether your prospective alliance is simple or complex, your next tool, the Modified ET Development Funnel, gives you a more structured approach to development when you need it.

TOOL #2: THE MODIFIED ET DEVELOPMENT FUNNEL

The roads to too many alliances have been paved with good intentions. As you can guess, good intentions can be a bad substitute for a reliable alliance-building process in many circumstances. While some alliances, like an ad hoc committee planning your annual company picnic, can be built just fine with a simple tool like Alliance Pillars Checklist, others might require a more structured approach to development: one that outlines contributions and draws, clarifies expectations, and allows flexibility for when the unexpected occurs.

For times when a structured approach is appropriate, you can use a modified version of the ET Development Funnel (Chapter 4) to build an alliance. Figure 5.5 should appear familiar to you, because you've used a similar approach in the last chapter. Notice that the three activities of the process remain intact:

Activity I—Ideation: You will gather the names of many potential allies and load them into the wide mouth of the funnel, remembering to take ample time to ideate thoroughly.

Activity II—Elimination: You will filter the prospective allies against predetermined criteria in three rounds of screening until your screeners confirm your single best ally choice. Consider the Concept of 100 > 7 > 3 > 1 to be a guide; you may start out with 70 and get 8 and then 4 then 1. The point is to shoot for a higher number than one would typically think.

Activity III—Development: You will build your alliance in four phases of development and use the Post-Launch Review and Post-Launch Review Gate to monitor progress, assess viability of the alliance over time, and determine next best steps, such as keeping status quo, making adjustments, or disbanding. (In certain types of mergers, the Post-Launch Review phase can actually span a longer period of time than the building of the alliance, sometimes extending for years.)

ET Alliance Development Funnel™

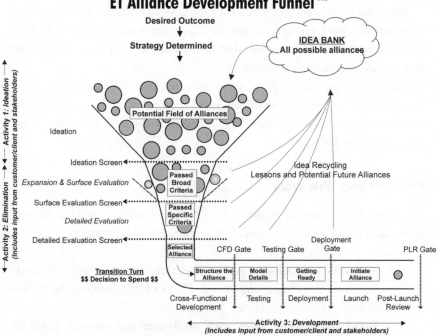

Figure 5.6—ET Alliance Development Funnel™

We will walk through the activities of the ET Development Funnel (using alliances instead of new product and service development as the output) so that you can use it to select a single best ally and develop an alliance with it from start to finish. Here are the six steps:

1. State your Desired Outcome and purpose
2. Perform your pre-work
3. Perform Activity I—Ideation
4. Perform Activity II—Elimination
5. Perform Activity III—Development
6. Determine next steps

Now that you've seen the tool, let's talk in general terms about how to use it.

State Your Desired Outcome and Purpose

State a clear Desired Outcome and purpose for establishing the alliance; make sure that it aligns with Strategy, Macro Tactics, and Tactics; and later share it with the people who will help you select and develop the alliance.

Know the *form* of alliance you want to build—ad hoc, consortium, project joint venture, joint venture, merger, or acquisition—and make certain that everyone on board understands what the alliance form entails—short/long term or low/medium/high resources.

Also, as you move through the three activities, keep the reason for the alliance in sight: entering a new market, gaining access to intellectual property, accelerating growth which may drive a competitor out of business, giving shelter to more homeless, etc.

Perform Your Pre-Work

As always, the Goldsmith Productivity Principle (GPP) is essential, so you must build structure into Ideation, Elimination, and Development.

- **Assemble your alliance group.** These are the people who will work with you from beginning to end. Think of this group as the NPSD group of alliance building.
- **Build screens and gates with predetermined criteria.** Look at your purpose, Strategy, Tactics, resources (human, time, capital), and external factors (economy, competitors, consumer trends) to

incorporate screening criteria that will eventually highlight your best ally option. Build your gates with criteria that will keep your alliance development on track with the original purpose for the alliance.

- **Choose your screeners.** Your screeners are the people who will scrub the names of potential allies against your predetermined criteria to make sure that your alliance group has played by the rules. Make sure you pick screeners who can be and are educated on being impartial in their judgment.
- **Select your gatekeepers.** Gatekeepers will ensure that all parties have met their responsibilities before your alliance moves to the next phase. If you've done a good job building the gates with clear criteria, gatekeepers can do a better job keeping your alliance on track with its intended purpose.

Perform Activity I—Ideation

Pull together the names of as many prospective allies as you can and load them into the wide mouth of the funnel. It's extremely important that you do a thorough job here, because too many leaders rush through this step before they even have their best "idea," in this case the name of their best ally, in the funnel. ET Development Funnel prevents you from falling in love with your own ideas.

If you remember from Chapter 4, a group of CEOs who were part of a consortium chose their best ally from the thirty-first and thirty-second names on their list, though initially they were ready to stop coming up with prospective allies when they had a list of only seventeen names, which later grew by twelve more and then finally expanded by three more after that. This exercise of thinking first only added two days to the entire process, which is right in line with the Economics of Thinking.

If you were to form an alliance in your organization, and your company employs 20,000 people, you would engage in the same type of ideation as an organization that seeks an alliance for the purpose of entering into another country to sell products.

Rushing through Ideation is likely to produce a mediocre alliance at best (or a disastrous one at worst), and put your ability to reach Desired Outcomes at risk.

Perform Activity II—Elimination

Your alliance group screens the one hundred names using the preset criteria and whittles the number of prospective allies down to approximately seven names, give or take. You want enough options so that after you have done further research later on, you end up with your most viable names. Then your screeners check to make sure that each one meets the requirements necessary to pass through the screen. Once satisfied, screeners hand the seven names back to the alliance group.

Next, the alliance group, depending on the type of alliance, does "inexpensive desk research" or complex detailed research (which may include on-site visits, getting nondisclosure agreements, and so on). The goal here is to do the right amount of thinking so that you can identify the three best names from the seven remaining names during the Expansion and Surface Evaluation phase. The evaluation may uncover additional new names, which is okay but not necessary. Keep in mind that any new names will have to be vetted to the first set of criteria. The goal is to exit this phase with three superior options that can be given to screeners at your second checkpoint.

In our previous example where the consortium sought out a new member, members of the group made some quick calls to their prospects, identified a few individuals who were not interested, learned that a few could not make it to the meetings, and realized that a few did not meet the criteria of operating a dual plant with separate financials.

Screeners decide if the three options meet criteria before passing them through the Surface Evaluation Screen and back into the hands of the alliance group. These three names undergo a Detailed Evaluation, an important phase that will enable one single ally to rise to the top of the list. This ally's name, along with evaluation data, is presented to screeners at the Detailed Evaluation Screen.

Note: If no names make it past this point, then it could be that none were viable, not enough alliance options were placed into the funnel, or the elimination criteria was too limiting. You need to determine which of these situations you're dealing with and make the necessary corrections.

If only one name makes it past the point, it could be that not enough ideas were in the funnel, the criteria was too restrictive, or that the criteria was set (purposely or mistakenly) so that only one name could be viable—people create single-source situations to force one idea to rise to the top, because that's what they wanted from the beginning, which may or may not be a situation of someone who has fallen in love with their own ideas.

If you find yourself facing one of these situations, you can pull out some of your other ET tools, like the Economics of Thinking or the Economics of Timing or Alliance Pillars to be sure that you are not allowing narrowly focused thinking to close off opportunities to you and your organization.

If screeners determine that the chosen ally has met criteria, they dispense your single "diamond-ball" ally. You will now begin developing your alliance.

Perform Activity III—Development

Follow the phases and gates of this Development process to cover the areas that make a good alliance.

- **Cross-Functional Development: Structure the alliance.** With your ally, bring together the people who will play a part in making this alliance happen. You're eliciting help from them as you build the GPP's 80% (systems and structures). The teams of people come from different departments, business units, etc., and offer cross-functional input and planning to ensure that the alliance will be successful. The HR representatives help to determine how staffing will be allocated, the IT department offers up its plan for integrating both parties technologically and systematically, the managers from finance outline budgetary issues, and so on. The cross-functional teams are building the structure—the Alliance Pillars—of your alliance. **Note:** *Be sure that the people you choose to help you with this function have the ability to see a larger picture and/or think at a level that will help you make your best decision.* Realize that a person's title doesn't mean that they have the right skills to help you here.

- **Cross-Functional Development Gate.** The gatekeepers match data and reports against the criteria you have given them. Gatekeepers make sure that the alliance in these early stages is still in alignment with its original purpose and Strategy. They perform the important role of keeping your alliance on track.

- **Testing: Model the details.** In this phase, members of your cross-functional teams and your alliance group are hashing out details, writing up floor plans, talking with people in production, etc., to try to devise some sort of model that will enable them to judge if their ideas and plans are realistic. This is the phase where the output from Structuring the Alliance is integrated together and put to the test: Will this alliance work? Mind you, this is a sort of mental game where options are explored so that you can create the optimum solution.

- **Testing Gate.** The gatekeepers come back into play here, but their role is strictly to test the Testing and see if it was performed properly.

Gatekeepers are asking, Did the testers test properly, and is this alliance in compliance with criteria?

- **Deployment: Get ready to launch alliance.** You need to be sure that all components of the alliance are in place before you pull the trigger. Ask if personnel are placed where they need to be, if the budget is in place, if your company is logistically prepared for the changes that are about to happen, etc. Your alliance group's main responsibility is to make sure that all cross-functional teams are in the ready position. If you pull the plug on working with someone at the very last minute, you've decided that the alliance, even with all the prep work having been completed, was not worth the effort.

- **Deployment Gate.** Gatekeepers read reports, communicate with key personnel, and make sure that the "ready position" of your cross-functional teams meets criteria. Say that you're about to acquire a company, and someone found a lien on the company in an obscure area that did not come up on the radar during legal review. If one criterion was that the lien had to be legally removed before you transferred funds for purchase, the gatekeeper would have to make sure that the lien had been removed before the alliance could pass through this gate and enter into the Launch phase. Remember, the Deployment Gate is the last countdown to launch.

- **Launch: Initiate alliance.** The alliance is official. Of course, Launch means something different to every alliance, because it is defined by the circumstances of the alliance. In a PJV, the Launch could be marked by the installation of a new deep-sea platform. In an ad hoc, the Launch could be the point where you and your two committee members exit your conference room with to-do lists in hand. In a merger, the Launch could be marked by the signing of a legal document or a ceremony signaling the beginning of the new entity.

- **Post-Launch Review: Assess outcomes and results.** This is an extremely important phase, one that too few organizations do well enough or often enough. The Post-Launch Review is essential, because you need real data and information that provides a measure of progress and results.

Determine Next Steps

- **Post-Launch Review Gate.** At this gate, you and your management team become the gatekeepers who scour all data from the Post-Launch

Review to judge how this alliance stands in terms of delivering the outcomes you intended for it. Based on your assessment (and the current needs of your organization), you will determine whether your next steps are to proceed without changes, make adjustments to the alliance, or to disband the alliance altogether.

At the appropriate time, the ET Development Funnel can be a useful tool that can optimize outcomes and mitigate risks involved in establishing alliances. At other times, the Alliance Pillars Checklist is a sufficient guide to building alliances. Which one is best? You be the judge on a situational basis.

There's a final piece of information you need in order to avoid confusion when you use the Modified ET Development Funnel to build alliances. It is the Pre-Development Funnel. Though it may seem like a somewhat advanced concept initially, it should make sense and help you save a lot of time later.

The Pre-Development Funnel

Sometimes you need to make some determinations *before* you're able to use the Modified ET Development Funnel for alliance building. Primarily, before you can select the right ally, you need to know which of the six forms of alliances would be most appropriate at this time, and you also need to be clear about the purpose of your alliance. When you must answer questions like these beforehand, you can actually initiate a mini Pre-Development Funnel whereby you engage in Ideation and Elimination to strictly select your "diamond" alliance form or purpose. In some cases, you would do two Pre-Development Funnels: one for the alliance form and another for the purpose.

Once you know the type of alliance and its purpose—"We are going to enter into a project joint venture to bring medical supplies to the disaster site," for example—you can incorporate them into your elimination screens—the ally must be able to contribute $125,000 within three days, the ally must have governmental clearance to travel into region, etc.—to be sure that you select your best potential ally.

Although the Pre-Development Funnel can be a useful way of clearing the mental clutter out of the actual process of selecting an ally and developing an alliance, *it is optional.* You might use the ET Development Funnel process for establishing alliances over the next fifty years and never once use the Pre-Development Funnel.

At the Time, We Thought We Were Doing the Right Thing

Gary and Audrina were responsible for making the acquisitions that their employer, a public Brazilian company bringing in $100 million in gross annual sales, needed to continue on its fast track to growth. The firm, with holdings in Taiwan, Germany, Argentina, China, and the United States, needed to maintain its current level of growth through acquisitions to keep its investors happy. The two acquisition managers studied eighty prospective companies and settled on seven of them to be acquired.

A year later, after Gary had learned some of the ET tools for establishing alliances, he looked back on past acquisition successes and failures with a fresh perspective and admitted, "At the time, we thought we were doing the right thing. Now, I can see clearly why four of the seven acquisitions from that year failed." His reasons were many, but they boiled down to three in particular:

1. Senior management gave two managers, Gary and Audrina, complete authority to make the selections. There were no screeners, no gatekeepers, and no screening criteria as part of the process to focus the managers' efforts.

2. Senior management was absent from the screening and gatekeeping activities, meaning Gary and Audrina didn't have the benefit of guidance and support to point out pitfalls.

3. Management had not thoroughly assessed whether the strategy for growth through acquisitions was the company's best strategic option. Without knowing for sure whether mergers or JVs would have been better options, management caused the firm to lose traction and time on potentially lower-yielding alliances.

Alliance Killers

Establishing alliances isn't just about coordinating concrete aspects like funding and logistics; it also has a human side. Statistically, over half of all organizational alliances fail, and according to Larraine Segil, a business-strategy consultant who's studied alliances for more than twenty years, most fail "not because of poor strategy and development or business mismanagement, but because partner companies are unable to work together effectively."[58] You can reduce casualties caused by human roadblocks by identifying early threats and overcoming them with your ET tools. Those threats, the opposite of Alliance Pillars, are called Alliance Killers, and they are what this section is about.

The ten Alliance Killers are the following:

1. Uncertainty
2. Apathy
3. Delusion
4. Grandeur
5. Ethnocentricity
6. Incompatibility
7. Selfishness
8. Sloppiness
9. Ignorance
10. Deceit

All six alliance forms are made between individuals, groups, companies, nonprofits, and organizations across industries, geographies, cultures, and more. Therefore, you need universal tools to attack the threats that can permeate the countless configurations of alliances, and you need to be able to adapt the tools to your unique circumstances.

Alliance Killer #1: Uncertainty

Uncertainty poses a real risk to alliances, whether it's born from mistrust between parties or from fear among individuals within one or both parties. You can obviously understand how doubts could come between allies and cause cracks in the relationship, but less obvious are the dangers posed to the union when one party's internal stakeholders feel threatened. I saw this play out in one company where a senior executive who was in the process of developing a joint venture suggested one of his high-performing managers with an impeccable ten-year track record to head the new alliance. He saw this as her opportunity for growth and possibly more income. She, on the other hand, feared failing at this new venture and risking the seniority, salary, and benefits that she had invested so much in earning over the past decade. Her uncertainty led her to reject her superior's offer, which in this case was probably better than accepting it, because a leader who isn't on board with an alliance has the power to consciously or subconsciously sabotage an alliance.

Internal resistance can often occur with other long-term/high-resources alliances like acquisitions and mergers, and it should be addressed early on. Less difficult to solve is the same type of resistance among short-term/low- or medium-resources alliances like PJVs and ad hocs, which may simply require parties to come to a small compromise.

Keep your eyes open to individuals, including yourself, who may allow their uncertainties to jeopardize the alliance. If you find that uncertainties are present that could undermine your success, you don't necessarily have to abandon the alliance, but you do have to look in two directions for solutions: inward to yourself, and outward to the alliance and the individuals involved. Inwardly, question whether you developed your CST Model well going into this alliance, defined clearly enough your Desired Outcome, and sufficiently "sold" the Strategy and Macro Tactics to your internal staffers or to the ally. Perhaps you have a weak history of project management with too few WSPs to your credit, and you haven't earned the trust you need to gain buy in.

In instances where staffers seem to be resistant to your alliance selection, you may have to delve deeper into the reasons why—after all, it could be an oversight on your part. Maybe your screening criteria weren't as tied to Strategy, Macro Tactics, and Tactics as you originally thought. Perhaps the ally isn't trustworthy, or the Alliance Pillars have some cracks in them that need to be filled before proceeding. Also, consider whether you just sold the alliance internally to your group; oftentimes so much time is spent on building an alliance that leaders forget to sell an alliance and its benefits to staff members. Then again, it's always good to place yourself in the position of the staffer and see from their perspective why they feel threatened, because the problem could either stem from "this alliance is bad for the organization" or simply "this alliance produces negative change for one individual on staff." Once you have explored these potential reasons for staff resistance and their threat level to the alliance, you can address the specific challenge.

Alliance Killer #2: Apathy

Apathy can hurt an alliance in several ways. If leadership is apathetic, this killer can wash through the alliance like a tsunami, taking the potential for positive outcomes with it. Typically, apathy exists on one side of the alliance, ending with the apathetic party unevenly shifting its responsibilities onto the other party's shoulders. As time progresses, fewer key responsibilities or tasks receive the attention they need, eroding the effectiveness and life of the alliance.

Watch for people who will go along with an alliance (or a project) without ensuring that key components are in order, because they plan to retire or leave the organization anyway and aren't concerned with the downside of the endeavor once they are gone. Processes like the one you're learning here safeguard organizations against the pitfalls of less-than-meticulous transactions like these.

Every aspect of the alliance needs focus and attention. If you're hiring a person to work on a PJV, leadership needs to get involved physically and mentally, agreeing on the type of person and the Tactics they will execute, and establishing outcomes, etc. Yet if apathy exists at the leadership and management level, it is unlikely that all Alliance Pillars will be addressed, putting the alliance at risk.

Alliance Killer #3: Delusion

There are many reasons why people delude themselves: ego, fear, ignorance, or committing too blindly to an idea to let it go are a few. Seeing only what you want to see puts your alliances in mortal jeopardy.

Two changes in approach will ward off delusion. First, install control mechanisms—like screening and gatekeeping criteria—that bring objectivity to your ally-selection and alliance-development process. It's difficult to ignore warning signs that something isn't right when you outline criteria in advance and have an alliance group, screeners, and gatekeepers keeping you on target.

Second, collaborate with colleagues who know your situation and who will be honest with you. For instance, you might feel that an acquisition is best for your Desired Outcome, but your colleagues might see advantages in a shorter-term alliance, like a PJV, where you can accomplish outcomes without the heavy commitment or drain on resources. Getting a grip on delusional decision makers—whether that's you or members of your group—will prevent your organization from losing traction and time.

Alliance Killer #4: Grandeur

Grandeur isn't always going to kill an alliance, but it can kill your hopes of achieving Desired Outcomes. If you're overestimating your return on investment, you could end up dumping money, time, and other resources into a relationship that isn't worth the bother. Again, keep your expectations about the alliance's outcomes realistic by ensuring that 1 + 1 will actually deliver an outcome that is greater than 2.

I have worked with some companies where leadership has overvalued their alliances, causing leaders to skew their perceptions of their organizations' growth. Growth figures can be misleading, because they combine organic growth from internal improvements and sales with inorganic growth that comes about by acquiring or merging with other companies. Therefore, you must separate the numbers from both types of growth to understand where your organization is growing and thriving and where it needs additional improvements.

Leaders whose egos are so large that they can't see a downside to an alliance are often prone to making mistakes like overestimating an alliance's capabilities to generate returns, neglecting to compose a backup plan, pushing manpower too hard to overcompensate for the alliance's flaws, and throwing good money after bad, all of which can crash down like a line of dominoes.

Alliance Killer #5: Ethnocentricity

Cultural barriers can kill an alliance, but you can overcome them. Being globally aware (which you'll learn more about in Chapter 8) can help you to understand how diverse groups of people work best and to be aware of how corporate cultures influence outcomes. When Oracle and IBM were in pursuit of Sun[59] as a potential ally, each firm conducted their own research to see whether Sun was a good fit. In the end, Oracle's laid-back West Coast vibe appeared to be the better match to Sun's corporate culture, edging IBM out of the running.

Randy, the owner of a 30,000-person company, concentrates heavily on cultural issues when he and his leadership team look for allies in other countries. To gain a global reach, his firm owns offices around the globe, and to make each office work successfully, he and his leadership staff use a collaborative approach to alliance building. Beyond location and skills, he and his team do due diligence to select allies that are accustomed to working with diverse individuals, companies, and markets, ensuring that cultural barriers will not be an issue.

Cultural killers can include ignorance of holiday schedules, avoiding eye contact, smiling too much, language barriers, or conflicts arising from opposing social morés. By the same token, putting ethnocentricity aside allows you to embrace differences and use them to fortify alliances. Just as products developed with an international perspective achieve an 85% success rate as opposed to domestically oriented products' rate of less than 43%,[60] cultural differences can make for stronger alliances, too.

Alliance Killer #6: Incompatibility

Like marriages, alliances can succumb to incompatibility issues. Finding the right ally is an obvious first rule, but having the sense and the tools to say no to a prospective ally once you've fallen in love with it is another matter altogether. (See Alliance Killer #3: Delusion.)

The success of an alliance can be derailed when certain factors of importance for each party are out of sync. Desired Outcomes don't have to be identical, but they must be complementary enough to make for a compatible alliance.

Say that allies disagree about the form of alliance they want to create. Agreeing on the actual form of alliance isn't always essential—as long as parties can agree up front to certain key details that are vital to a successful alliance (time frames, input, draws, benchmarks, etc.) the allies can still ward off the killer of incompatibility and form a successful union.

Sometimes the incompatibility is as black and white as financial issues that you can't work out. For example, major retailers often require that vendors be able to supply a certain amount of product before they will buy from them. To assist in the retailers' decision making, they look at the prospective vendors' lines of credit, cash on hand, etc. Other times, pinpointing and solving the problem isn't so clear-cut, especially when personalities clash or an ally lacks direction and clearly defined Desired Outcomes. If you believe that your incompatibilities are too much to overcome—and we've all been there—it's better to stop proceedings and end the alliance.

Alliance Killer #7: Selfishness

Even though many alliances are established between organizations, businesses, and entities, they're still created by humans, some of whom are selfish enough to be undisciplined, unethical, or greedy, putting alliances at risk. An ally who looks out for himself and leaves you in the lurch puts cracks in the relationship that allow many of the other Alliance Killers—uncertainty, apathy, deceit—to seep into the alliance.

Jason is an entrepreneur who built a business over a span of twenty years and was in negotiations to sell his business to a multibillion-dollar company. The transaction would mean that Jason could meet his retirement goals before the age of fifty, pay for his four kids' college educations, and cover the expenses of his ailing parent. Jason turned to a longtime ally, his accountant, for advice. "Don't do it. It's bad for you," the accountant told him. "You can make more money by keeping the business." What's astounding about this "advice" is that of all people, Jason's accountant had the financials to prove that it would most definitely be in Jason's best interest to take the deal. However, it would be in the accountant's best interest if Jason rejected the deal and stayed on as a client, because Jason's business composed 40% of the accountant's income. Sometimes your allies aren't looking out for you; they're only looking out for themselves. Under certain circumstances, if their selfishness doesn't kill your alliance, you should.

Alliance Killer #8: Sloppiness

Sloppiness is an entirely preventable Alliance Killer as long as at least one ally has the discipline to address necessary building blocks of the alliance and Alliance Pillars. Consider how some alliances need more elaborate or detailed systems and structures than others, how some rely on standard procedures for success, or how some require legal due diligence, and so on. You want to ensure that someone is meticulous in building a solid foundation under the alliance, and that no party's sloppiness is pervasive enough to weaken or break the alliance.

According to a June 22, 2010, *Bloomberg Businessweek* article by Tom Herd,[61] when more than 600 C-suite executives who had been involved in a merger or acquisition were surveyed by Accenture and the Economist Intelligence Unit, they "attributed success to mastering three stages of the M&A [mergers and acquisitions] life cycle: conducting due diligence, and most critically, planning and executing the merger integration process." Crossing your t's and dotting your i's is important.

Whether you need to adopt the Economics of Thinking and abandon old beliefs that mistake busyness for productivity or you need to build systems and structures into your alliance-building process, you must address all aspects of the alliance-building process to a certain degree of thoroughness if you expect the alliance to succeed.

Alliance Killer #9: Ignorance

Ignorance is an Alliance Killer born of two parents: lack of education about alliance building and lack of tools to ensure that alliances are built properly. Without the right tools—a good checklist of Alliance Pillars or a structured process like the Modified ET Development Funnel—you could be missing key components to building an alliance and not be aware that you're missing them.

Many leaders with little to no alliance-building education scan through a book on alliances as a last-minute crash course on the subject. Perhaps that's better than nothing, but it doesn't ensure that you know the process well enough or have the tools in place to be able to do the job right. Furthermore, the fear and stress that erode your confidence when you know you aren't as knowledgeable about alliance building as you probably need to be can be a distraction that prevents you from catching other problems until you're too far into the alliance.

In addition, you need to perform the ET activities in the Learning category well—general knowledge and leadership skills, insight into the competition, and awareness of global issues, three activities you'll be introduced to beginning in Chapter 7—so that you're equipped with the necessary mental reinforcements to enter into an alliance from a strong, knowledgeable position.

Alliance Killer #10: Deceit

Deceit has no place in alliances, period. If parties can't trust each other, the alliance is as good as dead. Any breach, ranging from some small incident to an illegal scam such as an unapproved draw of funds to an outright theft respectively, will eventually kill the alliance.

Since the potential for a prospective ally to deceive you is not always easy to detect, do your research and investigate any warnings that come your way, no matter how incredulous they may initially seem. In the summer of 2009, the New York State senate came to a standstill as alliances shifted in a Republican-led effort to gain majority vote away from the Democratic Party.[62] One of the Democratic senators switched sides, upsetting the party's majority and sending the senate into a tailspin. Whether you or I believe that the democratic senator was deceitful is not the issue; the bottom line is that people from his original party were counting on him and he gave them reason to lose trust in him.

■ ■ ■

Each and every alliance you establish will have a personality of its own and will demand very specific requirements to thrive and survive for its intended life span. Now that you understand some of the killers that can threaten the survival of alliances, you may see where a past alliance went wrong, and you can take steps to ensure that the same doesn't happen to any future alliances.

Together, we've covered a lot of ground about alliances in ways that should open doors of opportunities for your organization and provide you with new ways of solving your challenges. If you came to this chapter with a limited view of partnerships, your thinking is now expanded and your mind is now like freshly tilled soil, ready to sprout today's seedling ideas into tomorrow's harvests of possibilities. Take some time to reflect on the forms of alliances and those in particular that you can establish now or in the near future as tactical options to support your Strategies and reach Desired Outcomes. Obviously, you'll want to be sure that any alliance you spend the time and resources cultivating is one that delivers back to its parties greater returns than either party can achieve on its own, but now you have the tools you need to make those kinds of determinations and expand your options. In addition, these new ET tools and concepts are simple and universal enough that you can easily share them with others to multiply their benefits to your organization now and for years to come.

6

LEVERAGING TECHNOLOGY

AFTER PRESENTING A KEYNOTE ADDRESS to the California League of Food Processors, I was approached by one of its members, Chris Rufer, the president of the Woodland, California-based cutting-edge tomato processor, the Morning Star Company, which handles close to 30% of global tomato production. You've probably consumed one of Rufer's products on your last slice of pizza, spaghetti dinner, or ketchup-topped burger. Rufer, an innovative thinker, made an interesting statement: "People say that humans have changed over time, but I don't believe this is true. We've needed food, water, shelter, transportation, communication, and entertainment throughout history. Today, we still have these needs. So can you tell me what *has* changed?" After some thought, I realized Rufer had an excellent point. Our *needs* haven't changed at all; the only change that has occurred is how we've applied *technology* to those needs!

Citizens of industrialized societies grow, harvest, store, and retrieve food using more technologically advanced methods than their global neighbors residing in lesser-developed societies. Think about how technology has transformed shelter from simple huts to skyscrapers, and transportation from foot or canoe to automobiles and jets. Even entertainment has evolved from fireside stories to motion pictures to make-your-own movies for YouTube.

As a leader, you must look for ways that you can leverage technology so that you can maximize your organization's potential today and move it successfully into tomorrow.

What Technology Means to Your Organization

We have become so interwoven with and surrounded by technology that we don't always realize the enormous role it plays in our lives. Typically, we're reminded of this reality when technology fails to produce the outcomes we've grown so accustomed to receiving from it. Try getting to work on time when your car doesn't start or making a presentation when your computer won't link up to the Wi-Fi you need. Yet despite the pervasiveness of technology in our personal and professional lives, it's been my experience that the majority of leaders have a narrow-minded view of technology in terms of what it is and what it can do for their organizations. As a result of not seeing the vast potential that technologies have to sprout and support limitless opportunities, these leaders unknowingly rob their organizations of chances to grow and advance.

If you find yourself (or other colleagues) making statements like, "We already have state-of-the-art equipment throughout our organization" or "We're a service organization, so we don't use technology the way that a manufacturer does," start becoming aware that you are most likely not seeing a big enough or encompassing enough picture on the topic. Further clues that leadership's understanding may be too limited are references to technology that focus only on electronics or "advancements" items. Technology involves much, much more, and the ways in which you leverage it should involve cross-utilized, integrative, and innovative measures that both empower your people to do their jobs better and solve daily challenges.

Before we get into the meat of the chapter, let's lay the groundwork for new learning by expanding your definition of technology and exploring some self-limiting thinking you might have. As you read through this chapter, keep in mind that the activity of leveraging technology is not simply about technology; it is about how you as a leader can use technology in nontraditional and better ways to create more and better opportunities.

Advancing Your Organization by Leveraging Technology

Although technology in and of itself can be beneficial, it is actually the adeptness with which a decision maker leverages technologies that leads to opportunities and results. Understanding how to select and implement technologies in better and innovative ways expands your ability to maximize the potential of all of your organization's assets while simultaneously keeping ahead of the never-ending demand to do more with less.

Leveraging technology allows you to:

1. maximize the potential of all organizational assets.
2. continue to do more with less.
3. create change that your people will love.
4. have control over the inevitable evolution of technology.

Maximize the Potential of All Organizational Assets

As a first measure, let's expand your perception of technology and think beyond the concept of state of the art when it comes to technology. In actuality, technology is anything you use to maximize potential. In the case of human potential, consider how something as simple as a rock can be used to pound tent stakes into the ground at a campsite, how a pen is used to record thoughts on paper, or how a new standard-procedure model can increase the productivity of people who are working together.

As you increasingly expand your understanding of technology's ability to advance your organization, you will begin to integrate technology-driven solutions into all other activities of ET, too. Say that you decide to incorporate technology into your planning activities. When you are strategizing, you might consider how multiple technologies—devices, mechanisms, tools, or concepts—are plausible means for better achieving your Desired Outcome. For example, you might view your investment team as individuals who are constantly comparing financial data so complex that too many hours are spent on analyses. Your solution is to hire programmers to write software that helps you to make specific global data comparisons from information that has been automatically gleaned from online sources. Because technology has performed these gathering and comparison activities, members of your investment team can allocate more of their time to thinking activities like working on Strategy and Macro Tactics and less time doing busy work.

Take, for instance, Morning Star, which owes its title as the world's leading tomato ingredient processor to Chris Rufer's innovative leveraging of technology. In the past, tomatoes were harvested and then developed into a sauce that required temperature-controlled storage and transportation. Rufer mentally dissected the process into its simplest form, realizing that the majority of costs—warehousing space and shipping weight—were due to the water content in each tomato-paste container. Through strategizing, Rufer determined that he could remove the water from his product, ship paste only, and allow the product to be rehydrated by regional processing plants.

Using technology to change how his product was packaged, stored, and delivered would create two competitive advantages for Rufer's firm. One, tomato paste would no longer have to be stored and transported using expensive temperature-controlled warehouses and trucks, saving money for his company as well as for distributors and consumers on down the chain. Two, by removing the added weight and volume of water, Rufer would drastically reduce shipping expenses even more and increase the amount of product that could be fit into each transport—he was able to ship bulk quantities of paste to commercial/industrial customers like Heinz and Del Monte, first in 50-gallon containers and then later in 300-gallon containers. This revolutionized Rufer's organization and his industry. In addition, the competitive advantages for being first meant that Morning Star was able to reduce storage, packaging, and shipping costs, but also it was able to deliver a superior product, because the new containers could be stored outside, "marinating" the paste and improving its flavor.

Rufer is a trailblazer, and his innovative approaches to storing and shipping tomato products changed the way that all players within his industry conducted business. Eventually, old ways of handling tomato products were either modified or abandoned altogether as decision makers adopted these new and improved technologies and methodologies in a new era of processing.

Rufer is a modern-day leader who uses technology to maximize the potential of his organization's assets and who lives by the quote he once read from the ceiling of the Chicago's Museum of Science and Industry: "Science discerns the laws of nature. Industry applies them to the needs of man." At the time of our conversation, Rufer's employee base was 3,000, his volume was in the $600 million range, there was no management team, and he hired each person himself. Technology was Rufer's way of maximizing potential throughout his organization.

Continue to Do More with Less

In Chapter 2, I asked you to rethink your concerns about doing more with less, emphasizing how the concept is not a new or more pressing issue today than it has been in the past. Rather, this concept is one that has challenged historical and modern-day decision makers alike, and they will continue to do so as our world changes. Whether leaders need to streamline opera-tions to increase profits or to outpace competitors with better products and faster services, technology can provide the solutions. Eli Whitney's cotton gin increased productivity, improved quality, and decreased labor; it was not designed to eliminate slave labor. Andrew Carnegie, the steel magnate who sold his business for $400 million in 1900, used conveyor belts, overhead pulleys, and sophisticated furnaces to create operational efficiencies. About Carnegie, the website for the PBS *American Experience* history series notes:[63]

> He was possessed by technology and efficiency in a way no business-man before him had ever been. His relentless efforts to drive down costs and undersell the competition made his steel mills the most modern in the world. . . . His vast steel mills at Braddock, Duquesne, and Homestead boasted the latest equipment. As technology improved, Carnegie ordered existing equipment to be torn out and replaced. He quickly made back these investments through reduced labor costs, and his mills remained always the most productive in the world."[64]

The same could be said universally about great leaders of the present in all sectors and industries, in for-profits as well as nonprofits, across cultural and geopolitical divides, and from one management level, business unit, and department to another. More than a hundred years separates the Carnegies from the Rufers, and another 150 years will usher in many other great deci-sion makers who will continue the trend by turning to technology to do more with less.

In another instance where technology is used by leaders to do more with less, a transport ocean liner called *The Ebba*, owned by Denmark's A.P. Møller–Mærsk, holds 14,000 tractor-trailer containers, each large enough to hold all the contents of a three-bedroom house. Technology enables a crew of only thirteen to twenty people per ship to manage a liner of gargantuan size for months on end. As the doing-more-with-less trend continued, in 2011 Mærsk signed a $1.9 billion deal with Daewoo Ship Building and Marine Engineering Co. from South Korea to purchase another ten ships that are each larger than four football fields and can transport upward of 18,000 20-foot-long containers at once between Asian and European ports. According to a 2011 article by maritime news website gCaptain.com, technological advance-ments will enable these larger liners to reuse energy from engines' exhaust gas and will produce 20% less carbon dioxide per container than Mærsk's pre-vious vessels.[65] In addition, in comparison to other trading ships operating between Asia and Europe, these new ships will consume an average 50% less CO_2 and 35% less fuel per container.

[Order-Winner Technology]

MaverickLabel.com[66] in Edmonds, Washington, is a Web-based label company that has automated the process of delivering customized quotes. Back in 2006, when competitors were still manually producing quotes and automated online quoting processes were just emerging, MaverickLabel.com had the capacity to process 8,000 quotes daily. Its CEO, Mark Trumper, who was ahead of the technological curve, says he owes his firm's pioneering success to its IT department, which made it possible for customers to request and receive a quote based on computer-programmed algorithms and to place their own orders online, without the assistance of salespeople; in fact, the firm didn't have any sales force! Five of its twenty-four employees were IT people who developed a nearly hands-off system to process, ship, bill, and close out orders, thanks to their innovative use of technology.

This firm continues to shut out competition with its patented Order-Winner technology, the Uber Quoter patent; no other competitor can use this technology, which today empowers MaverickLabel.com to process an estimated 40,000 daily quotes with only thirty-four staffers and still no sales personnel. In addition, the firm does no in-house production, instead linking technologically to its network of vendor allies to provide products to its customer base.

Create Change That Your People Will Love

Another rethinking concept that I addressed in Chapter 2 was a challenge to the belief that people hate change. The truth is people love positive change, like flipping a switch and having heat or air-conditioning, a warm shower, or a quick ride in one's car to work. Technology enables leaders to effect the kinds of changes that both they and their people will love, even in instances where technological changes are not initially perceived as positive.

Nancy Rabenold,[67] president and CEO of Xcira (formerly Auction Management Solutions) in Tampa, Florida, has developed the exclusive patented technology for live online auctions—known as remote bidding supplement for traditional live auctions—and has built the infrastructure to support it. Owners of auction houses love her technology, because it empowers billion-dollar asset-auction firms such as Christie's and smaller businesses that sell products like real estate, art, heavy equipment, and automobiles to connect with buyers around the globe in a live experience. Buyers love Rabenold's change, because it eliminates the need for them to travel to auction sites, making the process of bidding and buying at auctions more convenient and less expensive. Her employees love the new technology, too, since it has an up-time of nearly 100%, and it's helped build a growing customer base that secures jobs. Rabenold has figured out how to leverage technology to produce winning changes that all her stakeholders love.

Have Control over the Inevitable Evolution of Technology

Technological evolution is an inevitability, regardless of whether new technologies are considered good or bad for people. In addition, when a technology exists, in almost every case someone will act upon it. It doesn't matter whether the idea is an action, a methodology, or a technology. In terms of the latter, if you aren't making mindful choices, others outside your organization, your precinct, your country, etc., will implement technologies that you may not initially consider to be viable (or ethical), and they'll do so whether you're on board with them or not. Pause and think before you discard an idea or technology to be sure you are not handing over an Order Winner to a competitor or eliminating solutions and opportunities to advance your organization.

As a leader, you can either let the inevitability of technological evolution be something that happens to you and negatively impacts you and your organization, or you can leverage technology to your advantage to create opportunities for the present or future.

I was dining with a client in Asia when I brought up an article in a recent international publication about how many countries around the region were using stem cell research to create new technologies to advance medical progress. (I'm not making a cause for or against stem cell research here; I'm simply illustrating how people will run with an idea or technology with or without you.) Without warning, a Canadian commented to me, "Why do Americans believe that because Americans are against stem cell research, the rest of the world feels the same way?" He then went on to name countries around the world, including Canada, where some form of stem cell research was being conducted. The same can be said for numerous other innovations, so beware that you don't deem a technology unfair or unethical without considering how your own points of view could be robbing your organization of chances to win. Once the word is out, the odds that someone will use a technology increase exponentially.

Technology for organizational leadership is no different. Keeping in mind that a technology can be anything from the most sophisticated and complex electronics to the most simplified and crude objects like rocks and sticks, once someone finds a new business technology or new way to use a technology, someone will move forward with it. Whether your organization becomes an innovator, a follower, or a nonparticipant depends on you.

Take a look around. Where might you be looking at potential opportunities through opinionated lenses, thereby limiting your organization's ability to progress forward? Think back to technologies that you may have deemed nonsensical in the past and consider their viability today. Just because a competitor hasn't used them yet doesn't mean that they can't advance your organization. Take this thinking a step further and try to identify technologies in *other* industries or sectors that you could utilize to give your organization an edge against competition, as well.

In addition, before you discount any technology as not being beneficial to your organization, challenge yourself to be more open-minded, perhaps even asking yourself, Why not? Keeping your mind open to different or unexpected technologies is a good starting point for performing this ET activity. As you read through the rest of the chapter, you will collect additional concepts and tools that you can use to seize opportunities and overcome challenges that accompany the inevitable evolution of technology.

The Leverager's Dilemma: Addressing the Downside of Technological Change

Though technology has the power to transform our lives, organizations, and societies for the better, it doesn't come without some challenges. It can be used for "evil" just as easily as it can for good, and it can be used irresponsibly to multiply errors and flaws rather than eliminate them. For a great number of leaders, technology's impacts on human labor—displacement of workers, negative changes, improper implementation that leads to more challenges rather than fewer challenges—cause fear among people, and with good reason. Michael Treacy, author of *Double-Digit Growth*, argues that technology, not outsourcing, is the primary displacer of U.S. workers. During a presentation he made to a tech firm in 2005, Treacy expressed that in the U.S. auto industry alone, productivity gains due to technological advancements from 1979 to 2004 eliminated 44% of jobs.[68]

So what do you do with this and other realities that point to the negative impacts of technology on people within societies and organizations? On the one hand, you may feel inclined to protect people by ignoring techno-logical opportunities, but on the other, you have a responsibility to grow and advance your organization as a whole. Since technologies will inevitably continue to evolve, leadership often feels conflicted with the *dilemma* of reconciling two seemingly opposing sides of an equation—"I can only do one or the other"—while keeping pace with the demands on them. Yet the dilemma is often nothing more than a self-inflicted roadblock that leaders can remove by rethinking their perceptions about technology. In essence, technology is neither good nor bad—it can be argued that technological advancements within Carnegie's steel mills eliminated jobs internally, but they also simultaneously made more jobs nationally, growing the economy, and improving quality of life for even more people—and with the right tools and knowledge, any leader can leverage technology to create win-win situations all around.

K. Dinesh, a founder and board member of India-based Infosys Technologies, once explained to me that society is a three-legged stool; leg one is the private sector, leg two is the public sector, and leg three is the nonprofit sector and community. His view is that when we have all three legs working to hold up the stool, we are able to offer a good quality of life for everyone. Let's be sure that we embrace the law of abundance by giving the workers, like the U.S. auto industry's 44%, the tools they need to contribute in all three legs of the stool. Decision makers, like H. B. Park from Chapter 3, who moved his tent manufacturing operations into Bangladesh, have the power to improve the human condition everywhere by bringing technology to areas where it can do the most good.

Using the tools you have already learned along with new ones from upcoming sections in this chapter, you will be able to successfully fulfill your responsibilities to both your organization and its people. Since I address the "how" more specifically in the sections about selecting and implementing technology, let's begin by addressing your mindset and focus.

Your job is not to protect every job as it currently exists, but to utilize tech-nology to grow your organization. If you do this properly, you will expand your operations to grow and create new and better jobs. Going back through what you already know, you will want to consider the Goldsmith Productivity Principle (GPP) by asking, How can I best use technology within my systems and structures to accelerate reaching our Desired Outcome? Immediately, you are shifting your focus away from the past—where jobs may be phasing out—and onto the future—where you can better match up the educational and training needs of the global workforce with tomorrow's technologies.

Leaders across the 7Crosses of ET—those in business, nonprofits, education, military, or government—are responsible for equipping people with the tools they need to evolve congruently with technological change and workforce trends. Leaders should have a sense of responsibility to evolve, but this is not always the case. Some organizations actually promote stagnation through ineffectual systems and structures and leadership's reluctance to leverage technology. This results in poor plans and tactics, both of which ultimately hurt all participants.

For example, over the years, business leaders have taken a lot of heat on the topic of outsourcing, and they have been tagged as villains for outsourcing jobs like those that went to call-center workers in India. This necessary step to keep service-delivery costs in alignment with customers' expectations may appear to be nothing more than offshoring work that eliminates jobs, but in reality, it is just the natural progression of activities that occur from the inevitability of innovative technological evolution. The responsible answer isn't to avoid outsourcing; if leaders did that, they'd only be clinging to jobs that will evolve whether people like it or not. Instead, the solution is to think a few steps ahead by forecasting the skills that tomorrow's workforce will need so that you can help prepare the workers to secure tomorrow's best jobs.

Still not convinced? Let's take a look at how the outsourcing trend evolves over time. As Country #1 exports lower-paying, labor-intensive jobs, Country #2 receives higher income opportunities. Country #1 is first in line for an evolution that brings a new kind of job to the market: intellect-based employment where education and training needs to adapt. However, Country #2 will eventually run through this evolution as well. India-based call-center employees are facing an exportation of their jobs just as American employees faced outsourcing years earlier. Indians want those call-center jobs less and less as time passes, recognizing that call-center customer service is giving way to new technologies and methodologies such as online chat and voice recognition systems that diminish the need for human call-center labor. There always will be call-center employees, but the numbers have diminished as new technologies enter the market place and costs of living rise in countries, producing a need for higher-paying jobs.

You must constantly keep an eye on how you can contribute to readying others in the face of technological change, whether it is an introduction of new technologies, a phasing out of old technologies, or the simultaneous occurrence of both. Over the more recent years, the number of manufacturers has declined, and this trend has taken manufacturing jobs with it; fewer workers are needed to perform manufacturing jobs as management output continues to increase. As a society, all of us have a responsibility to educate and train our masses from early education through adulthood, so that our workforce has the skills and knowledge to perform the jobs of the future, many of which have not yet been created.

At the same time, while automation has reduced manual-labor occupations, manual labor still has value to society as a whole and to the individuals who work with their hands. Manual labor will not disappear, but like everything else, it will continue to evolve as new technologies enter the market. Landscapers, carpenters, and painters provide value to society, but as we've already seen, they've changed over the years and will continue to do so with technologies such as wide-blade riding lawn mowers, cordless tools, and paint technologies that require only one coat.

In tomorrow's world, many of our manual-labor jobs will be performed in a virtual world, where workers use their brains and hands to deliver products via virtual technologies. A mining company in Australia is implementing a completely humanless mining operation, where all machinery will be driven by computer control, not unlike the way that drones are replacing pilots in the military. In your organization, whether you're using humans or technologies to get work done, your job is to ensure that both are leveraged to their fullest extent by supporting them with technologies and tools that keep them at optimal productivity levels. This in turn creates new jobs and opportunities.

You will always be expected to align your organization with the trends, or even better, be the forerunner ahead of them. Therefore, by seeing technology as the answer rather than as the enemy in this natural and inevitable evolution, you do your organization and society a service. That's because your improved perspective allows you to better identify opportunities to improve your organization's operations, products and services, and standards of work conditions.

The Upside of Solving the Dilemma

Another reason that fighting the evolution of technology is useless is because people love change when it improves their condition in some way, and technology, at the heart of how we live, work, and play, can do just that. Your municipal water and sewage treatment plants make it possible for you to enjoy the conveniences of indoor plumbing, while the World Health Organization

(WHO) uses technology to combat disease. Would you give up airbags in vehicles or refuse anesthetics during surgery in favor of either's predecessors? If your friend has HDTV and you have a 1959 RCA[69] black-and-white TV, who's hosting Super Bowl Sunday or the World Cup? Do you want to still wait several days for pictures to be developed and processed or instead use modern technology that allows you to snap and send right from your cell phone?

Improving health and safety and making something more enjoyable or convenient are among the ways technology can improve our conditions. This applies not only in your personal life but also in the workplace. For example, think about how the medical profession benefits from technology—advanced technology as well as more simple mechanical improvements. Research data from the Bureau of Labor Statistics (1998) showed that 12 out of 100 nurses in hospitals and more than 17 out of every 100 nurses working in nursing homes suffered from work-related musculoskeletal injuries, including back injuries from lifting patients out of beds and chairs.[70] This figure represents the highest rate of nonfatal job injuries of all other industries.

Now bring in the use of patient lifts and slings, like those produced by manufacturer Liko, that enable caregivers to lift patients out of a bed, into a chair, or onto a gurney more easily and safely than one can do manually. Providing patient lifts for nurses would be one of those positive changes that people love. In your role as a leader, you don't necessarily have to execute the changes, but you do need to be thinking and planning your next best leveraging of technology to propel your organization to reach its Desired Outcome.

In terms of convenience, think of trying to perform your job without a phone, computer, or e-mail. Thanks to the advancements in communications, we're able to connect with others faster, cheaper, and on more convenient terms than ever before. The Internet allows customers, patients, clients, patrons, and other stakeholders to tap into your organization's products and services at times and locations that are convenient to them. Newer phone technologies give people the flexibility to do their work at just about any place in the world with an Internet connection, as if they were sitting in their offices. You don't hear people complaining that they don't want access that will make their lives easier, but they do become unhappy when leadership fails to empower them with needed technologies to solve their challenges. Keep this in mind the next time you are tempted to stick with status quo as your safety net. You constantly want to be looking for better solutions through the leveraging of technology.

Leveraging Technology Levels the Playing Field

As you fulfill your dual responsibilities of leveraging technology to improve your organization and provide better options and conditions for members of your staff and of society, realize that technology can act as an equalizer, introducing opportunities that would have been inaccessible to people previously. And empowering other people correctly, as you will learn in Chapter 11, inevitably helps organizations in countless ways.

If barriers are preventing you from achieving an objective, you can use technology to overcome them more quickly and less expensively than with alternative solutions. Imagine a 16-year-old Russian immigrant to the United States who has not yet learned English. Although he is intelligent and hardworking, the language barrier prevents him from excelling in school, earning a job, and attending college. In today's world, he can still succeed, but he will have a steep hill to climb to reach his goal of becoming a contributing member of society. Enter technology.

Due to the rapid progression of voice-translating technologies tied to phone systems, in the not-too-distant future, this immigrant will be able to speak Russian into a phone and have someone on the other end receive his words in English. Phone translators will eventually move to ear translators. (Picture *Star Trek,* where everyone can understand everyone from different planets; they called the device the universal translator.) Technology will have removed the language barrier and leveled the playing field for people around the world. If you're the superintendant of a school system, how might a device like this enable you to maximize the potential of your teachers, streamline teaching methodologies to immigrant students, and accelerate the rate at which all of your students can learn?

Other equalizers include braille and optical character recognition software that enable the blind to learn new material. And consider artificial legs that empower amputees with equal or faster mobility than people with use of two natural legs. Technology opens job opportunities and enables people to live their dreams in ways that may have been considered impossible in the past.

And, of course, the digital world is a mass equalizer, because it provides information access to people globally, and it has removed certain obstacles to business for many people. Prejudices and logistical hindrances aren't impediments in cyberspace. For example, barriers once present for a disabled person, a person who doesn't own a car, or someone who needs a job with flexible work hours don't exist for an eBay seller.

The point I want you to keep in mind is that when you shy away from technology for the sake of protecting people, you may in fact be creating the opposite effect. Integrate technology into your thinking and planning, and combine it with other ET activities to provide people with newer and better opportunities.

An ET Tool for Selecting and Implementing Technology

Leveraging technology is how you develop a channel of opportunity, but the outcomes of your efforts are contingent upon your mastery of selecting and implementing the most appropriate, best, and right amount of technologies at any given time. The goal, says one director of corporate real estate for an industrial management firm, "is to use just enough technology to fit the bill: not too much and not too little." This means that in addition to including technology as a strategic and tactical option for advancing your organization, you also have to ensure that you strike the right balance so that you don't select and implement too much technology (which can waste resources) nor select and implement too little (which can make it more difficult to achieve Desired Outcomes).

So how do you do that? As I mentioned earlier in this chapter, you can consider concepts like the GPP—because it provides the systems and structures every organization needs—combine leveraging technology with other Enterprise Thinking activities, and use tools like the CST Model to come up with your plans and follow up using the ET Development Funnel to ultimately decide upon the best technology to support it.

Selecting Technologies Using the ET Development Funnel

Just as you were able to use Chapter 4's ET Development Funnel to select a single best product idea to develop, you can adapt the same tool to Ideate and Eliminate to find your single best technology ideas, too. Here is an illustrated adaptation.

ET Technology DEVELOPMENT FUNNEL™
(ideation and elimination activities)

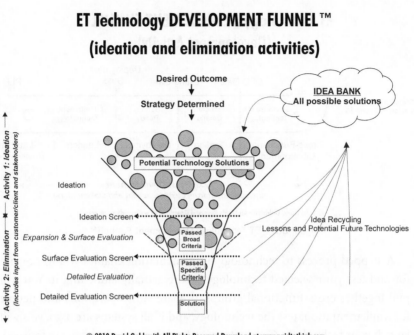

Figure 6.1—ET Technology Development Funnel™

To start, determine the criteria you will use to sort and select your best tactical options—in this case, technologies—at the three filtering screens: Ideation, Broad Criteria, and Specific Criteria. Then collect the ideas, although you might not start with as many as 100 here, and consider gaining input from others if you will need buy-in from them at any point later on.

Next, eliminate less viable ideas as they pass through all three screens, just as you would for developing products or improvements, and end up with one best idea. Now you can decide whether to make the decision to spend money and develop your idea or to stop.

Using the ET Development Funnel to Implement a Technology

You're already familiar with the ET Development Funnel process for developing a single best idea into a new product, service, or internal improvement. Now, you will follow the same process for taking your single best technology idea and implementing and integrating it into the appropriate place within your organization.

ET Technology DEVELOPMENT FUNNEL™
(Development Activity)

© 2006 David Goldsmith All Rights Reserved Download at www.paidtothink.com

Figure 6.2—ET Technology Development Funnel™

A stepped process to technology implementation enables you to prepare for and test your selected technology before actually launching it. You will pull together cross-functional groups, prepare your operations and people for implementation, test the technology, and if all systems are a go, you will launch your technology. Conduct a post-launch review and you are finished.

Once again the ET Development Funnel helps prevent you or your team from falling in love with your own ideas and from jumping to action before you've actually reached your single best idea. By slowing down, you give yourself ample Cyclonic Thinking Time even if it's brief, that you may need to determine your best moves along the way, leading to fewer mistakes and increasing the odds that your end result is successful.

In the case of a major international bank whose decision makers invested more than $20 million into a customer relationship management (CRM) software "solution" that failed within one month, the problem stemmed from two missteps: first, according to one senior manager, the team never spoke to any users before launching the software, and second, the team jumped to action without the input of a cross-functional group and without comparing this single technology to alternatives that may have been better for the organization. If they had at least spoken with stakeholders, they would have found out that many business units had already built their own CRM solutions and were not ready to switch. The structure of a process tool like the ET Development Funnel would have prevented these errors and increased the organization's chances of a successful launch.

Five Principles to Consider

Keep the following five principles in mind any time you are selecting a technology:

1. Select technology cross functionally.

Your situation—such as size and scope of a project or impact of a technology selection—should determine the level of involvement of cross-functional input you solicit and receive. A huge liquor distributor in the southern United States had thirteen different IT systems and sixteen different benefits packages that were not interconnected, because management didn't develop plans that were holistic and enterprise wide. They allowed individuals to make decisions that caused overlap and duplication throughout the organization. By selecting technology in silos, the firm was not working with a best technology, employees were confused about their roles, and money and resources were wasted.

2. Select technology with the big picture in mind.

In the 1980s, I attended a trade show to research some technology-related solutions for use in our facility and discovered three types of hydro sprayers, each with varying features that could help our employees do their jobs in less time. The salesperson explained that I would want sprayer #1 because my staff could clean twenty screen-printing screens with it per day, which would be a good fit for our office if I wanted to dedicate one employee to cleaning screens all day. When I inquired about other sprayers that might reduce cleaning times, the rep told me that I wouldn't be interested; in his view, sprayer #2, which cleaned fifty screens per day, and sprayer #3, which cleaned two hundred, would be "overkill" for my needs. I didn't share his point of view. The sales rep did not see my organization from 50,000 feet, but I understood its interconnectivity, which broadened my range of opportunities. Sprayer #2 would enable an employee to clean the same number of screens by lunchtime, which meant that instead of being tied up in the screen-cleaning room all day, he could help out with other areas of production each afternoon. I ultimately purchased sprayer #3 for $2,400, only an additional $1,100 over the recommended model, because its significantly more durable components, higher water pressure capability, and advanced automated parts allowed me to free up this employee in one hour, thus maximizing his value to our firm for the majority of time he spent on the job each day. This in turn had additional benefits like enabling job sharing and helping in job recruiting, because the dirty job was minimized.

3. Select technology that solves an actual challenge.

When selecting a new technology, make sure you're not making assumptions about the challenge you expect it to solve. I once met with a CEO of a $100 million business who spoke of how busy he was traveling around the country and working with his executives to improve productivity. When visiting one office, he looked around at the facility and immediately ordered the offices to be painted, believing that if he made a nicer looking office, his employees would enjoy their jobs more. A few weeks later, when the CEO returned to the office to view the progress, one employee approached him and said, "Thank you so much for the painting. However, what we really need in the office are more staplers, because we're constantly taking them from each others' desks, and for some reason, we can't get the purchasing department to buy us what we need." The CEO drove down to the local office-supply house and purchased a case of staplers for a couple hundred dollars: quite a small price in comparison to the paint job that cost thousands of dollars. The technology these people needed was staplers, not a paint job that provided a nicer looking workspace.

Believe it or not, many leaders take on a new technology without properly assessing if it's worth the time and effort or if there will be an ROI. This often happens when leaders forget that executing is not more important than strategizing, causing them to also overlook the fact that they may be focused on activities that will deliver back minimal returns without ever considering better alternatives. In the case of the several-thousand-dollar paint job, the organization had that much less to spend on other value-added projects, and that's not accounting for the inconveniences and lost opportunities associated with the consumption of assets during the paint project. Keep this in mind whenever you're using technology to solve challenges.

Jean, the owner of a Canadian firm, received a discount offer of $15,000 from one of his vendors on an upgrade to a new server. He was about to make the purchase when an advisor suggested that Jean push the salesperson to list some specific returns that the server would deliver to the firm. The advisor also reminded Jean that the $15,000 was just the beginning of a long line of expenses that he would have to recoup with this purchase; he would have to account for installation time, staffing commitments, etc. When asked about the benefits, the salesperson was unable to define any significant advantages that would solve Jean's challenge and help him reach desired outcomes. The new upgrade would slightly speed up some of his team's functions, but the improvements weren't noticeable enough to make the switch. So Jean and his leadership decided not to buy. Jean's firm was better off continuing to pursue its ongoing set of projects that they had already established rather than to jump on an offer because the deal sounded so good.

On the other hand, when technology is selected and implemented correctly, you can solve challenges optimally. This was the case when the Australian-based firm DataDot Technology Limited came up with a technology to help people retrieve their lost or stolen possessions. Boats, cars, planes, and computers are stolen every day, and it's easy for thieves and opportunists to remove serial numbers from various items and resell them without getting caught. DataDot's technology, a spray-on identification system that showers products with tiny micro-sized serial numbers, outsmarted thieves. Since the serial numbers can only be read by special police scanners and thieves can't possibly remove the thousands of dots on the items within their possession, DataDot's technology enabled many people to protect and retrieve their property.

4. Select technology with an eye on the future.

Obviously your organization will change over time, even if it's just slightly. Therefore, the technologies that you select must not only meet the needs of your organization in its present state, but they must somehow support your organization through transitional periods and times of growth and change. That's why you're going to service your organization better if you look down the road and into the future as you select technologies to meet your needs and solve your challenges.

For example, if you have three people in accounting who all need to access your accounting software at once, today it would be okay to purchase a three-seat accounting package to help them do their jobs. However, if you forecast the need for ten seats over the course of the next three years (even though at this point the forecast may seem like a guess or a dream), you would be wise to research the cost of those seats as part of today's package, because you could end up saving your organization additional expenses at a later date: the add-on costs of seven seats, time and money spent on contacting and implementing new seats, etc.

In other words, technology selected today should coincide with your organization's growth strategy. Scalability is a key component in your technology's ability to accommodate tomorrow's growth before it becomes a reality.

In Chapter 14, you will learn forecasting techniques to help you do your job better in multiple areas. Regarding technology selection, when you project your thinking farther into the future, you expand your scope of opportunities, you solve for tomorrow rather than just for today, and you're able to find better and more sustainable and scalable solutions. Considering that you are always going to be expected to innovatively improve your organization's operations, products, services, and standards of work conditions to keep pace with the world at large, selecting technologies with a forecasted view will increase ROI and place your organization in a stronger position.

5. Select technology based on its benefits, not because it's electronic or advanced.

Great solutions don't just come in the form of those technologies that are electronic or state of the art. Sometimes your best options include a range of other ideas from methodologies and models to crudely crafted objects and more.

Case in point: a business owner tried to transition her ten-person office from scheduling and managing priorities on paper to performing these functions digitally. Immediately, she and her team experienced a decline in productivity. Her colleagues said that there was a learning curve, and eventually she'd make the transition. Months later, she still could not figure out how her smartphone could help her be more productive and still work within her lifestyle. I told her to abandon the technology that hurt her and her organization and return to her original paper-calendar methodology. She was surprised at the advice. Everyone she had talked to said she needed to be digital, and yet for her, it wasn't the right fit for her at that time. At first she felt like she had failed, because she and her staff expended time and effort on this new process, but in the end, when she moved back to the paper version, her office was once again on the move.

Implementing Technology Successfully

You wouldn't buy a new car and then let it sit in your driveway unused any more than you would buy a computer for one of your staffers and never have them turn it on. Yet leaders every day obtain new technologies and let them sit idle, never implementing them fully enough to deliver a return on investment. Too often, leaders and their staffers get partway through an installation and never go any further, or they acknowledge that a technology fails to work from the start, but they do nothing to rectify the situation. Since people don't show up to work to screw up, I have to believe that the reason is that leaders don't always know how to implement technologies—whether it's the implementation of robotics, a new pylon driver for road construction, or the introduction of a new software—nor do they always understand their role in the process.

Now that you know that you can use the ET Technology Development Funnel to structure your implementation process, you are on your way to avoiding this problem. Along with this new tool, I want to give you a Technology Implementation Process to effectively implement technologies so that your organization can gain the maximum benefits from them. The process consists of five steps that mirror the CST Model from Chapter 3. These are the five steps of that process along with instruction and examples to guide you in its use:

1. **Desired Outcome:** State your Desired Outcome. "We want all students in our residence halls to be able to use the laundry facilities independently."

2. **Strategy:** Come up with your Strategy. "Our approach will be to first test and then do a campus-wide rollout."

3. **Macro Tactics:** Select the Macro Tactics that best support your Strategy. "We'll convert the Lawrinson residence hall's laundry room into an entirely independent and user-friendly pilot facility that provides posted information users will need to operate the equipment independently. We'll try to keep our instructions simple by explaining our approach in six steps or less. We will also install change machines and detergent vending machines within the facility. We will observe and talk to users and make micro adjustments along the way."

4. **Tactics:** List Tactics and fill in any necessary details about them. "We'll first create a master plan and CPM chart, then we'll follow the steps one by one, such as contacting XYZ Vending and ABC Vending to provide us with quotes on the vending machines and then contracting out the winning bid's services for one school year. We will provide a phone in the laundry room that links to the main desk at the residence hall so that if anyone has a maintenance issue, they can receive immediate service. We will install and maintain change/coin machines to ensure that people will always have the right change to operate the equipment."

5. **Execution:** Guide and support the people who will execute the Tactics. "We will walk through the procedures of using our facilities from start to finish, and then we will monitor students periodically to work out the kinks. We'll hire a person to maintain the equipment and notify management of any problems or improvements that we need to address."

To ensure a smooth implementation of your technology, spend time thinking through your process up front. This will give returns multiple times over. Be sure that your executors find you to be an approachable guide, and check in with people periodically as your circumstances require, to keep everyone on track.

During my early days in business, I used to get very frustrated that work would be interrupted, because people were unsure how to use simple technologies. For example, I would notice that the person nearest the fax machine was constantly asked, "Is it fax up or fax down?" The person fielding the interruptions could have been on the phone or working on a customer project that required concentration. I don't think the manufacturers of the fax machines realized that the vague image of a sheet of face-down paper they had stamped onto the machine failed to adequately instruct users. In addition to examples like this one, I also saw complex equipment being underutilized, because the learning curve to gain proficiency was too long. In both instances, the problem really came down to poor implementation, not poor execution. I want to make this distinction, because many leaders believe they have done a good job on execution by providing the technology like a fax machine to their people. However, when these leaders fail their users by not providing instructions for proper use of a technology, they have, in fact, failed in their implementation of that technology.

My frustration over the fax machine fueled my determination to find a solution. I challenged myself to take the complexity out of the technology by coming up with my own empowering tools. In this instance, I solved the problem easily by taping a sign above the fax machine. It simply read, FAX DOWN. Never again did anyone ask.

Later, I applied this simplistic approach to other processes and pieces of equipment, from how to turn on circuit breakers to light up the warehouse to turning on a 30-horsepower screw compressor. I would first play out the role of the user. Typically, I recommend to leaders that they convert any grouping of related activities to a six-steps-or-less process, and then write out or diagrammatically outline the steps for others to follow. I have found that most procedures or basic office processes can be sufficiently described in six steps or less—using any more than this can make your descriptions too cumbersome. When I used to post instructions for processes in my production facilities, the six-steps-or-less process became the tool that gave people their independence, because it empowered everyone, from longtime employees to new hires, to be instantly free to successfully perform functions on their own.

You can use pictures, graphics, videos, and short descriptions to accomplish the same results whether you're implementing repetitive activities or technologies. You can apply this concept anywhere. How many times has someone wanted to microwave a dish of food and stopped to ask someone else, "How much time should I cook this for?" If the person who fields these questions took the few minutes to jot down various items' cook times and post them next to the microwave, imagine how simple the process could be made for everyone. In addition to making your office work more efficiently, you'll make technology less fearful for others, too.

Tips for Ensuring the Proper Implementation of Technologies

From simple and common-sense solutions to more complex processes, your job is to provide people with the tools they need to successfully use technologies. In addition to the two new tools you now have to help you to help others—the Modified ET Development Funnel and the Technology Implementation Process—here are some useful tips that you can apply in a variety of situations and modify as you deem appropriate.

Provide the Resources, Guidance, and Realistic Support Your People Need to Use Technology Successfully

Give your staff the necessary resources and guidance to learn how to use a new technology and to integrate it into their daily work life: time, training, new tools, etc. Otherwise, you either put the implementation at risk for failure or you end up implementing a flawed technology or process that multiplies mistakes later on.

Sometimes leaders are overly optimistic about a new technology's ability to improve current conditions. They believe that because the technology is in place, any failure thereafter must be the fault of staff members. Too often, the failure is the result of leadership not properly addressing the GPP, and staffers get blamed just because they're at the tail end of the process.

I was in South America on business, and I had a window of twenty minutes' time to pick up a clock that I needed for an upcoming presentation. I was driven to a local big-box store, where I quickly picked up the clock, waited six minutes at the register, and dashed to the door with the shopping bag in one hand and my credit-card receipt in the other. I was a satisfied customer until I got stopped at the door by the person checking receipts. He told me that I would need yet another receipt before he would allow me to exit the store. At first I had no clue what he was talking about. When he slowed down, I understood that there were two receipts that the cashier should have given to me as proof of payment. Mind you, this was in Spanish, and it's my second language. I ran back to the cashier, disrupting him from ringing out the next customer, and asked for the receipt. He spun around and grabbed the second receipt from machine behind his processing location, apologizing the entire time. I took it and ran to the doorman and out the door. This oversight wasted time for both the cashier and for me.

In this scenario, most leadership would have blamed the cashier, believing he should be more customer-service oriented and more careful. He should have, should have, should have. . . . I didn't blame the cashier, however. If leadership had tried the procedure and worked the cashier's job and been required to pass out two receipts to each customer—even once—they would have realized that there was a flaw in the design of their process. The stations were laid out poorly by the managers. Remember, a leader's job is to design and build the systems and structures or at least approve them, even in cases where a design is created by so-called retailing experts. Instead of focusing on the people, decision makers should focus on the 80% of the GPP to ensure that details related to systems and structures aren't left to the employee to remember.

Regardless of the technology at hand, there will be times when not all users will get up to speed within your expected time frame. You will have to figure out the best approach to helping them become familiar and proficient with technology, and you'll have to continue to provide the resources they need. If you discover that you're having problems with any implementation process, you might find that you need to slow down and take a bit more time to teach staff members, because trying to do too much too fast can hinder progress.

Also, leaders find that breaking the implementation into steps is a good approach. So say that you're trying to teach people how to use a new CRM system. You can start with the basics of entering a customer's name, address, phone number, and current transactional data. Once your staff members are comfortable using these features, introduce them to more advanced functions, such as scheduling appointments, calculating profitability and probability figures, etc.

Create the Tools to Educate Others

Your people want to succeed, and they need your help to perform their jobs well. Provide your staff with training manuals, simple instructional sheets, in-house or off-site training programs, and other educational materials like standardized instructional videos.

The owner of a small tree-trimming company was unhappy that his three trucks were leaving the shop nearly an hour late each morning while crews would clean and prep the trucks for each day's jobs. The billing rate for *each* truck was upward of $1,500 per hour, so this lost hour was a considerable expense. The owner constantly told his staff that when they returned trucks to the company at the end of each workday, crew members should prep their trucks for the next day's jobs. After a long day cutting down trees, that was the last thing the crew wanted to do, so this routine of leaving unprepared trucks in the parking lot overnight went on for years.

The solution to such a challenge was so simple the owner could not believe he had not done it earlier. He hired a worker, at $10 per hour, to clean and prep trucks at night after the crews had left for the day. To speed up the new employee's learning process and to ensure that the trucks were properly prepared for the next morning, the owner supplied self-guiding tools—like instructions and accompanying photos—and he set up a prepping bay with drawers of supply parts within arm's reach of the incoming trucks. The new employee learned his job quickly, and within less than a week, all three trucks were out of the garage on time from that point forward.

You can use a similar approach to educate your staff whether you work in a doctor's office, a retail shop, a post office, a soup kitchen, or a warehouse. Put a picture of what a perfectly stocked drawer would look like; not only will it be a time-saving convenience, but it will also prevent costly errors. In aerospace, every tool belongs in a specific place, and if one tool is not where it should be, people will know that something is wrong. Obviously, the specific tools will depend on your organization's needs and resources, but it's still your responsibility to determine the best for your people. A one-page diagram might suffice for some groups while a more sophisticated digital tool, like the quickly updatable tablets used by airlines, is a better match for others.

Your aim should be to teach and guide people, all while empowering them to become independent and successful. You'll also save time by not having to answer the same questions repeatedly, because staffers will now have the tools to answer their own questions.

Watch for How Your Biases May Be Adversely Affecting Implementation

Quite often, leadership—not the technology itself—is the determining factor in whether a technology is successfully implemented or not. When you introduce a technology—which could be a plan, an alliance, a software program, an improvement to a process or product (like antiglare glass), and so on—your ability to guide and lead others through the implementation of it is most surely affected by factors such as your past experiences, biases, and skills. Becoming aware of your influence, both positively and negatively, can be enough to ensure that you are a catalyst to the process rather than a stop sign.

Three Types of Technology Adopters

A simple way to gain more clarity on how you might be affecting your organization's ability to implement technologies is to consider three types of technology adapters: enthusiasts, supporters, and avoiders. Regardless of your mindset, you'll find benefits and disadvantages to each perspective. Keep in mind as you read through the brief descriptions of each that you are probably a blend of each type depending on the situation, so your aim is to assess your tendencies toward any particular type and consider how a willingness to lean toward a different type from time to time could empower you to better facilitate the Technology Implementation Process in the future.

Enthusiasts are early adopters engaged in a constant quest for the next new thing. They enjoy learning about and trying new technologies, and as a result, give their staff members tools to improve efficiencies and productivity levels earlier than other types of leaders do. Early adoption can add up to serious competitive advantages, but it can have its downside, too. The overzealous enthusiast can select a technology too quickly, before having assessed its life expectancy, pros and cons, or any potential problems that could hinder a successful implementation.

If you consider yourself to be an enthusiast, you might be surprised to learn that you can be a problematic factor to implementation, especially if you're prone to overlooking others' limited skills or their resistance to change. To counter these tendencies, keep tactics simple—consider that people like most phone and tablet apps because of how simple they are to learn and use—and guide people at a pace that is reasonable for them until the Technology Implementation Process is complete.

Supporters fall within the middle ground between enthusiasts and their opposites, the avoiders. They accept technology as a necessary catalyst or tool. This type of leader doesn't adopt a technology as early as enthusiasts, so they're not necessarily leaping ahead of competitors, but they're not falling far behind, either. Supporters have their reasons for delaying the acceptance or use of a technology in comparison to enthusiasts, and these reasons can be varied. In some cases, they don't see an immediate need for the technology. In others, they want to be sure that the kinks have been worked out of a technology before they feel ready to take a chance on it. These leaders may want to allow enough time for the price of the technology to drop, considering that new-to-market technologies tend to be the most expensive.

Certainly, there are numerous reasons for supporters to temper their decisions about adopting new technologies. This additional time taken doesn't necessarily inoculate them against a poor implementation, however; they still need a process to ensure that their staff members reach the implementation finish line. Even if you're a supporter who treads the middle ground well, you should still use a process to ensure that you're covering all the necessary steps of a successful implementation. In addition, monitor your progress and tendencies, making sure that you're not leaning too far to the enthusiast's side or the avoider's.

Avoiders tend to be late adopters who are less likely than enthusiasts and supporters to seek technology to solve their challenges. Although their late-to-adopt tendencies can cause them and their organizations to lose out on opportunities, there is no direct correlation. Some of the best leaders I've met hate technology, and avoiders bring benefits to the table, also. Once avoiders see the need for a technology, they are very likely to vet out the options to ensure that they are viable, implementable, and beneficial both short and long term. Avoiders aren't necessarily *unlikely* to adopt a technology, although they can be more apt to be selective about the technologies that they introduce to their organizations. As a result, they're the leaders who can say, "I told you so," when a colleague rushes to action without taking the time to adequately think through a technology.

If you're an avoider, be wary of any tendencies to shy away from the Technology Implementation Process. You want to stay engaged in the process from start to finish and to be available and approachable in instances where others need your guidance. Try getting advisers who can help you through the learning, because it's easy to fall behind in today's world—when what you learned about yesterday is already out of date, it can cause you to be much further behind than you realize.

In Chapter 11, you will learn a process for empowering your organization's stakeholders that you will be able to use in the face of implementing technology, too. For now, just realize that when technologies are new to your organization, you have to approach implementation with an understanding of your own strengths and weaknesses to be sure that you are supporting your people and facilitating implementation, not hindering it.

Know the Level of Automation You Want to Achieve before You Bring in a Technology

Having a new "automation" technology in house doesn't mean that it's actually delivering ROI or performing the functions that it should. Though you can easily assume that your operations are automated when a computer or other type of electronic technology is involved, the mere existence of a technology doesn't guarantee that it's going to be utilized as an automated function to the extent that you originally intended, even after training sessions have taken place.

To be clear, you're not required to automate at all. But, if your objective is to achieve automation, then you really need to make sure that automation is your end result. I saw this misconception play out for years in businesses that made the transition from typewriters to computers, and then years later from data-collection computer programs to software packages with the capacity to integrate and interpret data. Leadership would invest in the technology as a means of achieving automation, but in reality, end up with nothing more than a glorified typewriter or an electronic storage bank for data. Employees at different stages of whatever process would still enter all data manually, fill out forms manually, extract and interpret data manually, and basically perform the same functions they always performed, just using a computer instead of a typewriter or a new manual software program instead of the old manual software program.

Three Levels of Automation

Different levels of automation—manual, manually automated, and automated technologies—serve many practical purposes, and once you match the best level to your current needs, you have to make sure that this level is achieved at implementation. Here are the definitions of each to ensure that your intentions match your outcomes:

Manual technologies require a high level of human participation. If you run your local food pantry, you might handwrite solicitations for donations, personally apply address stickers to envelopes, or assemble by hand the weekly food boxes for families. You're still using technologies like pen and paper, computers, or shelving and shipping materials, but basically the work is done manually.

Manually automated is when you perform manual activities with some automated assistance. This is where many organizations plateau, because when a keyboard or piece of equipment is involved, people assume that they're making great progress, although that's not always the case, especially when they're still doing much of their work manually. If you're receiving data on one form—customer orders, new-employee information documents—and then entering that data into a software program manually, you're manually automated.

Automated technologies remove most, if not all of the human element. Think for a moment about how you handle paperwork when you take on a new staff member. Does this person fill out a job application form or submit a resume, then upon being hired fill out W-2 paperwork, emergency contact forms, health and life insurance forms, and so on? Now contrast this manual/manually automated technique to an automated one, where you have someone enter all pertinent data onto a single digital form, such as an online order form or computer job application, and the data is *automatically* transferred to various end destinations such as CRM software, order-processing and billing queues, human-resources data banks, and so on. The work is done once, and redundant data is no longer handled multiple times by multiple sets of hands.

Microsoft Corporation uses one[71] such automated technology that breaks silos and automates the new-hire process. Employees or applicants enter at one location, and every department and location receives components of that data as needed. HR receives all payroll data, such as personal information, payroll information, vacation-time requests, health insurance requests, 401K data, etc. This automated system even orders the new hire's personalized door and desk sign from the original data.

A successful implementation does not require your operations to fit neatly into any one of the three categories above. What is important to keep at the forefront of your planning is that if you are aiming for automation, you must be clear about what that condition entails to avoid assuming you're automated when you're either manual or manually automated. This consciousness enables you to implement to the point that is right for your organization, and it keeps your expectations of others aligned with realistic conditions.

Technologies Aren't Just for Everyone Else; Include Yourself as a "User"

Frequently, leaders and managers bring in technologies for their staff members to use, but then they don't use the technologies properly for themselves. You don't want to be the person who is throwing a wrench into an otherwise well-functioning technology, process, or methodology.

The president of a midsized firm selected and implemented a new CRM application in his office as a way of integrating people and data across the organization. It was a great idea, but the president himself would not use the CRM program. One day, when a customer called him and spent an hour on the phone with him complaining about a defect in one of the company's products, the CEO apologized, promised to "make good" on the original sale, and returned back to work, never entering a bit of the conversation or the retribution the customer expected into the CRM program, although he had originally intended the CRM program to be a tool to record such information.

Two weeks later, when no amends had been made to the customer, and a salesperson—who had been using the CRM program proficiently—drove an hour to the customer, walked in and asked, "So, how has it been working out for you?" you can imagine the earful that this poor blindsided salesperson got. On top of that, the firm lost its credibility with that buyer altogether, and the employee no longer trusted the system as having accurate data, so he, too, stopped being as diligent in its use. There was nothing wrong with the technology; in fact, all the leader had to do was input the information in real time so as not to forget the details of his meeting. But in this and in many instances like it, the only problem with a technology is that the user misused it, negating any of the positive benefits that staff members could have otherwise enjoyed from that technology.

While visiting a national hamburger chain restaurant, I watched the staff as my order was prepared. All employees were wearing gloves to prepare the food . . . except for the manager. From what I could see, it appeared that he thought he could move the process along faster if he were unencumbered by the gloves. This manager touched the buns and condiments with his hands, in plain sight of the customers, while his employees wore gloves. What message does this send to employees and to customers?

In both instances, the failure wasn't in the implementation of the technology, but in leadership's failure to use the technology correctly. You've got to work the technology if you want it to work for you.

Use Modeling and Simulations

Modeling is a relatively inexpensive way of testing tactical options and selecting the best one to avoid dumping loads of money into something that disappoints you later. The aim is to achieve the highest return for whatever you do by putting your thoughts into tools that leverage your ability to think.

Modeling techniques can be as simple as moving plastic army men around in a sandbox or as complex as running a sophisticated software program for an architectural project. ProModel software was my first exposure to the phenomenal potential of modeling software. I was with a colleague who entered the number and location of his warehouses into the program, along with the capacity of each, supplier data, travel distances, and utilization rates for a fleet of chemical trucks. When the data was complete, he initiated the program to run several thousand cycles of what would happen during the scenario and within seconds the software revealed an end result: warehouses would run out of product and shut down distribution within a set period of time. By modeling, he and leaders like him become empowered with information needed to make important decisions.

The same type of modeling can be done for office work, work flow, manufacturing lines, and any other series of activities that you can conjure up. The value in using modeling is to give the user a sense of what will work and what won't before putting the thoughts into action. The value of observing, thus evaluating outcomes in advance, is that you minimize the risk of making a decision based on estimated outcomes and guesswork.

Modeling processes and modeling software are powerful but not foolproof. For instance, an insurance company VP can enter the number of claims her firm is currently processing into the software, add or remove an employee, insert a variable, run the program a million times, and observe the outcomes, enabling her to make better decisions. But if she works with flawed software or enters the wrong data, she will run the model incorrectly and base future decisions and tactics on the wrong statistics. One of the challenges with the financial markets relative to real estate in the early 2000s was that Wall Street relied on a model created by an academic person, and the model was wrong.

I expect that as you were reading these tips, you were recalling past projects where an implementation could have occurred more smoothly and successfully. And while the tools and tips will help you to leverage technology better in the future, it's also important to understand that you can make even greater positive outcomes happen when you become increasingly adept at leveraging technology in conjunction with other ET activities and tools.

Leveraging Technology in Different Ways to Advance Your Organization

Certainly, technology has the power to improve the ways in which we live and work. But your job as a decision maker is to do more than use technology in traditional ways. In order to really advance your organization, you need to think differently and smarter about the ways in which you can leverage technology to gain outstanding outcomes. Consider some of these advantages as you strategize your own ways of leveraging technology.

1. UNDERSTANDING TECHNOLOGY ENSURES THAT YOU DON'T TRY TO SOLVE CURRENT AND FUTURE CHALLENGES WITH YESTERDAY'S THINKING.

A big mistake that a lot of leaders unknowingly make is to assume that what didn't work in the past still won't work in the present. Translating this concept to technology, you have to be even more careful that you don't try to solve current and future challenges with yesterday's thinking. How many times have you heard it said that "we tried that before and it didn't work" in response to a proposed solution? The next time you hear that type of response, see it as a red flag and remind yourself that conditions, technology, processes, and beliefs change, meaning that the ways of the past don't always translate to the present or future.

Here's a concept that will help you rethink technology-based solutions. It's called Moore's Law (a term coined in 1965, after Intel cofounder Gordon Moore), which predicts that the processing power of transistors and resistors on a computer chip doubles every eighteen months. This has become an accepted trend in computing hardware. (The exact time span can be disputed as longer or shorter, but the point is still valid.) In essence, Moore's law, applied to advancements in technology at large, means that tomorrow will be vastly different than today due to the rapid rate of technologic change. In order to keep pace, you must anticipate tomorrow's conditions and solutions and lead your organization accordingly. You will learn how to prepare for the future in Chapter 14, the Forecasting chapter.

Another "law" that can help you make better technology-related decisions is Metcalfe's Law—announced around 1980 and credited to Ethernet co-inventor Robert Metcalfe—which states that the value of a network is equal to the square of its sum of users. Think of it this way: if there were only one cell phone user in the world, how useful would the cell phone be? Add a second user, and now the value grows. Add 2,000 people, and the value expands exponentially as each new user joins the network. If you apply this law to your organization in a general sense, what you're going to see is that many of the technologies that you select and implement will create a somewhat new condition or reality that could bring with it new "rules" and benchmarks for measuring progress, potential, and success.

A significant way of capturing opportunities is to continually look for ways to leverage the value of your organization's assets, from your customers/patrons/users to your internal team and external stakeholders. In medical research, a process or finding that would take years to develop can happen in days or months when one scientist develops a new technique, for instance. Within days, hundreds or even thousands of other scientists can utilize that development and potentially transform it into a new concept, technology, development or process, exponentially changing the face of medical research.

The Human Genome Project (HGP),[72] a project intended to identify all human DNA genes and to sequence their three billion chemical base pairs, was first initiated with a projected completion time of fifteen years from start to finish. The opinions of some doubters, who estimated that a time frame of fifteen years was too optimistic, seemed probable when seven years into the project, only a few hundred thousand base pairs had been sequenced. That's because people assumed that progress in the remaining eight years would unfold at a similar success rate as in the previous seven.

But doubters failed to account for both human learning—the project team was constantly improving techniques—and the rate of technological change. Therefore, the computers in year one were several times slower than in year seven. In the end, the three billion base pairs were sequenced and the more than 20,000 genes in human DNA were identified in only thirteen years.

Finally, when you use yesterday's thinking to solve current and future challenges, you miss out on numerous ways that you can cross-utilize or cross-breed technologies with each other and among different industries and sectors. Take, for example, the solar-powered ventilation systems that are available in Toyota Prius vehicles. Toyota televised a commercial advertisement where a young spokeswoman parks her car in a disaster site, exits her vehicle, and asks viewers, "What if we used the same energy that ventilates the inside of a car to ventilate a medical tent in a natural disaster zone?" Broaden your perspective, entertain new ideas and concepts, and see how you can solve current and future challenges more easily simply by updating your thinking.

2. TECHNOLOGY CAN GIVE YOUR ORGANIZATION 24/7/365 COMPETITIVE ADVANTAGES.

Leaders who adopt a 24 hours a day/7 days a week/365 days a year approach to leading and managing are often better able to leverage their organization's potential than leaders who don't, and they reach desired outcomes more quickly and more efficiently. Just as the 24-hour ATM has put control in the hands of consumers, advancements in communication, networking, and digital infrastructure (such as the Internet) give today's leaders the control over creating fully productive 24-hour days without working themselves to death.

Imagine that you are the VP of operations of an international architectural design team in Los Angeles. You need some work created for part of a building before a Monday morning deadline. You have options. You can assign all the work to your LA-based team, which will require them to work all night throughout the week, or you can expand your thinking to include a 24/7/365 perspective, which forces you to look at the world as a long time loop. Now you can include a second team of designers in Mumbai who are able to continue the design work during their day, which just happens to occur while your LA-based group is home for the night. Once the Mumbai team exits its office at six o'clock in the evening their time, production in your Stockholm office begins for the third eight-hour day of your operations, and it closes just as your Los Angeles office opens. That's 24/7/365 production.

This type of 24/7/365 production capability plays out in real life for Hong Kong–listed Techtronics Industries, Inc. (TTI), makers of popular power tools branded with the Milwaukee, AEG, Ryobi, and Homelite names, as well as floor-care tools including Hoover and Dirt Devil. Group EVP and president of the Asia Pacific division, David Butts described to me that TTI has research and development and design capabilities—from parts development to packaging around the world in such locations as Milwaukee, Wisconsin and Atlanta, Georgia in the United States; as well as Buckinghamshire, United Kingdom; Wennenden, Germany; Tsuen Wan, Hong Kong; and Dongguan City, Guangdong Province, China. By maintaining such a global presence, products can be developed across all these locations, and whenever necessary, staffers can capture global design. To some degree, it means that if the group in Milwaukee needs design work to meet a deadline, they can work on part of the design in one location and then have it completed in another, allowing for more than an eight-hour day, thus extending the workday.

Realize, however, that you can have a small operation and still utilize this 24/7/365 concept by hiring freelance workers based around the world to perform all or parts of functions within your production processes.

3. TECHNOLOGICAL CHANGE CAN MAKE THE SEEMINGLY IMPOSSIBLE POSSIBLE.

Today's advancements (and the many more on the horizon) allow you to integrate technology into your plans and create the type of future for yourself and your organization that just a few short years ago would have seemed unimaginable.

Seth Dechtman, a managing director of a speaker-booking bureau founded in California, used technology to achieve his desired outcome to live life fully, especially while he is still young. Dechtman wanted to be able to live in different parts of the world and still conduct business as usual. Over the course of two years, we worked through the selection of technologies that enabled him to be mobile without sacrificing business performance. Using cloud-computing technologies (where an outside vendor hosts and manages one's operating software), Dechtman managed his sales force and ensured that its members maintained access to pertinent data. He developed "intelligent" tools, allowing his sales staff to find speakers through the use of automated background searches and to process orders through automated document handling. He outsourced all accounts receivables to a service where incoming customer payments arrived at a lockbox and the service provider would deposit the checks into the firm's operating account. VOIP technology, Skype, and other means of digital communications were the final technologies that allowed Dechtman to close his physical office and maintain virtual operations from anywhere in the world, all the while growing the business. Today he lives and works in his wife's country of origin, Argentina, while doing business every day in the States.

Although your organization might not be the type that can go completely virtual, you can still utilize various technologies to create exciting results.

4. TECHNOLOGY EXPANDS OTHERS' ACCESS TO YOUR ORGANIZATION.

For increasing numbers of organizations, the future will demand that technology provide the channel for greater connections between businesses and people and other organizations. Just look at how technology allows you to go online and set up an oil change appointment for your car any time of the day or night, or to install a phone app, even after you've lost your cell phone, that will pinpoint the location of your lost mobile phone within a few meters.

Businesses in Louisiana, Mississippi, and Texas were hit hard by 2005's Hurricane Katrina. Many organizations, especially those that relied on tourism, were forced to close their doors forever. But that wasn't the unfortunate fate of Joey Sutton's signed-memorabilia store, Vintage 429, in New Orleans' French Quarter. Prior to the hurricane, Sutton, who was self-admittedly not a technophile when it came to his business, had built a sales "life raft" by expanding his clients' access points.

Understanding that leaders must meet their customers at multiple buying entry points, Sutton added an online catalog and a paper catalog that was sent to members on his mailing list well in advance of Katrina's arrival. When disaster struck, Vintage 429 closed the doors to its physical shop temporarily, but it continued to make sales through its two remaining entry points.

Now, and more so in the future, your organization will have to be transparent and connected both upstream to its vendors, downstream to its customers, and to all other stakeholders in between. Because technology will be the answer to this transparency and connectivity, you're responsible for selecting the technologies that will provide superior access points for others.

5. TECHNOLOGY EMPOWERS YOU AND YOUR STAFF.

If you think of yourself as a slave to your technology, you aren't managing it correctly. Think about the freedoms we gain from technologies such as convenient cash with ATMs, easy bill paying with online banking, precise navigation with GPS devices, and instantaneous connections to others with communication devices such as smartphones and tablets. There's no question that technology is empowering—if *you* control *it*.

Regardless of the type of technology you are attempting to leverage, the key is to constantly ascertain if it is the best and right technology to get you to your Desired Outcome. As your circumstances evolve and new technological options present themselves, the effectiveness of a current technology to meet your needs can diminish, which is why you need to be sure that you're not wasting time, money, and opportunities trying to utilize a technology that has essentially run its course. Questions like, "At this point in time, is this technology having the same level of positive impact on my Desired Outcome as it did when I first started leveraging it?" can help you keep up to date and on track.

In addition, while the technology may not change, your usage of it might have to in order to remain productive. For instance, simple activities like not checking your e-mail constantly (yes, you actually can stay on top of your work correspondence without checking your e-mail every thirty seconds), using junk e-mail screening devices so that your inbox doesn't become overloaded, and directing business contacts to reach you via an office phone number so that you aren't interrupted via your cell phone are ways you let technology help you rather than hinder you.

Technology is a tool that should empower us, make our work faster, easier, and/or better, and provide us the freedom to lead enjoyable, fulfilling lives.

■ ■ ■

You arrived at this chapter already knowing about developing plans, creating new products and services, and establishing alliances, and I'm sure that as you look back on those activities in comparison to leveraging technology, you already get the sense that this latter activity differs from the previous three in its direct and immediate impact on organizational and individual performance. While the human element in organizations will remain important, technology and its potential impact on your systems and structures is and will continue to be the most productive means of maximizing the potential and output of your organization's people, time, capital, and all other assets. In this chapter, you learned new concepts, approaches, and tools to strengthen your strategizing, enable you to make better decisions, improve your ability to solve challenges, empower your staff members, improve operational efficiencies, increase productivity, and advance your organization by leaps and bounds all through the single activity of leveraging technology.

As you become more proficient as an Enterprise Thinker, you will integrate the activity of leveraging technology into your performance of the other ET activities to intensify and accelerate results. In actuality, you already do this—for instance, when you use technologically gathered and calculated algorithms and data to determine Strategy and Macro Tactics—but now, when you view your organizational landscape from 50,000 feet, a plethora of new and improved opportunities will come into view. Combine your expanded vision with the tools you accumulate in this book and you will leverage technology more purposefully to achieve Desired Outcomes faster, better, and more efficiently than you ever thought possible.

CATEGORY 2:
[LEARNING]

Learning
Acquiring New Knowledge
Enhancing Global Awareness
Watching Competition

Forecasting
Forecasting the Future

Strategizing
Developing Plans
Creating New Products & Services
Establishing Alliances
Leveraging Technology

Performing
Leading the Charge
Empowering Others
Innovating Everywhere
Selling Continuously

I HAD JUST FINISHED READING a magazine article that really had me fired up, and I immediately started thinking about how I could put its contents into practice. The exciting feature story was about how the global tire-manufacturing firm Pirelli had begun an innovative way of servicing clients. Pirelli had made the leap from producing tires strictly within brick-and-mortar factories to creating custom-made tires inside mobile double-wide trailers it called "mini-factories." This newer and innovative manufacturing venue gave Pirelli employees the flexibility to produce custom tires on site in three steps instead of the usual fourteen, and to do so on demand and with shorter production times—down from six days to 72 hours—than traditional methodologies allowed. In addition, the mini-factories could produce numerous or few tires without the same need for midproduction storage space of raw materials; usually only 12% of materials are in production at any given time, requiring storage space for the remaining 88%, but in mini-factories, raw materials are processed throughout the production phase without the need for any storage space. Mini-factories, in comparison to their traditional counterparts, consumed 33% less energy, too, contributing to a decrease in manufacturing costs by 25%.[73]

I started wondering how I might be able to apply some aspects of this innovative example to my own business. The rather lengthy article appeared in a sophisticated trade journal known to provide detailed information within its articles like performance statistics, floor layout designs, and detailed photos and graphics. As I studied the details of the article and pondered how they might enable me to transform my way of doing business, I realized that I still couldn't duplicate the innovations myself.

The reason I couldn't is because I had a false sense of knowledge. Perhaps because the article was so well written, complete with photos and graphics, or perhaps because I had gotten caught up in my own excitement about the possibilities, I had initially assumed I had learned more than I actually did. But I had no answers as question after question came to mind: What were the inner workings of the facility? Did clients benefit from having an on-site manufacturer? What generation of facility was this—a ten-year success story or a six-month experiment in progress?

Then it hit me. I realized that much of my "learning"—not just in this article but in general—consisted of surface information or *awareness* that had been disguised as new *knowledge*. In this particular instance, the Pirelli article gave me no clarity, only concepts and no how-to instruction for duplicating the outcomes. Once I made this realization, I began to notice how even many of the books, papers, trade journals, and other magazines that I had been reading were nothing more than interesting accounts of what people had done but not how I could do the same on my own. Without having certain other information, like the profitability of an initiative, the timeline of progress, or the thinking behind a project, much of the information I accumulated was little more than nontransferable inspiration.

While both awareness and knowledge carry value and purpose, they enable you to produce vastly different types of outcomes. This is a huge distinction that most people never truly make, and it is the missing link to why people oftentimes can't duplicate ideas even though they are highly motivated to do so.

You've probably heard the statistic about how we receive as much information today in one Sunday paper as our ancestors received over the course of a lifetime a century ago. The exact quantity of information that bombards us daily doesn't matter as much as understanding how to extract the useful and valuable information from it. We are overloaded with daily opportunities to learn. It starts early, from the time we read our morning newspapers, it ends late, after we've watched the late-night news before bedtime, and we're hit all day in between with digital feeds and streaming news reports. Then there are the magazines, books, people, seminars, and training sessions that we seek out as a way of concentrating our focus on specific topics of information. But at the end of our continuous daily cycles of learning, do we really have that much *useful and valuable* information at our disposal?

Albert Einstein[74] once said that "the significant problems we face cannot be solved at the same level of thinking we were at when we created them." In other words, to effect any type of change, you need to elevate your thinking by feeding your mind in the right ways. I'm not necessarily talking about the sources by which you learn, since they can be quite varied from one leader to another. I know a business owner who hates to read books but who built a $50 million-per-year company just the same; he acquired awareness and knowledge through other means, that's all.

By the "right ways" to feed your mind I mean that in contrast to the spongelike continuous learning that happens by default as we interact with the world around us, leaders need to *consciously* learn, which entails more than putting oneself in the presence of the right people or watching the best trade-related videos. In addition, as a decision maker, you have to delineate your awareness experiences from your knowledge-building experiences to determine whether you are accumulating the appropriate brain food to solve your challenges. In some cases, awareness is enough, while in others, you need further exploration. Improving your ability to learn in ways that can produce necessary Desired Outcomes is the purpose behind the ET category of Learning.

Within this category, I will be describing to you three different ET activities—acquiring new knowledge, enhancing global awareness, and watching the competition—that will bring greater focus to your learning. These activities will enable you to adopt a mentality of perpetual and focused learning that will enhance your performance in all the other ET activities, ultimately "snowballing" into improved decision making, better solutions, and greater opportunities.

The possible momentum produced by constantly learning can be likened to the "snowball effect": the momentum that a small snowball gains by rolling down a snowy hill, getting larger in size and heavier in weight, causing the snowball to gather speed with each roll. Momentum to progress your organization can stop suddenly, also, if you do not dedicate yourself to learning. This stoppage of momentum is something I call the Stuck Snowball Theory.

The Stuck Snowball Theory is easily understood by those who have lived in cold-weather climates and who have most likely scooped up a handful of snow, packed it a bit in their hands, then rolled the ball across a snow-covered surface to pick up more snow as the ball rapidly becomes larger. If you leave the snowball stationary for a period of time, even for a few minutes, the snowball cements itself to the ground below, making it difficult, if not impossible, to get the ball rolling again (without uprooting the grass under the snow's surface). Your thinking, decision making, and therefore, opportunities for your organization can become cemented in a state of immobility if you don't keep the figurative ball rolling, because it is difficult to regain the momentum you lose when you stop Learning (or Forecasting, Strategizing, and Performing).

7

ACQUIRING NEW KNOWLEDGE

LIKE MOST LEADERS, YOU CAN probably recall an incident of your own where you read a magazine article, attended a seminar, or watched an online video and thought, "We should do that," but then, despite your enthusiasm and best efforts, you couldn't turn that idea into the outcomes you wanted. Chances are you have since thought back on these disappointments trying to figure out what went wrong. Wonder no more, because it's likely you'll find the answer you've been looking for right here in this chapter.

Different Levels of Learning

Oftentimes, we think we *know* something when in reality, we're only *aware* of it. Substituting awareness for knowledge is one of the reasons that you get frustrated with yourself or your staff when your ideas don't go anywhere. It's also the reason why seemingly well-thought-out plans veer off course or don't deliver the returns you expect. While awareness has its merits, sometimes the missing ingredient that hinders progress isn't a tactical plan, time, or money; it's in-depth knowledge.

Consider awareness to be a first level of learning, where you're using your five senses to gain an initial understanding of a situation. Awareness helps you identify challenges and opportunities, and it gives you a scope of options to address the various situations you face on a daily basis anywhere within your life. Awareness is abundant, because it comes from a variety of sources that are all around us every day. As trends in technology and communications indicate, we will continue to be flooded by this information overload that increases awareness, but that doesn't necessarily mean we will accumulate greater knowledge, a distinction that all leaders need to make. Over time, as you gather more information, connect dots, use Cyclonic Thinking, and do additional research, some of your awareness undergoes a conversion to knowledge, making it usable in different ways.

Knowledge, on the other hand, is an in-depth comprehension of subject matter, and generally an important element to making change happen. Without some in-depth knowledge, much of the information you've accumulated at the awareness level remains unusable.

Say that you manage a public works crew responsible for your city's snow-plowing services. Being aware of the five-day weather forecast helps you anticipate your crew's work schedule and better serve the public. If you're on your way to the airport, being aware of local road conditions helps you plan an alternative route around a construction zone to catch your flight on time. When a hurricane threatens your home town, being aware of evacuation instructions or shelter locations can save your life. Awareness is important.

But awareness is not a substitute for in-depth knowledge. I would not want someone who is *aware* of heart surgery to perform such a procedure on me. Nor would you want someone who is merely aware of gas lines to hook up a gas range in your kitchen. Outside of the office, the difference between awareness and knowledge seems obvious, but when leaders face challenges on the job, many of them try to address complex issues with little more than awareness-level solutions. And that could be one of the reasons why your past attempts to convert thoughts to reality have failed.

Attempting to use these two levels of thinking interchangeably is like trying to fix a flat tire with a circular saw. If you want to achieve Desired Outcomes, you have to select the right tool for the job. I have found that most leaders spend the majority of their learning time building awareness, all the while assuming they are building knowledge. As a result, too many of them don't have enough in-depth knowledge to make the kinds of transformational improvements to their organizations that they might need.

I once spoke before a group of equipment-leasing brokers about the future of their industry. In that presentation, I revealed five different sales channels that I had forecasted to exist in the near future, and I explained how two current channels would be disappearing based on my pre-keynote research, which revealed that several major banks were looking to displace brokers and lend directly to lessors using a completely different sales model. For a large part of the audience that was completely in the dark about this trend, my speech was their first point of awareness of this impending industry shake up. You can imagine that these brokers wanted to respond to the newfound challenge immediately, but to do so appropriately they would need more information and in-depth knowledge. The need to build both awareness and knowledge is a continuous responsibility.

Most experts estimate that within 18 months, much of what we learn today will be replaced by the next new thing. The rapid influx of new data often gives you too little time for in-depth analysis or comparisons unless you make use of the new video and audio (and one day holographic) learning tools that speed up the learning process. Still, you might not always have the time to do the research you want to do, but now that you're placing focus on the difference between awareness and knowledge, you're already in a better decision-making position.

The Five Enterprise Thinking Learning Triangles

Learning at the awareness and knowledge levels is as essential to your personal advancement as it is to organizational achievement. While being aware can help you make good strategic decisions about your career, many times the win-by-a-nose edge that lands you the job you want comes from the depth of knowledge you have in your field of study.

Due to the most recent recession, employment statistics from many countries around the world showed that there existed four unemployed people for every one job opening—a statistic that would lead you to believe that employers had their pick of qualified applicants. But in reality, most employers found themselves settling for not-so-qualified applicants who had not advanced their learning over the course of their careers, and, therefore, were lacking in knowledge. In job fields that required the highest level of concentrated knowledge such as computer and mathematical sciences, technical specialties, and health care, even fewer applicants qualified for jobs. Leaders need to evolve their knowledge and skills to meet the requirements of today's jobs, and those who do will have a competitive advantage over their less knowledgeable counterparts.

Knowing the difference between awareness-level thinking and knowledge-level thinking is an excellent starting point for focusing your learning time more wisely. My guess is that you're already planning to dedicate more of your learning time to becoming more knowledgeable about certain topics. This rebalancing will come back to reward you with better outcomes.

You, like the thousands of leaders I have worked with, are most likely very motivated to solve your challenges, but perhaps you hadn't realized until now that many of the difficulties in doing so could have been averted with a little more in-depth knowledge. Not until the difference was pointed out to these other leaders did they realize that they had been attempting to solve challenges and create opportunities using the wrong tool. What about you? Have you acquired in-depth knowledge in that past year to improve process flow and project management, take advantage of new technologies and discoveries, or learn to speak another language? Perhaps you can't think of at least one action you took to learn something in-depth enough to use it to solve current challenges more effectively. Then it's time to make some changes.

Once you become increasingly focused on these differences, it may be more apparent to you why you haven't been able to duplicate suggestions made by the author of that last business or leadership book you read. Many of these books disguise themselves as knowledge-building materials when in reality they offer little more than awareness-level information. To be clear, the authors of these books—like the professors in your classes, the mentors in your life, or the trainers in your OJT programs—are often genuine experts in their fields and are not intentionally trying to deceive you. Just the same, you owe it to yourself to make the distinction by asking, Am I gaining enough in-depth knowledge to execute the techniques and successes being presented to me, or am I simply becoming aware?

One way to assess where you stand is to make a mental list of in-depth learning experiences you have engaged in over the past year on any topic. I'm not talking about reading awareness books one after another; rather, I'm referring to specific topics such as improved process flow, project management, nanotechnology, biology breakthroughs, a new language, and so on. If you can't come up with experiences of any significance, recognize this as the wake-up call to inspire you to do so.

Include in your mental list traditional sources that are widely considered to be the keys to knowledge—books, classroom experiences, conferences, mentors—and examine how they haven't necessarily moved you beyond awareness. Long-running, best-selling, highly recommended books that recount stories about companies that have "tipped" and soared from good to great are excellent at building awareness, but don't necessarily give you the how-to instructions you need to duplicate their successes within your own organization.

I'm not suggesting that you stop reading these books, but if you want to use them to transform your organization or your career, ask yourself four questions: (1) Does the book deliver the promise of its title? (2) Can I duplicate the examples in this book? (3) Do I see others making transformations based on the book's information alone, or do they need additional information, skills, or knowledge? (4) Did I acquire enough in-depth knowledge that I can transfer what I have learned to other people and to different types of situations?

In addition, there are certain sources that may awe you, but that may never help you improve, because the information isn't transferrable to you. For instance, I loved the book *Freakonomics,* by Steven D. Levitt and Stephen J. Dubner, because it explained interesting facts and skills, but I also recognized that it would be very difficult to replicate the authors' methods, because they were out of sync with the way my brain is wired. That's not to say that you should shy away from material because it is initially uncomfortable for you to process, only that some people have unique skill sets (just as some leaders have certain attributes), that are not necessarily transferrable to others. A musician can hear slight pitches in a voice that the average listener misses, a wine connoisseur has a refined palate to detect slight nuances of flavor that the occasional drinker doesn't notice, and an editor immediately picks up spelling and grammatical errors that many people overlook altogether.

Another point to keep in mind as you focus your attention on learning is that if you initially don't understand something, be careful not to assume that you can't ever understand it, because you might just need a little time to mentally digest it. Also, be careful not to assume that because the material doesn't make immediate sense, it must be wrong. I have encountered numerous leaders who immediately dismiss a possible source of awareness and knowledge (thus eliminating certain opportunities), because they jump to the conclusion that something they have read, heard, or seen is just plain wrong when in fact it was just new or initially unclear.

It can also be easy to discount some good sources of learning considering how most of them tend to lean more heavily in favor of awareness building versus knowledge building, so you might not immediately recognize them as being as useful as they can be. But awareness-level sources work well as starting points, and from there you can seek out the aid of follow-up books, magazines, seminars, and other types of learning resources that teach you the how-to part of the equation.

You will learn some of those how-to tools here, because knowing that you need to continually feed your mind with new knowledge and awareness doesn't mean that you know *how* to do so. To illustrate the different levels of learning and their relationships to each other, take a look at your next concept tool, ET's 5 Learning Triangles.

ET's 5 Learning Triangles

The levels of learning—awareness and knowledge—are distinct from one another based on five criteria:

1. **Time Spent.** The amount of time needed to become aware differs from the time required to gain knowledge.
2. **Effort Needed.** The amount of effort an individual must dedicate to the learning process to either gain awareness or acquire knowledge.
3. **Number of Individuals.** The number of people who are aware compared to the number of people who are knowledgeable in a subject.
4. **Integration Needed.** The depth of learning is proportional to an individual's ability to integrate information from various sources.
5. **Usable Information.** The amount of usable information varies in relation to whether the learning is surface-level awareness or in-depth knowledge.

ET's 5 Learning Triangles

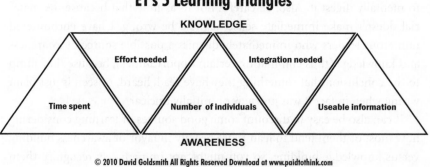

Figure 7.1—ET's 5 Learning Triangles

Figure 7.1 illustrates the differences between having awareness and acquiring new knowledge. Awareness spans the lower section of the five conjoined triangles. If you spend too much time building awareness and not enough acquiring knowledge, your mind may be full of information, but it won't necessarily be the form of information that you can use to make transformational change.

As you ascend the pyramid, you connect dots, use Cyclonic Thinking, and do additional research in order to reach deeper levels of learning (knowledge). The in-depth knowledge will convert much of the information that you accumulated at the awareness level into usable strategic and tactical material.

There are actually two levels of awareness and two levels of knowledge. As you spend time learning, your thinking progresses through all four levels. You begin with the lowest level of awareness, novice, and advance to the highest level of knowledge, expert. This progression opens up new options and opportunities to you. The four levels of advancement are:

1. **Novice.** The novice is the person who is only aware of a subject, but who really doesn't know enough about it to make use of it. If you're in your forties and took tennis lessons as a child, and you've begun to pick up a racquet again, you might consider yourself to be a novice tennis player.

2. **Intermediate.** This person is able to apply the awareness to his or her everyday challenges but only on a very surface level. Perhaps you've taken a year of once-a-week tennis lessons, and you now have a grasp of some basic tennis techniques. You could be an intermediate tennis player.

3. **Advanced.** The advanced learner has now begun to connect the dots. This person has integrated the subject matter into other information and can use the knowledge to either solve challenges or create opportunities. You're now able to strategically play the game, because you can put together a series of actions—serving the ball and driving toward the net—that cause you to win points more often and cut down your opponent's abilities to gain on you.

4. **Expert.** The expert is at the peak of knowledge. He or she has connected dots in ways that not only make the knowledge useful, but also create new knowledge. With a mastery of physical skills under your belt, your thinking accelerates to a strategic level where you understand the game in-depth enough to anticipate your opponent's current and expected next moves. You are able to create a master plan to win that includes adapting your Tactics throughout the game. Whether you have been a leader for decades or are at the beginning of your career, the right thinking tools can accelerate your learning to a higher level

faster than you might anticipate. The effort you have expended—
say that you held your first tennis racquet at age four and played
in tournaments throughout your childhood—combined with
your ability to integrate various elements of the game can result
in you becoming a nationally ranked tennis player by the age of
seventeen.

You can apply this progression of learning from awareness to knowledge
in any organization and across all aspects of life. The determining factors that
influence your progression are illustrated by the ET's 5 Learning Triangles.
Here we will explore each of these in detail.

Time Spent

Most of your time is spent learning at the awareness level.
This tends to happen by default, because you are alive and
surrounded by an abundance of awareness-type information coming from a
variety of sources (and trends in technology and communications will produce an even greater flood of data, reports, and mental tidbits than you have
today). You can't stop yourself from becoming aware as new information
presents itself to you.

Awareness is valuable in many ways. It protects you; you don't need to be
an auto mechanic to know that the squeaky noise coming from your brakes
means you need to get them checked out. It helps you identify opportunities; you catch a glimpse of a FOR LEASE sign posted on a warehouse that you
sense will be perfect for your expanding business. Awareness accumulates in
data banks within your mind, just waiting for the day when you use some
of it to connect the dots—make new connections between many pieces of
information, data, knowledge, etc., to reach new ideas and solutions—and
create in-depth knowledge.

When you're gathering awareness, except for those times when you're
actively seeking out awareness-building information—like when you read a
magazine article—you are likely to be in a passive state of learning. That's
why it is essential that from your awareness-building time you carve out
sections for knowledge-creation activities. You want to make the switch to
becoming more actively engaged in the learning process so that you acquire
transformative knowledge. It's often the difference between being able to say
a few words in a language and being able to have a conversation.

That's where the next learning triangle, Effort Needed, comes into play.

Effort Needed

The amount of information we receive can be as overwhelming as the task of determining how much of it we actually absorb, store, process, and use. By using filtering technologies like search engines, we can become rapidly aware of nearly any subject with little effort at all.

Becoming aware typically requires little to no effort on your part, but to become knowledgeable, you have to invest time and energy. Looking back at the instance when I read the article about the Pirelli tire company, I only gained awareness from reading it. In order to achieve results, more effort would have been needed on my part. It might be interesting, though admittedly a bit odd, if we could hook an electrode to our brains and receive an effortless and continuous feed of knowledge, but until then, be prepared to seek out in-depth information on your own.

Number of Individuals

The number of individuals who accumulate awareness is vastly higher than those who acquire knowledge. First and foremost, the disproportion exists, because most people have never really considered how different awareness and knowledge are from each other. Think about it: you spend your weekend reading a leadership book not because you're merely curious about its contents—awareness—but because you're hoping that it will give you the know-how to lead others to where you and they want to go.

When everyone on staff adopts a learning mentality and seeks out awareness and knowledge from a variety of sources, their increased awareness and knowledge banks multiply the potential of your organization. You may think that taking a step to make your team more aware and knowledgeable will be met with resistance—which is typically what leaders mean when they say that they can't get their people to learn—but usually that can be avoided with two measures.

First, it is your responsibility to seek out ways to provide quality learning experiences that are fun and exciting rather than boring or burdensome. Take a look at children's television programming and video games, and even use your ET tools to create some of the actual learning instruments that are powerful enough to engage your staffers in the same way that gaming software entertains kids and adults alike. Even if you're not a social gamer, don't rule out gaming software as a potential educational resource if you see a way that it can improve your thinking. And when you are hiring or selecting people to fill certain roles, keep your mind open to the ways that gamers might be able to contribute to your organization. I say this, because researchers have noticed that players of video games can sharpen decision making by up to 25% faster in making the correct decision compared to control groups, and can make choices and take action up to four times faster than the average person.[75] You can also seek out hands-on learning opportunities and incorporate them into your organization's educational programs. You can bring in guest speakers or send staffers on day field trips. For instance, offer an exchange program with a vendor or complementary organization in which each entity trades staffers for a day for the purpose of learning new ideas, efficiencies, processes, or methodologies that each group of people can apply to their own daily responsibilities.

I often ask leaders if they tend to take the courses they require others to take to enhance their knowledge, and most leaders say that they don't. If you're not engaged in some of these experiences, how can you determine if they are good or are meeting the needs of your organization? As a leader, you need to help elevate individuals from awareness to knowledge in a way that makes them engaged.

The second way to prevent resistance to awareness- and knowledge-building is to shore up operational efficiencies so that your people actually have the time in their schedules to partake in learning activities. By using your ET tools, you can create empowering systems and structures, implement the right technologies, align with the most appropriate alliances, and deliver winning (internal and external) products and services to ease the demands on your staff members.

If presently you're part of an organization that doesn't have time to groom learners, you can also hire new decision makers who are already knowledgeable and who already have a learning mentality. One of the wealthiest men in Brazil, businessman Eike Batista, believes that "over time you learn that knowledge is important. So [he] hired a team of executives . . . who had great knowledge."[76] In this way, Batista and leaders like him are able to quickly assemble a leadership team that can make greater contributions to the growth and prosperity of their organizations. Contrast this position of strength with the fifty-person leadership team of an organization for which I conducted an educational seminar. The majority of leaders had been employed at this organization for many years, so they were not getting new information from any recent hires. In an effort to uncover how steadily the organization acquired new awareness and knowledge, I asked how many of the fifty leaders had read a business book or had taken a course over the past year. Only two members of the team had done so, which immediately raised a red flag that these leaders may be lacking new ideas and information necessary to effect transformative organizational growth, especially if they weren't gathering new information from other sources like trade journals, business or science magazines, white papers, and other reports that would increase their learning.

An organizational culture that supports a learning mentality keeps your leadership team and staffers sharp, current on matters that impact your organization now and tomorrow, and able to make smarter decisions faster, all which can help you outpace your competition. Continuous and intentional learning is also important to the next factor of learning: Integration Needed.

Integration Needed

If your ability to solve a challenge is contingent only on being aware, then you may not need to connect the dots and integrate information from various sources and points in time. But in most instances, information by itself is useless until it is combined with other data, knowledge, situations, systems, or processes where it can work for you. Because you must make decisions at 50,000 feet, you can't solve challenges, create opportunities, or develop Strategy without seeing how all the pieces of the puzzle connect.

You need to be able to integrate data, statistics, experiences, current events, and other information to put your awareness into context. For example, if you learn that the annual tuition at Harvard University rose to $33,696 in 2009, up from $2,600 in 1970, that awareness alone might be pretty meaningless. However, if you're the head of a bank and you want to develop student-loan packages for prospective students five years from now, that information might be extremely valuable. Its value increases as you or your staffers integrate it into knowledge of your organization's products, services, and people. In addition, combine it with trends in lending and education, economics and politics, etc.

Can you recall the last trade magazine or newspaper article you read, its title, the name of the author, and five points that will transform the way you do your job? Perhaps the awareness you gleaned from the article piqued your interest and prompted you to learn more, but if you needed more information to integrate with the contents of the article and didn't take that step, much of the information you accumulated will remain unusable.

Now, can you name the last nonfiction book you read, its author, and five key points about the book? Chances are, your recollection of the book is better than that of the article, because the book forces you to be engaged with the medium for a longer duration of time, and because the book's length allows the author to provide more depth on a subject.

Both the magazine article and book are bound to increase your awareness and knowledge banks, and they'll provide value to your decision making in different ways. It's up to you to find a balance between the two types of learning.

Usable Information

Information in and of itself is not usable, but nearly everything you learn has the potential to be used at one time or another. In the 5 Learning Triangles diagram, awareness consumes a large portion of the Usable Information triangle, because all information is potentially usable at some point in time.

As your eye travels upward to the peak of this triangle, you see that less of the information is usable at the knowledge level, since you will have extracted only those pieces of it that support your deeper and more concentrated learning of a particular subject matter.

It can be easy to mislead yourself into believing that you have a wealth of usable information at your disposal, especially when you spend a lot of your time engaged in learning activities. You now know that you might have to recalibrate your definition of "usable."

The news and other popular media are great ways to become aware of current events that affect your organization. Although being aware of current events is often enough exposure to help you make better decisions about the direction of your organization, in some cases further investigation is necessary to get a true picture of what is really happening and to confirm that your information is accurate.

With more media sources offering nonstop, on-demand news and information, we're exposed to some misinformation that passes for fact. More than sixty years ago, broadcast journalist Edward R. Murrow recognized the benefits of rapid communications but also cautioned that ". . . it is also true that speed can multiply the distribution of information that we know to be untrue."[77]

The purpose of ET's 5 Learning Triangles is to help you make the distinction between being aware and being knowledgeable, and to understand that while both states of thinking have value, they are distinctly different and will affect your decision making differently, too.

We've established that the distinction between awareness and knowledge exists, and we've touched on how they both impact decision making, but we've yet to determine what topic areas you should be extracting from the information overload. Above all else, you need to have a true picture of your organization, its strengths and weaknesses, its systems and structures, and its people.

Gaining a 360° Awareness of Your Organization

Knowing your organization is crucial to good decision making. That's why I suggest that you take a good look at your organization from all sides and in as many aspects as you can, using a comprehensive assessment that I refer to here as the 360° awareness of your organization. As much as you may already know about its strengths and weaknesses and despite your concentrated pockets of knowledge about certain aspects, take the additional time and measures you need to ensure the information you work with is both complete and accurate.

Gaining 360° awareness requires that you understand your stakeholders' needs and expectations and how capably you are meeting those needs and expectations, in order to remain competitive. When you initially contemplated a 360° awareness of your organization, had you considered your organization from the perspective of all its stakeholders? Some groups, like the military, find that their people work better when they know each other better. I spend a good deal of time at the beginning of each NYU class's semester getting to know the students and making sure they know each other; we exchange our names, the names of our companies, our roles, and our expectations. We also eat lunch together, which allows us to learn about each other even more. The students say that by knowing one another early on in the class, they feel freer to open up, express their ideas, share feedback, and help each other learn and grow throughout the course.

Take into consideration the perceptions that others—from vendors and buyers to the general public and shareholders—have of your organization and use that insight to inform improvements you might need to make.

Branch out even further to the environment and world at large and include information about politics, the weather, the environment, and other factors that have an impact. Everything is connected, and the better you see the connectivity, the better you will be at Forecasting, Performing, and Strategizing, too.

The Interplay of Accuracy and Interpretation

In today's world, gaining 360° awareness requires you to have a new sense of urgency about getting accurate data quickly and installing the mechanisms to keep that information up to date. In years past, it may have been okay to view key performance indicators periodically, say monthly, quarterly, or annually, but the ever-accelerating pace of change combined with new legal pressures (such as laws that hold decision makers liable for financial reporting), demand that you keep your finger on the pulse of your organization's condition at all times. I say this because the vast majority of organizations don't pay attention to their numbers as regularly as one might think. Leaders tend to use last year's financial numbers to "guesstimate" the current year's performance with little validation that the approximations are on target. Strive to stay on top of more current and accurate information; if you had annual meetings to review numbers, schedule semi-annual meetings this year, or if you are used to conducting a midterm review, conduct quarterly reviews now.

A useful (but rarely developed) tactic for capturing your organization's current status is to create a digital dashboard that covers key performance indicators across your entire organization. In one firm that I visited, I noticed a running sales figure tally and other stats displayed at the bottom of key personnel's computer screens for all of them to see. Your digital dashboard must measure the right data and measure it correctly. You also want to monitor others' responses to it to ensure that it is actually improving your organization and not hindering it. For instance, if displaying running sales figures begins to push sales personnel to deeply discount products, but the discounts are eroding your profits, then you need to adapt your mechanisms to eliminate these negative effects.

The options for gaining an accurate 360° awareness are countless, and you will find specific suggestions of activities a little later in this chapter. Above all else, you want your interpretations of the data to be as accurate as the data itself. For instance, if you choose to use reports generated from the digital collection of data, you must first establish the aspect of your organization that you want to measure, such as gross revenue, a pipeline of forecasted activity, inventory, retention, attendance, or grant totals. A measure of gross sales may sound good initially, but if your mechanisms don't reveal which products are being sold—whether they are new products or older products that are already established in your marketplace—or that some services are only popular in certain regions and nearly dead in others, then you will need to make adjustments to your gathering techniques before you'll get an accurate story of your organization.

One of the ways you can ensure accuracy of reporting is to carefully create your collection mechanisms with people who have expertise in data collection. Be sure that the people working with you on this can actually produce accurate data-collection mechanisms they promise. Be careful, too, that if you're using the best practices or annual statistics from outside groups like your trade association, you do what you can to confirm the data, because often the people who are submitting the data are not taking the time to assemble their stats, they're just reporting their best guesses.

I experienced the challenges of data collection firsthand, when I was invited one year to write an article for the best-practices edition of a publication put out by the Spring Manufacturers Association. I set out to collect data by interviewing several members of the organization. My intention was to interpret the data to make recommendations and forecasts to the manufacturers for the present and future of their industry.

Within the first few interviews, I quickly realized that this task would be more daunting than I had originally expected. I had in front of me data from a wide range of spring manufacturers. Some produced springs for pens, others for cars, and others for mattresses. I also had to include the types of locations—urban, rural, stock shops, custom shops—and the geographical regions that affected average wages and building rental prices. Now add on top of these complexities the fact that few interviewees actually had accurate or consistent information to contribute to the interviews: inaccuracies were derived from the estimation of earnings and profitability rather than the use of actual financial calculations; inconsistencies were the result of trying to compare too many variables, like urban versus rural businesses or custom versus stock production, and so on. So be aware that data (and its interpretation) can be misleading.

Although larger organizations are often credited as being more advanced in the areas of data collection and interpretation than smaller organizations, truth be told, regardless of the size of any organization, *all* should have good data and interpretation methodologies in place to gain accurate and timely information for better decision making. Numbers give you a picture of your organization's performance that you don't always see, and they challenge your assumptions so that you can be sure that your decisions are aligned with the strategic direction of your organization.

What You Can Do Starting Now

The size of your organization or the funds available to you for research will not impact your ability to put into action the suggestions below. Furthermore, even if you're sure you already have a pretty accurate 360° awareness, trying the techniques here may uncover some surprising revelations.

Listen to People

As simple as it sounds, you can glean information just from listening to what the people connected to your organization have to say about it. With little effort, you can strike up genuine conversations with people who can offer insight into your organization's culture, products, marketplace, industry, and so on. (I'm not talking about the typical meet-and-greet type of tour that some executives do but rather a more in-depth talk with people who are really in the know.) Try to listen more than you speak, take notes, and approach these conversations with a sincere interest to understand what's going on and how you can help.

An auction house manager of a global organization who was responsible for producing and distributing catalogs to showcase items in upcoming auctions needed to speed up her team's production time. A large part of the auction house's high-ticket-item sales hinged on buyers receiving these catalogs well in advance of auctions; if a catalog's production ran too close to the auction date, sales were at risk, because bidders needed the advance time to plan their attendance and do their own research. Otherwise, they may not be able to attend an auction at all. This manager was tired of sweating out every production cycle and having her team of six work late just to keep up, so I recommended that she take a virtual climb to the 50,000-foot perspective by talking with other unit heads at the company and asking for their ideas for solutions.

She followed this advice, and to her amazement, a solution arose almost instantly from the VP of operations, who was responsible for receiving products for auctions. He shared with her the steps in his process, one of which was to take photos of soon-to-be-auctioned products as they arrived into their warehouses. He offered to add her name to the list of photo recipients so that she would receive photos of items at the same time he did. This would eliminate the lag time that had often delayed production. One conversation with a fellow manager had closed a month-long gap in production. Conversations with other unit heads expanded her organizational view, too.

In all her six years at this job, she had never considered taking time from her schedule to reach out in this manner.

Sagi Ashkevitz, president of Dental Savings, a 14-person dental supply company, began a simple exercise of asking his employees to submit quarterly improvement ideas for the organization. Their responses have provided Ashkevitz with phenomenal suggestions and information that he says he would never have received previously. The feedback has grown his firm in five years from a small shipping business operated out of his small, box-lined apartment to a thriving distribution firm housed in a 5,000-square-foot facility.

Too frequently, leaders assume that they know the ins and outs of their organizations better than they actually do. Whether you are collaborating with colleagues or engaging in dialog with people in a variety of capacities, the simple person-to-person interaction can provide you with the information necessary for good decision making.

Along these lines but in a more structured format is the interview approach to gathering information from both internal and external resources. Although it is similar to conversing with others, the "rules" of interviews—establishing a set time to talk, establishing the duration of the interview in advance, preparing a specific list of questions, securing a private time where the interviewee can focus his or her attention on you—better ensure that the time spent together will be free from most interruptions so that a lot of data can be accumulated at once. (Another benefit, one which I personally have enjoyed from hosting live interview series for two associations that are later posted online for their members to review, is that you can sometimes develop good friendships with your interviewees, and the input they offer you over time can be even more valuable than the answers you gathered in a single interview.) Most people are pretty willing to share their insights and opinions, so don't be shy about approaching them. Here are some basic steps that you can follow:

- Make a list of people that you think you need or want to know: colleagues, educators, industry experts, analysts, coworkers, etc.
- Craft a list of questions that you want to ask, but make sure you don't turn this opportunity into an interrogation. You want the interview to be flexible and organic—overplanning could limit the feedback that you get. You want to remain open to receiving information, even if it comes from not having asked a question. You can solicit help in assembling the questions to ensure they will uncover the kind of information you need.

- When you contact someone for an interview, share with them the purpose of the interview, the type of questions you'll be asking, and how much of their time you'll need.
- During the actual interview, play the role of the student, not the teacher, meaning you should *listen* to interviewees' responses. Take notes and/or record your conversations.

Notes are essential, because it is very easy to forget important points. I'm always baffled at how many people will attend a meeting without taking notes. They believe they'll remember the important items, but they don't! I once facilitated and presented at one firm's five-day conference during which time the CEO outlined to his 100 senior managers from around the globe what their new roles would be as the company underwent the implementation of new initiatives. As the facilitator, it was my responsibility to wrap up each session with a summary, so when the CEO concluded his presentation, I asked for someone in the group to give me three points that the managers could take away with them. No one could do it except one person who had been taking notes. My point to the group was that if they couldn't remember what was said just fifteen minutes ago, how would they remember what happened during the course of a week without note-taking. They got the message and midway through the event one of the planners came to me with a smile on his face and said, "We've run out of paper! They're taking notes." And although there's no guarantee that all participants will review their notes at a later date, at least with note-taking, a record exists that can be a valuable reference point for later use.

- After the interview, take the time to think about and convert the data from its raw form into something pertinent to your challenges or situation. This is an extremely important step, because we've all gone to the conference, collected a bag of brochures and notes, and then found the bag months later in the corner of our offices, never touched. What good is the material if it never sees the light of day? Human tendencies are to return to work and to move on, not to pull out the information and connect it to your daily responsibilities.
- Assemble your interview responses and look for patterns: similar issues, concerns, processes, outcomes, successes, and failures. Are you hearing a lot about customer service or returns or products or shipping processes? These patterns often highlight the areas that are most in need of improvement.

■ Sometimes interviews will point out discrepancies, like the interview I did with the president of a large association whose day job was CEO of a $300 million company. I was preparing for an upcoming presentation and had already interviewed many of his colleagues. After twenty-two minutes of telling me what he thought other interviewees had said, I shared with him that not a single person on my interview list had even mentioned these issues that he deemed important. Offended, he claimed that the others *should be* thinking and doing what he said, but his answers actually revealed that he was the clueless one. He had become married to his own thoughts, and he was disconnected from his people.

Because this was at a time when the economy was good, the CEO's missteps weren't apparent. Good economies can often disguise poor or mediocre initiatives as successful. After the global economy took a turn for the worse in 2009, his revenue plummeted more than 40%. Without an understanding of his organization and its marketplace, his strategies could not realistically be sustainable for the long term in any economy, however.

In short, interviewing is fast, inexpensive, and effective, and it can give you important insights into your organization and its industry.

Engage in Walk-Around Management

People toss around this idea of walk-around management, but have you ever thought about its greatest value to you as a decision maker? Sure, when you walk around and shake hands with people, they often feel more appreciated, and if you're heading a large organization, it's nice to show your face as a gesture of interest. However, its true significance is that you get to see firsthand how the people, facilities, and processes you've put in place are functioning. Walk-around management gives you awareness and knowledge that you can draw upon when you're Strategizing, Performing, and Forecasting, and even doing other activities within Learning, so that you can make better decisions.

In preparation for a project involving a manufacturing firm with several hundred facilities peppered throughout the United States, I interviewed its CEO, who described his facilities as clean and efficient and his employees as excited about some new processes they had just begun using. I decided to make an impromptu visit to one of the facilities located thirty miles from my office to get a firsthand look at it. To my surprise, the conditions were not at all as he described. During my walk-around visit, I saw a dirty workplace in need of a paint job. The employees were anything but excited, and most of them were reluctant to talk to me unless their comments could be given "off the record."

The discrepancy between the CEO's perception and the actual condition of his facility offered valuable insights into the organization. When I mentioned the disconnect (while being careful to protect the confidentiality of his employees), he answered, "Why didn't you tell me? I could have sent you to a nicer place." Obviously, he was missing the point, and he could have made a lot of strides on his own if he had just taken the time to visit the facilities in person.

We live in an age of advanced telecommunications, but digital and electronic techniques aren't always a good substitute for internal walk-around management or for meeting customers and vendors face to face. I once worked with a vice president of sales for a geographic region of an international European airline who had decided not to attend the organization's annual conference and instead made a virtual visit to it via teleconference and speakerphone. I attended one of those meetings and saw what he could not: his staff members' angry reactions as he addressed them about what he expected out of them. Later, one of his staffers told me that the impression the VP gave off was that he believed he was too important to spend the time getting to know his staff and to meet them face to face. The VP had no idea that this was the message he was sending.

Experience your organization firsthand to identify its plusses and minuses. Sometimes an organization needs the fresh eye of its leader to notice a problem that's escaped the attention of everyone who is exposed to it on a daily basis. I know of a company in Boston that spent hundreds of thousands of dollars over the years shipping packages via overnight air. One day, the manager walked around and asked some questions. To his shock, he discovered that many of their packages were being shipped using overnight air delivery service to the office next door, when (a) not all the packages needed to arrive the next day, and (b) even if they did need to arrive the next day, ground service or hand delivery by a mailroom clerk would have achieved the same result but for a lot less money. If someone in management (or even the front line) had seen the oversight earlier, they could have prevented the waste, and the misspent funds could have been redirected to organizational improvements.

This isn't a unique happenstance. Whether the waste comes from shipping or purchasing or from a number cruncher whose mathematical errors go unnoticed, walk-around management can help you make improvements.

Be Your Own Customer

You've probably heard about secret shoppers, people who pretend to be customers so that they can report their "typical" shopping experience to leadership. Usually secret shoppers are utilized as a tactic in retailing, but the secret-shopper model can be an effective research mechanism in any type of organization.

A New York state distributor and installer of office furniture and cabinetry had an agreement with the products' manufacturer that sales calls received by the manufacturer would be forwarded to the distributor/installer for follow up. This seemed like a win-win relationship until someone decided to test the process by using a secret shopper working on behalf of the distributor.

The secret shopper placed a call to the manufacturer and outlined a project that would have brought a hefty sum to the distributor. The sales personnel at the manufacturer's call center recorded the information and promised the shopper that he would receive information in the mail. The distributor awaited the lead from the national rep, but none came. So the distributor asked the secret shopper to call the manufacturer and complain that he hadn't received his information packet.

The rep apologized to the secret shopper and promised to send another package. Still, the distributor never received the lead on the "prospective shopper," nor anything from the national office, so after four weeks, the distributor decided to meet with the manufacturer's district manager to discuss with him how he could generate more sales within the region.

Initially, the distributor asked the DM for clarifications of the process as if suggesting only that sales leads weren't being forwarded to his firm as agreed, and intentionally leaving out the part about the secret shopper to see if the two could work out the problems. The DM insisted, "I've been here a long time, and this process works!" That's when the distributor described the secret shopper's two unsuccessful attempts to get the attention of the company's sales force. The DM was surprised by this revelation, to say the least. Had the distributor never taken the time to play customer, both parties would have missed out on an opportunity to improve business and generate revenue.

If you want to see how your organization treats its supporters—customers, patients, stockholders, citizens, students, etc.—*be* its supporter. If you can't go undercover, hire someone to do it for you so that you can gain awareness about their experiences.

Understand Your Organization's Financials

Financial reports reveal the health status of your organization. Numbers, like those found on a profit-and-loss statement and a balance sheet tell the story of your organization. They tell you how your decisions have impacted your organization, and they can highlight where your organization is sickest and healthiest. Understanding financials is one of the ways you get a 50,000-foot view of your organization.

Some people enjoy studying financial information, while others do not. Regardless of where you fall on the spectrum, you must pay attention to your organization's numbers, and you don't need a formal education in finance or accounting to do so. At the very least, you should have a general understanding of your monthly profit-and-loss statements (to see the relationships between incoming and outgoing monies to gauge profitability), your balance sheet (to get a snapshot of your organization's overall health and strength), accounts payable (bills that are due), accounts receivable (money owed to you), and the value and expected payment times of any work in progress. If necessary, hire someone to go through the financials with you and explain the information they contain. The time and money spent on this activity are worthwhile, and the data will help you make better decisions. For instance, you can't fill in the Project Evaluation Chart from Chapter 3 if you don't have accurate data.

At a consultants' meeting, a presenter conducted a random survey of the twenty-five participants to find out how they prepared their financial books each year. The majority of the group had no monthly reporting, and only a few understood the basics of accounting. One person commented that his system is to put all receipts into a box and hand it off to his accountant at the end of the year for tax preparation. This means that overall, the group had no financial dashboard to gauge their progress and to ensure that their businesses were running well.

Keep in mind that as a leader, you can multiply the benefits of improved decision making among your leadership team by teaching them how to understand financials. Not everyone has to see all the numbers, nor do they need to use them at the 50,000-foot view, but if they have the right financial data to enable them to better operate their business unit, department, franchise, and satellite location, etc. better, then why wouldn't you want to teach them how to acquire and utilize this information?

A past consulting client had a super salesman who grossed $3.5 million in sales every year. I asked my client about the profitability figures for that salesperson. After investigating the numbers, the owner was stunned to find that the company actually lost money every time the salesman made a sale. We asked the salesman how he priced his orders, and he told us that he simply added 10% of the cost of the goods as the sales markup. That 10% fell well short of covering the other costs associated with selling and delivering the product to customers, costing the company $600,000 annually.

You can't achieve 360° awareness without at least a general understanding of your financial progress. The latter might not be the key to high performance, but it is an indicator of problems and progress that needs your attention. Here's a tip: take a course at your local college or offer to buy lunch for someone in accounting in exchange for teaching you how to read and understand your numbers. This applies to leaders in small, medium, and large operations. The earlier you have this information and the more frequently you review it, the better, in order to make decisions that keep your organization healthy.

Look at Your Organization from Different Perspectives

Have you ever noticed that witnesses who describe an event recount details from different perspectives? To truly understand your organization from 360°, view it from as many different perspectives as possible. Here are two ways to broaden your awareness.

First, do someone else's job while they're on vacation. No matter where it is in the company, if a job frees up for a few days, step in and try to do it. You will gain a new awareness of your organization's functions, processes, and structures by experiencing this fresh perspective.

When my staff members took their summer vacations, I would step into each role to get a sense of how their functions were connecting with and contributing to the organization as a whole. During one such experience, I discovered that a manager who was always complaining about her workload despite the tools and processes we implemented to make her work easier was actually never *replacing* old processes with new; instead, she was *adding* the new processes to the old, and in turn, lopping hours of redundant work onto her daily schedule! In one day, I was able to eliminate these redundancies that bogged her down, and when she returned from her vacation, I helped her ease into the improved routine. Had I not gotten my hands dirty, we would never have recouped an average of fifteen hours per week being lost through this manager. I've always wondered what would have happened if I had done this earlier.

Doing the jobs of others allows you to see how people are performing, and what they need from you to do their jobs better. Perhaps some teams aren't following a new process as you thought they were, or that an idea you thought was working like a charm isn't working at all. **Note:** I have known executives who have taken a similar tact and a few times regretted the experience. You have to judge for yourself whether you are staying long enough to have a positive impact or lingering for too long and causing others to feel undermined and hindered.

Make Sure Everyone "Sees" the Same Organizational Structure

Have you ever traveled along the highway and followed another driver in his or her vehicle for hours? They pass another car, so you pass another car. They speed up to get by a large truck, you do the same. A real traveling team you are, until one of you steers onto an exit ramp as the other continues its path down the highway. A lot of leaders, managers, and coworkers operate in much the same fashion. They all think they're traveling toward the same destination, but when they're asked to describe even where they fall within the organization's landscape, most of them are nothing more than independent travelers.

Would you say that you and your staff are on the same page about your organization's operations, functions, and structure? Sometimes leaders, managers, and coworkers can work side by side for years, pointed in the same direction, and be heading for entirely different desired outcomes. Test your answer by performing the exercise that a couple of my clients tried.

We were at an executive retreat for thirty executives and managers of a nonprofit with eight hundred employees. After some preliminary discussion, I placed two easels, back to back, and asked the CEO and the executive director each to go to an easel and sketch out the company's corporate organizational chart while other members of the group drew their renditions on paper.

When we turned those two easels toward the audience, everyone saw two charts that were so different that they appeared to be describing two different organizations. Both the CEO and the executive director had forgotten several (but different) functional units. The executive director's reporting lines were wrong, too. One contained the board of directors and the other did not. The paper versions drawn up by audience members were no more consistent. This exercise was a real eye-opener for everyone in the room, including myself.

By acquiring an accurate view of your organization's structure, you can make better and unsiloed decisions for all of its departments, people, units, and other stakeholders by understanding how your decisions will impact every aspect of the organization.

So now you have some techniques you can easily use to gain a 360° awareness of your organization, and you can pass these techniques on to other decision makers by installing the mechanisms to keep them informed and by communicating directly with them the actions they need to take to gain the awareness they need to do their jobs optimally.

Since you know that you and your fellow decision makers must continually learn about your organization, the world in which it operates, and the competitors who affect its ability to stay operational, let's see how you and your leadership team can make the most of your learning experiences by exploring your learning preferences.

Looking Within: How Do You Prefer to Learn?

Much research has been conducted in the field of learning preferences and styles. There are advocates of the left-brain versus right-brain styles, supporters of the auditory-or-visual preferences, and people who favor testing tools such as Myers-Briggs Type Indicator. While these perspectives all have merit, they also have their weaknesses. One weakness in particular is that people end up labeling others, which is chancy, because it can limit potential. Whenever you place people into rigid categories, you risk never knowing the contributions they can make. The graphic artist deemed too right-brained to help with processes and systems might actually have a background in computer science or operations. By limiting your graphic artist's presentation to right-brained activities, you could miss out on the valuable input they could provide. Multiply this mistake throughout the organization and you miss opportunities both professionally and personally.

I believe that your next ET tool, the concept of Maps versus Words, won't present these same kinds of challenges, because it gives people a way of assessing their own learning preferences and helps them to better communicate and connect with others. Understanding the learning preferences of others through Maps versus Words enables you to keep the doors of opportunity open. In addition to using this simple tool to enlighten you to your own learning preferences, it empowers you to identify the preferences of the people around you so that you can work more effectively with them.

Maps versus Words

If I were to give you driving directions, would you prefer that I draw out a map complete with streets and markers, or would you prefer that I write out the directions in words? "Go to the town hall, take a left and keep going for about twenty minutes until you see the red barn, and then you turn . . . ." Even if you like both types of directions, you likely feel a stronger pull toward one or the other, but to what extent? I want you to think about the degree to which you prefer either maps or words before you circle your preference location on the scale in Figure 7.2 below. A marker of 10 means you have an extreme preference for either maps or words, whereas a marker placed closer to the 0 indicates a nearer equal preference for both. So, if you selected a 10 on the maps end of the scale, you are someone who needs a map and only a map, because using words would cause you to get lost. Conversely, if you place your marker on 10 for words and I give you a map, you'd find yourself pulled over on the side of the road twisting and turning the paper trying to make sense of it. A moderately placed marker for maps would show up on the left-hand side of the scale as a score of approximately 4. Now circle the number on the diagram that best represents your preference.

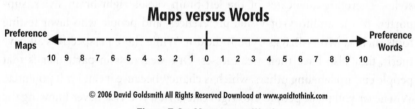

Figure 7.2—Maps versus Words

Without knowing it, you could be making incorrect assumptions about how people prefer to learn, but Maps versus Words, which is not a left-brain or right-brain test, takes the guesswork out of all that and gives you a starting guideline for communicating with or teaching others. Watch that you don't make assumptions about learning preferences based on others' positions—engineer, office manager, salesperson, copywriter—because I've met artists who prefer words and writers who ask for maps.

Because Maps versus Words reveals learning preferences, you can use it from the perspective of the student, who may want to seek instructors who deliver content in sync with the former's learning preferences, or from the perspective of the teacher, who may need to restructure parts of his or her course material to help those students with opposing preferences. If you've ever walked out of a course and said to yourself, "That instructor was horrible," only to hear the person next to you ask their friend, "Wasn't he fantastic?" you are most likely experiencing the duel of the maps-minded people versus the words-minded.

Translating Maps versus Words to your responsibilities as a leader, you have to learn to communicate with both maps and words, otherwise you lose your effectiveness. Mix up your methods of delivery using stories, graphics, definitions, and photos to be as inclusive of as many people as possible. While this takes practice, just being more aware can have huge returns.

Most leaders find that a safe bet is to develop a combination of both maps and words to connect with people across the spectrum. Sometimes the simple reframing of your delivery can make all the difference in the results you achieve. A longtime friend who helped to manage his family's pizza shop told me about a problem he was having with one of his drivers. The driver was a dependable friend and a conscientious employee, but whenever he needed to deliver to an unfamiliar location, he was late. "I just don't get it," my friend said. "I have a map right on the wall; I point out the location, he nods his head like he understands where to go, and then he drives away and gets lost. I like the guy and I don't want to fire him, but I don't know what to do."

It seemed that their learning preferences were on opposite ends of the spectrum. After learning about Maps versus Words, my friend went back to work with a new sense of compassion. A few months later, we bumped into one another and my friend excitedly told me about the progress he had made with his driver. "Right after you and I talked, I needed to show him where to go [for a delivery]. Instead of pointing to the location on the map, I wrote out the directions in words, and he didn't get lost. He hasn't gotten lost since!"

Your aim is to continually appeal to others using both maps and words to maximize your options for reaching Desired Outcomes.

Ways to Become More Aware and More Knowledgeable

Have you ever thought about the fact that you can't look at written words and *not* read them? The configuration of letters on paper, machinery, signs, and so on instantly force your mind into processing mode, where you can't help but put meaning to the words that your eyes see. In reality, the same type of mental activity takes place throughout the day when you see people, objects, and happenings unfold in front of you. Your mind begins to interpret them and assign meaning to them. So why not, when you're passing through a day, make sure that your brain is searching for information that is potentially valuable for improving your organization?

Learning opportunities are all around us, but to get you started here are some simple tips:

- **Read for awareness.** Peruse a daily newspaper or online resource to gain an awareness of current events influencing your organization. I read the *Wall Street Journal* daily, and when I'm on the road, I always read the national or local paper to learn different perspectives. Trade and nontrade magazines provide a quick snapshot—cross-function and cross-section—of what's going on in an industry, in arts and sciences, and in international and domestic business. I recommend you scan through the following business and/or future-oriented magazines—*Wired, Fortune, Inc., Bloomberg, Businessweek, The Economist, Technology Review, Popular Science,* and even *Scientific American.* There are thousands of different publications and resources in print or online, so you have a variety of options for learning and consistently gaining new awareness.

- **Read for learning.** Various studies have indicated a link between reading business books and earning more money. Books keep you engaged for a longer period of time than magazines and newspapers. This extra time enables you to think about material, integrate it into your bank of knowledge, and draw upon it when your organization needs you to do so.

  Fifty-one percent of leaders spend more than four hours a week reading to stay informed, but many others say they can't find that kind of time to read.[78] It's possible you feel the same way. And in reality, many people have built great organizations without reading books, so this is not an end-all solution. Selecting reading material wisely and intentionally is how you build your mental reserves for good decision making.

- **Participate in continuing-education opportunities.** Whether your classroom is brick and mortar or virtual, learning pursuits of any kind keep your mind fresh, your ideas percolating, and your solutions within easy reach. I mentioned earlier that I host two interview series for a couple of associations; both are centered around experts in two different industries, and I look at these series as my six hours a month to be a student.

- **Engage in child's play.** Playing video games is a fun way to peek into the future. It's especially great if you can play them with kids, because they adapt to and integrate technology better than adults do. Teenagers especially can teach us how to embrace the new as they introduce us to the most recent trends and technologies. You can even play games with players in other cities and countries through Internet connections. I played a game on Xbox 360 with my son and several youngsters from around the world. I was impressed with these kids' mastery of such sophisticated technology and how they learn to strategize collaboratively and act on their decisions in a fun learning environment.

- **Study great thinkers.** If you want to see our world with a fresh perspective, study the thoughts, values, and ideals of great thinkers, both past and present. Doing so can help you formulate innovative ways to approach your everyday life. I suggest that you read the first-person writing of great thinkers when possible or those of a person who worked side by side with the individual. This way you're getting the closest to the real information instead of an interpretation. One caveat, however, is that many authors write about experts that they have never met in person. This means you want to be mindful that you could be reading an author's assumptions and biases rather than about facts and reality.

- **Watch "junk."** Many of us remember our parents telling us to shut off the TV and go outside to play. And while we needed the time outside, today's world of TV has the power to teach us much more than we often give it credit for. How many world leaders have you met in person? Have you ever traveled to the Amazon or Australian outback or to the many wonders of the world? Yet we've all been exposed to many of these learning experiences through the portal of television. Now, the Internet with its YouTube videos and various podcasts offer even more opportunities for us to learn about faraway places and inspirational or historically significant people. I recommend Ted.com as one of the many excellent online sources for gaining awareness and in-depth knowledge.

- **Confirm the facts.** Studies, scientists, experts, and trade statistics are just a handful of the learning sources that we tend to believe without vetting them for factuality. We instantly assume that some sources are credible, because they've received a stamp of approval from a government, a prominent person, or a regulatory commission of one sort or another. But you have to be careful not to make your decisions based on unconfirmed data. For example, in November 2009, the world learned that the UN Intergovernmental Panel on Climate Change[79] had been releasing research findings that supported a dangerous trend of global climate warming. The panel had been making predictions based on unconfirmed stats they had received from various environmental groups about climate changes in places like the Himalayan glaciers and the Amazon forest and the world bought into those claims. (Note: This is not a statement about climate change; it's about awareness and leadership.)

■ ■ ■

My hope is that you leave this chapter with a better understanding that your role as a leader requires that you are perpetually and actively engaged in acquiring awareness and knowledge, because learning by default does little to improve a leader's decision making. You are taking away some new tools that will help you become both a better learner and teacher. Using these tools will expedite your learning, assist you in managing the information overload, and give you the mental fodder to identify and create new solutions and opportunities.

As you go about your day-to-day from now on, keep in mind the distinction between surface-level awareness and in-depth knowledge. Both of these are valuable to you as a leader, but remember that most leaders spend too much time on becoming aware and not enough time developing knowledge, a necessity when you want to effect transformation that advances your organization.

ENHANCING GLOBAL AWARENESS

THE MOMENT YOU TURNED TO this page, you formed an opinion of this chapter that quite possibly doesn't have a whole lot to do with what you're about to read. Your life experiences up to this point determined whether you thought, "This should be interesting," "I don't think I need this," or, "What does this even mean?" Realizing that every reader would bring his or her own impressions to the chapter, I knew when I wrote it that I would have to quickly convince you of the importance that global awareness plays in your life, because contrary to the misconceptions out there, being globally aware isn't an option reserved for executives at worldwide companies; enhancing global awareness is an essential activity that *every* decision maker must perform to keep pace in today's world.

Whether you're an entrepreneur who works alone or a franchisee who juggles a chain of restaurants, your level of awareness regarding how people, places, and things globally interconnect with you and your organization will impact the decisions you make. Take, for instance, Oscar, the small-business owner who has spent most of his life in a rural New England community. In the 1960s, he served in the U.S. Army, and in the 1970s bought a roofing business. Like many Americans of his generation, he threw his support behind American manufacturing whenever possible, buying American-made products like vehicles and supplies for his business.

To be certain, Oscar has always known that he has choices. As a lover of history and politics, he is equally informed about current events affecting his community, country, and the world at large, even holding a position in local government. However intelligent and well-informed he has been, Oscar, like many organizational leaders, was in business for several years before he

experienced an "aha moment" about the connection between global awareness and its impact on his decision making.

The connection has increasingly grown from "aha" moments, like the time
he told a customer that he offered only American-produced shingles when
she expressed an interest in some Canadian shingles she had seen. Moments
later, when he opened the door of his truck to get an item from its cab, the
customer inquired if he always bought American-made trucks. When he said
yes, she pointed to a sticker on the door that read, "Assembled in Canada."
After Oscar and his customer had a little laugh at his expense, he told her that
she could have her pick of any Canadian-manufactured shingle she wanted.
When this particular job was completed, he realized that the Canadian shingles were of higher quality at the time, and he used them on future jobs. Over
the years, he has ordered other high-quality, lower-cost items like sheet metal
from within and outside the United States to keep his business competitive
and his customers happy. Global factors creep into every organization; they
always have, and they always will.

Notice that when you read about the business owner's gradual connection
of the world to his business that at no time did you see that he was interested
in "going global" or expanding his business in any way beyond the community
where he lived. Yet his degree of global awareness affected how he led his organization. This point highlights the confusion about global awareness that exists
among leaders everywhere. Being globally aware is not about your organization's reach—whether your Desired Outcome is to have local, regional, domestic, international, multinational, or a global presence—it's about expanding
and enriching your thinking with real and current information about opportunities, solutions, and challenges that exist or that can be created.

Based on my experiences with a wide range of leaders worldwide, I believe
that you are already globally aware to some degree, but chances are, you're
not as globally aware as you could be, and you might not be as sure of how
to improve in this area as you would like. This chapter will give you the
tools and knowledge you need to enhance your global awareness, which will
expand your perspective, improve your ability to lead, and help you bring
more opportunities to your organization.

What Does It Mean to Be "Globally Aware"?

You don't need to be an expert in global affairs to be globally aware. In fact,
broadening and deepening your global awareness can be quite simple when

you know what to do. Here you will learn to shift your focus to four topic areas that will inform your decisions and create better outcomes.

Think of global awareness as the companion to the 360° view that you have of your organization; global awareness's external view completes the big picture. For instance, how might a political election, a crop failure, or an emerging technology from your region or from another part of the world impact the plans you have in place right now?

You can read any newspaper or news feed right now and find some of your next potential challenges, but that's only part of the equation. The other is to *connect* that information to your organization and *use* it to gain and maintain a position of strength now and in the future.

The Connection between Global Awareness and Career Growth

Global awareness will concurrently multiply your career options and opportunities. It is the raw material for connecting dots, creating new knowledge, and making strategically advantageous decisions—three essential components of those Wildly Successful Projects (WSPs) that enable you to prove yourself to others or to help you achieve a more fulfilling life.

As the world speeds up, you'll be forced to create opportunities, not just work off the ones that already exist. This is a reality for every decision maker, whether you're embarking on your career, grooming a successor before you retire, or managing a career that's somewhere in between these stages. Leaders who have the best mental tools, who can use those tools adeptly and creatively, and who continuously stay abreast of the external factors that can influence their careers and organizations will work from the greatest positions of strength.

Peter Felix, president of the Association of Executive Search Consultants, stated in 2010 that "leadership today is at a premium since organizations cannot ignore the challenges of new competition, evolving technology, industry convergence and globalization."[80] In addition, the firm reported in its midyear 2011 report that "the General Management/CEO/COO function is expected to see the greatest shortage of talent worldwide in the second half of 2011," and that emerging markets like Brazil, India, and China would see the largest deficiencies in executive talent.[81] Globally, the highest demand is for executives who have global awareness and experience. It makes sense when you consider how rapidly organizations worldwide are growing and how much more interconnected we all are.

For example, have you ever considered how the citizenship in a city like London or New York is a microcosm of the world? They're melting pots of diverse peoples from Brazil, Hungary, Italy, Korea, etc. The better their mayors understand the range of needs, values, and expectations of their culturally diverse populace, the more likely they are to make smarter decisions that provide better services to all citizens. Constituents reap the benefits of having globally aware leaders, and the mayors earn WSPs that they can use to sell themselves at a time in the future to advance their careers.

Say that you are a school administrator who wants to increase enrollment. You can use global awareness to reach out to a multinational market through exchange-student programs, or you can appeal to local prospects by copying an educational program used by a neighboring region's school system to graduate more of the students you already have.

You don't have to be in a management position to use global awareness to advance your abilities and career. In the past, physicians served the patients in their local communities. Today, physicians don't have to be in the same room, the same building, the same country, or even on the same continent to treat patients. On September 7, 2001, two surgeons in a New York City hospital used the robotic ZEUS Surgical System to remove the gallbladder of a woman who lay in an operating room of a Strasbourg, France, hospital.[82] This first transatlantic telesurgery, named the Lindbergh Operation after the first transatlantic flight pilot Charles Lindberg, shows that today's technologies and telecommunications are available for many types of global corroborations. Now it's just a matter of leaders in all industries and sectors setting their sights on acquiring a global mindset to identify, envision, and create opportunities that will advance individual organizations. You can adopt ideas, technologies, techniques, and solutions from other parts of the world or combine them with your own, but you've got to become aware of them first.

Do you study the ways that people in other parts of the world have solved their challenges so that you might borrow and apply their solutions to your own? Have you considered how changing weather patterns, fast-evolving societies, or emerging technologies in one part of the world will affect you, your suppliers, or your customers?

Global awareness is a key component to selling yourself and your ideas—not just in terms of WSPs and a track record of success—but also in face-to-face interactions. Not only does global awareness help you to negotiate better terms or gain buy-in, but being globally aware can enable you to bypass a range of barriers to entering new markets, working successfully with a diverse staff, and forging new relationships with all types of stakeholders. You'll be more successful if you're not just learning about others, but are also understanding the impression you are making on them. The more you know, the less likely you will be to offend others by standing too close to them, dressing too casually for their tastes, sending them roses when that particular flower is considered bad luck, or extending an invitation to a power breakfast to someone who frowns upon it.

If you do travel to countries or regions where the culture is not your own, having a global awareness will help you plan your itinerary around the host country's holidays, climate extremes (monsoons, hurricanes, etc.), special events, and other factors that may be foreign to you. Time and money can be saved by planning at a time that accommodates both parties, and you will likely make a better impression on the person you plan to visit.

When you are globally aware, you build knowledge stores that you can draw upon at any time, whether you're planning a future project or event, or find yourself unexpectedly caught in a present situation that requires your immediate response. In either instance, you can pro-act and react in ways that put you at an advantage and keep you there.

Global Awareness Improves Decision Making

Globally aware leaders make more effective CST plans for their organizations, choose projects that will more rapidly advance their organizations, create more options by working effectively with diversity, establish more productive alliances, identify and implement more appropriate technologies, forecast future challenges and opportunities more accurately, etc., to create and sustain more promising futures for their organizations. This is because they have broadened their scope of vision to identify not only opportunities and challenges, but to see, capture, and create options to address them.

A European businessman wanted to take his transportation company into Japan, but he was aware that an insurmountable obstacle stood in his way. The "players" in the Japanese market were a tight-knit group of men who had grown up together; their beliefs and values were shaped by their Japanese culture, they shared a lifetime of similar experiences, they were of the same social class, and they had a bond of trust and comradery that no outsider could penetrate. Rather than attempt to force his way through this cultural brick wall, he forged an alliance with a Japanese colleague who already had an "in" within this arena and who would be a trustworthy associate, instantly overcoming the barrier and entering the market.

Global-minded thinking leads to better decision making about all aspects of an organization, from marketing to hiring to operational procedures to new product development and more, whether you're running a mom-and-pop ice cream shop, a regional emergency-services nonprofit, or a worldwide corporation. Take, for instance, how one firm uses data about customer buying preferences to position sales staff in different locations. If you've traveled by plane, you've probably seen the Duty Free Shops (DFS) Group Limited logo on duty-free retail shops in airports and destination points around the world. The global business—which is even bigger than most people realize, with as many as ten additional retailers associated with this umbrella brand but not operating under the DFS name—owes its success to the global mindedness of its leadership. Michael Schriver, president of the company's Worldwide Store Operations, expressed in a conversation with me that understanding the buying preferences of Chinese versus Japanese customers drives some of management's decisions. Schriver explained that a purchasing difference between Japanese and Chinese customers is really a metal color preference. Japanese customers prefer platinum due to its perceived quality and durability. Likewise, in terms of metal color, they prefer white gold or platinum. Chinese customers, on the other hand, prefer yellow or rose gold. This affects each groups' choice of watches. The Japanese opt for sport watch models in stainless or white gold, while the Chinese opt for dressier styles in yellow or rose gold. In some cases, Chinese customers opt for two-tone or a combination of yellow and white gold or yellow gold and stainless.[83] This detailed information about customer preferences enables Schriver and his team to align associates who have certain language skills with the appropriate brand locations, such as concentrating Mandarin-speaking staff in their OMEGA boutiques and positioning Japanese-speaking staff at a brand like TAG Heuer.

On the flip side of the coin, not being globally aware can lead to mistakes that set your organization back. When one of the largest big-box retailers in the world entered Brazil, executives were unprepared for the resistance they would meet from locals who opposed the retailer's tactics to keep prices low. Instead of earning consumers' trust beforehand, the leadership went in somewhat blind and had a more difficult time attaining loyal customers in that country. This retailer also did the same for other countries such as Korea and Germany. In response, Nelson Fraiman from Columbia Business School commented, "Little details do matter. If a country like Germany doesn't like to smile, then don't smile when you say 'have a good day.' Little details are what usually kill American companies that forget to pay attention."[84] In today's world, globally unaware leaders will increasingly struggle to be successful.

But perhaps you don't run a multinational company. Maybe you manage an organization with a local scope. Global awareness will enable you to catch any changes on the horizon that could hinder your organization's ability to function normally or that could give you an edge in your local area. Being globally aware means that you learn about more options, and you can borrow the ideas and technologies that have brought success to other organizations, whether they do what yours does or not.

Say that you own a small business selling lawn mowers and tractors in Port Shepstone, South Africa. Your two nearest competitors are another mom-and-pop shop like yours and an internationally branded John Deere dealership two miles down the road. In the past, you might have guessed at what customers want from you and listed those services in the phone book and the local paper. Today, when you wonder how to attract more business, you look into different options. You don't have the R&D budget of a John Deere, but you can peruse its website and make some logical conclusions about what consumers of lawn mowers and tractors want. Perhaps you find that Deere's customers can book their own service appointments online. Right away, you can upgrade your site to offer the same convenience to your customers.

Even the route you take to enhancing your website can produce better outcomes when you're globally aware. For instance, since you're somewhat globally aware, you look outside Port Shepstone for a webmaster who can equip your site with the technology needed for online appointment book-ings, and you find one in Slovakia through an Internet-based company that matches freelancers to people in need of graphic-art services. Through the same site, you find a graphic artist in Argentina to design your next newspa-per advertisement, and this person's international perspective beefs up your ad beyond what the graphic artists at your local newspaper are doing for your competition. You are still reaching local customers, but now you're using the tools and options of the global landscape to do it better than before.

William Fung, managing director of Li & Fung,[85] attributes his firm's $14 billion a year "flat-world success" (a term coined from Tom Friedman's book *The World Is Flat* to describe how globalization has leveled the field in our global marketplace) to understanding that old-fashioned infrastructure has been replaced by exciting options of a global arena, where players can get any product or service twenty-four hours a day. Because of leadership's global perspective, the Asian company can reach way beyond its geographic borders to make use of designers, distributors, and manufacturers globally and accelerate its ability to manage supply chains for its worldwide customer base.

In addition to reaching outside your organization for the advantages of global awareness, you can build a culturally diverse staff from within. A diverse staff will bring many perspectives to the table and enable leadership to make more informed decisions. Two Americans and two Malaysians were dining together one evening when one of the Malaysians commented how a Malaysian will work a half a year to afford a cell phone. The American's gut reaction was, "That's so sad," but the Malaysian explained that in his home country, having a cell phone carried such a high level of prestige that working six months to have one wasn't considered sad at all; it was worth it—two cultures, two very different perspectives.

Think about how you can expand your options by working with a diverse staff. No matter what products you sell or services you provide, and regardless of whether you stay local or go international, if you keep lessons like this in mind, you are more likely to question your beliefs, see many of them as opinions and assumptions, and to challenge yourself with questions such as, "Is there a better way to reach others?"

At the leadership level, global awareness is no longer an extra advantage; it's a necessity. We've already discussed how being globally aware helps you earn and keep your job, but organizationally, you will increasingly need globally aware leaders on staff to keep your organization competitive. As *Wall Street Journal* management news editor Joann Lublin describes, "In rapidly growing countries such as Brazil, China, and India, tapping expatriates is becoming obsolete. Instead, global businesses are looking for leaders who have the ability to move easily between different cultures and have deep local roots as well as international operational experience."[86] Because the aging workforce will soon leave a huge gap in the availability of experienced leaders, you'll soon need to recruit from among the best worldwide or develop leadership using training and lessons from others globally. Do you currently have a hiring procedure that screens the best globally aware thinkers from the average? To stay ahead of this trend (and many others too numerous to list here), you might want to think about developing one.

Without a good grasp on global issues, you're more likely to churn out lower-than-desirable performance levels as you perform the other eleven ET activities, too. That's because global awareness is a piece of the ET puzzle that acts as a turbocharger that improves decision making as you perform all of your leadership activities.

How Global Awareness Turbocharges the Enterprise Thinker

Daniel Daswani is a master tailor and owner of a custom suit shop in Hong Kong. From an outsider's perspective, Daswani appears to be a local small-business merchant who could probably survive just fine without being globally aware. A closer look into Daniel Fashions' operations, however, reveals just the opposite. First, the store services a globally diverse client base, and Daswani, an American citizen born to parents from India and who was raised in Hong Kong, understands that winning over clients involves more than accurate measurements and snazzy suits; it's about knowing how clients' cultures drive their preferences for suits' styles and fabrics, too.

In addition to understanding diverse peoples, in order for Daniel Fashions to keep Order Winner fabrics in stock, Daswani must constantly be aware of events that impact his fabric supplies—from shortages in cotton driven by weather and natural disasters, to fluctuating prices of raw goods resulting from political activities or industry-related trends. Being globally aware informs Daswani's decisions to select appropriate vendors from around the world and establish alliances with them to keep his options open not just when shortages occur, but at all other times to keep stock of high-quality fabrics that please his clients and maintain his profit margins.

For Daswani and leaders like him, the 50,000-foot view of his world is as important as the one of his organization. His global awareness enables him to perform the Strategizing, Forecasting, Performing, and Learning activities better, producing higher returns for his business. Figure 8.1 illustrates the turbocharge effect that global awareness has on leadership performance. Even the slightest enhancement of your global awareness will positively impact your effectiveness as a leader.

Adding global awareness to your daily activities—from selecting and implementing technology to creating winning products and services—is like dumping a fuel additive into the gas tank of a race car. The outcomes are better and you might even get to them faster.

For example, think about the phases of building an alliance: Ideation, Elimination, and Development. During Ideation, you can do a *good* job collecting the names of prospective allies early on, but as you widen the mouth of the funnel to include more and better-suited names (possibly from beyond your geographic borders or your industry), you increase the likelihood of doing a *great* job of finding your best ally. Screening criteria in Elimination can take your search results from adequate to win-by-a-nose (or greater) margins when you incorporate lessons and ideas from other industries, technologies, politics, etc. Furthermore, when you better understand the morés, values, and business-practice preferences of your allies during Development, you are increasingly apt to negotiate contributions and draws that produce win-win outcomes for all parties.

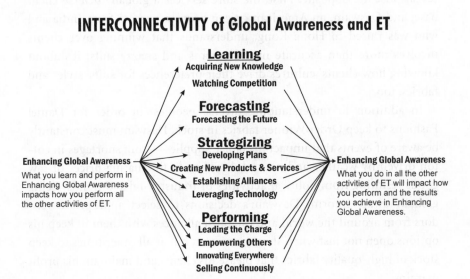

INTERCONNECTIVITY of Global Awareness and ET

Figure 8.1—Interconnectivity of Global Awareness and ET

Imagine the effects that global awareness can have on organizations when multiple activities are being performed by multiple decision makers simultaneously. Now, look at the right side of the InterCONNECTIVITY diagram (Figure 8.1) and think about how the other eleven ET activities can be used to enhance global awareness even further. For instance, you can leverage technology to help you to be globally aware faster by using an aggregator to collect content from the Web about your industry, countries you want to sell to, or for human resources data from around the world. You can program RSS feeds right to your desktop, tablet, or phone so that you don't have to search for the information. Every morning, the information is right there. As you (and others in your leadership group) become more proficient at interconnecting the twelve activities in this way, your organization can make improvements by leaps and bounds in no time at all.

The Approach to Becoming Globally Aware

Once you realize that you need to be (more) globally aware, the next question becomes how. This isn't so easy to answer. In fact, I've asked this question of executives around the world, and they give me the same answers: work in a country and travel. This is not how a person becomes globally aware. I know people who have traveled but are not globally aware at all. Some of these people have actually lived in a country (one in particular for almost fifteen years), and they can't speak but a few words of the "foreign" country's language.

Instead, I recommend that you engage in various types of activities with your staff members that focus your minds on becoming more globally aware. For example, you could hold weekly meetings, perhaps in a casual atmosphere like sharing lunch, where a person or two could bring a news story, a new invention, information about a cultural practice, or something that is interesting to the group. Then the group uses the topic to trigger ideas related to improving some aspect of your organization. This can be not only useful, but fun.

Already you can assume that reading a daily news feed or newspaper or watching news programs can help, but how can you be sure that you're getting the information you need? Furthermore, once you have the information, do you really know how to connect it to your organization for better decision making? I realize that it's far easier to say you should be globally aware than to actually become globally aware, which is why I have provided you with a tool that you can use to expand your thinking. In this section, you will learn about a simple yet effective approach to enhancing your global awareness, diagrammed here as the Roadmap to Global Awareness (Figure 8.2).

Looking at the bottom of the diagram first, notice the actual process that occurs in your mind (as represented by the three rectangular boxes). First, you Receive Global Information, which makes you Become More Globally Aware. Simultaneously, you Develop a Broader Perspective, which may or may not cause you to identify more global information that feeds into the cycle. The purpose, of course, is to Apply New Awareness to your daily ET activities so that you more surely and successfully reach Desired Outcomes.

The Four Components of Global Information

Let's go back to the top of the diagram and discuss the types of information that you need to be thinking about. When you hear the term "global

Roadmap to Global Awareness

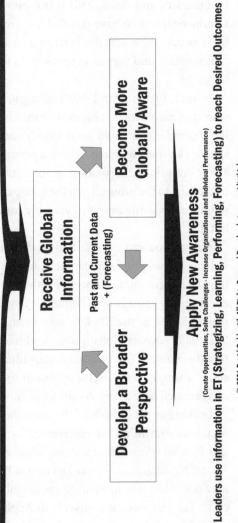

Humans & Living Creatures

Information pertaining to the differences between individuals/living creatures: Customs, Race, Religion, Beliefs, Values, Assumptions, Attitude, Family, Generations, History, Disease, Geography, Age, Creed, Color, Rituals, Height, Leisure, Disabilities, Genetics, Arts, Sex, Ecosystems, Modality, Size, Birthrate, Language, Species, Strength Adaptability, Life Expectancy, etc.

Physical Environments

Information pertaining to the universe: Land, Sea, Air, Planets, Chemistry, Climate, Nature, Physics, Resources, Time Zones, Plants, Geology, Weather, Acts of Nature, Seasons, Currents, Daylight/Night, Ecosystems, Wildlife, Temperature, Coastlines, Underground Resources, Minerals, Sun, Moon, Scarcity, Location, Force, Atoms, Space, Soil Composition, etc.

Governances

Information pertaining to the manner in which groups live and work together, including: Individuals, Groups, Societies, Geopolitics, Governments, Politics, Rules, Laws, Regulations, Policy, Economics, Structures, Individualism/Collectivism, Networks, Military, Countries, Regions, Borders, Taxation, Punishment, Alliances, Intelligence, Military, Social Policy, etc.

Technologies

Information pertaining to the technologies used and available in the universe: Business Practices, Supply Chain, Assembly, Financial, Weaponry, Infrastructure, Tools, Models, Fashion, Methodologies, Housing, Patents, R&D, Trademarks, Transportation, Food, Education, Energy, Nano, Health Care, Communications, Polymers, Sewage, Entertainment, Mathematics, etc.

Receive Global Information

Past and Current Data + (Forecasting)

Become More Globally Aware

Develop a Broader Perspective

Apply New Awareness

(Create Opportunities, Solve Challenges - Increase Organizational and Individual Performance)

Leaders use information in ET (Strategizing, Learning, Performing, Forecasting) to reach Desired Outcomes

Figure 8.2—Roadmap to Global Awareness

awareness," it is easy to conjure up an image of the globe and to assume that the topic is about the differences among peoples originating from specific geographic areas. In reality, however, global awareness encompasses four topic areas: humans and living creatures, physical environments, governances, and technologies. When you place your information-gathering focus on these areas, your mind will almost instantaneously begin to swoop relevant information into Cyclonic Thinking.

Humans and Living Creatures

Humans and living creatures impact all our lives in countless positive and negative ways, and some more subtly than we realize. For instance, did you know that if you have a leg ulcer that won't heal, you can get an effective prescription from your doctor for a wound dressing infused with Manuka honey, an antimicrobial honey made by bees in New Zealand that has been shown to speed up healing time?[87] On the downside, you might not initially see how a single bird could impact your life, but if that bird contracts the avian flu virus and makes its way into your food supply, industries and lives could be at stake.

On the human side, understanding our differences is a good starting point for finding common ground with people from all walks of life. To be clear, there are assumptions to overcome. Perhaps one of the most misleading assumptions of all is that diversity and global awareness are one and the same. They are not. Diversity is just one of the four components of global awareness. I want to make this distinction clear so that you don't focus only on diversity of people and believe you're gathering all the information you need to be globally aware. You still need to learn about physical factors, geopolitical and legal issues, and technologies and trends to round out the big-picture view.

Despite advancements in communications and increased international travel, the majority of people still see the world through the lens of their personal points of view. Before you can make room for learning about others, it's important that you learn about yourself—your assumptions, stereotypes, and preconceptions about people who are different than you—so that these factors don't become barriers to new opportunities. So let's clear the clutter that can prevent you from becoming more globally aware.

You can feel challenged enough to work collaboratively with people who share the *same* cultural background as you, so it can be even more challenging to find common ground with people of different backgrounds. Yet as our world becomes smaller, and we are increasingly finding ourselves working with people whose roots are from other parts of the world, we need certain knowledge and skills to help us navigate cross-cultural relationships with both internal and external parties more now than ever before.

One difference that leaders must learn to manage is preferences for working relationships—specifically, individual versus collective styles—that can be barriers to effective alliances, project management, and other cross-cultural endeavors. As Michael F. Tucker,[88] a personal acquaintance and 40-year expert in international and global HR issues describes in his publication *Applied Project Management for Space Systems,* the individualist is a person who prefers to take matters into his own hands and tends to make decisions without much input from others in contrast to the collectivist, who strives for group involvement and cooperation and puts the interests of the group above any single individual in the group.

Depending on the cultural roots of the person with whom you are working, you will find they have a preference for working individually or collectively, which may or may not be your preference. It's important to understand your own preferences, then to be aware of how they may or may not work in sync with others at different times.

The awareness of these preferences combined with knowing cultures helps you to become a better collaborator, because collaboration requires that you balance a coworker's or ally's style preferences for structure, trust, and values with your own to achieve mutually Desired Outcomes. So if you are from New Zealand and you are working with two allies, one from America and the other from Japan, you will be able to work more collaboratively with both of them, because you will understand that your American colleague tends to be more individualistic and your Japanese colleague prefers a more collectivist working relationship.

Even the smallest of differences in personalities and cultures can threaten business and working relationships or deals. In the aforementioned *Applied Project Management for Space Systems,* Tucker highlights how you can still work collaboratively through these differences by trying to find common ground on open-mindedness, flexibility, social adaptability, patience, and trust.

There are organizations that specialize in intercultural relationships and can provide you with the insight you may need to become more globally aware: SIETAR is the Society of Intercultural Education, Training and Research; IAIR is the International Academy for Intercultural Research; and the IJIR is a journal titled the *International Journal of Intercultural Relations.*

Other diversity issues can stem from generational differences within certain geographic boundaries. You can share a background with someone and still seem miles apart on your ideas, values, and aspirations, because you were born decades apart. Generational boundaries in the United States take on names like Generation X and Generation Y. People born between 1980 and 1989 under the People's Republic of China's one-child policy are known as the Little Emperors[89] for how their optimism and consumerism contrast to previous generations'. In India, you see clear distinctions between the loyalists born in the 1930s and 1940s and the "boomers" born after 1960 who associated success with leaving India and traditional Indian society. Generational divides span different generations, have different cutoff years, and carry different definitions, depending on who you are. Recognizing the differences can help you make better decisions.

For example, the innovation manager of a small thirty-person business once commented in the same conversation about a benefit and a disadvantage of two different generations, "If I give a challenge to a forty-something person, they want to sit around and talk about it while a twenty-year-old will within minutes tell me there's already a tool online to do what we want and fifteen minutes later they could be up and running." And then a few minutes later he summarized the younger generation's overall job performance based on criteria unrelated to technology as, "not [having] the same work ethic as the older group," even though they were very digitally inclined.

His quick jump to judgment is something you want to be cautious about, whether you're looking at a generational divide or a cultural one. What this innovation manager left out of the equation was the fact that the younger generation that he perceived as lacking a work ethic is approaching life with a different perspective. Keep in mind that broad, sweeping generalizations can cause your view to become narrow and myopic. Try to find where your ideas might be too limiting and to expand them. Case in point: in the United States, the generation of kids born between 1990 and 2000 have seen their parents work long hours to reach a "comfortable" standard of living, only to lose their jobs and watch their lives tumble backward within months. It would be safe to say that many members of this younger generation are asking different questions than their predecessors. Some youth in countries hard hit by the recession in regions such as Europe and the United States consider the comfortable standard of living to be a pipe dream, and these individuals are inclined to ask, Is it worth it?

While there is some fact to these observations, be mindful that these are not universal truths. Other youth do not feel this way, and regarding those who do share these perceptions, many will change their points of view over time. Their perceptions are not much different than those held by their once-hippie grandparents who were considered the free-living generation in the world of sex, drugs, and rock and roll in the United States during the 1960s and 1970s. And just as the grandparents' viewpoints evolved to where their generation ended up becoming the capitalistic builders and growers for the U.S. economy over the next few decades, so too may our current younger generation's thinking experience a similar evolution.

Generational differences, like any other diversity factors, can pose a threat to working successfully with others, and they can be clues to improving the relationships that you already have, which is why it is important to understand why groups of people collectively think the way that they do. When you're working with people of differing political ideals, languages, and religions, you want to know as much about them as you can so that you can appeal to their preferences, respect them, and develop rapport.

If you were to take a hundred people and divide them up into groups that reflect world population sizes, there would be 60 people from Asia, 15 from Africa, 11 from Europe, 9 from Latin America and the Caribbean, and 5 from North America. And how would you communicate with them? Twelve speak Chinese, 5 speak Spanish, 3 Arabic, 3 Hindi, 3 Bengali, 3 Portuguese, 2 Russian, 2 Japanese, and 62 speak other languages. Already, with this[90] limited amount of information, one's perspective changes and affects how they make decisions.

In addition, cultural differences and acceptances are opportunities for you to borrow and use ideas to improve your organization, its products, and its services. In Eastern Europe, people eat cut-up cartilage from animals' ears the way that Americans eat potato chips. If you're a food manufacturer who is looking to develop and launch a new food on the market, what other types of foods could you create that can be eaten like cartilage or potato chips? Having people on staff with different cultural backgrounds who are accepting of unexpected ways of thinking can provide you with a multitude of ideas and options.

Furthermore, if you are working with people from different backgrounds and socially accepted customs, be sure that you have an understanding of morés, acceptable forms of dress, customs, and norms that can make or break your dealings with them. You don't want to show up to a business meeting with Westerners dressed in sandals that are acceptable only to some Easterners. You also don't want to try to get down to business with people you don't know the minute you walk into a meeting if you're working with people who will only talk business with colleagues they have a relationship with and can trust.

Try to look at the people in this world from a figurative 50,000-foot view to broaden your global awareness and strengthen your organization's ability to compete and win.

Physical Environments

Our world is so intricately interconnected that global happenings—from weather patterns, natural disasters, and even time-zone changes—have an impact on various aspects of our lives and work. This reality applies equally to the world traveler as much as it does for the person who has never traveled beyond the borders of their home town. Though you might not recognize those influences all the time, they're there, determining the software on your computer, the engine in your car, the flu outbreak in your town, and the challenges on your mind.

Think back to how Daniel Daswani, the master tailor in Hong Kong, used his awareness of cotton crops' successful and unsuccessful harvests as compasses for selecting his vendors and stocking fine fabrics for his clients. Leaders are and will continue to be affected by global happenings either directly or indirectly, and those who take a proactive approach to working with and around those influences will position their organizations more strongly.

Look anywhere in the world to see how physical factors shape decision makers' strategies and tactics. In the past, cities arose along coastlines due to the prevalence of water-related travel and shipping. Today, a natural disaster's effects are not restricted to the residents of its geographic location. They have an increasingly negative impact on people and markets worldwide, too. An earthquake in Haiti might limit mango exports to Europe, prompting Belgian grocers to seek out new suppliers of the tropical fruit. Flooding in Thailand produces hard-drive shortages around the world. An earthquake and tsunami in Japan causes German decision makers to wind down nuclear facilities. Every part of the world affects another, which is why you must identify the challenges out there and convert them to wins.

Governances

Do you give much thought to the ways in which laws and political events from continents away are affecting your organization's present and future? Russia's trade embargo halts incoming shipments of wine from neighboring Georgia, forcing South Caucasus wine growers to seek new markets. India opens a 25-million-carat diamond mine, putting pressure on Canadian competitors to improve their marketing and sales, operational efficiencies, strategic alliances, and more. Any business seeking to enter certain markets must adhere to strict commerce laws and policies to avoid costly mistakes that jeopardize desired outcomes. Keeping abreast of geopolitical and legal issues is an effective way of heading off challenges before they happen and of creating new opportunities on the horizon.

A friend of mine set up a warehouse in India, and at the time was told he must hire local "unionized" workers, or Maharashtra. The businessman thought he had followed proper procedure when he hired eighteen workers, but when he was shut down—two times—for hiring violations, he finally learned that Maharashtra didn't just pertain to the union; it meant that a person's lineage in that geographic region goes back several generations. He's extremely globally aware and he's still learning. You really have to do your homework to reach your Desired Outcome.

Realistically, not every law or rule being made on the other side of the planet is going to change aspects of your organization. However, that doesn't mean that you can't learn from geopolitical and legal happenings in your community or from other parts of the world and use your awareness to do your job better. For example, when a friend of mine moved from Finland to the United States, he brought some interesting perspectives with him. One nugget of information that I will never forget was his account of how simple income tax preparation was in Finland as compared to how it is in the United States. In Chris's words, "Every year, when it was time to do tax returns, the government (without me having done anything) sent an extremely easy-to-understand form to me with a calculated suggestion on what all my taxes (pension, social security) were. [Because] I could not believe it worked, I went to a tax advisor two years in a row to get it checked out, and every time, it was the right amount, down to the euro. All you had to do is to sign it, put it into a prepaid envelope, and send it back. A tax return done in two minutes [a] year!" Imagine how many organizations could better service their customers, patrons, vendors, volunteers, or constituents if they learned about similar efficiencies from their global neighbors and implemented them locally. Global awareness opens up options for your Strategizing, Learning, Performing, and Forecasting, because you now have seen others achieve what you may not have considered.

The ideas that you hold in your mind as universal truths may often be just beliefs of your culture. Rethink, and look at yourself with a new eye to see where your beliefs, legal parameters, and political sympathies may be limiting your ability to make the best decisions for your organization. Then seek to advance your thinking to include ideas from other cultures that can improve your decision making.

Let's try a simple exercise to shake up your thinking a bit. Take a look at Figure 8.3 and see how long it takes you to figure out what it represents.

World Map

Figure 8.3—World Map

The number of seconds you spent deciphering this world map could have something to do with the location of your birth and upbringing. It's interesting to compare maps that are made in different parts of the world, because they tend to be egocentrically made. Europeans create maps that show Europe as the center of the world, the Taiwanese make maps that show the world from an Asian perspective, and so on. Whenever I hear the phrase Down Under, I can't but think, is Australia actually at the bottom of the world or is it that we've decided that the world is spinning with the North Pole at the top relative to the universe? I've been to Australia and I sure didn't feel like I was at the bottom.

Learning to accept this view of the world map is no different than reminding yourself that each governance and country has diverse laws and political beliefs that can both affect your organization and offer solutions that you can adopt to make better decisions. At times, understanding and even utilizing different ideas can be a matter of organizational survival.

In addition, realize that the boundaries that separate markets and their cultures are rapidly dissolving. If you want success in one part of the world—even if you never leave your own city or town—you must be able to elevate your perspective to a 50,000-foot global view and extend it around the globe to recognize opportunities.

┌─[Tying Components of Global Awareness Together]─────────

The idea "think globally, act locally"[91]—first conceptualized in 1915 for town planning by the Scottish activist Patrick Geddes—directs people to consider the ripple
effect that their local actions have on the world at large and to exercise responsibility
in their everyday decision making. Though the authorship of the phrase itself has
been disputed, the concept is most often linked to the idea that our actions impact
nature, and that if we're careful, we can protect and preserve the earth's natural
resources. However, modern-day leaders in business, government, education, military, and nonprofits have used the phrase to teach their people the importance of
global awareness and to remind staffers that regardless of whether the organization
is domestic, international, small or large, global ideas and practices can be adopted
to make the organization stronger.

Let's consider a new phrase: "local is global." No matter where you live and work,
whether you're in a small village or large metropolis, the global diversity of people
permeates your area. The world is becoming more and more diverse, and the playing
field is becoming more and more flat. You will build advantages into all that you do
when you can consider human diversity, all the races, religions, and cultures of your
employees, allies, and vendors, as well as when you can borrow ideas from organizations from around the globe to strengthen your own organization.

Technologies

Do you ever think about how you could take technologies or methodologies used for one purpose and unconventionally apply them for another?
In India, 81% of business leaders credit their business success to improvising new uses for existing items, techniques, and so on. The practice itself
is called *jugaad* (pronounced joo-*gahrdh*), and as IT entrepreneur Karan
Vir Singh describes, "It's like putting two spoons of turmeric powder into
your radiator if you spring a small leak. It works; it will seal the leak. In
Punjab, I have seen villagers buying an agricultural water pump at government subsidized rates, cannibalizing some other parts from here and there,
and turning it into a vehicle."[92] Just think about how powerful you or your
organization would be if you were able to direct your group with this new
type of thinking.

Encourage your people to address immediate challenges by improvising
new ways to use available resources. Global awareness provides you with the
mental data bank; all you need now is a dose of creativity. That's because
being globally aware opens the door to cross-pollinating and breeding ideas

to form new ones. Within seconds of a researcher publishing a medical report, researchers around the globe can begin to assimilate the report's contents into their own work, generate new information and knowledge, and rapidly disseminate new reports, which are then cross-pollinated with even more research findings.

The explosion of ideas and knowledge creation born of global awareness is limitless. Understanding this concept and becoming a cross-breeder yourself can be especially valuable when you're developing new products or implementing internal improvements. You probably already cross-pollinate ideas somewhat naturally, so if you make a conscious effort to do it and encourage your staffers to do it, too, your organization will benefit with many new options.

Reflect on how the Chairman of India's Tata[93] Motors strategized for world growth by considering the growing markets in Africa, China, and Southeast Asia. Exploding populations and climbing GDPs offered rich territory for a small, economical car. Tata's leadership developed a car that ships in pieces and easily snaps together once it reaches its destination. This means the car can be packaged into a much smaller space and assembled by a less skilled worker. Because the car's price tag is much lower than traditionally preassembled vehicles—$2,500 as compared to $15,000—the Tata Nano was affordable for more consumers, specifically the Indian middle class and people in lower-income-earning countries. Affordability to masses of people enabled Tata Motors to expand into more markets with ease. Tata Motor's leadership not only understood its local market inside and out, but it also leveraged its awareness of other developing markets around the world.

The Tata Motors example shows perfectly how when you develop products and services with an international market in mind, you tend to innovate and by applying those innovations—new efficiencies, new methodologies, new technologies—to existing products and product development processes, and you are more likely to end up with additional winners. Now that the snap-together car has been developed, the same applications can apply to other products and to existing products and services in all types of organizations: large/medium/small companies, single-person businesses, nonprofit agencies, government sector entities, and more.

This concept isn't just true for developing new products and services or for selling in international markets. It's also the case when you make operational improvements. You get a chance to see best practices at work by observing and learning from others on a global scale. This is not unlike applying the Finnish method of quick tax preparation to various operational efficiencies, or any other concept from different parts of our world to what you do.

Some globally influenced efficiencies and strategies, however, are bred from within as a result of diversity in the workplace. When you hire diversity, you invite different concepts to the decision-making table. The virtual melting pot of ideas can be used to ideate new and improved solutions and opportunities throughout every aspect of your organization.

Sources of Global Information

Amid all the responsibilities you have in a day and the numerous questions you ask yourself about solving your challenges, it can be easy to let the quest for global awareness become nothing more than a quick glance at the day's headlines or a few minutes of talk radio on your drive to work, but you'll want to make a greater effort than that, because leaders who continually gather updated information and incorporate it into their Cyclonic Thinking make better decisions and better plans.

So where do you look, and how do you make the most of the time you spend on this task? One of the ways that you can make the quest for global information easier on yourself is to use a tool that organizes the sources of global information by category.

Begin by imagining yourself in the world, and then expand your thinking beyond yourself to the world at large. Notice the ET Global Nesting diagram (Figure 8.4). It is a representation of where you stand in relation to the various levels of diverse groups that not only influence you but that you have the power to influence, as well. The concentric circles reach out beyond you to these influential global layers—groups, organizations, communities, territories, countries, regions, world (and one day, the universe).

As your mind flows from one stacked layer to another, you become aware of the different types of groupings that can impact you and your organization. Already you can see that if you were strategizing with a diverse group of people, this tool could help you to better tap into the intellectual capital of these individuals. You can also combine Global Nesting with subsets under the Approach to Global Awareness—humans and living creatures, physical environment, governances, and technologies—and ask your people to ideate within each layer. What do you and your staffers need to know about governances in a territory, what within the physical environment might impact your organization's offices in a particular region, and so on. Think about how you can gather new information from sources such as the media, colleagues, books, and more to expand your global awareness of each layer. All this thinking feeds and breeds new thoughts for ET.

ET Global Nesting

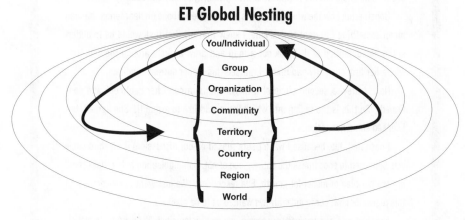

Figure 8.4—ET Global Nesting

Keep in mind that you're not just looking for differences between you and these categories of global awareness; you are looking for similarities, too. In addition, you're not just exploring groups, organizations, communities, territories, etc., to which you currently do not belong. You can expand global awareness by learning more about your *own* community or your *own* country, too.

Say that you want to start importing cocoa beans from Latin America, and you are looking for new vendors or allies. You will want to not only research the people, culture, and business practices of that region, but you will want to reflect your focus back onto yourself and find out what your prospective vendors and allies think about you, your culture, and your business practices. The awareness you acquire about yourself will allow you to strategize your approach before you ever meet them, give you the know-how to address potential barriers up front, and adapt your practices to put everyone on common ground.

[Clearing the Confusion over Vocabulary]

Ella, the head of Group Strategy for a larger lifestyle retailer, was trying to communicate to me her firm's growth strategy, but she struggled to define it. After several attempts and many minutes of conversation, Ella's tense expression eased.

[continues on page 324]

[continued from previous page]

"We want to be global," she announced. I questioned what global meant to her, because at this point her organization was primarily in only one country.

Considering how the word "global" is another one of those unclear terms that can mean something different to everyone, I knew that my first task would be to understand her definition of it. I took out a map and drew a circle around the countries where her firm currently had reach. I marked this as her current condition.

Next, I drew a second circle of a larger radius around her continent and confirmed, "So this is the region into which you would like to expand?" She agreed, but I sensed some hesitation.

I hesitated, too, because I wasn't sure (based on our discussion) if my third circle was supposed to encompass the entire globe or not. Communicating to her that I could not see her plan or model for growth, Ella responded, "We just want to concentrate on this region for now; our founder always wanted us to be global."

Aha, just as I had originally suspected; my mind interpreted "We want to go global" differently than Ella's did. To me, global was not just this particular region that Ella had outlined, it had to encompass the world. My next thought was that, if the same type of disconnect was happening throughout this 1,700-employee company, then strategy might always be a lose-by-a-nose challenge. I see this ambiguity over the definition of global everywhere.

Add terms like "multinational" and "international," and you've got a mixed bag of confusion that could be very costly to some organizations. For the record, the definitions of these terms are:

- **International:** The organization works or sells outside its home country. A website that sells its product to many countries could be considered international (as could it be multinational). "International" is not about footprint, though, it's typically about presence in markets.
- **Multinational:** The organization has representation in many nations. It might have offices in Mumbai to sell to the Indian market, offices in Genoa to sell to the Italian market, and so on. "Multinational" does not mean the organization sells around the world, although it typically holds offices in two or three locations to sell to specific regions.
- **Global:** The organization has a representation of staff around the world to allow for different types of distribution, ranging from local to multinational distributions. Organizations like Time Warner, Agilent, and Hyatt fit within the global category.

Imagine a situation where you want to recruit a senior executive to head up a division of your business. During your conversation with prospective VPs, you consistently make references to your organization "going global." A top recruit agrees to join your leadership team, comes up with a Strategy and Macro Tactics to move your organization into regions around the globe, but then after a month he realizes that you only want to expand from North America to South America. Imagine the conflicts that can arise internally and the financial consequences of this confusion to your bottom line.

To avoid miscommunicating your ideas to others, you need to be sure that everyone is on the same page when it comes to defining these terms. Otherwise, the price of mistakes may be too high to recoup.

Putting Global Awareness to Practical Use

It makes sense that someone who is worldly would already be on their way to becoming globally aware, because they have knowledge of cultures and societies and so on to give them a base. Perhaps that's a good starting point, but it's really not enough to become truly globally aware. Your learning must be continuous—reading the paper each day, interacting with diversity regularly, etc.—and active—communicate with others and be open to feedback that can erase misconceptions and false assumptions. Following are some ways that you can enhance global awareness.

Travel with Purpose

If you're in a position where you are traveling for work or pleasure, get to know the area and its people, not just the inside of an office building or conference center or touristy hot spots. Learn the weather, where people like to dine and why, what the natural resources are, when traffic is heavy or slow, what holidays are observed (and what they mean and when they occur), and really get a sense of the place before you even leave your home.

It would be easy to believe that by going on a few international trips, you will enhance global awareness, but I urge you to challenge that assumption. While it's true that travel to countries other than your own *can* contribute to global awareness, it doesn't always do so. Even people who are unencumbered by daily obligations that keep them rooted at home and work and who have the means to travel don't necessarily set out on their trips with the purpose of learning information that will improve their decision making.

Instead, the majority of work-related travelers tend to spend most of their time tied up in business meetings, so their travels take them on a closed-circuited route from airport to office building (or conference center) to hotel. Typically, if leaders do travel for pleasure, they are not talking, living, working, and otherwise engaging with the locals. More commonly, they're shopping, languishing poolside, and hitting tourist attractions. Rarely do I find organizational leaders who travel expending their energy learning about another culture and how it may one day influence them and their organizations. If you're curious about this, ask someone you know who travels a lot whether they have had a home-cooked meal in the country they've visited, how much of the language they know, and what was the last "non-touristy" thing they did while traveling. Then you'll see what I mean.

Of course, there are exceptions. Follow the example of someone like Eileen Campbell, CEO of the global research agency Millward Brown, who spends a great deal of time on the road overseeing more than seventy offices in forty-nine countries. Campbell does her homework before she ever leaves her office in order to meet the demands of her global organizations. She consults the *CIA World Factbook,* magazines like *The Economist,* her destinations' local newspapers, websites such as www.1worldglobalgifts.com that can provide her with a refresher in gift-giving protocols, and so on. Campbell has transferred the importance of global awareness to her staff, which multiplies the amount and quality of information she has at her disposal. Both Campbell and her executive assistant, Debby Stanley, may go as far as creating a dossier that also includes monetary exchange rates and current newspaper headlines. Campbell and Stanley understand the importance of having this information even before Campbell arrives at her destination, because it further enhances the information she gathers from interacting and working with the locals once her business trips are in full swing.

You can use these types of pre-travel resources to prepare yourself for your destination so your travels are productive and prosperous, and also you can use these same types of research to ramp up your own global awareness and the global awareness of fellow leaders on your staff so that you can focus your mind and energies on the Desired Outcomes you set out to achieve. The following Global Guidance & Travel Checklist will help you in accomplishing these two objectives.

Figure 8.5 Global Guidance & Travel Checklist

PRE-DEPARTURE

- ❏ Travel agents, corporate and online services
  - ○ Fees
  - ○ Secrets to purchasing travel
  - ○ Seat selection (SeatGuru.com)
  - ○ Policy
- ❏ Hotel ratings, displayed cost, and additional fees
- ❏ Currency and conversion
  - ○ Use of credit cards and fees
  - ○ International fees
  - ○ Exchange kiosks and banks
  - ○ Hidden charges in conversion
  - ○ Notifying credit card companies
  - ○ Tipping in taxis, hotels, and restaurants
- ❏ Weather, seasons, and the environment (+ / –)
  - ○ Humidity, rain, heat, sun, snow/ice
  - ○ Temperature
  - ○ Threats
  - ○ Safety procedures
- ❏ Packing requirements for women/men
- ❏ Baggage weight limits
  - ○ Fees for baggage: domestic vs. international
  - ○ Carry-on limits
  - ○ U.S. fluid policy
- ❏ Passport requirements
  - ○ Securing a visa and timing
  - ○ Procedure for entrance into a country
  - ○ Procedure for leaving a country

IN TRANSIT

- ❏ Airports and travel
- ❏ Frequent flyer sign-up
  - ○ Upgrade lists
  - ○ Alliances between airlines
- ❏ Lounges (business and first class)
  - ○ Showers
  - ○ What's free/what's not
  - ○ Credit-card access
  - ○ Speciality-card access
- ❏ Coach, business, and first-class offerings
  - ○ Leg room in exit row
  - ○ In-flight entertainment options
- ❏ Secrets to booking shorter flights
- ❏ Security checkpoints
- ❏ Traffic timetables
- ❏ Taxi/bus usage
  - ○ Hailing a cab, bus
  - ○ Paying for cab, bus
  - ○ Official vs. unofficial
- ❏ Light rail/rail/boat (Venice)
- ❏ Electrical power and converters
- ❏ Delays
- ❏ Reading/movies
- ❏ Pod sleeping facilities

ON THE GROUND

- ❏ Emergency numbers changes
- ❏ In-transit services for travel
- ❏ Traveling in groups or individually
- ❏ Political precautions
  - ○ Demonstrations, riots
- ❏ Baggage and personal belongings
  - ○ Security with hotel
  - ○ Safes
  - ○ Storage of luggage
- ❏ VAT and tipping expectations
  - ○ Taxis, restaurants, hotels, guides
- ❏ Language
  - ○ Different definitions in different cultures
  - ○ Languages spoken (primary language)
  - ○ Securing translators
  - ○ English spoken or not
- ❏ Telephone and data
  - ○ GSM, CDMA, quad-band
  - ○ Roaming fees
  - ○ Data fees
  - ○ Access to data plans
  - ○ E-mail, texting, video conferencing
- ❏ Touring and travel guides
- ❏ Finding alternative accommodations

Global Guidance & Travel Checklist Continued

PRE-DEPARTURE

- ❑ Framework for male/female behaviors
  - ○ Cultural awareness of difference
  - ○ Proper and improper activities
- ❑ Food and beverage challenges
  - ○ On planes
  - ○ In restaurants, hotels, open spaces
  - ○ Areas of concern
  - ○ Manners depending on situation
  - ○ Water challenges
- ❑ Medical information
  - ○ Insurance (travel specific or within policy)
  - ○ Shots
  - ○ Diseases
  - ○ Travel advisory
  - ○ Medicines to bring and on location
- ❑ Discount and travel cards
  - ○ Rail, boat, ferry, bus, subway
- ❑ Computer usage and Internet access
- ❑ Basic awareness of heritage, religion
- ❑ Economy and social class
  - ○ Poverty, class system, wealth
- ❑ Government, police, and military,
- ❑ Business and traditional customs
  - ○ Gifts
  - ○ Seating

IN TRANSIT

- ❑ Passport
  - ○ Frequent-visitor benefits
  - ○ Visas while traveling (personal and business)
  - ○ When to carry your passport
  - ○ Fast access cards (APEC, Global Entry)
- ❑ What's expected in downtime
  - ○ Drinking and eating expectations
- ❑ Major holidays travel advisories
- ❑ Car rentals and procedures
- ❑ Hotel recommendations
  - ○ Safety recommendations
  - ○ Pricing and fees
- ❑ Credit-card holds and final payment
- ❑ Jet lag
  - ○ Pills and medications
  - ○ Drinking on plane
  - ○ Impact of travel on others in group
- ❑ Cultural and behavioral
  - ○ Eye contact
  - ○ Asking questions
  - ○ Eating with or without utensils
- ❑ Drinking water
  - ○ Bottled or tap
  - ○ Food preparation in restaurants with water
  - ○ Airplane and ship meals using water
- ❑ Earplugs/systems
  - ○ Noise-canceling headsets
- ❑ Lost luggage

ON THE GROUND

- ❑ Currency conversion in transit
- ❑ In-country representation
  - ○ Consulate, embassy
- ❑ Electrical plugs and converters (multiuse)
- ❑ Access to over-the-counter drugs
- ❑ Local and regional news
  - ○ Television
  - ○ Newspapers
- ❑ Medical emergencies
  - ○ Hospitals
  - ○ Evacuations
  - ○ Using insurance
- ❑ Shopping
  - ○ Negotiations
  - ○ Bargains
  - ○ Safety
- ❑ Drinking water
  - ○ Bottled or tap
  - ○ Used to prepare food in restaurants, planes, ships, trains
- ❑ People you might meet
  - ○ Street, airport, cities/towns
- ❑ Local transportation fees
  - ○ Cab and cab colors
- ❑ Nightlife and entertainment
  - ○ Safe areas, scams, drug use, rape
- ❑ Police, military (Rights and privileges)
- ❑ Private security

Notice how the checklist is separated into three columns corresponding to the three phases of your travel: Pre-Departure, In Transit, and On the Ground. The checklist (in which many columns cross over to others) outlines the information you'll want to review before each trip. Preparing ahead of time can make your international travel easier and more productive. It helps if you sit down and review the secrets to great travel with others to better prepare yourself for international travel and note your findings on the checklist. For example, your travel checklist could note which countries' cabs take credit cards or where you need cash.

You also want to acquaint yourself with travel-related perks, conveniences, and efficiencies that could improve your performance on the road. I am often astounded to find international business travelers who know very little about these. A woman I met from Germany, for example, wasn't aware that her ticket status allowed her access to travel lounges where she could do her work between flights, although she had been traveling for work for eight years. Knowing how to travel more efficiently and what to expect upon arrival enables travelers to focus on the purpose of their trips and to spend extra time becoming globally aware.

Take the time to use the travel checklist before your travel. It can save you from wasting time and money later on. And be sure to share and review it with others on your staff to compound its benefits within your organization.

Maps versus Words on a Global Scale

Learning and teaching are two-way interactions. You are responsible for understanding your own learning styles and either seeking out like-minded teachers or adapting to their way of teaching. From the teaching perspective, when you are relaying information to others, try to appeal to learners who are both maps-oriented and words-oriented, so that your message is received by the people with whom you are communicating.

Of course, learning and teaching can be a challenging enough process when you're communicating with people who are like you, so you can only imagine how much more unlikely it is for two parties to get on the same page intellectually when they're separated by the boundaries of geography, politics, religion, and other cultural divides.

Chinese students who were taking a course at a well-reputed U.S. university were failed by their American professor, because he expected the students to engage in classroom discussion more often than they did. The professor interpreted the students' quietness in the classroom as apathy and lack of motivation, but his assumption couldn't be further from the truth. In reality, the students were a product of a Chinese culture that expects students to be respectful of adults and teachers, which in China means sitting quietly without talking. In China, to speak out or to question teachers or elders is perceived as disrespectful. If you're not of Chinese descent, you may wonder why the students didn't just adjust their behavior to appease their American professor. Breaking free from culturally ingrained behaviors can take a long time for some people, and it may never happen for others.

If the teacher had been both globally aware and understanding of the Maps versus Words concept, then he could have adapted portions of his curriculum to be more inclusive. Improved teaching techniques on his part would have prevented the misfortune of three of the Chinese students having to return home to their countries once their visas had expired without the much-needed business certification that they had worked so hard to gain.

That's why being aware of a concept tool like Maps versus Words can help both teachers and learners to overcome natural learning tendencies and cultural barriers. Whether you're working with a staff of people in another country, a culturally diverse workforce within your organization, or an ally who comes from a different background, consider Maps versus Words and try to find a common platform from which to work with the other party. In doing so, you can increase the odds of reaching both parties' Desired Outcomes.

Learn to Be an Aware Host

There may be times when you are faced with hosting a person or group of people who come from a country, culture, or region that is different than your own. Take this on as a project to not only be the host, but to learn from the experience. By learning about your guests' protocols, preferences, and so on, you show an interest in them, which is always great for facilitating positive relationships. It helps you when you're not playing host, too, because you can use the information that you have picked up, and then you can cross-breed it with your own ways of working and living. The extra time and energy spent on learning can produce innovative thinking, can improve operations, products and services, fund-raising, logistics, sales development, and many other aspects of your organization.

Take an Interest

Take the time to get to know people. Sometimes, just a few moments at the beginning of a meeting to have people introduce themselves is a great way to break the ice and open lines of communication.

In Chapter 7, I briefly touched on a measure I take to connect my students with one another at the beginning of each NYU semester. In essence, we go around the room and everyone introduces themselves—their name, their country, their organization, and what they expect to get from attending the class—and shares something unique that no one knows about them. (Generally, at least fifteen countries are represented in each class of sixteen to twenty students.) You don't have to go to great lengths in your meetings to do the same, but the time spent can be well worth it. In our classes, we find that by understanding each student's company, job role, accomplishments, desired outcomes, and country, we understand their perspective very quickly when they are speaking in class. Also, I find that the introduction puts students at ease and allows them to feel comfortable sharing feedback and suggestions with each other. Oftentimes, a suggestion from one student to another enables the recipient to go back to their jobs and gain a win-by-a-nose accomplishment.

How might taking an interest increase the value of your transactions with others, facilitate growth and learning, and earn WSPs on both sides? Whether your internal staff is diverse or not, how well do you know the people next to whom you work each day? Taking an interest in them could improve working relationships and increase all parties' performances.

In your instance, you might have three or four people in a room making up a pretty homogenous group. If that's the case, you can still get to know everyone, ask them to share their professional backgrounds, and to explain what assets they bring to the table. You may be surprised to discover previously unknown talents and knowledge bases that can be used cross-functionally within your organization, meaning the diversity is one of experience rather than culture. Taking an interest face-to-face is one way to learn about others. Another is to data mine it. An option is to search online to learn the extras. You can decide which method is most beneficial to you.

Be the Open-Minded Student

Being globally aware is easy to do if you know where to look, are committed to being open minded, and are willing to spend a little time accumulating information.

Although it seems like an obvious suggestion, take the few minutes each day to read some form of news that spans global issues. You will find that over time, you will begin to connect the dots of information and to formulate new awareness and knowledge about the world around you, how global happenings could impact your organization, and how you can use your newly learned information to make smarter and more proactive decisions.

The Internet has become an instant fountain of information that you can tap to discover just about anything, about just about anyone. Of course, the Internet, like all sources of information, can perpetuate mistruths, too, so if you're using it for research purposes, it's wise to occasionally confirm sources by doing a little extra homework.

Books can open your eyes about different cultures, economies, markets, and business practices. *Cross-Cultural Business Negotiations* by Donald W. Hendon[94] offers some interesting perspectives on how to work with different cultures. For example, if you want to negotiate a deal in Mexico, be prepared to establish a mutual relationship with Latino colleagues before moving into the negotiation process. But if you're preparing for the same negotiation in Germany, be ready to negotiate immediately. *The World Is Flat*, by *New York Times* columnist and Pulitzer Prize–winning author Thomas Friedman, is also an interesting read that provides valuable insight, regardless of whether you agree with some of the author's premises or not about what globalization means to all of us and our organizations.

You can also engage in other awareness-building activities such as watching foreign films, subscribing to international publications and online foreign news feeds, and talking to people from other cultures, to better communicate, negotiate, and work with global contacts. If you find yourself preparing for work-related transactions in another country, consider subscribing to an online European publication to gain insight into that culture. The broader understanding of a colleague's home country enables you to discuss more than business as usual, such as current events and how they may impact the other person. With a little effort, you can easily develop win-by-a-nose Tactics.

Learn to Speak to the World

A mother mouse is leading her young ones through a farmer's field, when a large cat suddenly leaps into their path. The mother mouse[95] stands up on her two hind legs and in her loudest voice shouts out "Bow, wow, ruff, ruff." The cat runs away in horror. The mother mouse turns to her children and says, "See the value in learning a second language?"

Learn someone else's language and doors of opportunity open. If you are fluent in more than one language, you already hold a ticket to working more effectively with others in different cultures and geographic areas, both of which will help to enhance your global awareness and attract opportunities. If you're not, you probably gained exposure to a second or third language in your schooling or in your community, and perhaps now you can develop that additional language into a tool that will help advance your organization.

I took only one year of Spanish in seventh grade, but over the course of my life, I've spoken to hundreds of people in Spanish to become conversationally fluent. While in countries where your native tongue is not the primary language, take out a pen and start to learn the words. Learning fifty words is not difficult and could change how people interact with you. A simple *ohayo* in Japanese, *jousahn* in Cantoneese, *god morgen* in Danish, and *dzien dobry* in Polish go a long way to start a connection.

You can take a course at a local university or private institution, use a computerized system, or study one-on-one with an instructor or friend in person or online. In some situations, you can learn the basics of a language along with another country's business etiquette and information about a locale.

Even when your command of a foreign language is rough, speaking to people in their native tongue is a great way to open doors and connect with others. Most people are willing to forgive grammatical slipups, but when you make no effort at all to speak their language, new contacts might take offense.

On the flip side, even when you're speaking the same language, the language can be a barrier. Especially when you're dealing with a colleague whose first language is not your own, try to keep expressions and slang to a minimum. I have a friend from the United States who nearly mastered the French language while working for months in France. But when her colleagues told jokes, she couldn't understand them and felt left out.

You might want to attempt a tactic that I call "speak international." It's when you must speak any language in a way that allows others to easily understand you. Sometimes this requires you to speak at a rate that allows others to catch your words. Other times, you have to speak in a more textbook manner, being careful not to rush or slur your speech and to avoid using contractions. Even duplicating the same phase in a few different configurations is a huge help to others. For example, I might say, "When the stars are in alignment," and then immediately follow with, "When all conditions exist for a successful outcome," so that people from other countries who may be unfamiliar with the phrase can grasp the meaning of my words without feeling left out of a conversation or misinterpreting my message, which could cause challenges later on. When you want to build relationships, small details in the way you speak can either foster or hinder progress.

Everyone Wants to Be Heard—Are You Listening?

Any time that you are working with others, whether your transaction is one-on-one or within a group, it's important that all parties feel like they are being heard, understood, or included in your directives. Otherwise, when you are ready to present your ideas, plans, and objectives to others, your words may not be taken as seriously or received as openly as you would like.

Resistance happens when people feel threatened—"I don't know your motivations and don't trust that you're looking out for my best interests"—or they feel disrespected—"Why should I listen to you if you're not interested in hearing what's important to me?" If you're not careful, relationships can quickly turn into tug-of-war battles of will, where one party figuratively tries to pull the other to their way of thinking and vice versa. An objective is to listen so that you can frame your message in a way that helps others understand you more clearly and to buy in to your ideas more cooperatively.

I was once talking with a friend who had just seen a movie about his religious group's true-life struggles to overcome prejudice and persecution more than fifty years ago, and he felt strongly that all people should see the movie to understand their tragedies. While I thought that it would be a nice idea, I also reminded him that many groups of people are struggling *today*, and most of them won't care about what happened decades ago until their current-day needs are satisfied. Will the North Vietnamese care about the plights of the Venezuelans as long as they are mired in their own challenges? Will the Somalis be of any help to the Croatians or Serbs, for that matter?

Now think about entering a new territory, embarking on a new endeavor, or commencing a new work-related relationship, and ask yourself what other people need you to hear. Ask yourself what they need from you *first*, before they can step up and meet you half way. Until you listen, your own words may fall on deaf ears.

Interact with People on Their Terms

According to Michael Soon Lee, author of *Black Belt Negotiating*, when it comes to international meetings, most people insult a counterpart within the first thirty seconds of meeting them![96] I doubt very much that insulting others is on the typical to-do lists of most decision makers.

In Eastern cultures, you are expected to have relationships with business colleagues that build over time in contrast to Western business approaches that are much more direct. A vendor in Shanghai will appreciate your asking about the photo of his family that you spot in his office, but an ally in Berlin may want to strictly talk business.

When Thomas Woo, president of city'super Group, a 1,700-person retailer in the Asia Pacific region, was strategizing about how to expand into Shanghai, he felt he could add a tremendous amount of value to the organization if he were physically located in the heart of the city, working and living there. Woo and his wife moved their base to Shanghai and commuted back to Hong Kong on a biweekly schedule. Actually submerging himself in the culture enabled Woo to gain a firsthand view of the Shanghai operations and achieve a deeper understanding of the competition and the market more effectively than he would have been able to do from a distance.

By studying people's diverse characteristics—genders, religious preferences, educational backgrounds, races, cultures, political beliefs, skills, etc.—you can gain the benefits of many new perspectives that help you avoid a social faux pas that could spell the end of a lucrative deal or of a chance to do work with someone in the future. According to Woo and experts like him, punctuality is important in Germany, so don't show up late. Latinos want to know you before they do business with you, so don't offend them by jumping into business topics too quickly. Arabs want to stand close to your face when they speak to you, whereas Europeans like to keep a distance of two to three feet. Leaders from both cultures need to understand such nuances up front and might want to meet somewhere in the middle when they interact.

An Israeli businessman explained how a group of business colleagues from different countries met in Japan to work on a project. The group entered a restaurant, where they were asked to remove their shoes before entering one of the dining rooms. One of the associates was embarrassed to have to reveal to the group that he had worn socks with holes in them that day. Even a small slipup like this might ruin a deal, or at the very least, embarrass you to the point of distraction where you might not be able to focus as sharply on the task at hand.

Working with global contacts doesn't just apply in situations with colleagues and allies. It's about reaching all of your stakeholders, whether they're board members, bank officers, media sources, customers, etc. ESPN held[97] the English-speaking rights to the broadcasting of the 2010 World Cup from Johannesburg, and leadership decided to take a global approach to assigning its broadcasters for the world's largest-watched sporting event. ESPN executives hired British football (soccer) announcers Martin Tyler, Adrian Healey, Derek Rae, and Ian Darke to replace American soccer broadcasters, a change that brought a different perspective to audiences. Decision makers who hired Tyler for the 2010 and 2014 World Cup did so because his personality and flavor as a native Brit (while tempering the colloquialisms that may be unfamiliar to a global listenership) add an authenticity and entertainment factor to their broadcasts. In addition, ESPN's globally aware leadership was able to jump up the organization's global presence and will continue to expand as the years advance.

Use Tools to Synchronize Cultures

Without realizing it, you can jeopardize a working relationship if you're unaware of your assumptions about yourself and the other party. A large U.S.-based global telecom business was implementing a secondary network in the Asia Pacific region—a move that required a substantial investment. The proposal moved forward for many months, and by the end of November, it was ready to launch. But in the final days before the launch, managers in Asia discovered that they were unable to reach their contacts within the United States. For four days, decision makers in Asia left several phone messages.

When they finally received a return call from their U.S. rep, who had taken a four-day Thanksgiving vacation, the Asian business leaders said, "It wasn't Thanksgiving here." These teams had been working closely with each other for months, and yet they still hadn't accounted for each others' national holidays.

One of the ways to overcome differences and to work through them is to systemize global awareness by using tools. So far, we've discussed the many ways that you can become globally aware and connect on a human side, but if you consider the GPP, in order to facilitate good relationships with multicultural colleagues, you need systems and structures. The Cultural & Geographic Synchronization Calendar is a tool to keep you in sync with others' holidays, important events, and even time-zone differences. On the calendar (see Figure 8.5) you can record special events that are expected to occur in other parts of the world, enabling you to deal more effectively with people around the globe.

Cultural & Geographic Synchronization Calendar

Month	Key Dates or Events in Any Given Month (Country and/or Culture)			
	You	1°	2°	3°
January				
February				
March				
April				

Figure 8.6—Cultural & Geographic Synchronization Calendar

Notice the column headings running horizontally across the top of the chart. The first heading is labeled, "You." In this box, write the name of your own country. In the boxes to the right of it, record the name of each country where you have a business contact. Running vertically in the left-hand column are the months of the year. What special events, noteworthy financial dates, seasonal weather factors, and holidays might impact your ability to do business with each of your global contacts? Record those events in the corresponding months' boxes for each country you have listed. Really, no event is too insignificant to list: locations where world events like the World Cup or Olympics are scheduled to take place, weekly or annual religious events, predictable seasonal occurrences such as monsoons or tornadoes, government holidays, and so on. You can transfer information from this tool to your travel list, allowing you to better map out your travel itinerary. For instance, schedule calendar meetings on heavier travel days, and travel to and from your destination when you know that heavier air and ground travel traffic has subsided.

When you plan your daily, weekly, or monthly schedules, refer to this Cultural & Geographic Synchronization Calendar, which one day will be automated so that you can manage all the important dates, times, places, travel, events, customs, and even individual likes and dislikes, as aggregators and spiders search online content and databases to be sure that you are on the same page with your colleagues. Many people find that it is helpful to post this calendar on the wall in their work space. Others make it available to the person who manages their datebook and schedule, and still others refer to it when they make travel plans and keep a copy of it with them when they travel.

Know When and How to Negotiate

At a couple of points already, we've touched on negotiations and a few books that have to do with negotiating across cultures. Much like designing products with an international appeal improves success rates even if the products are domestic, learning to negotiate cross-culturally will help you negotiate in any situation—foreign or domestic—as well.

For instance, if you're unfamiliar with Asia Pacific and Middle Eastern ways of doing business, would you consider that you're more respected if you haggle on pricing than if you just accept the first price thrown at you? In fact, the Chinese don't have a word for "no." They say *bu yao,* meaning, "I'm not interested." How might outcomes change if you replace "no" with "I'm not interested?" Instead of slamming the door shut on an opportunity, you might find the other party open to an alternative that meets all parties' needs.

During a trip to Manila, a friend took me out shopping among her local street vendors. We came upon some items that I had an interest in buying, so I asked the vendor how much they cost. As soon as I got my answer, I reached for my wallet. Fortunately, my friend caught me before I pulled it out and paid. She discretely pulled me aside and explained that shopping in the Philippines was different than shopping in the United States. "You don't want to pay the first price he gives you. Trust me, he expects you to negotiate with him."

I was initially taken by surprise by this cultural difference. Where I am from, you risk annoying and alienating a person if you argue about pricing. Just the same, I took her advice, approached the vendor with a counteroffer, and got the item for less than half of its original offer price. In many regions of the world, your capabilities as a leader are called into question if you can't negotiate effectively, but if you are an effective negotiator, you are perceived as a capable leader that others can trust.

Consider an Alternative to the 4Ps of Marketing

An alternative to the four Ps of marketing—product, price, placement, and promotion—is Abbot Chairman and CEO Miles White's 4Ps of global expansion: (1) people, (2) products, (3) presence, and (4) perseverance.[98] White attributes his international firm's ability to achieve successes on a global scale to the attention leadership pays to each of the following 4Ps:

1. **People.** When you make a decision to enter a foreign market, White believes that no matter how much you try to send in your

own team, you are better off employing people from the country you wish to enter. Build local operations in new markets to gain rapid credibility and access to customs, culture, language, and nuances you may never get otherwise.

2. **Products.** There's no excuse for missing the mark when it comes to selling products (or services) in a culturally or geographically new marketplace. If you think back to your NPSD Funnel, the whole purpose is to develop your best and potentially most successful products, and those with an international appeal will do better simply because our markets and cultures are so integrated, like those microcosms of diversity within major cities. While you must apply the same principle in new markets, you also have to make sure that you understand any nuances that could stand in your way to make necessary adaptation. New product developers at PepsiCo,[99] Inc. researched regional taste preferences before coming up with a customized flavor enhancement of Cool Cucumber for Lay's potato chips to appeal to consumers in the Asian market.

3. **Presence.** Presence refers to how you are present in the market. Are you in manufacturing, are you buying locally, or are you setting up offices in the market? Again, many of the suggestions offered throughout this chapter, from hiring practices to laws and regulations must be considered to make your entry and continued presence successful. Create systems that make this happen. By being a part of the community, you are more likely to gain cultural equity.

4. **Perseverance.** Consider your long-term expansion in this market, because short-term decision making will surely hinder your growth. You want to take a look at the overall Desired Outcome of your organization and make global-minded forecasts about how this new market will come into play as well as how you can contribute to the local market in various international locations. So, for instance, you may not learn the new market's language to the extent that you can speak or write it perfectly, but you can learn it well enough to prove to your international stakeholders that you are serious about making a long-term commitment.

When you take White's 4Ps into consideration, you gain a wider-scoped perspective of the challenges and opportunities before you. You also increase the odds that you will not let an important factor slip out of view, increasing your chances of success when entering new markets. This approach can work in for-profit, not-for-profit, governmental, military, and educational organizations.

Enhance Global Awareness Internally, from the Top Down

Look around your organization and ask yourself if your leaders and staffing are as culturally diverse as they could be. Strive to expand your organization's collective potential and create new options by becoming more globally aware from leadership to the front line.

The vice president of a large construction company (whose projects run in the hundreds of millions of dollars) became responsible for developing project-management leadership in the organization. The company is global and serves clients from different countries around the entire world. The training and development time for this industry's leaders is approximately ten years, but when I asked this VP how he was bringing in new talent, he said they had developed a curriculum at a college in Florida. When I asked him how diverse this pool of students was, he admitted that they were primarily Floridians. Can you see the disconnect? He was employing a monocultural workforce to serve a multicultural customer base. When I suggested he recruit hires from all over the world to ensure they'd be able to work effectively wherever they manage $100-million projects around the world, it was if he had experienced an epiphany. Clearly, he has some catching up to do. (This is quite a contrast to the hiring approach taken by the aforementioned ESPN executives during the 2010 World Cup games.)

Diversity's value in new product and service development, Strategy, competitive intelligence, alliances, and technology is unlimited. Combine these realities with the fact that our leadership population is shrinking, and you can easily see how organizations of the future who are most globally aware will be the ones to capitalize on globally driven opportunities.

In addition, the benefits to having a diverse internal staff are that their range of perspectives also feeds operational efficiencies, ideation, and decision making throughout your organization, which in turn keeps your organization from stagnating due to too much "sameness."

AnnaLee Saxenian, dean of the University of California, Berkeley's School of Information, released a study titled "America's New Immigrant Entrepreneurs" that revealed how in the past decade more than 25% of all U.S. engineering and technology companies were founded by immigrants. In California's Silicon Valley alone, more than 52% of companies are founded by immigrants, the greatest proportion coming from India, China, and Taiwan.[100] America benefits in any number of ways from this kind of vibrant economic and intellectual diversity.

Warsaw, Poland, native Janet Choynowski has understood the value of global awareness since 1992, when her home country was beginning to develop a free economy. She set up a real estate firm at a time when global investors started snapping up properties in Poland. Her diverse client base—buyers from embassies, banks, and construction firms in countries like Japan, Korea, Holland, Sweden, and the UK—required that Choynowski hire people specifically for their skills in communicating and doing business with people from other countries. Choynowski believes, "With all of the cross-border investment, even at an institutional level, it just seemed to make sense to me that a new client should not pose an emergency but an opportunity. Why not be ready for any client, from anywhere, right from the start?" Her successful company was eventually merged into Richard Ellis, now CB Richard Ellis.

Today, Choynowski is the CEO of Immobel.com, a California-based firm whose website offers multilingual real estate listings for properties around the globe. It is the largest, most comprehensive real estate mechanism in the world, using Choynowski's proprietary technologies and techniques to globally connect property buyers and real estate agents. Immobel.com now provides data-translation services to listings for 500,000 realtors in the United States via more than 100 realtor-association or MLS organizations, and to 100% of France through its Realtor Association, the French Association of Property Professionals (FNAIM). Going beyond cultural barriers where there is no single norm opens organizations to new opportunities.

When you enhance your own global awareness, you are able to incorporate it throughout your organization, positioning it to be stronger today and in years to come.

■ ■ ■

You don't acquire global awareness simply to be more tolerant of cultures other than your own, although tolerance will help you. You also don't do it for the sake of selling products internationally, although global awareness will make the endeavor easier. And you don't enhance global awareness by paying lip service to the concept of diversity and hoping that it will somehow magically turn into results later. In our increasingly integrated world, becoming globally aware and continuously staying updated has become a necessary component to good decision making.

And that's only part of the equation. The other is to incorporate what you gain by enhancing global awareness into your performance of the other eleven ET activities to give you and your organization more options for opportunities and solutions, ultimately creating a better future for your organization. Using the tools of this chapter will enable you to enhance global awareness and broaden the scope of opportunities available to you.

9

WATCHING COMPETITION

IN THE EARLY YEARS OF the nineteenth century, England dominated the textile-manufacturing industry. With the industry's exorbitant entry costs and laws preventing the exportation of technologies (and their designs), it looked like England would maintain its stronghold for generations. These barriers, however, did not intimidate Francis Cabot Lowell,[101] a successful Boston merchant with the drive and financial backing to turn the English textile industry on its head.

When Lowell visited England in 1810, he became captivated by the power loom, a technology that wasn't yet accessible to Americans, and he was determined to recreate the equipment back in America. Lowell memorized the power loom's inner workings, and upon his return to Massachusetts, shared the design with a mechanic named Paul Moody. Moody reproduced the technology, conceiving England's new competitor.

Now armed with the technology, Lowell set his sights on getting it operational. He approached other members of the mercantile community, including his five brothers-in-law, and in 1812 pooled $400,000, the working capital needed to charter the Boston Manufacturing Company. By 1814, Lowell's mill not only had the power loom in full operation, but it contained spinning and weaving processes, making it the first company of its kind to fully produce woven fabric from raw cotton in one facility. Yet the innovative side of Lowell's business would not be enough to challenge the English textile manufacturers.

English manufacturers probably weren't too concerned about a small company like Lowell's, because it still lacked efficiencies, economies of scale, and management expertise to compete at the same price points—but you should never underestimate a competitor.

In 1816, Lowell lobbied for and won "infant industries protection," a tactic used by American and German companies at the cusp of the Industrial Revolution. Essentially, the protection placed the first American tariff on foreign cotton products, limiting overseas rivals from competing in Lowell's market for a span of time. During the protection period, Lowell's firm (and other start-ups like it) would have sufficient time to grow and develop the operational efficiencies necessary to compete on par with already-established competitors without their interference. England's established textile manufacturers never saw what hit them until it was too late. In six short years, Lowell had changed an industry.

When you hear a story like this one, you realize how little the dynamics of competition have changed in 200 years. The Francis Lowells of our time continue to shake up industries, organizations, departments, and interpersonal relationship in ways that affect all of us. The question is what side of the scenario do you want to be on?

Every leader is watching and must watch their competitors, but how well are they doing it? Do you have some basic tools at your disposal to ensure that you're looking everywhere, identifying *all* your competitive threats, gathering the right kinds of information, interpreting your findings accurately, and then using data to make better decisions? When you improve the way you watch your competition—an area called competitive intelligence (CI)—you stay ahead of the pack and get what you want. *And you should be using CI in all areas of your life.*

Competition comes in different forms. It can be personal—like people who are vying for your job, trying to push their project ahead of yours or edge you out of buying a house you've had your eye on; departmental—such as departments that are attempting to edge yours out for a larger share of your organization's budget or resources; organizational—those entities fighting for the same grants, funding, market share, patrons, top management talent, and technologies as you; or global—countries jockeying for allies, territory, resources, money, and power.

Fortunately, you can adapt the tools and concepts of this chapter to any competitive situation, improving your ability to keep your eye on your competition without spending substantially more time in the process. You can integrate what you learn here into business intelligence, market intelligence, or any other type of "intelligence" that you already use. However, for the purposes of this chapter, the process of watching your competition will be referred to as competitive intelligence (CI).

The Typical Approach to Competitive Intelligence

There are many approaches to CI, and whether yours is informal, highly structured, or falling somewhere between the two extremes, the litmus test for a good CI approach is that it is appropriately matched to your circumstances and that it enhances decision making throughout your organization.

Think of the small-business owner who knows that there are two other local players in her field. She knows what they charge for services and what some of their general strengths and weaknesses are. She isn't focused as much on the competition as she is on the day-to-day operations of her business, because in her small community, if one of the competitors makes a change, she'll hear about it almost as quickly as it happens.

Some organizations build CI parameters into their strategies. Pepsi stakes a claim to "throat share," meaning it wants to be sure that it doesn't lose market share to any non-Pepsi beverages that pass down the throats of consumers. The firm makes sure that it knows about any newbie or existing player who brings a new beverage to market so that it can address those changes immediately.

Other organizations take an even more sophisticated approach to CI. Picture a military organization with its highly structured CI process, where lives can hinge on how well (or poorly) it gathers and interprets data to extrapolate impending threats from enemies. Or consider the high-tech company that must keep current on its CI to ensure that decision makers are forecasting the next new and best products and bringing them to market before their competitors. These types of groups have highly structured, oftentimes technologically supported networks for gathering, assembling, interpreting, and assimilating data for strategic decision making.

In addition to gathering and using intelligence to make decisions, leaders also have to decide the extent to which they conceal and protect intelligence about their organizations from competitors. There are entities that don't ignore their competitors, but they don't guard many of their activities and assets from them, either. In fact, they want them to know what's going on to show the industry they are the leaders, to instill an innovative environment, and to force their competition to play "catch-up." This is the case for UGL Equis Corporation,[102] an international facilities management firm with more than 43,000 employees. Its CEO is always pushing innovation and coming out with new products and methodologies. Unlike many decision makers who carefully guard their organization's secrets, this CEO doesn't hide the progress of a new product or service until it is ready to come to market.

Instead, he believes that as soon as his company comes up with an Order Winner, everyone—including competitors—should know about it through white papers, announcements, and other types of promotions.

With all the different types, levels, and degrees of CI, decision makers have many choices in terms of how they want to approach the process. Regardless of your choice, realize that some knowledge of competition is essential for deducing rivals' next moves and for determining your organization's next best strategic steps with accuracy. So if you don't have a CI process, you should. Typical approaches have some shortcomings that can lead to inaccurate assumptions, which is why you need a tool, in this case, a process—one not too complex or overly simplified—that doesn't allow you to miss key pieces of the CI puzzle.

Despite the vast variety of leaders who need a reliable CI process—people running for office, managing unions and associations, operating businesses, etc.—the majority don't know enough about CI to realize that they don't gather and apply competition-related data well. Sometimes an organization's application of CI focuses too heavily on collection of data, with very little attention on converting it into useful knowledge. Other applications enable you to collect data on the past and somewhat on the present, but don't give you any sense of competitive threats or opportunities coming in the future. Additionally, you need some way of filtering out the most useful and relevant from the plethora of information out there. Too many CI approaches ignore this key step. At times, these flaws won't hurt you, but at other times, the fallout from your blind spots can be devastating.

Removing blind spots is one of the greatest benefits of your new ET tool, the ET Competitive Intelligence Process (Figure 9.1). It gives you a view of your current and prospective competitors by forcing your data search in many different directions. As the Chinese military strategist Sun Tzu said in the *Art of War*, "So it is said that if you know your enemies and know yourself, you can win a hundred battles without a single loss. If you only know yourself, but not your opponent, you may win or may lose. If you know neither yourself nor your enemy, you will always endanger yourself."

How Well Do You Really Know Your Competition?

A few years ago, I was hired to speak to insurance executives at an insurance company, a billion-dollar giant in a market segment with only a few players. Its CEO wanted to give his eighty-person leadership team—composed of managers from all functional groups—some new tools they could use to manage their recent growth and to expand.

Prior to the event, I phoned ten of the managers to learn more about their current challenges. In each conversation, I realized that while they ran a great business, they were missing pieces of the puzzle that could help them grow market share.

Collectively, I believed we needed to get clarity on their competition. Once the group had settled in for part two of our work, I wrote the names of their competitors in each of the three column headings. Then I asked, "What are these top three competitors' annual revenues?" Not one person responded. After a short pause, I asked again. Surely, someone in the crowd had taken the time to look up these figures, considering how each of the three competitors are public companies whose estimated or actual revenue numbers are available to the general public and each company did a minimum of a billion dollars in revenue. The only person in the room that day who knew this basic information was the CEO. He and I had discussed his competition at length during our pre-presentation interview.

"Do you know an estimated number of customers these firms have?" Again, no response, so I filled in the blanks for them on the matrix.

"Do you know how many salespeople these firms have?" Sadly, the group couldn't answer that question either.

"What products and services are offered by these competitors?" A couple of managers gave some generic answers about products that I would place in the Order Qualifier category, which admittedly was better than nothing. However, the depth of CI really should have unveiled specific details to pinpoint why the competitors' products were Order Winners.

During a break in the session, I overheard one manager say to another, "We had to hire this guy to come in and show us how little we know. I'm so embarrassed."

Yet from the 50,000-foot perspective, it was the CEO who had the most reason for concern. With all the resources available to him and his leadership team, he knew that *he* hadn't allocated them in a way that gave his team a baseline of accurate data about their top competitors. There were some real aha moments for *everyone* in the room that day.

If you and your fellow decision makers were to list your organization's top three competitors and similar information about each one of them, what would be the extent of your cumulative knowledge? At first you might come up with some pretty thorough answers, but a deeper investigation might surprise you, because most leaders never consider *all the different forms of* competitors. Who's your competition when you're trying to secure a grant proposal for your research project? How many intelligence officers are out in the field? What deals are being proposed by your union to other organizations? Who else is vying for the same acquisition, and what's their plan? Who is applying for the same job that you want? By the time you finish reading this chapter, you probably will reconsider your original list of competitors, and you will most likely set your mind to gathering more information than you currently have about each one of them.

Where to Look: Your Competition Is Not Always Your Competition

Although we typically think of competition as coming from within an industry or sector, some of the most damaging competitors can come from outside it, perhaps because they're so unexpected that we don't even see them coming until it's too late. Industries and sectors other than your own have the potential to rob you of opportunities, even when they don't offer your same products and services. For instance, Netflix's competition is not just Redbox or even cable television movies. Its competition is any source that offers leisure entertainment to customers: YouTube, Apple iTunes, sporting events, someone's work load where they are stretched for time, and any other competition that detracts patrons from watching videos.

Take this concept a step further. Competition also comes in the form of "enemy" products or services that are in development from another entity that is either known or unknown at the time. The enemy of some governments could be information access from the Internet or electronic news sources. The enemy of the military might be public policy or an entity in the media that shifts behaviors. In some markets, the enemy of a breast-cancer awareness campaign could be a 5K run hosted by the American Diabetes Association, a direct-mail drive by the March of Dimes, or a telethon hosted by the National Multiple Sclerosis Society. Keep in mind that just as you are creating your plans, your competitors are simultaneously creating their own. These competing activities will undoubtedly force you to modify your plans or strategize new ones altogether to remain competitive.

How to Look: Outside-In, Inside-Out, Above, and Below

How is your competition penetrating your market? You might expect your competition to come at you through the same channels they've used in the past, but sometimes a player can surprise you by taking an entirely unsuspecting route.

That's what happened to colleges and universities across the United States when the University of Phoenix launched its Online Campus in 1989 and expanded its reach into communities around the world. If work and family obligations make it difficult for a prospective student to drive across town to attend night school, he or she can simply log in to the University of Phoenix's site at conveniently scheduled times to attend class and eventually earn a degree. Did all those local night schools, community colleges, and universities catering to the same market see it coming?

The reason that Outside-In, Inside-Out, Above, and Below works is that it expands your perspective and thinking, and changes the types of information you incorporate into strategizing activities while looking at your competition (*and* while they are looking at you).

- **Outside-In.** Gather intelligence from outside an organization from the perspective of looking into it. From the vantage point of looking in at your competitors, some questions your collectors should seek to answer are: Who's making decisions? What is being purchased? Where are they getting funding? To what destination is the VP of sales flying to today? Just as you will be looking outside-in to competitors, realize that they can be doing the same to you, so continually look for ways of protecting your private information, too. How does your competition see you, and if you catch them watching you, do you know if they're looking for any specific information? Sometimes a clue to what they're seeking reveals their next strategic moves against you. What weaknesses do you know about your competitors that could be advantageous right now?

- **Inside-Out.** Define how your organization feels about itself and then how you see the competition individually and as a whole. A question I propose is this: If you were recruited away from your current organization, what would you tell your new costaffers that would enable them to put your former organization out of business? From within your organization you can watch your competition, observing its strengths and weaknesses, its products, services, and operations from all different internal vantage points such as production, operations, HR, legal, engineering, safety, quality control, etc. I'm not just talking about the strategy, individual, or group. Ask how key players see opposing key players in the market.

- **Above.** Take a look at your competition from above when it is possible or advantageous to do so. This could require that you assume a literal position of height, say from a helicopter or the top floors of a skyscraper. You could also watch competition from a more figurative "above" position, from the 50,000-foot view of their departments or business units, or from the upstream point of view of a vendor or from an industry leader. By changing your perspective you may see a different footprint, sales locations, and/or flow of information. Look to where you can gain advantages over competitors in pricing, payment terms, delivery times, and so on. You might even look upstream to suppliers, researchers, and investment sources to understand their perspective. Where are competitors recruiting their newest talent, what's happening with research partners, are alumni donating? Once you've collected this information, turn your eyes onto your own organization to consider what your competitors would observe about your organization if their collectors looked at you in the same inside-out way.

■ **Below.** View your organization from underneath. Not sure what that means? Certainly, if you're building bridges, you could look at the physical underside of your competitors' work, but that is not typically what is meant by observing from below. This, too, is a more figurative translation that refers to studying your competitors' vulnerabilities and weaknesses, like security breaches, product recalls, or conditions that have forced layoffs. The other "below" perspective is the downstream look at competitors' customers, where you might steal market share from competition by learning how dissatisfied their customers are, giving you the chance to fill those gaps. Look at all people and organizations that could pose a threat to your organization's well-being, and don't discount anything. Once you've studied the competition, turn the view around to yourself: What are the vulnerabilities that your competitor might see? If you're in a high-risk security industry like intelligence or banking, you would want to be sure that someone can't overcome your organization physically from below by digging underground (think prisoners digging out from a tunnel). Or say you've recently heard that your landlord is experiencing financial challenges and you might be searching for a new place to set up shop if the landlord's property is seized by the bank or government; ask whether he might sell the building you lease from him and consider how that will impact your organization's ability to operate. How might a glitch in your software program enable a disgruntled employee access to delicate information that would be problematic in the hands of a competitor? Really, every area should be explored.

Oftentimes, by looking Outside-In, Inside-Out, Above, and Below, you are able to more easily uncover your next competitive challenge. One of the best examples of this multiperspective view comes from military defense strategists who must continually maintain protection and superiority on all fronts: land, air, and sea. These strategists understand that they must continually review their strategies, because obvious defenses won't protect their organization against surprises that arise.

In generations past, the response to enemy military strikes consisted of getting to land and finding safe havens to set up a base and go on the offensive. Then a somewhat controversial military strategy called seabasing evolved, where personnel set up a chain of flotillas at sea to serve as man-made islands for military operations. The supposed advantage of seabasing is that operations can move around to the best locations for sea defense while keeping troops out of harm's way. Seabasing, however, can leave troops open to a security threat coming from below, so measures have to be taken to maintain control and sea superiority by defending flotillas from below the water's surface.

With the passage of time and the evolution of technologies, the next major threats will come from space or space superiority, requiring strategists to provide security for their troops on the move, defend satellites that are already there, and to protect space stations and bases. In the movie *Star Wars*, the Death Star space station was supported by destroyers, fighters, and supply ships. In the future, this concept is not far off.

Now translate this concept to organizations and individuals across the 7Crosses of ET. Say that you are the owner of a computer center that installs and maintains computer networks for other organizations. You sell your services based on networks' abilities to improve productivity, lower costs, and shorten downtime. If you want to prepare your organization against its next unconventional competitor, you have to look beyond the obvious competitors and ask different questions. You can't just look at Johnson City Computer Specialists and ask how they'll outpace you in your local market. You have to look at online products that customers can download for free, overseas technicians who offer less-expensive 24-hour phone support, and other alternative resources that meet your customers' needs.

Take an Outside-In, Inside-Out, Above, and Below look at complementary industries, new technologies, developing countries, and emerging companies, and ask, how might these sources outpace us by better addressing our customers' productivity, costs, and down times? Take it a step further and explore ways to translate it to your demographic reach and depth in different markets, the coverage you get in the media, your online presence, event coverage, feet on the street, social networking, and promotional products.

Finally, try to apply the concept of Outside-In, Inside-Out, Above, and Below to all aspects of your organization, not just to how you are securing market share and capital. What internal networks are making you vulnerable? Which staff members give you an edge and which ones pose a threat? Is your geographic location the best for your organization at this point in time? And so on.

[Avoid Getting Bitten by the Unexpected]

There are some competitors you don't see until they have "bitten" you. They seemingly come out of nowhere, either because you don't suspect them or because they play by an unconventional set of rules.

When I was in college in the 1980s, one of my roommates brought me to a Japanese restaurant and introduced me to sushi. After that first bite, I was hooked, but dining on sushi was an occasional indulgence, because the food itself was extremely expensive, the restaurant was five miles from campus, and I rarely had two hours to spare for dinner. Luckily for me, a new sushi source popped up in town and made it possible for me to enjoy sushi more often.

No, it wasn't another Japanese restaurant. It was one of our local grocery stores. In addition to its deli counter and Chinese food buffet, our grocer added a sushi station where professionally trained sushi chefs prepared and packaged fresh sushi to go at less than a quarter the price I'd been paying at the Japanese restaurant. I can guarantee you those restaurant owners never expected they'd get "bitten" by the local grocer. We've become accustomed to finding sushi in grocery stores now, but remember that at one time it was a truly unconventional move for grocers to compete with specialty restaurants.

Try Biomimicry

One of the ways you can ferret out the unexpected competitor (or become one!) is to try a technique called biomimicry, in which you look to nature to observe how animals and plants compete, survive, and navigate their way through life. You can use biomimicry to improve the way you perform many of the ET activities, not just when you're watching the competition, as you will see again in Chapter 12 when we talk about innovating.

In terms of CI, think about Ravoux's slavemaker ant, a species of European ant whose queen fakes dead, gets herself dragged back to another ant species' nest, "wakes up," and kills that colony's queen. Essentially, she plays her own unconventional game to surprise and attack her competitor. How might this concepts come into play within your industry?

Sometimes, a new technology or an unrelated industry can appear to come out of nowhere and cut a swath through your industry or sector. Camera makers like Minolta and Canon, along with manufacturers of photography film, such as Kodak and Fuji, were hijacked by technologies that made it possible for consumers to use cell phones as cameras and to upload digital images to computers and online photo-processing vendors. Decades ago, the companies that helped consumers preserve memories probably never imagined that they would one day be attacked by the cell phone.

Other times, the challenge comes from your own decision making. This is the case when a competitor has given you ample notice that a new technology, methodology, or trend is either on the horizon or is already in circulation in the marketplace, and you have chosen to ignore it. For example, within the aforementioned memory-preservation industry, Kodak executives not only saw signs that competing technologies were approaching, they actually created some of the digital technologies and the company even owned intellectual property rights of them. Then, once the technologies were in the marketplace and rapidly gaining market share, Kodak execs didn't react with Order Winner counterstrikes. Throughout history there have been situations where individuals have identified threats and have not heeded the warning signs or have taken strategic measures that pushed opportunities away from their organizations instead of creating competitive advantages.

Be careful that you don't overlook or even create the "ants" that could invade you from within. Engineer-turned-salesman Sidney Harman and engineer Bernard Kardon were friends and coworkers at David Bogen & Co.,[103] a maker of public-address sound systems. Harman, in response to customers' needs, wanted to improve upon the company's existing products, but owner David Bogen was reluctant and slow to innovate. Harman and Kardon eventually left Bogen in 1953 to start their own firm, Harman Kardon. Together, they created new and innovative products—including the receiver, a single-unit device that combined a tuner and amplifier to make it easy for anyone to enjoy great-sounding music—and became a giant player in the audio/sound market. In 2009, the firm grossed nearly $3 billion, an amount that David Bogen & Co. could be adding to its bottom line.

You need to be watching the competition in many ways, and the right tools will give you that comprehensive perspective you need to begin the process.

Focusing on the Future

Your hands grip the steering wheel of a race car traveling at more than 200 miles per hour. For the past twenty minutes, you've jockeyed your way from eighth position to third, and once again, you're rapidly approaching the challenging curve known simply as "Turn 4." Throughout the race, you've kept a pretty good handle on other cars' locations in relation to yours, but the last time you rounded this turn, your attention lingered on the rear-view mirror for just a couple of seconds too long, and you nearly lost your position by two slots. This time, you're more focused. You remind yourself that you've spent months studying up on your fellow drivers and reviewing tapes of past races, and you can predict with some certainty how the driver of car #2 is going to enter this turn. Based on your combined knowledge of the past, present, and predictions of the future, you know exactly where you need to be entering the curve, how to bank the turn, and when to accelerate your way to the second position.

Seconds later, you career past your competitor and slide into second place, hot on the bumper of the first-place car. Though the rear-view mirror and in-the-moment decisions have helped, you credit your mini success on the future-focused planning you did before entering today's race.

Whether you're racing a car or leading an organization, getting ahead of your competition using information from the past and present can only get you so far. You also have to continually focus on the future ahead as you plan your next best moves.

Even if you believe that you are already future focused, chances are you will compete more successfully by extending your view farther into the future (which you will learn in more detail in Chapter 14). For now, you can make the improvement by looking beyond the future of your organization's products, services, and geographic factors to identify trends, patterns, cycles, threats, and opportunities presented by other industries and sectors, and from vendors, customers, and technologies that can render your offerings out of date, obsolete, or available through nontraditional channels both for external and internal offerings.

The ET Competitive Intelligence Process

By now, you can probably see how the ET tools that you have learned so far are designed to improve your decision-making capabilities. The ET Competitive Intelligence Process is a six-step mechanism that will make you a more effective strategizer by providing you with reliable and current information about your competition. Remember, the competition may be the person sitting in the next room or a business unit around the world. It's important to keep your perspective of competition dimensionalized in order to ensure that your thinking is broad enough to cover all types of competition.

This process contains effective CI activities derived from both the business and military worlds, making it a timeless ET tool that can be universally applied by people in any industry or sector, at any management level, across all cultures and geographic areas, and for any aspect of work and life. Whether your needs are simple or complex, you can use the model for multiple purposes, such as to get the information you need to secure a grant for research, to develop an incentive program in your office, to make your next personal career advancement, to pass your school district's annual budget, to fund and patent a new invention, and so on.

Look at Figure 9.1 and notice how the process begins and ends with strategizing, an important component of effective CI that is typically missing from models and processes. I first became aware of this gap in CI processes while seated on a plane next to a military intelligence expert. We were two strangers who struck up a conversation that eventually turned to the topic of competitive intelligence. It was then that my fellow traveler spoke of his life's work with the United States Central Intelligence Agency. He was an expert in CI, so I pulled out what must have been the eighth version of the ET CI Process in progress, and he shared with me how the military recently learned that if they did not start off with strategizing about CI, it could easily miss its mark. My immediate aha moment forced me to consider the role of Strategy within the context of the ET CI Process; what would you actually need in order to achieve your Desired Outcome?

With strategizing as an initial part of this process, you are forced to ask the hard questions up front about what you want CI to achieve for your organization, who is going to perform the various functions of CI, and what types of information you and your people are setting out to secure. In essence, the ET CI Process is a tool that enables you to plan your course of action much like playbooks and film help sports coaches prepare for their next games.

It's also important to understand that strategizing comes into play at two separate times for two separate purposes. In the beginning, your strategizing is focused on how you will use the CI process and for what purpose. In the end, the final step of strategizing is about plugging the competitive intelligence into your CST Model to empower you to make informed decisions for your organization.

Enterprise Thinking COMPETITIVE INTELLIGENCE PROCESS

Strategizing: who will collect the CI, what you wish your CI collectors to collect, how the CI will be used, to whom will they report

Types of Collectors

Individuals, Group(s), Team(s), Internal, Outsourced, Spies, Double Agents, Re-Double Agents, Triple Agents, Using Unsuspecting Individuals, etc.

Categories of Collection

Human (e.g., language, behavior) Signals (e.g., Internet, electronic, linguistic) Imagery (e.g., photo, satellite) Tangible (e.g., documentation, products)

Collect Data

Collected through:

Feet on street	Trade groups
Researchers	Associations
Alliances	Sales reps
Reports	Government records
Databases	Clipping services
Newsletters	Online searches
Direct contact	Competition
Interviews	Insiders
Consultants	Aggregators
Interaction	Social networks
Surveillance	Casual conversation
Trials	Staged conditions
Trade journals	Distribution channels
Speeches	Hiring / firing
Want ads	Security
Ad agencies	etc.

Example Observations:

Movement (also lack of)
Travel (freq. / destination)
Traffic (parking / geography)
Meetings (phone / secret)
Assets (people / equip.)
Filings (patent / copyright)
Purchases / sales
Acquisitions / sales
Equipment / technology
Observations
Behaviors / history
Security changes (IT)
Energy consumption

Data is confirmed

Assemble Information

Talent:

Integrators
Sifters
Data miners
Compilers

Responsibilities:

Condense and catalogue data
Eliminate redundancies
Convert to charts, graphs, etc.
E.g.: market mapping
Request additional data
Look for trends, patterns, cycles
Identify gaps in information
Build simulations and models
Break codes
etc.

Beware:

Planted information and misinformation
Improperly collected data
Incomplete data
Personal bias and assumptions
etc.

Communicate with leadership:

What's needed
What's missing
What's inaccurate
What does not make sense

Assembly is confirmed

Create Knowledge

Talent:

Interpreters of information
Analyzers

Responsibilities:

Look for connections
Extrapolate information
Interpret unknown
Compare differences
Identify conflicting information
Find similarities
Watch for cultural differences
Allow for 4D
Look for trends, patterns, cycles
Notify leadership of needed CI
Ensure accuracy

Beware:

Planted information and misinformation
Improperly collected data
Incomplete data
Personal bias
Assumptions
Counterintelligence
Identify assembly errors
internal competition
etc.

Predict moves
Identify weaknesses
etc.

Analysis is confirmed

Review products of Competitive Intelligence work
(e.g., reports, debriefs, media, summaries, presentations, etc.)
New intelligence is identified

Decisions are generated during Strategizing
(Cyclonic Strategic Thinking Model through Execution)

Figure 9.1—Enterprise Thinking Competitive Intelligence Process

Your new tool is composed of the following six steps of the ET CI Process:

1. **Strategize** about how to use the ET CI Process to reach your Desired Outcome. Determine who will perform each of the steps and how to ensure that you have reliable and useful decision-making "fuel."

2. **Collect data** about your direct and indirect competitors and be sure to include factors that could impact your ability to compete—political, legal, technological, consumer-driven, etc.

3. **Assemble information** that causes current and impending challenges and opportunities to jump out at you.

4. **Create knowledge** from raw data, so that you are you in a greater position of control over your organization's destiny.

5. **Review "products" of CI work** that you have identified to this point to confirm their accuracy. You want to connect the dots in hopes of creating more and better new knowledge.

6. **Strategize for the organization** by plugging the CI knowledge into your CST Model. Data alone means nothing, really. In order to make the ET CI Process work for you, you must integrate it into your decision making.

As you and your team follow the steps of the CI process—Strategize about using the Process, Collect Data, Assemble Information, Create Knowledge, Review, and Apply—you must be sure that the competitive intelligence supports your Desired Outcomes.

1: STRATEGIZE ABOUT USING THE PROCESS

The first part of the process, strategizing, requires those in leadership to begin to define certain parameters necessary to create targeted CI.

Before you even execute the other five steps of the process, you need to make some determinations about the use of the ET CI Process. You can't just tell people to collect information; you must first define the type of information and how you want to use it. Some, but certainly not all of the questions you might ask are:

- What is our reason—our strategic intent—for using competitive intelligence at all?

- What is our Desired Outcome of engaging in CI activities?
- What is the defined Strategy of the CI?
- Do the Desired Outcome and Strategy for CI align with our organizational (or group) CST Model's Desired Outcome and Strategy?
- What Macro Tactics are we considering: ie who will collect data, what data do we expect our collectors to collect, and how, when, and where will they collect it?
- What skills will our collectors, assemblers, analyzers need in order to gather, assemble, and interpret the right information correctly?
- Is our strategic intent going to make the best use of our resources?
- Are there technologies available that will enable us to automate any activities within the process?
- Are we accounting for challenges that may hinder collection and timing?
- Who should have access to competitive intelligence data at different stages of the process?
- How will we use the data to progress our organization toward our Desired Outcome/s?
- How will we guard data, and how will we determine the people who will have access to it?
- Do we have the right people on hand to help us convert raw data into usable knowledge?

Strategizing about how to use the process varies with different circumstances. Glancing at the step Collect Data, think about the guidelines and instruction you would give your collectors. If you're a private investigator, you might tell your team of collectors to shoot photos and videos, gain possession of contracts, or tail a mark. If you're producing a news program, you might instruct your reporters to secure documents, contact experts, and interview witnesses.

In addition, you must be specific in your requests for information. Be careful not to assume that everyone somehow understands what you want. Giving others a broad directive like "collect information about Company X" could fetch computer printouts, aerial photos, and organizational charts. You will surely be disappointed with the results, no matter how thorough, if you had originally wanted specs and prototypes of not-yet-launched products instead.

As you determine the content of CI, consider the following categories of information:

- **Human:** any information related to people such as behavior, language, eye movement, cultural traits, patterns, cycles, activities, repetitive actions, meetings, and travel.
- **Signals:** any message that identifies a trail, such as Internet histories, electrical signals like radar from submarines, or tracking phone calls, engine sounds, and linguistics.
- **Imagery:** any visual intelligence that gives you a quick snapshot of a condition such as maps, photos, drawings, videos, etc.
- **Tangibles:** any physical "data" such as documents, products, contracts, fabrics, samples, test tubes, chemicals, architectural plans, etc.

To use this process to improve the decisions you make, you need reliable information and knowledge, and that reliability hinges on the skill levels of your people and how well data is collected and handled. Taking this initial step will get your CI process off on a good foot and ensure that it is aligned with Strategy.

Strategize about Your "Collectors"

One of your first tasks is to decide who will collect data and how you want to organize collectors. Certainly, you can take an informal approach to getting your collectors together, keeping it as simple as asking one individual to find out certain information for you, or you can assemble a team to coordinate the activities involved in gathering information. Regardless of whether you have a complex or simple endeavor, you will want to make some determinations about your collectors at this strategizing juncture of the process.

Your gatherers can come from inside your organization or outside, depending on your circumstances and needs at the time. For instance, you might want to ask a friend working at another organization what she knows about the companies who are submitting bids on a construction job. Or, you might find it better to have a group of internal staffers working as a team to coordinate research on a local city revitalization project. As you decide which alternative is best for you, you will want to consider the systems and structures you put in place to coordinate their efforts so that they can easily report back to you.

Sometimes, keeping track of CI requires teams of people and support groups. Their involvement can be crucial to collecting the information you need, so be sure that you select the right people and give them all the tools they need to perform their missions successfully. Also, you will not only want to select people who have the highest chance of collecting the right types of information for you, but who can be trusted to work in the best interests of your organization. You don't want to one day discover that someone who is supposed to be collecting information for you has turned "double agent" and is feeding your information to a competitor. And since circumstances change, you'll want to assess your collectors' performances periodically to ensure that these people are meeting your organization's needs. Otherwise, oversight in this area can create a domino or chain reaction to occur, preventing you from getting the CI you need.

In the world of international espionage, superpower countries launch cyber attacks on each other, and they fund individuals and universities to research even better ways to conduct types of cyber surveillance and attacks. Japan, the United States, and the Republic of Korea cyber-attacked 8.9 million computers in China in 2011, up from five million in 2010. A 2012 *Wall Street Journal* article reported that the "U.S.-China Economic and Security Review Commission found that the U.S. telecommunications supply chain is particularly vulnerable to cyber-tampering and an attack could result in a 'catastrophic failure' of U.S. critical infrastructure."[104] In times of peace and in situations of heightened military tension, these countries want to be positioned to immediately collect data from strategic CI surveillance mechanisms to plot their next moves.

Selecting the right collector of this information is extremely important. Leadership must play out the scenarios as well as they can so that when the collector goes to gather information, they get what they need.

2: COLLECT DATA

 Now that you have determined who will collect the data—a single person, a team, an alliance, an outsourced organization—how they will collect it, and where it will be stored for your assemblers, you need to monitor the collection of information and be ready to adjust your methodologies so that the data remains relevant and accurate.

Here is why: Data collection can be a one-off activity, or it can occur on a continual basis. You must define your best collection method and then instruct others about how to collect what you need. Prior to 2008, a NYC boutique owner wanting to determine what to sell and how much to warehouse might have wanted to collect data as a one-off activity using traditional means—inventory figures, competitors' offerings and price points, trade journal stats, fashion and clothing shows, etc. But if the store owner had read an article in the newspaper ten months later that gave him new information to consider, he might have switched his method of data collection.

Say that the article offered a continual data-collection technique that might have been better aligned to the owner's needs. It reported that it monitored the increases and decreases in the number of turnstile turns at various subway locations throughout the city, and it cited a 14% decline at one station located near his boutique and other high-end shops in his area. Perhaps it would have been important for assemblers to know data like this.

Current data (or one-off data collection activities) can provide you with valuable information. However, it should be used only when appropriate, meaning you must realize that it may paint part of the picture for you when, in fact, you need information about what has transpired over time to get a complete understanding of a competitor. By identifying market changes, observing new legislations, scanning databases, talking with clients, attending trade shows, purchasing competitors' products at intervals to review improvements, or chatting up different suppliers, you are able to give data to your assemblers (and knowledge creators) that indicate possible cycles, patterns, and trends. Data that shows a change or progression of activity over time will help you not only with strategizing, but also with forecasting future challenges and opportunities, too.

Collection of data can occur in unexpected places. Long ago, our regular package-delivery driver from a well-known U.S. delivery company informed us that one of his area managers had been tagging along with him on our route, writing down the names of our suppliers off the boxes that were being delivered to our business, and then passing these names on to his son who was opening a competing business in the same industry.

The collection process itself can sometimes be as easy as observing happenings that occur out in the open. Collectors with a little time on their hands can produce valuable information just by watching online videos, trailing a competing CEO to the airport to find out the destination of his or her next business trip, or talking to a realtor friend about who is making recent real estate purchases in the area. The VP of a U.S. national company told me a story about how the organization was looking to develop some land, and they had been purchasing all the real estate quietly to keep the prices down until the CEO made the mistake of flying to a property on his private jet that had the company logo on the tail. Those looking for CI had their answer.

In general, a great deal of competitive intelligence is free and fairly easy to find, if you know where to look. Most often you can locate the data you need from databases, reports, newsletters, bulletin boards, direct contact, interviews, consultants, trade journals, trade groups, sales groups, government recordings, clipping services, suppliers, and other resources like these. Other times, just observing the happenings around you can provide collectors with appropriate and current data, such as monitoring the number of cars that are parked in a competitors' parking lot at various times of the day. Automated tools, like Google Alerts, that will e-mail up-to-date notifications to your inbox whenever your organization or its competitors are listed on the Web, require little time and free up collectors to engage in other collection activities.

Some organizations feel the need to take collection measures to a darker level and require their collectors to access bank accounts, pick through trash, install mechanisms that monitor activity on computers, hack into computer networks, tap phones, etc. Many of these types of collectors use technology— a virtual flip-of-the-switch technique—to gain instantaneous information. However, to gain valuable and useful data from organizations—with, perhaps, the exception of those involved in national security—you do not need to take such drastic steps, and some might find themselves in legal hot water if they do.

But before you rush to judgment, realize that most people have engaged in some sort of collection activity that another person or organization might find questionable, so the idea of ethics is certainly a subjective one. For example, have you ever retrieved a brochure from a competitor's trade show booth or called a competitor and asked for a price quote all while pretending to be a prospective customer? Some firms hire photographers to take aerial photos of a region to catch a glimpse of a competitor's operations below. And why do you suppose American football coaches feel compelled to cover their mouths with clipboards while speaking directives into their headsets during televised pro-football games?

Another method you can use to collect CI is to address people who are not internal to your competitors' organizations but who are affiliated with them just the same: for instance, by reaching out to consumers with surveys or through social networking. Companies like Communispace connect corporations to consumers for the purpose of providing feedback and data on CI. Communispace in particular gathers groups of 300 to 500 people who are interested in discussing a topic of relevance to a company—a product, service, image, brand, etc.—and these consumers' insights and commentary can be used by decision makers to plot their organization's next steps. For example, the consumer groups might shop a competitor, blog about a product, or take a photo of their pantries and send it to Communispace to share with its clients. Imagine the value of peering into multiple consumers' pantries and seeing your product (or not) in relation to your competitors' products.

The point: there are many different, creative, and effective ways that you can collect data on your competitors—talking with vendors, purchasing a competitor's product, researching political campaign donations on the Web, attending trade shows, keeping tabs on new legislative acts, etc.—and it's up to you to find and use those that most aptly fit your circumstances. Take a look at the ET CI Process again and read through the different collection approaches listed in the Collect Data step. With so many options, you're bound to find one (or many) to meet your needs.

3: ASSEMBLE INFORMATION

If you're like most leaders, once your collectors have collected the data, you will be eager to use it. While information alone can be valuable, most often, leaders need the gathered information to be assembled into a form for practical use. Typically, the collected data is just a clump of "stuff" like conference brochures, product descriptions, sales price lists, or online research statistics that needs to be organized in some fashion. Depending upon the amount, variety, and complexity of the data you've gathered, an individual or a team can properly assemble the information for you. The same people who gathered the information may assemble it, or in larger organizations, special teams or departments may take over the task. Often, these assemblers are hired specifically for their skill in interpreting data. (Many assemblers are versed in the activity of data mining, the process of looking through data for cycles, patterns, and trends to create more usable information.)

Like a team of investigators who have assembled information from a police scene, the information needs to undergo some transformation so that its meaning can be derived from it. In this step, assemblers sift through data, eliminate redundant information, highlight trends, uncover gaps, condense and compile statistics, and create graphs, charts, and other models that can help others to understand the data. In an attempt to extrapolate and deduce a true and realistic understanding of competition, assemblers may have to ask collectors to gather additional information to fill gaps left from previous collection attempts: photos don't reveal all working parts of an engine or static drowns out portions of an audio-taped conversation.

Assemblers should also be on the lookout for misinformation such as material that has been intentionally planted to mislead your collectors or bits and pieces of data that could be misinterpreted and subsequently lead to false conclusions. One of the ways to avoid being misled is by having skilled assemblers on board who aren't likely to jump to conclusions or to stop short of collecting complete information. Trained professionals are more likely to dig deeper, questioning motives of a competitor, trying to figure out the rationale behind a move, and accurately identifying abnormalities in normal patterns of behavior. The assembler who is skilled might say, "Hey guys, statistically there is an 84% chance the competitor would turn right and they turned left. Something's not right here. We need eyes on the street immediately," instead of taking a move at face value.

At the conclusion of this step, decision makers should end up with clear and accurate intelligence that they can use to make better decisions. Sometimes, the process is complex and occurs over a long period of time, but quite often, it is as simple and quick as collecting brochures, videos, and pictures from a trade show, spreading it all onto your desk, and putting some order to the information that will eventually heighten your awareness and knowledge of the competition.

4: CREATE KNOWLEDGE

Raw data does not usually provide the quality of information that you need for outpacing your competitors. You, your group(s), or other designated people who will become integrators, sifters, and data miners must interpret and analyze the findings and then create knowledge that will become useful to you as you strategize. Therefore, you and your group must connect the dots by looking at the findings from every angle and questioning every assumption, in order to determine how you and/or your organization can use the information as competitive intelligence.

Sometimes you will create knowledge but then realize that you must return to the collection and assembly steps to fill in missing pieces of information. Other times, you might need to take an action that forces your competitors to make a countermove, which in turn exposes to you what they are planning to do next. Think of the strategizing behind your moves as similar to that of a chess player who wants to take an opponent by surprise.

In certain instances, you might not uncover the information that you were expecting to find. That's often the case when you set the process in motion to confirm an assumption. If you find that you run into this situation, you should go back to the first step of the ET CI Process and re-strategize.

The knowledge you ultimately derive from the CI process relies heavily on how well you and your people have performed the first three steps. This is a somewhat "sketchy" example, but it proves a point. If I were to send you to look into a house and tell me about the family living in it, would you say that you could give me as comprehensive a report by peering into only one window of their home as you could by looking in many windows, listening to their conversations at open windows, sifting through their trash, monitoring their comings and goings, and trailing them each time they leave the home?

Then, of course, if you spied on this family for only a day, would you have as much quality information at your disposal as you would if you were to monitor them for three months, speaking to people in their community, and getting a handle on their current behavioral patterns? You need to think about not only where this family is and what they're doing today, but what they'll be doing six months or two years from now. Do they have kids in college, is someone planning on relocating for a job opportunity? And so on. The shift has to be into the future as well as you develop your knowledge for strategizing purposes.

5: REVIEW "PRODUCTS" OF CI WORK

The people who perform the Review step should be skilled and objective. They should be able to tell you if your teams of collectors, assemblers, and knowledge creators have provided you with an end "product" of material and knowledge that will empower you to make improved strategic decisions for your organization.

Here are some pointers about the Review step that you should know:

1. You have to account for what your organization's specific needs are. This is not a cookie-cutter activity, and if you approach it with an all-things-being-equal mentality, you're setting back progress, because all things are never equal. In other words, you will have to do some Cyclonic Thinking about whether the findings and knowledge meet your original purposes, and how you can use them in your decision making.
2. Look for decoys that will mislead you and your people. Specifically, you want to be sure that your competition hasn't sent out false information to intentionally derail you and force you to make bad decisions. For instance, a competitor might leak a press release about some fictitious product launch knowing

that if it can convince you that it is entering a new territory, you will get panicky, make a reactive move, and show your hand first. Distracting you gives your competitor the time to one-up you. Mind you, most organizations are so concerned about their own operations they are not really paying as much attention to CI as you may think. And even if they did get your information, they might not have the knowledge or resources to do anything with it. To prove my point, think about the last time you received information about another organization. What impact did it have on your next move? For the majority of groups and organizations, I'd bet not very much happened.

3. Try to find similarities and reoccurring data that indicates patterns or behaviors that might impact the interpretation of your findings.

4. Make sure the data is complete. One missing piece of the puzzle could mean losing by a nose. That's why looking Outside-In, Inside-Out, Above, and Below is so important. You can do all the steps seemingly right, miss one detail, and make decisions that leave your organization vulnerable. No matter how adept security strategists are, if they don't review all potential threat opportunities, they or their clients are in jeopardy.

5. Rewind your competitors' historical tape to uncover any information in their background, such as a training program, manager, or mentor, that could help you extrapolate their decision-making tendencies. Take a page from the sports world where coaches, general managers, and athletes can oftentimes predict the next move of a competitor based on the techniques that their trainers are known to teach and use. You can anticipate that a tennis player will return a lob near the fault line, that a quarterback will call a particular play under certain circumstances, or that a baseball player will swing at a curve ball if you are familiar with their trainers' special techniques. How can this be translated to your organization?

6. Acknowledge global and cultural differences. It is very easy to make incorrect assumptions by viewing your information through the perspective of your own culture. Be watchful, too, that the cultural norms of your knowledge creators doesn't cause them to come to false conclusions and then pass them on to you as valid knowledge, otherwise, your decision making will be tainted.

7. Don't assume tomorrow's decisions will follow yesterday's patterns. History is an indicator, but progress is such that you have to take into consideration technology and happenings that occur in the present and are projected to occur in the future, too. Technology, innovation, and emerging markets are accelerating traditional timelines and changing the ways in which we live and work. Would you have assumed in 1970 that you could "transport" an image instantaneously as we did with the first fax machines? And in the 1980s, when we were using faxes, could you have ever imagined the flexibility and freedom to send images and digital data right through your computer via e-mail or text? (The next time someone says, "We tried that in the past and it didn't work," remind them of this.)

Update your knowledge with the times. Your competition is not standing still, and yesterday's knowledge might not be accurate tomorrow. The person who's vying for the job you want could be accumulating new skills to outpace you, the country that you are in a space-program competition with might be securing patents of which you're unaware through subsidiaries or undisclosed arrangements, or the union might be making strides with legislation that will affect your bottom line next year. Everything in life is organic, even the thoughts and strategies of your competitors.

6: STRATEGIZE FOR THE ORGANIZATION

Finally, feed the data and the knowledge into your CST Model so that you're working with valuable and current information as you strategize. By now, you know that everything in Enterprise Thinking—its activities, tools, and concepts—are connected, and CI is no different. Plug it into other ET activities, like Forecasting (which you will learn about in Chapter 14), new product development, leveraging technology by creating new tools for collecting, establishing different alliances, and so on.

In addition, make sure that CI is shared with others in your organization when it is appropriate and safe to do so. In terms of appropriate sharing of CI, very often leaders don't think to distribute the knowledge to fellow decision makers, and their lapse can lead to missed opportunities to empower people throughout their organizations. Furthermore, (intentionally or unintentionally) withholding CI robs organizations of chances to break down silos—product developers possess certain knowledge that could help salespeople—and can run up costly expenses as different groups duplicate energies by conducting their own research. Keep in mind that you want all key players to have pertinent data so that they can make great decisions.

As far as safety and security are concerned, you want to be sure that certain sensitive material does not get into the hands of the wrong personnel. For example, if you know that a top-level decision maker has put feelers out for a new job, you might not want to share your most recent CI with her until you know more about her future plans. The potential for proprietary information to be transferred from one competitor to another is the reason why in 2005 Microsoft sued Google for hiring one of its corporate VPs, Kai-Fu Lee,[105] while he was still under contract with the former. Despite signing a nondisclosure agreement with Microsoft, Lee took on the position to spearhead Google's new research and development team in China. Microsoft's lawsuit was its attempt to protect such proprietary information. (In the next section, you will learn more about how your circumstances and competitors may force you to be protective of your information.)

The quality of the CI knowledge you now have is very much tied to the strategizing that you did in the first step by asking, Who will collect? or Who will assemble? and, For what purpose are we seeking CI? Throughout the rest of the process, if you continually checked in with the people who were performing the steps (to be sure that they were following the process as you had originally planned), you should have ended up gaining valuable decision-making material.

How Well Does Your Competition Know You?

This chapter has presented you with some of the ways that you can learn about your competition, extrapolate their next moves, and decide your next steps. However, CI is a two-way street, meaning that your competition is also looking at you, watching what you are doing, and seeking your secrets, technologies, and new products and services in progress. In response to this, you might be inclined to guard information.

But most organizations find it nearly impossible to protect their organization by playing defense. Your organization will always be vulnerable because someone—a disgruntled employee, nosy delivery person, unscrupulous supplier, etc.—will always have access to your information. That's why you have to play offense: to generate new Order Winners that keep your organization ahead of competitors.

In the 1980s, Rich Hoffman, a janitor working for a screen-printing manufacturer, frequently offered suggestions to the company's decision makers about improving the firm's products and services. His bosses ignored the suggestions, and the janitor became tired of observing from the sidelines. Armed with a great deal of knowledge about his employer, Hoffman left his position as a janitor and started his own company, M&R Equipment, to fill the unmet needs of his former employer's customer base and to put his past employer out of business.

His first press was a direct competitor to his employer's products, and Hoffman aptly named it the Challenger. Over the years, Hoffman's firm produced additional aggressively named presses like the Gauntlet, Conquest, Eliminator, Razor, and Renegade to continue his passionate rampage within the screen-printing equipment industry. M&R Equipment filled gaps left by competitors by introducing the first fully pneumatic presses, which were as good but less expensive than traditional hydraulic systems, allying with an aggressive leasing company to offer greater financing options to buyers, building his presses with more easily replaceable parts so that users could self-service their equipment, and innovating enhancements to presses that enabled his customers to improve productivity. Within the span of only a few years, Hoffman combined CI, innovation, and the drive to put out superior products to put his competitors out of business.

Of course, past employees are not your only threat. In fact, sometimes they are no threat at all. Threats and opportunities have the potential to arise from anywhere. What you do with them makes the difference between strengthening your organization or weakening it, which is why having a good CI process—whether you adopt one or source it out to an external vendor—is important.

When you think about the concepts and lessons that you have learned in this chapter, try to flip the perspective from you watching your competition to your competition watching you. Imagine that your competitor has the ET CI Process, and ask yourself, what might my competition be learning about me, and what would be the best way for my competition to put me out of business? In doing so, you (and your staff members) can begin to ideate on ways to shore up your defenses and to launch an offensive Strategy.

■ ■ ■

Watching your competition has the potential to improve your entire organization now that you have your new tool, the ET CI Process, which produces up-to-date and accurate strategizing knowledge about competitors.
When decision makers in your organization have solid CI, their performance
can improve in countless ways. For example, cross-functional NPSD teams,
screeners, and gatekeepers are better able to assess the viability of product
ideas and are more likely to develop Order Winners when they know about
the competition and consumer demands. When you are selecting alliances,
it's always good to know what your competitors are up to and who their
allies are so that you know who you can trust and how you can out-strategize
the competition without getting double-crossed. It can also be an important component when you are selecting and implementing new technologies,
because you can either imitate competitors' choices or, even better, improve
upon what they are doing. Later, you will see how CI comes into play while
you are forecasting, ensuring that your organization is a step (or more) ahead
of the pack and securing its future.

CATEGORY 3:
[PERFORMING]

Performing
Leading the Charge
Empowering Others
Innovating Everywhere
Selling Continuously

Strategizing
Developing Plans
Creating New Products & Services
Establishing Alliances
Leveraging Technology

Forecasting
Forecasting the Future

Learning
Acquiring New Knowledge
Enhancing Global Awareness
Watching Competition

IT WAS THE EARLY 1960S when a teenage boy from Pittsburgh's inner-city neighborhood of Manchester, Pennsylvania, passed through the halls of his high school and spotted the would-be inspiration for the life he would one day lead. Bill Strickland looked into a classroom and was so fascinated by a mound of clay being shaped into a form by art teacher, Frank Ross, that he became drawn in by the potter's wheel, instantly knowing that he wanted to learn the process. The teen talked his way into Ross's ceramics class, and the two developed a relationship that would change the direction of Strickland's life—and the lives of countless other people—forever.

Over the next two years Strickland cut classes so he could throw pots, but he was smart enough to give some of those pots to the teachers whose classes he cut—selling himself to those teachers and getting the results he wanted—passing grades. He took the next step and entered the University of Pittsburgh at a time when college was not the norm for people of any race in America, and certainly a rarity for people of color like Strickland. In 1969 he graduated cum laude in two disciplines. During his time in college, Strickland's love for art and desire to help others manifested itself into his involvement with an after-school program in a Manchester row house; that program became the Manchester Craftsmen's Guild (MCG), a community-arts center in Pittsburgh.[106]

In 1971, Strickland found himself at the helm of both the guild and another organization, the Bidwell Training Center, which specialized in providing vocational training to workers who had been displaced by Pittsburgh's declining steel industry. He eventually merged the two and now serves as president and CEO of Manchester Bidwell Corporation. As a professional speaker, Strickland tells his story to audiences and leaders around the United States to generate interest in his endeavors, thus gaining donations for his organization.

How has this inspirational leader's performance transformed so many lives? At the very core is his desired outcome to bring opportunity to members of his underprivileged community in a way that lends respect and dignity to Manchester Bidwell's members. In the organization's early days, Strickland believed that art and music changed people's lives, so he first set out to fill the center with beautiful and valuable art. Naysayers warned Strickland that he was setting himself up for disappointment, anticipating that inner-city youth who spent their after-school time in the facility would either steal or damage the art. Strickland didn't listen, and his art, including a handcrafted wood table, remained intact, undamaged, and appreciated by everyone. In Strickland's eyes, access to beauty and culture belongs to everyone.

In addition to a horticultural center that grows and breeds various strains of flowers and plants, the Manchester Bidwell Corporation boasts a student culinary program that rivals the best of the best worldwide. It was funded by John Heinz of the H. J. Heinz Company based in Pittsburgh after Strickland "sold" Heinz on the community benefits of his organization, which has served countless kids from the Pittsburgh school system, helping no fewer than 80% of them go on to college.

Strickland, an artist, entrepreneur, activist, educator, and organizational leader, is a living embodiment of the ET Performing category—a category that has to do with the harmonious marrying of one's personal Desired Outcome with the needs of their organization—showing how every leader has the potential to manifest his or her *inner personal* Desired Outcome into visible outward results. In Bill Strickland's case, his passion for art combined with his desire to fight poverty, crime, ignorance, and hopelessness created an organization that his website describes as the template for "education, culture, and hope" within community centers throughout the country.

As you approach the activities within the ET category of Performing, understand that these activities are different than those of the other categories in that they enable you to optimally address the human side of leading—the 20% of the GPP—in regard to the people you lead and to *you* as a leader. The Performing activities—leading the charge, empowering others, innovating everywhere, and selling continuously—come with their own set of universal tools like models, processes, and concepts that will open your eyes to ways in which you can improve as a leader. Here, the focus will be on *you*: how to improve your performance as a leader, how to understand and redirect your personal thoughts so that they manifest outwardly into better decisions, and how to cultivate and manage your relationships with other people to more effectively reach your Desired Outcome.

10

LEADING THE CHARGE

ON A SUMMER HOLIDAY DRIVE to Toronto, the city where he grew up, Sergio Marchionne scanned the highway looking at design features of other cars. The year was 2009, and only months earlier, the championed CEO credited with Fiat's stunning turnaround had been appointed to do the same for one of Detroit's Big Three automobile manufacturers, the financially distressed Chrysler. On this day, even though he wasn't in the office, Marchionne's thoughts turned to the daunting project before him: how to manage Fiat's new joint venture alliance with Chrysler and pull the latter—which had experienced a severe 25% sales drop in 2008—out of its downward spiral. Pinpointing the winning design features of competitors' vehicles and combining them with Fiat's technologies for fuel-efficient engines would help his team of product-design engineers back at Chrysler. However, Marchionne also knew that any contribution he brought to new product development would be a mere fraction of what he needed to accomplish in order to turn Chrysler around.

When he had first taken his post as CEO, Marchionne found himself strategizing about his next best steps as the leader of Chrysler. A year before, external stakeholders like the U.S. government had been less than impressed with Chrysler and its CEO at the time. Now that Fiat had brought a 35% ownership and new leadership into the mix, Marchionne had the task of selling himself as a credible leader to Chrysler's other two owners, the U.S. government and the United Auto Workers union (UAW). In addition, Chrysler now owed billions of dollars in loans to the U.S. and Canadian governments. Marchionne had to be the capable front man who would deliver on Chrysler's impending success—not only to investors but also to the millions of potential consumers who were watching. Armed with his auto-industry Wildly Successful Project, or WSP (Fiat's success), and a background in finance and law, Marchionne intelligently outlined his strategy and tactics, earning the trust and cooperation of the external stakeholders.

Internally, Marchionne had many challenges to address, perhaps none so pressing as updating Chrysler's outmoded product line. His predecessor had left only four new vehicle design models in the pipeline for the next few years, not nearly enough for a major player to survive on in the auto industry. Immediately, Marchionne wanted everyone to know that Chrysler, under his watch, was going to nourish its product pipeline. To show how serious he was about this change, he made bold statements with his actions that were touted in media outlets around the world. Rather than move into the traditional executive suite on the fifteenth floor of Chrysler's[107] headquarters, he took an office on the fourth floor alongside design engineers, showing that he was going to keep his finger on the pulse of Chrysler's challenge point (also its area of promising redemption), new product development. He traded traditional executive suits and ties for more comfortable sweaters and casual shoes to demonstrate through his attire that he was there to roll up his sleeves and get to work.[108] And after taking the aforementioned trip to Toronto, Marchionne took additional measures with his engineering and design staff to revamp the product line and make more fuel-efficient vehicles that were better aligned to increasing global fuel costs.

In addition to being personally available and involved, Marchionne wanted his team of people to have the tools, financing, and authority to do their jobs optimally. He empowered his CFO to approve operational funding requests under a million U.S. dollars, asking to be informed of requests exceeding that amount. He had capable people on staff, so as their leader, he only needed to ensure that he was building the systems and structures necessary to foster their success.

There was no need for inspirational speeches, pats on the back, or worker incentive programs. Marchionne's ability to increase Fiat's share of ownership, pay back billions of dollars in loans, and introduce the revamped Sebring as the Chrysler 200 were made possible with systems, structures, sensible plans, and guidance. The progress that the team was making instilled a greater sense of their confidence in Marchionne, and a belief that this progress and confidence would continue to grow was enough to motivate his people to work through weekends, over holidays, and long hours in between.

As was reported in a 2011 Reuters article, "Long-time Chrysler executives were energised [sic] by what was happening around them. . . . 'There was certainly a cadre of people here who were very hungry to go run a car company in the right way,' [senior VP of manufacturing Scott] Garberding said. 'He provided a picture for us that I think a lot of us said, "Yep, that's great, I'm in."' . . . The focus was now on cars, not costs, and Marchionne was leading the charge."[109]

"Leading the charge" is an expression one usually connects with action. But in ET terms, leading the charge is about the thinking that goes on in every leader's mind as he or she approaches daily challenges. More specifically, it is about the internal dialogue you have only with yourself and how those thoughts are manifested outwardly in your decisions and actions as a leader. Most people's perception of "leadership" typically centers on the image that leaders project to the rest of the world, yet as you see by the example above, that image is rooted in the thoughts that leaders have first: How will I approach this challenge? What strengths do I bring to the table? With whom will I work to reach Desired Outcomes? How will I dress and speak to appeal to stakeholders? And so on.

You've probably heard at one time or another that thoughts and actions create reality. This is true of leadership, too. As you read through this chapter, realize that Leading the Charge is not the "leadership chapter" of *Paid to Think,* because in essence, *all* of ET is about leadership. Leading the Charge is simply one of the twelve ET activities that focuses your private thoughts so that you can better direct your life and improve your organization.

The Building Blocks of Leadership: Activities versus Attributes

Think about a leader that you admire such as a coach, mentor, parent, or colleague, or a well-known present-day or historical leader. Why do you admire this person? Perhaps their upbringing, life's ambition, or path to success inspires you. If you were to describe this leader, you might use terms like determined, generous, ambitious, intelligent, or charismatic.

Even if this leader's personality traits inspire you, personality or leadership attributes alone mean nothing unless they're combined with action to create results. If you were to examine this person more closely, their actions and accomplishments are the true reasons they have grabbed your attention. You might say, "Clara Barton inspires me with her determination and generosity." But if Barton had not founded the American Red Cross in 1881, you probably wouldn't even know who she was. Yes, her attributes certainly played a role in her accomplishments, and her deep belief in her mission is inspiring, but they alone didn't build and sustain an organization that today trains and mobilizes more than 15 million emergency-relief humanitarians. She had to act on those attributes.

When you seek to improve yourself as a leader by following the popular approach of trying to adopt certain personality traits or even mimic leadership styles of successful leaders, you're heading out on a divergent path away from the outcome you're actually seeking. That's because transferring an attribute like "charisma" from one person to yourself or others is difficult at best, if not altogether impossible. And even if you could integrate some attribute that is not innately yours, research has shown that the trait would not likely help you produce better outcomes. A 2006 study by researchers at the Katz Graduate School of Business at the University of Pittsburgh found no correlation between a leader's charisma and a company's financial performance.[110] My own observations have led me to the same conclusions. Personality traits play a role but are not truly why people follow someone's lead.

So you have to ask yourself why people actually follow someone's lead. During speaking engagements where I've delivered keynotes to executives from all of ET's 7Crosses, I've asked volunteers to offer their reasons why people follow them. They've given responses such as their personalities, titles, educational degrees, and levels of experience. While these are all sensible considerations, I've seen only one concrete answer to the question: people follow you when they believe you will get them where *they* want to go. While people's desires can be varied—from needing the paycheck that you promise to deliver or wanting to service others through the means you can provide— their core reason for following you is the same.

So the next question becomes, How do I get people where they want to go? Well, you're already on your way by learning the concepts, methodologies, and other ET tools that you will use from here on out to transform your Desired Outcomes into realities.

An Improved Perspective about Leadership: The "White Horse" Leader

Earlier in this book, I talked about how we can't actually separate the functions of leading and managing, because they overlap and are complementary. You and I also took a brief look at the roots of leadership and management to better understand how they contribute to your perspectives about your role today. Now we are going to take a look at your role as a leader from the perspective that I call the White Horse Leader. Understanding your responsibilities from this perspective will help you to discern how you are either helping or hindering your own performance as a leader so that you can more effectively lead others to where both you and they want to go.

Historically, leaders generally learned how to become leaders through military experiences, and these leaders—*not management teams*—accompanied their troops onto battlefields, rode alongside their followers, and remained ever present to guide others through various missions. For a moment, I want you to visualize this type of hands-on leader sitting on the back of his white horse: the White Horse Leader who was leading the charge.

Many years later, industrialization emerged and with it came the discipline of management. While management has value, it has also figuratively pulled the leader off his white horse and away from his on-the-field command position and placed him or her in the seclusion of the executive office. This new post physically separated many leaders from their front-line people, concealing many of the daily realities and challenges of organizations from the view of leadership.

What this means to you is that you need to start looking at how your perceptions of yourself as a leader may lean one way or the other on this leadership-versus-management scale, and if you're finding that you're not spending enough time on your white horse, it's time to start using your ET tools to do so. Throughout the Performing category you will gain new tools and instruction on just how to lead the charge as a modern-day White Horse Leader and still maintain the leadership style you feel comfortable using. Becoming a White Horse Leader doesn't mean that you always have to be out front physically, however. I've met men and women who lead softly, lead from afar, lead through the assistance of other people, and who are all very successful examples of White Horse Leadership. Early on in his career, William D. Green, chairman and CEO of Accenture, a global management consulting, technology services, and outsourcing company, didn't feel comfortable standing in the spotlight. Yet over time, he learned to overcome the discomfort. As he explained it, "Now I lead a lot more from the front. I have a better appreciation of what people are expecting of me and how people are counting on me."[111] What you want to strive for here is to retain those aspects of yourself as a leader that have driven your success while improving upon weaker areas that create distance between you and your organization's stakeholders.

You can begin looking at yourself from the outside-in to seek out opportunities to improve. Perhaps you could go back to the "aha" moments you may have had when you learned about the CST Model in Chapter 3 and see if you possess one of the sure indicators of a disconnected leader; that is, have you found yourself displaying behavior common to disconnected leaders who say, "I came up with this idea—now you take care of it"? Some have the attitude that because they're leaders, they create vision, but any footwork, like developing strategy, and tactics, or thinking through the development of a product or service, etc., is the responsibility of others. Certainly, you have to tread the fine line between leading others and negatively micromanaging, but too much of this hands-off attitude threatens organizational success. This is because leaders with this mentality often don't develop plans based on their ideas, or if they do develop plans, they don't share their strategy with the people who are expected to execute these plans. You don't have to go to the extreme of sharing every strategy or tactical detail with your people, but if your tendency is to go to the other extreme and give your people ample room to work on their own, be sure that you are giving them enough direction and the right tools to reach the outcomes you expect. A Snapshot feature in *USA Today* in 2006 stated, "Of the companies with a formal strategy in place, 70% describe performance as better than their competition compared to 27% of those without it."[112] Just as interesting was the fact that only 5% of employees knew the plans developed by leadership. Evidently, you can increase the odds of organizational success if you have a plan, but you don't necessarily have to share the plan with everyone on staff.

Have you ever wondered about the connection between buy-in and leadership success? Someone once asked me about this, wanting to know if everyone at the leadership or management level needed to be part of the decision-making process in order for a top-tier leader to get buy-in. Although it seems sensible that including others will help you gain their cooperation, in reality, it is not a necessity. To illustrate my point, I previously asked you to think about this: When you drive, you tend to drive on public roads. Did you have anything to do with the development and construction of roadways and the transportation infrastructure? Those systems and structures were created for you without your involvement or cooperation in the decision-making phase of development. The same is true with the systems and structures you create in your organization.

As long as you're paying attention to the GPP and giving people the environment, tools, and guidance—such as one-on-one time, a single-page tactical plan, or a detailed CPM chart—to be successful, the plans don't always have to be outlined in detail for every person with whom you work. Congruently, you can get "on the field" with your people using technologies such as video conferencing and conference calling, collaborate software (shared desktops), intranets, and Web-based file-sharing services, further earning their trust that you will take them where they want to go and be there to guide them along the way should they need you. If you've ever had someone you're working with ask you a question via text while you were traveling, then send a video or picture for you to get a handle on what's in play, you're on the field.

As much as leaders have veered away from the White Horse Leader mentality in recent decades, I believe that they are coming full circle to where they are increasingly more connected and involved with the people they lead and with the people who contribute to their organizations' successes. This connectedness is made possible by the array of tools available to leaders and their people today. For example, internally, interfacing networks enable leaders to meet with project managers and to update development teams; externally, Facebook, Twitter, and other types of social networking tools keep leaders connected to customers, citizens, volunteers, patrons, and donors. At any time, the CEO of a public company can be called up and asked to answer to shareholders and the public through these media channels, making it much more difficult for leaders to hide.

Each day, as you approach your challenges and engage in that internal conversation about your next best moves, consider that sometimes you lead, sometimes you manage, and sometimes you must do both simultaneously. It's important that you know which role to play out and that you're always conscious of how taking on that role at the time is impacting your organization.

The ET Leading Process—Leading the Charge

Leadership isn't just born of the actions or attributes of certain individuals. Leadership goes deeper, to the core of the person, and it emerges from the thoughts and decisions that people make on a consistent basis. Now you may be thinking, "This seems very rudimentary. Of course my thoughts play a role in who I am and what I'm doing today," but consider for a moment that you've probably never seen the thought processes of leadership laid out before you as a multistep process. Therefore, you've never had the opportunity to gauge whether you typically follow all the steps, if you've done the steps right in the past, and if you've truly identified personal weaknesses that have perhaps robbed you of opportunities for years. With your new tool, you'll not only be able to do all that, but you'll also be able to link your personal strategizing to the type of professional strategizing you perform with the CST Model, making for a more compatible union of both aspects of your life.

Try to remember everything you've ever learned about making plans. In all that material, have you ever been shown how to integrate your personal needs and aspirations with the direction you set for your organization? Although your internal thoughts (and those of your co-leaders) definitely influence professional outcomes, they're rarely spoken of aloud.

You also make intentional decisions about how you want to present yourself to achieve your organizational Desired Outcome. Getting what you want professionally is influenced by what you wear, how you speak, the credentials you hang on the wall in your office, the vehicle you drive, the shoes or watch you wear, the way you address concerns with others, your fears, the accomplishments you share with others, and more. As much as both the personal and professional are connected through *you*, most lessons in leadership rarely address the influence of internal thought processes on leadership outcomes. Being aware of the connection and studying a diagrammatic process tool—the ET Leading Process—will help you realize four key benefits (outlined subsequently) and link your professional achievement with personal Desired Outcomes.

Four Benefits of the ET Leading Process Tool

When you use the ET Leading Process, you'll experience four key benefits:

First, you will see how the CST Model actually plays out in real life, not only from the viewpoint of strategizing for your organization, but also by taking into consideration your personal strategizing, too. In addition, you can use your heightened awareness about this connection to determine whether the personal strategizing of coworkers is influencing their participation and performance on certain projects and within your organization at large.

Second, the ET Leading Process is a stepped procedure that allows you to easily pinpoint areas of weakness that you need to improve within yourself to be a more effective leader. Using it as an assessment tool means that you will not have to guess where you're going wrong or where you've already mastered certain functions of leadership, because each step can be used as a self-performance checklist.

Third, this process is a universal tool that you can teach to others, multiplying its effects throughout your organization.

And fourth, your new tool will help you make use of the potential you have to be a successful leader.

Let's take a moment to consider what this actually means to you.

Years ago, our family hosted a few members of Korean-based tae kwon do demonstration team the Korean Tigers as they passed through our area on tour. The team consisted of college students who were majoring in tae kwon do at the university level. To earn their degrees, students were required to take courses in bioengineering, physics, and the mechanics of the martial art, all of which go way beyond what you would learn if you were to sign up at your local martial arts studio. As a black belt in tae kwon do myself, I was interested to learn from these students, particularly their coach. One day, I asked him how I could improve a specific kick. His lesson was an unexpected one, and I realized later that it universally applies to any endeavor, whether you're a martial artist or an organizational leader.

He asked me to stand up straight, arms to my side. As I stood there waiting for him to talk about the kick, he instead started talking about potential, explaining that while I stood in this position, I had 100% potential to deliver the perfect kick. He elaborated that once I engaged in each subsequent move, such as leaning forward, turning my hip, raising my bent knee, and extending my foot, I would either maintain or decrease my potential to hit my target. Therefore every move—lifting my leg, rebalancing my body weight, positioning my arms, etc.—had to be performed optimally for my body frame and my abilities if I were to deliver a kick as close to 100% as I could. That meant that if I initially bent my knee at a level of 89%, then every other move would have to be perfect just to reach a total performance rate of 89%.

In your endeavor to lead the charge, you start with 100% potential, too. Considering all the variables that you must deal with in order to reach your daily targets, wouldn't it be nice to know that the one factor that will not decrease your potential is yourself? The ET Leading Process, shown here in Figure 10.1, is designed to maintain your ready position at 100% and to help you stay as close to that level as possible as you lead your organization (and yourself) to your Desired Outcomes.

The ET Leading Process consists of five steps:

- **Step 1:** Develop plans on a personal level
- **Step 2:** Develop plans for the organization
  - ○ Desired Outcome
  - ○ Strategy
  - ○ Macro Tactics: including the decision to work solo or to bring on other leaders
  - ○ Tactics

Enterprise Thinking Leading Process

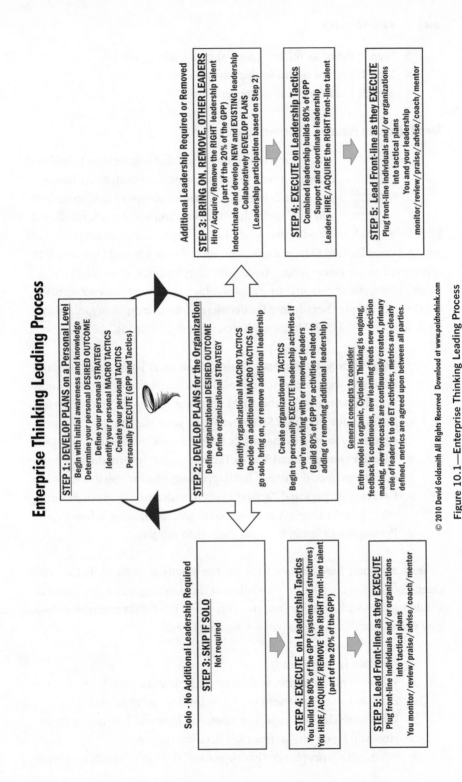

STEP 1: DEVELOP PLANS on a Personal Level
Begin with initial awareness and knowledge
Determine your personal DESIRED OUTCOME
Define your personal STRATEGY
Identify your personal MACRO TACTICS
Create your personal TACTICS
Personally EXECUTE (GPP and Tactics)

STEP 2: DEVELOP PLANS for the Organization
Define organizational DESIRED OUTCOME
Define organizational STRATEGY

Identify organizational MACRO TACTICS
Decide on additional MACRO TACTICS to
go solo, bring on, or remove additional leadership

Create organizational TACTICS
Begin to personally EXECUTE leadership activities if
you're working with or removing leaders
(Build 80% of GPP for activities related to
adding or removing additional leadership)

General concepts to consider
Entire model is organic, Cyclonic Thinking is ongoing,
feedback is continuous, new learning feeds new decision
making, new forecasts are continuously created, primary
role of leader is to do ET activities, metrics are clearly
defined, metrics are agreed upon between all parties.

Additional Leadership Required or Removed

STEP 3: BRING ON, REMOVE, OTHER LEADERS
Hire/Acquire/Remove the RIGHT leadership talent
(part of the 20% of the GPP)
Indoctrinate and develop NEW and EXISTING leadership
Collaboratively DEVELOP PLANS
(Leadership participation based on Step 2)

STEP 4: EXECUTE on Leadership Tactics
Combined leadership builds 80% of GPP
Support and coordinate leadership
Leaders HIRE/ACQUIRE the RIGHT front-line talent

STEP 5: Lead Front-line as they EXECUTE
Plug front-line individuals and/or organizations
into tactical plans
You and your leadership
monitor/review/praise/advise/coach/mentor

Solo - No Additional Leadership Required

STEP 3: SKIP IF SOLO
Not required

STEP 4: EXECUTE on Leadership Tactics
You build the 80% of the GPP (systems and structures)
You HIRE/ACQUIRE/REMOVE the RIGHT front-line talent
(part of the 20% of the GPP)

STEP 5: Lead Front-line as they EXECUTE
Plug front-line individuals and/or organizations
into tactical plans
You monitor/review/praise/advise/coach/mentor

Figure 10.1.—Enterprise Thinking Leading Process

- **Step 3:** Bring on other leaders (skip if working solo)
- **Step 4:** Execute on leadership tactics
- **Step 5:** Lead front line as they execute

Step 1: Develop Plans on a Personal Level

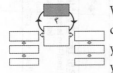 Whenever you face a situation that requires you to lead the charge—a new initiative, project, or current challenge— you actually begin an internal dialogue to determine how you will handle that situation. You wonder what skills and knowledge you have or will need to acquire, and how this situation plays into your personal Desired Outcomes. For instance, if your Desired Outcome is to climb a corporate career ladder, build your own business, or to direct a non-profit one day, these personal aspirations (which you might not ever verbalize to others) could play heavily into the decisions you make on an organizational level. Your personal CST Model might resemble the following:

- **Determine your personal Desired Outcome:** Long-term goals and what you want in life, such as owning a business, helping the educational system, making the world a better place, having an exciting life.
- **Define your personal Strategy:** Work your way up through management, job-hop to major job, travel and see the world.
- **Identify your personal Macro Tactics:** Gather information through interviews, modify style of leading, change the car you drive.
- **Create your personal Tactics:** Plans to purchase car, every morning select best clothing, get an advanced degree specializing in finance, etc.
- **Personally Execute:** Put your plans into motion.

Your attention then focuses back on the situation at hand. Before you enter a boardroom, walk into your office in the morning, call a meeting, call a vendor, meet with your banker, etc., you assess your skills and talents, and how you want others to perceive you. You might ask:

- What do I know already?
- What are my strengths, weaknesses, and areas of expertise?
- How do I want to present myself—clothing, attitude, etc.?
- What obstacles do I expect to meet, and how will I overcome them?
- How will I gain buy-in from key decision makers?
- What contingency plan do I have in place if I don't gain the support I need?

These types of personal questions are not necessarily ones that you would discuss with others. You may talk them over with your spouse, a relative, a best friend, your mentor, a coach, or an advisor, but not always.

It is in Step 1 that you toggle your attention between gaining an awareness of the situation and how you personally will handle it. The thinking process is cyclonic, and you want to quickly identify areas where you may need to fill in gaps within your knowledge bank about your industry, your project, or the people you might need buy-in from, by asking questions like:

- What is our true challenge? (Redefining tool.)
- What does my organization actually need from me?
- What do I know about my organization and the global and competition-related factors that threaten, influence, or enhance its ability to function?
- What framework (GPP) do we have in place and is it working?
- What resources and assets—financial, human labor, technologies, products and services, etc.—can we leverage in this situation? What are we missing?

The process of gathering new information and making changes is organic. You're trying to forecast potential outcomes for each decision and action even before you strategize on an organizational level. All this is happening in your mind. You've experienced this countless times during your life. Someone asks you, "Are you interested in the promotion?" and you tell them you need to think about it. The moment you heard their offer your mind started to swirl with questions and answers. Can you handle the promotion and the responsibilities considering the responsibilities you now have with a newborn at home? Do you want to travel more for work? Do you feel you have the skills, or can learn the skills, to manage such a large team? It's all a mental game where scenario after scenario is created until you're confident that one will work.

Step 2: Develop Plans for the Organization

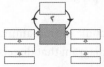
In this step, the CST Model that you learned about in Chapter 3 plays out from the perspective of the leader who is considering options for his or her organization.

Desired Outcome: You may already know, or believe you know, about the Desired Outcome of your organization, and now you strategize for this particular situation. For most leaders, their organizational Desired Outcome must be in alignment with or complementary to their personal

Desired Outcome. For example, an environmentalist wouldn't be likely to establish an organizational alliance with a party known to pollute air and water.

Strategy: Strategy is an extremely important starting point for all future decisions. It sets the direction of your organization, its resources, and end results. If you're working alone without the counsel of other decision makers, you can use thinking tools such as Redefining or many of the other Strategizing tools to ensure that your decisions will produce wins. Leaders who are weak at developing Strategy can find themselves searching for a job before they're ready to leave their posts, regardless of whether they're working in for-profit, not-for-profit, military, educational, or governmental organizations. It is at this juncture you make statements like, We should grow through acquisition," or "Our focus should be on new product development and markets outside of our region.

Macro Tactics: It is at this stage that you have two types of Macro Tactical jobs to do. First, you must decide whether you will work alone, as indicated by Solo in the diagram. Then, you will decide upon the overarching Macro Tactics for the project or initiative.

As you consider your option to go solo or work with a management team, a trusted colleague, an expert, a friend, or prospective and current customers and patrons, you should be asking questions such as:

- Will I need other people to work with me?
- Will I bring in leadership or front-line employees?
- Will I want to work collaboratively with others on Strategy or will I develop Strategy on my own?
- If I work with other management, will they function in the capacity of temporary decision makers for the duration of the project only?
- What systems and structures must I set up before I hire employees or accept new volunteers?
- How will I attract, select, and train these new participants?
- How will I guide these people and monitor their progress?

Whether or not you involve others impacts how you handle the remaining steps of the CST Model, as indicated by the arrow on the diagram that directs you to continue on as solo or with additional leadership.

- **Solo:** Complete the first four thinking steps of the CST Model alone. Working solo, however, doesn't mean that you can't solicit input from experts, consultants, or other people to help you strategize; it just means that these people will not perform in the capacity of additional leadership. A former historian of the U.S. National Park Service is thought to have once said, "The best leaders collect information widely, listen to everybody, and then decide by themselves." Consider this as a wise approach for yourself when you decide to go it alone.

Input from others is important, because it may cause you to reassess your personal and organizational strategizing in ways you hadn't previously considered.

- **Working with additional leadership:** Whether your organization is large or small, you may want or need to bring on additional leadership. I once asked Zig Ziglar, the international motivational speaker and sales expert, how he built his business. Ziglar said that he knew early on that his talents were in "writing books, preparing for speeches, and giving speeches," and that he would need to bring in other people to run the operational side of the business right from the beginning.

The decision to invite others to assist you can change from one project to another, one month to another, one business unit to another and more depending on your circumstances. In each situation, once you consider bringing on others, there are subsequent decisions to make, such as:

- What systems and structures (80% of the GPP) must I set up before I hire employees or accept new volunteers?
- What specific tasks should I expect the individuals to accomplish?
- What GPP do I need to establish to bring on other leaders?
- How will I attract, select, and train these new participants as leaders or front-line employees?
- What exactly do I expect others to contribute?
- How will I guide others and monitor progress?

Asking yourself questions like these is a good way to ultimately decide whether you will lead by yourself or lead with other leaders. No matter what your management level or type of organization, feeding questions into your Cyclonic Thinking is something that you are always going to be doing to make this determination

Now that you have settled on the Macro Tactics related to the structure of your management team—to work solo or with a group of other leaders—you're ready to address the selection of your overarching Macro Tactics for the project, plan, and/or issue at hand. Not only will you have to decide which of the remaining steps of the CST Model you will be performing on your own or collaboratively with your team, but you must also prepare Tactics targeted specifically to the management team so that they can work successfully. Therefore, you must:

- Determine how you will build the 80% of the GPP that will make the best use of everyone's talents. (Leaders need their own systems and structures, tools, and guidelines, different from those they develop for their front line; while the difference seems subtle, their impact on outcomes can be significant).
- Identify the educational needs of your team.

If you decide that you're going to act in the solo manner, you still need to develop the general Macro Tactics to ensure that when it's time for you to execute, you do it well. I've known leaders to wrestle with both the option of going solo versus working with others and with the question of, What Macro Tactics do I need to help myself or others to succeed?

The time you take to select the Macro Tactics depends on the Strategy and the type of endeavor you are planning. In addition, it can range from minutes to months or even years. Remember from Chapter 3 that Macro Tactics selection is not where you develop a tactical plan; it is a pre-thinking activity where you (and perhaps others) ask questions like:

- How can we reach Desired Outcomes in half the time, using half the resources?
- What would it take to achieve this Desired Outcome without human interaction?
- How might we benefit from working with a multicultural staff?

And you continue to ask questions while performing the necessary steps you must take to make the best decisions.

Tactics: Tactics are the tools that you develop so that anyone who is executing on your plans can do so successfully. These include plans, CPM charts, lists, blueprints, video instructions, etc. Tactics must be detailed enough to provide a road map, but not always so detailed that they obstruct the people who are executing them on either side of the ET Leading Process diagram.

Tactics must enable people to do the job at hand and are appropriately matched to the experience levels of the people who will execute them.

Not everyone wants to contribute input when you build tactical plans, nor does everyone have the skills to do so. Sometimes employees are happier when you create the Tactics and designate their role as executor only. I can't tell you how many times leaders look to their employees to solve the challenges their organization is facing and nothing happens. The reason is not because the group does not want to help; it's because it's not what they are best at or paid to do. You're the one who's paid to think as the leader.

Execute: In Step 4 of the ET Leading Process, once the leadership has been added, you will actually build and deploy the systems and structures that have been built. Your actions such as thinking, creating the GPP for the new leadership, sitting down with them to define roles, and conversing with them about direction, all happen within Step 3. It's as if you thought to yourself, I'm not going out tonight so I don't have to take care of laundry, clean the car, get a babysitter. These are no longer necessary.

Step 3: Bring On Other Leaders

 If you will be working solo without the assistance of additional leadership, skip Step 3.

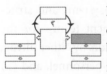 If you will be working with additional leadership, you will ensure that you hire/acquire the right people. You might be replacing leaders and managers who are not meeting the needs of the organization or the project, such as when venture capitalists or mergers and acquisitions specialists remove leaders, substitute job roles, or bring in whole new teams of decision makers.

Your situation may require you to indoctrinate management into your organization, team, or group by describing details to them, introducing them to others, supplying them with the right tools, sending them to meet with vendors, and by any other means you deem necessary.

You may work with this team to collaboratively develop Strategy for the remainder of the project, initiative, challenge, etc., or you may decide to perform this step on your own, depending on the Tactics you've developed to this point and how you decide to meet the needs of your organization. Most likely you have already selected many of your Macro Tactics and you may have already filled in the details of many of the Tactics, but with a new team comes new information, and their input may cause you to go back to some of your earlier decisions and revise them. Their level of involvement, of course, depends on your situation. For example, if you're hiring seventeen regional managers at once, your decisions about their involvement in strategizing will be different than if you hired one manager to handle shipping in one location.

In addition, one or more of the managers working with you may have to perform their own sub-strategizing activities—their own CST Models—to fulfill their responsibilities in relationship to the bigger picture: design their own systems and structures, secure talent to carry forth an initiative, and plug their own team or teams into their GPP so that they can ensure that Tactics are executed.

Keep in mind that you may be the sub-manager who is being introduced to a situation by a higher-level leader, and that you might have to take into consideration how well your plans mesh with the larger picture.

When Step 3 is completed, leaders should have a management team that has been brought up to speed so they are knowledgeable about Desired Outcome, Strategy, Macro Tactics, and Tactics as well as empowered with the right tools to perform their functions optimally.

Step 4: Execute on Leadership Tactics

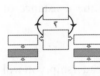 Up to this point, you have been engaged in thinking activities. Now you (and/or your decision-making team) will Execute some of the earlier decisions you have made. In this step, you will (1) build the systems and structures—solo or with involvement from your management team—for the people who will execute the Tactics, (2) line up the executors by either hiring, acquiring, or reassigning job responsibilities of existing personnel, and (3) coordinate your leadership team (if working with one) to ensure that all parties and activities of the project are synchronized.

Build the systems and structures (80% GPP): Give your people the systems and structures to succeed. It might be as simple as a one-page standard procedure or as involved as building a $2 million office. Then, be sure that the systems and structures are doable and that they will accomplish what you intend, even by trying them out yourself when possible. That way, if you find any flaws in the GPP, you can make necessary improvements before it becomes operational. It's your responsibility to review what's been created at the deployment stage, prior to launch, and ask, Will this work? Will this GPP help us to achieve our Desired Outcome as defined by the Economics of Thinking? Although this step is often skipped, give it your consideration, because it's a win-by-a-nose activity. Stop, think, and be willing to bet your paycheck that what you've accomplished to this point will work.

Line up the right talent (20% GPP): You must also hire and/or acquire the right front-line personnel who will execute the Tactics. It's not enough to say, "Get the right people on the bus." Getting the right people on the bus in the *right seat* requires planning, and the appropriate placement of executors is a measure too often performed without enough regard for the planning that drove its need in the first place. You really don't want to accept the few bodies that walk through your door by happenstance or because they replied to an ad placed at the last minute. Your future is in these decisions. If you're a one-person operation, you may have to execute, but you can still bring in other people, outsource to freelancers, enlist volunteers, or hire part-time help.

In cases where you will bring on people to execute, all organizations—small, midsize, and large alike—need management that ensures that the right and best people are selected. George and Bea Edelman, the onetime owners of Camp Idylwold, a boys' overnight tennis camp in New York's Adirondack Mountains, were leaders in their industry at the time they ran their camp. The husband-and-wife team understood the value of acquiring the best and right camp counselors to execute their Tactics, which gave Idylwold a competitive advantage over other summer camps. While other camps hired high-school-aged counselors, the Edelmans qualified only those candidates who had completed at least one year in college. They knew higher wages would attract more responsible and mature counselors who were worth the expense, since having the reliable and safety-conscious "executors" was a key selling point for gaining parents' trust and enrolling campers. Consider how you, too, can create a system that improves your ability to identify and secure the best and right people (in both leadership and front-line positions) for your organization's needs.

In addition, you can use several of your ET tools to help you position people appropriately. The Project Assignment Worksheet from Chapter 3 allows you to assign people to in-house projects from a big-picture perspective. It allows for cross-functional utilization of talents, which expands your choices of people beyond the silos of titles and departments.

Due to life's organic nature, you may find that your plans require modifications. For instance, if you're in the middle of your busy season and you know that operationally you can't afford to take current employees away from their everyday responsibilities, why not use the Project Evaluation Chart to assess the need of certain projects to be in progress at any one time based on their ROI and viability? Then you can meet with certain staffers to discuss reassigning upcoming projects on their Parallel Project Tracks to prevent you from Overcrowding your Canaries and overwhelming your staff with too many projects, all while addressing your organization's highest priorities. These, of course, are just examples of how you can use ET tools to put the right people in the right places to get the best outcomes, depending on your unique circumstances.

In the end, you want to make sure that the people you select are properly aligned with the Strategy of your organization and that they are supported with the right tools, guidance, and direction to ensure that each party is able to fulfill their responsibilities to the entire organization and/or project.

[Systems + People = Desired Outcome]

A ski school is one of the most lucrative profit centers of any ski resort, but one Vermont ski resort was running its school's registration process inefficiently, and management was remiss to find solutions. During the resort's busy season, each day would begin with the same unpleasant scene. Parents, expecting to fill out some paperwork, pay their bill, and drop off their kids en route to the slopes for the next several hours—a process that should have taken ten to fifteen minutes—found themselves waiting in line for more than an hour with their sweaty, crying, snow-gear-clad children in tow.

It wasn't unusual to hear customers groaning to each other that they refused to endure the wait again, even suggesting to each other the names of better-run resorts as future vacation options.

Although the problem was a mismanaged registration process—GPP's 80%—the ski resort's management team focused on training their staff—GPP's 20%—to give each customer a Disney-like "magic moment." Specifically, each staff member was required to sit with one customer at a time as the customer filled in every last detail on his or her registration form. Then the employee would offer ski and snow-board rentals for the youngsters, process payment for the customer, and finish up by informing parents about the lunch that would be served to their children and pickup times at the end of the day.

Management improperly addressed systems and structures, looking to erect a $300,000 building addition instead of streamlining the registration process, because Ray, the head of operations for 800 employees, and Nancy, the director of the ski school, mistakenly assumed that the "magic moment" took place in the registration lines, when in fact, it took place on the slopes!

It wasn't until management learned that the magic moment for snow-sports enthusiasts happens when they're outside enjoying their sport, not indoors filling out paperwork, that leaders began to understand that they needed to improve the paperwork process so that parents could move through their system rapidly.

After we discussed the new Strategy, Macro Tactics, and Tactics, two managers stayed at the school until 2 a.m. to reconfigure the facility. With the new system in place, one employee greeted entering customers and directed them to tables where they could fill out their registration forms. Another employee manned the tables and availed herself to field any customer questions. If customers needed rentals, they were given an additional form to complete before stepping into the payment line. Employees who were the fastest at processing paperwork and payments were stationed at the counter. Once customers had their completed paperwork in hand, they would step up to the counter and complete their transaction. Those customers who already had paperwork on file and were returning for a second or later day just made a stop at the counter and dropped off their children.

The new process reduced waiting time from an average of more than an hour to eleven minutes and eliminated the need for the $300,000 building. Not only were customers happier, but because they were no longer hostile toward the staff, and employee morale rose, too.

Not everyone on your team will share your 50,000-foot view, nor do they have to. Your job is to deliver the structures that will channel everyone's efforts toward the organization's Desired Outcome.

Step 5: Lead Front Line as They Execute

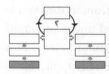 Based on your situation, you determine who will execute Tactics: front-line personnel, your leadership, or you. If you run a small operation or you're an entrepreneur working on your own, you may have to execute. Just the same, you must still allocate the time you need as a leader to strategize.

Now that you have established your Tactics and have some form of plan in place (80% GPP), the executors (20% GPP)—engineers, lumberjacks, teachers, maintenance workers, etc.—are plugged into those tactical plans. On some level, depending on your circumstances, you will review, praise, advise, coach, and mentor others—but with one difference. If you are working as a solo leader, you will guide the front line directly, whereas if you are working with a management team, you may be guiding this team of decision makers as they, in turn, guide the front line.

The entire ET Leading Process is organic. As you gather and learn new information—financial opportunities and challenges, changes in consumer buying trends, weather cycles, global events, competition's activities, new employment/unemployment patterns, emerging technologies—and you gain feedback along the way—financial reports, data, surveys, personal observations, one-on-one or group discussions—you will Cyclonically Think about new ways to adapt and succeed.

Continually review and revise tactics as the need arises. Get to know those with whom you work closely so that you're aware of their needs, can work in sync with the organization's culture, and are accessible and approachable in order to stay on target to reach Desired Outcomes. Whether you are directly or indirectly involved in tactical execution, the end outcome is still your responsibility.

The proficiency with which you perform each step of the ET Leading Process determines the potential you and your team maintain for achieving your Desired Outcomes—both personally and organizationally. Perhaps through the process or the examples you can already identify areas where you or others on your leadership team can improve upon existing skills, either by personally using the tools provided or by teaching others what really happens in the mind of a leader.

Five Ways to Boost Your Effectiveness as a Leader

Now that you have your new ET Leadership Process tool, undoubtedly you will begin to glean information about your performance from its use. And as you know, simply having information does you little good unless you know how to use it to improve your skills. That's why you are about to learn how to improve your performance in ways that will be as universally applicable in the future as they are today.

The sustainability of the following five suggestions is important considering how your role as a decision maker will evolve as technologies and advancements continually accelerate the pace of change and increasingly eliminate many repetitive and manual jobs in favor of more thinking-related ones. To keep ahead of the curve, you will have to constantly improve your performance of all ET activities, so heed these suggestions and return to them from time to time to meet the demands of tomorrow's work climates.

1. ALLOCATE TIME IN YOUR DAY FOR BOTH STRATEGIC AND TACTICAL ACTIVITIES

Most of us have a tendency to act upon our strengths instead of our weaknesses. You might notice that you have a natural preference to strategize or execute. Yet you must strike a balance and schedule time for both. Figure 10.2 offers recommendations on how to divide your time, based on your role in the organization. As you can see, even front-line employees do planning. They just do it to a lesser degree. For instance, the driver of a garbage truck must plan to ensure that he or she will have the supplies needed to complete a daily route on time, even though the bulk of this driver's day will be spent executing. The mid-level supervisor to whom the garbage truck driver reports will do a greater degree of planning—which might include next week's garbage route changes or hiring a new driver for a particular route—and a lesser amount of executing than the driver, although this supervisor will be engaged in the execution of Tactics that have been handed off by a higher-ranking decision maker. As one of those higher-ranking decision makers, your job is to make sure that you are allocating the bulk of your day to thinking (as you can see by Figure 10.2) and that everyone else is performing their roles according to the appropriate balance of strategic and tactical activities.

Time Division Recommendation for One-Role Chart

Position (Responsibilities)	% of Time Paid to Think "Thinking"	% of Time Executing Tactics "Executing"
CEO/President	90%	10%
Middle Management	60%	40%
Front-line Manager	40%	60%
Front-line Employee	10%	90%

Figure 10.2—Time Division Recommendation for One-Role Chart

In Figure 10.2, notice how the planning percentages decrease correspondingly with lower management levels. Use this formula as a benchmark to schedule your day's activities in your daily priority management planner, as you learned in Chapter 3.

Note: I'm often asked how to address dual managerial roles. For instance, someone might ask, "What happens if I perform two functions? I'm both the finance manager and the human-resource manager." In situations like this, since these are both middle management positions, the formula still applies where 60% of your day is dedicated to planning and 40% to executing. The only difference is that during the 60% of your day allocated to planning, you might have an even 30% and 30% split between finance and HR or an uneven split of 50% and 10% or some other variation. The same is true of your 40% of executing time. I've shown this in Figure 10.3.

Time Division Recommendation for Two-Roles Chart

Position (Responsibilities)	% of Time Paid to Think "Thinking"	% of Time Executing Tactics "Executing"
Finance Manager	30%	20%
Human Resources Mgr.	30%	20%
Total Time Allocation	60%	40%

Figure 10.3—Time Division Recommendation for Two-Roles Chart

The allocation of time for planning and executing applies to all organizations, because the need to spend time thinking is where leaders often short-change themselves and their organization. When leaders fail to split their time appropriately, either one function gets ignored or not enough time is spent strategizing. Determine where your position places you and start allocating the necessary time in your day for thinking-related activities.

In case you're not sure where you fit into all of this, I've provided a table (Figure 10.4) as a guideline for you. Chances are you can identify your exact position from those listed in this table, but if you can't, select one that is similar to yours and work with it for a while.

Allocation of Time for Thinking and Executing Chart

Profit Example Military Example Academic Example Not-for-Profit Example Government Example	% of Time Paid to Think "Thinking"	% of Time Executing Tactics "Executing"
CEO/President/Board General Chancellor Executive Director Mayor	**90%**	**10%**
Executive VP Captain Vice Chancellor Director of Operations Director of Administration	**60%**	**40%**
Sales Manager Lieutenant Dean Conference Manager Commissioner of Finance	**40%**	**60%**
Engineer Private Professor Waitress Auditor	**10%**	**90%**

Figure 10.4—Allocation of Time for Thinking and Executing Chart

As you become more proficient at scheduling your days' priorities according to this guideline and seeing successes come from your efforts, you will probably be excited to share this concept, along with the basics of priority management, with other leaders on staff. If you are developing other leaders or if your goals are to advance your career to a higher management level, allocating your time like this can facilitate and expedite the advancement.

Michael Gerber,[113] author of *The E-Myth*, recommends that leaders should *focus on* their organizations instead of *working in* them. What he means, in ET language, is that many leaders need to shift more of their focus toward strategizing and less on execution. In doing so, they also avoid the Squirrel Effect, an ET concept that you will learn about in an upcoming section of this chapter.

2. TRANSFER KNOWLEDGE AND SKILLS TO OTHERS

As our population ages, the number of experienced leadership and management candidates shrinks. This means that the ability to pluck key talent from one organization and drop it into yours is a dwindling luxury. Not only is our baby boomer generation of leaders retiring, but world populations are expected to decrease. In Europe alone, experts predict a population drop of more than fifty million people by the middle of the 21st century. Therefore, you must continuously build the leaders of your organization by transferring the knowledge and skills you have to the next wave of leaders. Just as you develop your own strengths as a leader, you must use all the tools and activities of ET to build these leaders of tomorrow.

Mark Lewis, CEO of Woodfold Manufacturing, Inc. in Forest Grove, Oregon, understands the importance of transferring what he knows and how he thinks to his successors who will lead his organization into the future. Lewis knows that he must plan well in advance if he is to meet his organization's long-term needs for a constant flow of talent. He recruits by reaching out to area high-school students and local citizens to find and develop leadership early on, inviting student interns into his company and teaching career and leadership skills to them long before they are ready to enter the workforce. Building leaders isn't something he believes happens overnight or on a whim. Lewis provides interns with college scholarships and personal guidance over the course of years until they are primed.

When I met Lewis, he had just attended the college graduation of one such intern and told me that he attends weddings and other special life events of the students he has helped, because they've become part of the Woodfold family. Lewis's efforts have benefited the community and placed Woodfold in a position to get first dibs on the talent he has groomed.

Knowing that leadership will be in short supply in the near future enables you to plan and act now to build strong leadership for the future. For Masayoshi Son[114]—chairman and CEO of SoftBank Telecom Corp. (which includes telecommunications companies SoftBank Mobile and SoftBankBB)—selecting tomorrow's leaders is a weekly endeavor that will span a decade. Son wants to retire by 2018 at the age of 60. To find his best successor, he meets every Wednesday with 300 leaders to improve leadership and identify "Masayoshi Son 2.0." Of these batches of executives, Son estimates that 10% come from outside of SoftBank and 90% are internal. Whether you decide to recruit from home or from around the globe, there are numerous options available to you.

3. USE YOUR WSPs TO PUSH YOUR ORGANIZATION FORWARD

As a leader, your role is to build a track record of Wildly Successful Projects (WSPs) and then use them in ways that progress your organization toward Desired Outcomes. That's a task that is often easier said than done.

People will often ask me, "I just finished this project, so it's a WSP, right?" My response is, "No, a WSP is not simply the completion of a project, nor is it necessarily a successfully completed project." You have to have the "wildly" aspect of the completed project in order to qualify it at a WSP, because a WSP outperforms the norm and exceeds people's expectations. The typically successful project might attract 100 new customers, whereas a wildly successful one brings in 326. Instead of a project that improves this year's inventory speed by 2.6%, your WSP yields an 11% improvement.

In the eyes of an Enterprise Thinker, to create WSPs you can't be a Jumper nor can you Overcrowd the Canaries. It is especially important that you think through your project in advance, taking the necessary Cyclonic Time to plan it out well in advance. When you're in the process of developing a WSP, you ask better questions about Desired Outcomes, you empower others properly, you're aware of competition, and you use your knowledge to forecast the next challenges and opportunities rather than react to present conditions, all of which increase the odds that your projects will be much more successful than you can anticipate. It's then that you gain the respect and trust of others, improve your organization, *and* gain buy-in from others when you're making your next decisions.

WSPs will travel with you your whole life. They're the equivalent of the back of a sports trading card touting the statistics of a successfully managed career.

4. AVOID THE SQUIRREL EFFECT BY STAYING FOCUSED ON YOUR PRIORITIES

In Chapter 3, you learned some valuable tools to keep yourself focused on the priorities at hand. Even with the best intentions, leaders are challenged to keep their eyes on the prize considering the number of responsibilities and distractions that creep into an average day. Yet, when you use tools like the CST Model to plan, the Project Evaluation Chart and CPM charts to select and move projects forward, and a priority-management system to organize yourself each day, you can stay on track to achieve your Desired Outcomes.

Any time you're challenged to remember the importance of your priorities, remind yourself of this true-life incident that happened to my family when I was about twelve years old. We returned home after a weeklong vacation to discover some weird destruction that an intruder had done to our home. I remember my parents' shock and dismay as they looked at the damage sustained to nearly every window's sills and surrounding molding. Who would do something like this, and why?

As soon as our dog bounded into the house and began its frenzied barking, my parents called the police. The officer on the other end of the phone suggested that the dog's reaction meant our intruder was of the animal type, and he recommended that my parents' next call be to an exterminator.

Based on my father's description of the woodwork damage, the exterminator surmised that the intruder was a squirrel and refused to pay a house visit, because squirrels are "too dangerous" and "climb up your arms and claw at your face." He told my parents to lock the dog in an upstairs room, open all the doors, and wait for the squirrel to leave. We were able to expedite the wait by baiting the squirrel with a trail of canned-tuna tidbits leading to the front door. Our intruder followed the trail out of the house, and left my parents to deal with the repairs.

Days later, when a contractor arrived to study the damages and give an estimate for repairs, he made a statement about the squirrel's behavior that I think is apropos for leaders, too. Looking at all the gnawed-up window frames, he said, "If this squirrel had just focused his attention in one area, he would have eaten his way out of the house in no time." Yet, because the squirrel had spread his efforts around the house, he failed to accomplish his mission to escape. I've since applied this type of unfocused activity to leading, and it was coined the Squirrel Effect by one of my NYU students.

Think for a moment about how much time you spend in a day gnawing away at one task, switching your focus to an initiative, then fighting fires and becoming disappointed that you're not getting the results you want. I'm sure that if this is your situation, you have a number of reasons why it is happening, but as you accumulate ET tools and learn how to use them to put yourself in the driver's seat, you can see how many of these reasons can disappear, giving way to a better tomorrow.

However, I recognize that you do not function within a vacuum. External factors can still pull you away from your desired target of focus. Quite often, people will ask, "What about my boss? I'm all over the place because he is all over the place," or they'll say, "I wish you could teach this to my boss." Certainly, knowing a better way of doing something but feeling uncertain about sharing it with a senior manager can be a challenging situation, but you still have options. For one, you can "manage up" by offering to share some of the tools in this book with higher-level decision makers. Or, if you're not comfortable doing that, you can always offer to teach these tools to your immediate peers and invite a supervisor to sit in on the sessions.

Regardless of whether you can sway a superior to use these tools, you can still benefit by becoming even more proficient as an Enterprise Thinker thereby maximizing your value to your organization in your current role. (Obviously, you can leave your current position, but that is not always a feasible alternative.) For example, a military captain who was overwhelmed and felt as if he was always fighting fires followed the recommendation to call in his superior and ask whether he thought the captain's prioritization was right. The general looked at the list and immediately eliminated several projects that were no longer important to the organization. Search your beliefs to discern whether they are actually hindrances imposed by other people or false assumptions that are causing you to hold yourself back.

By understanding the Squirrel Effect, you hopefully will stop and redirect your energies in focused ways that help you to perform better as a leader. All it takes is a win by a nose or a single WSP to make huge progress.

5. POINT TO YOU FIRST! (P2UF)

So often, when you're not pleased with an outcome, it's easy to find where someone else had contributed to the disappointing results. However, just as I have urged you to look at the GPP's systems and structures before addressing its human side, this time I'm suggesting that you look at the small portion of the GPP's 20% that represents *you*. Yes, when things go wrong, as they occasionally will, point to you first (P2UF).

I have found that many times, the people who initially appear to be the cause of a problem are actually people who followed leadership's instructions to the letter and/or they did the best they could with the incomplete plans, limited guidance, or insufficient tools provided to them.

That's why you are wise to look within and ask yourself some questions like:

- What did I do wrong?
- What was missing that I could have provided?
- Did I review the GPP first?
- Am I slowing down?
- Am I unfairly assigning blame to others?

Realize that leading others is a lifelong learning process, and although you will make mistakes, as long as you are willing to acknowledge your shortcomings and work to overcome them, your organization will benefit from your efforts. In addition, the more proficient you become at using ET tools, the more on target you and your staffers will be in your attempts to reach Desired Outcomes.

The Unspoken Realities of Leading

At the beginning of this chapter, I made the point that your personal thoughts manifest themselves outwardly as your decisions and actions as a leader. At that time, I was highlighting for you the link between your personal thoughts and the strategizing you do for your organization. In this section, I want your focus to shift onto the realities that come with the role of leadership but that no one tends to actually discuss. These are the nuances and truths that not only impact how you lead other people but that also threaten to impede your ability to reach Desired Outcomes.

People Don't Show Up to Work to Screw Up

One of the greatest unspoken realities of leadership is that people don't go to work to intentionally screw up. Over the course of the 1,800 interviews I have conducted, I've come to the realization that every person—from C-level leaders to front-line workers—wants to succeed. Regardless of whether the people were workers in businesses or volunteers in nonprofits or participants in any other type of organization, I've never met a person who intentionally set out to make mistakes, be yelled at, or create problems all day. (In fact, I've only come across seven people in all my years as a consultant and speaker who were indifferent toward their personal or organizational performance.) Most people want to do a good job, and if they're not performing well, it is because *they don't know how* to do well. In most cases, if people could eliminate fire fighting, enjoy their jobs, and earn the praises of those around them, they would.

Perhaps the reason why this reality is "unspoken" is because most leaders have an inkling that something is off, but they can't put their finger on the actual root of the problem. That's when blame can creep into relationships and organizations. But as you've learned throughout this book, if you're not getting results, you have to look at the systems and structures side of the GPP equation before you address the human element. That's not to say that the person who is "screwing up" isn't the root cause, but you can often rule out people as sources of challenges once you fix a situation caused by a problematic system or structure. Then, if you are still having issues with a person, you can either look at the training and development you've given them or look at the system you have in place for hiring the right people. In any case, realize that most people don't show up to work to screw up; they want to succeed as much as you do.

Someone Will Always Hate Your Decisions

I'm sure that there are times when you have been hesitant to pull the trigger on a decision—perhaps even to the point of paralysis due to analysis—for fear that your decision will be met with resistance. Yet, as common as this hesitancy is among leaders, rarely do they ever speak of it out of concerns that they will be seen as weak or incompetent. Leaders have to face two realities here: one, you are not alone in your concerns and two, when push comes to shove, someone will always hate your decisions. You can try doing everything right and still find that your decisions meet opposition.

The additional challenge that sprouts from this reality is the struggle to determine whether you should listen to your critics. If you've been doing ET right, your plans are well thought out and prepared, and you've taken measures to equip your people with the knowledge and tools they need to succeed, then you can proceed with a greater degree of confidence than you might otherwise have done in the past.

That's not to say, however, that there won't be instances where it would benefit you and your organization to pause and at least understand the logic behind the criticisms you may be receiving. Are others justified in their criticisms, are they unhappy, because they can't understand the factors influencing your decisions, do you fail to sell your ideas well, or are you just working with a difficult individual?

Certainly, using your new tools and performing ET activities optimally will increase your chances of gaining acceptance of others, but even then, there will be people who will not like some of your decisions. That's just a fact, so make peace with the reality that your role is not always to make everyone happy. Then, point to yourself first to be sure you're not part of the problem—if you find that a real challenge exists, solve the challenge. And only as a last resort, if you feel that you're working with a problematic person, consider replacing him or her. In my experience, it's the leader that needs fixing more often than the front line.

According to a 2008 Yahoo! survey, "43% of Americans don't like their boss's management style while 55% agree that the people don't leave companies, they leave their managers. [And] 32% of employees defy orders from their bosses."[115] While there is enough blame to go around, leaders have the authority and responsibility to effect change, while those who answer to them are usually not equally empowered. Therefore, use your authority responsibly and keep your ego in check.

At the same time, keep in mind that this is about seeing the 50,000-foot view and having the skills and knowledge to stick to the decisions when others, who may not have your view or understanding, dislike those decisions.

Notice how candidates who run for the position of U.S. president—or, for that matter, senior persons in many roles around the world—make a lot of promises to change status quo if they are elected, but when they take office, they often don't make those changes. Surely there are many reasons why this happens, but one overlooked reason is that newly elected presidents becomes privy to classified information they didn't have on the campaign trail, and the new knowledge and awareness shape the decisions they make moving forward, however unpopular those decisions will make them in the public eye.

There *Is* an *I* in Team

So often we hear the words "there is no *I* in team," an expression meant to honor the concept of teamwork and to remind people that they alone are not the single greatest reason why their groups, teams, or organizations succeed. And while the heart of the expression is well intended, I suggest you consider another point of view.

The truth is that successful groups are made up of individuals who take on a sense of personal accountability for their contribution to the whole. These are people who come to a project with the attitude that *I* will do my job right, *I* will come through for the team, and *I* will not let this organization down. Looking at the 20% of the GPP, these people prove the unspoken reality that there is indeed an *I* (or two or three or more) in every team.

You need an *I* in team to ensure that individuals pull their weight. When people are given the option to hide within the masses of the group, you'll always find the slackers who are all too willing to push their work load onto others and to avoid making their optimal contribution to the group as a whole.

Once you have addressed your 80% of the GPP, be sure that you seek out people who understand this unspoken reality and who are willing to step up and do their jobs well.

In terms of your participation as an *I* on your team, keep in mind that since language is extremely important to working effectively with others, you should pay close attention to your use of "I" and "we" in different situations. When your group succeeds, switch your language to "we"—we did it, we succeeded, we accomplished what we set out to do. Conversely, if circumstances go awry, the leader should take the "I" position publically—I take responsibility, I understand how we can turn this around, I will talk to the media, I

will help to make things right with the customer, etc.—and reserve addressing another person's errors with them in private. Seldom will you come out
on top if you do not use this formula.

Sustainable Progress Is Achieved Only When Leaders Consis-
tently Take Their People Where They Want to Go

At the opening of this chapter, I touched on the concept that people follow leaders who take them where they want to go. I've worked with numerous leaders, from senior management on down the chain, who think they're
doing a great job, because their people follow their lead and perform for
them. A closer look at these leaders' successes and some insight into their
people reveal another unspoken reality, which is that the results achieved by
their organizations occurred due to high-performing followers, not because
of high-performing leadership. A 2007 *BusinessWeek* poll of 2,000 American
middle- and senior managers revealed that 90% of managers think they're
among the top 10% of performers in their workplace [116] and 97 percent of
whom consider themselves shining stars. Think about that statistic for a
moment. What it really tells us is that the majority of leaders grossly overes-
timate their performance levels!

Many people will follow you for a paycheck, plain and simple. But let's
face it, you have a title—president, VP, director, manager, supervisor—and
the authority that goes along with it, which is oftentimes influence enough to
drive performance, at least in the short term. Yet meeting sales targets, gaining the cooperation of others, or reaching Desired Outcomes doesn't mean
that you're performing all the activities of ET optimally. It could just mean
that people are "making do" with what they have *despite* your shortcomings.
Perhaps they're holding onto a job, because they have a huge medical bill
they need to pay off, or maybe they're just biding their time until a better job
opportunity opens up somewhere else.

Typically what happens over time when leadership consistently underper-
forms is that good workers tire of picking up the slack and fixing poorly
thought-out plans or doing the work of both the executor and the strategizer, so they head for organizations where new leaders will take them where
they want to go. Along with their exodus goes the sustainability of success.
On-the-job success is important for most people, and a paycheck will hold
them for only so long.

When DuPont CEO Ellen Kullman was faced with pulling her organization
through the recession commencing in 2008, she was able to generate seven

straight quarterly earnings that beat analysts' expectations. "I am a much better leader because I had three kids." Kullman acknowledged to Businessweek. com. "With kids, they don't do what you want them to do when you want them to do it. Organizations don't necessarily, either. You've got to listen. You've got to learn how to influence."[117] With that philosophy in mind, Kullman focused her employees on matters that were within their control rather than on issues that weren't, and she led them safely and successfully out of the period of economic turmoil and into better times.

Your job is to continually improve your skills so that you're one of those organizational "I's" who is making your optimal contribution to the whole. In the next chapter, you will learn additional tools to help you empower other people, thus improving their odds of finding success within your organization. In addition, it's up to you to create an *authentic* track record of success (WSPs) and deliver value back to your people. Use the CST Model, ET Development Funnel, the Project Evaluation Chart, and Competitive Intelligence Process to select and develop winning projects that improve your organization and fuel others' trust in you. Only then can you be sure that your followers are there, because you're taking them where they want to go.

When Empowered People Fail, Leadership Is Usually at Fault

One of the most stunning of the unspoken realities of leading is leadership's obliviousness to their role in the failures within their organization. I'm always shocked at how many leaders complain about their people falling short of achieving targeted results without realizing that the people didn't have what they needed from leadership to succeed. When these leaders hand over authority and responsibility to others, they don't properly equip them to achieve success—typically, in lieu of providing plans and tools, they dole out a healthy dose of "you-can-do-it" praise—but when outcomes don't meet expectations, the leaders are left scratching their heads in bewilderment.

There are right and wrong ways to empower people (which we'll get into in detail in the next chapter), and if leadership drops the ball in the beginning, the whole endeavor begins at far less than its 100% potential mark.

Think back to Chapter 3 and the details of the Tactics portion of the CST Model. We discussed how you must appropriately match the tactical descriptions to the skill and knowledge levels of your executors. In addition, we've discussed the importance of tools for you, and that one of the great advantages of ET tools is that you can transfer them to others. Often, people need you to sit down with them, not even across the table but right beside them, and help them learn and develop just as you would ride next to your son or daughter in a car for forty hours or more, to make sure he or she has the skills to drive on back roads, highways, on city streets, and in heavy traffic. As you lead others, remind yourself that to avert negative outcomes, you need to properly arm them and guide them to success.

Leadership Can Be Taught, but Not Everyone Is Leadership Material

There are just some people—no matter how nice they are, no matter how much you would like to groom them for leadership—who will never be able to reach the level of leadership. The unspoken reality is that not everyone is cut out to be a leader, so your first step in developing your organization's next generation of leaders is to be sure you select the right people to teach and then know the right course of action to take with them.

There are essentially four types of people (and variations in between) from which to choose:

- those who stand out as potential leaders.
- those who will need to be sought out as diamonds in the rough.
- those who aren't capable of performing in leadership roles.
- those who simply don't want to rise to leadership positions regardless of any carrot dangled in front of them.

That's not to say that people in this last category aren't capable of performing optimally in leadership roles—they just don't want to lead within your organization. (This last group may enjoy coaching their child's little league team, but they don't want leadership responsibilities in the workplace.)

As you look to develop leaders in your organization, get to know people by observing how they handle situations: that means how they handle successes and failures, and opportunities and challenges. When it's feasible to do so, get to know your people personally, because the person you believe to be incapable of leading others based upon their performance within your organization might be a committee head at the local Rotary Club who regularly organizes successful community-centered events. Once you have a better understanding of a person's potential, you can then provide them with experiences to see how well they learn and achieve, remembering that leading often comes down to knowing how.

If You're Not Motivating, You're Probably De-motivating

All leaders have an impact on motivation, and the unspoken reality is that whether a leader is of the hands-on type or absentee type, they are in a perpetual state of either motivating others or de-motivating them. Undoubtedly, your actions, decisions, and comments have an impact on motivation, but like many leaders, you may not be fully aware of how they have caused certain conditions, both good and bad, to exist within your organization. The difference between the motivator and de-motivator comes down to the leader's proficiency at performing leadership activities and being able to sell his or her WSPs to instill hope.

In 1914, the following solicitation for twenty-seven workers appeared in a small European paper. After reading it, ask yourself if you would have applied for the job.

> *Wanted for hazardous journey.*
> *Small wages.*
> *Bitter cold.*
> *Long months of complete darkness.*
> *Constant danger.*
> *Safe return doubtful.*
> *Honor and recognition in case of success.*

Mind you, mass advertising did not yet exist, yet this ad drew more than 5,000 responses from Cambridge-educated scholars to seasoned sailors who were interested in going on an expedition to Antarctica under the leadership of Ernest Shackleton.

The response was favorable, not only because its leader held the promise of reaching new horizons, but also because it spoke to the heart and behaviors of people, who by nature are somewhat self-motivated. Consider for a moment the energy you'll see in a new hire. Typically, this energy is the motivation that comes from believing that an opportunity will lead one to their desired achievements.

After the seven months of training, *The Endurance* set sail. A few months into the trip, one evening in early 1915, the temperature at sea dropped very quickly, causing the ship to become stuck in ice in the Antarctic seas, where it was crushed by ice and sunk ten months later. Though Shackleton and his men were forced to live on the ice for five months, this leader was determined to save his crew.

He and five crewmen set out on a cross-ocean/cross-mountain trek over South Georgia over perilous terrain, battling snow, bitter cold, and lack of food to find help. When they came upon a whaling station on South Georgia Island, Shackleton organized a group of rescuers, and the newly formed band made its way back to the remaining members of *The Endurance's* original crew. In August 1916, all crewmembers were rescued and returned home alive.[118]

When Shackleton organized a second expedition, all crewmates from the first expedition who were still living enlisted. That's because Shackleton was a leader who knew how to lead others in such a way that he motivated them. His excellent planning skills and preparedness helped him build a track record of success, and he gave people the tools they needed to create their own successes.

Like Shackleton, not all your initiatives will work out as planned, but if you're a leader who can carve out successes and bring your people to where they want to go—whether their "destination" is to earn good wages, acquire health benefits, do fulfilling work, or feel prestigious—you will motivate and inspire them to follow you and to contribute to the successes of your organization.

Good Leaders Protect Their Offense with a Good Defense

Often, leaders place so much emphasis on sales or on the public face that their organizations project to external stakeholders that they overlook the importance that defensive mechanisms play in winning over customers, vendors, or shareholders. For example, they don't provide adequate backup support such as timely delivery from their production crew, accurate billing from their accounting department, or friendly service from their receptionists. The unspoken reality is that the best offensive moves can only get you so far if you don't have a good defensive network to back it up.

I liken this concept to a decision that was made by a head coach of one of my son's lacrosse teams. It was his freshman year in high school, and the team was leading its league due to a strong offense. Most games started off with a couple of goals from our son's team within the first two minutes, and it only got worse for the opposing team from there. So that the team didn't look like on-field bullies, the coach would pull his first stringers off the field in the first few minutes of the game so the second- and third-string players got most of the in-game playing time.

Our son, a defender on the first-string squad, continually voiced his concern that if his team were to come up against another with similarly skilled offensive players, his team would be at a disadvantage due to the fact that the first-string defenders had little to no ball-handling time during games. His solution was that when the offense was pulled off, the coach should leave the defenders in to get the practice they needed.

His concerns were realized when the day came to play his team's most aptly matched rival. As usual, in the first few minutes our son's team scored. Then the other team scored. Then our son's again, then theirs. For the first time that season these defenders had to play the entire game. The game ended with a win for our son's team, but only after going into a nail-biting double overtime. The lesson for the coach should have been that regardless of how well the offensive team was doing, the desired outcome—the win—was jeopardized because the defensive team wasn't given what they needed to be as strong as their offensive counterparts.

The same holds true in any organization. Be sure to strengthen all aspects of your organization so that you can draw upon any part of it when you need to.

Great Leaders Know When to Lead from the Front and When to Lead from the Rear

This chapter opened with a vignette about Fiat/Chrysler CEO Sergio Marchionne, a leader who seems to know when to get out front and represent his organization in the media, to governments, and to financial backers when he is called to do so. At the same time, Marchionne knows when to get involved behind the scenes, both strategically and tactically, as proven by his decision to work from the operational core of Chrysler's headquarters. The unspoken reality is that the majority of leaders have a preference for leading either from the front or from the rear, but rarely do they like equally leading from both places. There's no shame in having a preference, and I believe that you're far ahead of the game if you can acknowledge your liking for one over the other as a starting point for learning to figure out a way to accomplish the benefits of having both done well.

That does not mean that you must actually do both. You can create mechanisms and hire co-leaders who can perform one or the other if you find that you have weaknesses in one of these areas. For example, I once worked with a turnaround manager for the United Way who quite successfully remained in the rear, but who was able to train and support a staff of leaders who led out in front. This manager is one of six employed by the United Way whose job is to enter underperforming United Way offices and make them viable again. The way these turnaround experts approach their missions is to do the jobs quietly, away from any media attention, and even distanced from the front office. Their responsibilities are to find talented leaders and nurture them into their roles, phasing out their own positions as the organizations become strong enough to function without them.

Although the turnaround specialists don't typically announce their time-line for staying with an organization, they tend to work on a three-year cycle. For that reason, they want to lead from the back and build up the leadership that will be staying on to be able to lead from the front, teaching the up-and-coming leaders how to attend media functions, speak to the public, conduct effective meetings, and run the organization. The turnaround team, there-fore, stays out of the limelight and primarily advises new leaders so that the latter can work on their own one day.

I've learned over the years that most leadership books focus on theory, leadership style, and leading from the front. However, these resources seem to ignore the fact that many leaders can't extrapolate the practical from theo-retical, they have their own leadership styles that are oftentimes not like those being touted by the gurus, and they need alternatives to leading from the front if that's not their strength.

There is no one cookie-cutter approach to leadership, which is why you need alternatives to leading from the front or back if one or the other is not your strength. Bottom line: your organization needs leadership that is effec-tive both in the front and the rear, and it's up to you to be sure it gets it either from you or from people and systems that you put in place to suit your par-ticular circumstances.

Leaders Are Like Coaches Who Create Playbooks and Assign the Right Players to Execute Their Plans

Think of yourself as the coach who strategizes and creates playbooks and of your staff as the players who execute under your guidance. Coaches don't typi-cally ask athletes to help them assemble playbooks. That's not to say that while trying out a play an athlete doesn't provide feedback so that the coach can modify the play to make it stronger. But the unspoken reality is that the leader who functions as the coach has one set of responsibilities, and the followers, who act in the capacity of players, have another.

In addition, coaches and players generally do not perform interchange-able roles, yet there are situations where this does occur. Even if you lead a small operation where you wear the hats of both a coach and a player, you still need to separate out the responsibilities of each so that you don't fall into the trap of executing Tactics without giving ample attention to strategizing. For example, when a Hollywood actor directs a movie and acts in it too, he is creating strategy with a collaborative team *and* he is executing, by acting out one of the roles. However, the actor/director is not collaborating with all the other actors, per se; he is performing two distinct jobs and has two sets of people—strategic to write the playbook and tactical to execute it—and he keeps those functions separate.

Leading Takes Practice

Are you ever surprised at how difficult it is to find good leadership or management? Aside from the many, many reasons we've already outlined, this is due to the fact that throughout life, people in most cultures are taught to play by the rules, listen to their elders, stay seated in class, and obey authority. But then, seemingly instantaneously, when they're put in a position of leadership, they're somehow supposed to forget all that's been ingrained in them and act like a leader. Being a leader requires a different mindset and additional tools, and you have to practice if you want to have strong leadership skills.

Becoming a great leader is a lifelong journey. It can be an unforgiving job of sometimes unpredictable rewards and consequences, meaning that you might take action believing that it will deliver a positive return only to churn out a negative one. There are times when you have to admit that you've erred, and sometimes people are forgiving and supportive, other times they're not. The lessons you learn by trial and error are invaluable and necessary to your growth as a leader.

Most educational systems are not designed to build leadership and encourage innovative thinking. They are meant to equip the masses with basic information needed to gain non-leadership employment. The condition stems from educators who don't know what it is to empower others and who don't know that it's their responsibility to do so. In addition, education is siloed, and not until high school, and only within certain disciplines, do educators sparingly crossbreed courses—a history teacher integrating art or science into their curriculum, for example. Therefore, students aren't getting skill-building instruction on how to integrate information and connect the dots the way that leaders must in the real world.

If you examine any society in history that has done well, the parents did not know if they would survive, so they taught their children the skills necessary to continue on if something happened to them. Maybe something is missing in our education where practicality of leadership and real-world utilization of that education has been lost. Yet you can give opportunities to others in a similar fashion by utilizing your ET tools to become a better leader, practicing them in conjunction with each other and with all ET activities, and by transferring those tools and concepts to others so that they can become empowered, too.

Successful Leaders Choose Their Own Captains

Has anyone ever said to you that you can choose your own team? How did that make you feel? A little nervous? A little excited? A leader's achievements often come down to the captains they surround themselves with, whether those captains came with the job, or the leader went out and handpicked them.

Sometimes you take on a new position and inherit a group of leaders that you wouldn't necessarily select if given your druthers. In these instances, you'll probably find yourself constantly assessing individual leaders to ensure that they are carrying out your Strategies and Tactics. In many instances, leaders are forced to let some of these inherited leaders go to make room for people who are better suited for their team and plans. In the end, you choose your own captains.

As head coach of the Northwestern University football team, Gary Barnett was asked by a television reporter how he was able to take the team to a college football bowl game after its twenty-year losing streak and after just two years on the job. His reply was that when he first took the position, he realized that none of the team's coaches had ever been to a bowl game, so he started by replacing them. The new coaches improved current athletes' performance levels immediately, because winning coaches have winning tools. The impact affected recruiting, because better coaches recruited higher-caliber athletes in subsequent seasons. The combined effect was more wins. Within two years he had a winning team.

Now look around at your leadership team. Do you have winners? Would you go to battle with the people around you? Can you teach them to win? Do you have the skills to elevate their performance? In response to these questions, I'm often told "No." If that's your situation, then it's your role to make the changes. While hiring is an obvious solution to building a team of winning captains, there are four ways that you can accomplish the same outcome.

The easiest way to have a winning leadership team is to step into a position where one already exists. It's great when your decision makers already understand each other, can work cooperatively toward solutions, and can help you execute on Tactics that reach Desired Outcomes.

The second-best situation is that you acquire a group of decision makers to replace less-effective ones. Depending on your situation, you may have to promote people from within or hire them away from other organizations (such as when headhunters are used to find already-skilled talent).

The third way is to create your own group by bringing on all new people. While this option can be exciting, there's more effort involved. The payoff, of course, is that you get the team you want and that will buy in to your initiatives from the onset of your relationship with them.

The last and least-appealing option is to acquire (or inherit) a group of leaders who are challenging to win over and who will demand that you prove yourself before they're willing to buy into your ideas. These situations exist all the time, and they challenge leaders to figure out how to work with groups that are uncooperative or incompetent. Sometimes you have to really struggle to get anything done until you can make changes to this type of group.

In any one of the situations, you still have to perform leadership activities to ensure that you can make progress and lead your organization optimally.

Leaders Who Walk in the Shoes of Their People Make Better Decisions for Their Organizations

One of the most painful unspoken realities of leading is to admit that leaders can be clueless about the challenges their people face. That's why I have always felt that there are few opportunities better than stepping into the actual jobs of your people to see firsthand how these individuals are being supported or hindered by leadership—leadership meaning you.

The television show *Undercover Boss,* launched in the UK but since released in a number of countries around the world, features a senior-level executive, usually a CEO, who conceals his identity from subordinates while stepping into a front-line job within his own company. As the leader works alongside unsuspecting "coworkers," he learns the challenges of the job and quickly identifies how most of those challenges exist because of shortcomings from management. Prior to this clandestine work experience, these managers assumed that the challenges at the front line were caused by employees, but their perspective changed as did the decisions they made after revealing their identities during an apologetic speech.

As recommended in Chapter 7, try doing a subordinate's job when they go on vacation. It's a great way to learn how you can improve your organization. Be the receptionist, the purchasing agent, the shipping manager, or the order-entry clerk. See where repetitive tasks could be streamlined, notice where mistakes are consistently made, pay attention to where bottlenecks in processes exist, and take note of where people seem frustrated with their jobs. These are all opportunities for management to make better decisions and improve the organization.

Getting your hands dirty can reveal a lot more about the impact of your decisions than walk-around management can, and the changes you make in yourself as a result can bring long-lasting benefits to your organization.

Tomorrow's Success Is Directly Tied to How Well You Think and Decide Today

One of the most exciting unspoken realities of leading is the power that today's decisions have to create the future of your organization. If you've never considered this reality, take a moment to consider how the strengths and weaknesses of your organization today are the result of leadership and management decisions that were made in the past. You inherit conditions that are the result of past leaders' decisions, and you are currently creating the tomorrow that either you or the next leader will have to work with.

Cheng, the owner of a Chinese takeout restaurant near my home, learned early on in life that his thinking would shape the future of his family and his business. He came to America from China with a limited knowledge of the English language and opened a restaurant in Syracuse, New York. One day several years ago, Cheng explained that he wanted to build his business into multiple restaurants, and he asked me to take a tour with him of some property that he was considering buying. I remember one building in particular. To the everyday onlooker, it looked like nothing more than a three-story dilapidated fixer-upper sporting a caved-in roof. It was in a less-than-desirable part of town, but Cheng saw none of that. Instead, he envisioned what it would be in the future—its first-floor restaurant and two floors of apartments to house his nuclear and extended family members.

Fast forward a year later: Cheng invited me to visit the completed structure housing a new restaurant on the first floor and at least a dozen apartments throughout the rest of the building for his nuclear and extended family. There was also a central gathering area, a laundry room, and even a prayer room. The decisions that Cheng had made twelve months earlier had led to this incredible reality.

The better you are at performing the activities of your position and integrating factors that affect your organization—its products and services, employees, competition, industry-related changes, global and geopolitical issues—the better able you are to make and create an improved tomorrow for your organization, too.

The Majority of Leaders Fear Their Flaws Will Be Exposed

In the beginning of this book, you read statistics revealing that very few businesses and organizations are actually run by people with a business-school education. An unspoken reality of leading is that countless decision makers are not confident about their decisions, actions, and their organizations, while outwardly projected as highly functional, are not well run, and oftentimes unstable. I call it the Wizard of Oz Syndrome due to its likeness to the wizard in the famed 1939 movie *The Wizard of Oz*, who outwardly projected an image of mightiness and power, but who in reality was nothing more than a cowering man pulling levers behind a curtain while braying into his microphone. An overwhelming number of leaders and organizations pose as skillful, confident, and "together," but pull back their curtains, and you wonder how these organizations continue to function. I often ask myself, how do boats float, planes fly, and restaurants not make more people sick considering what I've seen behind the scenes at organizations.

One way to overcome the hindrances associated with this reality is to feed your mind with the right types of information so that you can make smart decisions, lead your organization to success, and ultimately breed a sense of inspiration and motivation among your people. That's because when you make decisions based on facts and acted upon by skills rather than from making guesses and taking chances, your decisions tend to have a longer-lasting positive impact on your organization, which instills trust and hope in your people.

With the right data in hand, you can make better financial decisions, even if you decide to up the risk level, because you can more accurately calculate the impact that your decisions will have on your organization. The owner of a chain of jewelry stores believed that 80% of his business came from referrals by satisfied customers. It wasn't until we conducted some research that he realized approximately 80% of his business came from passers-by who saw his signage and decided to walk in for watch batteries, ring repairs, or new purchases. His business was built on walk-in customers who like his signage, not on existing customers making referrals. Even though his business was doing okay, imagine what opportunities he could have captured earlier had he known the actual data.

Slow down, accumulate and assemble the information, then take some time to process it so that you can make realistic and smart decisions to steer your organization into a brighter future.

■ ■ ■

Leading the Charge is about you and the thinking that impacts how you lead others. While previous chapters have addressed the more practical aspects of leading, this chapter has focused on the human factors involved in leading and managing others.

After looking at the historical roots of leadership and management, your view of your role as a leader and manager should be expanded, and you should be challenging some of the beliefs you've held as truths so that they no longer hinder your ability to perform. Through the ET Leading Process, you became aware of the need to reconcile personal Strategies with organizational ones and the importance of focusing your thought processes internally in order to improve the skills and image you project outwardly to others. And while the tools you have learned are static, I do realize there is an organic nature to how your professional life unfolds. As you incorporate your new awareness, knowledge, skills, tools, concepts, and activities into your daily work life, you will make the kinds of win-by-a-nose decisions that eliminate fires, free up your time to think, enable you to generate WSPs, and inspire you to continually build a better organization, career, and life today and tomorrow.

EMPOWERING OTHERS

IMAGINE THAT YOU ARE THE parent of a sixteen-year-old son who wants to learn to drive the family car. Picture yourself walking past your son as he plays basketball in your driveway with his friends. You toss to him the keys of the car and tell him that you have complete confidence in him and his ability to drive himself to school the next morning. Your logic is based on three facts: (1) he drove with you in the car for ten minutes last weekend and seemed focused, (2) he's a good student in school, so you know he's responsible, and (3) he's watched you drive him to school for the past several years, so it's no big mystery what roads to take. (I think you know where I'm going with this scenario.) When your son inadvertently miscalculates a turn and runs the car into a ditch, who are you going to blame? Him, for not knowing how to drive, or yourself, because you didn't properly empower him with the skills and education he needed to operate the vehicle safely?

Most people would never thrust a loved one into the driver's seat before adequately preparing them for the challenges ahead. Yet when it comes to their work environments, leaders put their people in the same kinds of risky situations by handing over authority without having sufficiently established the 80% of the GPP, including well-thought-out plans, specific skills, tools, systems, processes, knowledge, and more to support their people's success. Yet once you can see that the solution begins with you—because leaders have the authority and means to build an environment that empowers others to reach Desired Outcomes—you will experience far fewer disappointments and enjoy many more successful results.

What I want you to get out of this chapter is that empowerment involves more than the handing over of projects and tasks to others, and once you're equipped with the right leadership tools to empower people properly, you'll no longer have to rely on the ineffective default method of simply motivating people with encouragement—what you'll see referred to as "hugging and kissing" your people. There are definitely right ways and wrong ways of transferring authority and responsibilities to the people who help you achieve your Desired Outcome, and if you want better outcomes than you've gotten in the past, you can make an immediate change by using a tool that you will learn here called the ET Empowering Process. It doesn't have a fancy name, but it will improve your results and help you strike that balance between the extremes of letting go too much and of hovering to the point of suffocating progress. In addition to this tool, you will learn some tips that you can use to help others to help your organization be the best it can be.

Now that you have the first ten chapters under your belt, I'm sure that you're increasingly seeing the interconnectivity of all the ET activities, so as you read through this chapter, try to do some Cyclonic Thinking of your own about how you can use some of the tools you have already learned in conjunction with the ones you learn here to give your people the 80% of the GPP that will foster their successes.

Empowering Others at 50,000 Feet

Every leader must rely on other people to manage some portion of their tactical activities, even if the leader operates within in a small organization and executes at times. So it makes sense that the better you equip executors with the tools they need to be successful, the better off your entire organization will be.

As the president of a small financial institution, Fred hired a government-recommended consultant for $10,000 to develop a disaster plan for his bank. I doubt that Fred really anticipated having to use the plan, since most of us don't when we're taking such prudent measures, but he did the responsible thing and followed regulations just the same. After he received the completed plan, Fred filed it away for safekeeping in the event of a "rainy day," and to his surprise, that rainy day actually arrived in the form of a major flood that wiped out his bank's infrastructure and that of numerous other institutions across the Midwestern region of the United States. Assuming that the 600-page tactical plan had adequately prepared his institution to handle these sudden challenges, Fred and his staff pulled out the plan and got ready to use it. Disappointedly, they discovered that the plan was nearly useless. It did not contain the information that they all needed to minimize damage to the bank and to get operations up and running smoothly soon after the flood waters subsided. The consultant had failed to provide a tool that empowered Fred and his team to reach Desired Outcome.

Months later, Fred and other banking presidents joined up at a statewide conference to discuss disaster plans and the flood that affected all their banks. Within two hours, they identified twenty or so realistic disaster-plan tactics that they could roll into a simple disaster-recovery plan consisting of no more than five pages. Within their roles as leaders, they worked together to develop a plan that was concise, precise, and realistic. Different than Fred's first emergency plan, this new version included the cell-phone numbers of key staff members so that everyone could communicate should landlines go down. It also outlined the actions that leaders would need to take if team members couldn't physically reach the bank, another obvious directive missing from the 600-page plan, probably because the consultant had likely never been in the position of a leader having to pull together a team in a real disaster.

If you were to consider all the people that Fred and his leadership would have to address in the event of a disaster, you would quickly see that the scope of the tactical plan extends beyond the bank and its employees. External stakeholders, like patrons and board members, and disaster-service people like plumbers, carpenters, locksmiths, and local government and public-works officials would have to be addressed as well. Even in the best of times, Fred and leaders like him are constantly in a position where they need to empower others in order to protect and grow their organizations.

Take a moment to consider the people who play important roles in the success of your organization. Who must you entrust with responsibilities such as tasks and projects? There may be other decision makers, front-line workers, staff members, volunteers, teachers, officers, or technicians, depending on the type of organization you lead. Typically, when we think about empowering others, we look at the people who function within our organizations. However, I'd like you to expand your perspective to the 50,000-foot view so that you can realistically include all the people that you depend on to a certain degree: suppliers, customers, allies, lawmakers, and bankers, the janitorial service that keeps your restaurant's restrooms clean and the landscaping company that trims hedges in the summer and plows your parking lot in the winter. What kinds of changes can you make to the ways in which you work with them that will empower them to do a better job for your organization?

In essence, your decisions affect *all* of the people who have an impact on the results you achieve as a leader. Therefore, when you place your next order for a product, I want you to see that order as an act of empowering the vendor to provide your organization with what it needs. So if your business specializes in installing tile in commercial buildings, how can you more effectively tie your vendor—the supplier of your marble tile—to the customer orders you have in house? What systems can you put in place, and what tools can you use to ensure that you and your staff members can track when the marble will arrive and how it will be transported to a specific job site on time and in quality condition?

From 50,000 feet, you can set up a digital tracking system linked to your primary vendor's order processing system so that you can view where the order is in production. The system also connects to the fleet management systems of major carriers so that your team does not have to look up where your shipment is in route—their digital dashboard supplies them with daily updates. All this is linked to your own scheduling system, which you tie to project CPM charts. Knowing where your marble is in route enables you to have trucks and manpower at the right location at the right time so that the marble is moved as quickly as possible to the job site and installed. The result is reduced inventory, improved product delivery, early warning tools for staffing needs, elimination of phone calls and e-mails, increased productivity by reduction of nonvalue added actions, and improved cash flow because of faster invoicing and collection.

When you realize the responsibility is yours to empower external stakeholders as well as internal staff members, you make greater strides in your working relationships with them. You begin to ask, Are our purchase orders easy to read? Do we give our vendors ample time to do their best work for us? Are we helping our vendor help us? and so on. You create infrastructure that allows vendors to tap into your organization through computer portals for the purpose of systemizing and expediting shipping and billing functions, or when you make it possible for clients to manage their accounts 24/7 from their home computers, you are empowering your external stakeholders to do their best job for you.

Since the process of empowering others (either in their everyday jobs or for specific projects) requires you to go beyond the simple transference of authority to them and then sitting back and hoping for the best, you need a way of ensuring that you have created and installed the appropriate 80% of the GPP. Certainly, you contribute to this aspect of empowering others just by performing all the activities of ET, which result in complete plans, improved products/services/internal improvements, reliable allies, appropriate technologies, up-to-date information about global happenings and competitive intelligence, and so on. But above and beyond all of that, you must specifically provide others with what I call "building the entire package" of tools, systems, structures, knowledge, skills, and guidance they need to be able to make good decisions when necessary and to carry out your plans, even if they don't share your 50,000-foot perspective.

The Enterprise Thinking (ET) Empowering Process

Regardless of whether you're an involved leader or one who prefers to be hands off, when you empower other people with responsibilities, the final outcome of their work still rests on your shoulders. I'm sure that there have been times in your life when you passed the torch to another person expecting a certain outcome, and later you were disappointed in their performance. It happens to all leaders at one time or another. Whether someone misunderstood what you wanted and messed up a plan or they intentionally cheated you in a deal, if your trust in someone else didn't yield the results you wanted, it's up to you to take the steps needed to prevent a repeat of the situation in the future. And like all of us, when you know better, you do better.

That's why the ET Empowering Process can be such a reliable go-to tool for you. It consists of steps you can easily follow to ensure that you, in your role as the leader, take the right actions up front to produce optimal conditions that stand a better chance of producing the outcomes you want: a win-win for your entire organization. And it helps you to avoid taking nonproductive and even counterproductive measures, like those listed here:

- "Hugging and kissing" people to motivate them, improve morale, or instill confidence as a primary means of securing better results. Too much emphasis on this 20% of the GPP can sidetrack leaders away from producing the 80% of the GPP necessary to foster success.

- Ignoring the 80% of the GPP, resulting in leaders supplying an incomplete system that demands repeated intervention to avoid perpetual doubt, confusion, and mistakes. A sure sign that you have developed an incomplete system is when you continually receive the same, avoidable questions like, "How do I log into the intranet from home, again?" or "Do we have to dial 9 to get an outside line?" or "Do we remove the compound before or after the process is complete?"
- Walking away and letting employees struggle to find solutions. Some call it the sink-or-swim method, while others use the phrase, "feed them to the wolves." Neither sounds pleasant, and surely there are better ways to be more helpful when people need assistance to move from point A to point B on their own.
- Smothering and negatively micromanaging. Smothering occurs when leaders fail to lay out a solid plan and when they overlook the task of providing tools that appropriately match the skill levels of executors. Your job is to remove some of the obvious obstacles to others' progress and replace them with the appropriate support that empowers people.
- Offloading dirty work that leaders don't want to do themselves. Remember, your job isn't just to assign busywork and tasks; it's to ensure that members of your organization are making value-added contributions to projects and processes that strengthen the whole organization.

Oftentimes, these misguided measures will mask the ineffectiveness of the leader and unfairly place blame on the people the measures have supposedly empowered. Yet everyone shows up to work day after day and tolerates the situation, usually because they need the paycheck. If you want to see improvement, you have to change yourself first by developing certain leadership skills and by using effective tools.

The best leaders are those who recognize the need to continually improve their skills. Just look at the person who oversees a committee or a group of volunteers where the followers don't receive a paycheck. These leaders are forced to gain buy-in and cooperation from people, often based on their sheer skills as a leader. If they want people to stick around and participate, they not only have to set direction and instruct people to execute on tactics, but they have to make sure that they're empowering people in ways that give them hope they can succeed and that eventually lead them to where they want to go. They have to give their volunteers the structure and supplies they need to perform their jobs, and they have to be available to guide and steer them should they stumble or veer off course. The people working typically aren't being reimbursed. Instead, they've found some value in performing as a volunteer and it's up to the leader to ensure that the results they achieve are commensurate with what the leader brings to the environment.

The "magic" these leaders use to build success among volunteers is actually a bundle of steps they've found to be effective in reaching their desired outcomes. The ET Empowering Process is also a bundle of steps designed to produce better results than you would have achieved otherwise. Not only will *you* have the direction that *you* need to integrate other people into your strategic and tactical plans, but your people will receive the direction and guidance they need to reach the outcomes you expect of them.

Below, you will see a diagram of the ET Empowering Process (Figure 11.1), consisting of four steps: (1) Develop Plans, (2) Build the Package, (3) Transfer the Power, (4) Monitor Progress and Adjust the Process. Through this process, you will make sure to:

- Tie empowering to the plans that you develop so that you are transferring power to the right people and so that those people truly fulfill a purpose. This process starts with developing plans so that you are able to align your people and resources with Strategy and focus them in the direction of reaching Desired Outcomes.

- Build a package of necessary "supplies" that your people need to do their best work for you. This includes building the systems and structures as well as providing tools, guidance, and support.

- Transfer power and responsibilities to the people you have determined to be the most appropriately skilled and knowledgeable to produce the highest returns.

- Keep everyone's momentum and progress on track by monitoring the progress of your people, offering your guidance, and adjusting the process so that everyone comes out a winner.

Enterprise Thinking Empowering Process

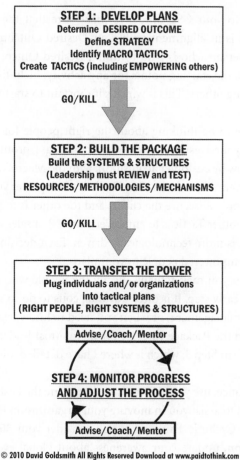

© 2010 David Goldsmith All Rights Reserved Download at www.paidtothink.com

Figure 11.1—Enterprise Thinking Empowering Process

Notice that in addition to the four steps, you have GO/KILL points between the first two steps that serve as your opportunity to decide whether proceeding forward is in the best interests of your organization. These points cause you to pause and assess whether the Empowerment Package you are building will or will not produce your Desired Outcome. If you find that it will not, you are always better off stopping—stopping altogether, stopping and going back to the previous step, or stopping and starting over again. Taking the time to think through your actions early on—the Economics of Thinking—will pay off in the end.

So here are the four steps in detail.

Step 1: Develop Plans

Go back to your CST Model to make sure that the Tactic of using executors is in alignment with your Desired Outcome and Strategy. For the person who is paid to think, Desired Outcome and Strategy are always the starting points for any activity, including the ET activity of empowering others. This is why it's important to start with developing your plans.

You also have to be thinking about the right people for the situation at hand. Let's say your Desired Outcome is to increase profits by 12%. Your Strategy is to grow by customer acquisition, with the Macro Tactic of securing 46 new clients over nine months. One Tactic is to empower your VP of HR to hire two new people to secure the clients and the other is to pick up the production load. Another Tactic is to empower your VP of sales to develop a new sales model that is more technologically driven. Each decision you make ties the soon-to-be empowered people to your plans.

In some cases, you may actually specify the people who will be working with you at this early step. It is often advantageous to do so when you're hiring or selecting management, or when you need to know who the people are before you Build the Package (Step 2) for them. Most leaders, however, hire and select people in Step 3, which is where I have detailed for you how to hire and select them.

In either instance, use your ET tools to determine the best people, groups, or organizations to assist you in moving your organization forward. Perhaps you'll engage in Cyclonic Thinking as you consider your 360° awareness of your organization, update your awareness about global events, and revisit data from your competitive intelligence activities. If you will be developing a new product or establishing a new alliance, you can pour this information into your ET Development Funnel to determine the direction of your organization, unit, department, or group, depending, of course, on the details and needs of your situation.

I caution you to control any impulse you may have to jump to action before thinking through your plan—hmm, where have you heard that before? I recall a conversation I once had with the owner of a sales-based company who did not yet understand the Economics of Thinking and took the fast-shooter approach to addressing an issue he was having with his top saleswoman. He had previously promised all of his salespeople the full support of his marketing department, but he had never really followed through on that promise, prompting his number-one salesperson to hire her own marketing person and later approach him and ask for a higher commission rate to cover her increased expenses. His solution was to tell his marketing department that they needed to "step up their game" and help out sales, but he never discussed any of the details with them. He didn't give them a plan with tactics, and that's because he didn't think to tie their efforts to strategy. Without better direction and tools, the marketing department had been insufficiently empowered to play a pivotal role in the sales teams' efforts. And although the owner blamed the marketing department, it was the leader's fault that it remained a siloed and ineffectual department for the company.

These activities are part of laying a solid foundation under people so that when you empower them, they know what the Desired Outcome is that they are expected to reach.

Step 2: Build the Package

Next, build an environment that breeds and supports success. The package is your collection of systems and structures and other resources that empower people to carry out their responsibilities. Leaders tend to overlook this step, but it is a huge component of successfully empowering others.

If you are continually teaching new tools to your staff members and giving them opportunities to build skills and acquire knowledge, this step will only require you to provide any additional tools that are well matched to the specific situation. For example, if people already know how to use a CPM chart, then any detailed plan you give them containing one will be easier and faster for them to use. If, however, you are working with people who lack knowledge or have skill gaps, take the time early on to bring them up to speed or ensure that someone else does. This small measure pays off both in the short term when your group achieves its Desired Outcome, and in the long term by building intellectually advanced individuals who may one day become future leaders.

Look through any plans and make sure that they contain enough detail to act as a guide, but not so much detail that they bog people down. Keep in mind that the "road map" should suit the ability levels of the people who must follow it, and it must be a realistically achievable guide that ties directly to Strategy and Desired Outcome. You may recall the point I made in Chapter 3 about how important it is to match your Tactics to the skill and knowledge levels of your executors. In that chapter, I made mention of how you would need different types of Tactics to prepare a novice cook in contrast to directing an experienced chef; the person who lacks cooking skills might need you to provide instructions on *how* to sauté vegetables whereas the experienced chef would only need to be told *to* sauté them. You want to choose the best tools for the situation, so if you had to teach a project to military engineers, for instance, you might decide to include Tactics like training videos and documents that outline key deliverables so that executors are equipped to proceed on their own, and if they need a review of instructions, the materials that you have provided to them are available whenever necessary. The same concept applies, obviously, for any organization, whether you're supplying a CPM chart to educators for converting their math lessons to a new curriculum or linking admissions officers at your university to your recruitment staff using an advanced customer-contact software program and showing everyone involved how to use it.

As you may have already realized from these examples, the transfer of authority or responsibility doesn't always involve a plan. Sometimes, you're entrusting people with tasks that contribute to a larger project or that service your customers one at a time. In many situations, the Empowerment Package becomes the tools of the trade: the best carpet steamers for your cleaning staff, the hydraulic lift for your moving crew to reduce injuries and complete jobs faster, and iPads for your waiters so that you can update dinner specials quickly and easily.

Another point to consider whenever you are about to transfer authority and responsibility to others is that, as I mentioned in Chapter 10, people don't show up to work to screw up, so chances are, when there's a failure in Execution, the cause stems from a poorly built Empowerment Package or lack thereof. On the leadership side, the inadequate or missing package is typically the result of poor planning, which causes leaders to overlook the 80% of the GPP or focus too much on the 20%.

My wife and I encountered one such flaw many years ago when we took our then-young sons to a restaurant in New York City. We'd visited the place before and enjoyed the food and service, so why not go back again? Well, if this second experience had been our first, there might not have been a second visit at all. We were greeted, seated, given drinks, and then . . . nothing. We watched and waited for our food as one family after another arrived, placed their orders, and ate their meals.

The waitress—who we later learned had years of experience waiting tables—apologized time and again. Then her manager stopped by our table to explain that she had discovered why our meal order had failed to process and corrected the problem.

Apparently, this was the waitress's first day working at this particular restaurant, and when she keyed her employee number into the computer system, it didn't take. That's because the manager had erred and not activated the waitress's key code. The waitress entered her customers' food orders just the same, because the system had no kick-back mechanism to alert users when their orders were denied. The flaw in the software meant that no one was able to detect that the order never transferred to the kitchen. Now that the manager had identified and rectified the problem, the meal order was being processed.

Although the empowering process had failed due to a technical glitch, management was still responsible, and this is why. First, the decision makers selected (quite possibly unknowingly) a computer system that did not work as it should, and second, the manager on duty did not jump in earlier to solve the challenge when table after table was complaining about not being served. This is how organizations lose by a nose.

It's important to address this issue of leadership responsibility, because leaders have both decision-making authority and purchasing power to which subordinate staff members don't necessarily have access. Therefore, blaming others is futile. The improvements must begin with you, and the first and best question to ask yourself is, Did I build the right GPP that will successfully empower my people to reach successful outcomes? If you build the Empowerment Package well, the answer to this question will be yes.

Step 3: Transfer the Power

For leaders who have never used the ET Empowering Process, this third step will probably be the most familiar, because this step is usually a leader's starting point for empowering people. Notice how completing the first two steps of this process forced you to lay the groundwork for your people before you even brought them into the picture!

Now that the groundwork is set, you will select your people and transfer power to them. You may find that this is a time when you must develop a hiring (or selection) process that enables you to bring on the right people. This is the early part of transferring power.

Review your hiring process to ensure that its screening criteria will ultimately result in the selection of the right people for your organizational culture or special project. In the first phase of Southwest Airlines'[119] process for hiring flight attendants, peers screen candidates based on their energy levels by requiring candidates to energetically proclaim why they want to work at Southwest. Picture yourself taking part in an interview with this airline company. How comfortable would you be if you had to stand up in front of a panel of employees and express your excitement about working for them? If the thought of this scenario makes you cringe, then their system would eliminate you, because your personality would not be in alignment with their corporate culture. The hiring process gives Southwest Airlines a slew of flight attendants who are predisposed to carrying out desired behaviors.

Disney sends[120] job candidates on a walking tour through a creative-looking building for the purpose of educating candidates about the employee experience at Disney. Those who take the tour are actually scrubbing themselves against broad criteria without knowing it. Every prospective employee is introduced to fundamental guidelines, such as no facial hair for men, and if they're still interested after the tour, they move on to additional phases of Disney's hiring process. You've surely done this yourself in many situations. Think of a time when you've walked into a nightclub, hotel, store, party, or office, immediately concluded, "This is not for me," and promptly left.

It almost sounds too obvious, but since I've seen many leaders make this mistake, be sure that if you are selecting people from a pool of internal leaders or staffers, you know them well enough to detect whether they are right for the task at hand. You can't just make assumptions. You also have to ensure that if they don't have the skills today, they will be able to develop them in time to carry out the responsibilities that you have given them. You wouldn't tell a factory worker on his first day at work to oversee the quality control until you were sure that he knew what he should be looking for.

Be especially careful when you select other leaders to avoid finding yourself in delicate situations later that surface from making wrong choices. For instance, if you assume that you are surrounding yourself with leaders who have certain skills and you just let them proceed without taking necessary measures up front, their lack of skills could become evident at a most inopportune time. I recall a colleague of mine who was working on a promotional package and had hired a PR team, consisting of the PR company's owner and right-hand woman, to assist him. The PR group continually made recommendations that did not serve my friend well, and after nine months of trying to work with people who ultimately showed that they couldn't be trusted to make smart decisions, he had to part ways with them. He not only lost a lot of time where he could have been generating opportunities, he also lost the money he had invested in the firm and damaged the relationship he had with the PR owner prior to their working together.

Another perspective to consider is that just because you know how someone performs on the job, you don't necessarily have a true picture of who they are and what they're capable of achieving. The person who appears to be unproductive or unmotivated at work may spend their weekends managing their bowling league of twenty-four teams or building sophisticated surveillance technology that they sell online for additional money. Like I say, although you can't always know what assets people put to use in their off time, when you do know, it helps you to place the right people in the best positions for them (and you).

In addition, Step 3 is where you must make sure that everyone on board understands what is expected of them. Regardless of whether you are working with senior-level managers or a group of Girl Scouts, everyone involved needs to know the particular destination you have assigned to them, and they need your guidance and support at varying degrees to get there.

This brings to the forefront an issue that you may have faced, since it often perplexes leaders. Many have asked me if it's necessary for the people who will be empowered to be involved in decision making. That depends on your situation. I can understand if you're concerned that other people won't buy into your ideas if you don't include them at decision points, but it doesn't have to be that way, either. Certainly, there are some circumstances that warrant others' involvement in decision making, but as a general rule, the answer is no. Others do not have to take part in developing Strategy, building the GPP, or addressing any smaller questions that may arise, as long as your plans are appropriate, you're selecting the right people, and you're providing the type of support they need.

For the most part, leaders themselves struggle to make good decisions, and they have the experience (and now tools!) to do the job better than the people they manage, so why would you risk inferior Strategies, Tactics, and systems and structures for the sake of gaining buy-in? A report by Wharton School[121] of Business associate professor Iwan Barankay suggests that the majority of people prefer to receive a limited amount of feedback and information from their superiors. In two advertisements placed for an identical position where one ad mentioned supervisorial feedback, prospective applicants were three times more likely to respond to the second ad that made *no mention* of feedback. Not all people need to play your role, nor do they necessarily want to see your 50,000-foot view. Typically, in regard to sharing decision making, Strategies, and the big-picture view with the people you empower, you will encounter three types of people:

1. **The people who need to know:** In some situations, people need to share in decision making, Strategy, and the inside knowledge in order to execute on the plans you have given them.

2. **The people who don't need to know but want to know anyway:** There are those people who feel most comfortable when they understand where they fit within the scope of the grander scheme. Although these people don't necessarily need to know the details, sharing with them enables them to do their jobs without the distraction of uncertainty.

3. **The people who don't need to know:** This group of people will perform for you if you give them the plan, some direction, and any additional support, but they don't need to share in decision making or strategizing in order to carry out your plans. They don't need to know, don't want to know, might not understand if you told them, or all of the above.

At the very least, the way to gain buy-in is to give people their plan, explain their function within the context of the larger picture, and give them everything they need to make a successful contribution to the whole.

A final factor that you need to consider when transferring power involves the question of *how*. Depending on the skill levels and involvement of the people, you will adapt your methods of transferring power to them accordingly. Just as you must provide appropriately matched Tactics to the individuals to whom you will be transferring authority, you may find that at times you will have to walk through a process or project with your people, whereas in other situations you can hand off the task to an experienced manager that you've worked with in the past and know that a few progress updates here and there are all you need to keep the initiative on target.

Every time you empower others and you are building the GPP, keep in mind the small subset box on the GPP diagram that represents you; you as a leader are always responsible for building the 80% of the GPP so that you can properly empower people who make up the 20%, ensuring that they always have their best understanding of their roles and expected outcomes.

Step 4: Monitor Progress and Adjust the Process

Your responsibilities don't end once you have transferred power to others. This is where the work of monitoring their progress and making necessary adjustments along the way begins. Your role in Step 4 is very similar in approach to your activities within the Learning category. Not only might you be monitoring your organization, global happenings, and competitors to stay abreast of matters important to your organization, but in a similar fashion, here you are also monitoring your people, their progress, and the unraveling events that influence the overall initiative to make sure that these variables aren't steering your intended plans off course.

Since at this point you're constantly becoming aware of new occurrences so that you can readjust to the conditions if need be, you may find that you will need to create new plans on how to accelerate progress, correct any misconceptions that may have arisen, or retrain, replace, or terminate people who were initially involved in your initiative. Just because you devised a plan doesn't mean that it is set in stone. Evolving situations will require you to determine what individuals and systems and structures need to be modified by you to maintain levels of productivity and to ultimately yield the results you want.

Regardless of whether your situation changes or remains the same from the start, the degree to which you are involved with your people will vary based on a number of factors unique to your situation. For some people, being led by a positive micromanager will foster progress, whereas other people will only rise to the occasion once a more demanding leader raises the level of expectations and follows through to ensure that people have met preset benchmarks. Others still may respond more favorably and produce results faster if they're left alone to do their work, and say, have to apprise you of their progress through weekly reports.

Furthermore, your circumstances will dictate the role you play in monitoring progress and making adjustments. Geographic culture and corporate culture also influence whether you act in the capacity of advisor, mentor, coach, or something else. Regardless of the role you assume or name you assign to it, you will continue to act as a guiding support person for the people you have empowered. Here are some common examples of the roles you may opt to play:

Reviewer: As a reviewer, you are looking at a number of indicators that tell you a story about the progress of an initiative. Some of the indicators include: KPIs (key performance indicators), financial reports, the feedback you get from face-to-face conversations with others, and so on. In the capacity of reviewer, your findings reveal that an adjustment needs to be made to a nonhuman component such as a system or process. In these cases, you may not have any need to communicate your adjustments to the people you have empowered.

Positive reinforcer: Although I normally wouldn't encourage you to run around "hugging and kissing" everyone as a primary means of making progress, you may find that there are often occasions during which the people working with you are doing a decent job, but they need some positive reinforcement from time to time to let them know that they are on track. In these instances, you are checking in to confirm that they are making the progress you want, and since you don't need to make any adjustments to what they're doing, you give them encouragement before moving on. Obviously, I can't predict all the different situations, types of organizations (for-profit, not-for-profit, government, military, education), and cultural and geographic factors that determine whether positive reinforcement is helpful. But I can tell you that in my experiences working with decision makers around the world, I have never encountered even a single organization where some type of encouragement does not work, that is, when the GPP is in place.

Advisor: The very name often denotes a level of confidentiality, but confidential or not, the advisor is someone who offers guidance after they've collected some background information about a situation that impacts their advisee. An advisor is usually someone who is sought out by others for their insight and advice. The advisor can offer direction, lessons, stories, and instruction to help the other person (persons, or groups) to reach the Desired Outcome. The role of advisor is helpful when you're working with people who are receptive to outside advice, who want to accelerate their progress, and who are open to receiving tips on how they can personally improve their performance. To be clear, working in the capacity of advisor can range from a relationship that is complex, long-running, and confidential to one that is as simple, fleeting, and open as a laborer asking a foreman, "Can you give me some advice on how to handle this customer's problem?"

Coach: In an organizational capacity, a coach is usually someone who walks you through the stages of performance; many times he or she is assigned to a person or group of people to increase performance levels. The challenge with the word "coaching" is that it has become a buzzword of the 21st century that can carry negative connotations, although coaching in and of itself is not necessarily negative. After all, what credentials do you need to be a coach, and who certifies them? Life experience, business experience? But does experience alone qualify you to be a teacher of sorts? The CEO of an $800 million firm confided in me that his organization had spent millions on coaching over the years, but not until the economic downturn in 2008 did the CEO realize, "In good times, we appeared to have excellent coaches, but when things went bad during the recession, we realized that we had wasted our money."

A good coach has the insight to know when the timing is right to push someone and when to leave someone alone and let them put to use what they have learned for themselves. In general, however, most people do not make great coaches.

A side note: In some organizations, coaching has too often become synonymous with the quasi-performance review. In some of these de-motivating scenarios, the "coach" meets on a weekly basis with the person they are supposed to be coaching, but instead of acting in the capacity of a coach, these leaders take notes, ask questions, and then shoot off verbal criticisms or (primarily negative) letters of performance-related feedback to the people who are being "coached." Under the guise of "coaching," they tend to decrease productivity, the antithesis of empowering others. This type of coaching is always bound for failure. Job and performance reviews (not to be confused with the aforementioned type of review) are after-the-fact assessments of performance, whereas coaching should enhance performance while the individual is engaged in the activities of their job. If you want to guide, coach. If you want to scold, do a job review. But if you want to guide people and make them distrust you simultaneously, confuse the two.

Mentor: The mentor acts in a similar capacity as the advisor, but generally the mentor guides and advises someone because of some personal attachment he or she has with the mentoree. Being a mentor shouldn't feel like something that is forced. This type of empowerment should arise from a relationship based on trust, where it is apparent that the mentor wants to bring another person under his or her wing and tells them not just what they should do, but how they can improve their ability to think and make better decisions so that the mentoree is able to make better decisions independently. Mentors help someone improve performance, because they care about that person.

---[**My First Mentor**]--

I met my first business mentor when I was 21 years old. At the time, I was a recent college graduate, and he was the CEO of Tilcon, a rock quarry supplying more than 90% the stone used in the New York City area. John Gillespie hired me for a summer position on a day that began with his calling my home at 5:30 a.m. His schedule dictated a change in time for our originally scheduled 9 a.m. interview. Could I be there by 7 a.m.? I quickly calculated I'd have seven minutes to shower and another couple to down a quick breakfast. I was soon in my car heading down the highway to a destination that was more than an hour's drive away.

[continues on page 436]

[continued from previous page]

At the interview, John asked me a series of questions about previous work experience and any knowledge I may have had of quarries, of which I had absolutely none. After the questioning, he offered me a job at above minimum wage. When he was about to leave, I told him I had a few questions of my own. I guess he liked my moxie, because from that moment on he treated me differently. Little did I know that it was then that he decided to take me under his wing and mentor me, even giving me a pay raise that day.

I didn't immediately realize that his approach to grooming me was to show me the big-picture view of the entire facility (rather than to pigeonhole me into a single, siloed position). John's way of empowering me was to give me the right exposure so that I might potentially be a successor to his role. He quickly put me on a kind of rotation that would give me a full tour of the quarry's systems and structures, and he met with me once a week to give me the guidance I needed, answering my questions so that I could fill in any blanks that were left after my experiences in a particular area of the company. My mentor had given me access to more information than most people who were working there for years, and he put people in charge of helping me when he couldn't do so.

He was never a "hugger and kisser." At times, the lessons were hard learned; more than once, he gave me a general framework for what he expected in terms of outlines, and then let me go. On one occasion, employees intentionally let me make a mistake by allowing me to unknowingly drop a rock the size of two sedan cars into one of our machines, a move that clogged up the system. John knew that my growth would come from a combination of one-on-one instruction and the freedom to err.

At the same time, he had a plan for me and personally watched over my progress so that he could elevate my perspective to the 30,000-foot view, and then to the eventual 50,000-foot view and keep it there. For example, my first job at the company was to work in the dispatch office. He wanted me to understand how the network of 250 semis moved upwards of 22,000 tons of stone a day as well as how the organization would move nearly 15 scows each transporting 1,000 tons of stone daily.

There was one notable moment that marked John's progress as my mentor. It occurred shortly after he overheard me ask the dispatcher about the costs of each shipment. In my mind, I was trying to calculate the quarry's overall sales volume, but the dispatcher could only offer, "Mr. Gillespie doesn't want me to know that information." Both of us were unaware that John was around the corner and had overheard my inquiry, but I learned of it later that day, when my mentor pulled me aside and told me he wanted me to be thinking this way. "Keep putting together the pieces," he encouraged. Whether I was working in dispatching, the scale house, or any other function alongside the other workers, John encouraged me to ask questions and challenge myself to learn continuously. Within no time, he promoted me to assistant supervisor, his encouraging stamp of approval motivated me to keep on progressing.

My relationship with John began as a boss to an employee and expanded to a mentor to mentoree. As the years passed, I stayed in touch with him, keeping him updated on my career and listening to any nuggets of wisdom he had to offer along the way. Through the years he attended my wedding, joined our extended family for special holidays, and stayed in touch long after I had made the decision to venture out on my own into other business endeavors. He has always been someone I could count on for great advice.

Regardless of the role you want to play, follow the concepts of the Learning category and be sure that you are providing new information and the opportunities to keep your people abreast of on-the-horizon happenings that can help them make their best contributions to your organization. By continually monitoring the progress of your people, you send the message that you're interested in them and that you're accessible to them whenever they need your input. By staying connected to the people you empower and asking yourself how you can better serve them, you increase the chances that the results you achieve are in alignment with your Desired Outcome.

The Misnomers of Motivation and Morale

Motivation and morale are misunderstood. They are not achievable as long as your focus remains on them. In fact, trying to make people motivated and trying to build morale will actually have the opposite effect. By now, you understand the GPP and its premise that without first building the network and environment that breed success, the pursuit of motivation and morale is counterproductive. Encouragement and compliments are like salt and pepper—they can make the dish more palatable, but they alone won't make the meal.

If you're finding that morale or motivation are dwindling, look at how *you* are empowering (or not empowering) your people before you cast blame. Jeff is a frustrated unit manager who oversees 142 total employees and 7 direct reports. He complains of low morale within his unit, and attributes the problems to corporate leadership's unrealistic demands on him and his staff to increasingly produce more. Corporate decision makers crunch numbers in a room, ask themselves what they want the next year, then wield crazy demands without considering new project initiatives, product or service price compression or reductions, currency fluctuations, or population changes, and without accounting for corporate mishandling of product and service initiatives such as the delay in a mobility platform, distribution center, or the reality that they have yet to fill the VP of finance's job, vacant for eight months, which is delaying all reporting. In one year, they wanted Jeff's unit to deliver a 19% increase in volume on top of the 106% increase he produced last year without providing any more resources to Jeff and his people.

When Jeff tries to explain that corporate's goals are burning out his people and drying up his resources, Jeff's supervisor tells him to "figure it out." The senior management team that oversees Jeff and his unit have failed to properly empower Jeff to do his job. It's not enough to tell your people that they're smart enough to come to their own conclusions. If your people are struggling, it's up to you to help figure out the real challenge and to contribute to the solution.

Yet time and again, I see senior managers drive away outstanding talent, because they don't know how to properly empower their people. The problem is exacerbated, too, because when Jeff finally jumps ship one day, the firm will have a real struggle to entice someone else to take his place. Not only does word get out about an organization's climate, but good talent can often tell with one look whether the corporate culture is one in which they can develop successes.

Until leaders recognize that the problem originates with them and needs to be addressed by them, they will not get the results they expect from this particular business unit.

Think back to Sheila, the manager I told you about at the beginning of Chapter 2 who did some rethinking about her responsibilities to empower her staff members, and specifically in the example, a staff member who was having issues with his computer. When Sheila decided to look into the 80% of the GPP instead of the human side, she discovered that her employee had a valid complaint. His computer was three years old, and it was unable to process many of his new software's functions without continually crashing. Realizing that only she had the clout to push through a purchase order to upgrade her employee's software and hardware, Sheila adopted a new perspective of her role, thus opening more and better opportunities for her organization. Not only was she happier when she found this key to empowering others effectively, but everyone on staff—both up the corporate ladder and down to the front line—was happier with outcomes, too.

People need hope that they can make tomorrow better than today. For the same reasons I don't call myself a motivational speaker, hope doesn't come from rah-rah speeches and pats on the back. It comes from knowing that you have the skills, tools, and knowledge to perform the activities of your job exceptionally well. One such tool that leaders can use to build Order Winners within their organizations is the Transparent Career Ladder, a mechanism that can separate the serious achievers from the dreamers and elevate the people who want to rise up the ranks by giving them a formula they can use to accelerate their performance.

The Transparent Career Ladder

While many people are content working the same job year after year, many others look for opportunities to grow and advance themselves and their careers. That's not to say that everyone wants to climb the corporate ladder to a higher-ranking position, but the majority of people do seem to be motivated by the possibility of gaining some sort of achievement, whatever that means to each individual. Think for a moment about what kind of career ladder, if any, that you have at your organization that motivates both (1) the up-and-coming leaders and (2) the people who want growth, but not in the direction of management positions. If you do, in fact, have a career ladder, is it transparent, meaning everyone understands how it works?

Just as important as the actual career ladder itself is leaders' and staffers' knowledge of how it works. A good career ladder allows people to advance their careers at their own pace. It must be a vehicle that delivers reliable rewards, but it can only do that if you build it without the all-too-often subjective and arbitrary benchmarks that give some career ladders a bad name. To truly empower people, you must create a mechanism that goes beyond offering the promise of hope; it must guarantee outcomes. A sports coach tells his team of athletes that if they work hard, they'll play in Saturday's game. In the ears of many athletes, the message rings, "Hard work equals playing time." In this scenario, some athletes take on the challenge, work extremely hard, and expect to play. But when the time comes to reap the rewards of their hard work and their coach doesn't make good on the promise to play, the athletes can become disillusioned, stop putting forth the extra effort, potentially leave the team, or all three.

In another scenario, the coach outlines specific goals that athletes must achieve in order to get game time: jump 24 inches and sprint 40 yards in under 5 seconds. The athletes hear the same thing, but the specifics motivate them to go home and practice even more on their own, long after team practice has concluded. When athletes meet these requirements, they are acknowledged, and they get some playing time. These athletes, who are driven by clearly defined targets, continue to achieve and provide value to their team, much like employees who strive to reach specific benchmarks. In fact, you'll even see the Escalator Theory in action, since some managers and employees will work harder and faster to reach the benchmarks sooner.

Building a Transparent Career Ladder in Your Organization

Some of the best decision makers and staff members have a fire under them to excel. When you combine these go-getters in groups, they can synergistically motivate and inspire each other to perform at optimal levels. The powerhouses who are driven to win in their careers can create wins for your organization, but only if you can attract them to your roster and retain them over a period of time. One of the best ways to entice and keep high achievers is to give them the hope that they can continually advance themselves within your organization, which is why having a Transparent Career Ladder is so important.

It's important that any career ladder you develop has benchmarks and metrics along with corresponding rewards. Consider the Career Ladder Development Guide in Figure 11.2 as your instruction manual for building your own Transparent Career Ladder or improving the one you already have.

Overview of the Career Ladder Development Guide

Most of the process tools that you have learned about in this book have started with instructions at the top of the diagram. Your beginning point for the Career Ladder Development Guide actually starts at the *bottom* of the diagram, then branches out into two ascending tracts—one on the left for people who want to advance their careers but are not interested in leadership positions and another on the right for people who want to develop as leaders of your organization. As your eyes pan upward, you read the next set of instructions and information until you end at the top of the diagram with the box titled Meets Forecasted Talent Requirements.

Strategizing Completed

Here we go again starting our process with planning, but as you know, planning is a culmination of all the activities of ET, so when you plan, think bigger than you might expect to initially. You will want to review the strategic direction you have set for your organization, business unit, or group

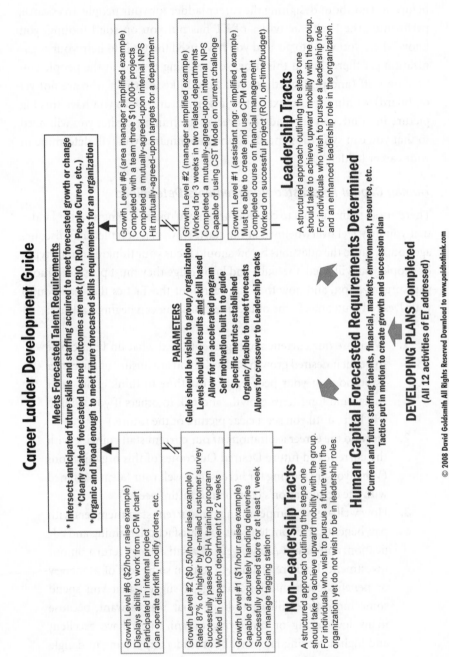

Career Ladder Development Guide

Meets Forecasted Talent Requirements

* Intersects anticipated future skills and staffing acquired to meet forecasted growth or change
* Clearly stated forecasted Desired Outcomes are met (RIO, ROA, People Cured, etc.)
* Organic and broad enough to meet future forecasted skills requirements for an organization

Leadership Tracts

Growth Level #6 (area manager simplified example)
Completed with a team three $10,000+ projects
Completed a mutually-agreed-upon internal NPS
Hit mutually-agreed-upon targets for a department

Growth Level #2 (manager simplified example)
Worked for 3 weeks in two related departments
Completed a mutually-agreed-upon internal NPS
Capable of using CST Model on internal challenge

Growth Level #1 (assistant mgr. simplified example)
Must be able to create and use CPM chart
Completed course on financial management
Worked on successful project (ROI, on-time/budget)

A structured approach outlining the steps one should take to achieve upward mobility with the group. For individuals who wish to pursue a leadership role and an enhanced leadership role in the organization.

PARAMETERS

Guide should be visible to group/organization
Levels should be results and skill based
Allow for an accelerated program
Self motivation built in to guide
Specific metrics established
Organic/flexible to meet forecasts
Allows for crossover to Leadership tracks

Non-Leadership Tracts

Growth Level #6 ($2/hour raise example)
Displays ability to work from CPM chart
Participated in internal project
Can operate forklift, modify orders, etc.

Growth Level #2 ($0.50/hour raise example)
Rated 87% or higher by e-mailed customer survey
Successfully passed OSHA training program
Worked in dispatch department for 2 weeks

Growth Level #1 ($1/hour raise example)
Capable of accurately handing deliveries
Successfully opened store for at least 1 week
Can manage tagging station

A structured approach outlining the steps one should take to achieve upward mobility with the group. For individuals who wish to pursue a future with the organization yet do not wish to be in leadership roles.

Human Capital Forecasted Requirements Determined

* Current and future staffing talents, financial, markets, environment, resource, etc.
Tactics put in motion to create growth and succession plan

DEVELOPING PLANS Completed
(All 12 activities of ET addressed)

Figure 11.2—Career Ladder Development Guide

before you go about designing the career ladder for your people. In essence, performing the twelve activities of ET has put you on solid footing, you know where you want to go, and you have used the tools to help your organization get there. But at this time, you're going to look at the people you have on staff (and perhaps those you would like to attract who are not yet on board) within the context of the larger picture. Once you have this big picture in mind, you are ready to forecast the human capital you will need so that you can sync those needs to the benchmarks you will determine in your career ladder.

Human Capital Forecasted Requirements Determined

There are so many factors to consider when you're developing a career ladder that you may feel overwhelmed at the start. However, don't let that discourage you, because the questions below should focus your thinking on the types of people you will need, the skills and knowledge they must possess to move your organization, and how they can carry out the Tactics that lead you to your Desired Outcome. Some of the questions you can begin to ask are:

1. What are our current staffing talents, and what do I anticipate to be their desired growth paths? (If you are unsure of the career aspirations of your people, take the time to think about your short- and long-term growth, and talk to others if you think it will help, until you see a clear picture of the future.)

2. How do the career aspirations of our current staff coincide with the current and future Desired Outcomes of this organization? (What you are looking for here is how well your talent is aligned with the organization's current and future needs.)

3. How well are we compensating our current staff members with pay, benefits, freedom to grow, job satisfaction, training and education, and so on? Are we getting a satisfactory return on our investment? If you're inclined to rely on some sort of monetary or benefits compensation package, I suggest that you spend some more time thinking about what people want, because many low-paying or no-paying organizations have excellent and high-achieving talent without leadership having to dangle the "carrot" of financial rewards.

4. If our people reach certain benchmarks set forth on the career ladder, will we be able to deliver on the rewards that we have promised them? Any career ladder that offers a false hope or

that consists of constantly changing rules will be nonproductive. If you can't or won't deliver on your promises—if, for example, you cut a geographical territory and leave a salesperson hanging, never promote people to the positions that they've "earned," or fail to realize the opportunities that you told others you would—then your career ladder is as good as dead.

5. What are the current and forecasted market conditions that could affect our people's abilities to reach benchmarks and that could reduce our ability to keep up our end of the bargain?

6. What type of staffing will we need to meet our long-term strategic objectives, and how can we translate those needs to benchmarks and metrics within the career ladder?

Two Tracts of Personnel Development: Non-Leadership and Leadership

Notice as your eyes move up the guide that you have an option on the left to develop a career ladder for employees who are not interested in management—Non-Leadership—and on the right, a career ladder for up-and-coming leaders and managers—Leadership. Be sure you include tracts for each category, because it is easy to assume that everyone hopes to develop into leadership roles, when, in fact, there are many people who don't want to lead, they just want to do what they're doing at a higher level and at a capacity where they can offer higher value to your organization. That's why, when you're developing your career ladder, you must include both categories of people, so that you can determine up front not only the contributions your people will need to make to the progress of your organization for both the present and future, but also how you will ensure that you follow through on your promises.

Growth level examples are provided to help you with ideas and guidance, but you will base the specific growth-level benchmarks for talent development on needs and Desired Outcomes. Notice that in the guide, under Parameters, you have factors that you need to consider regardless of which type of career ladder you are developing; these parameters must be visible to everyone, because you don't always know who in your organization wants to grow and climb.

Pay special attention to the fact that you don't have to follow the typical systems out there that are focused on time-specific benchmarks, keeping in mind that often you don't want to discourage or de-motivate people who are excited and ambitious enough to work harder and faster to reach their personal goals rapidly. Key people who offer exceptional talents and who want to advance their careers faster than a six-month timeline or an annual timeline could leave and work for a competitor if you hold them back.

Forecasted Talent Requirements

All the while, you must synchronize the benchmarks and metrics of working up the ladder with the forecasted finances, resources, and Strategy of your organization to ensure that you will be able to compensate people as they climb the career ladder. Once you have this information, you can have a better idea of your Forecasted Talent Requirements so that when people want to rise quickly, they don't end up outpacing your resources in terms of how you're planning the strategic direction of the organization.

Here are some factors that you need to keep in mind when you are building a Transparent Career Ladder to ensure that you are accurately determining your Forecasted Talent Requirements:

1. You must see into the future far enough to be sure that if someone hits career-ladder benchmarks, you will be able to make good on your promise to promote them and that their promotion will be good for your organization. This is where the 360° awareness of your organization and a true understanding of its financials can be especially important for you to have.
2. Give people who want to advance their careers and who are willing to do the work another level of visible guidelines to succeed. Don't try to only advance the careers of people who are happiest in their current positions.
3. Address equally the needs of people who want to grow and those who don't. Uncover what motivates both kinds of people to perform their jobs optimally and supply the necessary Empowerment Package so that managers and front-line employees alike can excel.

Provide to people across the board specific goals to shoot for, and then deliver when they reach those targets. Any time in the future if you find that your organization's Transparent Career Ladder needs modifications, you can consult your Career Ladder Development Guide to improve your ability to do so.

Techniques and Concepts for Empowering Others

When you consider all the stakeholders who must be empowered to some degree or another, the options for making a successful transition of authority and responsibility are nearly endless. There are a number of techniques and concepts suggested here that you can use, adapt, and expand upon to fit your particular needs. Keep in mind that at the core of it all, you as a leader must continually perform the twelve activities of ET in conjunction with empowering others to be sure that your people are empowered with purpose. In other words, you empower people in alignment with your plans' Strategy and Desired Outcomes.

Be Accessible and Approachable

If a situation veers off course or if people don't understand something, they should be able to turn to you for guidance without penalty. You don't want to allow an impending problem to unfold, because people are afraid to speak up. Be consistent and true to your word. If you say you welcome questions, be open and helpful to people when they approach you. And if you've never offered to field questions or offer guidance, consider doing so.

Consider these examples:

The vice president of operations for a South American software business unit was handed the responsibility of growing her market share in developing island countries around the region. After several months on the job, she came to the conclusion that many businesses, specifically the very large prospects, refused visits by her team and would often request American salespeople and technicians. What she was encountering was cultural bias against her team. The prospects felt that South American salespeople were inferior to those from America. When she went back to leadership with this discovery, they told her to fix it herself and that no Americans would be sent to support her, despite there being million-dollar deals on the table. She told me the whole experience frustrated her beyond measure. She was a very capable manager, but if her leadership wasn't more accessible and ready to support her in the future than they were then, they risked losing her eventually.

A high school football coach would give his team and their families an introductory speech before the start of every season. Some of the topics he would cover had to do with coming to see the coaches on matters that could affect an athlete's ability to play. "If you are injured, see one of the trainers and let us know. We don't want anyone going out there when they shouldn't." Yet throughout the season, when student athletes sustained extreme injuries like those to the knee requiring orthopedic care (or surgeries in some cases) and concussions that were serious enough to take the athletes out of school for a period of time, any attempt by parents or students to communicate with the head coach or his coaching staff were treated with disrespect, and the student athletes were either punished by coaches or treated like they were whiners. One student with aspirations to play college football and who had a severe enough concussion that he couldn't attend school for two-and-a-half weeks and couldn't drive for a month, was told by one of the coaches, "If you didn't want to play, you should have just told us." The disconnect between leadership's message and reality posed dangers to health, morale, and the achievement of Desired Outcomes.

Realize that questions can be great symptoms of where you need to improve. For instance, if you're finding that your staff members often avoid speaking up, chances are they don't feel safe saying anything that could be offensive to you or that could cause you to perceive them as incompetent, lazy, or unreasonable. However, when people don't have the answers or tools they need to do their jobs optimally, it's usually because leadership hasn't provided the package in the first place. You may find that your instructions were unclear, that your GPP is not functioning, or that a process that you assumed had been thoroughly organized was not. It goes back to pointing a finger at yourself first rather than casting blame onto others.

By acknowledging to others that you are willing to improve on their behalf, you can actually make people feel safer in talking to you. This is important, because the fact is, most people don't feel comfortable bringing negative topics to their superiors. So what you need to be aware of is that you can push or intimidate people enough that they won't speak up for fear of the retaliation and consequences that they have seen dealt out by leaders who rank higher than them in the authority hierarchy. Furthermore, a point worth reiterating is that you must keep in mind how *you* have the authority to make the improvements, whereas your subordinates may not. Knowing where these kinds of challenges exist enables you to identify and address them, which keeps your organization functioning smoothly and safely.

Use a Variety of Training Methods

Remember Maps versus Words? Keep that concept in mind as you develop training and education methods to get your people up to speed. That's because everyone has their own approach to learning, so the more proficient you are at seeking out or developing a variety of teaching methods that appeal to different learning preferences, the more likely you are to connect with your learners. These methods include courses, training and rotational programs, tactical plans, step-by-step processes, standard procedures, hands-on experiences, one-one-one encounters, and so on.

For example, some players in the multibillion-dollar-a-year cosmetics industry understand that training is key to repeat sales and referral business. Competitors who sell their cosmetics through high-end department stores offer free makeup applications as a way of enticing customers to buy. Quite often, women will purchase makeup, take it home, and because they don't have the skills to properly apply it on their own, end up not using the product. That mistake by competitors is an obvious opportunity to win by a nose for Nicoleta Barac, the regional trainer for cosmetics firm Trish McEvoy Ltd., and her staff members who make sure that they empower clients differently than competing brands' makeup artists do. They take an extra Order Winner step toward securing repeat and word-of-mouth business in the long term.

At Barac's cosmetics counter, which carries the Trish McEvoy line of cosmetics, makeup artists apply product to only one side of a client's face as the client watches the process unfold in a mirror. (Men, you might not realize that most women who have had a professional makeover don't learn how to repeat the application of makeup that their makeup artists have performed on their faces.) The artist describes what she is doing each step of the way as a first measure to teaching the process to the client. You may have seen or experienced other brands' techniques, where the client sits passively in a chair and allows the artist to apply a full face of makeup. After Barac's artists apply makeup to one side of a client's face, they encourage the client to complete the application process on the other side. As the client mimics the artist's procedure, she is walked through any difficult patches she encounters while applying the makeup. That way, when she gets home, she can apply the product expertly and be happy with her purchase. The hope is that her friends will like the way her makeup looks and stop in to duplicate the process (and the purchase) for themselves. The goal is to empower the customer to be independent and still achieve successful results.

Empower Intentionally

There are times when overly ambitious people decide that it's their time to seize a slice of the power in an organization. If this person reports to you, chances are you have good reasons why they don't already have that authority, so you need to keep your eye out for when these individuals overstep, and yet you do want individuals to grow. A balance is needed so that the people who want to grow can do so, but individuals who require supervision to a higher degree receive the guidance that they need, too.

Your stakeholders are counting on you to empower others selectively based on their ability to contribute value and to work in the best interests of your organization. I once witnessed an incident where the CEO of a company lost control of his VP of HR. She acted as if she were CEO and involved herself in matters well outside the realm of hiring, which in some companies would be okay, but in this company was a problem. Stepping on toes, she went on a rampage of allocating funds, delegating other decision makers' daily activities, and often blocking senior management decisions by inserting herself between the CEO and other members of the leadership team. Her interference and micromanaging had become counterproductive.

To regain control and correct the situation, the CEO reworked his organizational chart, with board support, to rebalance the VP of HR with other business units. This measure limited her access to certain information and gave back control to each business unit.

Be mindful of the fact that empowerment is just as much about letting people know where they are not needed as much as where they are. Make your selections wisely and keep everyone informed.

Take-the-Fork/Give-a-Spoon

There are many paths to the same outcomes, and it's your job to decipher which ones are the best for any given time. Cheerleading, hype, false praise, or empty promises don't motivate people. People are motivated when they feel hopeful of success and certain that they have the knowledge and skills they need to reach whatever they wish to pursue. Many also thrive under a healthy dose of pressure: not too much, not too little. In the face of no pressure, people may sit around and underperform. On the other hand, too much interference from management, and people can become frozen in their tracks.

Be wary of ways in which you may be de-motivating your staff, too. When you see the people you've empowered engaging in unproductive behavior or making unproductive decisions, approach the situation as you would a toddler wielding a fork in an attempt to feed himself. Have you ever watched a parent with a child in this situation? For the most part, they know if they take the fork away without offering up a good alternative, the child will scream and yell. So what do they do? They wave a shiny spoon in front of the child and gently take away the fork. I call this the Take-the-Fork/Give-a-Spoon technique, immediately stop the undesirable, perhaps dangerous behavior— the fork—and replace it with better and more productive alternatives—the spoon—so that you're still positively encouraging others to move in the direction of the Desired Outcome.

In this situation, the child sees the spoon as another exciting and positive experience. Now you may see this concept as some overly simplistic attempt at a solution to use within your organization, but some of the best leaders do this all the time. Imagine that your staff are manually tossing packages around the warehouse in a way that is dangerous to both the product and the people. If you were to install a new process that increased efficiency or provide a new technology, like a pallet jack that eased the work of lifting all the packages, the entire challenge would disappear.

Keep in mind that people are motivated when you lead them to where they want to go. Become aware of where your people want to go within your organization, and then build the Empowerment Package so that they can get there.

If You Must Choose, It's Better to Transfer than It Is to Tell

When some activity doesn't go as you expect it to or you don't get the responses you want from others, don't point fingers of blame at other people. Stop for a moment and consider that the disappointing results likely stem from something you did or didn't do.

Maybe you didn't think through the situation as well as you should have in the initial planning stages, which blinded you to pitfalls that you should have identified at that time. Or perhaps you failed to empower someone properly by not giving them the tools they needed to do their job to your satisfaction. You can come up with dozens of areas where you may have misstepped if you examine the situation.

So here's the answer. First ask yourself, Do I just want people to do what I want, or do I want to develop leaders who can think for themselves? Depending on the situation at hand, you can go one way or another on this option. Just remember that there's a time and place for both.

If you think that it's best to have people think on their own, you have to shift your approach to a side-by-side technique where you transfer your thinking process to others by giving them tools, skills, and knowledge. As you teach them, continually assess if the information you are transferring will best equip them to make good decisions (even in your absence) when they're confronted with challenges. Obviously, the skills and knowledge levels of your people will vary with each circumstance, but that doesn't excuse you from being the strategist first, deciding on your best approach, then being the teacher who transfers lessons to others.

Every Organization Needs a Leader Who Micromanages the Right Way

From the leadership perspective, you want to stay abreast of happenings and progress to keep everyone on track, head off and solve challenges, and maximize resources like time, energy, and money without smothering them. In this chapter, I've already discussed how establishing systems and structures—which enable you to micromanage in a positive manner—is one of the ways that you empower others, maintain productivity, and positively lead and manage, but in the larger scope of Enterprise Thinking, by performing all the activities of ET you become a better leader who by default will provide better guidance and opportunities for your people to succeed.

Just look at a leader like Joseph Wakim, former head of catering at Miami's ultra-hip Delano hotel. On one of my trips to South Florida, I had the opportunity to watch him in action, and I was impressed by his ability to be an active and visible leader to both new members of his staff and those who had been working at the Delano for a long time. He seemed to know what people of each skill level need, and he knews when to let his group do their jobs. At the same time, Wakim understood that his organization depended on him to give personal attention to the hotel's patrons, so he remained an ever-present White Horse Leader without being resented for being a micromanager. Wakim always provided his team with the systems, structures, and tools they need to do their jobs optimally. He did so successfully, because he not only did his homework, but he did his research on a daily basis through walk-around management. I met Wakim years ago as an intrigued traveler. I watched him in motion as he ushered new employees through the systems and worked alongside his staff members, all the while gaining the realistic feedback he needed to perfect his organization's superior systems and structures. I was impressed by Wakim's ability to support his catering team, even knowing how many wine bottles were delivered to each table, yet still able to maintain his position as a leader who provided tools to others, not executing their tactics for them.

Wakim understood the importance of face-to-face contact with patrons as a way of providing them with the high level of service they expected at the Delano and assuring them that they were receiving the utmost care and attention. Wakim also understood that his on-the-floor presence enabled him to collect a 360° awareness of operations to incorporate into his planning and to make improvements that kept the Delano ahead of its competitors.

The challenge for most leaders is determining when to get involved and when to step back. As a general rule of thumb, if you're collecting information to build the 80% of the GPP or you are engaged in building the GPP, then involvement is important and usually necessary. At the same time, if you find yourself constantly directing the 20% of the GPP once you've put systems and structures in place, then you may be negatively micromanaging, especially if you're getting a read on people that they seem annoyed or flustered in your presence. David, a manager at a biomedical technology company, would receive e-mails throughout the day, every day, asking for progress and financial reports on his unit from his VP. Some days he'd receive more than a dozen such requests, and they were bogging him down and eating up valuable time. The challenge was that the VP's interruptions affected David's performance. It was as if the VP would assign a four-hour task and then within an hour forget that there were three more hours to go. David left the organization. Are you like this VP?

Have Realistic Expectations

How often have you heard the phrase, "Let's give it 110%"? Have you ever really thought about this suggestion? The fact is, no one and nothing can function at a 110% performance level. Period! Engines burn out. People burn out. Casual references to the expression deflate morale by placing too much pressure on people to push themselves too far. People need ample time to adopt new skills, habits, responsibilities, and tools. If you want higher productivity, create a better GPP, leverage some technology, change a process, create new alliances, be a better leader, and do your job better so that your people can excel.

In addition, when you give people the directives of an initiative or of their everyday responsibilities, be realistic about your expected outcomes. Not only is it good for your organization when you're not burning people out or making them feel unappreciated and resentful, but it is morally a good measure, because too much pressure and stress are not only signs that you're doing something wrong, but lead to chaotic environments. A Swedish study that followed 3,100 Swedish men for a decade reported that leaders who negatively impacted their workers increased their employees' chances of suffering a heart attack by 60%, as compared to positive leaders whose employees were only 40% likely to suffer emergencies.[122]

And what about you? In reality there are days where you've worked an entire day and have said you've accomplished nothing while on other days you get one big success at 2 p.m., and you can say you've made the week. The same holds true of those around you. Being realistic keeps you focused on your purpose and helps you fulfill your responsibilities to your people. You're all there to achieve a Desired Outcome, not to work at 110%.

One way to keep your expectations on par with reality is to be a good planner. If you plan well, your expectations will be based on accurate thinking that results in accurate Strategy, Macro Tactics, and Tactics. When you don't take the time to think things through, you end up expecting others to deliver on unrealistic expectations.

Encourage Stealing

Whenever I'm in a group situation, whether it's with my NYU students or facilitating an organization's internal strategy session, I encourage people to learn from each other. Jokingly, I tell people to steal from each other, by which I mean they should take the best ideas from each other and apply them in their own lives to create new opportunities. It is really no different than seeing a person wear a certain style of clothing and going out to purchase a similar article for yourself, but at the same time, making it your own. As long as your "stealing" is legal and ethical, it can be a great way to move forward quickly.

This "stealing" concept is something that you probably already do if you're not a forerunner in your industry or sector, anyway. You gather competitive intelligence, extrapolate information from it, forecast what your competition's next moves will be, and either follow suit or, better, try to beat them to the punch. In many cases, "stealing" from other industries is a great way to gain a competitive edge over unsuspecting competitors.

So while "stealing" externally can be beneficial, I find that some people frown on it when it is done internally, and I want you to question why you wouldn't want some internal staffers to learn from others. After all, some people call this stealing "best practices," but by most industry standards, "best practices" sounds like a more politically correct way of gathering ideas to mimic.

In my strategic planning sessions with executives, I tell them they are all working together, and that if they all improve, the organization improves. This translates to if they see something that they feel was presented better, approached stronger, and/or would yield a better outcome, then they should use it. You can't imagine how many people are shocked at such a suggestion when they initially hear it but who end up seeing the value over time. They see how a simple shift in their perspective enables them to stop limiting their organization's ability to grow and develop by leaps and bounds, too.

I'm not just suggesting that you steal, however. I really want you to take it seriously both by gathering improvement ideas from external sources, and by developing silo-breaking systems and methodologies that open the floodgates for great ideas to flow across departmental and business unit lines in a way that allows for a lot of cross-functional sharing of ideas. One way to accomplish this is to use a modified version of the ET Development Funnel for NPSD, alliances, and technology, except in terms of empowering others, you create the environment that brings together the best minds from throughout your organization to collaborate, communicate, and transfer information. If someone on staff makes an outstanding presentation, why wouldn't you want others to follow the example and use the same format, style, process, methodology, or language in other areas of your organization to strengthen it now and in the future?

Ask Two Questions

A colleague once shared with me his personal adaptation of the concept of Return on Investment (ROI) that he calls Return on Bother (ROB). Jim Gilmore,[123] author of *The Experience Economy*, sizes up situations and opportunities and asks, "Is it worth the bother?"

The great thing about creating a culture where people feel comfortable and empowered enough to ask questions is that it can lead to another important question that not enough organizations are asking, Does this look right or is something "off"?

The VP of sales at CBS television in the 1980s would always look for employees—from management to the front line—who were thinkers and who would speak up when something seemed off. In her department, advertisers were promised a certain number of viewers for each commercial time slot they purchased. If the Nielsen ratings came in at lower-than-anticipated numbers, CBS would have to make up the difference by offering clients additional commercial time.

Considering that any miscalculation made by one of her employees could translate to hundreds of thousands of dollars, the executive needed to know that her staff members could pull their thinking back from the details, take a look at the bigger picture now and then, and assess whether the figures made sense to detect any errors in their calculations. Had she taken a tyrant's approach to managing, she may not have empowered her staff members to feel safe speaking up, and that could cost the network countless millions over the course of a single year.

Being able to look at a situation, size it up, and determine if it seems worth the bother or if it looks right is how you and your group can collectively judge whether your organization is on the best path or if changes need to be made. If the something in question is a project, you can fill out the Project Evaluation Chart from Chapter 3 and assess its true ROI. Then, if it is a winning idea, you can develop the project using your tools like the CST Model, a version of the ET Development Funnel, and so on. Now when you consider empowering your staff members (or stakeholders in general), keep in mind that you must decide whether the Return on Bother makes it worth your deploying assets on an endeavor and moving forward.

Beware: Build the Empowering Package or Someone Else Will

One of the most significant tips you can keep in mind when it comes to empowering others is that it is your job to build the Empowerment Package to ensure that others will find success. One of the pieces of advice that I give to my clients and students is that if you don't build the Empowerment Package, someone else will out of sheer need for the 80% of the GPP in order to "survive" on the job.

I've worked with numerous leaders who, upon learning about the ET activity of empowering others, will say that this was a real moment of realization for them when they finally understood that it was *they* who were at fault when their people didn't achieve expected outcomes.

I've also heard the sad stories of excellent mid-level managers who became fed up because upper management did not build the Empowerment Packages the subordinate managers needed in order to succeed on the job. Due to senior-management negligence, these mid-level or front-line managers took measures to leave their jobs and relocate to places where they could launch their organizations ahead fast. This was the case for Shawn, a division head for a major hotel brand, who had a better understanding of how projects propel organizations forward rapidly than his boss did. When Shawn approached a superior and asked what projects she would approve for him to complete, she said that there were none in house at the time. For a couple of years, he made every effort to select and assign projects, but without the support of his upper management team, he became discouraged and took a higher-level position at a competing hotel chain, which was a huge loss for his previous employer.

The other problem with leaving the building of the Empowering Package or the GPP to your people instead of doing it yourself is that they don't necessarily have your 50,000-foot view of your organization, which means that their attempts to fill the gaps left by leadership could result in your initiatives being out of alignment with Desired Outcome and Strategy. When you use the CST Model and tie it to the ET activity of empowering others, you ensure that your Macro Tactics and Tactics are selected and developed (respectively) in a way that moves your organization to targeted outcomes better than if you leave the building of the two to your people.

■ ■ ■

Leaders can build (or destroy) faster than any other staff member, depending on how well they empower others to execute Strategy and Tactics. View the activity of empowering others as much more expansive than the simple act of handing over authority. Empowering is an activity that you're doing at every touch point within and external to your organization. Every decision and action you make, from the time you plan your schedule to when you conclude your day, has an impact on how empowered all your organization's stakeholders are.

Empowering others is not a touchy-feely activity, but one that's strategic in nature. The approach you take to empowering others must be holistic and unsiloed, and it is the same whether you're preparing them to handle massive objectives or to make minute, quick decisions. Use the tools, concepts, and principles you've learned in this chapter in conjunction with those throughout ET to empower internal and external stakeholders in ways that enable them to deliver maximum value back to your organization.

INNOVATING EVERYWHERE

I'M GOING TO TELL YOU a little story. On the surface, it will not appear all that interesting. Therefore, you'll have to pay close attention to it, because I am going to quiz you at its conclusion.

His first meeting of the day took longer than he had allocated, and Sean had only twelve minutes before the next one to grab an espresso, phone his wife to confirm that a colleague would be joining them for dinner that night, and brief one of his managers who was out sick the day before about a new purchasing form.

He hopped the elevator to the second-floor café, ordered his shot of caffeine with a splash of milk, and dashed to the elevator with cell phone in hand. "Yes, thanks for taking care of the reservations," he finished while exiting the elevator. Just then, he spotted his manager.

"Hold up," Sean motioned to the manager. "I want to show you the new purchasing form. Andrea will fill you in on the details later."

Moments later, Sean slipped behind his desk and dialed up his Skype call. The next meeting would start on time.

Are you ready for your quiz? Perhaps you expect me to ask you what Sean did wrong or what he did right. Nope, neither. Here's your question: How many innovations did Sean encounter in those twelve minutes?

Even if you go back to the story and begin counting—(1) the concept of office meetings, (2) espresso, (3) elevators, (4) the cell phone, (5) restaurants, (6) purchasing processes, (7) forms, (8) desk chairs with rolling wheels, (9) the Internet—you would still never accurately include all of them in your response. For example, what about the innovation of domesticating animals so that the splash of milk in Sean's coffee didn't require Sean to chase down some poor cow in a field? Or consider all the processes involved in the mining, harvesting, and manufacturing of raw materials needed to build the elevator. We are completely enveloped by innovation, and throughout each and every day, innovations influence everything we do, think, and experience. Throughout the history of mankind, one innovation has built upon another—or displaced it altogether. Yet when you look at your organization, how often do you see its components within the context of innovation? If you're not consciously *innovating everywhere* in order to drive the activities of your stakeholders and secure the survival of your organization, I expect that your outlook will be different by the time you finish this chapter.

Encouraging Creativity

All people are born innovators, but as they journey through childhood and into young adulthood, they become conditioned to "color inside the lines" both literally and figuratively. Research shows that people tend to lose their innovative spirit in early childhood. Advice from well-meaning parents and teachers channel most people away from free-spirited thinking and toward the conformity sold to them as entry tickets to good colleges and decent jobs. Society rewards the kids who don't question authority, who won't ask aloud why or why not, and who are willing to play along. If you want the letter of recommendation to gain entry to a college or job, being a renegade won't get you a very good one.

Perhaps looking back on your life, you can see how you bought into the fallacies that diminished your innovative tendencies until you tried to stand out as a go-getter, someone special or unique, to a college-admissions officer, a person interviewing you for a job, or a financial backer for your business. Although you may not have seen your need to stand out rather than to fit in within the context of innovating, that's just what it was. And today, when you want your organization to edge out competitors, grow, and prosper, you are continually required to innovate, whether it's with products, people, departments, use of equipment, financing, or any other aspect of running your organization.

In this chapter, you are going to learn tools and options that will help you to generate innovative thought within yourself and within others throughout your organization. As you progress, you will realize what a high-ranking priority innovating is, and by chapter's end, you'll see that there are better ways to drive innovation than just asking people to "be innovative."

We'll lay the foundation for learning by addressing underlying concepts of innovation and the rationale behind the ET activity of innovating everywhere. As Rob Cook, Pixar emeritus, once told me, "Undermanage or over-manage, you lose creativity," and I believe your new understanding will expand creativity and jump-start innovation so that new opportunities will open up for you and your organization.

Before we really kick off this chapter, it's important that you understand why this ET activity is called "innovating *everywhere*" and not just "innovating." Even great leaders have often made the mistake of limiting their opportunities by assuming that innovation is primarily related to new product development. In reality, innovation is like a fuel additive that should be applied to every ET leadership activity and every aspect of your organization to make them much, much better than they already are. Innovation alone does nothing, but add it to other leadership activities, and you instantly turbo-boost their effectiveness.

Innovating throughout your organization may happen quickly in some areas and take some time in others. However, when you develop the mindset of innovating *everywhere*, you will make explosive improvements throughout your organization.

What Does "Innovating" Mean to You?

As I just mentioned, leaders tend to assume that innovating is an activity reserved for new product or new service development teams. That's simply not true, and if you don't expand its uses beyond the area of product and service development, you'll surely miss out on a lot of opportunities. So right up front, let's get clear about what innovating actually is.

Think of all the tools and activities of Enterprise Thinking as engines. Also picture every aspect of your organization as an engine. Innovating is the fuel that feeds all of them. Innovating expands strategizing, improves alliance building, accelerates new product and service development, and redefines how you leverage technology. You can be innovative when engaging in competitive intelligence (CI), when becoming globally aware, in the approach you use to forecasting, etc. When it comes to performing ET activities, just remember that innovating by itself is a *useless* activity until it is plugged into another activity.

Innovating is an excellent way to address challenges. If you want to anticipate disastrous weather conditions such as hurricanes or tornadoes so that building-supply companies such as Home Depot or Lowes can insure that much needed supplies are available to certain store locations after a disaster, you can take an innovative approach and develop algorithms to anticipate those weather conditions. By being innovative, you can improve farming practices exponentially. Just tie GPS satellites to farming equipment so that individuals who drive harvesters no longer have to steer the machine and the machine is piloted by the GPS, which increases yields and enables the farmer to do more with less.

Innovating combined with other ET activities can change a good opportunity into a great one. An assistant director within Scholastic Books can ally with regional groups to gain publicity, but when she strikes an agreement with the Lance Armstrong Foundation, visibility for her public projects goes through the roof. And, of course, being innovative with new product and service development can yield outcomes that run the gamut from incremental product improvements to the development of radical and/or disruptive new products, technologies, ideas, and processes improvements. Sometimes incremental adaptation of an existing product or service is a more successful innovation than a total redesign. For example, triangular tires would be a total redesign, but would you prefer them over an incremental improvement like a better tread?

Innovating with a Purpose: Square Watermelons?

When I received an e-mail one day that described a square watermelon, I was intrigued, but not entirely convinced that square watermelons were really being grown and sold or if the e-mail was a hoax. It said that square watermelons were grown by the Japanese to make it easier for people to fit the fruits into their refrigerators, since living spaces in the country were small. I first wanted to find out if this was true, and if so how it was accomplished. After a bit of research, I learned that the square watermelon was created by a Zentsuji farmer, whose process entailed placing watermelons while they're still small into square, tempered-glass containers. As the fruits grow, the containers act as molds, constricting the form of the growing watermelons to the glass walls. What I then learned from my research was a little different than the spam e-mail had led me to believe.

A square watermelon is not for the average consumer; the cost of just one watermelon could be as much as the equivalent of U.S. $80 in comparison to the round watermelon retailing at U.S. $12 to U.S. $20 each. Because food gifts like tropical fruit are highly cherished in Japanese culture, the square watermelon did find a small niche market as a gift item, but since most people could achieve the same result (i.e.

[continues on page 460]

[continued from previous page]

fit the fruit into their refrigerator) by cutting up traditionally shaped watermelon into pieces, the square watermelon didn't hold much widespread appeal due to the price point and didn't take off as a mainstream grocery item.[124]

Innovating for the sake of being different doesn't necessarily mean that the outcome is better than what you already had. Always remember that innovating should occur to improve your outcomes.

Concepts and Rationale Behind Innovation

Most of the leaders I meet know that innovation is important to success, yet few know the rationale behind innovation so they can make better choices, be more impactful when innovating, get their people to be innovative, and assess whether innovation is appropriate at certain times. The topic of innovation can be hazy, even confusing for some, but it doesn't have to be. We're going to briefly explore some underlying concepts about innovation to lay the groundwork for performing the activity of innovating everywhere. It is essential that you learn about all four concepts, because they play off one another, affecting the outcomes of your decisions. The four concepts we will cover are:

- Concept #1: The Innovation "S" Curve
- Concept #2: Leadership's Challenge with Innovation
- Concept #3: The Curse of Disruptive Innovation
- Concept #4: Innovation Challenges Born from Our Modern-Day World

Once you understand the rationale behind innovation, you will begin to see opportunities for it everywhere. As you read about the concepts, keep an open mind. You may grasp some of the concepts quickly, whereas others might require a second or third read-through. My approach is to give you a simple lesson in layman's terms so that you can make sense of innovation's importance within the larger context of ET activities. Though the four concepts here should be enough background to inform your decisions, your industry or sector may demand that you acquire more in-depth information on the topic of innovation.

Concept #1: The Innovation "S" Curve

Innovation takes place throughout the world all the time, yet many decision makers don't fully understand how it impacts their organizations. The accelerated pace at which change occurs in today's world means that leaders can't afford to be ignorant about innovation, nor can they wait around to get up to speed—for they may never catch up. If you use the concepts and follow the directives in this chapter, you can begin to rapidly infuse every aspect of your organization with innovation so you won't lag behind others.

Sometimes leaders will say, "But we don't have products, we're in government," or "We don't need to change our products, because consumers love our unique brand and don't want us to change a thing." And in many cases, these leaders are right not to change their actual products, but they can still take an innovative approach to production processes, delivery methodologies, packaging, and fulfillment of their products and services. They can also be innovative in their approach to hiring managers, training front-line workers, and gaining access to competitive intelligence (CI). Innovating is everywhere. You have to look at more than just the products and services alone. You need to look at all aspects of your products, services, and operations to see where they can be improved so that you can keep ahead of the "S" curve of innovation.

The recipe for French's Classic Yellow Mustard is the same today as it was when it was first introduced in 1904 at the World's Fair in St. Louis, Missouri. Although the product itself remains unchanged, the components surrounding the condiment have evolved to keep pace with the times. The product's ownership has changed hands, the packaging has been updated, plastic containers have replaced glass bottles, bar codes and nutritional labels have shown up over the years, and its distribution has expanded in scope and improved with modern logistics. Think about the changes in farming methods to grow the mustard seeds and the different tools used to crush them. Also consider the inventory controls and technologically driven systems that handle order processing and billing. Within the processing plant, one person running the bottling of the mustard produces 112,000 bottles in one shift all by himself, because technology has been innovatively devised and incorporated into the production process to leverage the employee's performance.

Had the management in charge of producing, selling, and distributing French's Classic Yellow Mustard failed to innovate, the product wouldn't be on store shelves today, regardless of how much people love the product. If we were to diagram the progress of just one of French's Classic Yellow Mustard's innovations, we would be looking at its Innovation "S" Curve.

The Innovation "S" Curve is a means of diagramming the progress of any innovative idea from its inception and development within your organization and through its life cycle in your marketplace.

Take a look at the Innovation "S" Curve diagram (Figure 12.1) and refer back to it from time to time as you read its description. Although you can apply this concept to alliance development, technology creation, CI collection, and countless other activities, for educational purposes, we will discuss the S curve in terms of product development.

Expanded Innovation "S" Curve

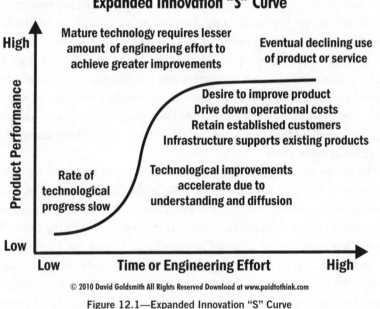

Figure 12.1—Expanded Innovation "S" Curve

The x-axis running horizontally along the bottom of the diagram represents the amount of time or engineering effort expended on your innovative idea. The y-axis represents the stage of performance/development of your product.

The inception of your product occurs in the lower left corner of the diagram. If your organization is a company that has invented a new computer chip, this location on the diagram is where you are investing resources into the chip's new design, production facilities, marketing, engineering, sales, and so on. As these activities take place, your innovative "idea" moves up the S curve, which is in essence, the life cycle of your product.

As product sales of the chip increase, investments in producing, marketing, and distributing the chip mount, until at some point, the chip claims its optimal condition. That's where the S curve crests. For a while, all is stable. You continue to invest in the chip to improve its speed, decrease costs, and increase sales to customers.

By now, you've wrapped your business around the chip. Your infrastructure is built around it, and your R&D is devoted to it, so why shouldn't you ride the wave? Minor and periodic enhancements in the chip's design, process improvements, and in its marketing and advertising keep everything flowing at a steady pace. But you realize something else has been happening at the same time.

While you've been growing and tending to your product, a competitor has been developing a revolutionary new chip technology that works as effectively as your chip, is smaller, produces less heat, is more durable, and is easier to manufacture, yet it sells at one-third the cost. Your competitor was starting its own product's S curve, and some of your customers have already switched to using the competitor's product.

You now face a challenge: How will you will you handle this new situation?

Concept #2: Leadership's Challenge with Innovation

In just about any marketplace, you can expect to compete against a certain amount of emerging innovation. New competitors enter the market, different products are developed, and improved ways of operating organizations emerge. So while a rise in *your* innovation's S curve means that your product or idea is progressing forward, a rise in your competitor's S curve means that you have a competitive threat that will need your attention.

Figure 12.2 is my interpretation of this progression; I call it the Natural Progression of Innovation. It is based on the "innovator's dilemma" concept from the work of Harvard professor and innovation expert Clayton Christensen in his book, *The Innovator's Dilemma*.[125] This diagram illustrates your product's innovation status (the lower of the two S curves) in relation to that of your competitor (indicated by the higher of the two S curves). Notice the intersection point between your S curve and your competitor's.

Natural Progression of Innovation

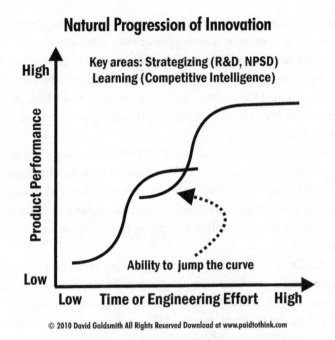

Figure 12.2—Natural Progression of Innovation

Notice that at this intersection point, your innovation's life cycle has flattened out whereas your competitor's innovation is on the rise. Typically, this means that your competitor's innovation is gaining momentum in the marketplace in contrast to yours, which is steady. (In many instances, products in this "steady" phase are referred to as cash cows.) Although everything seems okay, steadiness is not necessarily an advantageous position for you to be in—at least, not for long, because you can never be entirely sure about exterior factors that could impinge on your innovation's future.

You basically have three counter responses, all of which can be effective depending on your situation's variables such as timing, technologies, capital, etc. You can:

1. **Continue to support your existing chip without making any changes.** When organizations' leadership chooses status quo, the innovation is said to be "riding the innovation curve." Sometimes you can ride the innovation curve without any immediate consequences, but you have to ask yourself how long you can do so. Would you still like to be selling typewriters today?

2. **Create a "me-too" (copy of your competitor's) product.** Some me-too products do well in the marketplace, but unfortunately,

they typically deliver low profitability and market share.

3. **Invest in research and development and launch a completely new product.** This can be a very viable option, but you have to be realistic about your organization's ability to catch up and surpass your competitor. Can you afford to pull resources away from your existing product and dedicate them developing a new one? In many cases, the sooner you take this option, the better, because if you wait too long, you might not have the money or the time to ever catch up.

The option of standing your current ground doesn't seem viable and whether you invest in a new innovation or not, you lose customers. You're caught in what Christensen coined the *innovator's dilemma.*[126] It seems that whether you stay the same or move forward, you are taking a risk, and that risk could become chancier if you're unsure of when to make the jump away from status quo and toward innovating.

As you're weighing these options, your competitor's product is moving farther up its S curve (as indicated by the vertical up arrows), making it more difficult for you to catch. The longer the competitor's S curve is allowed to grow without any interruption from you, the more difficulty you will have jumping the curve and either catching up or surpassing your competition. Your cost to compete with the new product rises. Soon, there will be no catch-up option left for you. The innovation wave will pass, and your organization may die. Christensen outlined in his book how companies engaged in every industry—from disk drives to excavators to metal processing—all faced the same conditions, then supported their existing products while driving down costs and increasing quality and output. He showed how these companies eventually closed and new market leaders took their place. That's the scenario organizations face every day.

[Winning by a Nose with Innovating Everywhere]

Only a few short years ago, the synthetic (or plastic) wine stopper became the hottest new thing in winemaking due to its ability to prevent cork taint, a condition caused by cork wine stoppers that ruins the taste of wine but that has gone unaddressed by cork manufacturers despite numerous complaints by retailers and bottlers about the problem. The innovation of the synthetic wine stopper seemed like the imminent demise of the traditional cork stopper as the former grabbed a rapid 20% share of the wine stopper market by year's end in 2009. Some experts, like internationally

[continues on page 466]

[continued from previous page]

known wine critic Robert Parker, estimated the cork stopper's eradication by as early as 2015. But that's not what happened. The trend seemed to reverse in 2010, when the sales of cork stoppers rose by 7% and then jumped again in the first quarter of 2011 by an increase of 12%.

So what happened? Two things, really. Cork-stopper manufacturers had both "snobbery" and innovation on their side. According to a 2011 article from the *Portugal News* online, "studies have shown that bottles with a natural cork are assumed by consumers around the world to be better than those with a synthetic cork or screw cap," so consumer support was on their side.[127] In addition, natural stopper manufacturers improved their production techniques so that the issue of cork taint was diminished greatly, satisfying retailers and bottlers, too. So although it appeared that synthetic stopper manufacturers were making strides at one point, their innovations in product material and design weren't enough to sustain their growth.

Concept #3: The Curse of Disruptive Innovation

A difficult type of innovation to safeguard your organization against is *disruptive innovation*. When you are hit by a truly disruptive innovation, you are completely taken off guard and your own innovations become displaced. The disruptive innovation is like the bogeyman who attacks you in the dark before you even know he is there. Here is Christensen's rendition of disruptive innovation.[128]

Disruptive Technology S Curve

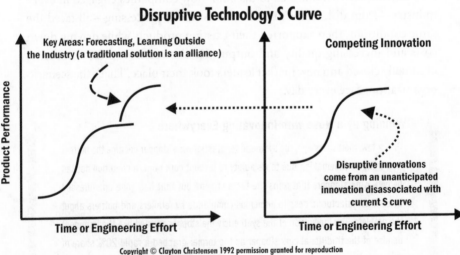

Copyright © Clayton Christensen 1992 permission granted for reproduction

Figure 12.3—Disruptive Technology S Curve

Let's break down the events that Christensen says occur when your innovation is displaced by a disruptive innovation. The left-hand graph in Figure 12.3 shows an S curve of your innovation. See how your innovation has leveled out, as indicated by its flat horizontal line. Now cast your eyes on the S curve in the right-hand graph; this represents a disruptive innovation emerging from a competitor (which could come from within or outside your industry or sector). As you can see, the latter innovation's S curve began at a higher and faster performance rate, and you didn't see it coming, so you were not positioned to react.

The dotted horizontal line pointing to the left from the disruptive innovation's S curve to your innovation's curve indicates its (often rapid) attack on preexisting innovations in the marketplace. Looking back at your S curve, you now see the disruptive innovation's crested curve sitting atop your flat line. Your innovation has been displaced.

The recording industry is one that has been plagued or progressed (depending on your point of view) by multiple disruptive technologies. Records and eight-tracks were displaced by tape players, which were displaced by CD players, which eventually gave way to downloadable music. Few in the entertainment field prepared themselves for the disruptive technology that came along to convert and transmit information digitally, changing the way people buy and listen to music.

This is my take on disruptive technology: The bad news is that once you've been snuck up on by a disruptive technology, your options for a counterattack are very limited, but the good news is that there are measures that you can take to *prevent* falling prey to disruptive innovations. These measures typically fall into one of four categories:

1. From the ET Strategizing category: Set your sites on alliances like joint ventures, mergers, or acquisitions as an approach to innovating—like Google's acquisition of Motorola's cellular phone business and the 17,000 patents[129] (7,000 in progress) that came along with it—that place potentially disruptive technologies on your team and change your status from victim to victor.

2. From the ET Learning category: Adopt a learning mentality. Know about your organization, your competitors, and global factors that might signal blind spots and impending threats. In addition, you can establish an autonomous R&D facilitator from outside your organization's culture and thinking to deliver information and knowledge back to you. Remember, R&D is a

state of mind, not a building or floor in an office. Anyone can do it if they see the value.

3. From the ET Forecasting category: Forecast the futures of your own industry and of other industries so that you can identify *potential* disruptive technologies before they have an impact on you.

4. From the ET Performing category: Utilizing the development funnel approach when addressing these types of disruptive innovations doesn't work. Instead, create a culture that encourages people to hunt for innovative ways to improve the overall organization. This conditions your staffers' minds to continuously search for solutions and opportunities in innovative ways. From the Enterprise Thinker's perspective, you can see how fueling your new product and service development activities with innovation can strengthen your products and services as well as your internal improvements, further fostering the growth of competitive advantages throughout your organization. All of this sets the stage for positioning your organization to react and be proactive when confronted with emerging disruptive innovations.

Keep in mind that as you improve your thinking skills as a leader, you will more often be proactive rather than reactive in your strategizing and your approach to solving all challenges, including those associated with innovation.

Concept #4: Innovation Challenges Born from Our Modern-Day World

Let's recap before we move any further. Any time you develop and market a new "product," a competitor is likely to be developing the next competing or differentiated product simultaneously. The competitor's innovation poses a risk to your innovation, which is why you must continually be working on the next "new thing," which could be the product itself or the numerous components that contribute to its success: packaging, financing, distribution, delivery times, marketing, alliances, and so on. The basic rule is this: Without innovating to keep your product on its S curve, a competitor will inevitably displace your innovation, whether it takes them five months or 50 years to do so.

---{ **Overcoming Innovation's Challenges with New Awareness** }---

Denmark's Oticon, Inc.,[130] a world leader in hearing-aid manufacturing, is a firm that values input from smart thinkers, wherever they may be. Oticon's U.S.-based marketing manager Rasmus Borsting and his team were challenged with how to market a groundbreaking hearing aid that used Bluetooth technology.

The European marketing team sought to solely promote the product's Bluetooth technology, a marketing move that put the focus on the technology itself. Unfortunately, they were reaching out to a target market of elderly people who might assume that a blue tooth was a condition warranting a visit to the dentist.

Borsting, on the other hand, wanted to be sure that he had the optimal marketing approach to successfully introduce this advanced product to the market, so he encouraged his father to try the device and give honest feedback about it. When Borsting's father remarked that the new technology's surround-sound capabilities and dual sound in both ears enabled him to *see* better by allowing him to more easily identify the direction of incoming sound, Borsting had the marketing hook he needed.

Rather than focusing on Bluetooth technology, Borsting's team touted the benefits of it, and the marketing campaign was hugely successful. This is just one example of how leaders' newfound awareness can influence strategizing and ultimately the selection of tactics.

Even organizations that appear to be exempt from this rule are not. Mars, Inc. has made candy for nearly 100 years in large part because its leadership innovated with improvements related to packaging, logistics, new markets, advertising, ingredients, and more to keep the company's products competitive. Just as I outlined with the example of French's mustard, if leaders had not innovated, their product would not be sellable. Today's point-of-sale (POS) systems require bar coding for calculating inventory. Tomorrow's POS may require printable radio frequency identification (RFID) with specialty inks instead of utilizing a tagging system. If you don't innovate, consumers— or those in your business channel (manufacturers, distributors, retailers, etc.)—may turn to one of your "new and improved" competitors. And while leaders have always had to deal with oncoming innovations, their challenges are multiplying in recent decades.

In the past, innovations were somewhat incubated geographically. Your most threatening competitor may have come from down the street, and the only restrictions you may have had were imposed by your region's commerce laws. Now, technology and communications have made our world smaller and flatter. They've also opened a vortex of rapidly emerging innovations from around the globe that were unheard of just ten years ago. A person with an idea in Mumbai may have carried that idea to his grave, having absolutely no impact on your operations in Cape Town. Today, that person's grand-daughter could introduce an innovation that displaces innovations and organizations around the globe.

In addition to dealing with a greater number of competing innovations, you have less time to react to them. To illustrate this point, I have come up with the Macro Reality of Innovation graphic. Take a look at Figure 12.4. In it you will see your innovation's S curve in the lower left section, and you will see the numerous emerging innovations on top of it. My purpose in illustrating this concept with a graphic is to give you a deeper understanding (than most existing literature in this area provides) of how, as the number of competing innovations multiply, their life cycles get shorter.

Time compression is increasing, forcing you and other leaders to make faster and more accurate decisions about your next steps. Ten years ago, you may have had two years to bring a new product from inception to launch, whereas today, you might have four months. In many high-tech industries, leaders are forced to keep multiple products in their development pipelines at any one time, and they have to decide whether they are going to invest in technologies that grow their organizations organically or whether they're going to acquire existing technologies to keep pace.

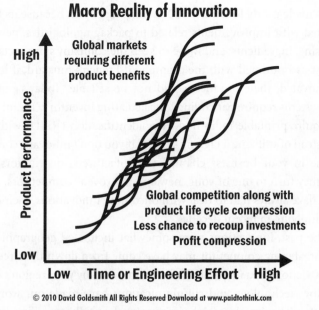

Macro Reality of Innovation

High — Global markets requiring different product benefits

Product Performance

Global competition along with product life cycle compression
Less chance to recoup investments
Profit compression

Low

Low   Time or Engineering Effort   High

Figure 12.4—Macro Reality of Innovation

Although examples of this condition are visible in every industry, leaders in consumer electronics are very much under pressure to innovate faster than ever before. In early 2010, Sony, Panasonic,[131] and Samsung released news that by June they'd all be offering 3D televisions in the $3,000 price range that would require users to wear 3D glasses. The race was on to see who could make product changes and advancements faster than their competitors to snatch market share from one another. Almost instantly, buzz of advancement number one from Toshiba's Masaaki Oosumi unveiled the company's new 3D TV, which does not require the use of glasses. This feature positioned Toshiba with a clear advantage, despite some reports that the picture quality was slightly lower than competing products. Toshiba's pitch also included a launch date of December. The breathing room for the competition now was that the televisions were only 12 and 20 inches in size, that there would be only 2,000 units produced per month, and that the sets would only be released in Japan initially. That said, there is a 56-inch screen in development.

Ideally, leaders in all industries and sectors should be proactively forecasting and planning to be ahead of competition. Unforeseen forces can shift the economic, political, or environmental scene and change consumer demand. Think of the rapid expansion of countries' social and digital revolutions, a war, or high inflation or an economic depression, all of which has happened around the world in just the past decade.

In Figure 12.5, the triple-arrowed contact points along your innovation's S curve represent these types of unforeseen forces that require your attention. One of your responsibilities is to continually maintain R&D—gaining awareness and knowledge organization-wide—so that you can forecast and strategize to keep ahead of competing innovations. And while there is no "right" answer in how to see the inflection points, an Enterprise Thinker is better prepared to make good decisions at these points, because they are not thinking linearly like the majority of leaders tend to do; instead, they are thinking at the 50,000-foot level and performing ET activities like establishing alliances, acquiring new knowledge, or watching the competition. These activities make the traditionally unforeseen threats visible, and early on. But if you're not performing the ET activities, you may not have the time to react quickly enough to protect your organization when the marketplace demands dramatically new technologies, distribution channels, new pricing structures, new sales models, continuous innovations, new product launches, a complete redefining of your Strategy, and more.

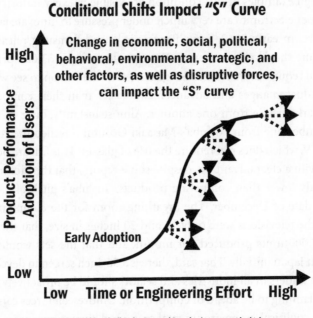

Conditional Shifts Impact "S" Curve

© 2008 David Goldsmith All Rights Reserved Download at www.paidtothink.com

Figure 12.5—Conditional Shifts Impact "S" Curve

You don't want to be in a position of getting caught off guard without any new innovation in your pipeline, because at that point, no matter how hard you struggle to rapidly change course, you might not be able to recover. This happened to numerous companies and organizations when the recession hit. Those who had some innovation in their pipelines did slightly better than those who choked and died in the storm, but still, they didn't fare as well as those organizations that were committed to innovation.

In my own business, I used ET tools and activities to ensure that we were not one of the recession's victims. Even before the financial distress became public knowledge, my wife and I noticed subtle changes in the buying environment that pointed to greater problems on the horizon. Government jobs that we had lined up were cancelling well before anyone was talking about a suffering economy, and that sign prompted us to do more research. I spoke with experts in the financial markets, reached out to decision makers in large organizations, and asked questions of people in government about trends, buying patterns, and other changes they were encountering. Therefore, instead of just looking at the current global economic conditions, our global awareness, competitive intelligence, and acquisition of new knowledge combined with forecasting informed our decisions to direct our marketing and sales efforts away from the domestic U.S. marketplace and focus on the Asian market, a geographic locale that we determined was more economically promising. When the U.S. economy took a hit, we were already gaining a foothold in the economically securer Asia-Pacific region.

While you're riding the S curve, your hungry competitors—who might not be as bogged down by heavy overhead expenses and staffers accustomed to the status quo as you are—are better positioned than you to stop, retool to meet the new demands, and reenter the marketplace with relative ease. Before you can make a similar type of shift, your customer base can dry up. Almost overnight, you're faced with an immediate challenge for which you are unprepared, because you were expecting the slow decline of the typical S curve model.

How do you know you're in this position? Your products are no longer needed, you get slammed by new business or requests, you're now in the news whereas in the past, you weren't, and the reports about your organization (or products, etc.) are not necessarily positive. The optimal response to being in this position, obviously, is to prevent getting into it in the first place. As you can see by now, the activities of the Learning category, combined with the Forecasting category's tools and activity have the potential to protect you and your organization from this S curve challenge. Your proficiency as an Enterprise Thinker will automatically improve your ability to see how everything is connected—the European markets' health impacts the United States, and the outcome of the political shift in Korea's leadership impacts industries throughout the world, and so on—and to identify opportunities and solutions that would have been previously invisible to you. New and better thinking is how leaders everywhere can use innovating to their advantage instead of allowing innovation from the outside to threaten the health of their organizations.

High-cost private universities were caught off guard in 2009 when an onslaught of college-bound students opted for going to low-tuition community colleges and living a bit longer at home with Mom and Dad. And not until U.S. gas prices crept up around the $4 mark did consumers truly begin to pressure and support auto manufacturers' investments in alternative solutions, such as in electric and hybrid vehicles or more efficient gas engines like the one that can currently operate at more than 120 miles per gallon. This despite that our first vehicles in the early 1900s were running exclusively on electricity. You never know when the next surprising innovation will cut your innovation's S curve short, so you have to be prepared on all fronts. That's where Enterprise Thinking can give you the advantage, because you'll be more prepared for the change than you would be otherwise.

At the beginning of this chapter, I made note that innovation alone is useless. It must be combined with other "engines" like your ET tools, ET activities, and multiple aspects of your organization in order to turbo-boost their effectiveness. At this juncture, we will begin to connect the activity of innovating everywhere to your role as a person who is paid to think.

Decision-Making Factors

Every day, you look out over the landscape of your organization and think about the best ways to move it forward. Some of the earlier innovation concepts you've added to your ET toolkit will now become a part of your decision making at 50,000 feet, which is a real plus considering how important the activity of innovating everywhere is. According to a 2010 *McKinsey Quarterly* survey, 84% of executives reported that in the wake of the global economic rebound, innovation has become a top priority once again. At the same time, only about a third of these leaders admit that they include innovation in their strategic planning processes, and they experience difficulties finding the right innovative people, developing a culture of innovation, and organizing processes that foster innovation.[132] If you can relate to these leaders in that you recognize the important role innovating plays in your organization's development and growth but you aren't sure what measures to take to create a more innovative organization, the tools you learn here will be most helpful to you.

To progress your organization innovatively, you need to be able to (1) select the right type of innovation to reach Desired Outcomes, (2) commit the appropriate level of resources and time to make the innovation a success, and (3) communicate your plan clearly to others through the use of shared vocabulary.

Selecting the Right Type of Innovation

The level of innovation you select depends on the development and growth needs of your organization at any given time. Though there are many types of innovations out there (and a great deal of information about them to learn), I want to give you a simple description of three types so that you can decide which is right for meeting your Desired Outcome.

- **Continuous innovation** is the adaptation of an existing product or service through incremental improvements, typically requiring little or no behavioral change to use. If you add rollers to a chair, you improve the chair without changing its function. Continuous innovation is a common way to satisfy existing customers and grab new users. Fluoride in toothpaste and extended store hours are continuous innovations.

- **Dynamically continuous innovation** represents a dramatic change in the way we use a product, without changing the technology behind the product all that much. Minimal behavioral change is required. The Sony Walkman bundled well-known magnetic cassette tape and player technology into a new, portable device. The laptop computer enables consumers to use an existing technology in a new way.

- **Discontinuous innovation** (sometimes called Revolutionary Innovation) requires significant behavioral change. The Internet and digital data storage as a replacement for physical data storage are discontinuous innovations. Discontinuous does not always mean disruptive, because the latter (like its name) disrupts the market significantly in a short period of time, whereas a discontinuous innovation may take years for the market to adopt.

While you are still making decisions and before you actually take action, it is important that you select the type of innovation that is the most in alignment with your Desired Outcome and you commit an appropriate level of resources and time to the innovation to make its success realistically achievable.

Committing the Appropriate Level of Resources and Time

Now that you have some understanding of the types of innovation you can choose, you can also see that certain types of innovations require more resources, time, and energy from your organization than others. Be sure to commit the appropriate level of resources and time to the innovation to ensure its success.

Basically, the three innovation commitment levels are low, medium, and high. Figure 12.6 is a visual representation of the options you have when it comes to determining your level of commitment to any innovation-related project.

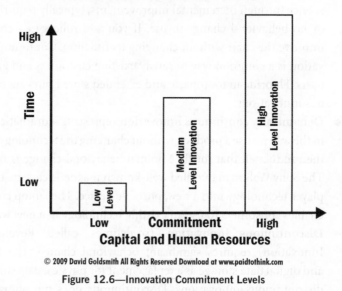

Figure 12.6—Innovation Commitment Levels

Interpreting the diagram is simple, but determining the right level of commitment for the type of innovation you want to develop can be extremely challenging. When you consider the accelerating life cycles of all types of innovations and the rapid influx of competing innovations, you quickly realize that you have little room to waste time or resources. When the stakes are high, the innovation commitment decision can actually make or break not only the innovation, but the organization that has invested in it, too.

Therefore, if you're looking to develop an innovation that requires a high level of commitment—typically, some type of disruptive innovation—but you are only willing or able to commit a low or medium level of resources and time to it, you could be dooming the innovation before it even gets off the ground.

In addition, you must consider the human factor. I'm not just referring to the number of people or the cost to put them on the project. Leaders who can innovate and produce WSPs gain greater buy-in from their people on future projects, an "asset" to which you can't easily assign a value to. In addition, you must decide who you will assign to develop the innovation and how you will approach describing your plan to them.

Communicating Your Plan through a Shared Vocabulary

When it's time to explain your plan to others, teach to others the vocabulary—continuous innovation, dynamically continuous innovation, and disruptive innovation—and use it to clearly communicate your Desired Outcome to them. There are many advantages to using the vocabulary.

First, your expectations become clear to others. What would you rather hear from a superior: "Be innovative" or "I want a dynamically continuous innovation, and we're committing a medium level of resources and time to it."

Second, the vocabulary forces you to define the parameters and scope of the project in order to be able to share it with people. Taking the time to add a degree of specificity also forces you to double check that your decisions are in alignment with Strategy and Desired Outcome.

Third, your people will be able to alert you sooner if they get into the project and find that the level of resources committed to it is not high enough (or is too high) for the type of innovation they are expected to achieve.

When everyone involved shares the same vocabulary, your CPM charts, tactical plans, and other means of directing others are easier to understand, making them more likely to reach your Desired Outcome on target, on time, and within budget.

You can enjoy the rewards of the Economics of Thinking by taking the time to make innovation-related decisions early on in any endeavor.

Developing the Mindset of an Innovator

Having a mindset of an innovator will open your eyes to the opportunities right in front of you as well as enable you to create opportunities that are yet to materialize. Here, you will take the first steps to developing the mindset of an innovator so that you can more effectively innovate everywhere throughout your organization. Earlier in this chapter, I touched on the fact that by the time we reach adulthood, we have been conditioned to adopt status quo, letting go of much of our childhood spirit to naturally innovate. I can't think of a better starting point to regain some of the courage and creative thinking we've lost than to ask the question that once appeared on the desk of Regina Dugan, then-director of DARPA, the Defense Advanced Research Projects Agency (Dugan is now a senior executive at Google), that read: WHAT WOULD YOU DO IF YOU KNEW YOU COULD NOT FAIL? When Dugan shared the quotable question with me, I couldn't help but wonder if it wasn't some sort of mantra for many of the people working at DARPA, an innovative U.S. Department of Defense agency that develops new military technologies, like its unmanned glider in the works that is expected to have the capacity to fly from New York City to Los Angeles in eleven minutes at a speed of Mach 20.

Innovating Is an Ongoing Activity

Innovation is not an end-all objective; it is a continuous flow of "fuel" that turbo-boosts the effectiveness and performance of entire organizations. Leaders who understand that innovating everywhere is an ongoing activity that needs to be performed in conjunction with the 11 other ET activities, dramatically improve outcomes, and conversely, if leaders do not innovate, they put their organizations at risk.

Arie de Geus—former head of strategic planning for Royal Dutch Shell turned professional speaker, and author of *The Living Company: Habits for Survival in a Turbulent Business Environment*—is a globally known expert on why some companies survive for decades and others die before their time. He explains that multinational corporations have an average life expectancy of only 40 to 50 years and that "a full one-third of the companies listed in the 1970 Fortune 500 . . . had vanished by 1983 [having been] acquired, merged, or broken to pieces."[133] Standing the test of time involves more than product innovations. The ways in which products are brought to market must evolve, too. Think back to French's and Mars; they've both enhanced or revamped their call centers' support, their packaging to include today's bar coding and labeling requirements, their financing needs, and much more to ensure their ongoing survival. If they hadn't done these things and even one of these areas experienced a failure to keep pace, their products, services, and entire organizations could have faced extinction. When you're continually thinking about ongoing innovations within the context of the ET framework, your thoughts and decisions move your organization forward purposely instead of haphazardly, putting your organization in a stronger position to forge its best future.

Innovation Occurs Everywhere

We don't always recognize the innovations that surround us, yet when you become aware of how innovating occurs everywhere, you can recognize opportunities to make even simple improvements through innovating, like changing the way your staff answers the phone, bills your clients, applies for funding, or generates leads.

LG Electronics[134] is known for its innovations in mobile phones, TVs, appliances, and other products, but in recent years, it applied that same innovative expertise to its new supply chain, and in doing so, earned the Institute for Supply Management's annual award for leadership and innovation in procurement. Chief executive Nam Yong set out to break silos and integrate business units' procurements when he took over in 2007, leading him to hire the firm's first chief procurement officer, Thomas Linton, who successfully centralized purchases, saving $2 billion from its cost of goods, which previously grossed at $30 billion annually. Trading out copper for aluminum in many of the firm's electrical products added up to a savings of $25 million in 2009, and consolidating orders for silicon disks used to make chips shaved another $1 billion off the top. Innovation promises to deliver huge benefits when it is woven into the fibers of organizations.

Whether your organization sells products, offers services, or plays the role of support arm for another organization or group, innovating is essential to its growth and survival. Look around your organization and consider the many areas of it you can improve by innovating. Legal partners can innovate by creating an online database to enable their staffers and clients quick access to information resulting in improved client services. A university research library can adopt data-mining software that empowers researchers to compile data in minutes rather than days, giving the researchers more time to examine and use the data. A sales person can use a wiki, a type of software that allows several people to edit website content, to help manage a group project. If we thought more about the innovations that surround us every day, we might stop thinking of innovation as some difficult or occasional activity.

Booz, Allen, & Hamilton, Inc. research shows that only 10% of new products are actually new; 26% are improvements to existing products, another 20% are new product lines (created from existing products), and 26% are new additions to product lines. Of the remaining product innovations, 7% represent repositioning and 11% are cost reductions.[135] While these figures are significant, they rarely include non-product-related innovating, so you can apply these statistics to operations, technologies, alliances, and more to get an idea of how limitless your options are.

Order Winners Come from Innovating

Innovation is intrinsic to generating (and maintaining) Order Winners. If you remember from Chapter 3, Order Winners, which impel people to select your organization and its offerings over those of your competitors, eventually slip off their pedestals and become mere Order Qualifiers—characteristics that allow you to participate on par with competitors—as your competitors either mimic your Order Winners or come up with unique Order Winners of their own. Can you see the S curves in your mind? You can't always avoid having an Order Winner retrogress to becoming an Order Qualifier, but you can continually innovate so that you keep a couple of paces ahead of competitors just the same. A patented pharmaceutical product can remain on the market as an Order Winner until the patent expires and competing pharmaceutical companies launch their own versions of the same product. To remain ahead of the pack of followers, you would need to breathe life into your next new Order Winner by innovating.

Keep in mind that innovating keeps you winning in areas that go beyond simple products and services. When the recession put many retailers out of business, Toys "R" Us saw an opportunity to double its number of store locations for the 2009 and 2010 Christmas buying seasons by renting out vacant mall spaces at bargain prices. The firm's chief executive, Gerald Storch,[136] and his management team applied innovation to its distribution channel, expanding locations by 90 temporary pop-up stores in 2009 alone.

Innovating Is Not Synonymous with Being Creative

Innovating and being creative are not the same. Innovating improves a condition or product and helps you reach your Desired Outcome. Being creative doesn't mean you accomplish either objective.

If you're having difficulty making the distinction, many of the ET tools can systematically point you in the right direction. For example, when you use the CST Model to strategize, you create clearly defined Desired Outcome. When you're innovating, the tactical options you entertain will align with your Desired Outcome. But if you were just being creative, you could be pulling any idea out of the air without any certainty that it will be strategically advantageous to your organization.

Everyone Should be Thinking about Innovating

You might have your doubts that everyone can or should be an innovator, but even the most unexpected potential contributors on your staff should not be discounted. (That's why later in this chapter, you will learn techniques for fostering innovation throughout your organization.)

For example, you may not want the person who transports a tanker of hazardous material be innovative about driving or unloading the contents out of fear that his attempt to change things up could result in disaster. But if you think about it, this guy works most closely with the task at hand, and perhaps he can offer insight that you could not anticipate. Perhaps he has noticed that the seal used to cap the liquid inside his tanker leaks slightly in cold weather. Encouraging him to innovate could lead him to suggest that the cap needs to be replaced with a material that doesn't contract with decreasing temperatures during winter months.

People in management and in the field should always be thinking about innovation. It's just that some of them still need to follow strict guidelines or continue to work within highly structured environments so as not to confuse innovation with haphazardness.

[The Gold Standard of Innovation]

If you're looking for a culture of innovation, look no further than Israel, a country that lives and breathes it. The world's Warren Buffetts and Bill Gateses revere this small country for its high aggregation of innovative leaders, and the results speak for themselves. Innovation turned a country with limited resources into a thriving agricultural success and a technological powerhouse even under the cloud of constant war with its neighbors. Its population is just 7 million, yet Israel is second only to the United States in terms of patents and research activity.

We can look to several factors responsible for spurring innovation in Israel. For one, culturally, Judaism encourages the questioning of status quo and conventional wisdom, fueling the search to develop new and better ways of living and working. Notice how many hospitals, research facilities, educational institutions, scientific discoveries, inventions, and Nobel Prize winners have come from this innovative culture. Second, mandatory military service exposes every citizen to leadership experiences, arming youth with lessons about problem solving (some of which could make the difference between life or death) that they take with them throughout their adult lives. Almost every single person has a military experience that provides them with leadership training at a very young age, and they continue to get ongoing leadership experience for much of their adult life, because citizens are required to fulfill reserve service for upwards of a month a year until the ages of 43 to 45. The experience forces individuals to lead and to solve challenges that are often life threatening, forcing them to learn to make calculated decisions and to learn to think for themselves. In addition, Israel provides its commerce and government with the highest percentage of R&D funding of any country in the world. The melting pot is home to people from more than 70 countries, because Israelis recognize that diversity fuels innovation. In fact, Israel's government even subsidizes language-immersion programs for new immigrants, sending the message that cultural diversity is welcomed and making it possible for newcomers to become greater contributors to society. Education is valued, and a high level of emphasis is placed on math and sciences. If you could take a page from this tiny but highly innovative country, imagine how much more innovative your organization could become.

Creating a Culture of Innovation

At this point, you have a foundation for understanding what innovating everywhere can do for your organization and your responsibilities as a leader to perform this essential ET activity. Now you are ready to learn how to build a culture of innovation within your organization through two avenues: facilitating innovation and triggering innovative thinking among your people. When innovating becomes a part of your organization's culture, everyone realizes that innovation isn't some occasional task that you awkwardly ask everyone to do. Instead, it becomes a community mindset that gives birth to a continuous flow of improvements.

Facilitating Innovation

Facilitating innovation is as much an inside job as it is an outside one. You want to embed a mindset of innovation simultaneously among internal stakeholders—leaders, customers, support staff—and the network of external sources—vendors, customers, officials, lenders, media—who contribute to your organization's successes.

For example, some organizations use social-networking tools to reach out to both types of groups and solicit innovative ideas from them. Papa John's chain of pizza restaurants launched a contest for its Facebook fans to submit recipe ideas for the next great pizza. Winners get free pizzas for life and 15 minutes of fame in return for their innovative entries.[137]

Start asking yourself how you can facilitate innovation, then try some of the tips below.

Fill the Idea Bank

Encourage staff members to deposit innovative-improvement ideas into your physical or electronic Idea Bank, introduced in Chapter 4, on a regular basis so that great ideas are captured before they are forgotten and are relevant to the needs of your organization. A staff member who has just encountered a problem with her computer will submit a more valuable idea—buy software updates so computers don't crash when we are servicing customers— than the employee who is brought into a room once every six months and asked, "What innovative ideas do you have for our organization?" Creating the 80% of the GPP for innovation collection by offering tools such as an e-mail address to send ideas, a wall individuals can write on, a drop box, and a shared spreadsheet for ideas to collect real-time thinking can do wonders for innovative contributions. Leaders who implement some of the innovative ideas they glean from the Idea Bank reinforce innovative thinking among their people and tend to more easily gain the cooperation of others, too.

Collecting ideas for an Idea Bank can be as simple as requesting that each staff member write one suggestion per day onto a sticky note and attach it to a wall or window before they leave each evening. Other methods, like online and phone services that allow your people to submit their ideas anonymously are advantageous for many organizations. Keep in mind, however, that if you request suggestions and never use them, people will become discouraged and less likely to put forth the effort in the future. It's useful, if you choose not to use some of the ideas, that you show those who submitted them that you considered them seriously. One way to do so is to show people a Project Evaluation Chart that contains some of the Idea Bank ideas; that way, even if the idea doesn't rank as a project #1 or #2, your staffers understand that there were concrete reasons, perhaps losses by a nose, that informed your decisions.

React Positively to Curiosity

Curiosity is the seedling for innovation, and if you can recognize it and react positively to it among your people, you can multiply innovative ideas everywhere. However, you might have to earn people's trust before they'll express their curiosities. That's because just as they have traded innovation for the acceptance and approval of authority figures, adults have traded curiosity for safety and convenience. Most adults can think back to a childhood incident where they or a peer dared to ask an adult why, only to be reprimanded for challenging authority, even when the questioner's intent was innocent.

Consider any idea or question as a potential starting point for innovation. For example, you operate a foundry and one of your laborers wonders aloud what it would be like to have a break room on the premises for him and his coworkers. If your first reaction is to shut him down, because you think he wants a place to slack off, you might miss an opportunity to increase productivity. Then again, if you encourage him to expand on his idea, you learn that he has noticed employees sitting around on the equipment during their breaks, slowing down the work pace of other workers who were not on break at the same time. A break room would allow operations to function without pause during break times. By reacting positively to the curious remark, the idea of a break room becomes an innovative improvement that enhances workers' performance.

As I said at the beginning of this chapter, people are born with an innate sense of innovation, but throughout life, they are discouraged from standing out in the crowd and rewarded for conformity. You sit in a position to either build an innovative culture within your organization or foster the suffocation of innovation that is so prevalent in most societies. Simply becoming aware of your role in encouraging innovation can be huge for your organization, unlike situations where people in positions of authority seem oblivious. For example, when I was in college, a student put forth additional effort to complete an essay about deer that had been assigned by his professor. Instead of just consulting books and magazines as references, the student actually went in to the woods to study the behavioral habits of deer. When the student cited his experiences in the bibliography of the paper, the professor penalized this A-level student for pursuing his curiosity about deer and reporting his firsthand findings. Instead of encouraging the student's curiosity, he accused the student of trying to manipulate him, returning the paper with the note: "If it looks like bull___, sounds like bull___, and reads like bull____, then it probably is bull____." Ouch! In the future, how likely might this student be to offer up innovative ideas to an employer?

Embrace Workplace Diversity

Maintaining a diverse workforce gives you access to a broad range of ideas, opinions, and perspectives. The more variety in your workforce, the more experiences, viewpoints, histories, attitudes, and expectations you have to innovatively inform your ideas and initiatives.

Bloomberg Businessweek's 2010 listing of the top fifty innovative companies worldwide[138] highlighted the trend that U.S. firms are losing spots on the list to companies based in countries around the globe. Making it to the top twenty-five were five companies from China, India, or South Korea. Five of the seven newcomers to the list were from developing countries, so consider how diverse companies can provide a plethora of innovative opportunities.

One of the ways that you can hire diversity is to set up operations in different markets. Thomas Connelly, DuPont's chief innovation officer says, "Emerging markets have been our most consistent source of growth over the past decade. They will continue to be a major factor not only for growth of the company but also the source of our innovations. It is no coincidence that our new innovation centers are in China, India, and Brazil—where the new customers are and where we need to be with our technical resources."[139]

Because our populations are so mobile today, you don't have to go to the ends of the earth to attract a diverse group of people to participate in your organization. A wide variety of thinkers are out there just looking for opportunities to make contributions to their organizations. It's your job to find them and give them a chance.

Allow Time for Ideas to Germinate

Have you ever thought about *when* you get your best ideas? I'm betting they usually come to you when you're enjoying down time, like while you're cooking, biking, listening to music, taking a shower, or away on vacation, and are less likely to surface while you're at your desk, in meetings, or managing others. The typical timing of idea generation highlights two points.

One, although working longer days can help you increase output, it can hinder your performance as a leader, because it robs you of ample time to think.

Two, when the focus turns to innovation, oftentimes the most progress is made not during meetings where attendees are asked to be innovative, but after work, when Cyclonic Thinking allows ideas to germinate. Google and 3M's[140] leadership understand this concept, which is why they encourage their employees to spend roughly 15% to 20% of their work time engaged in self-directed solutions to work on projects not associated with the core business. W. L. Gore, which specializes in manufacturing fluoropolymer-based products, is another company that urges its employees to set aside time to work on new ideas. Gore engineer David Myers, whose primary job was developing plastic heart implants, used this time to find a way for smoother gear shifting on his bike. This led to the development of Gore's Ride-On line of plastic-coated bicycle gear cables, which in turn led to Myers creating improvements on cables used to operate large animated puppets like those at Disney World, and on guitar strings.[141] Innovative thinking time enables Myers and employees at organizations like his around the world to solve complex challenges, come up with new products to offer, and to solve customers' experiences. The famous story of the Post-it Note's development came from a researcher who accidentally discovered the technology while working on a self-directed project.

Fostering innovation doesn't happen in a single meeting or even in a month; it's something that evolves over time when you purposefully include it as part of everything you do. From planning to hiring to ideating and collaborating, you can introduce opportunities to innovate to your people on a regular basis and let their ideas germinate over time.

Get Outside Help

External contacts can sometimes see innovative solutions more easily than internal workers who are too close to challenges to see them objectively.

When leadership at Chiquita Brands International wanted to improve profitability, it turned to GEN3 Partners, Inc.[142] for innovative solutions. GEN3 found that people would eat more of Chiquita's bananas if the bananas were readily available and were not damaged or over-ripened.

Based on their findings, GEN3 encouraged Chiquita to expand its point-of-purchase locations beyond grocery-store produce sections. Today, Chiquita offers individual bananas for sale at kiosks, near candy counters, and at healthier fast-food restaurants such as Subway or Panera Bread.

Chiquita also contracted with engineers and scientists to develop a plastic bag that would suspend a banana's ripening process at the attractive yellow stage. By reaching out to experts, engineers, and a new network of distributors, Chiquita solved its challenges innovatively.

Connect the Front Line to Upper Management

You already know that you can elicit innovative thought from your management team, but have you been thinking about ways to connect your front-line staffers—who are in contact with your members, customers, attendees, buyers, and suppliers and who use your systems and procedures—to your upper management so that they can share with decision makers their gold mine of innovative improvement ideas?

In many organizations, time, geography, and patterns of work behavior separate the people who have the authority to make changes from the people who work in the trenches and are figurative sponges of experiences that could sprout limitless innovative ideas. You can develop a process on your own, or you can follow my suggestions here for forming a connective corridor between your front line and upper management:

1. **Create an Idea Bank.** If you sense that people feel uncomfortable about providing honest feedback at first, you can allow them to make anonymous deposits. Be sure that upper management acknowledges innovative ideas and gives credit where it is due.
2. **Create a culture of innovation by supporting ideation.** Once people begin contributing to ideation, whenever possible and in the best interests of the organization, make the effort to implement ideas. Your actions (more than your words) will encourage frequent and willing ideation from your staffers. In addition, you can elicit innovative suggestions by using some of the triggers in the next section to put the thinking process on track.
3. **Give feedback.** When you select an idea that you want to develop, share with people some of the factors that determined the winning idea. This way, people can begin to understand why their idea worked and how they can make valuable suggestions in the future. Knowing that they're being listened to and

appreciated will encourage people to think innovatively and to share their ideas with leadership.

4. **Keep criticism in check, and don't dismiss ideas as bad before doing your research.** If innovating is new to you, be aware that you may perceive some of the ideas as outlandish. You should give deeper thought to these ideas, because they just might hold the answer to winning-by-a-nose solutions. You want to encourage, not discourage people.

5. **Be open-minded to the inexperienced.** Pay close attention to the recommendations you receive from younger staffers, being careful not to discount them because of their lack of experience. The president of a company told his twenty-six-year-old daughter that her suggestion wouldn't work. She tried it anyway, and it worked. He felt foolish for having immediately rejected the idea, but he learned to be more open to new and innovative ideas. Stay in tune with younger generations, and borrow innovative ideas from how they spend their leisure time, too.

6. **Know your people.** Take the time to get to know your people by simply talking with them and listening to their ideas. Even if their initial ideas or needs are not innovative, you can use their feedback as launching points for your own innovative twists on them and to deliver improvements within the work environments or any other aspect of your organization.

Allow for Open Innovation

Open innovation is a means for allowing people who are external to your organization or your particular group to participate in its innovative improvements. This concept is based on the premise that everyone gains cumulative value when they're able to tap into your intellectual property and trade secrets, and share proprietary technology, research findings, and more. You are able to spread the seeds of your work by opening channels and allowing your technology to link to another technology, which links to another, and so on. This is very common today in the Web space when a firm releases the programming code for their service so that others can create new services. Sometimes the services become cumulative and an organization wins, which is what happened with Twitter and the apps developed around it. Twitter's code allowed other individuals and organizations to write their own programs that added value, improved ease of use, aggregated information, etc., which in turn aided Twitter to gain more popularity.

Steven Johnson,[143] the author of *Where Good Ideas Come From: The Natural History of Innovation,* describes how Nike released more than 400 of its patents on the website GreenXchange. Nike shared technologies that are connected to the green movement in an effort to offer a civil service and to facilitate the exchange of ideas.

Engage in Social Ideation

Social networks give you access to people from multiple backgrounds whose ideas are generated by a variety of interests and experiences. Frequently, connections formed in social networks are stronger than the relationships that people have with their next-door neighbors or coworkers, because social-network connections are based on similar thinking, not close physical proximity.

Social ideation is a two-way form of communication that businesses and nonprofits can use to achieve desired outcome. A 2009 SmartBlogs.com interview with Craig Newmark[144]—the "Craig" in Craigslist—revealed that many government agencies such as the Pentagon and the U.S. State Department, under Hilary Clinton, used social media internally so that staffers could communicate ideas to each other through their intranet and could communicate externally with outsiders about public diplomacy topics.

In a January 2011 interview with Piers Morgan on Piers Morgan Tonight,[145] Kourtney and Kim Kardashian discussed the impact that social networking has had on their rise to fame as reality stars, spokespersons, and businesswomen. Kim alone had more than six million Twitter followers at the time, to whom she tweets for feedback on products she's contemplating developing. For example, followers will tweet their choice of shoe color, providing instantaneous free-market research. Although negative publicity can certainly generate challenges and lost followings, on the positive side, imagine the kind of Idea Bank of innovation you can build with that volume of dedicated fans.

Follow Your Gut

With all the technologies and trends available today for gathering information and feedback to use for making innovative improvements, there is still something to be said for natural-born skills, hunches, instincts, and intuition. In other words, innovating can still come down to following your gut. Sometimes, when your "gut" needs a little knowledge, you can feed it with information from people like Steven Levitt, co-author of *Freakonomics,* who are just wired in ways to see what others don't and can conclude intuitively what others need data to understand. Great innovation can be just as much internal as it is external. We're not throwing out thought, rather we're taking in observed behavior and saying, "I've witnessed your history, heard your call, seen your results. I've got confidence in you based upon your prior WSPs." The more WSPs an individual has in a variety of areas, the more confidence you can have in that individual to connect the dots and create more value.

Use Crowdsourcing

Years ago, gaining market research information was an expensive and time-consuming endeavor for many organizations. Depending on the size and circumstances of the organization, outside research firms would have to be called in to conduct extensive surveys and perform lengthy assessments of the data. Today, digital technologies allow many organizations, both large and small, profit and nonprofit, from private and public sectors, to inexpensively and instantly tap into their target markets through a process called crowdsourcing, the outsourcing of tasks to the external masses that are typically performed by internal employees or dedicated research firms.

Earlier, I mentioned Papa John's Facebook contest asking consumers to submit their recipe ideas for their next specialty pizza in the Papa's Specialty Pizza Challenge. Contests and other means of inviting the public to weigh in on your products, services, ideas, plans, and so on are forms of crowdsourcing. When viewers of television shows like *American Idol* and *Dancing with the Stars* call and text their votes in favor of program participants, these viewers are participating in crowdsourcing activities.

While the customer is not always right, the data that customer input provides can save organizations from making costly errors. From Steve Jobs came this perspective: "You can't just ask customers what they want and then try to give that to them. By the time you get it built, they'll want something new."[146]

In 2010, retailing giant Gap released its new logo, expecting that its progressive and updated look would receive a warm reception from the public. The results were not as expected. Within hours, a flurry of responses poured into the company, prompting leadership to abandon the new logo and revert back to its tried and true navy blue. Gap execs admitted that the process of developing the new logo did not involve crowdsourcing. Their comments inferred that while Gap physically owned its brand, it would have been wise to consult with consumers before taking any innovative liberties with its highly recognizable logo. Used in the right way, crowdsourcing can give you the information you need to make better decisions on behalf of your organization.

Triggering Innovative Thinking

Every time I hear the phrase "think outside the box," I cringe, not because there is no box or even because if one existed you wouldn't know if you were inside or outside of it anyway, but because when leaders use the phraseology as a directive to their people to think innovatively, they're being too vague and they're not typically giving their people the tools to operate innovatively. Telling your people to think outside the box yields disappointing, if any, results, because your people don't know what to do.

If you're really interested in jump-starting innovation within your organization, use some of the "triggers" described below. Some of them are going to seem out-there to some of you, but that doesn't mean they won't work. In fact, if you really want to make some rapid progress, stretch beyond the limits of your comfort zone and go for the ones that seem the most challenging.

These triggers are suggestions that you can use to help the people around you think differently and more innovatively. Certainly, some triggers will appeal to you for instant use, while others may seem more useful at a later point in time. Either way, the next time you sit down for a meeting or send someone out to be innovative, use the trigger list to illicit ideas and to spur new thinking.

Don't Just Role-Play or Wear Someone Else's Hat . . . Be the Person!

Everyone has heard of role-playing. It's an activity where you pretend to be another person, and then you mimic their personality, thoughts, actions, speech, and perceived reactions to various situations. As a way of triggering innovation, I want you to take traditional role-playing to an entirely new level. I don't want you to pretend to be the other person; I want you to become them.

Wearing someone else's hat, walking in their shoes, and thinking about the customer does not work as well as you might think, so try this approach to getting inside the minds of others instead. For this activity, our target will be the customer/client/member/patient/constituent or whatever noun you use to describe the type of person who receives products or services from your organization.

First, think about someone whose hat you're supposed to be wearing and now let's change the condition. Think of the responsibilities they face on the job each day, the people who report to them, the pressures they have from their superiors, their family relationships, their finances, the challenges they face with their aging parents' health issues, their concerns about paying for their kids' college educations, and any other factor that you see as relevant to them. Once you have this information logged into your mind, I want you to BE THE PERSON. I want you to sit at their desk, live in their homes, face their challenges.

If you're like the thousands of people I've worked with, your perspective about the other person has changed dramatically in only moments. (You may have even realized that you don't know much about this other person at all.) By taking role-playing to this extreme level, your revelations are significantly different and can change the ideas you generate about addressing this person from here on out.

You can now try this trigger with your team in numerous ways. For instance, you can hand out a list of customer names to a group of staff members that you have assembled together, assigning one customer to each staffer. Then, you can ask each participant to perform the exercise just as you did, and later ask everyone to share their conclusions and realizations with the group.

Another option is to select a category of stakeholder to become or have your people become someone within that category—the happy customer, the potential hire, the vendor's VP, or the litigious patient—and watch how participants immediately view these stakeholders in a different light.

You can also ask people to become famous or historical people like great thinkers, inventors, villains, or politicians. If you direct a staff member to become Albert Einstein and strategize, that person may turn to formulas. A person who has become Steve Jobs might engage in radical thinking, and the participant turned Leonardo da Vinci may draw images to express his ideas instead of speaking or writing them.

When you become the other person, your entire perspective changes and you trigger innovative thinking.

Spend More Mental Time in the Future

All management exists in the future, because planning is actually future-focused thinking. You can trigger innovative thought when you spend more mental time focused on the future. Forecasting takes you well beyond imagination, because when you consider current data, trends, patterns, and cycles, you're still in the world of reality, but you're now playing out what you know to be true a few steps forward. You can do this by reading magazines, watching videos about far-fetched ideas, or by having a monthly get-together to discuss what life will be like five or ten years in the future. By forcing yourself to be in the future, your mind will begin, as will others', to see new connections.

Salespeople use this technique to their advantage, because they know that if you are thinking about your future, you may see yourself in a different light.

Try Jugaad

As I mentioned in Chapter 8, in India, business leaders use the word *jugaad* (pronounced joo-*gahrdh*) to describe how people innovatively address immediate challenges by improvising new ways to use available resources, as when you attach a hand towel to the end of a broom to dust cobwebs off the ceiling or use a screwdriver to pry open a can of paint. If someone were to extend the pull chain on a ceiling light by tying their shoelace to it, they are using jugaad, too. Perhaps you've heard that some medicines developed to treat a particular medical condition are found to have "beneficial" side effects that cause doctors to prescribe a medication for ailments that it was not originally intended to treat. This, too, would be a form of jugaad.

Whether you've spent your life in a geographic region that has offered an abundance of resources or a shortage of them, you can still apply the concept of jugaad to your organization and your career to devise innovative solutions.

Connect the Dots

Connect the dots is a term used to describe the mental process of drawing connections between related and seemingly unrelated objects or concepts to develop new knowledge and to derive innovative solutions.

Connecting the dots is a natural thought process, but in order to *elicit* innovative thought, the process needs to be brought to your conscious mind and played out. Bring people together and ask them to draw connections between items or concepts. For example, ask them relevant questions like, How does the price of wheat affect the shipping industry? or What similarities exist between the rampant famine in Somalia and the investment in harvesting equipment in neighboring Kenya? Some connections between a tape recorder and a textbook could be to put them together to record notes or to make books on tape.

UPS management connected the dots to develop operational efficiencies that saved 3 million gallons of fuel in 2006. A 2007 ABC News online article explained how UPS used package-flow technology, computers, codes, and programming to plan routes where trucks would make as many right-hand turns as possible, saving 28.5 million driving miles, time, and money.[147]

Artist Alex Beard, known for his paintings, children's books, and "impossible" puzzles, connected three dots to market his products and services. The dots were that (1) he had created an aquatic-themed painting that was so enormous that few homes would have room for it, (2) he wanted to help a nonprofit organization, and (3) he wanted public exposure for marketing purposes. Beard contacted the Audubon Aquarium of the Americas, located near his studio in the French Quarter of New Orleans and offered to donate the painting. The aquarium's leadership accepted the painting, and Beard received excellent exposure. Another time, Beard volunteered to paint a mural for New Orleans where the city's mayor, well-known players from the New Orleans Saints football team, and local businesspeople came together to celebrate the new art addition to their facilities, complete with media coverage.

Try connecting the dots to solve any of your challenges on a daily basis, and you will become better and faster at using it to trigger innovation.

Mimic Nature

Try biomimicry, the discipline of looking to nature for new technologies and designs, to trigger innovative thought. Did you know that a spider's web with strands the thickness of a pencil could stop a jumbo jet? The shape of turbines is similar to the structure of DNA.

CAMP, an Italy-based sporting-gear manufacturer, improved upon its ice axe when designer Franco Lodato asked,[148] "What is the best example of a hammer in nature?" Using the woodpecker as his model, Lodato lowered the pitch of the pick and angled it downward like a beak. Lodato's innovation became a best-seller.

At the Shanghai Jiao Tong University's[149] State Key Laboratory of Metal Matrix Composites in China, scientists looking for more efficient ways to produce hydrogen are studying photosynthesis in an attempt to mimic the ways in which plants produce food.

For eleven-year-old Aiden Dwyer of Northport,[150] New York, a winter hike with his family a couple of years ago triggered a nature-inspired innovation for solar energy. After noticing the configuration of bare tree branches as they seemed to reach out to capture the sun's rays, Dwyer crafted his own rendition of the "solar tree" and compared its sunlight absorption rate to that of a traditional flat-paneled solar instrument. His discovery: his tree-shaped figure absorbed more light! Dwyer has received global recognition, requests for speaking engagements, and awards for his innovative thinking. Though some of the attention Dwyer has received has been negative from people who want to see more proof, he just may be onto something.

Bring a leaf or a rock from outside into your office. Ask your team how one can innovatively mimic the leaf's ability to transport and retain water or the rock's ability to withstand some of nature's harshest elements. Observe images of nature you've gathered from online sources, visit a museum, or hike a trail to trigger innovative thought. Try to incorporate nature's innovative efficiencies into aspects of your organization. Just as springtime grows new plants to feed animals and the seasonable cycles enable every silo of nature to balance, foster, and bolster, see how you can generate the same types of unsiloed benefits within your organization, too.

Play Like a Child

Awaken your childhood consciousness by playing games in your mind all the time, not just at times reserved for innovating. For instance, today observe everything in nature that's red, and tomorrow listen for everything musical. When you change your orientation to that of a child, you see the world differently, and new ideas come to mind. The Shell Oil Company sent out a promotional DVD[151] featuring the company's newest oil-extraction technique. It enabled drillers to access oil resting in underground pockets alongside major oil-well shafts, using what Shell termed snake well technology (later registered as Smart Field Technology). The film started with a field technologist interacting with several work colleagues. He was stumped in his search for a new way to extract oil from those pockets.

The scene shifted to a diner, where the field technologist was eating a lunch of burgers and milkshakes with his son. At one point, the boy removed the flexible straw he'd been drinking with and turned it upside down to use the angled end to suction up the last drops of milkshake from the curved walls of his glass. The technician experienced an "aha" moment, returned to his office and began designing the flexible "snake well" extractors that could drill in multiple directions.

To get people to use the trigger of playing like a child, think about Outside-In, Inside-Out, Above, and Below—have them get on the floor and look around when thinking. Say that you're managing an entire floor of an eldercare facility. Why not lie down on a gurney or sit in a wheelchair and ask someone to push you through the halls? As you take on this fresh perspective, how does your view from below enable you to see where changes could help your residents? For example, lowering the television to eye level to prevent neck strain, changing out harsh ceiling lights with softer-glowing fixtures to set a more serene tone, replacing floor strips between carpeted rooms and bare floors to make smoother room transitions for patients being transported on wheels or using walkers, and so on.

Change Your Physical Workspace

Modify your workspace, even quickly and inexpensively, to wake up people's minds and trigger innovative thought. Hang new art, repaint a wall, bring in new plants, or rearrange furniture. Think about how beneficial it might be for you or others in your organization to leave the office altogether and work offsite using wireless and a laptop.

MVP Collaborative, a Michigan[152]-based advertising agency, triggers innovation with six themed rooms: a futon room, whose futons make for a relaxed atmosphere; a "ball" room—a small gym that uses large exercise balls for seating; a theater room, where employees can act out their ideas; a traditional conference room; an Idea Café, where groups congregate in small workspaces among a big-screen TV and foosball table; and a client room, where clients can work on long projects and enjoy a pool table and lounge chairs.

Reverse Engineer

With reverse engineering, you break down an existing product, service, methodology, or approach to its individual steps, processes, or other "parts." As you reassemble those elements, your mind generates ideas for a better, more efficient, or more profitable end product.

By reducing your organization's products or processes to their smallest individual elements, you create an opportunity to put everything back together to form a newer, more innovative solution. When was the last time you reverse engineered your own products? If you wait for your competition to do it, it might be too late to innovate fast enough to overcome a competitor's strike.

Storyboard Ideas and Collages

Walt Disney created storyboarding,[153] a technique for movie development where each scene is laid out in blocks to offer a scene-by-scene illustration of ideas before filming actually begins. The technique allows for groups of people to discuss a sequence of events prior to deployment in order to work out any kinks beforehand and ensure a smooth execution. You can use storyboarding in business and organizational settings to outline an acquisition, define an entry into a market, or to dictate the motion of goods or people within an office, a yacht, or a subway.

Any time you have a sequence of events to think through, try to see your idea play out in this way in order to expose its weaknesses while triggering innovative ways of adding depth and value to that idea. Storyboard when you develop an innovative product, alliance, process, or Strategy. Then share your storyboard with your team to identify gaps in your reasoning or to tie up loose ends.

A similar approach to triggering innovative thought is putting together a grouping of items or ideas into a collage. A collage is a compilation of items that you can assemble onto paper, whiteboard, or other substrate according to some logical relationship—"logical" being subjective here—that they have to each other. The compilation could be based on culture, texture, color, geography, products, or any other topic you can imagine and can contain a number of different types of items like photos, newspaper articles, or other pieces that trigger thinking.

By asking others to put together a collage, you're inviting them to think differently. They are able to connect ideas through imagery, just as interior designers do in the planning stages, when they assemble fabrics and images from magazine clippings onto a board or as teachers do when they display photos, brochures, and entry tickets on a classroom bulletin board to capture memories of a student field trip.

Mind Map Ideas

Mind mapping is an activity that works on the basis of relationships. In the center of a whiteboard, tablet, or other writing space, write out a word, short phrase, or sentence that describes your idea. Next, write related ideas in the surrounding white space. Use lines to connect the related ideas to the central idea and to each other.

Sample Mind Map

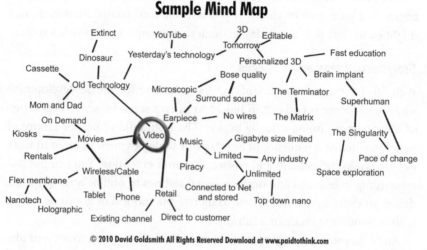

Figure 12.7—Sample Mind Map

Here, you can see how a single idea could spread into hundreds of related idea branches to help you understand how ideas connect to each other. The next time you have a meeting, pull out a gigantic piece of paper and draw an idea on the page. Next, ask people to immediately share their connecting ideas so that you can record them on the paper (similar to Figure 12.7) and watch their ideas begin to flow. You write "customer," someone connects their word "bad" to it, and another person says "invoice." When you feel you've exhausted the exercise, you will have a visual representation of potentially innovative ideas in front of you.

After hearing this idea, one of my students went back to his office, ripped the panels of a cardboard box apart and reconfigured them into a single large "canvas" for the purpose of mind mapping. He brought his team together, and then wrote down a starting thought on the canvas, adding a few subsequent thoughts alongside of them to get his staff members going. Then he left them alone. A few days later, after his staffers had some time to contribute to the ideas, he revisited the canvas and saw that it was full of brilliant opportunities that he could utilize as new fixes, ideas, and projects that would help his business.

Engage in Wordsmithing

Wordsmithing is the simple act of playing with words to alter meaning. Here's an example of how one word changes not only the meaning but your reaction to the meaning. Would you rather be *pulled* by a magnet or *pushed* by a magnet? The words "pull" and "push" suggest different forces at work, even if the forces result in the same movement. The changes are significant to the person being asked, but the outcome will still be the same (unless we get into the physics of body pressure being exerted and how this might be achieved). The value in wordsmithing for innovation is that it's a skill that can work in your strategizing, your copywriting, letters, speeches, instruction guides, and labeling.

Here's how you can use wordsmithing. Let's say you've come up with your Five Reasons Why and they include special packaging to preserve a product's freshness. By wordsmithing, you can convert the five reasons to more specific descriptions: Our product is vacuum sealed, allowing it to last four weeks, twice as long as other products on the market. Or, our product stays fresh 87% longer than competing brands' food, saving families an average of 23% more money on their annual grocery bills. Wordsmithing makes the messages you send to others stronger.

Play with the words in a document, letter, title, or product name by substituting synonyms, tweaking word order, and creating conflicting statements. Sam Horn's *POP! Stand Out in Any Crowd* contains[154] wordsmithing ideas that trigger innovative thought.

Cross-Pollinate

Hybridizers cross-pollinate plants to produce new varieties with specific kinds of advantages: higher yields, improved disease resistance, climate adaptability, etc. Organizations also benefit from the cross-pollination of ideas between industries, companies, departments, and individuals.

Cross-pollination helped Procter & Gamble develop Crest Whitestrips.[155] Engineers in the dental-care division tapped the expertise of those in the laundry division who already understood the whitening process. Mastermind groups often are cross-pollinating by bringing different people together. You can do this by sharing individuals across your organization, shadowing a vendor, or asking if you could swap one of your VPs with someone else's to gain additional input during a strategic planning session. Cross-pollination can happen everywhere from departments to countries, militaries to educational institutions. The sharing of ideas gives people new insight that can trigger innovation. Spend time thinking about how you can cross-pollinate internally as well as externally. You may ask a vendor or a noncompetitor to allow you to visit their facility or to also share employees as a way of triggering innovative ideas.

Use Bricolage

In 1970, the crew aboard *Apollo 13*'s[156] spacecraft, along with members of mission control, were forced to do some quick problem solving after an oxygen tank exploded, damaging the craft's electrical system and leaving the crew nearly 200,000 miles from Earth without a ride home. Details aside, the group devised an alternative plan that safely transported them back to earth using the spacecraft's lunar module.

Though not as dramatically, we've all been stuck in a situation where the supplies we need are not on hand, so we've had to improvise. Your car slides off the road in a snowstorm, and you have to throw your floor mats under a couple of tires to gain the traction you need to get back up onto the road. Or your copy machine's door starts to fall off, so you use a safety pin and duct tape to secure it back into place.

Without knowing it, you were practicing bricolage, a word with French origins that's used to describe developing or creating something from the supplies you have on hand. Similarly to jugaad, bricolage is often practiced in impoverished nations where people are forced to make do with limited resources.

You can use bricolage to prompt those around you to be more innovative in their approach to solving challenges by asking them different questions:

How would you do this if you only had these resources to work with? What would you do differently if you were in this other situation? How can we apply this concept to our product, service, methodology, etc.? Try the technique by asking members of your team, If we only had these three items, what would you do to accomplish our Desired Outcome?

Look Outside-In, Inside-Out, Above, and Below

As creatures of habit, we all have tendencies to search for solutions using the same patterns of behavior. Yet the "same old, same old" approach to problem solving can mean that you're leaving viable options on the table without knowing it. As you recall from Chapter 9, one way to examine your competitors and for you to gain insight into their impressions of your organization is to trigger different thinking through observations that come from Outside-In, Inside-Out, Above, and Below. For example, if each time your financials show a dip in profits your first instinct is to bear down on your sales staff, you could be overlooking some significant causes that need your attention, such as changes in buying patterns, soaring costs of goods, new technologies that are displacing your products, and so on.

The best way to break your rote thinking is to force yourself to look at your challenges from all different angles. This is what is meant by Outside-In, Inside-Out, Above, and Below. One of the fastest ways to adopt this multidimensional approach is to travel and experience other cultures. An experience like a guided tour through a jungle or safari where your guide says, "Make sure to shake out your boots in the morning because of spiders," wakes up your mind in ways that spill over into other areas of work and life.

Also, from Chapter 9, you may recall the military Macro Tactic based on Outside-In, Inside-Out, Above, and Below–type thinking called seabasing, which involves decision makers setting up a military security base on an island-like flotilla.

Just as military leaders build superiority from the air, land, sea, and space, you need to innovatively look at your organization and its offerings from all angles, not just from 50,000 feet above but from the perspectives of customers, vendors, or allies. Observe from the inside-out by taking the view of your front-line employees, janitorial staff, or management team. From below, you might see vulnerabilities to safeguard against, like theft and fraud.

For example, you can use this exercise to make your parking lot more efficient and attractive—try to park in it yourself, go up to the top of your building and look down at it, view it from down the street, count the paces from your accessible spots to your closest door—and see how your ideas start to flow.

Think Upstream and Downstream

The terms upstream and downstream refer to your position in the product or service chain relative to your final user. Thinking upstream means considering your supply network and vendors. Thinking downstream refers to customers, franchisees, clients, etc.

A multinational general-contracting firm ran into "upstream" legal trouble when several of its "downstream" subcontractors failed to submit employee-data forms to the U.S. government. The subcontractors weren't trying to break the law. They just didn't have the computers and software necessary to comply. The GC's first reaction was to tell the subs they had to fix the problem, and while this initially seemed like an attractive option, it didn't work. Then someone came up with the idea that if these subs can't afford the systems, why don't we give them terminals into our systems, and we can help them to ensure they are legally doing the right background checks, getting identification, etc.? The GC's leaders installed terminals in subcontractors' offices, providing access to software so that subs could meet compliance requirements—a less expensive solution than replacing their entire subcontractor network.

Mimic Ethnographers

Anthropologists who study cultures and human social behavior and then write narratives of their findings are ethnographers. Business and organizational leaders have used ethnographers' expertise to gather information on buying patterns, consumer uses of products and services, and various factors that drive consumer behavior. However, to trigger innovation, you could actually mimic the process of ethnography yourself or ask your fellow leaders, group members, board of directors, etc., to do the same.

New automated technologies are now being put in place to supply leadership with analytics on current happenings within their stores. The analytics bring new insight to decision making, which is the case with Alexei Agretchev's RetailNext software; it films patrons in retail locations and automatically feeds data about patrons' behaviors to leadership. For example, the minute a customer walks through a store's doors, the cameras that seem to be merely scanning for shoplifters are also tracking individuals' movements. Data from the cameras is sent to decision makers in retailing so that they can discern the most trafficked areas and the effectiveness of particular promotions or displays by observing facial expressions, eye movements, and other reactions from shoppers, and by calculating the length time they stayed at a particular location. The cameras, without human interference, can record details such as, product X was viewed 53 of times, there were an average of 37 visitors in aisle Y at any given time, buyers looked to the right side more than the left side of a display. Armed with this data, leaders can create better tools to assist salespeople, and they can suggest certain improvements: floor plans and layouts that best attract buyers, product displays that should be altered by eliminating specific items and adding others with a greater response from patrons, and so on.

You can easily and inexpensively put the same idea into action by working with an informal focus group of consumers. Working from a survey or list of questions, you can tell participants that you are collecting their responses for later review. Here's the twist: You're not just reviewing their answers, you're also observing consumer actions and comparing them to a second (and possibly third) wave of data. You can capture this comparative data by planting observers in retail outlets to watching how consumers pass by, look at, touch, or talk about your products when they're unaware of being watched. You might also look at consumer-complaint reports and see if discrepancies exist between those reports and the survey data that you have collected.

Take Field Trips

Visiting a customer, vendor, or colleague is one way to observe firsthand the challenges that you're trying to solve. The front-line observations that feed innovation can take many forms, as you notice the behaviors, environments, tools, and situations that impact your challenges.

David Speer, CEO[157] of Illinois Tool Works, once told me about an incident in which a customer of one of his organization's units, Miller Welding, couldn't get welds to hold whenever workers welded in isolated areas of Canada. The team at Miller tried everything they could to figure out why their equipment (and the equipment of their competition, incidentally) was not working in these specific locales, but they were unable to uncover an answer. It wasn't until Miller Welding sent a team to the location that the unit was able to identify the problem and come up with one of its solutions. The welding equipment was in top working condition, but the generators that powered them had been delivering an inconsistent flow of electricity, which caused the welds to be weak. The field trip helped Miller's team pinpoint the challenge and create new technologies for managing the power supply. It resulted in the development of a whole new product line.

Be a Contrarian

Sometimes you can trigger innovation by refusing to go along with the crowd. Become your negative customer, employee, or observer. Complain about what won't work and what doesn't work, and observe what kind of opportunities your negativity reveals. While this is a simple trigger, it's not used—not because it does not work, but because it's easier to say, "think outside the box." And yet you can see how pinpointing challenges and opportunities would be so much more powerful!

Emulate Your Heroes

We all know that how we think affects the realities we create for ourselves. So it makes sense that if you're having trouble triggering innovation, you can ask yourself how the people you admire might handle a similar challenge.

Steven Spielberg and George Lucas talked about their love of American painter Norman Rockwell's work in a feature story that ran on American television's *Sunday Morning* on CBS.[158] Both directors admitted that Rockwell's work influenced their own and that they had often drawn upon those iconic paintings to set the tone for many of the scenes in their movies.

The next time you're stumped for fresh ideas, think about how another leader, a mentor, a friend, or a grandparent would have approached your situation. It's a fun and effective way to trigger innovation.

Observe Your Points of Light

Points of Light is a visual tool you use to assess what is transpiring inside and outside of your organization. Mentally take the climb to 50,000 feet and start thinking about the relationships that your organization has with its customers, employees, allies, vendors, or within its internal departments.

I want you to visualize that every action is connected. If your customers call you, imagine this incoming call as a beam of light that is directed at you. If you reach out to a customer, then the light beam projects outwardly away from you. The greater the volume of connections, the more light or connections you see. In similar fashion, think about all the interactions that you and your customers have with each other; what do you see? As a next step, expand your contacts to all of the people who are connected to your organization or who are in some way associated or impacted by it.

The Middle Eastern regional manager for a multinational technology firm said the first and most surprising observation he made from performing this exercise was how few beams of light were outgoing to prospects and customers and how many more beams of light were dashing internally between departments. In seconds he realized that he had a huge and immediate challenge to solve. And he's not alone. Every time I walk someone through this exercise with leaders, they make realizations that they did not anticipate.

Perform this exercise considering process flow, relationships with allies, package flow, marketing efforts, document handling, regulation compliance, and more. Once you have performed this activity, consider the totality of the Points of Light and what story it tells you about your organization. If you see most light streams moving toward your organization and fewer flowing back to the sender, you might not be marketing or you could be receiving a lot of complaints. Do the lights zip back and forth, or does the light project in a one-way flow? If you had the benefit of computer animation, would each light flash rapidly, or would the streams of light mimic a flashlight with nearly dead batteries?

When Jeff Hurt[159] was the director of education and events and the meetings architect for the National Association of Dental Plans, he transformed the association's conferences and meetings by changing how people exchange information. At traditional events, speakers transmit information to their audiences. Hurt changed the model so that the exchange of information for conferences started several months prior to events via blogging, webinars, videos, and forums. During conferences, a back channel was managed with Twitter. Attendees tweeted to one another and to speakers using a hashtag (#), which enabled them to provide instant feedback and would steer the direction of the presentation. Hurt also conducted live-streaming videos so that attendees who couldn't attend in person could tune in on their computers. The result was one big discussion about the topics and a higher level of retention of the content.

If you were to look at Hurt's conferences through the lenses of Points of Light, you would see the streams of light darting in many directions as opposed to traditional events where the light flows from the speaker to the audience with only occasional two-way streams representing question-and-answer sessions.

Points of Light help clear mental clutter so that you can more easily trigger innovative thought and filter out distractions, aiding you and your team in developing new and innovative ways of building better relationships with stakeholders.

Invite Radical Thoughts

To trigger innovative thought, ask yourself, What would be the most radical thing that we could do with this organization?

Sidney Craig, the creator of the Jenny Craig[160] weight-loss company, hired controversial spokesperson Monica Lewinsky near the height of her scandalously earned notoriety. At that time, Craig's move was considered radical. Now look at the weight-loss industry's spokespersons. They're from all walks of celebrity and include individuals who have less-than-stellar track records. What was once considered innovative is now the norm, which is why every so often, you need to reassess your definition of "radical" and start from scratch.

Ask everyone in your group to come up with one radical thought for your next planning session or for your Idea Bank. You will find that the task isn't as easy as it sounds, but it's a good measure just the same, because it focuses people on more innovative solutions that will help keep your organization ahead of the innovation curve.

Try Processes that Let You Work Less

Many of the tools in the book are specifically designed to enable you to achieve more in less time, allowing you to work less. Processes are a great way to innovatively streamline groups of activities and spare you and your people from wasting time.

Different transformative management processes can be used as innovation triggers. Certainly, most people have heard of Six Sigma, but there are numerous others, too. One modern manufacturing practice that has proven successful due in part to its innovative nature was born in Japan from the mind of engineer Shigeo Shingo, the prominent expert on manufacturing processes who helped to develop Toyota's acclaimed production system. Shingo's SMED (Single[161] Minute Exchange of Die) is a lean production method used to reduce waste in the manufacturing process.

In his book *A Revolution in Manufacturing: The SMED System,* Shingo described how his method was used in the search for a solution for the change-over of a ten-ton press that originally required hours of work. To reduce change-over time, the press was positioned on a lift right behind the press it would replace so that when the first was removed, its replacement could immediately move into position. Because positioning had to be exact, the team installed cones on the bottom part of the press that would slide into perfectly milled cone-shaped holes below. Now a press could change over in less than a minute.

Shingo's SMED production method—a concept I've used countless times in my own career for every area of business, from the front office to manufacturing, and in every sector—is based on the philosophy that with the right tools, the right thinking, and the right engineering, the time it takes for any manufacturing changeover to take place can be drastically reduced to less than ten minutes (single digit minute). So a two-hour changeover can become a two-minute one, and a six-month changeover can become a six-hour one. In other words, ask yourself, What would it take to work less to trigger innovation so that whatever I do is brought down to a very fast process?

By asking "What (process/es) would it take?" (Redefining tool from Chapter 3: What Would It Take . . .) and adopting an anything's-possible attitude, you are able to stretch your imagination and trigger innovation. Think of a schoolteacher who enters a room, clicks a switch, and brings all learning materials instantly within reach. Or picture a document-processing program that allows a new hire to enter payroll data on one form, then automatically propagates all other forms, including computer documents, company credit-card data, and so on, in a matter of seconds.

Take the International Perspective

Look at every aspect of your organization through an international lens. How would you market your ideas to an international audience? How would your processes stand up to international competition? What solutions would be available to you if you were facing your challenges in a country or culture foreign from your own?

You can begin by assigning to different people on staff a country or a culture or a religion to research and represent to see what ideas they can bring back to your group for triggering innovative thought. During one of my NYU classes, Shilla Valentina Ghersi, a student and the owner of Retail Trading Solutions, explained to the group that luxury goods are big business in the Muslim countries that she sells products to from her Miami, Florida–based business. In fact, she told us that women often wear the most stylish clothing and accessories you can imagine under their burkas, though they only reveal them at private luncheons with other women or in their homes with their families. This information is something your organization can plug into its competitive intelligence, use for developing new channels of distribution for products, or consider when it's time to establish a new alliance, whether your decision makers are entering Muslim countries, high-end product ventures, or doing something entirely different.

Being myopic has its costs, so asking others to think internationally changes every point of view. New consumers, allies, and vendors who emerge in our global marketplace can show you innovative ideas and opportunities that you can adapt to meet your current challenges.

Ask "Why Not?"

Asking why not takes you out of the norm and into the realm of possibilities. It thrusts you out of your comfort zone, and encourages you to challenge rules and status quo. When you take on a why-not approach to triggering innovation, you're free to explore ideas that you may have been too inhibited to try previously. All you need to do is train yourself to ask this question first before you discount any off-the-cuff or out-there idea.

[Why Not: Breeding Innovation Sensibly]

I was immediately impressed by Mort Grosser when I first met him. Over the course of 40 years, he built a successful venture capitalist career out of asking, Why not? But what intrigued me the most was his thinking. A sensible man, Grosser understands that there is naturally trepidation over risk, but he says you have to start with an open mind. He describes his approach, which he calls Why Not Plus, as a "habit" that allows him to keep an open mind toward new ideas without thinking about it or consciously forcing himself to do it.

Grosser also doesn't think that "Why not?" is all good, either. He says it is a potential "two-edged sword" that can come back to cut you off at the knees if you don't combine it with the right blend of additional thinking tools to vet out the imposter opportunities from the genuine ones.

In 1978, Grosser was invited to join aeronautical engineer Dr. Paul MacCready's Gossamer airplane team in its quest to build the first human-powered plane that could fly across the English Channel. Grosser thought, Why not?, and accepted the assignment. On June 6, 1979, pilot Bryan Allen completed the mission, which Grosser described as "a thrilling and inspirational experience" and a "a major confirmation of my why-not instinct."[162]

Fast forward to March 18, 2012, when Grosser opened an e-mail and watched a video of a Dutch engineer taking off and flying with battery-powered birdlike wings attached at the shoulders; the video had received more than eight million hits when Grosser first watched it. Though other viewers comments were "Brilliant!" and "Inspirational!" Grosser told me that he wasn't instantly convinced—so he watched it about twenty times—and deemed it a hoax. Two days later, his suspicions were confirmed. When people asked him how he knew it wasn't real, he explained the two-part process of Why Not Plus: first comes your why-not response followed by the "plus," which is a combination of critical thinking skills.

Grosser likens the Why-Not-Plus approach to the Chinese proverb of Look and See, where your first "look" allows you to get an overall take on a situation, but the second "see" enables you to delve into the subject matter deeper and look at it more critically. "Why not?" served as Grosser's first *look* at two aeronautical situations that could potentially open the door of possibilities, and the "plus"—all of those thinking skills that the venture capitalist pulled upon from his engineering and business backgrounds—enabled him to *see* the viability (or lack thereof) in two prospects. Sounds pretty sensible to me.

Triggers of innovation like the ones you have read about here can greatly help you to develop a culture of innovation within your organization. Not only do they force you and other decision makers to ask different and better questions when addressing your organization's challenges, but they serve as powerful tools and concepts that you can transfer to others as a means of gleaning innovative ideas from them. Whether you choose to start with just one or decide to try a few, use these triggers of innovative thinking to put your organization miles ahead of where it is today.

No matter how much you facilitate innovation or how well you're able to trigger it, all of your efforts will go nowhere unless you manage it effectively within the greater context of your organization. You have added many tools to your ET toolkit that will enable you to innovate everywhere in conjunction with all the activities you perform as a leader. Here are some parting thoughts as you leave this chapter and begin to seek new opportunities to strengthen your organization through innovation.

Dennis Hong, the founder and director of RoMeLa,[163] a Virginia Tech robotics lab that has pioneered several breakthroughs in robot design and engineering, gets his inspiration at night when he goes to bed, seeing lines and shapes that form mechanisms. He keeps a notebook with a pen with an LED light on it at his bedside to record what he sees. Then first thing the following morning, Hong deciphers his writings, rushes to the office to add them to a database of ideas that he keeps, and eventually finds a match between his ideas and problems so that he can then write proposals.

Hong acknowledges that this free flow of innovative ideas, their capture, and their use might not happen if not for the "safe" environment of his workplace, where brainstorming sessions are encouraged and people don't criticize each other's ideas. "If they do, people clam up," explains Hong.

As seemingly obvious as Hong's description sounds, I see time and again too many well-intentioned leaders impede progress by ignoring opportunities to innovate or by unintentionally discouraging innovation in their organizations. But you can initiate innovating everywhere by taking the following four measures into consideration:

1. **Allow yourself to be wrong.** Invite others to challenge your ideas by asking them to come up with innovative alternatives. When you loosen up a bit and allow others to excel, you not only earn their trust, but you also come up with some great innovative

options. Encourage open debate that can spur people to generate innovative ideas and share them with others.

2. **Systemize innovation.** Give people the tools to record their ideas and then to share them with you and other members of your group. Keep in mind that the lack of a system *is* a system, so be sure that yours fosters and captures innovation. In addition to recording and storing ideas, you need means by which people can convert their innovative ideas to realities. For example, use your Idea Bank to store ideas so that they're readily available the next time you and your cross-functional teams decide to develop a new product, service, or improvement or engage in other ET activities.

3. **Allow people the time to think about innovation.** When your team feels rushed, burdened, or overworked and overwhelmed, the last thing they're probably going to want to hear is you asking them to be more innovative. By teaching others how to use ET's tools, especially those that open blocks of time, like the priority management planner from Chapter 3, you're helping others to alleviate common pressures and you're giving them a chance to schedule time on a daily basis dedicated specifically to innovative measures.

4. **Keep your focus on the big picture and strategically incorporate innovation throughout your organization.** Innovating everywhere expands the effectiveness and impact of everything else.

■ ■ ■

Innovating everywhere is an ET activity that has a turbo-boost effect on other activities and their tools, because the outcomes of your efforts are typically better than they would have been otherwise. And although innovation is generally considered as a new-product development or strategic-thinking additive that helps you leap ahead of competitors or drive your plans into new territories, when you infuse innovation into every corner of your organization, the opportunities for explosive growth and development on an organization-wide scale are countless.

When it comes to innovating everywhere, I see your responsibilities as threefold. First, you need to develop an innovative mindset to improve your own performance as you engage in the thinking activities that you do. Use the tools in this chapter to help you recapture your innovative spirit and utilize it on a daily basis.

Second, you need to transfer the concepts and tools in this chapter to other decision makers in your organization to multiply the opportunities of innovating everywhere. Not only does this set precedence for the present, but it can help you build a stronger group of next-generation leaders to guide your organization into a brighter future.

And third, you and any other leaders within your organization must create a culture of innovation where people not only feel safe speaking up with innovative new ideas, but they also have the tools to be able to do so successfully. Furthermore, your responses to the feedback you get from staff members will have to be monitored and tempered to ensure that people don't feel that they're being asked to engage in activities for the sake of busyness. Too often, I see decision makers who feel it's important for their people to "participate" and "do the work," but then leadership drops the ball by not taking all that groundwork a step further and producing results with it.

As you leave this chapter, pay special attention to the "everywhere" part of the innovating everywhere activity. It's not just something reserved for strategic planners and new product developers—it's an activity that is essential throughout organizations as they make the leap from a 60-mph world to a 200-mph one. Be sure to distribute it generously in your organization.

13

SELLING CONTINUOUSLY

FROM THE TIME HE WAS a sixteen-year-old office boy working for an upstate New York newspaper, Bob Danzig had heard about David Yunich, an ambitious young salesperson who set annual records for selling newspaper subscriptions door to door. Yunich had become a sort of icon for Danzig, although the two had never met face to face.

Seventeen years passed, and Danzig, now a newspaper publisher in his thirties, was asked to go to the Albany, New York, airport on behalf of the chamber of commerce to pick up the honoree at their black-tie event that evening—the new chairman of Macy's who had ties to the community. His name was David Yunich.

Danzig was thrilled to finally meet the go-getter and put a face to the name that had set all those subscription records. Soon after the men had shaken hands and Yunich insisted that Danzig refer to him by his first name, the two set out for the old neighborhood, where the tuxedo-clad Yunich gazed upon the humble second-story flat of a two-family home where he grew up.

"I heard your name year after year as you set those records, and now here you are, the chairman of Macy's. Do you think there was a link between the two?" Danzig asked.

"No doubt about it," Yunich answered. "I went to Harvard for an MBA and was recruited to the Macy's training program like many other young graduates. But while the others brought sophistication to the program, I brought something else. When I was selling those newspaper subscriptions and someone said 'no' to me, I wouldn't hear 'no,' I would just say to myself, They're not ready yet. I never let them discourage me, even if I got 20 nos in a row. I brought the same mindset to Macy's, and today, the sophisticates work for me." Yunich just kept selling.

Danzig, who later went on to serve 20 years as the president of the Hearst Corporation, never forgot the lesson he learned from David Yunich that night:

> The success of every leader hinges on his ability to sell . . . to sell himself as capable and credible, to sell his ideas (the way a salesperson sells products and services), and to sell others on the promise that he can take them where they want to go.[164]

But even when you know that you must sell yourself and your ideas, you may not realize that to do so successfully, you need to go beyond convincing words and sales pitches. Your performance and your track record—both of which hinge on how well you perform the activities of Enterprise Thinking—typically do the selling for you.

The Role That Selling Plays in Great Leadership

Leaders are on display all the time, sometimes selling products and services for their organizations, but more often, selling themselves and their ideas in a non-stop quest to move their careers and their organizations forward. If we were to lump all the sales and selling situations of your organization into one large iceberg, the tip of the iceberg would represent the products and services that your salespeople sell, and the massive chunk remaining would encompass all the other selling situations that ultimately fall under the responsibility of leadership. In other words, selling plays a huge and comprehensive role in good leadership, although most leaders have never looked at it that way.

The approaches you take to selling your ideas, successes, and plans must be as varied as the individuals to whom you are making your appeals. Having a number of ET tools to draw on gives you the ability to be more flexible, and, therefore, more successful, in gaining approval and buy-in. For example, if you decide to relocate part of your operations to another region 300 miles away, the pitch you give to the business-unit leader will differ from the one you give to the banking loan officer, and that pitch will differ once again when you get home and have to pose to your spouse the prospect of moving your family to another city. With each initiative, your perspective must rise to 50,000 feet, so that you not only address every aspect of the whole in your strategies and plans, but also so that you tailor your approaches to gain buy-in from each player who has a role in the initiative's success.

Consider how many times in a single day you are selling:

- You sell to people and groups outside your organization who play a role in its success when you apply for financing and lines of credit with lenders, negotiate with vendors, establish alliances, persuade government officials, and talk to the media and the public.

- You sell to your insiders—your leadership team, heads of business units and departments, your board of directors, managers, and front-line workers—each time you share your ideas or plans with them, present health benefits and incentive programs to them, or guide them through their everyday challenges.

- You sell to your family and friends, whether the "sale" is strictly personal or it involves balancing life and work. "I will be working late to make sure this project wraps up on time," might be music to the ears of a demanding boss, but to your family that wants you home by dinner, you might need to take a different slant by adding, "which means we'll all be able to leave for our vacation on Friday as planned."

- You sell your reputation and credibility as an individual through every walk of life by highlighting the most appropriate assets at the time. Think about the words you've chosen, the clothing you've worn, and the achievements you've mentioned each time you've transitioned from one position to another or needed something from another person. That's why building a career track record of Wildly Successful Projects (WSPs) is so important to success. WSPs say to others, "Yes, I can, because I already have," even at times when you're selling ideas that have yet to come to fruition.

- And here's the eye-opener for most leaders: you sell yourself and your organization each and every time you complete projects—especially WSPs—that transform your organization and make it stronger. This requires you to see the big picture, address challenges and opportunities from the 50,000-foot perspective, and use ET tools. For example, when you add Forecasted Winners such as advanced technologies, a near-perfect on-time delivery record, or revolutionary intellectual property, you can attract customers, funding, tax breaks, outstanding employees, and more, all of which helps you to win people over and gain buy-in for future endeavors.

You are the quintessential salesperson who is selling continuously. Have you ever looked at your role in quite this way before? Despite the fact that selling is as vital to your success as oxygen is to your survival, if you're like most leaders, you've never considered selling to be an essential leadership activity. Fewer than 8% of the leaders that I've worked with have ever taken a single sales course, and that's probably because they've only considered sales from the perspective of selling products and services. This chapter is designed to expand your thinking, redefine the role that selling plays in your life, and give you the tools you need to forge an improved future for yourself and your organization.

{ Who Do You Think You're Talking To? }

Why is it that some messages seem to go over well in certain circumstances and flop in others? Chances are, when other people are listening to you and seem cooperative, it's because you're speaking in a manner that appeals to them. Even as a young child, you learn to tailor your messages to the audience—speak to your teacher in one voice, your friends in another—but sometimes in organizational situations, you can be unaware of different perspectives and how a single tone, manner of speaking, or message requires some tailoring.

One of my first work-related experiences that required me to customize my speech came when I was a managerial assistant in a rock quarry and I was asked to make sure that the intra-quarry roadways were clear of large rocks that could potentially damage the $70,000 tires on equipment. This task required me to approach one of the bucket-loader drivers so that he could drop his blade (which was the width of two city streets) and swoop up all the rocks, some the size of a typical car tire.

I found very quickly that any attempt to direct my crew by asking, "Excuse me, could you please scrape the road?" fell on deaf ears. No one moved at all. I tried three times to get a reaction. Frustrated, I turned my hard hat around, put on my 1980s mirrored glasses, closed the gap between me and the men, and bellowed, "Get the #!*%-ing rocks out of the road!"

I was surprised to hear the driver say to me, "If that's all you wanted, why didn't you just ask in the first place?" This approach to selling would have yielded very different outcomes if I'd used it while applying for a telemarketing job or asking my friend for a lift to the airport.

Certainly, I'm sure you can recall an instance or two when afterward you thought to yourself, I could have approached that (situation or topic) better. Obviously, the words you use make a difference, but your actions surrounding

[continues on page 514]

[continued from previous page]

circumstances make a difference, too. That's because your title can only get you so far. For example, try working alongside people for a while so that they see you're trying to understand their situation before you make decisions that affect them. Or, as I've mentioned throughout this book, spend some time thinking and researching ideas and plans up front before you propose them to others so that you're not just dropping one idea after another without bringing any of them to fruition. In this way you can earn others' trust, and when you say, "This is a good idea; it will work," people can believe in you.

The next time you're in a position where you're seeking buy-in, approval or cooperation from others, remember to ask yourself first, Who do you think you're talking to?

The ET Leadership Sales Approach

You already have a framework that helps you influence others, whether you've recognized it as such or not. This framework consists of your organizational environment and everything in it, your title, and your reputation built on past experiences. To have achieved the successes that you've earned to date, you've also probably figured out a routine, some tips, and maybe a methodology that you use when you want to persuade people and gain their cooperation. But do you have a structured model for selling continuously that you can rely on in a multitude of instances to get you and your people where you want to go, and does it help you pinpoint areas of weakness that could prevent you from gaining future successes?

The ET Leadership Sales Methodology (Figure 13.1) is a standard model that is easy to learn, use, and transfer to others to gain the types of outcomes you need in order to advance your career and your organization. You can modify it to suit your style or use it as is. It leverages other Enterprise Thinking tools, breaking down silos that hinder progress and opening doors to greater opportunities.

The ET Leadership Sales Methodology consists of two phases:

- Phase 1: Planning, which is the first four steps of the CST Model
- Phase 2: Execution, which guides you through the steps to closing your sale

This methodology, as diagrammed below, is a breakdown of the common components of every sales process. You first think about the strengths

ET Leadership Sales Methodology

YOU BRING EVERYTHING TO A SALE

TOOLS: Models, Products, Concepts, Infrastructure, Capital, Staffing, Land, Law, Portfolio, Services, Processes, Patents, Specific Tools, etc.

SKILLS & INFORMATION FROM: ET Strategizing, ET Learning, ET Forecasting, ET Performing, Education, Sales, Negotiations, Persuasion, Redefining, Engineering, Business, Pilot, Nano Technologist, Physician, etc.

EXPERIENCES & STRENGTHS: Relevant and Irrelevant History, Homework, Conclusions Generated, Personal Style, Attributes, Risk Levels, Alliances (Supporters, Influencers; Network) Battlefield, Classroom, Leading, Graphic, Speed, Hand Eye Coordination, etc.

Phase 1 Strategizing
(Including Mental Modeling, Testing, etc.)

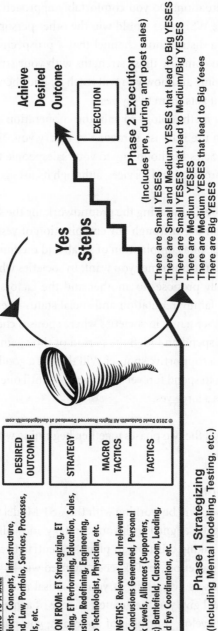

DESIRED OUTCOME

STRATEGY

MACRO TACTICS

TACTICS

Yes Steps

Achieve Desired Outcome

EXECUTION

Phase 2 Execution
(Includes pre, during, and post sales)

There are Small YESES
There are Small and Medium YESES that lead to Big YESES
There are Small YESES that lead to Medium/Big YESES
There are Medium YESES
There are Medium YESES that lead to Big Yeses
There are Big YESES

Figure 13.1—ET Leadership Sales Methodology

you bring to the situation: Do you comfortably approach people you don't know? Do you have WSPs that would win the other person over? Does your organization have a distribution channel that a prospective ally would like to access? Then you combine those strengths with your strategizing (look at your Desired Outcome and how you will reach it) and then engage the other person in a way that gets them to say yes.

You can use this methodology to gain the cooperation of your managers as easily as you can use it to ask someone to marry you. You can also teach the ET Leadership Sales Methodology to your salespeople to use for the traditional selling of products and services, although its uses go way beyond that purpose alone.

Essentially, you begin by laying the groundwork for the sale, and then you win the other person over through any combination of yeses: multiple small yeses, medium yeses, or a combination of small and medium yeses, and large yeses that bring you the outcomes you want. In societies where marriages are arranged, one family proposes to another and the factors that precede the proposal—such as family reputation and social status—tend to lead to one large yes. On the other hand, in societies where spouses choose each other, a man and a woman spend an indefinite period of time gaining small yeses— Will this person be a supportive spouse? Will they be a good parent? Do I like this person enough to spend forever with them?—until one of them pops the question that yields a large yes.

Let's walk through the two phases together, beginning with what you bring to the sales process.

Phase 1: Planning

In this first phase, you will be working with the CST Model to ensure that the steps you are taking are aligned with your Strategy and will lead you to your Desired Outcome. Taking this time to plan is essential, because you want to be sure that your time, effort, and expense are used wisely.

Your aim is to assess everything at your disposal and select those assets that you estimate will give you the greatest chance of achieving your Desired Outcome. As you develop your plan of approach, you may realize that you can just walk into someone's office and ask for what you want, but more likely, you will see that you need a plan that involves various steps in it to get you to that ultimate end. I've found that people can relate to a personal example here, so let's try one to show you how you can plan a mini-step approach to gaining small yeses.

After three years of dating, you want to propose to your girlfriend. Your plan includes the following: As you plan, take a look at your strengths, skills, WSPs, and organizational wins to determine which of these factors you want to bring to the sale. In addition to covering the four parts of the CST Model, you will incorporate your bucket of assets into this process. In the ET Leadership Sales Methodology, choose your Tactics based on their ability to help you gain yeses—those small approvals that progress you toward the ultimate agreement you seek—from the other party. Bring everything you've got to the table if it means that you can rack up the yeses.

- Small yes #1: Her family is traditional, so you meet with her father a couple of weeks beforehand to gain his approval.
- Small yes #2: You buy an engagement ring.
- Small yes #3: You make dinner reservations at her favorite restaurant. This is where you will pop the question.
- Small yes #4: You plan the specific events of the dinner—at what point during dinner you will you ask her, how you will present the ring to her, what you will say leading up to the big question, etc.

Now, surely, these immediate plans are important, but in reality, you've been making this sale for the past three years. Your track record as her boyfriend is what got you to this opportunity today.

In this instance, and in many others throughout your career, the plan is just the final stage of the sale, but it is essential just the same. And not only can a series of small yeses be as effective as one large yes to closing your sale, both scenarios can take the same amount of time. For instance, you might need twelve business unit heads to buy into a new initiative, and it takes you six months to get all of them on board. Then again, you could be working to establish an alliance with one party, and you have to spend two years getting that one yes. Or, you might want to enter a new market, and you need many yeses from different government officials and suppliers in that region before you can close the sale. The combination of small, medium, and large yeses might take you three months or three years.

In the end, whether you gain a series of small yeses or one large yes, as long as you close your sale within the time period allotted, you've successfully reached your Desired Outcome.

Looking back at the diagram (Figure 13.1), you can see that your Tactics come from the list titled You Bring Everything to a Sale. The three categories of Tactics are:

- **Tools:** You can make use of all of your ET tools, models, products, concepts, infrastructure, capital, staffing, and so on to win over the other person or group.
- **Skills and Information:** Perform your ET activities optimally to build strengths that you can sell when you need to and realize that any skills and information that you have accumulated throughout your life can be utilized to close a sale.
- **Experiences and Strengths:** Look back at the experiences that you have had over the course of your career and life and think about how they may come into play now to reinforce your message and win the other person or group over. Be sure that you include everything here: friendships built on common experiences, religious or extracurricular associations, and so on.

Keep in mind that with each action you take within this phase, you have opportunities to win by a nose. By the same token, doing any of the planning phases (Desired Outcome, Strategy, Macro Tactics, Tactics) incorrectly or rushing them can lead to losses by a nose.

Phase 2: Execution

Once you have your plan in place, you are ready to Execute on it. This is where you actually seek out those yeses you will need to close your sale and achieve your Desired Outcome. As I mentioned, sometimes you have to build one yes on top of another until you ultimately reach your end destination, and at other times, a single yes is all you need to move forward.

Let's look at this phase with an example. Say that you want to free up cash flow by asking a vendor to extend the period of time it gives you to pay your bills. Currently, your payment terms are 30 days, but you've calculated that an additional 15 days will help your organization meet its cash-flow needs. Certainly, you might have to take smaller steps to get this yes, beginning with gaining credit references from some current vendors who have offered you a higher limit and longer payment terms (each of those references represents a small yes), then progressing to setting up a line of credit from your bank (another small yes from your banker), and finally ending with your using these yeses to negotiate a new credit agreement (the final yes).

Mike Critelli, retired CEO of Pitney Bowes,[165] once explained to me how he and his team developed a fitness facility on premises and the reasoning behind its creation. Research showed that healthier employees performed better, and Critelli saw an opportunity to drive economics and shareholder value through better health and well-being among his workers. From their many Macro Tactics and Tactics options, leaders chose to develop systems and structures—specifically the internal improvement of building an on-site health facility, along with changing policy around behaviors to create a cultural change. In order to do this, they had to sell the initiative to their employees.

Leadership developed a six-part package that they could incorporate into a larger plan, thus formulating the foundation for future leadership and employee buy-in. This package included:

1. Providing a state-of-the-art on-site fitness center staffed with professional trainers
2. Hiring their own medical staff
3. Providing privacy protection to employees so they could use the health facility without fear of their medical information circulating throughout the company
4. Offering employees incentives to set and reach health objectives
5. Delivering a well-prepared message that would encourage employees to use the facility
6. Redirecting wasted money by (a) eliminating reimbursements for unnecessary expenditures at breakfast meetings, (b) changing the venue of corporate meetings from restaurants to on-site offices, and (c) capping the budget on food and alcohol expenditures at gatherings

These changes made individually would not have been valuable. However, taken together they fit into a larger plan that incorporated the many small yeses Pitney Bowes' leaders would need in order to make the sale. First, they needed agreement, buy-in, and cooperation from management as they built a new health facility and hired qualified people to run it. Critelli was able to share the research, proving that healthier employees performed better, and that prevention of illness was cheaper than treatment. This research sold the facility's value to the organization, especially since the firm's health-care costs had risen 14% in five years, taking a chunk of profits. Second, they needed to gain yeses from the employees, who had to agree to use the facility. Again, organizers of the project tied health insurance and health-care costs to the value of the facility, and as a result, they sold the package.

Whenever you are engaged in selling, in order to achieve your Desired

Outcome, you must strategize and build a plan first, create the systems and structures next, then plug in people, and finally, monitor and adjust as necessary based on new information.

It's important for you to not just know about your new tool, but to internalize it and make it a habit in the course of your everyday dealings with other people. Initially, it may take a little effort on your part to refer back to the ET Leadership Sales Methodology, but when you do, you will be forced to engage in planning, Cyclonic Thinking, and the Economics of Thinking, ensuring that each measure you take has purpose and leads you and your organization to its Desired Outcome.

Pathways for Selling Continuously to Other People

In addition to knowing the right approach and being able to carry it out, you need to know where to direct your energies in order to advance your organization the fastest and most reliably. I've found that many leaders have the right ideas, but they pitch them to the wrong people. Other times, leaders don't gain the buy-in they need, because they don't consider all the people that they have to talk with in order to push their ideas and initiatives forward. Think of these different people and the possibilities they offer for success as pathways for selling continuously.

Pathways for selling continuously are common to all leaders. What's not so common is the ability to navigate through them as well as you might need. The Pathways within Leadership Sales diagram (Figure 13.2) details the numerous directions in which you can and should constantly sell yourself and your ideas. The imagery is intended to give you a reference so when you are considering how you'd like to sell, you don't forget the myriad options available to you.

As you can see, there are many routes to "yes," and it's up to you to determine the appropriate pathway for your situation at any given time. These pathways can help you get around obstacles and increase your chances of earning more wins for your organization. Do realize that you may be engaged in several pathways at once? For example, if you're a VP and you're attempting to put a new manufacturing process in place, you may have four pathways to navigate. You might start with the CEO, presenting your idea to him in terms of how it has improved productivity and increased profits for other organizations and how it can do the same for yours. Second, you navigate the pathway of the line manager by proposing your idea to her, showing her how it promises to reduce her paperwork, decrease errors, and improve quality. You also might invite her to watch you try out the process with one of her machine operators. Third, you want to get the machine operator to accept your ideas, so you meet with him, briefly introduce your idea, try his job function to show him that you understand his current challenges with his job and how the new idea will improve his performance and make his job easier. Indirectly, you might be navigating the pathway to your organization's banker for financing by putting together a comprehensive package that shows how the investment in the process will ultimately reward the organization and enable it to adhere to a repayment schedule.

Pathways within Leadership Sales

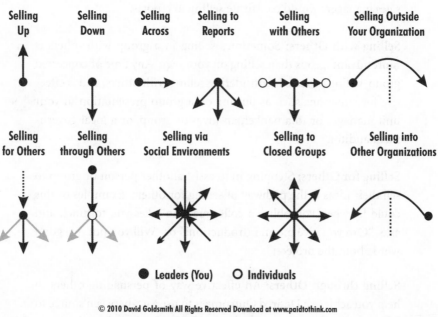

Figure 13.2—Pathways within Leadership Sales

Here are the different pathways that can help you to get where you want to go:

> **Selling Up:** Selling your ideas to decision makers such as your board of directors, supervisors, investors, and councils, in order to gain their approval and/or support in one way or another is called selling up.

Selling Down: Even though you have the authority to make decisions and steer your organization's ship, there are times when you must gain buy-in and cooperation from the people who report to you or buy from you or otherwise need your approval. Selling your ideas to this group of people is called selling down.

Selling Across: Selling across is the act of selling to colleagues, peers, and other decision makers who are of equal rank or position to you.

Selling to Reports: When you sell down to a group of people whose rank on your organizational chart falls below yours, you are selling to reports. Pitching your ideas to your three marketing directors, your team of six legal councilors, two generals, or seventy global pre-sales managers would constitute selling to reports.

Selling with Others: Sometimes selling in a group with others is more advantageous than selling on your own. Any type of concerted group-selling process is considering selling with others, and is effective for situations such as putting on a group presentation to your unit manager or to a banker, an investor group, or a local government auditor.

Selling for Others: Stepping in to assist another person or group to sell their ideas is the pathway of selling for others. Examples of this could be when you oblige a colleague who takes you to lunch and asks, "Can you give me an introduction?" or "Will you put in a good word about the project?"

Selling through Others: An effective way of persuading others to help you achieve a Desired Outcome is to use a go-between source to deliver your message. In an instance like having your logistics manager tell your vendor that if the latter doesn't get a shipment of yours to its destination on time, you will be replacing said vendor, you are selling through others.

Selling via Social Environments: When you sell your ideas in open forums, when a CEO speaks to the media, when you speak to masses of people through a blog post, or when you work a room at a company get together, your public efforts are how you are selling via social environments.

Selling to Closed Groups: Presenting your ideas in quasi-public or public groups can be an effective way of gaining support and yeses from others that is called selling in closed groups. You are taking this pathway when you sell to larger groups of people who may or may not be your equals or who may nor may not be in your industry. Forums for this pathway might be press conferences, trade industry conferences, or small conference room meetings.

Selling Outside of Your Organization: Selling outside of your organization happens with a multitude of sources, such as vendors, governments, other countries, etc.

Selling into Other Organizations: There are times when you have to penetrate an organization to gain influence of some sort within it. Although selling into other organizations is an action taken by salespeople who sell products and services—copy machines, janitorial services, raw goods—leaders can use this pathway to sell their ideas, too. Examples include supporting a cause or funding a project.

When you look at Figure 13.2, try to see more than the obvious. You know how you typically sell yourself and your organization to others already, but maybe you want to use the Pathways within Leadership Sales to sell using nontraditional avenues or perhaps you will use a variety of pathways in sequence or collectively to achieve a Desired Outcome. If you currently put out press releases to announce new products—a means that requires you to go through others and outside your organization—choosing a different pathway might enable you to reach more of the right people sooner.

⊣ Navigating Pathways Creatively to Win Over Unlikely Supporters ⊢

Oftentimes, you'll meet resistance from people not because they don't like your ideas, but because you haven't navigated the right pathways in the right way. When that happens, you end up dealing with people who don't understand your ideas or don't understand how your ideas will benefit them. If you truly think that what you have to offer is in the best interests of you and another party, by all means, explore that particular pathway.

In some situations, especially when you're reaching out to people that you don't typically deal with, a little creativity can go a long way in getting your message across. The year was 1886 when the world's first automobile powered by an internal-combustion engine took to the streets of Munich, Germany.[166] Its inventor, Karl Benz,

[continues on page 524]

[continued from previous page]

was facing resistance to the vehicle from citizens angry about its noisiness. According to them, Benz's invention was so noisy that it frightened children and horses, leading local government officials to set a speed limit of 7 kilometers per hour (3.5 miles per hour) within city limits. Benz knew that he could never establish a market for his product if the speed limit remained that low, so he devised a plan.

The inventor knew that *speaking* his point of view would get him nowhere, so he would have to be creative about the message he delivered by offering the mayor a ride in a brand-new Benz as it came off the production line, to make a nonverbal case for why the speed limit should be raised. Not realizing that Benz had an ulterior motive, the mayor accepted the offer and Benz's plan was set in motion.

That day, while the men were traveling the streets together and the mayor was waving to onlookers as the car drove along, Benz's co-conspirator, a milkman driving a horse-drawn wagon, strolled up next to the mayor, screamed offensive remarks to him, and then took off rapidly past the automobile. The mayor ordered Benz to take after him, but Karl Benz reminded the mayor of the city's speed limit and kept the vehicle at its steady but slow stroll. Guess what was changed the next day?

Perhaps you can think of some ideas that you would like to set in motion but that will require you to take a nontraditional pathway to gain the approval and cooperation that you need. Rather than shy away from it, go back to your ET Leadership Sales Methodology and include this new pathway in your plan.

Building the Type of Organization that Sells Itself

Another approach to selling involves using your organization as a sales tool in and of itself. As Larry Ellison, CEO of computer-technology company Oracle, said in his autobiography, "in a great company everybody sells—not just the salespeople."[167] That doesn't mean that your shipping manager or executive assistant are peddling product, but when you build the 80% of the GPP, each person on board can perform their jobs optimally and ultimately affect the relationship all stakeholders have with your organization. Therefore, every person should be hired and every system should be designed to support those relationships.

I often say that salespeople should be grateful that management and leadership make mistakes. Otherwise, organizations wouldn't need salespeople at all. Imagine if you never lost a customer, because your organization was exceptional at innovating, adapting, and achieving zero defect rates.

Beanie Babies, the stuffed toy phenomenon in the 1980s with billions in sales, became so much in demand that salespeople became order takers.

The product was right, it was marketed right and distributed right, and was even withheld at the right times to create demand. When employees couldn't keep up with demand and the volume of calls, leaders had to turn off phone lines that had been open to the general public and instead set up private phone lines for staff to conduct business with vendors and sales reps to avoid overload.

Larry Ellison's quote about everyone in an organization having an influence on sales is dead on. If you're a restaurant owner, you needn't force your head chef out of the kitchen and into the dining room to greet each patron as they arrive. If this chef is fulfilling his function properly—offers a varied and interesting menu, ensures that the kitchen staff are cooking meals properly and on time, meets health department standards, orders the right quantities of ingredients, etc.—he makes a positive contribution to the collective experiences diners have with your restaurant and ensures that your clientele are likely to return to your restaurant. As I mentioned in Chapter 10, there is an *I* in team, and if your head chef understands this concept, he also understands that he contributes to the sales process by doing his job exceptionally well. Your job is to make sure that you are empowering him to make his best contribution by providing him with the tools and environment that foster success.

Now multiply your chef's contribution to the contributions made by all of your staff members. The holistic inner workings of the organization contribute to its success.

By doing your job exceptionally well so that everyone else can do theirs well, you actually turn your organization into a huge, holistic WSP. In addition, salespeople who are backed by strong organizations can sell products and services more easily in the marketplace. Facility managers who have proven records of profitability are able to negotiate lower rates on leases. A reputation of offering superior employee packages like great health care, paid vacations, and on-site child-care facilities helps human resource managers attract high-performing managers to their organizations over competitors' HR departments. The credibility that comes from excellence is the payoff of selling continuously done right by leadership.

All organizations—even nonprofits—survive by "selling" something. Educators trying to set up a charter school sell the educational benefits of their school to communities, governments, and parents. Cities, states, provinces, countries compete for residents, tourism, and new commerce by building better communities than neighboring governments. The rewards go to locales that can best sell benefits like low crime, exceptional schools, tax breaks and incentives, natural resources, public transportation, low pollution, and great parks and recreational facilities.

The locals who managed the Beijing Olympics realized that they had an opportunity to show the world that their country was a place to invest in and to visit. In order to secure these opportunities, the government had to be sure that Beijing's smog would not pose a threat to capturing these opportunities. To head off international disapproval, government and businesses temporarily suspended manufacturing in many parts of the city to cut smog levels. Those responsible for the fireworks digitally altered them so that they would be visible through the remaining smog on television. People from different areas came together to make Beijing's experience as a host a success.

Nonprofit organizations sell to their donors, both individuals and groups, that they are the best investment. Associations that rely on membership dues to survive sell their benefits to lure new members and entice existing members to renew.

Every organization that survives and achieves long-lasting success sells collectively as a unit and does so continuously. By the same token, if even one part of the organization fails or loses by a nose, the whole is at risk of losing, also.

[Building the Engine that Sells Itself]

I had just boarded a U.S. Airways plane headed for Phoenix, Arizona, in the coach seat just behind first class, when flight attendant Tina Costanzo approached my seat, politely confirmed my identity, and told me that if I needed anything, she would be pleased to help. Puzzled by the special attention, I wondered why and then asked the person next to me, a vice-president of sales who managed 15,000 people, what she thought. We were both baffled. Why me?

When Costanzo passed my seat again, I quietly asked her the same question. Her answer was quite simple. When the passenger list is distributed before takeoff, Tina reads passengers' Dividend Miles (US Airways' frequent flyer program) status, and she noticed that I was a Chairman's Preferred—status flier, which means I fly with the airline a lot (and, therefore, give them a lot of money). When she notices a passenger with high-level status she takes extra care of them. Both the woman next to me and I were very impressed.

It's easy then to take Costanzo and put her on a pedestal, to say she's the type of person you'd want working for the organization. True, she is an excellent employee, but from 50,000 feet, you should also see that she is one part of a larger and more intricate system that supports sales for the airline.

US Airways' leadership, not Constanzo, has set up systems and structures that empower employees to schedule flights, create pricing models, send marketing materials, develop relationships with travel agents and, in the end, persuade customers to purchase tickets from them.

When I fly, their system captures my travels in a way that categorizes me as a frequent flyer, and on each list, my status is noted. Costanzo, who understands the value of repeat customers, uses this list to provide exceptional customer service and to support the sales process.

If not for IT, engineering, the call centers, maintenance, food services, the people that hire people like Costanzo, and tens of thousands of others behind the scenes, Costanzo would not be able to do what she does so well. Performing sales comes from building the 80% of the GPP, the systems and structures, and from providing the tools to make your entire organization a success.

Leading well enables you to create an organization that can sell itself in many ways. As we explore this and the other ways that you are selling continuously, you will learn new ET tools to be able to do your job optimally. First, let's take a look at some of the challenges that can affect your ability to sell and what you can do about them.

Overcoming the Challenges of Leadership Sales

Considering all the diverse challenges that you address in a day, it's not surprising that many of those challenges will be better solved as you improve your ability to sell yourself and your ideas to others. At the same time, selling continuously brings with it its own set of challenges, many of which can be categorized by their similarities and solved with some very specific ET tools. Whether you're hitting a roadblock as you attempt to push through an initiative or having difficulty getting others to envision your yet-to-be reached Desired Outcome, the right combination of techniques and tools will enable you to overcome sales-related hurdles.

Gaining Buy-in and Cooperation

The best-laid plans can be sidetracked by resistance, whether it takes place in the open or behind the scenes. Buy-in is often essential to achieving your

Desired Outcome, but there are times when gaining buy-in is challenging, even when you have all the elements of a winning idea. Sometimes you need to surround yourself with your strongest supporters, and elicit help from them to win over the people who are resisting you.

Greg, who works in management for the U.S. Air Force, needed the approval of fourteen of his colleagues before embarking on a project. His tactical approach to selling was to gather all of them into one room and to show them his PowerPoint presentation.

After viewing his slides and having him give me a shortened version of the presentation, I could see that his idea was a good one, but his message had holes in it: holes that he couldn't fill in for me when I asked him about them in a private one-on-one setting. This told me that if he were confronted by his group of peers, his presentation would have yielded disastrous results. As we talked about the challenge ahead of him, Greg told me that he had doubts about gaining the buy-in that he needed, yet what concerned me was that he was scheduling the meeting anyway, because he was afraid he'd lose the opportunity. Think about that. He was going to enter into a nearly no-win situation under the logic (or illogic) that waiting would harm his case.

Luckily, Greg was willing to follow my recommendation to scrap his plan for a single meeting and try a different approach. We decided he would gain support from people he could count on one at a time, *before* presenting his idea to the entire group, thereby minimizing risk. We used the Buy-In Chart (Figure 13.3) just like the one you see here.

BUY-IN CHART

Name	Relationship Likes me personally	Alignment Supports my ideas	Total Score	Final Ranking

Figure 13.3—Buy-In Chart

The Buy-In Chart is a sales-approach tool that enables you to gain the support of one person at a time. Although we will walk through its instructions for use when you are approaching individuals, you can use it to approach entire departments, units, organizations, governing bodies, and even countries, depending on your project and its scope.

In the first column, list the people or groups from whom you'll seek support. In the second column, assign a ranking to each of the people you've listed, based on the strength of your relationship with them, giving the most supportive person the ranking of 1, and the least supportive person the last-place ranking.

In the third column, apply the same kind of ranking to rate each person's level of alignment with your idea, with the score of 1 going to the person who is most likely to agree with you, and so on. Finally, add up each person's scores from columns 2 and 3, and enter the result in column 4 (Total Score), then record their final ranking in column 5.

A note of caution: The Buy-In Chart's effectiveness is as strong as its design is simplistic, so resist any urge to add more columns or to change the headings of the columns. Otherwise, you risk diminishing this tool's ability to elicit the cooperation and support you are seeking. I have seen a few leaders try to play around with the design of the tool, but in doing so, they've not received their anticipated results. If you recall, I made this same note about the Project Evaluation Chart you received in Chapter 3, explaining that many of these tools, though seeming to be very simple, have been developed over a period of time so that they are easy to use and are reliable in their outcomes.

The person with the *lowest score* is your strongest supporter, and therefore, the person that you will most likely want to present your idea to first. The concept isn't any different than the tactic you used as a kid to get something that you wanted. If you wanted a treat from the ice-cream truck vendor, and you knew that Dad was the parent who would most likely grant your request to catch the driver as he passed through your neighborhood, then it was Dad you approached first. The last thing you wanted to do was ask Mom, who was cooking dinner and didn't want you to spoil your appetite.

Referencing the chart in Figure 13.4, Baxter is your top ally. Begin gaining buy-in by approaching Baxter first. From a purely quantitative position, he is most likely to be in alignment with your ideas *and* to like you, and therefore, he will offer you the best feedback, helping you to spot and fill holes in your idea and prepare for challenges. Your top ally can ask tough questions in a safe environment, and in general, help you hone your presentation before you take it on to the second-ranked ally on your list, then the third-ranked ally, and so on. Each time you meet with any ally, you improve with practice, clarifying your idea, polishing your presentation, and gathering support. However, if you have a list of 20 people, you do not need 20 one-on-one meetings, just enough to gain momentum.

Buy-In Chart Example

Name	Relationship Likes me personally	Alignment Supports my ideas	Total Score	Final Ranking
Kyle	3	5	8	3
Santiago	4	6	10	5
Monique	6	4	10	6
Chelsea	1	3	4	2
Kim	5	4	9	4
Baxter	2	1	3	1

There are 6 people in the group, therefore, the numbers in the first two columns are 1–6, since the score/rank goes up to 10.

Figure 13.4—Buy-In Chart Example

Greg gained project approval by using the Buy-In Chart. Without this Tactic, Greg's pre-work and the project itself would have failed.

You can experiment with the Buy-In Chart to fit it to your personality, style, and your environment.

Selling More than "Relationships"

You've probably heard that "relationships are the most important part of selling." In other words, people buy from people they know. Is that actually true? Think for a moment about the number of insurance agents you know. Do you do business with *all* of them? How about attorneys and real-estate agents?

Of course you don't, even though you have relationships with them. Maybe you don't have enough business to spread around or you don't want too many people knowing your private matters, so you have to select the person—friend or not!—who can service you best. If you took a closer look at the people who get your business, you'd realize that the reasons for your buying decisions boil down to the same as everyone else's—you buy from people and organizations who fill your needs best . . . period.

Your sales staff probably won't be very happy to hear this news. If you spent your time kissing up, running ragged, and shaking hands, you'd want to know it paid off, too, wouldn't you? Unfortunately, the reality is that none of that matters if your ideas, plans, or products and services don't meet the other party's needs and expectations.

Do you know the owner of the grocery store where you purchase the bulk of your food? How about the owner of the subway or pizza shop, dry cleaner, gas stations, or car dealership? You might know one of them, especially if you live in a small town, but honestly, most of us don't know our primary vendors well, if at all.

When you purchase from Amazon.com, Tesco, Carrefour, Nordstrom, Audi, Toshiba, or Bridgestone, you rarely (if ever) do so because of a personal relationship. In fact, few people have ever spoken to an Amazon customer service representative or even known that there are any. As you assess your own buying habits and patterns, you'll most likely conclude that you don't purchase much of anything from people you know. The matter of "relationship selling" really boils down to two realities.

First, buyers must trust that your organization, offerings, brand, etc., will deliver on its promised value, otherwise you have no foundation for a sale. This is true even if you're a leader who is selling an idea or a plan that has yet to materialize. Perhaps you can occasionally win someone over based on a relationship, but if you don't deliver value, you will not be able to do so continuously.

Second, relationships open doors of opportunity. If you have a relationship with someone who can connect you to a particular individual or group, your relationship can pave the way for bypassing gatekeepers and getting the third party to take your phone call or meet you to hear your ideas. Yet even though there is a relationship, this does not mean you'll buy. Imagine your good friend who works in banking has changed his employment from an internationally known bank where you have all your accounts to a regional banking institution. He calls you and asks you to move your accounts to his new place of employment, but if you were to do so, you know that you would suffer specific losses: the close working relationship you have with a lender who offers you lines of credit with just a phone call and the conveniences of free ATM usage and foreign currency conversion when you travel internationally for business. Do you move to the new bank? Most likely, you're going to pass on your friend's offer, no matter how much you like him, because he can't offer Order Winners to you.

So let's just establish for now that people don't buy relationships—they buy what works for them. At the same time, you can make relationships work in your favor, because they can play a role in selling continuously, as you'll see below.

Making Strategic Connections: Understanding *Guanxi*

You are probably familiar with the concept of six degrees of separation, which simply means that everyone is linked to just about everyone else through a chain of no more than six people. The concept is one to keep in mind when it comes to selling continuously, because you never know who in this world might help you facilitate progress for your career or your organization.

In the Eastern world, relationships and connections are viewed slightly differently. *Guanxi* (pronounced gwan *chi*) is the term used for deeper relationships connecting family and friends that go back several years or even generations. *Guanxi* circles of trust are not always easy to break into. However, that doesn't mean its underlying concepts can't help you sell yourself and your ideas, because these concepts aren't restricted to geographical areas; you can apply them no matter where you live and work. And, since it's always easier to use a concept as a tool when you have a specific formula, process, or set of steps to follow, I've developed your next new tool, the ET *Guanxi* Mapping Tool, as a straightforward means of converting your connections into strategic advantages for yourself and your organization. Think of this tool as a combination of the two concepts of six degrees of separation and *guanxi*.

So, even if you don't have connections to people that span generations of relationships, your new tool will enable you to still access the benefits of *guanxi* by showing you how to quickly access the right allies. Furthermore, even if you only have a couple of *guanxi*-type relationships in your life to date, the ET *Guanxi* Mapping Tool will show you how to build upon the personal connections you have with others to progress along your chain of six degrees of separation.

In 2008, Compass Advisers, a Manhattan-based investment bank, opened a small four-person Shanghai office and hired a native Easterner, Ivan Cheah, to be its managing director. As described in a *New York Times* article, Cheah "became Compass's passport to the region."[168]

In late 2009, Cheah set up a dinner meeting between Compass's partner

Ze'ev Goldberg and Ren Jianxin, the chairman of ChemChina, a state-owned firm in need of financial backing. At one point during the meal, their business conversation turned to the topic of one of Goldberg's family members who had been diagnosed with a neurological disorder.

Ren put Goldberg in touch with a close friend, the Chinese minister of health, so that Goldberg's relative could receive specialized herbal treatments for the disorder. The relationship between Ren and Goldberg evolved rapidly.

In January 2010, ChemChina announced that it had purchased a 60% stake in the Israeli-based agrochemical company MA Industries. Its only financial backer in the deal was Compass Advisers.

If you trace back the steps leading to this transaction, it all began with Compass's hiring of Ivan Cheah. The trust of *guanxi* had been *accessed* rather than *earned*—a faster way to gain initial contact with prospective associates such as ChemChina—accelerating Compass Adviser's foothold in China. On the flip side, Ren's trust in Goldberg enabled him to extend a personal favor that won Goldberg over and earned the financial backing that ChemChina so desperately needed. And now you can create the same kinds of access points for your organization using the ET *Guanxi* Mapping Tool.

In addition, you can use it on a personal level to promote yourself. I was struck a few years back by the cover photo on the September 24, 2006, issue of *New York Times Magazine* depicting a series of people responsible for football player Michael Oher's rise to success. Oher, the subject of the 2009 film *The Blind Side*, was adopted by a family that guided him to coaches and opportunities that eventually led to his rise to NFL fame. Oher's ascent in life, which reads like a textbook example of *guanxi*, was visually summarized by images of allies dotted on the magazine cover. If I were to ask you to illustrate your strategic connections in a similar fashion, what faces of *guanxi* might you see? Most people don't necessarily know the real answer, but your new tool will channel and focus your thinking so that you can identify connections that you can tap into to create opportunities.

The ET Guanxi *Mapping Tool*

Reaching out to potentially helpful contacts is only one component of *guanxi* within the context of Enterprise Thinking. You need to develop a plan in which you identify and select the right people and then formulate the best approach to gaining their cooperation before you ever reach out to them. The ET *Guanxi* Mapping Tool is a stepped process for creating that plan. It will slow you down so that you're spending more time thinking before taking action, a fundamental component of the Economics of Thinking.

Follow these six steps:

1. **Gather names.** Make a master list of all the key people you know today and people from your past that you may have less contact with today. This may take some time to develop, but keep at it, because some surprising names that you may have forgotten in recent years may make the list. Include on this list the names of people you don't yet know but that you believe you will need to know in order to help you to achieve your short-, medium-, and long-range Desired Outcomes. Also gather the names of any people who are close enough to you that they would be willing to contact a third party to make a soft-sell introduction for you. This seemingly insignificant win-by-a-nose move could be all it takes to bypass gatekeepers and get someone to listen to your ideas. (Remember, although developing *guanxi* can take many years, accessing *guanxi* can be rapid.)

2. **Categorize names by level.** From your master list of names, assess the level of closeness you have with these people and place their name into one of the categories listed here:

    Level 1: *Guanxi* is deep and long established.
    Level 2: The relationship is close enough that the other person can call you if they would like.
    Level 3: You share friendly ties where the other person would take your calls.
    Level 4: You have surface knowledge of the other person and/ or they have the same of you, but if you have any relationship, it is at the acquaintance level.
    Level 5: You and the other person are not connected.
    Level 6: The conditions between you and the other person are negative due to prior experience(s).

3. **Pre-plan your approach.** Think about your most important endeavors and start to select names from the list that you think might be helpful to you. Determine how you can help these people get where they want to go before you ever ask them to help you. In some cases, you may just have to ask them or the people you feel can connect you to them. Always err in the direction of not assuming that they will feel they have to help you, and your help will be noticed.

4. **Establish a plan.** Now it's finally time to establish the plan for reaching out to the new extended list of the people you want or need to know by doing some basic research. As you develop this plan, look for conditions where you can wow someone and then situations where you just keep in contact. Like Ren's ability to assist Goldberg, you want to find opportunities to help your contacts improve their lives professionally or in some instances, personally, to form deeper connections with them.

    If you're a Maps versus Words type of learner, you might want to write a person's name on a piece of paper, then draw three circles around that name, which remains in the circle like a bull's-eye. The outer circle contains general information that you could find in your newspaper or online. The middle circle contains more personal and in-depth information, the types of which can be gleaned in a coffee-shop conversation or through occasional contact with the person. The inner circle contains more private information that you may have to dig around for or earn others' trust before learning. Once you've assembled your information, reach out to newer contacts on a regular schedule that you have determined is appropriate for your circumstances.

5. **Take action.** Begin by reaching out to the people you know and that you have had recent years' contact with, because communicating with them tends to be easier than breaking the ice with occasional contacts or those from your past.

6. **Be patient.** Don't expect anything in return, even if your culture expects reciprocation. Being genuinely helpful to others without pressuring them to pay you back will eventually lead to the kind of trust that opens doors of opportunities, even if it takes years to earn that trust.

Note: Don't abuse the ties.

While using the ET *Guanxi* Mapping Tool, keep in mind that *guanxi* is not about selling. It's about developing long-lasting deep connections like those between people who have gone to school together, shared family outings, or are tied together through other personal experiences. The history people have with each other is the key to traditional *guanxi*. For short-term results, you are going to work at accessing contacts à la the six degrees of separation, but for long-term outcomes, expect to work a lifetime on relationships, realizing that some will yield fast opportunities while others will never produce a return for the effort. In the end, remind yourself that in the realm of *guanxi*, it's not who you know, it's who knows you. A big difference. So review where you've been, who you have known, and where you would like to take the direction of your life and organization. Then apply what you've learned here and see your relationships flourish.

Collaborating to Strengthen Your Sales Impact

Picture a single stick that you find on the ground. Alone, it's pretty easy to snap into two pieces, but bundle that stick with twenty others, and it's a bit more challenging to break it apart. Organizations run on the same concept. A unified group of collaborative workers can give each other information, support each other's efforts, and move the organization forward faster and stronger than its individual members working alone typically can.

Now imagine that you and your leadership group (or even front-line people) have a room in your organization where they can come together to work in unison on a single sales-related project. The concept here is a take on the war room, where military minds come together to strategize next moves to overcome an enemy and achieve a common desired outcome. For our purposes, we'll call the concept the Collaboration Room, and it will serve as a meeting platform to share information that enables you and your people to sell your products, services, organization, or ideas better.

Say that you want to acquire twelve new salespeople during the calendar year. Selling for recruiting is also leadership sales. You could tell each of your six salespeople already on staff that each of them is responsible for recruiting two new salespeople over the next year. The plan could work, but chances are, your plan will work better if you craft it using the Collaboration Room.

Now imagine that you've brought your six salespeople into this room and asked them to come up with a list of forty prospects. Each person will go out into the field, do Internet searches, work their connections, consult their *guanxi* contacts, and gather as much information about these forty people as they can to bring back to the Collaboration Room for your next meeting.

You place a photo representing each prospect on the wall in your Collaboration Room. Each photo is adhered to a sheet of paper, giving you enough room to write notes about prospects. Onto each photo, draw three concentric circles, each of which represents a different facet you must address. The first circle represents a prospect's organizational life, the second is their known activities, and the third is any personal information that may help in the acquisitions. Then you task the group to fill in the data to build a profile for each prospect, and encourage the group to provide specific information like where a prospect goes to the gym, who they hang out with, who their best customers are, where they love to eat, the name of their spouse, where they like to vacation, and so on.

As the data comes in, you and your team sit down together and start to develop plans for moving forward based on the new information and your organization's assets, skills, and connections that could put you in touch with the best prospects and eliminate other prospects as unviable. Say that one person on your staff is a member of a gym where one of your prospects goes to workout; assign that staffer to visit the gym at a time when the prospect will be there and to strike up a conversation with him. Another staff member may be connected to a prospect indirectly through family members. This affords you another opportunity to put someone from your organization in contact with a targeted prospect. The sum of these various connections builds a plan that helps you gain the outcomes you desire.

The reason that I urge you to try this tool is that in too many organizations, I find executives saying to salespeople, leadership, and board members, "You need to recruit/secure/win over, at least two people." Then these leaders walk away without empowering their staff members with a plan, package, or appropriate transfer of power. But if you create a Collaboration Room, you can do all of this and get better results.

Just think about how useful the Collaboration Room can be in moving your plans ahead quickly and with a greater potential to succeed. You can use the concept of the Collaboration Room for many purposes, such as searching out allies, headhunting new managers, securing new locations, or targeting members of the media who can promote your organization.

Selling the Invisible

When it comes to pushing your ideas forward, being able to sell all things invisible can be as important (if not more so) than selling products and services. Unlike tangible products that the consumer can touch, see, and try out, ideas require the seller to gain a certain degree of trust and faith from their audiences. Unless you have an amazing track record of WSPs (and even then there's no guarantee of a sale), you'll need one of the great powers of persuasion: making the invisible visible.

There are a number of tools you can use to paint a picture of what your idea means to others so that you appeal to both types of Maps versus Words learners. You can use language tools like analogies, metaphors, blueprints, models, photos, stories, etc., so that the other person can form a frame of reference. For example, if you're accustomed to saying something like, "This initiative will bring innovation to our department," try instead saying, "This initiative is the jolt of innovative espresso our department needs to get up to speed in one month." Go back to your ET toolkit and pull out tools like Redefining and the Five Reasons Why—two tools that yield better outcomes when you involve wordsmithing—to convert your ideas into mind pictures for others to visualize.

Home builders, designers, and decorators are all people who have to sell their ideas without always having the benefit of a sample to show. Like them, you can use illustrations, past accomplishments, and testimonials to help others understand what it is you can do for them.

They use visuals to win over their buyers: builders show model homes, designers and architects present blueprints and drafted plans, and decorators reveal color photos. What might you present visually to gain the buy-in you need from your stakeholders? Can you express your ideas using a storyboard of how a new process would work in the warehouse, how users will interface a department, how the final rendition of a clothing line will turn out, or how the outline of a previous landscape design has played out in real life?

If you don't have models and other visuals, concrete data can be your sales visual. When you say, "Customers are complaining," you might get some response, but when you follow it up with, "There were 137 errors in our last 89 orders," you get people's attention fast. Stats and stories are persuasive.

The point is, don't go into situations empty handed when you're selling a concept or idea that others can't see. Find or create the tools you need to make the invisible visible, and you are more likely to close your sale.

Overcoming the Barriers of Organizational Politics

Not unlike Greg's situation where he needed the buy-in of fourteen coworkers before launching a project, Glen, a printing company manager, was having trouble getting his crew to understand that change was imminent. His staff members had been printing the same types of print runs with the same old equipment for decades, and the time was long overdue for upgrades in equipment and procedures. From management to the front line, everyone on board was stuck in their ways, and Glen couldn't see any way around the politics that stood between status quo and progress.

He had calculated that one single project alone could bring an additional $1 million a year for his firm, but he couldn't get even one of the VPs to sign off on the upgrades. In all the discussions we had, the VPs were to blame—they did not want to change. We discussed, however, that in the end, it was still Glen's responsibility to sell the project despite the challenges that he was facing. The truth was if the sale was not made, it was not because of the politics, it was because he had not figured out the plans necessary to create the acceptance.

Sometimes, overcoming the barriers of politics begins with changing yourself, not necessarily changing others. Keep in mind that you might have to point to you first (P2UF) before you take next steps, as described in Chapter 10. If Glen had not made the sale, it would have been Glen and his thinking that needed to change. Conference planners can complain that some of their sessions are poorly attended, but they're quick to take credit for sessions that are jam-packed. Yet, the conference planner is as equally responsible for selecting good speakers who fill the room as they are for booking bad speakers who fail to draw a crowd.

If you're finding that you can't get past certain people-created barriers, there are steps you can take to blast political barriers and get to "yes."

1. **Identify your true political foes and find out what drives them to say no and yes.** Appeal to both responses by offering something in your presentation of ideas that's "in it for them." One way to prepare for presenting to challenging people is to try the innovation trigger exercise from Chapter 12 called Become the Person to gain a more accurate perspective from their point of view.

2. **Don't take "no" as a dead-end answer.** Instead, as David Yunich from the opening story in this chapter did, consider "no" to mean that your opposition is not ready just yet, and then make the necessary conditional changes to put opposition in the ready position. Great salespeople know that getting to yes sometimes doesn't take the easy route from point A to point B, but instead, takes some time.

3. **Ask if you are the problem.** If you don't have WSPs, if you've been dishonest in the past, if you have a history of stopping short and not following through, these negative factors will follow you until you convert your professional rap sheet into an impressive resume. Point to you first, because people could be resisting you based on their past negative experiences with you.

4. **Build the framework and then fill in the pieces.** It's easy to blame the stalling of progress on politics, but sometimes the

plan isn't complete enough, the Tactics aren't clear enough, or some other factor is causing people to resist you.

5. **Know the big picture, the 50,000-foot view, and sell the pros of your initiative to senior management.** People often believe they have a great idea, but because they haven't proven that they can see its big-picture impact on the overall organization, they fail to discuss the specific details that earn the trust and buy-in of senior-level executives across and organization. And beyond content, you need to consider the mode of communications you use, too. In an age of e-mails and texts, I can't tell you how many times I've had to ask, "Have you spoken to them directly?" and the answer is no. In addition, you may need to acquire new knowledge so that you can provide the details that you need to convince upper management that you truly understand the impact your ideas will have on your organization. Isn't it better to say, "This will not only improve the performance of our IT team, but I've taken the extra step to ensure that this will not negatively impact the marketing department, too"?

6. **Try to nail down a couple of reasons for the politics.** Your best-laid plans can be derailed by politics that exist surrounding your organization, your circumstances, or both. Before you take additional measures to sell your ideas, try to pinpoint the reasons for the politics and assess whether you can work around them. Sometimes, certain types of politics are ingrained in the culture of an organization, and until staffing (usually senior management) changes, you have to create plans that deal with these conditions. As a reminder, you're paid to think and part of this role involves dealing with human nature.

These are just some of the ways that you can overcome barriers to buy-in and cooperation when you think that politics are blocking your progress.

Knowing Your Role in Regard to Traditional Sales

The tools and concepts you learned for achieving internal buy-in also work effectively for external sales, like when you want to establish alliances, set up shop in a new region, or sell actual products and services.

If the organization is small, a business owner can be the lead sales person on staff. If the organization is large, top management might be called in to sell products and services to buyers on occasion, because they see the bigger picture, or because they can use the clout of their title—CEO, president, owner, director, etc.—to win a sale. In these larger organizations where executives are stepping into the role of the traditional salesperson on occasion, too much of their time is spent on meet-and-greet sessions that don't result in the direct sale, most often stemming from a lack of understanding that selling continuously is an essential leadership activity, and therefore, they don't work on building selling-related skills. Far too many executives confide in me that their time is often wasted when they step into the salesperson's role, and I believe that the reason so few do anything to prevent the problem from occurring in subsequent situations is because they are unaware that their role of the leader is not to just go through the routine but to intentionally seek out opportunities to advance the organization. The next time you're to be face to face with a client or customer, you can let them know in advance your intentions: that you want to sit down with them to help them open an account, make a bulk purchase that will give them better unit pricing, or make some other form of sale.

If you're a decision maker in a nonprofit organization where the "sale" entails winning a grant or other form of funding, the responsibility of sales might fall to a single decision maker or to a committee, but the lesson is still the same. So whether you're in a large business or in the back office at a "complex" or "installation" organization, stating your intentions up front and using selling tools like the ones you will take from this chapter will help you to win what you need for your organization more often. Just tailor the tools and concepts to your particular situation, and you will get better results for the time you put into selling.

The airline industry is a small community of fiercely competitive companies that build, sell, and buy planes. Executives are often key salespeople. For years, Airbus's chief of sales John Leahy was a step ahead of his rival, Boeing, until Boeing's CEO Alan Mulally, stepped out of the executive office and into the sales arena.

Mulally's team began monitoring and forecasting the whereabouts of Leahy very closely. In April 2005, Boeing's staff learned that Leahy was about to visit the chairman of Korean Air, Yang Ho Cho. Knowing a deal was sure to be written at that meeting, Mulally quickly contacted Cho and arranged to meet with him before Leahy's arrival. During their meeting, Mulally and Cho negotiated that Boeing would buy plane parts from Korean companies in exchange for Cho's business. The tactic resulted in the purchase of ten Boeing 787s and options on ten more planes.[169]

Let's not forget that making the actual close was not Mulally's only role in this sale. From 50,000 feet, Boeing had to have the right products and a credible reputation, among many other elements, to earn Korean Air's business. Mulally knew when it was right to step out of the executive office and contribute to external sales, but not everyone sees how their involvement can help or hinder their staff.

While consulting to the executive and his management team responsible for managing and leading an $800 million national company, I found that many regional and area sales managers were doing ride-alongs with their sales staff as frequently as four days a week. Sales records indicated that when executives accompanied their salepeople on sales calls, sales increased, and when sales personnel worked alone, sales dropped. The real issue was that managers were not supporting sales by transferring skills, nor were they building new systems, tools, or processes that would properly empower sales personnel to be independently effective in the field.

Another reason for salespeople's ineffectiveness boiled down to an issue that had been masked. No one really paid attention to how the leaders were using their elevated position on the organizational chart to influence buyers. Because executives were relying on the influence of their titles to close sales—something that was not duplicable by or transferrable to salespeople—decision makers weren't dissecting parts of the sales process to find out what other tools and selling points their salespeople needed to overcome barriers to sales. Salespeople could not say, "I'm the regional VP." The leader was unaware of how he was hindering his sales staff's performance. He had improperly allotted his time—too much tactical work and not enough thinking—causing him to do his salespeople's work for them instead of coming up with ways to provide more effective sales support and empower the group to become better and more independent salespeople.

Sometimes, your role is to engage in direct sales of products and services; other times, your role is to act as a guide to those who do the selling, and still at other times, your role is to think and strategize so that your organization is a strong entity that can sell itself based on its merits to take people where they want to go.

Cornerstones for Engaging Others

No leader can accomplish all that he or she needs to without the help of other people, be it internal or external to the organization. (And even a one-person operation relies on outside resources to survive and thrive.) Therefore, having the skills to win over others to your way of thinking is an essential part of your success. Surely, you already possess many of these types of skills, because they have allowed you to rise to the position you already hold. However, it's always nice to have a reference tool that reminds you of the ways in which you can perpetually sharpen your skills in this area.

Here, you will learn about the four types of skills that form the Cornerstones for Engaging Others: behaviors, oratory skills, writing skills, and interpersonal skills. I have offered some suggestions within each cornerstone. However, you can use the reference chart supplied online at www.paidtothink.com to come up with many of your own that will fit into your unique circumstances.

Behaviors

Get Accepted

Tailor your sales pitch and your style to your audience. If you're a contractor, your presentation and style will depend on whether you're selling a new addition to your client, selling the idea of working overtime on Friday night to your work crew, or having lunch in the lunchroom with others. If you're meeting someone new, do some homework ahead of time to uncover what they want, need and like, as well as how to speak with them.

An HR manager gave a presentation on leadership skills to a group of trucking safety managers. Her audience looked on unimpressed as she placed a red ball on her nose like a clown in an attempt to infuse humor into her presentation. She didn't connect with the managers, lost credibility, and failed to sell her ideas to the group.

Learn the Game

When you sell, you're often working in an environment of unspoken rules in addition to legal regulations. It's important to know what you're going getting into before you present your ideas, make plans to move forward, put people in motion, or otherwise expend resources and time.

For instance, in certain parts of the world using the term "domination" in a sentence, such as, "We want to dominate the market," means nothing more than an aggressive approach to building business. But not everyone is so nonchalant about the same terminology. In Europe, for instance, saying you want to dominate the market could cause the EU to investigate if you're working toward a monopoly. Substituting "industry leader" or something similar would be more appropriate in that region.

You want to be in sync with the morés and customs of the culture around you, whether you're dealing with people of another country or people within your own organization. Sometimes the messages are conflicting, and it's difficult to know what is the right action to take. Too many of the organizations that I've worked with say one thing and do another. For example, they'll say, "Give us something on innovation, because we're a very innovative company," but then, they'll force every presenter to use their standard PowerPoint presentation format, because, "This is the way we do it." Not too innovative, is it?

Every industry, country, sector, religion, culture, business unit, and even family-run business is driven by sets of written and unwritten rules. Knowing them can help you plan effectively so that you can close your sale.

Be Timely

Pay attention to deadlines, seasonal opportunities, and cycles. Your actions today will determine how trusting, cooperative, and receptive people will be toward your ideas now and in the future.

A school superintendent who seeks state funding to fill budget gaps must take measures to finish their paperwork and submit it on time, or they lose the sale. An engineering firm's manager worked six months to complete a proposal, but submitted it twenty minutes late, blowing all chances of earning the project. The consequences of not being timely can last for years.

I'm often asked how to get buy-in from others and, behaviorally, if you're late for meetings or arrive late to work, you immediately start off in the red. There are exceptions, but in general, being on time says a lot about your ability to deliver results as promised, and trust is a huge component to winning in sales.

Learn New Sales Tools

Leadership skills and sales skills walk hand in hand. Always remember that your ability to sell comes down to how well you lead and vice versa. Since leaders don't typically develop and hone selling skills, you need to take the initiative and self educate.

Take a course, read a book, watch a sales video, travel *occasionally* with your sales force. Listen to great speeches, watch successful people work a room. Build selling skills by learning about related subjects, such as persuasion, negotiations, and human behavior. While this isn't true in every instance, knowing more about how to sell can help you eke out more wins, even by a nose.

Step Out of Your Comfort Zone

Everyone has certain preferences for how they learn, how they work with others, and how they present themselves based on their personalities and strengths and weaknesses. In an ideal world, all of us would be able to approach our everyday challenges, even those that involve selling continuously, in ways that feel most comfortable for us. But realistically, that isn't always possible. Sometimes, meeting people on their terms in order to sell your ideas or products means that you must step out of your comfort zone.

While it's certainly not as pleasant to do, you can still work effectively in these circumstances. For example, you may prefer e-mail and texting as convenient and comfortable forms of communication, but in some cases, they are not appropriate substitutes for phone and face-to-face communications—especially if the other party has told you they want to talk directly with you—and you need to make the compromise.

Years ago, a particular speakers' bureau booked me on several jobs, but its owner missed numerous opportunities to close sales for me and other speakers, because the guy wouldn't pick up a phone and make a phone call. He would rather spend his time and everyone else's on nine e-mails over the course of two days, when a five-minute phone call would have cleared up all the details. In some instances, clients who wanted to book their jobs quickly would call the speakers instead of the bureau owner, pushing the administrative responsibilities onto speakers when they should have gone to the bureau. Needless to say, his business suffered over the years when speakers grew tired of doing his work for him.

Acquire new skills and hone up on current skills in a number of different areas by using the tools and practicing the activities of ET. Then, when you have to perform in an environment that seems foreign to you, you can make the switch more easily and still accomplish your outcomes.

Temper Your Temper Strategically

Anger can ruin your chances of selling yourself and your ideas, whether the emotion is exhibited as one large outburst or as a subtle glint of irritation. It's always great when a person has a true passion for their idea, but if the passion is coated in anger, take a step back and assess the situation for improvement-making opportunities before you move forward.

In politics, it's believed that the angry guy is the loser when it comes to negotiations. That's why you typically don't see politicians expressing their anger openly. If you do feel anger when you are trying to sell your idea, fight the urge to allow emotions to cloud your judgment and cause you to say things you'll regret later or talk to the wrong people about your challenges. I know of a business owner who shares his anger about business matters with his customers and his employees, even when his anger stems from employee-related issues. If you have to address anger in order to sell your ideas, at least root your complaint in fact, then quickly turn your message in a positive direction by explaining the benefits and advantages that your ideas will have on others.

If you can't do that, then remove yourself from the situation and dissect why you feel angry. Usually, anger is a sign that something needs your attention, because clearly, when everything is running smoothly, there's no need for anger. You can actually break down the elements of any sale, internal or external, into pieces to determine where you need to improve. Spend time rehearsing the words you will speak to deliver your message. Review your plan to be sure that you have addressed all areas that could produce resistance from others. The Macro Tactic should be that you put yourself in control and avoid being reactive, because the more you're *in* control, the less frustrated you will be and the less likely you are to produce a game-losing slip.

Use Techniques to Overcome Selling Weaknesses

You can vastly improve your outcomes by improving your ability to deliver your message. Videotape or audiotape yourself to gain an accurate observation of your delivery and to improve upon your weaknesses (small room, large room, one-on-one). You might even want to tape one of your own meetings to see how you actually perform on the job. Many people find this exercise helpful, because it shows them that they need to become better communicators, and watching a recording of themselves reveals specific areas where they can begin to improve.

If you just can't sell well, sometimes stepping aside is best. Look at your staff and identify people who have the skills to promote your idea capably. Then, you can assign different selling-related responsibilities to people based on their talent rather than by their title, just as you do when you use the Project Assignment Worksheet from Chapter 3 to place the right leaders on the right projects.

If that's not an option, change the format altogether by offering visual aids and written materials, or involve others in your sales presentations the way some leaders do when they set up a question-and-answer session.

Deliver Wildly Successful Projects (WSPs)

From a sales perspective, this is how you should look at your next WSP. First, it moves your organization ahead fast in the short term. Second, when you take on a project and complete it so successfully that you build a reputation as a winner, the perception that others have of you adds weight to your ideas and improves your ability to sell, because people follow winners.

Here are some approaches you can use to generate WSPs:

1. **Be exclusively exceptional.** Take on a project and do it so exceptionally well that others will not only take notice, they will consider you the go-to person for that particular type of project in the future. When the BP oil spill occurred in 2010 off the southern coast of the United States in the Gulf of Mexico, John Wright was the[170] obvious and only choice for a solution. Wright is a relief-well expert who drilled the relief well almost 3.5 miles beneath the ocean's surface to put an end to the disaster that gushed nearly 5 million barrels of crude oil into the Gulf. His target: a pipe so relatively small—only seven inches in diameter—that it would be an easy target to miss. Yet Wright's precision is dead-on, one disaster after another, which is why he doesn't have to seek out customers; they find him.

2. **Do the job that no one else wants to do, and wow others with its successful outcome.** Want exposure in your community? Go to a local nonprofit, volunteer your time on a project that no one else is willing to give their attention to, and turn it into such a WSP that you'll have tongues wagging. Want to rise up the ranks within your organization or industry? Follow the same methodology within those arenas. Here's the mistake that many people make: They take on a job that others want, expect to get a lot of exposure, then do an okay job with it. Their expectations are off kilter, and they don't do anything that's stellar enough to make it a real Order Winner on their resume of achievements. Remember, this is about Wildly Successful Projects (emphasis on the word *wildly*).

[WSPs Sell!]

Karen is a manager who had to reduce office space across multiple locations of her company. Her solution was to have employees trade their private workspace for a smaller and more open work environment—not an easy sell. She used a type of Buy-In Chart to work with engineers, architects, and equipment suppliers to create a more efficient workspace in one of her locations. With a handheld camcorder, she

[continues on page 548]

> [continued from previous page]
>
> recorded stages of the process and enthusiastic staff responses, and posted them online. When she had to gain buy-in from workers at other facilities, Karen shared before-and-after video footage of her project to win over even her harshest skeptics with proof of what she'd accomplished. Everyone wanted the conversion, because the WSP spoke for itself and earned people's confidence.

Oratory Skills

Practice Speaking Clearly and Logically

People have asked me how I learned to speak in public, and I've explained that the premise of my approach has actually been quite simple. I realized a long time ago that there are two components to being a good speaker. The first component is related to thinking, and second is related to speaking clearly. Both components have to be strongly executed in order for me to speak effectively, otherwise, I could have a lose-by-a-nose moment in front of hundreds of audience members.

My solution was to visualize my face in two parts—the upper part where my brain is and the lower part where my mouth is—and then work on both parts independently so that I could improve my overall performance. For the brain, I made sure to organize my thoughts before I spoke. This would require me to do the pre-work of doing research, talking to people about their challenges, and making sure that I assembled the right combination of content to deliver solutions to people. Then, for my mouth, I became conscious of how I enunciate my words, practicing speaking clearly all the time (and not just when I was ready to present) so that while presenting, I wouldn't be concerned about saying ahs and ums or displaying other flaws. Considering how often you are selling, practice frees your mind from distractions and allows you to have the focus of a chess player who is thinking many steps in advance so that you can stick to the purpose at hand and get the results you want, which is an advantage you want when selling continuously.

Know When to Remain Silent

Although speaking up gains recognition, shows intelligence, and demonstrates authority, there are appropriate instances when saying less (or nothing) will produce better outcomes. Sometimes, persuading others happens more easily when you sit back, listen, and make assessments before you speak. In other words, an effective selling experience sometimes happens because of what you don't say.

If you've ever taken a sales course or read a sales book, you might have been instructed to not speak until a prospect has spoken. The idea behind this directive is that the person who speaks first puts himself at a disadvantage by playing into the hands of the silent party. You'll often see it written as, "He who speaks first loses." While this may be an effective technique for forcing others into buying whatever it is you're selling, that's not the intent of this section.

For leaders who are selling continuously, the urge to do all the talking can get in the way of truly understanding the needs of the other party. If you fail to listen, you may be inclined to take action or to pose benefits to others based on your assumptions about what they want to hear instead of actually knowing what it is they want and need.

Here is a simple exercise you can try over the course of your next ten meetings: Don't talk until everyone else has spoken on a topic. Take notes as they speak to see if you can find an "aha" moment or to gauge whether you need to redirect some of your message to meet the needs of the group. Sometimes, even in those few moments where you are listening to others, you can have a small amount of Cyclonic Thinking Time during which you swoop up ideas, swirl them around in your mind, and decide which ones require your attention first.

When you do speak, you're not repeating or contradicting anything that's already been discussed. You want to be able to ask questions that take the current discussion deeper or that progress your group further ahead. By asking good questions, you prompt people to rethink their initial ideas and assumptions. Asking great questions is just as important to your endeavors as giving the answers.

You can also use the tactic of expressing a number count before you speak to ensure that people are listening. You might say, "I would like to make two points," or "I have three suggestions," and then state your points briefly and succinctly to keep people's attention, make an impact, and move on without wasting anybody's time. When you incorporate a number count into your presentation, most people will think, "I can listen for four minutes," or "Okay, that's two points, now what is the third one?" It also helps people to remember what you say.

Another exercise involves more time, but when the conditions are appropriate, it can deliver real benefits to you and those on your staff. The next time you take on a new position or huge project, take thirty to sixty days to focus primarily on asking questions and retrieving information instead of advising people on what to do. Asking questions is a sales technique as much as it is a way of finding out information.

This measure in patience allows you time to explore and work on your planning, just as it did for IBM's leadership in the mid 1980s, as outlined in the book *The Silverlake Project*.[171] This book explains the story of an IBM-owned plant and its leadership in Rochester, Minnesota, that had made some huge errors in the advancement of the System/36 (S/36) and System/37 (S/37) midrange computer systems. The employees had begun to think that they knew more than their customers when it came to customer product needs, but the wrong assumption caused the firm to sink money into one technologically advanced machine after another that failed, because developers had actually lost sight of their market. To make matters worse, these assumptions resulted in the creation of products that made the customers' previous investments obsolete or incompatible. Both their vendors and their customers were furious with the decision making.

In a perfect example of Enterprise Thinking, IBM's top leadership switched tactics and brought in new leadership, Tom Furey, an outsider from the East Coast who, in the first few months of being at the helm, only listened and asked questions. He did this with employees and with customers. In effect, he moved from being product-driven to customer- and market-driven. When he finally started to make changes, the changes were vast and fast. He brought in the best customers to aid in development and testing, created parallel processing of work, moved to rapid prototyping and manufacturing, and when all the dust settled, after only two short years, the skunk works created the AS/400, a computer system that would be the lead product for IBM for years to come despite its $200,000 price tag.

When the product was launched it was launched globally all at once in multiple languages with a sales force completely trained and production set to meet demand. Due to leadership's willingness to be quiet, listen to customers, and develop a product that people truly wanted, this product launch was the most successful of its time, earning the plant the Malcolm Baldrige National Quality Award, a huge WSP to help IBM sell more machines.

Sometimes, silence really is golden. Look for the golden moments to be silent, listen to others, and allow the plans that you have developed to unfold.

Win People Over with an Engaging Story

Don't underestimate the power of a good story to sell your message. Stories are not only entertaining, they're a great tool for getting a point across in a way that engages the listener. They can quickly tip the scales in favor of the case you're trying to make, and serve as a call to action in ways that persuasion and negotiation can't at times.

In the late 1990s when Magic Johnson and his business partner Ken

Lombard approached then-Sony CEO Peter Guber[172]—who is now the CEO of Mandalay Entertainment Group and was a producer of *Rain Man, Batman,* and *Midnight Express*—to strike up an alliance, Johnson took the reins in the meeting by telling Guber a story to sell his idea. In my personal conversations with Guber (reiterated in his book *Tell to Win*), he recounted how Johnson asked him to close his eyes and picture a "foreign country . . . a promised land," where Sony could find a partner with established inroads to the culture, where there was ample real estate, an English-speaking audience, consumers ready to purchase, and a competition-free market in which to open more Loews movie theaters. By the end of the story, Guber was begging Johnson to tell him where this country was and in what part of the world it resided. He then discovered that Johnson was describing the promised land of Los Angeles, a mere six miles from their meeting location. Despite known gang activities in that particular part of the city, Guber and Sony were won over by Johnson's engaging story—and were enamored with finally breaking into a powerful purchasing community just around the corner—and decided to enter into the deal.

If stories are so effective, why don't more people tell them? I believe it's because they're not confident they can pull them off. They don't want to appear phony or manipulative, they just don't think storytelling is their style or forte, or they don't know how to craft a great story. Yes, there is some art in telling a story, but the reality is that the only shame in telling a story is telling a bad one. If you're telling the story with the intention of improving the other party's lot (as well as your own), the story may or may not be artfully told, but it won't be a bad story.

To help you to get started, especially if you believe that storytelling is difficult, think about that fact that you tell stories all the time. At dinner with your family, on the phone with colleagues or while meeting in a small group with your leadership team or spending time with your friends, you've probably never been told to stop talking, because your storytelling abilities are so horrendous. So already, you should know that you're probably better than you thought you were. All you may need is to organize your thoughts before you begin to speak, then refine your message by clarifying any points that might be confusing to people and by wordsmithing to make some points more interesting.

If you happen to believe that you're not a naturally gifted storyteller, don't worry. There's an ET tool for that, and it's the Selling Your Ideas with Stories formula (Figure 13.5). Just include a component from each category—Story Origins, Reasons, and Lesson—in any order that works for you, practice your key points, and let your stories sell your message.

SELLING YOUR IDEAS WITH STORIES (Getting Rapid Buy-In)

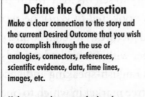

Story Origins	Reason	Lesson
Personal Stories Life/Family/Youth/Travel/Fun Friends/Encounters/Etc. **Organization/Group Stories** **Outside Stories** News/Friends/Competitors/ Research/Family/News/History/ Legends/Heros/Etc. *Stories may explain what to do, what not to do, be positive, negative, or neutral.*	**Define the Connection** Make a clear connection to the story and the current Desired Outcome that you wish to accomplish through the use of analogies, connectors, references, scientific evidence, data, time lines, images, etc. Make sure to be aware of cultural differences, age, gender, political views, upbringing, religious beliefs, etc. because a person's makeup will influence their perception of what you say and what you mean to say.	**Bring It All Together** While you may think you are perfectly clear, you may not be. Make sure to tie all the messages together so that everyone is on the same page. HINT: Don't overdo this part. The better the storyteller, the less you'll need to reiterate the lesson. The better crafted the reason, the less time necessary here. The Desired Outcome is that by this point everyone knows what you're talking about.

Figure 13.5—Selling Your Ideas with Stories

Basically, you want your story to illustrate the reason that you define, which is why you don't simply have the one category titled Story Origins. Select a story that is appropriate, interesting, and that will be positively received by your listener. (**Note:** this is not to say that the story itself has to be positive, just that it is something that is acceptable to your listener.) The story's origin can come from personal situations, organization or group happenings, or topics outside the two.

You also want to determine the connection this story has to your pitch and purpose. In other words, you must determine the Reason for your storytelling. Although Reason is placed in the second position in Figure 13.5, remember that you can perform any of these components in any order that works best for your situation. Therefore, you might want to determine your Reason before you select your story or vice versa.

The third component in Figure 13.5 is the Lesson that you want your story to impart. The Lesson is most effective when you find common ground with your listener, and incorporate the common element into your story. The key to engaging others and getting them to buy into your message is being able to weave these three components together. In the end, your story should be compelling enough that your listener wants to take action that leads you to your Desired Outcome.

Here are some additional tips to remember when crafting your next story:

1. **Make it fun and exciting.** Consider telling it with a twist to further engage your listener.
2. **Give it a beginning, middle, and end.** All good stories need a plot, so set up the characters in an appropriate setting, have them do something, and then bring the story to a conclusion.
3. **Be detailed.** You want to pepper in the right amount of detail to engage the other party—but don't go overboard and bore him or her. Details should spice up the story, not bog it down.
4. **Guide your listener.** If your story contains several concepts, be sure that you transition from one to another in a way that doesn't lose your listener. The listener needs to be able to follow your message throughout the story.
5. **Check out the story from multiple angles.** You want to make sure that the story will be well received, so be sure that the idea or initiative that you're proposing isn't going to meet with resistance, because it poses a threat to someone else, be it their job, their profitability, their comfort zone, etc.
6. **Prop up the story with facts.** Be sure that you back up the story—no matter how engaging it is—with concrete data and facts. Even if there are no facts, if you're selling an idea that you expect to drive your organization forward, make sure that you illustrate why and how your ideas have substance.

A good story can turn even the most mundane of messages into interesting lessons. I remember working with a newly appointed marketing manager of a team of twenty-one employees who needed to get across a message to his team that it was time to make some radical changes. What he wanted to do was to set the stage for his new role within the organization. When I asked him what message he wanted to impart, he immediately opened up a corporate PowerPoint presentation with thirty slides. To say that his message was boring would be an understatement, and it seemed ironic that a presentation to promote change and innovation was couched in such dullness.

I asked the manager if he would be willing to step out of his comfort zone and try a different approach for delivering his message. Within seconds of suggesting that he kick off the meeting with a compelling story to capture his team's attention and get them to associate with him as a person rather than a boss, I could see his discomfort. On my end, I was fortunate to have already helped his organization with a few WSPs so he allowed me a little leeway, listened to my request, and attempted to come up with a story from his past that he could describe to the group as an opener for his presentation.

At first he drew a blank, but after an hour of searching he came up with something that synced with the lesson he wanted to impart, and we crafted a story that included all three components from the Selling Your Ideas with Stories tool that you just learned. As we worked to plan his presentation, he periodically mentioned his concerns that his team wouldn't want to hear anything personal and that he doubted that they would have any interest in listening to his three-minute story. He was still uncertain about the storytelling component of his presentation when we both concluded our work for the day, but we met again the following morning to polish it up in his conference room before his team arrived.

One by one the group entered the room and sat around a large conference table. They were all prepared to hear what their new leader was to impart, and to me this was a good sign, since he was taking a very important first step and was wrestling with his message on both a personal leadership level and organizationally as defined by the ET Leading Process. As I looked over at him, I could see in his eyes that he was about to revert back to his slides. He looked at the group and back at me. In a split second, he made the decision to take a leap of faith, and he began to tell the story I've abbreviated here:

"Through my career, I've lived in over nine countries around the world and each time we've moved, my wife and I have had to return home to figure out what we would need to leave behind and what we would need to bring with us on the next journey. So, if the weather is cold, we need to bring along cold-weather clothing, if we're planning to live in an apartment, we need to limit what we carry. In business, we often do the same thing. We have to decide what is necessary for us to continue doing and what we should stop doing. Today, we're going to spend our time figuring out what we need to be doing as a marketing team and what we should stop doing from this day forward."

You could see listeners' reactions in their body language. His group was engaged. I noticed people nodding their heads when he talked about having to leave behind household items in his moves to new homes. The group not only understood the message he wanted them to take away from the meeting, they associated with him, bought into the message, and were interested in knowing how they could turn a new page for their department.

The approach was simple: Tell a story, connect it to what you want to happen, and then bring the entire message together. In my client's presentation, he brought the message together by actively engaging his group in an activity. He split the group into two and gave each group a different task. Group one had to compile a list of actions they should no longer be doing: what they had to leave behind. Group two determined what actions they needed to perform better. Then both groups switched tasks. In the end, the leader made them all winners by purchasing breakfast for them the next day. He was shocked at how much his team participated. The engaging story sold his ideas much better than his corporate PowerPoint presentation could.

Regardless of the order you assign to the three components of a good story, as long as those components are present, you can engage others, deliver your message, and win them over to your side. Storytelling is a fun and memorable way of selling continuously.

[Storytelling Sells: Lessons from One of Amway's Top Distributors]

Thousands of hopeful salespeople gather throughout Asia to hear the inspirational stories told by Holly Chen, a sixty-eight-year-old former teacher and a grandmother who, along with her husband, Barry Chi, owns one of Amway's highest-grossing distributorships. According to Chen, one of the secrets to selling is that, "You have to know the inside of people, rather than the outside of people. . . . You've got to know their hearts."[173] And knowing the hearts of other people is what this storyteller banks on to motivate the 300,000 people who are part of her multilevel marketing distributorship.

Whether Chen, who earns close to $8 million a year from the personal-products company, imparts a story from her personal past or draws upon the experiences of more widely known people, she knows that her "most powerful weapon is to move somebody emotionally."[174] In one presentation, she might tell people about her humble beginnings in a small fishing town in Taiwan, and contrast those experiences to the ones she enjoys today, such as flying in a private jet and being a regular buyer of Chanel products. In another presentation, she excites audiences with tales of how human perseverance pays off, highlighting impressive accomplishments like the Great Wall of China to the Egyptian pyramids. Whatever the story, Chen is sure to make it an interesting one, which is how she not only captivates thousands of audience members for hours at a time, but also how she built a distributorship that includes one in every ten Amway representatives.

It doesn't take much to see that for leaders like Holly Chen, storytelling is a powerful selling tool.

Writing Skills

Present Written Material Well

Some people can read a couple of paragraphs that are littered with grammatical errors and not notice any of them, while others can't get past the first couple of mistakes without having them become major distractions to the message they are trying to understand. Since you can't be sure whether the readers of your material will be from one group or the other, you have to make sure that what you write is appealing to both types of readers.

The written material you send to others is a representation of you. If you can write clearly and without grammatical errors and misspellings, others may perceive you positively. Poorly written work, on the other hand, can send the message that you're unintelligent, sloppy, or incompetent—even if you're the exact opposite of that. It may not seem fair that your capabilities are judged based on a skill that challenges many people, but it's a reality. Personally, I don't see errors in grammar or punctuation; my focus is almost entirely on content. And though I'd like to think that I can express my points in writing somewhat clearly, I wish I could personally thank the unnamed person or people from Microsoft who developed software that generates a red line under misspelled words.

If you can't write well and don't see your skills improving any time soon, get writing or editing help from someone who can write for you or edit your material so that it is the best representation of you that it can be.

Collect and Use Testimonials

Your history follows you wherever you go, so make sure that you're putting your best successes out there for others to see by collecting written, audio, or video testimonials. Great testimonials are a way for others to validate your ability or your organization's ability to perform.

Collecting testimonials is easiest when you follow the tips here. The approach starts with securing testimonials while people are still excited about you and before you lose touch with them. Otherwise, enthusiasm wanes, people move away and switch jobs, and with their move goes your chances to get the testimonial. If you've ever tried to get a testimonial years after the fact only to find the person's moved on and you can't reach them, you understand this frustration. Yet, despite the fact that many leaders know this, they still don't pursue individual or organizational testimonials in a timely fashion.

Here's an option that will enable you to build a collection of testimonials.

First, pay attention to what people are saying about you or your organization: "What a fabulous job," "We could never have done this without you," "You've doubled our volume." These are signals that someone could be a potential testimonial giver. When you recognize these cues, take action by offering two options to the person from whom you would like the testimonial.

Here's what I say: "I'd be interested in knowing if you'd be willing to write a testimonial for our firm (or me personally) based on what you've just said." If you've done a great job, this is typically responded to with a "sure." Next, instead of waiting for eternity for something to arrive, you make the following offer immediately: "You can write a testimonial letter for me, and I'd be very happy to have it, or I can write a sample letter using the words you've just said, and then send it to you in a document that you can alter any way you see fit and send it back to me. Which would you prefer?"

Fifty percent of the people will choose to write a letter from scratch on their own, and the other 50% will agree to await your sample letter for them. The majority of people who opt to write their own letter don't take the time to actually do it, because, quite frankly, they're busy and they've moved on. For this group, I wait two to three weeks, and then I call them. They are always apologetic, and they usually agree that it would be best if I send a sample letter for them to review. I make sure that before I have called them I already have a letter written up so that when they ask for it, I can immediately e-mail it to them and they can look it over while our conversation is still fresh in their minds. Usually, people will edit the letter and return it right away. **Note:** Be sure that when you write the letter, you don't go overboard with compliments. Stick to the facts. For the second group of people who opt for a sample testimonial letter from you at the start, write and send a testimonial in a timely manner, and they will return it as expected.

Lastly, testimonials, even those that say you are great, are nearly useless unless they contain specific and differentiating information about you or your organization. You want people who read your testimonials to see Order Winners, not that you're "vanilla" like everyone else. Examples of Order Winners are: "XYZ organization serviced 78 pumps in 41 hours—the fastest we'd ever had the work completed," or "John was the youngest and first person to manage a project over $4 million and he finished the project three weeks ahead of schedule, something no other employee in the organization has ever accomplished before." Again, like the statistics on the back of a sports trading card, you want the types of comments displayed in your testimonial letters to tout your best assets. That way, you can later add the comments to your CV, resume, marketing materials, media interviews, hiring solicitations, website pages for recruiting good talent, or any other medium you use to secure new opportunities.

Follow the technique and follow up on the letters, because the testimonial letter you get today could be the win-by-a-nose sale tomorrow.

Interpersonal Skills

Be Your Most Credible You . . . and Maintain Your Credibility

As I've said before, leaders sell themselves and their ideas by selling their ability to convince others that they can deliver on their promises. So, what's your "credibility" rating? Surely, we've all seen snakes who've gone on to win multiple rewards in business and in life, and although these people highlight the fact that life isn't always fair, are you really willing to take a risk with a valuable asset like your reputation?

What is fair is that you have the opportunity each day to make decisions that can build your image and credibility, both of which you can use to sell yourself, your ideas, and your organization to others. You just have to figure out what you want to be known for, and follow through on what you say you'll do.

Not all leaders agree how they want to use their authority to build their image and credibility. There are leaders like Genghis Khan who made decisions that probably wouldn't go over well in today's world, but that at the time helped him to get his people where they wanted to go and to reach desired outcomes. Legend has it that once, when he was traveling with fifty of his men, a pack tumbled off the back of one of their horses. When Khan, who built one of the largest empires of all time, saw that none of the other 49 men stopped to help retrieve the bag, he took their lack of participation as a sign that they were disloyal to the group and killed every one of them except the guy who lost the pack. His reasoning was that the one soldier who lived would return home and tell the story to everyone—a leadership sales pathway that certainly got Khan's point across, wouldn't you say?

You also have to consider how wildly *unsuccessful* projects can erode your credibility and throw up barriers to future success. Back in the early 1990s, a large shopping mall developer didn't pay all of his contractors and vendors upon completion of several mall construction projects, which put several of these establishments out of business. I personally think the developer thought that there would be no repercussions. Years later, when mall leadership tried to create a massive expansion for one of their existing malls, local contractors, government officials, and citizens living in the area hadn't forgotten the questionable business tactics of the past. One individual, a government official whose family member lost his business in previous dealings with the developer, made it his mission to not let the developer move forward with the project. Leadership at the shopping mall tried for several years to get tax breaks, find reliable contractors, and extend payment times for lines of credit, but the people to whom they made their appeals—local lawmakers, vendors, and lenders—did not trust the developer and would not cut the mall's leadership a break. Eventually, plans for the large buildout were scrapped, and a smaller project took many more years to push through.

Your life is one big selling experience that not only leads to credibility but needs it to move forward.

Think Before You Act

Selling requires Cyclonic Thinking. Use the tools we talked about in this chapter to slow down, take calculated steps, and look at systems and structures first, whether you're dealing with an employee, selling a project that requires two years of work, or making a simple request of a team of people. Leaders make the mistake of taking a lot of time to plan a project, but then never give the project a chance to survive, because they haven't spent any time planning how to sell the project to the people who can make it a reality. The few minutes, hours, days, months or years spent planning can take an idea and move it from the "file" category to, "Let's do it."

Andrew Warner began an online greeting-cards business and grew it rapidly to more than $38 million.[175] When he started his firm, he realized that if he labeled his company Greetingcardsbusiness.com, the name alone would suggest to administrative assistants that his phone calls to their managers were sales related, and since their jobs as gatekeepers are to reduce the number of interruptions their bosses receive in a day, he'd have trouble bypassing the assistants and doing business. Forecasting that there could be issues, he named his company Bradford & Reed, believing that if he made a phone call to prospective buyers, their gatekeepers might believe that they were fielding a call from a law firm or a venture capital firm and be more willing to pass his calls through to executives. As a result, Warner's calls were taken, and when he left a message with a gatekeeper, his messages were passed on.

Give People Options

All day long, you're reaching out to others to get your ideas heard, to get behaviors to change, to execute on your role, and to get your questions answered. One approach to gaining cooperation from other people is to give them a few options, because options give people a chance to do what they like, which is to have the freedom to make their own decisions. For example, you can suggest that your front-line manager make a call to the head office or you can say to him, "There are three options. The first is I make the call. The second is you make the call. The third is we call together. Which would you prefer?" If you don't say anything immediately after offering the options, the other person will tend to eliminate less favorable options and then select the one they prefer.

You can do this for anything. If a vendor delivers product late, you can give them three options. One, they discount the item. Two, they can come and pick up the merchandise. Three, you can get a credit on the account. I've had individuals try this time and time again, and they find that regardless of whether the person they are working with is above them or below them, or outside or inside the organization, the person will tend to select one of the options.

According to business consultant and author Alan Weiss, by preparing three options, you channel the final outcome within an area that works for you and you give the other person the ability to decide what works best for him or her, a win for both parties.

In different circumstances, you may want to offer more than three options—as long as you don't overwhelm people with too many options. Tests have shown that when the number of options a person has to choose from becomes too high, he or she will either make poorer choices or will avoid selecting options altogether.[176] The aim should be to offer enough that you get people to say yes without going so far as to cause them to reject you and your ideas.

Consider Your Image and Adapt to Your Audience

When dealing with colleagues, close allies, or peers, you have to consider the whole-package image that you're projecting to others to gain their buy-in. Sometimes you make the most immediate connection by mirroring the style of the other party. At other times, you need to stand out as a unique representative or expert and embrace your unique style.

Katherine, a new-product-development consultant, thought that dressing like the engineers she presented to and worked with would earn their respect. When she underwent a makeover and upgraded her wardrobe, the engineers still respected her expertise, but leadership also took notice and her sales increased.

Mirroring others can result in positive benefits within any environment. A sleeve tattoo might help you sell more motorcycles. A chic necktie might inspire a wealthy patron to buy a piece of art from your gallery. A foreign accent might tempt tourists to dine in your restaurant. But beyond these simple tips, you have to look at how your image plays out internally within your organization, too. I've seen it many times: leaders who are oblivious to the fact that the image they believe they are projecting to their staff members is perceived totally differently by their people.

This happens frequently with leaders who place too much emphasis for organizational success on their people—the 20% of the GPP—without giving their people the tools and guidance they need—the 80% of the GPP—to attain those successes. In one particular company, leadership would constantly tell their staffers, "You need to support this effort," as a way to gain support for their newest initiatives. Over time, not only did staff members lose motivation, because they knew the initiatives wouldn't go anywhere, but they lacked trust in leadership, because the empowerment packages they provided (if they provided any at all) typically missed key components that were essential to reaching desired outcomes. Either tactics were absent or unclear, or a plan was missing altogether. Keep in mind that when you have the urge to ask for support, you must point to you first, and ask if you have authentically earned others' confidence enough to actually get the support you seek. Even though people will go through the motions of appearing to support you, especially if their paycheck depends on it, they can't really follow you if the image of you as a winning leader is one that only exists in your own mind.

Whether you intentionally project an image or not, people are either drawn to or repelled by the image that you and your organization display online, how you respond to them on the phone, what you say to a vendor's front-line workers on the phone, what you drive, how you speak, where you went to school or did not, etc. In some instances where adapting to your audience is authentic and serves a purpose, it is wise to do so, but just the same, you still want to remain true to who you are and what your organization represents. Sometimes, simply being aware that someone is always looking is enough to cause you to make an improvement that allows you to sell yourself and your organization.

Deliver Solutions, Not Complaints and Challenges

Persuade with solutions that can move people and organizations forward. Just as I discussed in Chapter 3 in the section about Redefining where we suggested new thinking in the form of What Would It Take . . . , asking why and looking over your shoulder at the past is as effective as pointing fingers of blame, but looking into the future and offering solutions is one way to get people to take notice and buy into your message.

I once presented to a health-care association servicing rural communities. The group's members were unhappy that the state health-care director wouldn't respond to their suggestions for improving health care. I decided to prove a point by rapidly going around the room and asking the good-sized crowd of participants one by one for their suggestions on how the health-care system could be improved. When we reviewed their list, very few suggestions were actual solutions. They were complaints disguised as solutions or generic statements that didn't take in the big-picture perspective, rendering them useless to the director. Receiving a list of complaints rather than solutions is probably why he had not responded to them, but the participants were totally unaware of the image they were projecting to the health-care director. Whining, "We aren't innovative," wasn't going to sell them or their ideas. Proposing something like, "We should consolidate all the IT infrastructure of reservation facilities into one office to gain economies of scale and allow the state to have up-to-date software," would undoubtedly be much more effective. Sometimes when you don't get your message across, it's because you haven't fully considered how the image you're projecting discredits you.

Take the time to do more than devise a plan or prepare a presentation. Look at all aspects of your image to see where you need to mirror your prospects and where you need to stand out as a capable and unique personality.

Attempt to Understand Others Before You Ask Them to Understand You

The credit for this lesson—seek first to understand, then to be understood—goes to St. Francis of Assisi, a Catholic saint of the 1200s. His message is similar to that of many great leaders and "people persons" who tend to get along well with others. Yet, although leaders know that they should try to see the other person's perspective and give them a chance to express their ideas and concerns before imparting their own opinions and requests on others, they fear that in doing so, they will lose control over the progress they want to make in selling their ideas to others.

There's a way of putting people at ease, letting them know they're being heard, and being able to gain their cooperation when you have to push forward with a project or task. Your tool consists of two simple sentences that pack a lot of punch.

Begin with, "I hear you, and you are telling me _____."
Follow up with, "I chose to _____, *because*
_____."

Sometimes, taking the few seconds to let another person rest on the rationale behind your ideas before marching forward with your plans results in people feeling more at ease with you and being more willing to accept your ideas.

During the interview process before speaking to a division of a multinational company, I kept hearing complaints from interviewees that their superior, Marcia, was a real steamroller of a manager. No matter what input anyone ever offered, Marcia seemed to ignore it and immediately followed up with her plans for the group. Marcia's associates had become so de-motivated by the pattern of behavior that they would go along with her ideas simply because anything they offered wouldn't be considered of value anyway.

When the day had arrived for me to interview Marcia, I instantly experienced what her coworkers had been complaining about. Every time I made a comment, Marcia ignored it as if the only thing she could hear was the next thought that she wanted to share. So I decided to give this tool to her—although you can use it when working with external stakeholders, too—and walked her through it.

At first, we played out a scenario that would have been typical in her office:

Me: "Can we discuss next year's health-insurance provider?"
Marcia: "I've got it under control. We'll be going with XYZ."
Me: "Their out-of-pocket expenses are too high for most of the staff."
Marcia: "I'm taking care of it."

Then we framed the conversation using, "I hear you, and I chose to _____."

Me: "Can we discuss next year's health-insurance provider?"
Marcia: "Sure, what's up?"
Me: "Well, ABC has lower out-of-pocket expenses than XYZ."
Marcia: "I hear you; you're saying that ABC has lower out-of-pocket expenses, and I agree that for simple office visits, paying $15 is more appealing than paying $20. However, I chose XYZ, because their premiums will save each staff member an average of $650 per year."

Right away, you can see how a few extra seconds to let others know that you hear them—not to mention to explain how you actually arrived at a sound decision—can improve your ability to sell an idea to others and gain cooperation.

Preparing to Succeed

You're about to walk into a set of negotiations for a major deal. You've done your homework, you know the numbers, and you've spent time on the selling point. Your counterparts have done little if any of this. Who's most likely to have the upper hand and to direct the discussion to their advantage? The obvious answer is, you do.

But if this seems obvious, why don't more leaders prepare themselves to handle relationship dynamics as meticulously as they can in order to give themselves and their organizations certain advantages? I believe it's because they don't see themselves in the role of leadership salespeople who are selling continuously throughout their everyday dealings with others. From a 50,000-foot perspective, the less prepared a person is, the more vulnerable and disadvantaged they are in almost every setting, because they are put in the position of reacting to someone else's directives. The better-prepared person is almost always steering the conversation, and he or she tends to own the option of deferring authority to someone else or taking control when it works to his or her organization's advantage. When one party says, "I've been working carefully on this idea, and I believe we have three options which are X, Y, and Z. Which one do you think we should start with first?" that person has immediately seized control of the situation and placed the other person in the position of being reactionary. The key to getting into the driver's seat and staying there is to plan ahead, knowing the optimum Desired Outcome before you ever enter the meeting. This way you can devise each of your options to direct the other party toward your Desired Outcome.

Now let's turn the tables. You're about to walk into an interview scenario with the media, and you've done your homework about the interviewer, their questioning style, what you want to answer, and how you will redirect questions that could put your organization in a negative light. You are exercising PR at its best, and the other party is now reactionary, because you've positioned yourself to set direction throughout the course of the interview. Being prepared has its advantages.

Then there are situations where two parties show up to the discussion, both well prepared. In this instance, you may be on par with each other as far as preparedness, in which case, the victory will likely go to the person who has the better plan, even if it wins by only a nose. Say that you've prepared a presentation for creating a medical treatment facility. Your plans allow for medical treatment of 200 people, but you don't realize until the meeting that this number is low. If the other party has prepared a plan that can adequately service 3,000 people under similar conditions, you're going to have difficulty coming out on top, despite showing up prepared to set direction.

Figure 13.6 is a simplified formula that will help you understand the important role that preparation plays in your ability to sell effectively.

Managing the Situation (Sales, Negotiations, Persuasion)

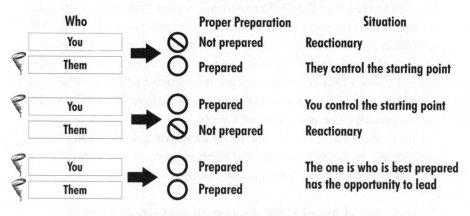

Figure 13.6—Managing the Situation (sales, negotiations, persuasion)

- If you are not prepared and someone else is prepared (someone could be a group), someone else controls the starting point of the sale.
- If you enter prepared and they do not enter prepared, you control the starting point, even if you let them begin in order to show that you know more.
- If you both enter prepared, then both of you have the opportunity to lead. At this point, it's many of the other skills that take over.

This tool is intended to show you that you have the ability to set direction and move your organization forward, but you have to be prepared for all the opportunities where you can either influence or be influenced, otherwise you can't sell as effectively.

Show Them "The Beef"

In 1984, Wendy's, known for its famous hamburgers, ran a television advertisement in the United States featuring[177] Clara Peller, an elderly woman who scoffs at the small size of competitors' burgers with the famous catchphrase, "Where's the beef?" Peller pitched the idea that only at Wendy's would you find a burger substantial enough to be worthy of her approval. In reality, when you're selling your ideas, others are seeking the substance behind them, and you don't want to part ways with them asking where the "beef" was in your idea.

Bob, the CEO of an 800-bed hospital, revealed to one of his mid-level managers that he would soon be replacing his CFO. The manager, Cheryl, who had worked with the CEO at another company years earlier, expressed her interest in taking over that position, and went so far as to say that she had some ideas in mind for improving the organization. Bob asked her to expand on them. She told me that she made mention of three improvements: redesign the layout of the offices to improve productivity, add new software to operations, and make a couple of organizational changes. The CEO nodded, and six weeks later, someone else got the job.

Cheryl asked me where she might have gone wrong. I offered an alternative response to the approach she had taken, in case she met with the same situation in the future. It went something like this:

> Bob, I'm glad you asked that question. I'd like to set up a time to sit down with you for about ninety minutes where I can go over my plans. I want to get the material together that I've researched over the past few months on software that can improve our profitability. At home, I also have sketches of an improved floor layout that I believe will increase productivity. And I also have come up with a few organizational changes that we can easily implement to restructure our flow of data to make it more readily available in real time.

If you were Bob, which set of suggestions would you want to hear from your next CFO? Frequently, leaders try to sell their ideas, but the ideas have no substance behind them. Replace vague suggestions with "beef," and you just might make the sale.

If You Want to Be Noticed, You Have to Sell

Networking can only work if you make yourself desirable enough to other parties so they want to deal with you. But too often, leaders attend networking events think they are making an impression on others by showing an interest in them and then leave without making an equally memorable impression on the people that they meet. As a result, these leaders go back to their offices, return to work as usual, and don't have anything to show for the time they spent on networking activities.

Paul, a transportation executive from France, attends a community networking event. While he is there, he meets Guillaume, the president of a regional travel agency. Paul sees opportunities to work with Guillaume, so he spends about fifteen minutes asking Guillaume several questions and intently listening to his answers. Finally, Guillaume says that he's enjoyed their discussion, excuses himself from the conversation, and sits down at a table with a couple of people that Paul doesn't recognize. Paul looks at his watch, tucks Guillaume's business card into his jacket pocket, and heads for the door.

The next day, Paul decides to follow up with Guillaume by phone. Guillaume's secretary puts Paul on hold, then returns to the phone to say that Guillaume is unable to take his call. She takes a message, but Paul never receives a return phone call from his new networking contact. Why is that?

Every time I survey a group of decision makers about similar circumstances, and I ask them if they would take a call from someone like Paul, they all tell me that they would not. And each time, they give the same reason; if they don't see a person as offering any value to them or their organization, they're not going to invest any further time into them.

Consider an alternative approach. They next time you're meeting with someone, do both: ask questions and contribute to the conversation. If someone hears what you say, and, therefore, understands that you can help them, they will be willing to pursue further contact with you. In other words, if you want to sell later, you have to sell initially to get noticed.

Be Culturally Conscious to Sell Yourself and Your Ideas

In certain parts of the world, especially in countries like Ireland, Australia, Thailand, and Denmark, it is frowned upon to stand out in the crowd—you need to align yourself with cultural behaviors before you can attempt to sell yourself and your ideas to other people. That's not to say that in these cultures leaders don't sell continuously—they do—but their idiomatic expressions, slang terms, mannerisms, approaches, methods, and tactics differ from culture to culture depending on what yields a desired outcome.

Consider the challenges facing the president of Dole Asia, James Prideaux, whose responsibilities stretch as far as from New Zealand to Japan to Egypt when it comes to selling continuously. Not only are he and his management challenged with different norms, customs, languages, and time zones, they, like many other multinational, international, and global organizations, are challenged with learning to sell internally, also. In Prideaux's Middle East office alone, there are fifteen employees from seven different countries. In such environments, leadership is always working through the selling methodology while carefully considering how each individual is interpreting leadership's intended messages. Idiomatic expressions, cultural experiences and references, and body language must all be addressed to ensure that what Prideaux and his management team want to impart is what is heard by his staffers.

You have to be careful that the intentions behind your words and actions are actually being interpreted as you would like, otherwise you risk your ability to sell to people. In a personal experience, I luckily learned a lesson about literal translations in a private environment when I misspoke to a group of Latinas after exercising. The workout made me really warm, so I said, "Soy caliente," which literally translates to, "I'm hot." After much laughter, the ladies I was with shared with me that the correct expression is, "Tengo calor," which translates to, "I have heat." Apparently, in my first attempt to describe how I felt, I had inadvertently said, "I'm horny."

By becoming globally aware, you can make sure that you don't misstep and offend the people you're trying to sell to. For instance, the Danish follow the Law of Jante, which encourages humility and group achievement and discourages seeking and talking about one's individual successes. If you were to work with people who value this social moré, you would still sell continuously, but you would have to tailor your messages about your organization's potential to help others in a way that would be palatable to people who value collective achievement. All you have to do in any culturally new environment is do your research ahead of time and incorporate cultural and social preferences into your plans.

Put Your Best Foot Forward

So often when working with leaders and managers, I find myself asking them, "Is it the message or the messenger?" What I'm trying to find out is whether the person has the right ideas but just isn't presenting himself or herself in the best light. While the question can apply to you as the person who is doing the selling, it can also apply to you as the person who is resisting the sale that's being made by someone else to you.

The CEO of an enormous cable-channel conglomerate made a presentation about new programming during a visit to Syracuse University. His presentation was open to the public, so I attended and was shocked at this guy's manner of presentation. He opened with a thirty-minute monotone introduction that he read from a piece of paper. Then he stepped away from the podium to deliver the heart of the presentation, a subject that he was excited about, and became animated and engaging. At the conclusion of that ten-minute segment, he returned to the podium (and the monotone voice) to read his final remarks. Be aware of how you appeal to others.

A corporate manager responsible for 5 million square feet of retail space tells me he has a way to balance his firm's portfolio, but every year after he submits his ideas, senior management turns them down. He complains that no one wants to listen to great ideas. If what he's saying is really the case, then his inability to get buy-in is his fault, not theirs, because there is always a sales approach if you plan well enough.

An insurance executive says that she has a better way to approach managing the projects within her unit, but when she presents her idea to her board of directors, she gets push back from them. She needs to gain buy-in from other units and present a plan of action to the board instead of vague suggestions. Otherwise, she'll always be seen as the person who talks but never says anything.

A corporate nonprofit executive has an issue, comes up with an idea, presents it to her director, and instead of getting support, she's told to "pull her own weight." She needs some WSPs in her back pocket as well as a list of specific items, guidance, resources, etc., from her director. The executive needs to conduct herself like an intellectual peer unless she's satisfied being perceived and treated as a front-line worker bee.

Each of these scenarios can be solved by selling the right image to the right people in the right context. You can probably think of several personal scenarios where you tried to sell your ideas to someone who flatly refused them. Chances are, you didn't engage them well, either in image or content.

The Theoretical Jump

Selling continuously doesn't occur in a vacuum; sometimes you have to set a mental stage for your "audience" in order to get your message to be understood, let alone accepted. That means that even the best-prepared presentations can fall flat if your audience doesn't have enough foundational knowledge about a subject to be able to recognize the value in your message or offerings. And really, it makes sense that there will be times when the presentation of your ideas isn't enough, especially considering how people have different experiences, opinions, and knowledge levels about certain subjects.

Furthermore, how your message is received depends on what you're selling, to whom you're selling, and the environment in which you're selling.

The editor of an international organization was once reading over the facts that I had outlined in the beginning of this book about how the majority of leaders have never received a degree in management and that they learned everything on the job. She questioned the validity of the statistics that I reported, even going as far as to say that I was wrong, and challenged me to substantiate my claims. A day or two later, I presented her with pages of research to support my statements, but I could tell that she still hadn't come around. During the next call I had with her about a week later, she blurted out, "I've been looking at CEO lists, and I'm seeing exactly what you said. It's amazing how many leaders don't have degrees." For the next 30 minutes, we discussed the stats.

But what astounded me about her was that when it came to editing the piece that I had written for other readers, she completely eliminated all the supporting evidence that she had needed to convince her of the validity of the claims, as if none of it might matter to the readers, thus robbing other readers from access to the same information that had enabled her to make a theoretical jump and buy into the point I wanted to make.

Here's the secret: the journey that you and other people take to learn something and the theoretical jumps that everyone occasionally takes have to be considered when you're planning how you will sell to others. There will be times when, in order for other people to understand you, they will need to take a mental journey to become aware or knowledgeable in order to even consider what you're offering to them. It is a mistake to believe that you can cut out steps. Next time you're about to think about selling, remember that often the buyer is like you and needs to take the journey.

The Assumed Buyer May Not Be Your True Buyer

It is too easy to make false assumptions about people that could sabotage your ability to sell to them successfully. Since you can't always be sure whether the person next to you is a potential buyer, it's probably a good rule of thumb to consider anyone around you to be a possibility.

If you've ever seen the movie *Pretty Woman*,[178] you are likely to recall a famous scene in which Julia Roberts' character, Vivian, has been tasked with finding some new clothing for a dinner engagement with billionaire industrialist Edward Lewis, played by Richard Gere, who has hired the young woman as his escort. When Vivian, clad in her usual prostitute-like digs, enters an upscale Beverly Hills boutique in search of dinner attire, the shopkeepers are condescending and won't sell to her. Edward discovers that Vivian has been disrespected, so he takes her shopping at another boutique and spends a fortune on new designer outfits. Later, when Vivian strolls past the original boutique dressed in expensive clothing and carrying a lot of shopping bags bearing the names of the boutique's competitors, she glimpses the saleswomen who humiliated her and brought her to tears. That's when the following dialogue takes place:

> *Vivian, smartly dressed and carrying many bags, stops in at yesterday's clothing store.*
>
> **Vivian:** "Do you remember me?"
>
> **Salesperson:** "No, I'm sorry."
>
> **Vivian:** "I was in here yesterday. You wouldn't wait on me?"
>
> **Salesperson:** "Oh."
>
> **Vivian:** "You work on commission, right?"
>
> **Salesperson:** "Ah, yes."
>
> **Vivian:** "*Big* mistake. Big. Huge! *(Turns away.)* I have to go shopping now!"

You never know where your next opportunity to sell will arise, so consider everyone a possible prospect. In days gone by, there was a dress code that used to more clearly separate people, but today's casual work environments can be misleading, and the Silicon Valley multimillionaire isn't necessarily the dapper guy in the Ferrari, she's the dressed-down lady in the Prius. The person sitting in first class on your next flight may be using his brother's mileage points, while the person seated in row 14 may own four thriving businesses.

Don't be misled by appearances. Realize there are very unique cultural behaviors that may make you think you know who you're looking at, but that guy next to you may be the one person in your life that can make all the difference in your future.

Don't Take Your People for Granted

Leaders often forget to sell to the one group of people they rely on most: their internal staffers. Yet, you have to convince your managers and frontliners that they should stick with you rather than go to another leader. Even if they're just showing up for the paycheck, if you don't win them over, you risk losing some of your best talent. In 1956, Dorothy Carnegie (wife of famed *How to Win Friends and Influence People* author Dale Carnegie), advised in her book *Don't Grow Old . . . Grow Up!*[179] that if you want to keep a spouse happy, give them an abundance of gratitude and express it frequently. Surely, the recipe for keeping people happy involves the entire GPP package, but I'd say that a dose of appreciation goes a long way, too.

Linda Heasley, CEO of national clothing retailer The Limited says, "I believe that my associates can work anywhere they want. My job is to re-recruit them every day and give them a reason to choose to work for us and for me as opposed to anybody else."[180]

Sometimes re-recruiting, leading, and supporting others must be done face to face, and at other times it can be done through different channels.

As a leader you must understand that your job is to make sure your organization is *the* place to work—it's a work environment people enjoy or maybe the pay is so high that people would love to work for you. Fire departments have volunteers who love the role. I used to do protective security at concerts, and I can tell you the team I worked with did not do the work for the pay. They did it because it was fun.

Within the Cornerstones for Engaging Others, your options to sell through behavior, oratory skills, written skills, and interpersonal skills are nearly endless. With a little thought and a degree of dedication, you can improve your ability to sell to the many different types of people you encounter each day.

■ ■ ■

Selling continuously is one of the twelve ET leadership activities that you perform every day of your life. From the time you wake up in the morning and select the clothing you will wear to the end of your evening when you take a last glance at the priorities you've scheduled for tomorrow before turning out your light, you are making decisions about selling yourself, your ideas, your organization, and perhaps your products and services to a wide range of people.

Despite the numerous situations you constantly experience that require you to sell, there's a good chance you've never taken a sales course. And if you think about it, even colleges and universities don't offer degrees in sales, which is a pretty astounding fact given the immense role that selling plays in a leader's success.

It's especially important to understand as you assess the differences between leadership selling and salesperson selling that your audience comprises a wider range of people and groups, and that your approach to selling continuously is devised at 50,000 feet. This elevated perspective allows you to integrate this activity with the other eleven ET activities, giving you the ability to create organizational-wide WSPs that become self-selling mechanisms, too.

As you exit this chapter, you add several new tools and concepts to your ET toolkit that will help you perform this activity and all other ET activities easier and more effectively. Remember that as you become more proficient as an Enterprise Thinker, you can combine the tools from selling continuously with all your other tools to improve your ability to win over internal and external stakeholders, the media and public at large, your family and friends, and any other person or group who can advance your personal and career aspirations.

CATEGORY 4:
[FORECASTING]

Forecasting
Forecasting the Future

Performing
Leading the Charge
Empowering Others
Innovating Everywhere
Selling Continuously

Learning
Acquiring New Knowledge
Enhancing Global Awareness
Watching Competition

Strategizing
Developing Plans
Creating New Products & Services
Establishing Alliances
Leveraging Technology

WE HAD JUST FINISHED LUNCH when one of my colleagues, an executive of a $100 million global consulting firm said, "We never thought we could teach forecasting to our clients, yet in twenty minutes, you showed me that not only is it possible, it is very doable once you have the right tools." Perhaps as a person who leads other people, you have not only felt somewhat challenged to do any type of forecasting beyond calculations involving a spreadsheet and some statistical data, but you haven't even been sure how to really forecast. Don't worry, you're not alone. Furthermore, if you've been under the impression that forecasting is something that only strategists, governments, and scientists do, or that it's just a numbers game for executives in large companies, you're about to be pleasantly surprised. Forecasting is for everyone. It's an essential leadership activity—one that can be performed with or without numbers—and it enjoys a two-way relationship with all other ET activities so that enhancing your performance as a forecaster improves all activities' outcomes and vice versa.

Just as you have done throughout this book, in this chapter you will continue to accumulate tools that will enable you to make better decisions in the present so that your career and your organization gain optimal outcomes in the future. You will learn how to improve your all-around performance as a leader and how to make informed decisions that will stand the test of time and forge a much better future for yourself, the people in your life, and your organization.

FORECASTING THE FUTURE

THE SPEAKER AT THE PODIUM announced the ten-minute break to his audience of 1,000 or so retailers and exited the stage. The venue was in Colombia, South America. I was slated to speak to the same group later that day, but at this time, I blended in and appeared to be another retailer attending the conference. (Oftentimes, I like to sit in on presentations to hear what other speakers are presenting and how the audience is responding to be sure that my presentation addresses participants' most current and pressing challenges.) I stood up to stretch my legs as three managers of big-box home-improvement stores who were seated behind me started talking about how they didn't get much out of the presentation, because, "It's impossible to plan for the future." I guess the reason for their comments were that several of the speakers had asked the audience to "think about the future," to "be prepared for the future," and to "consider the future." I couldn't help but ask one of the men, "How do *you* plan for the future?"

"I don't have time for that, I'm so busy handling everything else," answered one of the three who each managed just over 200 employees. "When I try to look into the future, I can't plan any further than a month at a time." Moments later, he added that to plan a quarter of a year in advance was impossible in his line of work.

Mind you, these men didn't yet know that I would be presenting later on, so we were chatting as retailing peers. I knew that he could look much farther into the future than one month—even farther than one year; he'd just never learned the tools to do so. When people talk about "the future," they put the topic into one massive outlook without knowing how to approach it.

My Macro Tactic would quickly show him and his colleagues that they could *see* and *predict* the future. After all, he was in retail, an industry of predictable annual cycles and seasons: the Christmas holiday season, the spring and summer landscaping seasons, etc. I decided to try something to help him by changing the subject very slightly, because I knew that in order to help him understand this next concept, I would have to slowly pull down some of his mental barriers.

"Do you have children?" I asked.

"Yes, three sons, (ages) 7, 4, and 1."

"When you learned that your wife was pregnant with your first child, did you think about what it would be like to be a father? Did you start planning for the arrival of your new baby—setting up a nursery, selecting a pediatrician?"

"Sure. We had the whole baby shower thing and got the house ready."

"And when your son was born, did you begin to imagine where he would attend elementary school and whether he would attend college one day? Maybe you pictured him as an adolescent, and you even thought about how he would one day marry and have children and grandchildren of his own."

"Yeah, I guess I did. You know, you can't help but think about how their life is going to be."

"So what you're telling me is that you were able to think up to 50 years into the future about your child, but you can't think more than one month into the future of your business?"

As a smile crept across his face, I knew that he understood the connection. He probably *could* extend his thinking forward beyond a single month at a time. When you look into the future, you obviously can't predict every detail, but you can extend your thinking forward much farther than you believe you can. For example, this man might not have known exactly which school his children would one day go to. Some details come into view as you approach certain time frames. But he realized that by having a vision deeper into the future, he could make better decisions today.

By removing two barriers that had previously stood in his way, he would be able to translate the skill of forecasting from his personal life to his professional one. Namely, both of the barriers— being bogged down in the day to day, which kept him focused on the present, and having never been taught how to forecast—would require him to gain new thinking tools.

I told him that I would be presenting later in the day, that I would be giving him and his fellow retailers the forecasting tools to extend their thinking into the future and that I would show them how to use the tools. And that's exactly what I'm going to do for you in this chapter.

The underlying premise of forecasting the future is to learn concepts and tools that enable you to bring into conscious view the vast number of solutions that already surround you. When you complete this chapter, your vision will extend farther into the future than it does today, and you will be able to use that forward focus to make a difference in all areas of your life.

The Art and Science of Forecasting

The decisions you make today create your organization's future. So it makes sense that your ability to anticipate tomorrow's challenges and opportunities will directly impact how well you strategize today and that in turn will determine your organization's preparedness to operate and compete in the months and years ahead.

Right now, look at your entire organization—its operations, products, services, staff members, cash flow, assets, and relationships with stakeholders and allies. Currently, each of these areas is either thriving or struggling based on decisions that you or your colleagues made in the past. An underlying concept of forecasting is:

You are where you are today based upon decisions you've made in the past.

It's important that you understand how this concept affects your career and your organization, because, as I say to so many leaders, the challenges you face today are most likely the result of some leader's decision a month ago, a year ago, or a decade ago. Although you may think you already realize this fact, I've found that once people truly come to see their current challenges and opportunities as products of past decision making, they become more interested in how to forecast so that their current decisions have the greatest chance of producing excellent opportunities in the future.

So as you engage in Cyclonic Thinking and you develop plans, try to imagine what your organization will become five or ten years from now should its decision makers continue making similar decisions. Even if you like what you see in your mind's eye, you can probably admit that there's room for improvement. Now it's only a matter of having the right thinking tools to do better.

We've talked a lot about good decision making coming from the top down. While the 50,000-foot perspective is an essential component for good decision making, it doesn't stretch your thinking very far into the future. For that, you need forecasting, an activity that informs your decision making, launches your thinking forward, and empowers you to make the types of anticipatory decisions that secure your organization's stronghold in its future, not just its present. And like all the other activities of ET, you perform this activity every day, throughout each day.

Forecasting is not guesswork. It's a blend of both art and science. While you have to be creative and innovative, you also have to make your decisions based on data, observations, knowledge, and facts if those decisions are to have long-term power.

In essence, forecasting will enhance your decision making the way that high-beam headlights enhance your nighttime-driving vision. When you switch your headlights from low to high beam, you immediately see farther into the distance and you identify the sharp curves, bumps in the road, and other would-be surprises ahead of you. High beams also widen your vision horizontally, illuminating objects such as pedestrians and animals on the sides of the road sooner. Having better information and more time to decide how you will handle what's coming at you puts you in an advantageous position both on the road and within your organzation.

Living Mentally in the Future

Already, you look into the future every day. You forecast hours, days, weeks, months, and years into the future. Each time you search for an answer to a challenge and you ask yourself a "what-if" question, you're playing out a future-focused scenario in your mind. What if I can secure the funding for the equipment this month instead of waiting until next quarter? What if I consolidate two work crews on the larger job's site tomorrow and wrap up work there four days early? You may be figuring out human resource needs, identifying capital market changes, anticipating troop movements, calculating where the next hurricane or disease may strike, or anticipating next week's payroll.

A passage in the book *McDonald's: Behind the Arches*[181] describes how the forward-thinking solution to the company's cash-flow challenges was derived by an accountant named Gerry Newman during McDonald's early years. After calculating that there would not be enough funds to cover payroll at the end of the week, Martino changed paycheck distribution to a biweekly schedule and kept McDonald's running. Whether you're forecasting about tomorrow or about twenty years from now, this type of mental modeling is one of the ways that you "live mentally in the future."

Your organization, career, and personal life are all greatly impacted by your ability to live mentally in the future, yet, if you were to estimate how much time you spend doing so compared with focusing on present issues or past experiences, where would you say you spend the majority of your mental time?

The Forecasting Orientation diagram (Figure 14.1) is a visual representation of three types of leadership thinking—Retro, Current, and Forward—that correspond to a leader's focus on the past, present, and future respectively.

Forecasting Orientation

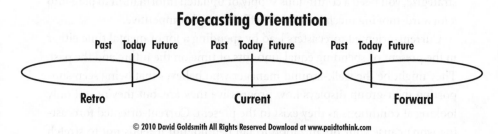

Figure 14.1—Forecasting Orientation

Most leaders will admit that they aren't sure how to forecast accurately and don't believe they can stretch their thinking as far into the future as they probably should. When they see this diagram, the majority of them identify their ways of thinking as somewhere between the Retro and Current orientations, because they tend to live mentally in the present and the past. You might associate with their tendencies if you're apt to make statements like, "It's impossible to plan 60% of my day, because my industry is so unique that I can only realistically schedule 10% of my days in advance." (As an evolving Enterprise Thinker, you already know that no industry or sector is too "unique" for ET tools.) Ideally, you want to live in the Forward Orientation, but it takes extra effort to stay there, because the future is always moving, which requires you to continually think, read, learn, listen, model, and so on to advance your thinking.

Retro-oriented forecasters are leaders who spend more mental time in the past than in the present or future. They might believe they are looking forward when they say, "We need to review our stats," but they're only looking at information from the past and trying to guess what the stats mean for tomorrow. When they don't innovate, update operationally, or bring new products to market, they are not leaping out of the past. Some leaders' thinking is so entrenched in the past that even when they are given a proven way of, say, increasing productivity by 40%, they will insist that the old way is better. If you are a Retro-oriented forecaster, you find yourself holding onto old ways of thinking, saying, "We tried it that way in the past and it doesn't work." As I've said before, you can't solve tomorrow's challenges with yesterday's thinking. A Retro-oriented perspective puts your group or organization behind others, in a position of playing catch-up. It hinders your organization from offering anything more than me-too products and forces your people to function with outdated equipment and technologies. Although you shouldn't discount the importance of reviewing historical successes and failures when you strategize, you need a continuous supply of updated information to plug into a forward-moving mechanism to be efficient and competitive.

Current-oriented forecasters lead by spending a lot of mental time either in the present or spending equal amounts of time on the future and the past. They might be the walk-around manager who believes that being seen supporting their group displays how progressive they are, but they're still only looking at conditions as they exist in the present. Current-oriented forecasting won't cause your organization to fall behind, but it tends not to stretch your thinking far enough into the future to consider long-term opportunities and challenges, and therefore, won't propel you and your organization forward as advantageously as is possible. For example, if you're a Current-oriented forecaster, other people are likely to consider you to be on top of your game, because you can still make good decisions about which projects to develop, but those projects aren't likely to make the big-enough movements to hit aggressive targets or to protect against longer-range challenges. Current-oriented forecasting will not place your organization in its best strategic position long term.

Forward-oriented forecasters spend most of their strategic thinking time living mentally in the future. They click on their mental high beams and look everywhere down the road, seeking their best future options for both their professional and personal lives. If you're a Forward-oriented forecaster, you research data and then extrapolate and calculate to seek new and better techniques, products, services, technologies, and more. You are not primarily focused on the past and the present, like the Retro- and Current-oriented thinkers are. As a Forward-oriented forecaster, you're seeking stats on population shifts, consumer needs, and behavioral changes as ways to live in the mental future and bring a fresh perspective to your decision making.

Note: Be careful not to confuse leadership's Forward-oriented forecasting with projects' future-focused outcomes. For example, if you're working on a project that you expect will preserve the environment for future generations, that project is different than your internal operations, and no matter how much your thinking stretches into the future to protect the environment, if you're not planning, innovating, establishing alliances, implementing technology, etc. as a Forward-oriented forecaster, your decisions could remain seated in Retro- or Current-oriented thinking, and therefore, be so short term that they put your organization at risk of not surviving to see the effects of your project's outcome.

After learning about the three orientations, where do you fall on the orientation scale? Already, your awareness about the three forecasting orientations will begin to evolve your perspective, so if you believe that you're not yet at the Forward Orientation, at least you can begin to make strides to advance your thinking in a direction that focuses you on the future.

You're going to strive to move yourself into the Forward Orientation position using the tools and concepts forthcoming in this chapter. In addition, you will begin to see how you can apply forecasting to all of your other ET activities, which will enhance your performance and create a stronger future for your organization. You can learn to forecast innovatively just as you can forecast for innovation. You can use forecasting knowledge to plan, just as you can utilize planning to forecast more frequently, more precisely, and more effectively. As you learn more about forecasting and its accompanying tools and concepts, your Forward Orientation will advance, also, to the Optimum Forward Orientation, which not only projects your thinking forward, but it also widens the scope of your vision to uncover and make even more opportunities and sustainable decisions than you ever thought possible. The Optimum Forward Orientation is diagrammatically represented in Figure 14.2.

Think back to the analogy of using high beams on a vehicle at night, and envision how your headlights on high beam not only spray the illumination ahead, but also widen your vision on each side of the road so that signs and obstacles become visible earlier. By forecasting an Optimum Forward Orientation, similarly, you see more of what is coming at you sooner and with a greater breadth of information at your disposal than you would have with low-beam light, so that you and your organization stay on the road to Desired Outcome. This new orientation enables you to view opportunities and challenges in improved ways, too. For instance, a Retro- or Current-oriented forecaster might run a cash-flow analysis using the previous quarter's financial data, spending most of their time analyzing what happened and then making a few projections, whereas Forward-oriented forecasters will use some historical data and, in addition, look to gather real-time data about today and then spend the bulk of their time extrapolating farther into the future with it, all the while realizing that what they project must tie to real-life conditions and the ability to actually do what's projected. Then, as Forward-oriented forecasters learn additional tools, the orientation expands to that of the Optimum Forward Orientation, where advanced tools and more data—experiences from the past, awareness and knowledge of the present, and forecasted data about the future—lengthen and broaden the scope of vision and improve decision making even more.

Optimum Forward Orientation

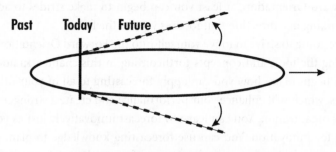

Figure 14.2—Optimum Forward Orientation

With Forward-oriented forecasting, every activity you perform yields better outcomes, because when your decisions are made with an accurate eye on the future, they are more on target with your Desired Outcome, and therefore they have longer-lasting impact on your entire organization. Think of the impact you can have on developing new products and services when your organization is able to set its competitive intelligence in motion earlier. Imagine what kinds of results you can achieve from your plans when they contain specific project-related details that offer insight into government oversight changes happening a year ahead of others in the industry, enabling you to progress your organization ahead faster than it would have progressed otherwise. Consider how the arsenal of information at your disposal for establishing alliances can help you select allies that are not only useful for your current needs but will help leverage patents currently under development months or years into your future, too. These are only a few examples of how the Optimum Forward Orientation improves leaders' ability to perform all ET activities, even if the outcomes improve only by a nose!

When you optimize your forecasting orientation, opportunities and advantages increase in number while anxiety or firefighting diminishes, because you are prepared to address any reality you foresee in the future.

Alternately, as your forecasting orientation regresses toward the past, your focus slips into that rear-view mirror thinking, and once-available opportunities and advantages dwindle. Keep in mind that you need to work to achieve and maintain an optimal forecasting orientation. Think of it like losing weight and keeping it off; once you get to your optimal condition, the only way to maintain it is with sustained effort. Forecasting is a continual activity.

Forecasting Tools

People can become confused about what forecasting is and how to do it, so a good rule of thumb is to think of a good forecaster as more like a meteorologist than a wizard looking into a magic ball. A meteorologist uses tools that combine knowledge, theories, technologies, patterns, and so on, to predict future weather conditions with some degree of accuracy.

In contrast is the pseudo-futurist who doesn't use these types of tools to gain a precise prediction. In fact, anyone can play the pseudo-futurist by looking out their window on a cloudy morning and "predicting" that they might need an umbrella that day. It doesn't take much skill to deduce rainy conditions when you look at the sky and see a dark wave of gray clouds moving in. Some go as far as to wait for rain sprinkles to hit the pavement before announcing their "prediction."

But the meteorologist, a more credible (albeit not perfect) source of forecasting information, can't take the liberty of repackaging current or retro weather conditions and presenting them as tomorrow's or next week's forecasts. She needs real substance behind her forecasts so that we can plan next week's road trip, decide whether to rent a tent for next weekend's barbeque, or board up our windows and evacuate before a hurricane hits. You provide more value as a leader when your decisions are made based on some degree of forecasting.

Forecasting tools work in conjunction with all of the other ET activities and their corresponding tools to really pack a punch no matter what you're trying to accomplish.

One of the most exciting changes you will experience from becoming a better forecaster is the ability to discern the credibility of forecasts and reports from the outside world. For example, there will be times when you hear something in the media or at a conference that may contradict what your own forecasts are telling you. In some instances, you will find these reports to be useful "compasses" that awaken your awareness to factors that you hadn't considered in your own forecasts—I caution you against abandoning your forecasts without further investigation—although at other times, you will identify so-called experts as less accurate than they may have appeared before you learned your new tools.

When you are a better forecaster, you will catch those people who label themselves as futurists but who do not really forecast the future in the act of pseudo-forecasting. These are the people who learn about events that are in the budding stages of development or that have already happened (but that are unknown by the general public) and then either report on or repackage those events in speeches, white papers, articles, newsletters, blogs, etc., as if they're going to occur in the future. The great thing about seeing these falsities early on is that they won't poison your planning or derail your plans, because you will have the tools to look past them and stay focused on the road your organization needs to take to reach its Desired Outcome.

In addition, when you detect these types of people, remind yourself that you are just as capable, if not more so, of forecasting on your own by using your ET tools and incorporating them into your daily activities. You already know how to look at information closely, connect the dots, and incorporate your new knowledge into your strategizing.

Cycles, Trends, and Patterns

Cycles, Trends, and Patterns is an ET forecasting tool that directs your focus on indicators of potential future events. Each can be used to extrapolate into future scenarios. If you were to look at just the activities of the Learning category—acquiring awareness and knowledge, becoming globally aware, and watching competition—you would also identify Cycles, Trends, and Patterns that you can feed into your planning activities. As long as you connect the dots between Cycles, Trends, and Patterns with your new awareness and knowledge about the potential future, you are advancing your thinking from Retro and Current orientations to a more Forward-oriented perspective. Therefore, the more you are able to analyze data and identify these three types of indicators, the better your decision making becomes.

Cycles: A cycle is a repeated occurrence that happens over a period of time, usually at regular intervals, as an indicator of future activity. Cycles are recurring and timely events, such as those that take place within political, consumer, biological, natural, and financial markets. We know when election years are approaching. We turn to economists for their ability to predict "bulls" and "bears" based on past cycles. Seasonal cycles tell us when to expect hurricanes or snowfalls, anatomical cycles are the impetus for new pharmaceuticals, and economic cycles impact interest rates and home sales. Biological cycles help leaders plan retirements, understand medical services, underscore research funding, and aid in urban planning.

Trends: A trend is a tendency in a particular direction. Human behavior, clothing preferences, travel, religious attendance, music selection, and a society's shift to new perceived enemies and allies are all trends. Kids under the age of eighteen who live in many industrialized countries have trended toward cell phone and messaging technology in every aspect of their social life: e-mailing their teachers for missed assignments when they're too sick to attend school, watching movies and videos on portable devices, and sending a text in lieu of ringing the doorbell when they arrive at a friend's house. Skirt lengths for women, tie widths for men, UGG boots, bell-bottom jeans, "bob" haircuts, and chunky-heeled shoes are trends in clothing and fashion. Yes, technology can also be trendy, so, too, can be lawn care, beer selection, nightclub attendance, types of watches and types of countertops used in homes, industrial design, chemical usage, breeds of pets, mobile phone brands, games played, and so on.

Patterns: Patterns are repetitive activities, characteristics, or occurrences. You can find patterns in shapes, figures, letters, colors, numbers, and activities in human behavior. The ways in which employees communicate with one another, customers walk a floor, leadership engages with staff, markets fluctuate, geopolitical wars occur, molecules structure themselves, water flows, and diseases infest populations are patterns. When you observe patterns, consider whether they are long or short term, limited or unlimited in scope, repeatable or unique, and so on. Years of consistent human behavior offer very different information than does last year's layoffs, and you must balance the two. You can look for patterns in an office's arrangement of desks, the tiles arranged on the floor, or roadways within a community. All of these patterns might give you indications of future happenings.

The benefit of understanding Cycles, Trends, and Patterns and using this understanding as a tool is that it can help you to be proactive when making decisions, improve your accuracy, decrease costs, increase productivity, and empower a greater number of people. It can boost your ability, too, to sell your ideas. If you say you see a cycle and it's actually a trend, you could make significant investments and be completely wrong. Let's assume you use a lot of petrol in your fleet of trucks. You see a trend in pricing that you interpret to mean the cost of fuel will rise significantly next year, so you lock it in now at a price rate for the next year. Then, throughout the year, you see that prices are dropping to well below the price you prepaid for next year's petrol. You misinterpreted what ended up being a twelve-month cycle as a longer-range trend, and you made a costly error as a result.

You want to assess whether you're facing a cycle, trend, pattern, or combination of them and make decisions based on this starting point. A toy manufacturer who wants to develop the next winning product among "tweens," kids in the eight- to twelve-year-old range, monitors trends in leisure time to discover that this group increasingly prefers technology, music, and fashion over traditional toys of the past. No longer are dolls for tween girls as lucrative. Competitive intelligence data reveals a change in consumer buying patterns, prompting your marketing team to replace billboard ads with an aggressive online campaign. It used to be that "Black Friday" marked the beginning of the Christmas shopping cycle in the United States, but over time, retailers pushed back the start date to the midnight hour of Thanksgiving's close, and now to during Thanksgiving Day. Identifying Cycles, Trends, and Patterns uses the past and present to extrapolate the future.

Forecasting Triggers

When you are forecasting, you must avoid being so myopically or linearly focused on products or aspects of your industry that you don't notice other factors that could impact your organization's future. Forecasting Triggers is a tool, in the form of a list, whose purpose is to force you to think beyond just your typical thoughts about the future and to extrapolate into new frontiers. Forecasting Triggers are intended to wake up your mind and make the invisible visible, so be careful not to select particular triggers solely because they are familiar or interesting to you. Instead, go for triggers that are unexpected, and see where your exploration of them can reveal surprising challenges or opportunities for your organization or its industry.

Depending on your circumstances, you will determine whether it is more advantageous for you to explore Forecasting Triggers on your own or with a group. The instructions for using this tool vary slightly for individuals and groups.

Forecasting Triggers

View these from the perspective of YOU, your ORGANIZATION, your CUSTOMERS/CLIENTS, your COMPETITION, your SUPPLIERS/VENDORS, and the WORLD

Globalism	Emerging markets	Social awareness	Interest & exchange rates	Transportation
Geopolitics	Digital 24/7 lifestyles	Trust	Taxation	Social networks
Climate (global & local)	Robotics	Individualism	Gaming	Customized production
Energy	Relations/Diversity	Social applications	Automation	Economics
Water shortage	Shelter	Technological convergence	Talent	Education
Bio growth	Language	Video	Leadership	Retailing
Aging society	Space exploration/Travel	Communications	Health	Entertainment
Virtual world	Commodities	Nanotechnology	Terrorism/Piracy	Employment
Unretirement	Fashion	Cashless society	Migration	Communications
Work life	Seasons	Weather	Happiness	Thought
Feminism	Generations	Biological factors	Family	Arts
Wealth	Governance	Food	Nature	Marketing
Performance	Nanomedicine	Real estate	Mobile convergence	Forecasting
Research	Bioengineering	Agriculture	Weaponry	Portability
Regulation & oversight	Anti-aging	Transportation	Air & space flight	Emerging markets
Mergers & acquisitions	Urbanism	Sports	Music	Cloud transformation
Branding	Data & big data	Marketing channels	Publishing	Sustainability/Scalability

Using Forecasting Triggers Individually

1. Identify a trigger/select a trigger.
2. Generate your projections about the industry and its future.
3. Once you've identified the future of several triggers, look to connect a series of projections in a manner that may give you insight into your own future.
4. Don't be selective about which markers are important or not, because the world is connected. You must learn to make the connection where there appears to be none and then identify opportunities.
5. Utilize the new insight for future learning and for all areas of ET and record the new insights and information for future reference.

Using Forecasting Triggers in a Group Setting

1. Separate your group into subgroups.
2. Assign a random set of triggers for each group to explore.
3. Have the groups extrapolate into the future about what may happen to the trigger and the impact. Look for Cycles, Trends, and Patterns.
4. Ask the group to share a summary of their thoughts with the other groups.
5. The groups should collectively discuss highlights and new thoughts. You must learn to make the connection where there appears to be none and then identify opportunities.
6. Utilize the new insight for future learning and for all areas of ET and record the new insights and information for future reference.

Figure 14.3—Forecasting Triggers

Exploring Forecasting Triggers Individually

Let's say you're trying to strategize about the future of your group, and you'd like to get that wider headlight view or to force yourself to think differently. Individuals who are exploring Forecasting Triggers on their own can follow five steps:

1. Select at least one trigger of your choice, or better yet, randomly select an item on the list, perhaps the first that you see. This will force you to think outside of your normal frame of reference.

2. With the selected trigger, make some projections about what you think the future of the trigger will be. You can think about how it will affect all kinds of areas like countries, individuals, animals, oceans, etc. Think about the new technologies that may be in place, how the products will change, or how people will behave. You may want to do some quick research if you're unfamiliar with the trigger and explore how it might be impacted by weather, robotics, or urbanism so that you're not making assumptions but, instead, are collecting facts.

3. Connect the dots between your trigger and your organization, between two or more triggers, and/or among triggers and the factors that will influence them in the future.

4. Identify potential opportunities by looking at your triggers, the research you've done about them, and the connecting of the dots. You don't have to make determinations that some triggers are more important than others, because you don't want to limit your possibilities.

5. Record your new insights for future use, or immediately use them to improve your performance of ET activities.

Exploring Forecasting Triggers in a Group Setting

A group of people who are exploring Forecasting Triggers can initially work in small groups and follow similar steps to those for individuals. However, working with a group involves more steps, because you want members of the group/s to exchange information and provide input that can generate new ideas and knowledge.

1. If your group has enough people to substantiate smaller conversations that will enable everyone to participate, separate your group into subgroups; otherwise, work as a single group.

2. Assign a random set of triggers for each group to explore.

3. Ask each group to collect projections about their triggers and to extrapolate future conditions, events, and influences related to their triggers and to your group or organization. Ask questions like, what are the futures of taxation and nanotechnology, and how will they impact our RV manufacturing company? Keep in mind that at first, people may not see any connections at all, so wait and let them think.

4. Bring the groups together so that they can share a summary of their findings, insights, and thoughts with each other.

5. Encourage the groups to collectively discuss highlights and new thoughts.

6. Record the members' new insights for future use, such as placing them into an Idea Bank (as discussed in Chapter 4) where you collect ideas for new product and service development, selecting technologies or allies, or planning for your next project.

The insights gleaned from these types of exercises can be used by cross-functional decision makers throughout your organization or by you either now or at some point in the future to improve performance of all ET activities. In addition, exercises force individuals to expand their thinking in ways that are different and better than their norm.

Forecasting Triggers in Action

Decision makers use triggers to inform their decision making. The headmaster of a private boarding school faces dwindling enrollment over a three-year span of time. He wants to stop the downward trend by recruiting new students for the upcoming school year and beyond, so he consults his Forecasting Triggers and decides to explore four of them: economics, family, video, and virtual world.

He thinks about how the economy has hurt families financially, how pressure on kids to perform academically has hit all-time highs, and how these two factors are influencing parents' decisions to enroll their children in local schools rather than to send them to boarding schools. He starts to get into the minds of the kids to understand what they like, and he observes how kids enjoy watching TV shows and movies on their computers, how much of children's and teens' leisure time is spent playing in the virtual world of video games, and how kids easily move between traditional communications of face-to-face interaction and digital correspondences like texting and

Skype. He goes on the Internet, picks ups some gaming magazines at his bookstore, meets with IT and administrators of college online programs, and consults with his school's psychologist in an attempt to collect projections about his triggers and a wide range of other factors that could affect his ability to enroll students.

The headmaster wonders how he may be able to develop an innovative approach to education based on the methodology used by the creators of the popular animated children's program *The Magic School Bus*. The TV show, based around the likeable teacher Ms. Frizzle and her small band of curious young students, makes science education fun and engaging. How might the headmaster develop a comprehensive curriculum from the marriage of education, technology, and entertainment to attract students and their parents to his progressive type of school? He realizes that it is plausible, but he would have to be sure that this new product and service fills the gaps left by traditional education and that challenges unique to the demographic are addressed so it will work at the grammar- and high-school levels as effectively as online education has worked for some institutions at the university level.

If you were to think beyond your organization for more information, the potential ways in which the Forecasting Triggers list can help you to forecast is multiplied. You could talk with a colleague or vendor about any of these topics in casual conversation, with or without informing them about the list. You could observe stakeholders, competitors, and prospective consumers as they relate to any of the topic areas. The manner in which you decide to work from the list is best determined by your particular circumstances at the time.

Forecasting the Evolution of Your "Buyers" Options and Preferences

If you came to this chapter with limited forecasting experience, I'm guessing that your perspective of forecasting—specifically what you can forecast and how you can do it—is expanding rather quickly. At this point, I'm going to show you how to forecast the future of your organization's "buyer," a term that might mean retail consumer to you, or, depending on your organization, could be students, citizens, distributors, countries, and so on. For the sake of simplicity, the examples we will use in this section will pertain to the traditional customer, but you can adapt the concepts to fit your definition of buyer.

The better you can forecast buyers' behaviors from watching Cycles, Trends, and Patterns and connecting them to triggers, the more on target and long lasting your decisions will be. And while it would be nice to make forecasts about buyers in general and apply them worldwide, the truth is, despite globalization, certain areas of the world experience these changes at one point in time, while other areas may not experience the same changes until five or twenty years later or may never experience some of the same changes at all. Therefore, what I will share with you are concepts about buyers' evolution to enable you to adapt these concepts as universal tools to your industry or sector, your geographic location, and your current point in time.

The Multi-Dimensional Buyer

If you had grown up in the 1800s and even into the 1900s in the United States, you would have most likely walked down to the corner store, traveled to a market, visited a street vendor, had someone visit your home, or sought the wares of a traveling vendor for many of your purchases. The method you used to purchase your items was simple: a one-way, one-location process. You had to be on site to view a product, negotiate the terms of the sale, and determine if you were going to bring the product home with you or have it delivered later. The progression of time brought with it additional buying options, including catalog sales like those introduced in 1888 when Richard Sears, founder of Sears, Roebuck and Co. distributed a mailer to advertise the sales of watches and jewelry.[182] Then, as different technologies entered certain marketplaces, they were utilized to create yet another access for consumers to buy. Alexander Graham Bell's invention of the telephone in 1876, for example, made phone purchases possible.

Although these advances meant greater conveniences for consumers, they also meant that retailers had to make sure that they were keeping pace, offering the additional access points for their customers to buy, and ensuring that those access points were operating well enough that their conveniences were keeping buyers coming back as loyal customers.

Fast-forward to today. You have a plethora of ways in which you can do business with a retailer: in-store shopping or by phone, fax, e-mail, text, instant messaging, Internet, cell phone, automated purchases, etc. Your preferences for multiple methods of purchasing define you as a new kind of buyer, one I call the Multi-Dimensional Buyer, or MDB.

As an MDB, you expect the retailers you buy from to provide you with stellar service, whether the buying method is face-to-face with a store clerk or it's your cell phone connected flawlessly with a retailer's website. In each case, retailers must provide you with a near-flawless shopping experience, because if they fail you at any one of these access points, you may not come back to them. An online shopping cart that doesn't process your order as expected breaks your trust in the retailer and causes you to jump to another vendor whose shopping cart works the way it's supposed to, right? Sometimes, no matter how well a retailer does its job, you're still going to research prices at the local store and then go home and buy the product via your computer. Your range of choices puts you in greater control than ever before, and you and your fellow shoppers are constantly evolving in ways that keep retailers on their toes.

To be clear, the MDB is not about online versus brick-and-mortar purchasing. At its core, the concept of the Multi-Dimensional Buyer is about constantly evolving buying options and the expectations that go along with them. MDBs expect all touch points to work well, and because there are so many options, these buyers are not very patient or forgiving. So from the perspective of the leader who is selling products, services, ideas, and more to the MDB, how does this change your perspective on how you will meet expectations of your buyers in the future?

Have you ever considered your organization within this context? Would you have ever considered it to be a multidimensional vendor (MDV)? Consider why a buyer may purchase from Amazon over another vendor, even waiting a couple of days for shipping in order to save a few dollars. Could it be that the buyer believes that Amazon "gets" the MDB, which translates to a great buying experience?

When I was younger and I wanted to get a new vehicle, I would drive to a couple of dealerships within a 10-mile radius of my home, talk to salespeople, study their brochures, take a couple of test drives, contact my bank's loan officer for financing options, and finally make a purchase. But that was twenty-five years ago. One of my most recent vehicle purchases was conducted through very different channels. I visited the eBay website, searched photos and descriptions of different options, contacted a banking rep at USAA in Texas 1,500 miles from my home for financing, and bought a Chevy Suburban from Walters Elkland Chevrolet, a dealer in another state. The owner of the dealership delivered the vehicle 130 miles to my driveway, and I never left the seat of my office chair.

I first introduced these concepts of the MDB and the MDV at the 2006 Terry Lundgren Retail Conference in Tucson, Arizona, after having researched buying Cycles, Trends, and Patterns from a variety of industries, not just retailing, to forecast some next moves by this modern-day buyer. My desired outcome was to arm audience members with a concept tool that would pull their thinking out of the typical cross between Retro and Current orientations and move it into the Forward-oriented perspective regarding buyers and also shift thinking toward future upstream and downstream channels, buyer, behaviors, the GPP for staffing, and needs for improved systems and structures in anticipation for tomorrow's opportunities and challenges. Since this was a primarily American audience, the forecasts were geared for the American market, although the concepts, as I mentioned, can be adapted for any region in the world.

To expand your thinking, consider how the MDB evolution has impacted buying preferences in all industries, even sectors, in recent years. While people may use the services of a real estate agent to find a new home, they also can play a more active role in the selection process by using search engine filters to narrow their list based on specific criteria, and they may select the real estate agent based upon how well their organization's tools work. It used to be that when someone wanted to secure a new job, they would look up ads in their newspaper's classified section and make calls. Now, these same people can "shop" for their next potential employer by reviewing ratings from past employees, scouring social sites, reviewing employers' histories, and connecting with existing employees on blogs, Twitter, or via e-mail. In tomorrow's world, you'll expect to see pre-interviews done via video so that job hunters can filter out potential job opportunities before spending time traveling to each location.

Figure 14.4 illustrates many ways the MDB can touch and be touched by an organization. Notice how there are many more access points today than there were just 30 years ago. When you see a diagrammatic representation of your buyers, you automatically begin to draw conclusions. For example, if today's buyers are accustomed to accessing my organization on their own timetable more so than in the past (remember the days in the United States when you had to get to the bank by 3 p.m. if you wanted spending money for the weekend), how much more impatient might they become in five years, and what do I need to do to ensure that our organization keeps pace with my buyers' expectations tomorrow?

Depending on your organization and its geographic location and reach, these access points and channels are expanding every day. Tomorrow's diagram of the MDB's access points might include augmented reality systems, holographic marketing, or biology impressions. Augmented reality, the overlaying of a computer-generated image onto a real scene, could provide innovative marketing solutions to capture the MDB both

Access Points for the Multi-Dimensional Buyer

Just a sampling of what impacts a Multi-Dimensional Buyer's decisions.
You must do them all correctly. One mistake and they move on.
(Examples include: coupons, discounts, repair history, billing, lighting, smell,
cleanliness, attitude, checkout, online checkout, credit card processing, etc.)

Figure 14.4—Access Points for the Multi-Dimensional Buyer

today and tomorrow. (You have likely seen augmented reality if you've ever watched a televised American football game; that yellow line you as a viewer see "magically" placed onto the field as a yardage marker is augmented reality. It is not visible to the athletes and officials on the field.) Adam Broitman, chief creative strategist for the digital and social media marketing company Something Massive, uses augmented reality in marketing and advertising programs for clients, like one for Red Bull where consumers can link their cell phone to a path of bottlecaps and to the firm's website—as a way of staying ahead of the curve in terms of attracting today's and tomorrow's MDB.[183] Holographic marketing is another innovative way of capturing the attention of the future MDB. An example of holographic marketing might be a 3D display of products that provides potential buyers with a full grasp of a product's usability. In the future, biology impressions that happen when your body gives off a signal (mental or physical) could notify your product's suppliers that you are in need of a particular product, you need a refill, or that you are happy or uncomfortable with a service.

The purpose of the Access Points for the Multi-Dimensional Buyer diagram is not to assess the current access points of your organization's MDBs. It is to give you a visual tool that extends your vision forward to help you forecast future access points.

FORECASTING THE EVOLUTION OF YOUR MULTI-DIMENSIONAL BUYER

Perhaps you never considered your buyers in the context of their access points to your organization before, but it's an important consideration to make when you need to forecast buyers' future needs and your ability to meet them.

If you were to draw a diagram of access points for your organization's Multi-Dimensional Buyer, what would it look like? Keep in mind that if you were to illustrate these points as they appear in the present, you are not yet forecasting. You would need to add on to your diagram your predicted access points, based on anticipated technologies that will become available to you and your buyers, evolutions that are projected to occur in your industry/sector and complementary industries/sectors, experts' forecasts that appear in trade journal articles or at conferences, and more. Gather this type of information and see how many new access points you need to add to your diagram.

You want to consider all aspects of your organization, from its internal operations to your Forecasted Winners, as you customize the diagram for your purposes. For example, a North American bookseller is very likely to draw an online-sales access point as a current access point, but a South American bookseller is more likely to draw an online-sales access point as a possible forecasted point, because buyers in the South American market don't tend to buy their books online at this time.

The conclusions you draw when you finish drawing your organization's rendition of this diagram can be plugged into your CST Model for improving your plans. This simple addition to planning activities helps to extend your vision farther into the future, ensuring that you are not basing tomorrow's decisions on yesterday's conditions, but making decisions that have long-lasting positive outcomes.

Forecasting the Evolution of Your Industry or Sector

Even if you've never thought that you could forecast the future of an entire industry or sector, there are some rather simple considerations you can make that will enable you to do so. And even if you're not sure you can come up with a 100% accurate projections, simply going through the exercise of forecasting will open your eyes to potential opportunities and challenges that are coming your way.

Certainly, your strategies must evolve in response to or in advance of changes in your marketplace. But ideally, you want to evolve any Strategy at the beginning of the changes, or even better, effect the changes yourself. There are numerous subject areas you can study that are relevant to your industry or sector.

Let's walk through a simple example related to the banking industry to see how you might adapt it to your own forecasting activities. If we were to forecast the preferences of the banking customer twenty years from now to get a feel for the types of decisions we should be making today, we would look at current customers' definitions of good customer service and project those definitions into the future. Here are the responses we might realistically expect to get from customers in three age groups:

- Seniors age 60+: Preferences are for high personal contact services like face-to-face interaction with tellers and customer service reps. They like to enter their bank to make deposits and withdrawals with tellers.
- Mid-range ages 40–60: Preferences are for a combination of face-to-face contact and some digital services like ATMs and online bill pay services.
- Young patrons age 20–40: Preferences are for primarily digital and 24-hour services with little value placed on face-to-face interaction. They also like phone apps and online services that are quick and easy to access.

Considering the different preferences, expectations, and behaviors of the three types of groups is essential for moving your banking institution forward. You not only address current buying Cycles, Trends, and Patterns of patrons, you forecast with some certainty what these groups and the upcoming groups behind them generationally will do and will want in ten years, twenty years, and beyond.

Consumer Preference Over Time

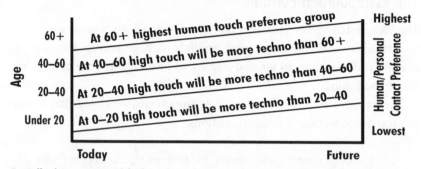

Typically, the perception of high touch is relative to one's age. In 2012, a 60-year-old will consider high touch to involve more human contact than that of someone under age 20 who would consider high touch to be more technology driven, such as online banking. Then again, a person closer to age 20 will be more likely to prefer more human contact than someone 10 years their junior.

Figure 14.5—Consumer Preference Over Time

Looking out ten and twenty years into the future, you can see the trend's direction, but you also know that if you were to abruptly shift your model to the strictly self-service model preferred by the ages twenty-to-forty demographic, you would exclude your over-sixty patrons. In addition, you and the leaders who create plans must account for exceptions to the model, where some customers in the over-sixty category mimic behaviors of those in the twenty-to-forty category.

Can you see already how these considerations can impact your decision making today? This is the beauty of forecasting, and as you're seeing, forecasting isn't necessarily a difficult activity to perform once you have the tools and concepts to get started.

Notice how many dots were connected in this one-example exercise, and how many activities and tools from every ET category came into play:

- Strategizing category: planning, new product development, alliances, technology
- Learning category: awareness, global, competition
- Performing category: leading, empowering, innovating, selling

Leadership has to blend all the elements of ET together to forecast for their organizations, in the same way you just saw for this single forecast within the banking industry.

The Extrapolation Formula

The Extrapolation Formula is a basic tool that allows you to see future opportunities and challenges from multiple vantage points. You can use it alone and in groups to forecast one set of future conditions or multiple future conditions.

The Extrapolation Formula has three components, which together add up to a forecasted picture of future conditions:

Current Conditions + Cycles, Trends, and Patterns + Technology = Future

This is how it works: First assess some current conditions, and try to get a more complete picture of your situation by looking beyond the simple in-your-face circumstances you encounter. You can use the tools offered in the Learning category (Chapters 7–9) or with innovating everywhere (Chapter 12) and use the Outside-In, Inside-Out, Above, and Below trigger outlined in Chapter 12 to be as comprehensive as possible in collecting information.

Next, try to identify as many Cycles, Trends, and Patterns as you and your group can think of that may be happening using the Forecasting Triggers. Be exhaustive in your approach, because a push to go beyond the common and well-known Cycles, Trends, and Patterns will yield valuable information that you can use to inform your decision making and make truly transformational changes.

Lastly, add the technology component to your thinking by considering how the future would play out if you leveraged your ideas. Then take this information and write a few new rules to govern your organization, to create new products or services, to establish alliances, to lead differently, to empower others, and so on. While the Extrapolation Formula appears somewhat obvious at first glance, its application can drive very deep and impactful thinking if you use the formula to its fullest potential.

Here's an example of how decision makers put their country at a certain advantage by making a decision based on the forecasted conditions using the Extrapolation Formula, rather than trying to plan for tomorrow using yesterday's rules and conditions. Malaysia has a history of water shortages, and its leadership recognized that with increased population growth comes increased water shortages. Hyflux, an Asian integrated water management and environmental-services company, built a desalination facility to transform ocean water into clean water for human use. Let's plug this example into the Extrapolation Formula:

- Malaysia's current condition was its water shortage.
- Decision makers combined the current condition with its cycles/trends/patterns of a growing population to see that the shortage would only continue to worsen.
- By searching technologies that could influence change in conditions, leadership decided to use desalination plants to solve their challenge.
- The future for Malaysia is less likely to include a water shortage, despite having a larger population than it has today.

Now that you've seen how the Extrapolation Formula works, you may be thinking that it's not so new and that you'd take these measures anyway. Whether or not that's actually the case, would you also be likely to teach this formula to others if you hadn't learned about the tool? The tool is the fulcrum that helps you lead differently. Without it, you'd be saying, "Let's think about our options."

Forecasting is an activity that has the potential to radically transform decision making within your organization, and the better able you are to transfer your forecasting tools, like the Extrapolation Formula, to others, the better able you are to expand the potential of your entire organization.

There are countless ways that the Extrapolation Formula can be integrated into other ET activities to forecast future conditions that will inform your decision making. You can look at sales figures or the number of people being served; cash flow; resource reserves like inventory, availability, and skill levels of current labor; competition; big data such as the information supplied from Facebook or Twitter; etc. What you're going to be looking at is how the entire package can create a future that is different and more accurate than the circumstances you see in the present and that you previously anticipated for the future.

Activity-Based Forecasting

Considering how complex forecasting can appear to be at times, one of the ways you can gather more specific information is to break down your projects, processes, and initiatives into separate components, then predict the future of each component individually. In this next section, you will learn a tool called Activity-Based Forecasting that will enable you to get specific in your forecasts by focusing your thinking on detailed predictions that you can later use as you engage in developing plans.

Activity-Based Forecasting is an ET tool that projects your mental vision of your organization, products, or plans farther into the future than most leaders believe is possible. Essentially, it works in two parts and delivers two types of information to you.

- **Part 1 – Determine the minimum amount of time you must look into the future:** Select a topic like your organization, product life cycle, or plan. Then break the topic into its individual activities, assign a time frame to each, and then string them together in chronological order so that you can see where the cycle of activities ends on the timeline extending into the future.
- **Part 2 – Create a forecast:** As you examine the various activities, you make projections about each activity to determine how the topic might play out in the future.

Now you might say once again, "I can do all of that in my head. It's a no-brainer," but be careful about jumping too quickly to that conclusion. Activity-Based Forecasting actually delivers to you a more comprehensive picture of the packaged activities than most leaders initially anticipate seeing. Once you understand the origins of your new ET tool and read some examples about how others have used it, you will better understand this point.

Part 1 – Determine the minimum amount of time you must look into the future

I was out to dinner with a mid-level manager one evening in New York City when our conversation turned to forecasting. He told me that in his industry, a decision maker can't forecast more than a year or possibly two years into the future. Although I knew better, I let the comment slide, because I was hungry and didn't want to delay my meal with a debate about forecasting. Once we had been seated and had a chance to order our meals, the conversation resumed. He said that his sales cycle was between six and twelve months. Realizing that he could be making some major missteps if he continued to make decisions based on these false assumptions regarding timing, I decided to walk him through the process that has since evolved into Activity-Based Forecasting.

I first asked him, "How long is your production/development cycle: the time it takes to make your product once an order is committed to by a buyer?" To this, he responded, "Twelve to twenty-four months." Already, we had jumped to his original forecasting time frame of twenty-four months; soon, we would exceed that span as we looked at additional activities.

"How long is the installation?"

"Anywhere from six months to a year and a half," he answered.

I followed with, "Do you support the product after a consumer has purchased it? And do you offer warranties for your product for an extended period of time?"

Yes, and yes, they offered a two-year support package and an additional year of warranty protection.

All in all, if you added up his product's life cycle from start to finish, you would have to include the following activities:

1. Sales Cycle = 24 months
2. Production/Development Cycle = 12–24 months
3. Installation = 6–18 months
4. Tech Support = 24 months
5. Warranty Coverage = 12 months

Total Life Cycle = 78–102 months

Adding up the individual activities brought this decision maker out of his myopically focused two-year view and showed him that he could actually project his thinking six and a half to eight and a half years into the future.

That meant that he and his team had to be anticipating staffing needs, capital, insurance coverage, equipment, and a host of other components for each contract over the course of an eight and a half-year span of time, yet he was only looking two years into the distance.

I realized that he had only been thinking about the technology, nothing more. But forecasting is not just about technology; it's about looking into the future in all areas of your operation, from warehousing to sourcing natural resources. Leaders need to see the 50,000-foot view and take in everything when they forecast.

When leaders at the global forest-product firm Weyerhaeuser Company need to forecast tomorrow's ways of utilizing trees to create opportunities and solve challenges for people and organizations around the world, they are not just looking at the technology used to cut down trees. Decision makers at all twenty of its businesses need to consider paper needs, recycling, lumber trends, weather influences, and more as they make long-term decisions for their organizations. They can't just look at what type of buildings are being made today or what kinds of real estate is selling well in today's economic climate. They have to forecast the state of these conditions thirty years or more from now because to remain a sustainable organization and to create sustainable forests, where trees take decades to grow, one needs to be thinking this far into the future.

Part 2 – Create a forecast

While Activity-Based Forecasting can be used as a means of determining how far you can see into the future, it can also give you a view into the future so that you can make more accurate forecasts. When you see forecasting as a compilation of the activities making up your processes, products, projects, etc., rather than as one massive and daunting question mark, you can more easily understand why past attempts to get your people (or yourself) to visualize the future produced more blank stares than answers.

Instead of addressing an entire subject matter all at once, which is difficult to do even for the experts, Activity-Based Forecasting helps you to break the subject into its individual activities, assign a time frame to each, put them back together to get a long-range picture, and then to forecast each activity's projected opportunities and challenges. Activities in Activity-Based Forecasting could include selling cycles, production cycles, technical support subscriptions, warranty periods, financing contracts, etc. Forecasting isn't as daunting when you break it down into smaller parts. Here are some simple steps to follow to do your own Activity-Based Forecasting:

1. **List the "activities" of your project or initiative.** Begin by making a list of the components within your project or initiative; these components are called activities, although they are obviously different from your ET activities. Your project can be the mapping out of your career, operational improvements, or an entire process from design through launch.

   Example thread:

   If you're a nonfiction writer and you want to use Activity-Based Forecasting to learn of challenges and opportunities that are likely to impact your writing career over the next twenty years, you could break your writing projects into the following activities:

outlining	examples	references
writing	editing	printing
story development	layout	distribution

2. **Predict the future of each activity.** After you have made this list (by yourself or with the help of other people) of activities, bring together the other people who will help you with your forecasting, and as a group, either discuss the future of each activity or, if your activities require more

in-depth investigation, assign individual activities to different members of your group. In instances where your group will disband and meet at a later date to discuss predictions for each activity, give everyone a deadline for their research and regroup for the following step in the Activity-Based Forecasting process.

Example thread:

As a writer who works alone, you may research your activities alone or you may reach out to experts that you know who can help you with your predictions. For instance, an informed person may have already told you that new, automatic outline-building software will help you create outlines faster and more accurately than you do now, and an article in your most recent trade journal might have provided you with additional forecasting information that will affect your decisions about your future. How might the following forecasted information begin to change how you are planning your future projects?

SAMPLE OF CHARTING ACTIVITY-BASED FORECASTING

Activities	Forecast future of activity
Outlining	auto outline builder, contract outline writers, statistical reader satisfaction, title suggestive software, voice recognition/hands free
Writing	voice conversion to improved writing, language conversion, reading age leveler, transition writing software, real-time suggestive software
Story Development	topic slant, supporting evidence aggregator, ego removal, character development, idea recommendation, excitement-building software
Examples	instant example creation, story-finding software, video-to-text search, crowdsourcing ideation and writing
Editing	auto editing, phrase-meaning sensor, plagiarism stopper, auto layout software, rewording for stronger content, auto add content
Layout	auto layout graphics insertion tools, intelligent layout selection, crowdsourced design, font recommendation specific to readership
References	citation builder through linkage, auto reference tool for voice/print, auto updating/organic reference lists, artificial intelligence indexing
Printing	desktop conversion to multimedia and multiple format, auto layout software, paper and digital, price quoting for print and digital
Distribution	social distribution, list builder, direct to consumer, opportunity finder, book chapter singles, analysis of self- or commercial publish

Figure 14.6—Sample of Charting Activity-Based Forecasting

3. **Discuss predictions for each activity.** Ask group members to share the details of their predictions and encourage everyone else to provide positive suggestions. One reason that I suggested working in a group is because you never know what tidbit of information could become a value to forecasting. Someone on staff who has observed a trend in the making or who catches wind of a political event that could potentially impact one or more of the components could help to change the direction of your strategizing and give your decisions lasting power.

The group tasked with reporting on how the sales cycle will change in five years might look at current trends that would suggest changes in purchasing. They might also look at how 3D imagery platforms might improve the way you show your products, and how rapid prototyping may enable small firms to own equipment.

The group charged with bringing in information about product development changes within five years could be looking at time compression with robotics, continued advancement in object-oriented programming, or adhesive technologies for building supplies that will minimize architectural damage in natural disaster zones, and factors like those that could define the way products are developed in years to come. They might show your group how your product will be made smaller and should take half the time to build.

Example thread:

> You can run your findings by people with futuristic points of view, but be careful that you don't rely on the advice of people just because they have a title or experience. This is the exact scenario for Clayton Christensen's innovator's dilemma (first described in Chapter 12), where often those within the industry or sector are so connected to their own future that they can't evoke new ideas for a new reality. For example, your agent, other colleagues, or close associates may initially appear to be knowledgeable, but you really want to consult people who may have Forward-oriented knowledge about your industry or any other industry that could provide you with additional predictions or assist you in assessing the accuracy of the predictions you already have.

4. **Summarize predictions into a comprehensive forecast.** Once you have acquired the individual predictions for each activity, bring them together to form a big-picture view of your project's future. This is information that you can incorporate into the CST Model when you are strategizing your next best moves and developing plans for other people to execute on at a later date.

Example thread:

> Now you can assemble each activity's predictions into a summarized, big-picture view of your future and incorporate the information into your plans. These items can be useful in any aspect of the CST Model. For instance, you may decide that a Macro Tactic is to gain as many advantages through technological enhancements as possible, so your Tactics are to add the highest-rated editing software to your computer and to research options that will enable you to make a smooth conversion into the future.

Activity-Based Forecasting is a more effective means of forecasting than the typical scenario in which a leader asks a group to think about the future or to create a "vision." You can use the tool on its own, or you can use the information that you have gleaned while engaged in Activity-Based Forecasting to make even more accurate forecasts for your career, individual projects, or your organization. Just plug the information into your next tool, Forecasting Horizon Markers, and see how the future becomes more visible.

[If You Break It, Don't Come Home]

When you think about the job of an astronaut, you don't imagine a person wearing heavy gloves while practicing how to use a wrench. But that's exactly what mission specialist Dr. James Newman did on several occasions in preparation for the Hubble Space Telescope's fourth servicing mission in March 2002.

Newman's job on the upcoming mission would be to assist in replacing and upgrading older equipment to increase the telescope's imaging capabilities. Planners and crew members worked together preparing, planning, and forecasting activities and possible challenges. In essence, they performed Activity-Based Forecasting, breaking each task into separate activities, predicting best- and worse-case scenarios for each, and taking measures to ensure that the mission was a successful one, otherwise, a fellow NASA astronaut joked, "If you break it, (MEANING THE HUBBLE) don't come home." And that's where the wrench comes in.

Surely you've heard of stripping a bolt, something that happens when one gets too enthusiastic about turning a wrench before properly aligning a shaft's threads with the hole the bolt is meant to go into. It can happen to anyone under the best of conditions, but imagine how tricky it can be to avoid doing this in space while wearing those protective gloves. When such an important and expensive mission is at stake, you don't want a little thing like a stripped bolt to be your loss by a nose. That's why Newman and his fellow crew members practiced the task continually until they could immediately feel if the threads of the bolt were misaligned.

[continues on page 608]

[continued from previous page]

> Newman told me that the practice paid off. He recounted how he was making one of the replacements when he felt the wrench's familiar tug of resistance. Carefully, he counter-turned the wrench, realigned the threads, and successfully tightened the bolt, a "simple" task that could have gone horribly wrong if not for the benefit of good forecasting behind him.

Forecasting Horizon Markers

Let's begin by revisiting the concept of the Optimum Forward Orientation shown earlier in this chapter and how having a broader and longer view into the future allows you to see more opportunities and challenges earlier than if your thinking remains in the Retro and Current orientations. Although you know the importance of Forward-oriented thinking, you need to know how to get it and use it to make improved decisions. That's where Forecasting Horizon Markers comes into play. It is another ET tool that extends your vision forward, adds structure and specificity to forecasting, and helps you establish benchmarks that align with Strategy and Desired Outcome. You use Forecasting Horizon Markers to strategize and make plans.

Look at how the Optimum Forward Orientation in Figure 14.7 is accompanied by a timeline marked with specific points in time; these points are Horizon Markers that serve as benchmarks for progress. When you can see your benchmarks in front of you, everyone involved gains a big-picture view of the future and can focus energies on meeting benchmarks by their specific targeted dates.

Establish Horizon Markers for Forecasting

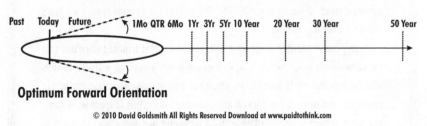

Figure 14.7—Establish Horizon Markers for Forecasting

An entrepreneur who wants to get his business to $4 million in three years so that he can sell it and retire in five years could place time-sensitive

Forecasting Horizon Markers on his forecasting timeline. A multinational strategic team may use Forecasting Horizon Markers to inform others within their organization of specific dates in the future so that everyone can see the bigger picture and better understand their place within it. Government agencies can model simulations about trends in their cities or provinces, and then use Forecasting Horizon Markers to determine cash flow needs and budgets years in advance, allowing people to negotiate contracts with suppliers.

To create your own Horizon Markers, begin by drawing your own timeline by placing the Optimum Forward Orientation image on the left and extending a straight line, which will be your timeline, away from it toward the right as you see in the above diagram. Then, take some time to determine the points in time you feel are best to mark on your timeline as important forecasting benchmarks. The timeline points and the spans in between can start as soon as in a few days, with spans between as short as a few days, and can extend into the future for as long as you believe you can *realistically* see your future based upon the tools you've already learned about. If you're concerned about how to set your Horizon Markers, know that you will be getting more tools in this chapter to help you establish and place them on your timeline.

At the opening of this chapter, I told you about the conversation I had with the big-box retail manager regarding the outlook he had for his son's future. He admitted that he could envision his son's first fifty years of life. If this man had said that he wanted to pay for his son's education in full, we could forecast the anticipated educational path of his son and overlay it with the anticipated career progression of the father, using Horizon Markers to forecast how much money the father would need to earn and save by certain benchmarks.

In addition, we would look at factors that could impact this progression of activities: trends in education, educational costs, technologies that could influence the father's ability to earn, advancements that might help the father earn more money faster, etc. As their lives and the father's career unfold, and as different external factors and new information becomes available to this family, they can make adjustments to their Horizon Markers and their tactics to ensure that they stay on target to meet their financial desired outcome.

Each industry and sector will have to consider various factors that determine a realistic timeline. A large firm that supplies cogeneration plants, establishes wind farms, or builds nuclear facilities must have leaders who are looking ten to fifty years into the future to make decisions because of government regulations, population shifts, demand curves, etc., so their timeline might look a lot like the one in our diagram. Yet, a technology firm's decision makers may be able to look no more than three to five years forward, as is the case with companies like the India-based Infosys Limited. When Sanjay Purohit held the position of Group Head, Planning and Assurance at the firm, he explained to me how the tech company used Horizon Markers for planning.

At Infosys, the planning team marks the firm's timeline with six Horizon Markers. The farthest reaches five years into the future, and the rest extend between the current date and the five-year benchmark. Long-term thinking at Infosys ranges from three to five years and no further, because leadership needs its people to anticipate potential opportunities related to rapid changes in social trends, emerging markets, and more, as accurately as possible. When Purohit's team of twenty-two sits down to make projects at the five-year mark, they know that they are stretching their thinking as far as it can realistically go for their industry. They must consider that new events, unexpected technological advances, and new information will potentially change the decisions they make. As they progress over time to a place closer to their five-year mark, they must move their thinking beyond that point in time and place a new Horizon Marker at the updated five-year mark. In this manner, the leadership team at Infosys will always have a five-year forecasting window.

At the three-year Horizon Marker, leadership is looking at creating a sustainable business and a competitive advantage, because their decisions are expected to ultimately become reality. The team might be looking at investment opportunities, hiring and leadership talent needs, products that must be developed, or markets they need to pursue.

At the one-year Horizon Marker, Infosys's focus is more on projects and initiatives for products and services that are already in the pipeline or that are considered short-term opportunities, like how to maximize return on what they have already decided or how they can best use resources to maximize revenue. Decision makers' monthly and quarterly Horizon Markers can be useful in many ways, such as helping its finance team and accountants who are asking how the firm can maximize revenue with activity that is already in progress, leverage investments, etc. This is no different than when you say to yourself: We have only a month. What can we do with our borrowing and investments to maximize the securing of customers, our marketing results, and inventory utilization? Having clarity about the future is how Infosys nearly tripled the size of its workforce in less than a decade to more than 100,000 employees.

Determining Forecasting Horizons

So how do you determine the Forecasting Horizons that are right for your organization? Now that you know about Activity-Based Forecasting, you can incorporate the activities that you separated out from your process, product, project, etc., into your Forecasting Horizon Markers timeline. In addition, some of the research and forecasting associated with each activity may make its way onto the timeline, too, such as information from your sales cycle, product/service development cycle, repeat sales and replacement cycles, support services cycles, and external cycles from vendors, customers, governments, and seasons.

Establish your timeline

To establish your timeline, take out a clean sheet of paper or open a new document on your computer. Draw a horizontal line from left to right. On the left, write the minimum amount of time that it takes to produce and deliver your product or service. Include time that is spent internally performing these activities and those performed by parties externally. This is the shortest range of view you should have into the future.

On the right, write the longest distance you believe you can see into the future on behalf of your organization, which should be at least twice the timeline of the delivery of your product or service. (Now, after reading to this point, this is no longer as challenging as it would have been before, because you now have better tools with which to forecast. In essence, you've been given high beams that will help you to see much farther into the future.) Although I suspect that you will revisit the timeline at a later date to extend the time written in this position, using the longest-running cycle is a good enough start. Notch off the time increments of the other cycles on the timeline.

Sample Formulas

If you sell your product then produce or deliver it to your channel or your end user:

> (Sales Cycle + Product Development + Product Life and Support + Liability)
> x 2 = Minimum

If you first design your products and then sell the item to your channel or to the end user:

(Product Development + Sales Cycle + Life Cycle + Product Life and Support + Liability) x 2 = Minimum

Your formulas can be as short as you can make them for your group or as long as necessary for the entire organization. The purpose is to force your mind to reach as far into the future as is necessary to make quality forecasts that impact decision making effectively and to connect your thinking to other industries (or sectors) to your industry (or sector). In the field of nanomembrane technology, for example, leaders will need to include the speed of technological change in their forecasting formulas in addition to the research being done in nanotechnology and membrane technology and the potential to merge with other technologies such as biotechnology, health-care technology, garment technology, and hydro technology. If a membrane technology were to be used for water desalination, then a forecaster must be looking at population shifts, too. Although the product cycle falls into a five-year Horizon Marker, the Horizon Marker for population changes might force the forecaster to look five to ten years forward to ensure that the firm is selling to people in geographical areas that want desalination plants.

We've worked through this exercise from the vantage point of the entire organization, but realize that you also can establish Forecasting Horizon Markers for departments, product sales, IT, acquisition time frames, warehousing, etc. Additionally, although much of the language references product sales and product development, you can make the adjustments to fit your industry or sector if you're working in a nonprofit organization that doesn't make product sales.

One parting note about Forecasting Horizon Markers: This is not about being 100% accurate. We have to work with the realities of leading, so we're striving for improved decision making, not perfection. Perfection is not possible, because as you look further out into the future, the variables are too great to always be correct. Establishing Forecasting Horizon Markers is great for helping you fine tune your decisions cyclonically. If you're looking five years out, and you approach your third year within that original span of time, you can measure progress thus far and make adjustments to year five and beyond. Having the additional time to prepare for your organization's future in advance makes your decisions more proactive, giving you more options for improved outcomes.

The Pentality of Forecasting

Over the years it's been my experience that despite their good intentions, leaders easily overlook many opportunities for forecasting, and as a result, instead of living mentally in the future, they stay stuck in the present or past. But it's unrealistic to expect that anyone will live mentally in the future simply because they're told that it's a good thing to do. Instead, they need to know what to be looking for and where to look, which is why I developed the next tool, the Pentality of Forecasting. Just as a pentagon has five sides, this tool consists of five topic areas intended to direct and focus your attention to key realistic factors affecting the long-term well-being of your organization. These categories are:

1. You/Your Group/Your Organization
2. Customer/Client (member, patron, sponsor, etc.)
3. Competition
4. Supplier/Vendor
5. World/Universe

Either alone or with other leaders in a group setting, all you need to do to get started using the tool is to select any one of the five categories and discuss the future of that category as it pertains to your organization's long-term well-being using preset Forecasting Horizon Markers. Typically, people like to choose the category that they are most comfortable with, which is fine, but you want to be sure that you address the other categories, too. Otherwise, you could potentially fall into a rut of ignoring categories and missing opportunities and challenges that have an impact on your organization's future. So if you want to forecast your Customers/Clients one, two, and five years into the future, select a different category based on data and extrapolations the next time you forecast, eventually covering all of the categories.

Let's take a look at each of the five areas and how you can explore them for potential forecasted opportunities and challenges.

Pentality of Forecasting

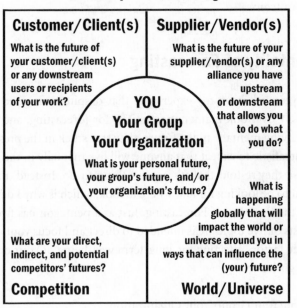

Figure 14.8—Pentality of Forecasting

You/Your Group/Your Organization

What's going on within your organization and among the people who play a role in its successes?

You – Each time I work with an individual on their organizations, the conversation inevitably comes full circle back to the topic of what all the changes and challenges going on with the organization mean personally to the leader. They might say, "Yeah, our revenues are down within our business unit and we're getting pressure from corporate to make some fast changes. What this means to me is that if I can't light a fire under this sales staff soon, I'll be looking for a new job." The "you" here represents you personally. What is your future? This may mean your career, health, family, interests, age, abilities, etc. Anything about your future is always something to be considered when forecasting.

Your Group – In this forecasting category, you're making projections about your group's future. What will happen to its members, its lifespan, its leadership, and its products? The multiple dynamics that happen among the people in a management team, unit, small business, committee, or department affect not just that group but the organization as a whole. Is your group thriving and in need of measures to support an expansion, or is it in danger of being absorbed or eliminated altogether? Are there key decision makers within your organization who are battling personal issues that will impact their on-the-job performance? Do you see some up-and-coming new hires that are hungry for a promotion and are willing to bring new information, leads, and opportunities to the table? All of these issues and more factor into your organization's ability to grow, compete, and survive in the long term.

Your Organization – This forecasting category pertains to your organization's future based upon your Forecasting Horizon Markers. What will your organization be like in two, five, and ten years? Address factors such as personnel, cash, and assets as well as all the activities of ET in your answers, such as what you see in the future in relationship to planning, alliances, and innovation. Take in the big-picture view of your organization to be sure that you're considering as many new challenges and opportunities as possible.

Customer/Client

What will happen with your customers or clients in the future? Think about how they might change, how they might be challenged, what behaviors they might exhibit, how they may do business, what's happening in their markets, and more. Do you see some changes that will affect their relationships with your organization in the months and years ahead? How will they use technology to either increase or eliminate their need to use your products or services? Consider how issues like increasing or decreasing unemployment figures and confidence changes in worldwide market conditions will impact their future dealings with your organization. It's not always just about the products and services, either. Think about recalls, ethics challenges, greed, community support, environmental initiatives, and anything else that might impact their future so that you can make better decisions for your organization. What if you learned today that your customer has been looking to acquire a company just like yours to provide itself with your type of service internally? What would you do differently? You can substitute in member, patron, sponsor, recipient or whatever term you use. The concept is still the same.

Competition

First, when it comes to forecasting the competition, the obvious places to look are at direct competitors, those parties who offer the same products and services that you do, vie for the same customers and funding resources that your organization does, and who oftentimes use the same vendors. However, the types of competition you face aren't always so apparent, as you learned in Chapter 9 when you read about competitive intelligence. Forecasting and competition take on a whole new dimension together, because now you must look at complementary industries, emerging technologies, and any other factors that threaten to displace your products and services or that could bolster them. While forecasting your competitors, you may foresee that several of them could potentially move out of the business, because they can't make a high enough gross profit on their current products to invest in up-to-date operational improvements that are essential for carrying these competitors into the future. The earlier you can forecast these types of changes, the better decisions you can make now to grab their share of the market before someone else does.

In education one might think about the school or university next door. The military might consider the countries vying for the same ocean waters or for natural resources. Government has competition for industry, trade partners, and the purchase of debt. If your country has a higher borrowing rate than another, you may find that capital markets leave you with less funding than you need. Furthermore, have you considered how vendors can become competitors, as was the case when it was announced that China would build more than 9,700 miles of high-speed rail track by 2020? Vendors were excited to be able to bid on the job, but their excitement was short lived when they learned that the Chinese government had assembled its own groups that would be fully capable of completing the project without the use of traditional vendors.

Supplier/Vendor

Make a list of your most commonly used vendors, and then gather data about them to predict what their futures will look like. What factors are affecting or will affect their long-term ability to provide you with the resources you need to remain profitable and functional? Do you believe their long-range plans are to continue manufacturing the supplies that you buy from them? Based on historical data, can you predict with some certainty that they will continue to deliver superior products or services, or are you anticipating that quality will suffer? Have you heard anything about them that would indicate that they will be going out of business or expanding the business in different markets or into your market? If you're planning based on forecasts about their future, you can make more strategic decisions.

World/Universe

If forecasting about the universe's impact on your organization seems far out, remember the lessons from Chapter 8 about becoming globally minded. Take the same mental leap if you need to, because forecasting the world's—and universe's—impact on your organization's future is not only practical, it's essential. If you're a fisherman, for example, you may need to look for predictions about tides, currents, and the effects of chemical dumping and pollution to make solid long-range plans. Do you have your finger on the pulse of big-picture world events that will ultimately factor into the long-term health and survival of your organization?

No leader can afford to operate with his or her head in the sand, because more than ever, our world is so interconnected that news on one side of it instantly affects activity on the other. If you have a tendency to be egocentric, it's really beyond time to get yourself up to speed on current happenings and to learn from people like analysts (even historians) who can offer insight into what is likely to happen next so that your organization can take a proactive approach into its future. The U.S. housing fiasco and subsequent market crash, along with the tumbling of economies among members of the European Union, affected consumer buying patterns worldwide. This alone should be example enough that you need to catch the markers for change in time to make decisions that safeguard against their ill effects.

Also think about how the moon orbit, solar flares, air temperature fluctuations, rising and falling sea levels, and the ozone layer's depletion impact how we live and work. Did you know that when a solar flare occurs, the earth is bombarded with charged particles from the sun? This universe-related occurrence can impact power grids, satellites, and ground communications. Given that airlines rely on satellites for GPS and communications, experts advise that aircrafts avoid polar routes (those over polar ice caps connecting Asia and North America) during solar flares. If we could forecast the solar flares, however, organizations that use these routes would be able to plan an alternative route or method of travel for personnel and equipment. Forecasting forward, it's likely that these types of changes in the universe will be less and less problematic to air travel.

Share your findings with internal and external stakeholders, and invite them to come up with their own forecasts. By sharing and utilizing the Pentality of Forecasting with other decision makers, you can help to focus their thinking on the five categories, which in turn will enable them to provide you with more wide-scoped insights and forecasts that you can incorporate into your plans for your organization's future.

Ways to Improve Your Forecasting

While everything you do is viewed by other people as occurring in the present, in truth, today's outcomes are products of yesterday's thinking. And in order for you to make decisions that yield the best long-range solutions to both your current and predicted opportunities, you need to place your mind into the future now and let it live there. I understand that the realities of leading sometimes pull your focus back to present-day thinking—which is fine since it's the best you can do under some circumstances—but as long as you're spending most of your thinking time in the future, the solutions you forecast will be more accurate in months and years to come.

Given that we rarely work within perfectly ideal situations, there are still ways that we can mitigate risk and maximize results—hence the art and science of forecasting. Here are some forecasting suggestions that will empower you to create your best solutions and opportunities.

Use Technology

Forecasting is not just about thinking about the future, it's about *building* it, and that can sometimes require you to play out numbers, scenarios, and models to get new insight into tomorrow. Technologies are forecasting vehicles that allow you to do just that, and they can be used in two ways: directly for making forecasts and indirectly to gather and assess data that you can use for forecasting.

There are certain software capabilities, like modeling software, that will give you actual forecasts. Simply enter the data needed, and your technology will provide you with a predicted long-range outcome that you can use for strategizing and planning for your organization. For instance, you can run a program to find out if a competitor is likely to be out of business in ten years. Then you include this information in your Cyclonic Thinking to make more informed decisions about the direction of your organization's future.

Then there are technologies that will gather, interpret, and even create new information from which you can make extrapolations and predictions; it's as if you're engaged in forecasting-related functions even when you're not focused on forecasting. For example, a technology can collect big data about changes in purchasing rates of flu medicines within a supply chain, combine this information with school attendance records and comments made on social media about children feeling sick and calculate your future purchasing and stock requirements, enabling you to utilize the data at a time when you're trying to determine your next moves.

Working with a Forecasting Team

Many leaders have found that working with a "think tank" of fellow forward-thinking people improves their forecasting outcomes and for this reason I recommend that organizations set up a forecasting team whose sole responsibilities are to think about the future. This is a group that does not have to think about solving the future but rather what may or could happen in the future. In selecting the team, consider how you assign staffers to various functions and roles within your organization because of the skills they possess; the same should be true of this group. You select individuals based on the way people think so that when they participate in the team, you get the highest return for their work. Don't make the mistake of including individuals because of their title or position, because their role does not necessarily mean they are forward oriented. These individuals may come from internal or external sources. Your forecasting team should be a group of people capable of seeing many aspects of your organization at one time, and they should have a broader perspective than the typical front-line worker.

A forecasting team is *different* than your current management team or board of directors, although the team may include forward-thinking people from either group. A common mistake that leaders make is assuming that their boards of directors, who may be great at making decisions, have ample time to forecast. Sure, board members can often plan well, but without forecasting, their planning is too short term, limited in scope, and incomplete. Besides, often boards and senior teams have to spend time on issues related to HR, budgeting, or legal matters that chew up their thinking time, whereas a forecasting team's purpose and focus are hugely different than those of most boards of directors.

The same mistake applies in small businesses, too. Oftentimes, a husband or wife goes into business, solicits their spouse to perform bookkeeping activities, and maybe brings on a sibling to work as a laborer. Although these family members provide value, they're not necessarily helpful to the owner in the area of forecasting.

Pull together a group that can strictly focus on "what-if" issues as Forward-oriented forecasters, regardless of who they are or where they're located. Think of this group as your limitation-free dream team with a single task: providing forecasted information for your use. Therefore, if you must choose between an internal manager who is not much of a forecaster or an excellent forecaster who lives on the other side of the world, pick the latter. With today's technologies, such as video conferencing, distance should not be a factor in your selection process anyway.

Decide on the Right Degree of Openness

The information that you work with during forecasting can sometimes be sensitive, even damaging if it ends up in the wrong hands, so you have to determine what degree of openness is appropriate for your organization, individual projects, and specific situations. The owner of a chain of dry cleaning stores won't be as likely to have to protect information in the same way that the military strategist who handles sensitive documents does. Even within a single department, your level of openness can vary from one situation or person to another.

Do you include others in the decision-making process, or do you work alone to create plans? Leadership styles, staff members' levels of trustworthiness, and sensitivity of information within an industry or sector are determining factors in how much openness is appropriate. The time to make these decisions is before you start collecting data, not after the fact when crucial information is circulating all over the organization or worse, into the hands of competitors who can use your information to their advantage. Then again, if you're forecasting for a socially conscious movement, doing science research for the betterment of mankind, or creating policy that helps struggling nations, then letting everyone in on what you've found could be a great way to make progress. It's up to you to make these judgment calls.

Engage in Social Forecasting

The ET Social Forecasting tool borrows its framework from the realm of social networking. Just as leaders can use social networking as a mechanism to connect people and groups for the purpose of distributing and receiving information, ET Social Forecasting involves the development and engagement of a particular network for the purpose of transferring information that you can use to predict future outcomes. The members of your ET Social Forecasting group can be customers, internal staff members, vendors, government agencies, or any type of stakeholder who is relevant to your organization's operations and survival. You have a great deal of flexibility in how you build this tool, whom you invite to participate and what kinds of information you seek, but remember that ultimately, the purpose of ET Social Forecasting is to enhance your performance as you forecast.

Your new tool can advance your thinking from the perspective of the typical Current-oriented forecaster to that of the Forward-oriented forecaster. Let's compare how the two types of thinkers might anticipate their customers' future buying needs. The Current-oriented forecaster waits for incoming orders from customers to determine when products are brought into inventory and distributed to buyers on a current as-needed basis. Although I've labeled this person as a "forecaster," he really isn't forecasting much at all. He is reacting and providing product on a short-term anticipated cycle. The Forward-oriented forecaster who has developed a social forecasting network that asks customers to provide their anticipated product needs four weeks in advance, can order product in bulk, prevent delays in delivery times, and act more proactively on behalf of the organization's customers, is better positioned to meet demands this week, next week, and for the next two weeks after that. So how might this transmission of information take place?

Let's look at a simple scenario. You're in the freight business and you need to have trucks and containers available to your customers for moving their goods. If you don't have them available, you can't ship your customers' goods when they need you to do so. As a way of gathering data that you can use to better anticipate how many containers you will need on hand for shipping customers' goods, you create a social forecasting group composed of your customers and you ask each of them to simply submit a form onto which they've recorded their estimated shipping container needs over a given period of time, say weekly for the next month. This data enables you to make more accurate projections about what you need to do based on what you know is going to happen in advance: cash flow, on-hand supplies, equipment availability, and other factors of preparedness.

When the data comes in, you can then tally the needs and place containers and arrange to have trucks to meet this demand. In the following weeks, you ask the same question, but now that everyone is paying attention from a Forward-oriented perspective, each week's submission should be a more accurate estimate of customers' shipping needs. This type of anticipatory planning moves you from reacting to planning.

If you want to improve the process, and you've built the right 80% of the GPP, you can advance social forecasting to a science. You can have your system track the accuracy of your customers' predictions and then (1) adapt incoming forms' estimates accordingly or (2) share with each customer his or her accuracy rates so that they can adjust their reporting procedures accordingly. It's human nature to want to improve, and with this new information, customers will be able to do better next time.

You can multiply the benefits of ET Social Forecasting by thinking upstream and downstream and connect not only those using your equipment but those who drive the need for equipment. You can calculate in consumer behavior, holidays, currency fluctuations, stock market figures, contracts, bankruptcies, wars, and more to fine tune the analysis so that the predictions are more accurate. The result will be fewer fires, superior customer engagement, and an improved work environment with trucks, equipment, and product moving when they need to move.

You can engage in social forecasting regardless of your industry or sector. Just be sure that you don't request information that is too complex or time consuming for other people to gather, or no one will do it. Remember, the people you request this data from are working also, and you put yourself in the other people's shoes ("Be the person" from Chapter 12) as you develop the requests for data and Build the Package—a basic premise for empowering others from Chapter 11, where you, as the leader, don't just request others to perform activities, you try out the systems and structures yourself to see if your requests are realistic so that your users can more easily follow your lead.

ET Social Forecasting allows you to involve more people, organize the transfer of information better, and accumulate more accurate and pertinent information than you would have had in the past. Your proficiency at social forecasting enables you to come up with more accurate forecasts at various technological levels. The four levels of forecasting are:

1. **Level 1 – Human-Generated Forecasting.** At this level, a few people, typically staff members within an organization, make predictions about the future for themselves and others.
2. **Level 2 – Technology-Supported Forecasting.** Individuals make forecasts using manual systems to collect data from internal and external sources. (Remember that just because you use a computer spreadsheet does not mean what you're doing is automated.)
3. **Level 3 – Semi-Automated Forecasting.** Automated systems gather information that is used to make predictions about the future by humans.
4. **Level 4 – Automated Forecasting.** Automated systems that have the power to gather information from a wide range of data sources (such as distributed groups of people and organizations) that computers, instead of humans, use to make more accurate predictions.

If you're now thinking that only the big organizations engage in social forecasting, think again. Very few organizational leaders, relative to the number of global leaders in the world today, are thinking this way. They are limited in their forecasting skills and very much suffer the Wizard of Oz Syndrome, which, as I explained in Chapter 10, is when leaders and organizations take on an outward appearance of strength, power, and confidence, but in reality, are not sophisticated and "together," and are sub-par or average at best.

Regardless of the size of your organization or the funds you have at your disposal, you can either develop a sophisticated ET Social Forecasting network or you can simply utilize the concept of social forecasting to improve the information you have on hand to make better decisions about the future of your organization.

Determine Appropriate Level of Scalability

As you integrate forecasting into strategic and tactical activities, there will be times when you have to anticipate how much more of something you will need in the future than you need today, based on calculated projections. How much more inventory will you need in order to handle higher-volume orders? How much more credit will you need to be able to finance new projects? How many more people will you need on staff to service customers in the new markets you plan to enter? As we touched on before, forecasting is not an exact science, and your estimations are not always going to be 100% on target. In addition, you might feel cursed with the knowledge that you need something that isn't feasibly acquirable in the short term, but the upside is that at least you know earlier rather than later that you need it so that you can be taking steps to move in that direction early on.

You might decide to keep the computer program that your five-person staff is presently using, because cash flow dictates that you are unable to finance an upgrade at this time. However, you still know that one day, perhaps twenty-four months out on your Forecasting Horizons timeline, you will need that upgrade. As long as your eye is on the future, you can make decisions now to improve productivity or to ramp up your credit rating so that you can either purchase or finance that upgrade down the road.

Factor in Sustainability

The importance of forecasting is that it allows you to make decisions with lasting power. That's not to say that every decision you make when you're forecasting needs to last the duration of, say, your Forecasting Horizons. Even though you might have a six-year outlook, today's decision might need to be sustained for only one year, and after that time, you adjust your Strategy, Macro Tactics, or Tactics to meet current and future needs at that time.

Thinking about sustainability may help you to select your next best project off your Project Evaluation Chart. When assessing options for the most sustainable project among them, you might select the project that gives your organization longer-term results, or you might need a project that gives you greater returns in the short term. Either way, you determine which level of sustainability is right for your organization at the time.

Consider Your Best Engagement Models

Proper forecasting helps you to consider long-term engagement models to connect your organization to its stakeholders and vice versa. Thinking back to the Multi-Dimensional Buyer, consider how many access points organizations have now provided to their stakeholders that were unheard of even a decade ago. Forecasting allows you to see technologies, trends, and more to engage your stakeholders—or when appropriate, to disengage them and seek new options for engagement.

With a Forward forecasting orientation, you need to ask yourself, and fellow decision makers, how you can engage customers, employees, media, and suppliers; people who are ancillary to your products, services, and internal operations such as legal and governmental entities; competitive-intelligence allies; or even people to whom you outsource services, to be able to build a strength in the future.

Learn from Other Forecasters and Futurists

You can learn from futurists such as the author Alvin Toffler and creators of science-fiction entertainment like Gene Roddenberry who look at the future with a different eye. Forty years ago, Roddenberry's *Star Trek* previewed many of today's modern technologies, including the cell phone, Bluetooth technology, holographic communication, laser surgery, digital books, and the sonogram.

Your forecasting abilities improve by reading magazines such as *Scientific American, Discover, Popular Mechanics, Popular Science,* and *Wired*; watching videos on TED.com, which is devoted to presenting ideas from new and innovative thinkers in the areas of technology, entertainment, and design; participating in organizations such as the Association of Professional Futurists and the World Future Society; finding an online futurist discussion group; and studying past and present theorists, such as M.C. Escher, Stephen Hawking, Leonardo da Vinci, and Albert Einstein, will help you to discover patterns in their thinking. As you observe how others forecast the future, you'll immediately start to create your own extrapolations.

Don't Base Tomorrow on Yesterday

When you're forecasting, keep in mind that many of the systems and structures, technologies, and even jobs of tomorrow may not be in existence today. Forecasting with data and tools the way that meteorologists do helps you to account for this gap within the accelerating pace of change.

The pace of innovation and performance jumps exponentially when technology comes into play, so if the span of time between points A and B is ten years, you can't assume that the same amount of time will separate points B and C. The same degree of improvement might take only a period of months.

As mentioned regarding the Human Genome Project (Chapter 6), yesterday loses relevance in forecasting. In a conversation with a former director of a water and sewage municipality, I learned about a 1960's forecast for a U.S. region's increase in water usage (40%) based on an anticipated population increase of 40%. While the population bumped up by 36% within the time frame, water usage only increased by 20%.[184]

Great forecasters disconnect themselves from yesterday's thinking to make room for the future.

Think in 4D, Not in 3D

When you're forecasting, shift your figurative perspective from 3D thinking—more than just the length × width × height of objects as they appear in the present or appeared in the past—to 4D—which also includes the aspect of time—so that you break free from a current- or retro-oriented focus and allow yourself to see an immeasurable number of new possibilities before you.

In Figure 14.9 the arrow points to the same location on the planet using the same date but in different years: 1964, 2010, and then again in 2029. Say that you were to describe where you are as you read this line of the book in 3D terms—flying in a plan over the Pacific Ocean—you would be telling only a part of the story. But if you were to explain your location in 4D by including time, then reading it on April 25, 1964 versus the same date in 2029, would mean something different in many aspects—the book's content, the uses for the book, etc.—due to geographical, physical, political and other changes that occur from one point in time to another. Adding this additional dimension of time enables you to more accurately defines where you are and the possibilities available to you. Furthermore, the 4th dimension enables you to escape present or past thinking—"we did this in the past and it didn't work"—and envision or predict potential happenings on the horizon.

The Universe in 4D

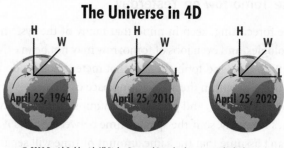

Figure 14.9—The Universe in 4D

So let's look at a scenario—a road construction project—from different perspectives based in three different points in time.

In the United States during the 1940s to 1960s, infrastructure projects were huge employment generators. Building roads put thousands of people to work on construction sites and in factories that manufactured construction equipment, plants that made concrete or blacktop, and organizations that drafted road plans. If we were to fast-forward to 2012, these same projects would require a fraction of the workers due to automation's impact on equipment manufacturing, stone production, paving techniques, and so on. Take these changes along with what you already see on the horizon from other industries, extrapolate new possibilities from them, and fast-forward your thinking to 2029, where you might anticipate that road construction has cross-pollinated with the farming industry; more specifically, that motor graders, asphalt pavers, dozers, and dump trucks are given self-directed navigational instructions via satellite and harvesters are operated by a combination of computer programs, PS, and an on-board operator to supervise the equipment during operation.

If we were to take the same road paving condition from the perspective that time has changed, we might say that in 1952 a single-lane road was needed in a portion of northern Canada to supply products from the interior of Quebec to Montreal or to Halifax. Fast forward to 2012, and you might find that the towns may no longer be shipping the same products or the road has been removed. Take one more jump forward in time to 2029, and you may discover that the same spot has become a reserve for protecting an endangered species.

When you assess your organization's current pluses, minuses, opportunities, and challenges, look beyond where it stands today, and consider where it stands in terms of its time: past, present, and future. When you are working together with people who limit themselves mentally, help them make the shift to 4D forecasting by encouraging them to consider that economic, technological, and consumer changes that leave yesterday's failures behind and give way to today's possible successes.

The 2006 YouTube video "Did You Know," researched by Karl Fisch, Scott McLeod, and Jeff Brenman,[185] illustrates the number of years it took for new forms of media to attract an audience of 50 million people. As you can see, current media establish a market faster today than they did decades ago:

Radio: 38 years
TV: 13 years
Internet: 4 years
iPod: 3 years
Facebook: 2 years

Be careful how you're limiting potential by not looking forward enough on the timeline, because what wouldn't have worked in 2009 might work in 2013.

While you forecast, take into consideration the factors of real-time information and real-time results. For example, in small-business accounting, we began with a manual ledger and gradually improved it over time, but it never yielded more than an after-the-fact categorical tally of expenses that we would use for future study. The Excel spreadsheet brought in an electronic calculating factor, which eased up time and helped to make the switch from waiting for financial information to getting it sooner for evaluation purposes. When software programs such as QuickBooks came about, decision makers were able to receive financial data closer to real time, and to use it for making improved decisions. The jump from Excel to QuickBooks was much faster than from the early ledgers to Excel. Tomorrow's jump to the next financial-computing software will most likely be more drastic and rapid.

Today, real-time accounting is not uncommon. Tomorrow, we will have tools that not only collect data, but also interpret data and competitive intelligence. The combination of data and factors will enable leaders to extrapolate information and make better-forecasted decisions. Start to look at all aspects of your organization in terms of the rate of improved technologies and advancements that can help you make forecasted decisions more accurately and more rapidly based upon 4D thinking.

Improve Your Tools

Forecasters must never be complacent with the tools they are using to fore-cast because what's good for today technologically may not be good for tomorrow. Therefore, as a forecaster, your job is to improve the forecasting tools you have and to innovate with new products, or services so that your leadership team can forecast better. Today you have spreadsheets and tomor-row you may have an aggregation software that pulls from 200 online sources to give you much more precise data, or even better yet, a set of options for the future that you could not see on your own and that will help to analyze information.

Anticipate Three What-If Scenarios

Because forecasting is not an exact science, even the best future outlooks tend to evolve with the passage of time. So although you're using forecasted information to develop plans, you still have to be flexible in your approach to certain forecasted situations. One way to balance the need to follow plans and to remain flexible as new information presents itself is to anticipate three what-if scenarios as you develop plans. There are three groups of what-if scenarios you can play out.

What-If Scenario Group #1

The first group of what-if scenarios is: (1) What if the forecast comes to frui-tion exactly as I anticipate? (2) What if the forecast comes to fruition partially as I anticipate? and (3) What if the forecast comes to fruition vaguely as I anticipate?

While the first two scenarios allow you to follow your plan to varying degrees, the last scenario would likely require you to make a major detour from your plans, even to develop new plans altogether. Regardless of how your scenarios play out in the end, it's a good measure to develop plans that account for a range of forecasted outcomes to ensure that your organization is adequately prepared as circumstances unfold.

What-If Scenario Group #2

The second group of what-if scenarios is (1) What if forecasts are perfectly successful? (2) What if forecasts are reasonably successful? and (3) What if forecasts fall short?

In preparation for the perfectly successful forecasts scenario, you develop plans from Desired Outcome and Strategy to Execution as if your forecasts play out perfectly as anticipated. To prepare for reasonably successful forecasts, you develop plans that have a contingency factor, and that account for the future playing out slightly differently than anticipated. And for the falling-short forecasts, your plans leave greater room for flexibility and adaptation depending on how differently you think the future might play out in comparisons to the forecasts you have made.

What-If Scenario Group #3

In this final grouping, you develop forecasted plans based on three extremes of outcomes: (1) What if the future brings quick and/or drastic changes? (2) What if the future brings gradual changes? and (3) What if the future remains similar to the present?

In this case you're developing plans based on what you currently know and what you can reasonably predict. You are creating three plans or three versions of a plan that provide direction and guidance regardless of the extremeness (or lack thereof) of the outcomes that the future brings.

Any time you are strategizing and forecasting, you can consider your options from these three points of view to better prepare your organization for its future.

Use Modeling

Despite their ability to improve forecasting, modeling techniques and software are rarely used because leaders typically don't do much forecasting and don't realize how modeling can help them with their forecasts. If modeling techniques are used, they may still not work for a variety of reasons. They may be very crude or limited, the data plugged into them may be flawed or incomplete, or the users may not run their simulations out long enough to gain accurate conclusions.

For example, a person may draw a model on a white board but never run the model over and over to realistically simulate a true-life situation. Maybe the forecaster wants to see if a particular toy that is in development can withstand a certain amount of rough play by a child. A model could be set up to bang the toy around 100 times, but if the reality is that the toy will be banged around 100,000 times, then the model should simulate the latter condition to deliver an accurate forecast to the testers.

Modeling is fairly simple. All you have to do is come up with a set of conditions that come into play for your particular forecasting needs and play them out in as many ways as you can to get a sense of what would happen if this set of conditions were to exist. What could happen if you build the order-processing center in a certain manner, if you place the distribution center in the location you're considering, or if you were to expand from two check-out lines to six? Modeling also helps you to share with other decision makers your potential outcomes so that colleagues gain a more accurate grasp of your forecasting and can provide better feedback to you.

If you use spreadsheet forecasting, from a leadership perspective of modeling, your thinking is far from reality. Spreadsheet forecasting or planning involves people sitting in a room and extrapolating for the next year. The danger with spreadsheet planning is that leaders tend to make projections without basis. For example, if you've projected 11% growth on a spreadsheet without basing this on employment figures, pricing trends, consumer behavior, competition, etc., and then you pass down this information to others, all the while thinking you've modeled the future, you've done nothing but frustrate your people by charging them with a job that they can't necessarily accomplish. Think about modeling this way: If those people to whom you sent your planning forecasts come to you and say, "How do we do this?" and you don't have any answers, or you say, "It's your job to figure that out," you're not forecasting or modeling—you're dreaming.

Build CPM Charts

Critical Path Method charts are tools that force you to forecast, because in order to accurately define a future plan, you must think through not only what you anticipate to happen but what outside influences might impact your plans. Creating a CPM chart (Chapter 3) ensures that you go to 50,000 feet and build part of the 80% of the GPP, your plan, before you introduce it to the 20% of the GPP, the plan's executors. This single reason is why I prefer the CPM chart over Gantt charts. The CPM chart brings your thinking to the 50,000-foot level and requires that you address Macro Tactics before adding Tactics. Gantt charts, on the other hand, make it too easy to react in a knee-jerk fashion to current issues or wants, and Gantt chart users are notorious for extending deadlines and altering timelines with the change of a single cell in a spreadsheet program. Your plans are always better when you make forecasts up front and think out the plan steps in advance.

Surround Yourself with Forward-Thinking People

Are the employees, colleagues, friends, and family that you currently spend time with forward-thinking? Although we've already discussed the development of a forecasting team, oftentimes the people with whom you spend your down time (both on and off the job) can have an influence on you and your ability to be forward-thinking.

If you make up your mind today that you want to surround yourself with forward-thinking people, incorporate this objective into organizational and personal situations. In the office, you can use the ET Development Funnel to design a hiring process that surrounds you with a forward-thinking management team. Screen candidates based on predetermined broad and specific criteria that eliminates anyone who is not a future-oriented thinker. You need forward-thinking people who can strategize and forecast, so ask job candidates what successful strategies they've created in the past to gain competitive advantage, or pose a challenge and ask them to brainstorm with you to generate potential solutions.

Look Upstream and Downstream for Cycles, Trends, and Patterns

It's important to forecast from a number of different starting points. Look upstream to vendors, look downstream to customers, and look sideways at industry competitors and complementary industries that could revolutionize and change the face of your industry. All the while, try to identify Cycles, Trends, and Patterns from what you see today.

The Five-Years-Ahead Exercise

Imagine that you're standing five years in the future from today. A reporter asks you to explain the one major accomplishment you achieved over the past five years that enabled you to become an industry leader so quickly.

When I pose this exercise to leaders in my audiences, they come up with vague answers like, "We offered great customer service," "We were innovative," "We worked together as a team," or on the other extreme they say they never really thought about it. But actually, the answer to becoming exceptional in one's field has to do with projects (as defined in Chapter 3) that move organizations forward: for example, transforming customers to a wireless grid, converting legacy computer systems to current technology, etc. What leaders should be saying is, "We implemented a new hand-held, crystal platform that created flat multidimensional images of our systems, enabling engineers to build in a completely different 4D environment." That's the winner.

Then after more discussion, leaders inevitably realize that in order to be standing five years in the future having achieved their accomplishment, they would have had to have begun working on their endeavor years before our discussion. I once guided 300 energy-sector CEOs who were coming up with ideas to reposition themselves better in their industry through this exercise. At the end of the exercise, they realized that in order to reach the outcomes they wanted at a five-year mark in the future, they would have had to have begun their projects at least ten or twelve years ago. In other words, they were already five to seven years behind schedule before beginning!

Performing this exercise is an eye opener, because it's one thing to dream and another to lead based upon forecasting. When you connect the dots from a forecast to planning, the "aha" moments happen. Your job is to make sure what you're projecting as a future outcome from your projects can actually happen according to your plans.

The Five-Years-Ahead Exercise works, because it allows your mind to seek and identify current and future opportunities through the observance of Cycles, Trends, and Patterns and the extrapolation of them forward in time. And although looking five years into the future doesn't allow you to control the future, the exercise does allow you to make decisions that will control how your organization will thrive within it. It's simple; your future outlook must be connected to the projects you're working on so that you intersect tomorrow as planned.

As you can now see, there are many ways in which you can extrapolate the information you have today into a forecasted picture of tomorrow's opportunities and challenges. The Forward-oriented perspective increases the odds that your plans are more accurate and proactive, as long as you avoid certain mistakes that some forecasters can make.

Avoiding the Eleven Mistakes of F-O-R-E-C-A-S-T-I-N-G

The tools that you have learned so far should enable you and other decision makers within your organization to work collaboratively together to develop forecasts that will strengthen your organization's ability to grow and thrive both in the present and in the future. However, there are some mistakes that could plague your ability to forecast well if you're not aware of them. Here are the eleven mistakes of forecasting that you will want to avoid:

F – **Falling in love with your own forecasted ideas.** Because your conclusions from forecasting are projections, be sure that you are not tempted to follow through on a forecasted idea simply because it's one that you hope to have happen.

O – **Overestimating the accuracy of your forecasts** or of the data you are using to make your forecasts. One of the reasons why it is so helpful to have other people working with you is so that they can pitch in on the research needed to confirm the accuracy of your data and forecasts. A sign that you're an "overestimater" is the plans you make based upon your forecasts never pan out as anticipated. Solving this challenge may be as simple as including others in your forecasting so that you're not thinking in silos.

R – **Reacting to the past or present** instead of proactively forecasting for the future. As tempting as it is to react to a past occurrence when forecasting, you have to try to push some of the past events out of your mind and remain focused on the future. That's not to say that you don't take the past and present into consideration when developing plans to prevent repeating errors, but the activity is forecasting, and that requires you to look forward, not back.

E – **Expecting other people to do forecasting without your participation.** Don't waste your staff members' time by asking them to accumulate data and report spreadsheet projections to you if (a) you're not giving them the guidance to provide the right information and (b) you're not going to use their information at all. I've seen leaders make this mistake too many times. As a result, they end up discouraging their people, wasting time and energy, and diminishing the effectiveness of forecasting over time.

C – **Confining the scope of topics or time frame** in your forecasting activities. As I mentioned at the beginning of this chapter, frequently leaders assume that they can't project their thinking too far into the future or that they can only anticipate certain aspects of their organization's future. As you've learned, with the right tools and people, you can expand the scope of topics and extend your thinking forward, allowing you to come up with better forecasts that will inform your decision making.

A – **Acting like you're an expert** in the area of forecasting when you don't know what you're doing. You now have the tools to become a better forecaster and to teach forecasting to your staffers so that they can multiply the benefits of forecasting throughout your organization. There's really no excuse for not practicing the tools and performing this activity. Even if you're not at an expert level initially, over time your forecasting skills will improve.

S – Solving tomorrow's challenges with today's or yesterday's thinking. It takes consistent and sustained effort to live mentally in the future. It's easy to regress into Retro- and Current-oriented thinking, so you have to catch yourself if you have a tendency to default to those conditions, and keep your mind focused on the road ahead.

T – Trusting the wrong people as forecasting collaborators. Put aside titles and silos and look for people who are willing to put in the work to forecast, who enjoy being Forward-oriented thinkers, and who have something to offer to forecasting efforts. Beware of "yes" people who tell you what you want to hear or go along with your forecasts without ever challenging you and offering alternatives. If everyone on your forecasting team agrees with you, it's likely you're not gaining any real input or different perspectives and data that you might need to ensure that your forecasts are as accurate as they could be. If you trust the wrong people, you'll fall prey to making poor decisions. Case in point: Look at the headlines of forecaster articles over the past few years and you'll read about economists who one week will say the recession is over and the next week say the exact opposite. You must make your own decisions.

I – Ignoring the signs of impending challenges, because they are not what you want to see. The job of the leader is just as much one of courage as it is hard work, and there will be times when you won't like what your forecasts are telling you. However, these forecasts aren't going to be as daunting to overcome as they once were, because you can go to your ET toolkit, pull out the right thinking tools, and proactively lead your organization to better future outcomes regardless of how challenging the future may initially appear.

N – Navigating through forecasting exercises without tools. Earlier in the chapter, I mentioned that forecasting is not guesswork, it is an activity based on data that enables you to predict with a degree of certainty the future your organization is facing. Therefore, to ensure that your predictions are as close to reality as possible, you have to take the guesswork out of the game and use tools that give you a realistic snapshot of the future so that you can take measures now to navigate successfully tomorrow. Forecasting takes time and tools to help you to perform your role and to incorporate forecasting into your life on a whole new level.

G – Generating conclusions based on awareness-level information when additional research is needed to confirm your assumptions or predictions. Don't conclude too quickly that you possess the truth about a topic and don't assume that you are knowledgeable about something before exploring the possibility that you're merely aware of it. Just as you learned in Chapter 7, there is a huge difference between acquiring awareness versus developing knowledge, and while awareness alone will be enough at times, when you do need a deeper level of understanding, you have to be sure that you're not fooling yourself into thinking you have knowledge when you don't.

No matter how great your forecasting tools are, if you don't blend them with a degree of honesty and realism, you could potentially lead your organization off its road to Desired Outcome.

Forecasting and the Other Categories of ET

Enterprise Thinking appears to be about the present, but from a big-picture view, it's really about the future. Yes, its activities and tools help you solve daily challenges, but actually, when you combine all four categories of ET, you're able to project your thinking beyond today and make decisions that are good for your organization's future.

If you maintain an Optimum Forward Orientation, you elevate yourself and your performance as an Enterprise Thinker, because forecasting is an activity that you perform in conjunction with other ET activities. By seeing farther into the future, you are using higher-quality mental power to perform those activities.

Take, for instance, all the thinking you do when you use the CST Model to develop plans, and how the information you use going into the process will impact the end results coming out of it. The plans you come up with in your CST Model will be different if you consider where you want your organization to be in five years as opposed to only where you see it in five months. Planning is made stronger when you can accurately extrapolate global Cycles, Trends, and Patterns, too. When you're selecting Macro Tactics and Tactics to play out your Strategy, you open up numerous and potentially better options—like advanced technologies, improved products, new hires, etc.—by seeing beyond your available options today to those that will be available in twelve months or two years.

Your perspective at 50,000 feet also needs to extend years into the future. Let's say that the year is 2004, you are the director of an elder-care facility, and you've seen the impact that today's increasingly mobile workforce has had on the extended family. You meet with your futurist group, and one of your members tells you that a fairly new technology, today's version of Skype, is on the horizon for mass use. You gather this concept into your Cyclonic Thinking and consider how it might help many of your residents whose children and grandchildren live miles away and therefore, don't have the benefit of family members stopping in frequently for face-to-face visits. How might the trend toward increased mobility and decreased direct access intersect with this technology to shape the future of your organization and your industry?

If you combine this trend with that of each generation's increased comfort with technology, you might forecast how families that can't travel for a Sunday visit with grandmother could still pay her a visit via a video conversation. If you had been a Retro-oriented forecaster, this new option to keep residents and their families connected may not have been adopted as quickly or at all by your organization. Yet, because you were more progressive in your approach, you might outsell a competing health-care facility, because you're coming up with solutions that please all generations.

The use of forecasting tools enables leaders to make progressive and long-lasting decisions for their organizations. Let's take a look at how forecasting influences the other three ET categories' activities:

- **Learning** – Forecasting extends your vision forward and gives it a wider scope, making you realize that you can't just settle for awareness and knowledge that keeps your perspective rooted in Retro- and Current-oriented thinking. This understanding impels you to seek awareness and knowledge—about your organization, its competition, and the global arena in which both exist—that are not just an accumulation of data from the past and present, but that are also an extrapolation of data about future challenges and opportunities, too. Through forecasting, you gain a longer-range vision that empowers you to make decisions that are more often proactive versus reactive, giving you more control than ever before over the future you forge for your organization.

- **Strategizing** – Developing plans based on where you are today and what you intend to accomplish in the near future are typically too shortsighted to have the positive impact they need on your organization. So if you find that you are constantly revising plans and/or your plans tend to fail to deliver the outcomes you set out to accomplish, chances are your thinking is too Retro- or Current-oriented. But when you can forecast future opportunities and challenges more accurately, you develop plans, establish alliances, and utilize technologies in ways that deliver more positive and sustainable outcomes down the road. For example, think about the activity of developing new products and services: Considering how many products spend less time on the market today than they did in the past, leaders must be faster and more precise in their decision making than they've ever been. Forecasting allows you to predict how the world around you will impact the reception your products and services will have in years to come, and it informs your decision making so that your products and services can evolve to stand the test of time.

- **Performing** – A leader who can regularly live mentally in the future is one who can envision better options for synchronizing personal aspirations with professional Desired Outcomes, because they have a long-range view of possibilities in both areas. In addition, forecasting gives you a better handle on not only today's leaders but on what the next generation of leaders will need, allowing you to take measures now that will empower them in years to come. Additionally, knowing about a multitude of opportunities and challenges on the horizon focuses your measures to innovate and triggers new ideas for better innovating, too. And finally, when you are making decisions from a Forward-oriented position, you increase the chances that you can develop WSPs that enable you to sell yourself and your ideas, further enhancing your ability to excel personally and professionally.

By engaging in forecasting, you can enhance your performance of all ET activities and build a brighter future for your organization than you could have imagined otherwise. Forecasting is such an essential activity that it can spell the difference between decline and growth for many organizations. Dr. Martin Apple, president of the Council of Scientific Society Presidents, described to me the happenings in an ongoing IBM study of 1,500 CEOs that showed how during 2008 and 2009, 30% to 40% of IBM companies saw a drop in growth while 20% enjoyed an increase.[186] The difference, according to Apple and the researchers involved, is that the latter group had leaders who immediately shifted gears and overcame the "change gap" by redirecting their planning. Their approaches were to increase transparency, look towards growth markets, acquire bargain priced assets, hire talent that was released into the market, generate new and distinctly better alliances than in the past, and be innovative in their infrastructure development. All of these measures translated to growth. So, while you can be proficient at performing activities within the Strategizing, Learning, and Performing categories, you can better ensure that you reach your Desired Outcomes by bringing ET full circle and becoming an expert at Forecasting, too.

NEXT STEPS...

REDEFINING YOUR FUTURE

AT THE TIME WE MET, Oksana Sobol, a manager at a global market research company, was grappling with a business issue at work. She told me how one of her new hires had entered her office and complained that all of his incoming calls were requests from clients who wanted their forecasts to be delivered faster than the firm's typical ten-day turn-around schedule. Sobol had been previously aware that clients were unhappy with the time it took to deliver forecasts to them, because this had been an ongoing challenge. However, she also knew that her analysts already felt they were maxed out. Before learning about ET, it appeared that the only way Sobol would be able to please her clients would be to and reduce delivery time by asking analysts to work longer hours and at a faster pace. This is how Sobol described using ET to solve her challenge.

> "Initially, I could see no solution that could please everyone; either the clients would be unhappy, or the analysts would burn out. But then I learned about ET, and it got me thinking about my role as a leader. It was my job, not the analysts responsibility, to figure out what to do in this situation.
>
> "I started by using Redefining to identify my real challenge, and then I deconstructed the forecasting process and developed a CPM chart of the process as it currently played out. I found that the biggest chunk of time on the critical path—five days—was consumed

by waiting for in-market data that our analysts needed for benchmarking. I knew that if I could eliminate his step, we could shorten the entire process by five days without accelerating any of the actual analytical work.

This revelation prompted me to shift the activities involved in the collection of in-market data from mid-stream to the beginning of the process by creating a structured repository using past projects and requesting up-front what we thought we would need in the future. With this change, we could meet and often exceed our clients' expectations. That was the Economics of Thinking in action!

It's been many years since I learned Enterprise Thinking, and I still return to my notes about the tools whenever I face an issue that needs solving. ET has changed the way I approach everything."

And she's telling the truth when she says "everything," because she uses ET on the job and in her personal life all the time. I remember her saying to me that just as Microsoft has a Start button in the left bottom corner of computer screens, she wishes there were a MyET Toolbox button, because in reality, she knows with certainty that the right ET tool is always there when she's faced with her daily challenges and opportunities. It's just a matter of selecting and utilizing the most appropriate one at any given time. (To download your copy of MyET Toolkit, visit www.paidtothink.com.)

Sobol was promoted to a role with more responsibility and is a living example of how, regardless of you management level, geographic location, industry or sector, when you're armed with ET tools, you have more and better options at your disposal. Prior to acquiring her ET tools, her default option would have been to try to work it out with both parties—20% of the GPP as a first (and maybe only) measure—which never would have delivered to her a real solution like cutting the delivery time of forecasts by over half. ET changed Sobol, and it has and will continue to change you and the people with whom you come in contact for years to come.

Think back to the first time you cracked open *Paid to Think*, looked at the number of pages you would have to read, and made the decision to invest in yourself just the same. How have some of your past beliefs about leadership and management been reshaped by the understanding that your primary role is to think? What assumptions did you challenge, and how has your approach to problem solving changed by having thinking tools? Now you create better plans by using the CST Model rather than the old approach of "strategy and tactics." Using the ET Development Funnel, you make product selection and development decisions that are less random and more tied with overall Desired Outcome; you guess less and win more often by feeding your decision making with competitive intelligence data; you multiply successes throughout your organization by understanding how to properly empower others; and you make decisions that better position your organization now and have longer-lasting positive effects, because you have the tools to keep your perspective heightened at 50,000 feet and stretched farther into the future.

Of course, you've changed so much more than these examples can express. My guess is that you have been experiencing new kinds of successes as a result of more and better thinking that you wouldn't have experienced before you learned about Enterprise Thinking. And as much as you've changed since you first picked up this book, you will change even more as time passes. You're only at the cusp of understanding what you can do with ET and what it can do for you.

What You Can Expect Moving Forward

Every individual is going to experience the changes brought on by ET differently and at different rates, but one area of irrefutable change that every Enterprise Thinker experiences for sure is a change in thinking: how you think, what you think about, and the amount of time you put into thinking. These factors have surely already advanced your thinking past many of your competitors and contemporaries who may only "pine for more solo time to think and strategize" as mentioned by the performance-expert company SuccessFactors, Inc.'s CEO Lars Dalgaard, who "tries to dedicate as much as 25% of his week to thinking by making time on flights or blocking out time on his schedule—occasionally retreating to a quiet room or driving on the highway to let ideas crystallize,"[187] two points that reiterate the value of Cyclonic Thinking and scheduling the appropriate amount of time in your day for thinking and priority management. Regardless of where you are in your transformative process, you're ready to take a different kind of journey, one that reveals six underlying premises of ET that will shape your thinking as you take your next steps into the future as an Enterprise Thinker.

ET Makes the Invisible Visible

Ask anyone on the street to name a few reasons for the $2 billion success of the blockbuster film *Avatar*, and you'll get a variety of answers: award-winning cinematography, innovative visual effects, excellence in editing, 3D technology, PR and marketing, etc. But ask an Enterprise Thinker and you'll get a different kind of answer. From an ET perspective, it's all of these elements, intricately woven together into one mega-WSP by world-renowned director James Cameron.

Cameron spent fifteen years Cyclonically Thinking about his project. He knew that a good storyline wasn't enough to launch an innovative new product like *Avatar* onto the global marketplace. He would have to learn about advancements in technologies and forecast trends in moviegoers' preferences—would people pay a higher ticket price to see a 3D movie? The director had a collection of WSPs in his back pocket, including *The Terminator*, *Aliens*, and *Titanic* that enabled him to sell himself as a deliverer to alliances like 20th Century Fox, who bought into his ideas to the tune of hundreds of millions of dollars for one of the most expensive films ever produced.

To the general public, the end product seemingly speaks for its success. To the Enterprise Thinker, the end product is only the visual representation of countless behind-the-scenes puzzle pieces coming together. *Avatar* grew from a single idea that sprouted branches of other ideas, people, organizations, capital, technologies, systems, structures, and good decisions . . . and it all culminated in a breakthrough Order Winner under the planning and direction of Cameron, the man who was leading the charge.

Not only did Cameron perform his leadership activities proficiently, but the end product of his efforts is also a symbolic representation of Enterprise Thinking's ability to make the invisible visible. If you were to sit in on a 3D version of *Avatar* without wearing the 3D glasses, you would not see the special effects that brought the movie its accolades. Yet the special effects are there, because they have been built into the screen. The difference between being able to see them or not is whether the viewer has the glasses—the right "tools"—to see them. The same clarity happens to you through Enterprise Thinking. The twelve activities and accompanying tools enable you to see the opportunities that have been in front of you all along. In other words,

Enterprise Thinking makes the invisible visible.

Like other Enterprise Thinkers who say that they see ET everywhere, you probably find that you can never look at your own organization the same way again, because now you have the ability to see what has been before you all along. Nineteenth-century author and physician Oliver Wendell Holmes has often been quoted as saying, "Man's mind, once stretched by a new idea, never regains its original dimensions."[188] With the tools and concepts you've learned in *Paid to Think*, your mind has been stretched. Now it's time to take everything you have learned to a new level.

ET Eliminates Siloed Thinking

Previously, you may have seen your organization as a collection of silos, but with your new perspective comes new and unsiloed decision making. Now you understand that these silos are more like integrated tentacles that connect and twist around each other, impact one another, and have the power to strengthen or weaken your organization as a whole. This new awareness forces your perspective to 50,000 feet and highlights opportunities as never before. In many ways, you're seeing what many IT experts have known all along: Organizations are simply networks of departments, people, products, systems, ideas, etc., that need to be coordinated properly to reach Desired Outcome.

This concept played out in real life when Guy Chiarello was first offered the position of chief information officer for JPMorgan Chase. CEO Jamie Dimon didn't get an immediate "yes" from Chiarello that day. Instead, Chiarello wanted to be sure that his approaches would align with Dimon's plans and those of other leaders on the team. He told me that he relayed to Dimon, "We're going to have to figure out how to leverage this business horizontally across all business units, or I don't want the job."[189] His background in IT was proof enough that gaining buy-in from all other business units and functions would be an essential component his success. Once Chiarello was sure that he was a fit for JPMorgan Chase's culture and overarching plan, he accepted the position and was able to deliver value to the firm.

ET Is Practical: It Is Your World

Of course, seeing the previously invisible can initially come with its own challenges. When you are first exposed to ET, you can feel like your mind is trying to drink a flood of ideas rushing at you with the force of a fire hose. Some people complain that they want to shut off the flow of ET into their brains so they can sleep at night, but they can't. They may describe a series of frequent and unexpected "aha" moments happening to them both within their organizations and when they're going about their daily lives. For instance, people see the GPP not only in their organizations, but in the restaurants where they dine with their friends and families, while traveling to and from work, at their doctors' offices, while watching sporting events, and everywhere else they look. That's because ET is practical; it not only fits into your world, it *is* your world.

For example, a simple ET principle like the Economics of Thinking extends beyond the walls or borders of your organization. Surely, it increases your value as a leader by aiding you in focusing an appropriate amount of time on thinking activities before you engage in actions, resulting in better outcomes. But you can apply the principle in all areas of your life: your home, social life, community involvement, and more.

[The GPP Puts an End to Brothers' Bickering]

When our sons were young, they would occasionally bicker over which one could use the TV when they each wanted to watch a different program airing at the same time. We had one television and saw no reason to get another one, since we wanted to limit television viewing anyway. For a while, it didn't seem like much of a problem. When conflicts arose, the kids would tend to try to bargain with each other first—"Okay, you get it this time, but at four o'clock, I get my show"—and if that didn't work out, they would plead their cases to my wife, their referee. When the frequency of the bickering increased to an almost-daily occurrence, I knew that this "hugging and kissing" approach needed to be replaced by a look at the 80% of the GPP.

I decided to create a TV chart on an Excel spreadsheet. It would cover a two-week period of time starting in the morning and ending at night (even though they wouldn't be in front of the TV the entire time), and it would alternate viewing times at half-hour intervals. I also rotated the intervals every other day, so that if one boy had the 8 am time slot on Monday this week, his brother would have the 8 a.m. time slot on Monday next week, ensuring that everyone got a fair shake on popular time slots.

When I presented the TV chart to the boys, it was accompanied by a digital clock to ensure that they could keep accurate track of their viewing times. Then I explained that they would have to follow two additional rules: (1) you can change or swap out times, and (2) if there are any future arguments, we go by the chart. The arguments stopped immediately. The boys never came to us with a TV-viewing issue again. By addressing the 80% of the GPP at home, we empowered our children and solved our challenge to everyone's satisfaction.

ET Is the Umbrella Approach Over Everything Else

As I mentioned in Chapter 1, ET is unlike other approaches to leadership and management, not just because it focuses on the twelve activities, but because it is an umbrella approach that works cohesively with the various types of performance-related processes you may already have in progress, such as Six Sigma, Lean, ISO, Balanced Scorecard, Myers-Briggs, etc. For example, consider how ET is compatible with Six Sigma and Myers-Briggs: Six Sigma is a planning tool that you can incorporate into the activities of the ET Strategizing category, and Myers-Briggs is an awareness process that you can incorporate into the activities of the ET Learning category. In essence, the universality of ET means that ET doesn't compete with your other tools. Rather, ET is the umbrella leadership framework, and other tools, concepts, methodologies, and so on fit under it.

ET's Universality Creates Synergistic Value

As the concept of the 7Crosses of ET states, your title, industry or sector, geographic location, culture, etc. don't matter when it comes to becoming an Enterprise Thinker, because the challenges of leadership are universal. Judy Smith, medical director for the Roswell Park Cancer Institute in Buffalo, New York, touched on this truth when she said, "We are coming to grips now with the fact that we are much more similar to other businesses than we are different."[190] And so far, I've discussed the universality of ET as the reason you can use it *within* and *for* your organization. Now, what we're going to do is take the topic of ET's universality a step further and examine it within the larger context of a network *outside* your organization, and what this network means for you and your future.

When I say "outside," I'm not just talking about the vendors, buyers, and people from various places around the globe who might come to understand ET concepts and contribute to your organization's growth and survival today from any sector. I'm talking more in terms of ET as a global leadership style that becomes a network of sorts that can deliver an even greater synergistic value as defined by Metcalfe's Law.

Metcalfe's Law states that as the number of people involved in a network increases—networks like those involving mobile devices, the Internet, apps, intranets, and more—the greater value the network provides to its members. For example, what would be the value in owning a phone if you were the only person to have one? As soon as someone else owns a phone, however, the value of having the phone increases. Add ten people or ten thousand or ten million, and the network of phone users increases in value. Apply this law to ET, and you begin to realize how much more value you can gain from ET by teaching it to people within and outside your organization.

In the present and near future alone, imagine how your life would change if the people around you followed the same basic principles of ET. You'd get plans from senior management that were well thought out, which would provide greater value than simple spreadsheet expectations. Your vendors would empower you to help them by participating in building better systems and structures within the 80% of the GPP. And although you can already make a move from one job to another and transfer your knowledge, skill set, and tools to that new position quite successfully (though you may still have to learn the nuances of that particular industry, sector, or organization), consider how much more easily you can make the transition if the people at the new job already understand ET, too!

On your journey to becoming a more proficient Enterprise Thinker, realize that you are becoming one of the people who understands this global style of leadership and who will add value to the ET network. Whether you're talking with a prospective ally in another country or meeting with a nonprofit organization in your local community, the more people who speak ET's common language and understand how its tools are used, the more synergistic value will be gained, because it will be possible to work more collaboratively and cohesively together, to enjoy higher levels of performance and productivity by breaking out of silos, and to more assuredly reach professional/organizational and personal/life-related Desired Outcomes.

ET Focuses Your Thinking on the Future

Being proactive instead of reactive is a good position to be in when you're a leader. And to be proactive, you have to be living mentally in the future, which is what all four categories of ET do for you. Each tool is designed to push your thinking forward, whether you're using a tool from Learning to increase your global awareness or one from Performing to help your staffers think more innovatively. In other words, it's not just the tools from Forecasting that focus you on the road ahead; every tool by nature makes you stop and think before taking action, bringing you out of the day-to-day current and reactive focus many leaders find themselves sucked into and directing your attention on thinking activities that will position you to build a better tomorrow.

Having said that, keep in mind that focusing on the future doesn't just mean you need to be thinking about the extended future. The short-term "future" is important, too. Your future includes what's going to happen when you get on next week's job site just as much as it includes your five-year plan. Say that you are looking at your department's sales figures and you are concerned about hitting the target numbers. You're concerned because missing the targets could mean that you have to let go of a staff member next month, you will struggle more to secure funding for projects next year, and a particular lost sale could hurt your organization for the next three years. In each instance, you're still forced to look at the future, and the better you can do that, the better off you and your organization will be. ET puts you in that stronger position, because you see what's coming and can create your destiny with more certainty as opposed to reacting to events that are happening to you.

Five Stages of Becoming an Enterprise Thinker

Enterprise Thinking is not a magic trick. You don't just learn it one day and somehow have the skills to lead and manage at a figurative 200 mph. It takes time to move through the process, although you've most likely begun applying ET to your own life, both professionally and personally. Eventually, you will learn to be more proficient in all areas of ET, because you now have the framework to enable you to do so, and your higher level of proficiency will drive results.

Teresa King Kinney, CEO of Realtor Association of Greater Miami and the Beaches (RAMB)—a trade association for realtors in Miami, Florida, is the embodiment of great Enterprise Thinking leadership. Kinney took a position with the association at a time when it was functionally average, and transformed RAMB into one of the leading real-estate organizations in the world. When I met Kinney and her COO, Deborah Boza-Valledor, she had already developed a team of reliable captains and had begun building a loyal membership base for RAMB by offering an incredible list of proprietary products and services to its members. Our work together was to build on those successes, much as this book will allow you to do, by ramping up Order Qualifers, even if only by a nose, so that they became Order Winners that would solidify the Miami-based organization's position as a focal point for global real-estate transactions and enable RAMB to keep its promise to members to help them "list more, sell more, and make more."

Kinney secured top services for her membership that no other association of her type provides. She innovatively sold her ideas to establish exclusive alliances with vendors and has played a matchmaking role in developing the most exclusive alliances network of any realtor association in the world between Miami-based real-estate agents and their colleagues in thirty other countries. The leaders accomplished this achievement despite having to combat an aggressive, low-priced competitor association that RAMB eventually merged with, creating the largest local realtor association in the United States. The combination of Kinney's ability to create superior systems and structures and her talents as a smart forecaster have put RAMB in a position of success for years to come.

The Five Stages Explained

The complete transition from *learning* to *becoming* requires you to execute on a process that will integrate ET into your life. There are five steps in this process to becoming an Enterprise Thinker:

1. Learning
2. Applying
3. Adopting
4. Integrating
5. Becoming

The Five Stages to Becoming an Enterprise Thinker

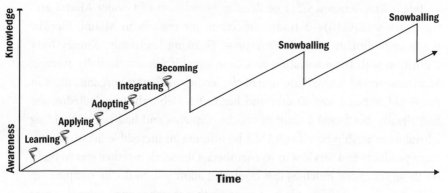

Figure 15.1—The Five Stages to Becoming an Enterprise Thinker

As you can see from Figure 15.1, you experience the five stages over time—rapidly for some people, longer spans of time for others—until you are performing many of the activities and using many of the tools to increasingly proficient degrees. Execute these five steps, and Enterprise Thinking becomes a part of you.

1. **Learning:** You have already exposed your mind to a new set of skills, tools, and concepts, and you can always reference sections of this book whenever you need to polish up on how to use them.

2. **Applying:** Knowing what to do isn't enough to create transformative change. Use your new tools, even on a small scale, so that you can achieve new successes. You can't read yourself into a state of leadership proficiency.

3. **Adopting:** Once you have applied ET and you have a few experiences under your belt, you will begin to unravel old habits and replace them with new ways of thinking. The adoption of new thinking will deliver a huge reward, you will begin to see how easily you begin to create new knowledge, which translates to new opportunities for you and your organization.

4. **Integrating:** With each success—both large and small—you will find yourself integrating ET into your thinking almost subconsciously. You might begin with a simple exercise such as Points of Light, which you learned about in Chapter 12, Innovating Everywhere. Say you want to improve how your organization meets the needs of its buyers. You would observe from 50,000 feet the flow of activity as flashes of light, both incoming (new orders, complaints, returns, referrals) and outgoing (advertising and marketing messages, product shipments). Then you might decide to use the ET Development Funnel to address your Desired Outcome, using observations from the Points of Light exercise to build criteria for screens and gates.

5. **Becoming:** You won't be able to see your organization, your industry, or your global community the same way ever again. You will see everything through the lens of ET. When you read a newspaper, talk with colleagues, meet new people, and so on, you will internalize the experience as an Enterprise Thinker. Just as when you see something in print and you can't help but translate those words into meaningful messages in your brain, you won't be able to stop seeing everything from the bigger picture and almost instantly uncover real challenges and envision new solutions.

After you have become the Enterprise Thinker, you will see that your skills and abilities will continue to improve over time. Notice in the diagram how the lines swoop down and then back up to a higher level of proficiency. These swooping lines indicate how the process of being an Enterprise Thinker continues in cycles as you learn nuances of the ET approach, combine the activities and tools in your own ways, and discover new and exciting ways to reach Desired Outcomes.

For instance, have you ever liked a movie so much that you wanted to see it again? And then when you watched it a second or third time, you noticed a number of "new" details that you hadn't caught the first time around? The mind captures what it is ready and able to absorb in the present moment, so it is good for people to revisit a source of knowledge in order to gain the full experience they need. If you were to reread this book, you would discover even more information and tools that you hadn't quite grasped during the first read. As you refer back to the book's contents, you will realize that ET is like peeling off the layers of an onion, each layer revealing something new and fresh. After reading *Paid to Think,* marketing expert Jay Abraham (who wrote the foreword to this book) said that he knew he'd have to read the book three or four times to get all the subtleties and depth of material. I suggest that you revisit portions of *Paid to Think* to reinforce what you have learned and to develop solutions as new challenges arise in your professional and personal life.

Irene Rosenfeld, CEO of Kraft Foods once noted, "Leaders tend to focus on 'what to do,' but the real issue is more often 'how to do it.'"[191] Integrating ET into your daily life is a matter of applying both the "what" and the "how" through the constant use of your new tools as you perform your twelve leadership activities.

Gauging Your Personal Progress

In the early stages of becoming an Enterprise Thinker, you might not know how to gauge your level of proficiency. To help you track your progress, look for indicators—positive and negative—within your organization in the months ahead. As you see occurrences from either the positive or negative list, you will be able to gauge how effectively you've inculcated ET.

INDICATORS OF ET PROFICIENCY
Positive Symptoms

- People want to work with you
- Your projects are coming in on time and on budget
- You're reaching Desired Outcomes
- You're being promoted
- Media is recognizing your achievements
- You can sleep at night
- You feel in control
- Fires are limited and for just cause
- Questions from others are strong
- You're excited to go to work
- Progress is moving as planned or improved
- Plans are being executed properly
- Others, both internally and externally, want to partner with you
- You're generating innovative products
- Staff is growing, learning, and taking on new responsibilities
- People are using the tools of ET
- Everyone is speaking the same language
- Meetings are productive
- The right technology is being selected and used accordingly
- Performance from others is greater than expected
- Work is done in half the time, with half the resources
- Your organization grows faster than the industry
- You begin to deliver disruptive products or services to other industries
- Forecasting has been an integral part of decision making
- You are globally minded (even if your organization only operates locally)
- Alliances are formed and managed effectively
- The components of strategizing are improved
- You've improved your sales abilities
- Competitive intelligence is done with precision
- Leadership knows its role and acts accordingly
- Your ideas are accepted with less resistance
- You have time to think
- Profits, or whatever benchmark used, are improving
- You're now in control of your own time, and are not just reacting

INDICATORS OF ET PROFICIENCY
Negative Symptoms

- Projects or assignments go in the wrong direction
- Deadlines are missed
- You hear people asking questions that seem obvious to you but they are still lost
- What you get back is not what's expected
- Leaders are executing before thinking through the action
- Frustration is prevalent
- You're spending nonproductive time talking about how to get everyone together on the same page
- Requests for "thinking outside the box" don't deliver
- You need conference calls regularly
- People are surprised at what you're saying or doing
- Micro teams form in a coalition to support each other against you
- People are renegotiating what's fair and workable
- You're making threats
- Everyone seems to be going in different directions
- You feel that your job is at stake
- Your organization's effectiveness is declining
- People are second-guessing you
- Discussions about leaving the organization or never working for you again are heard
- You feel undue pressure
- Numbers are no longer adding up
- You're unsure you're going to reach your Desired Outcome
- You're micromanaging where people don't love the changes
- Leadership is making late-stage changes to projects
- Negative media coverage
- You're working all the time
- Others don't want to work with you
- Profits targets are missed or declining
- Those you service or vendors are giving you some "advice"
- Others would rather avoid you than tell you what they think
- You're shooting off nasty e-mails in the middle of the night
- Bickering over little issues escalate
- You blame failure on others
- Your health starts to suffer
- You're losing support on initiatives
- Me-too products are continually created
- The word str--ss* is used frequently by you or others
- Alliances fall apart and you think it's them

*I never use this word and don't even like to see it in print, because it's so negative that the moment you say it, you feel bad.

Refer back to this chart in the months ahead to be sure that you are using ET proficiently to be a better leader, to optimally solve your challenges, and to build the promising future that your organization needs.

Today's Thinking Creates Tomorrow

At various times throughout this book, I've touched on the point that the decisions you make in the present will ultimately forge your future and that of your organization. That's because there's one undeniable reality that you must take with you as you embark on every new day:

All management exists in the future!

Outwardly, your words, actions, and behavior give the impression that you are providing value by what you do in the present. But that's only partially true, because although what you're doing today helps to guide and direct your organization and its people, the overall condition of your organization in this moment is not as much the result of what you did this morning or last week. It's quite probable that your contribution to today's successes took place as a result of the thinking you did months and even years ago and the decisions you made based on what you had learned, strategized, performed, and forecasted at the time. The current reality is a manifestation of all your past thinking-related activities as they are being played out by the lower-level managers and front-line staffers during execution-related activities, and this fact is the reason why having the right tools and the right thinking as essential to success. And the cycle continues, because as others are executing on your past plans, you are engaged in the twelve ET activities that will advance your organization into the next phase of its future.

Creating More Time

So often I meet people—smart people—who tell me that they feel "buried" under the burdens of their job and don't have the time in their daily schedules for even the most basic of pleasures, like having dinner with their kids or spending a single uninterrupted hour of time talking with their significant other. It's sad, and hopefully now you see that it doesn't have to be this way. You have tools at your disposal that give you power over your schedule and enable you to prioritize your entire life. Jeff Weiner, CEO at LinkedIn, expresses the importance of "carving out time to think, as opposed to constantly reacting." More specifically, Weiner points out that "during that [thinking] time, you're not only thinking strategically, thinking proactively, thinking longer-term, but you're literally thinking about what is urgent versus important."[192] Use ET to pull you off what one of my sons calls the "hamster wheel" of life, to focus your mind on what really matters and to allow you to achieve more, earn more, and live more. (And by "earn more," I don't necessarily mean earn profits in all cases; you can earn more influence, more free time, or more meaningful experiences.)

ET Is about Knowing What *Not* to Do

ET has just as much if not more influence over determining what you *should not* do as it does over what you *should* do. That fact can be as beneficial to your life as it can to your organization. For instance, the ET Development Funnel weeds out lesser options for new product development and reveals a "diamond" idea; lacking this type of process could prevent you from focusing your attention on Order Winners and waste your time on me-too products or new products that are nothing more than Order Qualifiers. Whether you're strictly applying this tool to product development, or you're applying the tool to decisions in your personal life, focusing precious time a Forcasted Order Winner that helps you achieve Desired Outcomes will enhance the quality of your life both within and outside your organization.

The same is true for working with all of your tools, like the Squirrel Effect, the Escalator Theory, Jumping the Tracks, Overcrowding the Canaries, the 51% Rule, Alliance Killers, the Cultural and Geographic Synchronization Calendar, Selling Your Ideas with Stories, or *Guanxi* Mapping, and so many more.

Becoming an Enterprise Thinker allows you to create the type of life now and in the future that you've always dreamt. You can't get past time back, but you do have another chance tomorrow to get it right. In other words:

You can't fix yesterday; you can only create tomorrow.

You now have the tools you need to create the tomorrow of your dreams.

Empowering Yourself to Live Your Best Life

Many years ago I spoke with Jack Covert, founder and president of the bulk-order business-book firm 800-CEO-READ. During that discussion, I told him about the ET approach to leadership and how I wanted to put it into a book at the request of clients for use as a how-to guide. At that time, Covert said, "Wow, it would be great if you could get all of that in one book," but considering how much information ET covers, we both knew that it would be a challenging task to produce such a work not to mention get people to commit to reading an atypically large book. Well, I want to thank you for taking this journey and to congratulate you for investing the time to learn ET. It is an extensive Empowerment Package that now belongs to you and that will enable you to build value into your life, not just into your organization.

Performing all twelve activities well will result in blocks of time opening up in your daily schedule that you will be able to fill with enriching experiences that make all aspects of your life more enjoyable. Do something that you've always wanted to do either for yourself or for other people, like serving your community or eliminating struggles and conflicts in different areas of life or in the world, so that you're contributing to the well being of all people. Incorporate ET into what you do every day, and see what incredible results you can achieve.

As I've said, you don't have to perform all twelve ET activities exceptionally well to see a huge change in your organization, career, or life. Due to ET's connectivity, improvement in one area yields results in other areas as well. Case in point: A few years back, I met an executive named Stephanie whose career had stalled and who felt like she had stopped living. She had learned some of ET—not nearly as much as you have in this book—and through some of the same tools you've been learning, she started to ask herself different questions, which produced different answers. I looked at her situation holistically and shared with her that career and life are connected, so one suggestion I offered was that she create a "wall of life" in her home. All she had to do was go out, engage in experiences that were meaningful, fun, and/or interesting to her, have someone take one photo of her having each experience, and over time, fill this wall with individual 4" × 6" photographs depicting her living life.

About a year after our conversation, I received an e-mail from the new and improved Stephanie. Not only had her career opportunities exploded—she had recently accepted an offer to become the president of a new company—but she was on her way to enjoying a new adventure: "I can tell you that the wall is filling up, and that I'm off to Ireland by myself tomorrow. No reason, just had a friend double-dog dare me that I'd never go alone, so I'm catching the first flight to Dublin in the morning."

Be sure to continually use all your ET tools to sharpen your skills so that you keep your focus on the future that you want to create for yourself and your organization. You'll want to be sure not to let this book just sit on a shelf or hide in a box, because it is a toolkit and reference guide that will help you build a better tomorrow.

Now is your time to build tomorrow.

In the end, for me fulfillment comes from working with purpose and enjoying everything life has to offer. For example, I'm happy to discover how to do something in five minutes that would have previously taken forty minutes, and I'm thrilled when I take a business trip to another part of the world and can spend a few hours dining or walking through a market with its local residents. But to have the time and opportunities to enjoy these kinds of experiences, you need the right tools, because try as you might, there is no guarantee that anyone will build the life of their dreams, especially if they don't know how. As my wife has said, "You don't get As for effort; you get As for results." (In the United States, an A is the ideal grade given to students who perform optimally.) So although exerting effort in your organization and in your life is admirable, the universe isn't going to reward you for not achieving Desired Outcomes. My hope is that you use Enterprise Thinking to enjoy your life more, too, both when you're in and out of your organization. You may be surprised to learn that high-performing leaders are not all workaholics. Outside of certain situations and projects that will occasionally take up more of their time than usual, many leaders can actually sleep eight or more hours a night and still spend time with friends, family, or by themselves. Now that you have better tools and *Paid to Think* as your reference guide to look back on from time to time, you can continue to cultivate your skills, boost your proficiency, and achieve more, earn more, and live more.

■ ■ ■

Throughout the years that I studied tae kwon do, I always considered the earning of my black belt as a sort of finish line. The journey wasn't always an easy one. There were days when I would drive to the *dojang* dead tired from a grueling work schedule to learn new forms, perform conditioning exercises, and spar with classmates. From time to time, I'd have to figure out how to give everything I had during these practice sessions despite a broken knuckle or torn muscle. Then there was the whole work/family/self balancing act. Tournaments and tests kept me and my classmates on our toes, too. Yet through it all, I kept my eye on the prize, the coveted black belt.

The day of the black-belt ceremony finally arrived, and with it came an eye-opening experience. Obviously, it was a proud moment to receive the belt and certificate from my master, Korean champion and U.S. Olympic tae kwon do coach Master Sun Chong. Not so expected was what Master Chong said in his speech to us:

"Now, you are beginner students. Now you will learn tae kwon do."

I was stunned. What? Did he just say *beginner*? Wasn't I was a beginner way back when I had to wear that white belt?

That was a humbling but eye-opening moment for me, and one that I will never forget. I wasn't crossing a finish line. I was beginning anew.

In essence, Master Chong was explaining that the stages from white belt to black belt had provided us with a basic foundation of skills and knowledge. Now that we had our black belts, we would be moving into a new phase of learning and development. Master Chong's words made progressively more sense in the ensuing months and years as I continued on this marathon-like journey to grow and develop as a martial artist and in my career and my life.

Consider this point in time as your black-belt benchmark in Enterprise Thinking. You have learned the basics of ET, and now you have the foundation you need to take yourself and your organization to another level. This is where *you* begin anew.

NOTES

CHAPTER INTRODUCTION

1 http://www.gurufocus.com/news/91848/buffett-gates-and-munger-tell-fox-business-that-united-states-future-economic-outlook-is-positive

2 "Digest of Education Statistics," *National Center for Education Statistics*, 2001. http://nces.ed.gov/programs/digest/d08/tables/dt08_010.asp and http://nces.ed.gov/fastfacts /display.asp?id=40
UNESCO: United Nations Educational, Scientific, and Cultural Organization—Institute for Statistics.

3 Chad Moutray – personal phone conversation with author on Dec. 3, 2009.

4 Association to Advance Collegiate Schools of Business (AACSB)—author's personal experience, March 2001.

CHAPTER 1 ENTERPRISE THINKING

5 Hay Group. "Facing the Leadership Crisis." Powerpoint Presentation, Jan. 2007.

6 Lane, Kevin and Florian Pollner. "How to Address China's Growing Talent Shortage." *McKinsey Quarterly*, July 2008.

7 Ibid.

CHAPTER 2 RETHINKING

8 George, Claude S. Jr. The History of Management Thought Second Edition Prentice-Hall, Inc. 1972 vii

9 The CEO Exchange Episode 502 Safeguarding the Future: Heroes and Villains of the Computer Age. John W. Thompson Chairman and CEO (Watched on Television) http://www.pbs.org/wttw/ceoexchange/episodes/ceo_jthompson.html

10 Rubado, Meghan. "Michael Heagerty, who forgot to sign his own petition, loses Syracuse Democratic line by Falling one name short," *The Post-Standard* , Jul. 30, 2009.

11 http://www.spacex.com

12 Ibid.

13 http://money.cnn.com/2010/11/22/autos/oprah_winfrey_vw_beetle/index.htm

14 http://www.manpower.com.tw/newsPress20090804.do?menuId=3-7-18

15 Byrne, John. Business Week "How Jack Welch Runs GE" 1998 McGraw-Hill Companies Winning Jack and Suzy Welch Harper Business (384 pages Hardcover)

16 Schechner, Sam. "NBC Bets on Gaspin to Remake Prime Time," *The Wall Street Journal*, Aug. 3, 2009. http://online.wsj.com/article/SB124925735440500275.html

17 Boeing Buttons: http://www.reuters.com/article/2011/06/21/us-air-show-button-id USTRE75K1XR20110621

18 Sonya Misquitta and Geeta Anand. "India Hopes for Rain, and an Accurate Forecast. *The Wall Street Journal*, August 13, 2009 H.R. *Hatwar, the head of India's meteorological department*

19 *Manual of Political Economy*, by Vilfredo Pareto, 1906, English trnsl. 1971; http://management.about.com/cs/generalmanagement/a/Pareto081202.htm

20 Koch, Richard. The 80/20 Principle: *The Secret of Achieving More with Less*, Currency Books, Doubleday & Company, Inc., 1998.

21 http://en.wikipedia.org/wiki/Gordian_Knot

CHAPTER 3 DEVELOPING PLANS

22 http://www.youtube.com/watch?v=-hxX_Q5CnaA

23 http://en.wikipedia.org/wiki/Undercover_Boss

24 Oprah's Big Give Television Show Episode 4, The $100,000 Giveaway http://www.oprah.com/slideshow/seriesandspecials/oprahsbiggive/pkgoprahsbiggive/slideshow1_ss_episodes104/2

25 Personal research by author while conducting interviews for a presentation.

26 Business.com "Critical Path Method" http://www.referenceforbusiness.com/encyclo pedia/Cos-Des/Critical-Path-Method.html?Comments[do]=mod&Comments[id]=1

27 Hill, Terry. *Manufacturing Strategy: Text and Cases*. 3rd ed. Boston: Irwin McGraw-Hill, 2000

28 Maura Webber Sadovi. "Sherwin Stays After Deal Sweetened." August 26, 2009 http://online.wsj.com/article/SB125124207557658661.html

29 Friedman, Thomas. "The Lexus and the Olive Tree" (Hardcover 469 pages 2000 Farrar, Straus and Giroux) http://www.amazon.com/Lexus-Olive-Tree-Understanding-Globalization/dp/0374185522/ref=sr_1_1?ie=UTF8&s=books&qid=1258916301&sr=1-1

30 Wheelwright, Steven and Kim Clark. "Revolutionizing Product Development: Quantum Leaps in Speed, Efficiency, and Quality" Free Press (Hardcover 1992 Page 90) PERMISSION GRANTED

31 Berry, William L. and D. Clay Whybark. *Manufacturing Planning and Control Systems*, 2nd edition Homewood, Illinois, Dow Jones-Irwin 1988 (Canary Cage Approach John Bennion of Bain and Company).

32 http://www.brainyquote.com/quotes/authors/a/alfred_a_montapert.html

33 Priority Management® Time Text® Methodology and graphics with permission John West Partner

CHAPTER 4 NEW PRODUCT

34 Deutschman, Alan. "The Enlightenment of Richard Branson." Fast Company 108 (Sept. 2006).

35 Cooper, Robert G. *Winning at New Products: Accelerating the Process from Idea to Launch.*(Perseus Publishing, 2001), 10.

36. Ibid, 67.

37 http://www.brainyquote.com/quotes/quotes/n/nolanbushn130640.html

38 David Annunziato. Idea Bank – personal conversation with author

39 Mark Victor Hansen – personal conversation with author

40 Miller, Mark. "1,600 People Apply for One Meter Reader Job." KomoNews. com, Feb.12, 2009, www.komonews.com/news/39498372.html.

41 http://en.wikipedia.org/wiki/Eating_your_own_dog_food.

42 Sherwin Williams paint can tested in Syracuse John Nottingham

43 Domino's Pizza – personal conversation with author.

44 Man Made National Geographic "Nuclear Plant" UK Sellafield Nuclear Plant Controlled Demolition, Inc. CDI http://channel.nationalgeographic .com/series/man-made/3500/Overview#ixzz0XQHTliRj (Confirmed Quote Stacy Loizeaux)

45 Cooper, Robert G. *Winning at New Products: Accelerating the Process from Idea to Launch.* (Perseus Publishing 2001), 67.

CHAPTER 5 ALLIANCES

46 Keeley, George. "Strategic Alliances Why Go It Alone?" Published on Website of law firm of Keeley, Kuenn & Reid, accessed Mar. 17, 2012, www.kkrlaw.com/articles/alliance.htm.

47 Lorange, Peter and Johan Roos. "Strategic Alliances: Formation, Implementation, and Evolution (Paperback 1993 Wiley), 14.

48 Ibid, 14.

49 R. Thomas Umstead. " HBO Rings in A PPV Knockout: 'Golden Boy' vs. 'Pretty Boy' Nabs 2.15 Million Buys" May 13, 2007 Multichannel News http://www.multichannel.com/article/128996-HBO_Rings_In_A_PPV_ Knockout.php
R. Thomas Umstead " Lewis Tyson Pays Off Big" June 16, 2002 Multichannel News http://www.multichannel.com/article/68664-Lewis _Tyson_Pays_Off_Big.php

50 ABC26 "Alliance to Create Louisiana, Florida Aerospace and Aviation Corridor Launched" Associated Press October 26, 2009 http://www. abc26.com/news/local/wgno-news-aviation-corridor-story,0,6763432 .story

51 Hotz, Robert Lee. "More Scientists Treat Experiments as a Team Sport: Massive Collider, a Global Collaboration, Has a Bumpy Start; But

Sometimes the Work of Crowds Yields Wisdom," *The Wall Street Journal*, Nov. 20, 2009, A23.

52 Cox, Lauren. "Blind Woman Sees With "Tooth-in-Eye" Surgery," ABC News, Sept. 17, 2009. http://abcnews.go.com/Health/Technology/woman-regains-vision-tooth-implanted -eye/story?id=8595589

53 Goldsmith, David. "Organizational Design: The Hollywood Model," Jan. 2000. http://davidgoldsmith.com/hotarticledetails.php?topicid=149

54 http://www.unitedspacealliance.com/about/default.asp

55 Washington State water-district mergers – personal conversation with author.

56 Pepitone, Julianne. CNNMoney "Dell to buy Perot Systems for $3.9 Billion," *Money.cnn.com*, Sept. 21, 2009. http://money.cnn.com/2009/09/21/technology/dell_acquires _perot_systems/?postversion=2009092111

57 Svensson, Peter. Associated Press. "Kindle display maker E Ink to be bought for $215M," *USAToday*, Jun. 1, 2009. http://www.usatoday.com/tech/products/2009-06-01-eink-kindle_N.htm

58 Segil, Larraine. "Making business alliances work," *Management Quarterly*, Summer 2008.

59 Clark, Don and Ben Worthen. "Oracle Snatches Sun, Foiling IBM," *The Wall Street Journal*, Apr. 21, 2009. http://online.wsj.com/article/SB124022726514434703.html

60 Cooper, Robert G. *Winning at New Products: Accelerating the Process from Idea to Launch.* (New York, NY: Basic Books, 2001), 68.

61 Herd, Tom. "M&A Success: Beating the Odds," Bloomberg Businessweek, Jun. 22, 2010. http://www.businessweek.com/managing/content/jun2010/ca20100622_394659.htm

CHAPTER 6 TECHNOLOGY

62 Clancy, Michael and Victoria Cavaliere. "GOP Coup Upsets Balance in NY Senate," NBCNewYork.com, Jun. 9, 2009. http://www.nbcnewyork.com/news/local-beat/GOP-Gains-Control-of-State-Senate-after-2-Dems-Switch-Sides.html

63 "Andrew Carnegie," *The American Experience*, Public Broadcasting Service, 1997. http://www.pbs.org/wgbh/amex/carnegie/index.html

64 "Andrew Carnegie: Making Money the Old Fashioned Way: The Steel Business," PBS American Experience series Website, accessed Mar. 27, 2012, www.pbs.org/wgbh/amex/carnegie/sfeature/mf_flames.html.

65 "Maersk Expected to Order 10 More Giant Triple-E Class Ships," *gCaptain.com*, Apr. 18, 2011. http://gcaptain.com/maersk-expected-order-giant-triple-e/?24022.

66 Personal conversation with author—Mark Trumper, MaverickLabel.com in Edmonds, WA http://www.mavericklabel.com/

67 Personal conversation with author—Nancy Rabenold

68 Author's personal experience: Michael Treacy speaks at Infosys Conference 2005.

69 http://www.tvhistory.tv/1950-1959.htm

70 "Table 12. Number and Median days of Nonfatal Occupational Injuries and Illnesses with Days Away from Work Involving Musculoskeletal Disorders by Selected Occupations, 1998." *Bureau of Labor Statistics, US Department of Labor*, Aug. 2010. www.bls.gov/iif/oshwc/osh/case/ostb0791.pdf.

71 Gates, Bill. *Business @ the Speed of Thought* (Warner Books Ltd. 1999), 41–44.

72 http://www.ornl.gov/sci/techresources/Human_Genome/home.shtml

CHAPTER 7 NEW KNOWLEDGE

73 Ferrario, Giovanni. "The Pocket Factory." *World: the quarterly magazine for Pirelli's management throughout the world 22* (Jan. 2000), 3–4.

74 Ferrario, Giovanni. "The Pocket Factory." World: the quarterly magazine for Pirelli's management throughout the world 22 (Jan. 2000), 3–4.

75 Holtz, Robert Lee. "When Gaming Is Good for You," *Wall Street Journal*, Apr. 6, 2012.

76 Rose, Charlie. "Eike Batista: Rich Man. Richest Man?" *Bloomberg Businessweek*, Feb.22, 2010. http://www.businessweek.com/stories/2010-02-10/eike-batista-rich-man -dot-richest-man

77 On receiving the Family of Man Award, 1964. http://en.wikiquote.org/wiki/Edward_R._Murrow

78 Bersin & Associates. "How Executives Stay Informed: A Study of Resources Used and Time Spent Locating Critical Business Information." Research study, Nov. 2005, www.learningdirectorsnetwork.com/refdocs/bersin_how_execs_stay_informed.pdf.

79 Walsh, Bryan. "Himalayan Melting: How a Climate Panel Got It Wrong," *Time Science*, Jan. 21, 2010. http://www.time.com/time/health/article/0,8599,1955405,00.html

CHAPTER 8 GLOBAL

80 Association of Executive Search Consultants. "Year of Resurgence for Executive Search Consulting." Press release, Mar. 3, 2011, www.aesc.org/eweb.

81 Association of Executive Search Consultants. "2011 AESC Member Mid-Year Outlook Report." June 2011, www.jofisher.com.au/pdf/AESC_MidYear_Report_2011.pdf.

82 "Surgeons Perform Trans-Atlantic Operation." CNN.com, Sept. 28, 2001, http://articles.cnn.com/2001-09-28/tech/telecom.surgery.idg_1_france-telecom-robotic-arm -surgeons?_s=PM:TECH.

83 Michael Schriver, e-mail message to author, Dec. 19, 2009 at 9:53 pm.

84 Blackman, Stacy. "Why Wal-Mart Failed in Brazil," CBS *MoneyWatch. com*, Feb. 23, 2010. http://www.cbsnews.com/8301-505125_162-31041902/why-wal-mart-failed-in -brazil/.

85 Fung, Victor, William Fung and Jerry Wind. *Competing in a Flat World*, (Pearson Education, Inc. Publishing as Prentice Hall, 2008).

86 Lublin, Joann S. "Finding Top Talent in China, India, Brazil," *The Wall Street Journal*, Apr.11, 2011, http://online.wsj.com/article/SB100014240 52748703696704576223124193736768.html.

87 Voiland, Adam. "5 Health Benefits from Bees, and 5 That Call for Caution," U.S. News & *World Report*, Oct. 8, 2008, http://health.usnews.com/health-news/family-health/articles/2008/10/08/5-health-benefits-from-bees-and-5-that-call-for-caution.

88 Tucker, Michael F. "Managing Projects Across Cultures," Applied Project Management for Space Systems.

89 Reese, Lori. "*A Generation of Little Emperors,*" Time World, Sept. 27, 1999. http://www.time.com/time/world/article/0,8599,2054392,00.html

90 http://www.100people.org/statistics_detailed_statistics.php

91 http://en.wikipedia.org/wiki/Think_globally,_act_locally

92 "What's Culture Got to Do with IT?" *Straits Times* (Singapore), Sept. 29, 2002.

93 www.reuters.com/article/2008/01/08/us-tata-car-idUSBOM93788 20080108

94 Hendon, Donald W., Rebecca A. Hendon and Paul Herbig. *Cross Cultural Business Negotiations*, (Quorum Books, 1996).

95 Mother Mouse story—Author's conversation with a fellow traveler.

96 Author's interview of Michael Soon Lee, March 30, 2011.

97 "ESPN convinced US soccer audience has knowledge," *FoxNews.com*, June 30, 2012. http://www.foxnews.com/sports/2012/06/30/espn-convinced-us-soccer-audience-has -knowledge/

98 White, Miles D. "The Four Ps of Global Business Expansion," *The Wall Street Journal*, Nov.12, 2010.

99 Deemer, Andy. "The Great Chinese Chip Taste-Off," *Asia Oscura*, Dec. 18, 2011. http://asiaobscura.com/2011/12/the-great-chinese-chip-taste-off.html

100 Wadha Vivek, AnnaLee Saxenian, Ben Rissing, and Gary Gereffi, "America's New Immigrant Entrepreneurs." Joint study conducted at University of California, Berkeley, School of Information, and Duke University, Pratt School of Engineering, Master of Engineering Management Program; Jan. 2007.

CHAPTER 9 COMPETITION

101 http://inventors.about.com/od/indrevolution/a/Francis_Lowell.htm

102 UGL Equis Corp – personal conversation with author.

103 http://www.harmankardon.com/en-us/aboutus/history/pages/history.aspx

104 Gorman, Siobhan. "U.S. Report to Warn on Cyberattack Threat From China," *The Wall Street Journal*, Mar. 8, 2012, http://online.wsj.com/article/SB10001424052970203961204577267923890777392.html.

105 Greene, Jay. "Microsoft Sues over Google's Hire," *Bloomberg Businessweek*, Jul. 20, 2005. http://www.businessweek.com/stories/2005-07-20/microsoft-sues-over-googles-hire

CHAPTER 10 LEADING

106 Bill Strickland: author's personal experience and Manchester Craftsman's Guild. http://www.manchesterguild.org/
107 Boudette, Neal E. "Fiat CEO Sets New Tone at Chrysler: Marchionne Shuns Executive Suite for Office Near Engineers; 2010 Jeep Model Highlights Challenges," *The Wall Street Journal*, Jun. 19, 2009. http://online.wsj.com/article/SB124537403628329989.html
108 Jucca, Lisa, Deepa Seetharaman, and Soyoung Kim. "Special Report: Can an Italian Elvis Make Fiat-Chrysler Dance?" Reuters.com, Mar. 25, 2011. www.reuters.com/article/2011/03/25/us-fiat-chrysler-marchionne-idUSTRE72O15P20110325.
109 Ibid.
110 Agle, Bradley, et al. "Does CEO Charisma Matter? An Empirical Analysis of the Relationship Among Organizational Performance, Environmental Uncertainty, andTop Management Team Perceptions of CEO Charisma." *Academy of Management Journal*, Feb./Mar. 2006. http://images.usnews.com/usnews/biztech/features/CEOcharisma.pdf.
111 Bryant, Adam. "68 Rules? No, Just 3 Are Enough: Interview with William D. Green." *New York Times*, Nov. 21, 2009, www.nytimes.com/2009/11/22/business/22corner.html?pagewanted=all.
112 "Snapshot," *USA Today*, Nov. 15, 2006. Based on data from a survey by the Cognos/Paladium Group.
113 Gerber, Michael. *E-Myth*, Harper Business (paperback) 1988. http://www.amazon.com/E-Myth-Michael-E-Gerber/dp/0887303625/ref=sr_1_2?ie=UTF8&s=books&qid=1258919945&sr=1-2
114 Wakabayashi, Daisuke. "Softbank to Groom Executives," *The Wall Street Journal*, Jun. 27, 2010. http://online.wsj.com/article/SB10001424052748704569204575328592696159832.html
115 http://www.fastcompany.com/welcome.html?destination=http://www.fastcompany.com/1008704/fast-facts-about-americas-bosses October 1, 2008
116 "Ten Years From Now . . ." *Businessweek*, Aug. 20, 2007, www.businessweek.com/maga zine/content/07_34/b4047401.htm.
117 Kaskey, Jack. "A DuPont Chief 's Days of Future Passed." *Bloomberg Businessweek*.com, Jan. 13, 2011. http://mobile.businessweek.com/maga-zine/content/11_04/b42120 17598520.htm.
118 George Butler 2000. "The Endurance: Shackleton's Legendary Antarctic Expedition" http://www.amazon.com/dp/B0000A7W16?tag=thelandoferic&camp=14573&creative=327641&linkCode=as1&creativeASIN=B0000A7W16&adid=094XRGSGG0DT45GYANFY& and http://www.amnh.org/exhibitions/shackleton/

CHAPTER 11 EMPOWERING

119 Carbonara, Peter. "Hire for Attitude, Train for Skill," *Fast Company*, Aug. 31, 1996. http://www.fastcompany.com/26996/hire-attitude-train-skill

120 Disney hiring procedure – author's personal experience with Disney staffers.

121 Barankay, Iwan. "Rankings and Social Tournaments: Evidence from a Crowd-Sourcing Experiment," *University of Pennsylvania CEPR and IZA*, July 2012. Gould, Tim. http://www.hrmorning.com/is-your-review-process-actually-killing-motivation/ August 20, 2010

122 Nyberg, A., et al. "Managerial Leadership and Ischaemic Heart Disease Among Employees: the Swedish WOLF Study." Occupational and Environmental Medicine 66 No. 4 (2009): 51–55.

123 Personal conversation with author—*The Experience Economy* author Jim Gilmore http://www.strategichorizons.com/jimGilmore.html

CHAPTER 12 INNOVATING

124 http://www.japanfortheuninvited.com/articles/shikaku-suika-square-watermelons.html

125 Christensen, Clayton. *The Innovator's Dilemma*, Harper Business Press, May, 1997.

126 Ibid, xiii.

127 "Cork Wine Stoppers Making a Comeback." ThePortugalNews.com, June 25, 2011, www.theportugalnews.com/cgi-bin/article.pl?id=1118-18.

128 Christensen, Clayton. *The Innovator's Dilemma*, Harper Business Press, May, 1997, 41.

129 Associated Press. "Developments in Google's $12.4B Motorola purchase," *MSNBC.com*, August 13, 2012. http://www.msnbc.msn.com/id/48649687/ns/business-us_business/#.UCmMT6D4Lcx

130 Oticon – Personal experience with author.

131 Takenaka, Kiyoshi and Franklin Paul. "Sony, Samsun detail 3D TV plans," *Reuters*, Mar. 9, 2010. http://www.reuters.com/article/2010/03/09/us-sony-3d-tv -idUSTRE6280H920100309

132 "Innovation and Commercialization, 2010: McKinsey Global Survey Results." *McKinsey Quarterly*, Aug. 2010.

133 http://en.wikipedia.org/wiki/Snake_Well http://www.shell.com/home/content/innovation /meeting_demand/smartfields/

134 Ihlwan, Moon. "Innovation Close-up: LG Electronics," *Bloomberg Businessweek Magazine*, Apr. 15, 2010. http://www.businessweek.com/magazine/content/10_17/b4175037784791.htm

135 Cooper, Robert G. *Winning at New Products*, 2nd ed. (Cambridge, MA: Perseus Books,1993), 14-15. (Referencing Booz, Allen & Hamilton / PDMA best practices study, Drivers of NPD Success.)

136 Case Little, Margaret. "Toys 'R' Us CEO shares keys to staying competitive over holidays, during economic storm," *National Retail Federation*

Retail's Big Blog, Dec. 20, 2010. http://blog.nrf.com/2010/12/20/toysrus-ceo-shares-keys-to-staying-competitive-over-holidays-during-economic-storm/

137 http://www.papajohns.com/pizzachallenge/index.shtm

138 http://www.businessweek.com/interactive_reports/innovative_companies_2010.html

139 "Lessons on Innovation from DuPont's Thomas Connelly," interview with Thomas Connelly. SmartBlogs.com, Oct. 29, 2010, http://smartblogs.com/leadership/2010 /10/29/smartbrief-qa-tom-connelly/.

140 Goetz, Kaomi. "How 3M Gave Everyone Days Off and Created an Innovation Dynamo," *Fast Company/Co.DESIGN*. http://www.fastcodesign.com/1663137/how-3m-gave-everyone-days-off-and-created-an-innovation-dynamo

141 Deutschman, Alan. "The Fabric of Creativity." *Fast Company*, Dec. 1, 2004. http://www.fastcompany.com/51733/fabric-creativity and http://www.fastcompany.com/magazine/89/open_gore.html?page=0%2C2

142 Abelson, Jenn. "Yes, we have one banana: Boston firm helps Chiquita find a way to keep delicate fruit ripe and ready," *The Boston Globe*, Mar. 6, 2007. http://www.boston.com/business/articles/2007/03/06/yes_we_have_one_banana/

143 Johnson, Steven. *Where Good Ideas Come From: The Natural History of Innovation* Riverhead Books 2010

144 Colaizzi, Merritt. "Live from TWTRCON '09: Craig Newmark on the Power of Real Time Communities," interview with Craig Newmark. SmartBlogs.com, Oct. 22, 2009, http://smartblogs.com/social-media/2009/10/22/twtrcon-keynote -highlights-from-the-craig-newmark-interview/.

145 http://piersmorgan.blogs.cnn.com/2011/01/25/piers-morgan-tonight-preview-kim -kardashian-gives-10-of-her-money-to-charity/

146 Burlingham, Bo, and George Gendron. "The Entrepreneur of the Decade." *Inc.*, Apr. 1, 1989. http://www.inc.com/magazine/19890401/5602_pagen_2.html

147 Rooney, Brian. "UPS Figures Out the 'Right Way' to Save Money, Time and Gas." *ABCNews.go.com*, Apr. 4, 2007. http://abcnews.go.com/WNT /story?id=3005890& page=1#.T4iAs47Z7uY.

148 Rockwood, Kate "Biomimicry: Nature-Inspired Designs," *Fast Company*, Oct. 1, 2008.

149 http://en.wikipedia.org/wiki/Biomimicry

150 Hollander, Sophia. " A Youngster's Bright Idea Is Something New Under the Sun," *The Wall Street Journal*, Jan. 5, 2012.

151 van Vallegooigen, Jaap. Snake Well Technology. Link to video http://davidgoldsmith.com/wordpress/?p=1353

152 MVP ad agency with different rooms for innovative thinking – author's personal experience.

153 http://en.wikipedia.org/wiki/Storyboard

154 Horn, Sam. *POP! Stand Out in Any Crowd*, Perigee Trade (a Division of Penguin USA), September, 2006.

155 Kelly, Tom. *The Ten Faces of Innovation*, (Doubleday, 2005).

156 http://nssdc.gsfc.nasa.gov/planetary/lunar/ap13acc.html

157 David Speer – personal experience with author.

158 Braver, Rita. "Lucas and Spielberg on Norman Rockwell," *CBS Sunday Morning*, July 4, 2010. http://www.cbsnews.com/2100-3445_162-6645543.html

159 Jeff Hurt – personal conversation with author.

160 Hays, Constance L. "The Media Business: Advertising; Monica Lewinsky Meets jenny Craig, and a Spokeswoman Is Born," New York Times, Dec. 28, 1999. http://www.nytimes.com/1999/12/28/business/media-business-advertising-monica-lewinsky-meets-jenny-craig-spokeswoman-born.html?pagewanted=all&src=pm

161 Shingo, Shigeo. *A Revolution in Manufacturing: The SMED System*, Productivity Press, 1985.

162 Mort Grosser, e-mail message to author, Mar. 26, 2012 at 3:20 am.

163 "Dennis Hong: My seven species of robot," *TED Ideas worth spreading* (video), Sept. 2009.

CHAPTER 13 SELLING

164 Bob Danzig – personal conversation with author.

165 Mike Critelli – personal conversation with author.

166 http://genforum.genealogy.com/benz/messages/145.html

167 Symonds, Matthew, and Larry Ellison. *Softwar: An Intimate Portrait of Larry Ellison and Oracle*, first trade paperback ed. (New York, NY: Simon & Schuster, 2004), 175.

168 Rusli, Evelyn M. "When Competing with Big Banks, Smaller Can Be Better." *New York Times*, Jan. 24, 2011.

169 Oneal, Michael and David Greising. "It's schmooze or lose in air wars," *Chicago Tribune*, Apr. 13, 2005. http://www.chicagotribune.com/news/nationworld/chi-05041 30177apr13,0,3860796.story Lunsford, J. Lynn, Daniel Michaels and Christopher J. Chipello. "Boeing Beats Airbus For Crucial Job," *Wall Street Journal*, Apr. 26, 2005. http://online.wsj.com/article/0,,SB111442901315815867,00.html

170 Hatcher, Monica. "Master driller aims to bring relief to oil spill/Disaster in the Gulf," *Houston Chronicle/chron.com*, July 11, 2010.

171 Bauer, Roy A., Emilio Collar, Victor Tang, Jerry Wind, Patrick R. Houston. *The Silverlake Project: Transformation at IBM*, Oxford University Press, 1992.

172 Peter Guber – personal conversation with author.

173 Berman, Dennis K. "Inside the Amway Sales Machine." *The Wall Street Journal*, Feb. 15,2012. http://online.wsj.com/article/SB10001424052970204062704577223302734609434.html.

174 Ibid.

175 Warner, Andrew. www.mixergy.com

176 Iyengar, Sheena. "How to Make Choosing Easier." TED Talks video, 16:05, Nov. 2011, www.ted.com/talks/sheena_iyengar_choosing_what_ to_choose.html.=

177 http://en.wikipedia.org/wiki/Where%27s_the_beef%3F

178 Lawton, Jonathan and Stephen Metcalfe. Pretty Woman, March 23, 1990.

179 Carnegie, Dorothy, *Don't Grow Old . . . Grow Up!* E.P. Dutton, 1956, 123.

180 Bryant, Adam. "Re-Recruit Your Team Every Day." *New York Times*, July 3, 2010.

CHAPTER 14 FORECASTING

181 Love, John F. *McDonald's Behind the Arches*, Bantam Books 1986, 177.

182 http://search.ancestry.com/search/db.aspx?dbid=1670&o_iid =46256&o_lid=46256 &o_sch=Web+Property

183 "Red Bull Augmented Racing," *YouTube*, Mar. 18, 2011.

184 Akers, Frank, et al. "Charting New Waters," The Johnson Foundation at Wingspread, Sept. 2010, 14–15.

185 Fisch, Karl, Scott McLeod, and Jeff Brenman. "Did You Know," *YouTube*, Oct. 21, 2008. http://www.youtube.com/watch?v=cL9Wu2kWwSY

186 Dr. Martin Apple, e-mail message and phone conversation to author, Mar. 2012.

CHAPTER 15 CONCLUSION

187 Silverman, Rachel Emma. "Where's the Boss? Trapped in a Meeting." *The Wall Street Journal*, Feb. 14, 2012. http://online.wsj.com/article/SB10001 424052970204642604577215013504567548.html.

188 http://www.brainyquote.com/quotes/authors/o/oliver_wendell_holmes _jr.html

189 Guy Chiarello – personal conversation with author

190 Porter, Jane. "Doctors Seek Aid from Business Schools." *The Wall Street Journal*, Dec. 22, 2009.

191 "Irene Rosenfeld serves up new 'rules of the road.'" *The Wall Street Journal World* Business Forum online, accessed May 11, 2012. http://online.wsj. com/ad/article/wbf-rosenfeld.

192 White, Erin. "Four CEOs' Tips on Managing Your Time." *Wall Street Journal* online edition, Feb. 14, 2012. http://online.wsj.com/article/SB1 0001424052970204883304577221551714492724.html.

GLOSSARY

4Ps of global expansion a tool from Abbott Labs chairman and CEO Miles White that helps leaders (and members of their organizations) to become more globally aware by focusing their attention on people, products, presence, and perseverance from a global perspective

4Ps of marketing a framework used by marketers to ensure they address product, price, placement, and promotion in the marketing of goods and services

4D four-dimensional; how the universe is defined, using the four dimensions of length, width, height, time, and location

7Crosses of ET an Enterprise Thinking concept used to specify the leadership model's universality as cross functional, cross level, cross industry, cross sector, cross culture, cross time, cross life

51% Rule an Enterprise Thinking concept stating that the likelihood of an individual or group to take on an endeavor or take a next step increases when they perceive they have at least a 51% chance of success

100 > 7 > 3 > 1 an Enterprise Thinking tool used in conjunction with the ET Development Funnel suggesting that during a selection process one should begin with as many ideas as possible (100 being an optimal target) and then narrow down the options to a single best option in increments from 100 to 7 to 3 to 1

50,000-foot perspective figurative terminology used to describe one's comprehensive and overarching "view" of an entity, geography, situation, etc., to understand the interplay, interactivity, and interconnectivity of smaller components within a larger context

Acquisition one of the six forms of alliances also known as a takeover or buyout; occurs when one entity takes complete control over another, either by purchasing it outright or by buying up more than 50% of its shares

Activity-Based Forecasting an Enterprise Thinking tool used by leaders to predict future occurrences accurately and more easily by first separating out individual activities within processes and then extrapolating the potential future of each activity rather than by attempting to address entire processes at once

Ad hoc alliance one of the six forms of alliances in which an impromptu committee or group is pulled together to fulfill a specific purpose, then disassembled once the group has served its purpose

Affiliate a type of joint venture alliance in which an association is established between parties and which requires fewer resources than mergers or acquisitions

Alliance Killers an Enterprise Thinking checklist tool used to prevent two or more parties from entering into potentially ineffective or bad relationships by indentifying early threats to an alliance, namely uncertainty, apathy, delusion, grandeur, ethnocentricity, incompatibility, selfishness, sloppiness, ignorance, and deceit

Alliance Pillars an Enterprise Thinking checklist tool used to ensure that two or more parties (1) are suitably matched to enter into a relationship, (2) enter into the right type of relationship, and (3) define parameters of their relationship up front to ensure its success; the eight pillars are form, risk, ally, objectives, financials, budget, controls, and human resources

Allocation of Time for Thinking and Executing Chart an Enterprise Thinking tool used by leaders as a guide for scheduling an appropriate percentage of their time to thinking-related and tactical activities depending on one's management level

Paralysis due to Analysis a concept describing the immobilization that occurs when one spends too much time thinking and misses out on opportunities as a result

Automated Forecasting level 4 of the ET Social Forecasting tool; predictions are executed by automated systems (rather than humans), which have the power to gather information from a wide range of data sources, such as distributed groups of people and organizations

Automated technologies any instrument used to leverage human potential that functions entirely (or almost entirely) without human intervention

Basic Strategizing informal and unstructured two-phase planning process that includes strategy and tactics

Be the Person Enterprise Thinking tool used by leaders and their stakeholders to trigger innovative ideas in which an individual, in a figurative manner, assumes the identity of another individual in order to understand what the latter is thinking and how he or she is behaving

Build the Package Step 2 of the ET Empowering Process where leadership builds the 80% of the GPP—a collection of systems and structures and other resources necessary to support the 20% of the GPP—prior to transferring power to others

Buy-In Chart   an Enterprise Thinking tool used to identify one's greatest supporters for a prospective idea or initiative so that they can gain buy-in from the supporters before pitching ideas and initiatives to other parties, increasing the odds of acceptance

Career Ladder Development Guide   an Enterprise Thinking tool that serves as an instruction manual for building an organization's Transparent Career Ladder or improving upon an existing one

Challenge Statement (CS)   the true challenge one identifies through the multi-step process of Redefining

Cloud-computing technologies   software applications and storage that are external to an organization and managed/hosted by an outside vendor

Collaboration Room (war room)   any physical or virtual location where two or more people assemble for the purpose of creating strategy or working together on a mutually beneficial strategic project or activity; within ET, suggested use is in selling continuously, but it can be used in any ET activity

Collectivist   a person who strives for group involvement and cooperation and considers group interests and needs to be of higher importance than those of any individual in the group

Competitive Intelligence (CI)   the awareness and knowledge about one's competition that comes from collecting, assembling, and analyzing data

Conditional Shifts Impact "S" Curve   an Enterprise Thinking diagrammatic tool that shows how changes in economic, social, political, behavioral, environmental, strategic, and other factors, as well as disruptive forces, can impact the S curve

Consortium   one of the six forms of alliances in which a band of groups or individuals pool a limited amount of their resources in the pursuit of some type of leverage and shared desired outcomes

Continuous innovation   the adaptation of an existing product or service through incremental improvements, typically requiring little or no behavioral change to use

Cornerstones for Engaging Others   an Enterprise Thinking tool directing leaders to develop skills in four areas—behavioral, oratory, writing, and interpersonal—as a way of enhancing their ability to gain buy-in, elicit cooperation, and win sales

CPM Activity-Planning chart   an Enterprise Thinking tool used as a companion to the CPM chart that indicates activities and their designations, immediate predecessors, and time they will take to finish

Critical Path   the longest path, indicated by the longest time it takes to finish activities in the Critical Path Method chart

Critical Path Method (CPM) chart   a tool used by planners and project managers to organize and track projects by highlighting interdependencies and chronologies of projects' activities in graphic form

Cross-Functional Development   a phase occurring in Activity III (Development) of the ET Development Funnel, during which participants making up subset teams from various departments or areas provide input from their areas of expertise and collaborate to perform preliminary steps leading up to a product/service/improvement launch and begin engaging in their own parallel development processes needed for an eventual, successful launch.

Cross-functional Group   Activity III of the ET Development Funnel, after leadership makes the decision to spend, individuals from across an organization participate in the development of an initiative so that multiple inputs are represented and the odds of the initiative's success increase

Cultural & Geographic Synchronization Calendar   an Enterprise Thinking tool used to enhance cross-cultural and cross-geographic relationships by highlighting and synchronizing key dates or events that might otherwise conflict and impact the ability for parties to work effectively together

Current-oriented forecasters   an Enterprise Thinking term used to describe leaders whose thinking tends to focus so heavily on present matters that their forecasting capabilities yield short-term decisions

Cycles   repeated occurrences that happens over a period of time, usually at regular intervals that can indicate future activity; within the ET tool Cycles, Trends, and Patterns, a factor to consider for making more accurate forecasting predictions

Cycles, Trends, and Patterns   an Enterprise Thinking tool that reminds leaders to study a collective grouping of three time-related occurrences to identify change indicators and make extrapolations to forecast potential future events

Cyclonic Strategic Thinking (CST) Model   an Enterprise Thinking tool used to create superior plans over traditional strategic-planning approaches by guiding leaders through five specific decision-making phases—Desired Outcome, Strategy, Macro Tactics, Tactics, and Execution—ensuring greater outcomes

Cyclonic Thinking   a metaphoric Enterprise Thinking term comparing the way that one's mind takes in ideas, gives them consideration, and "spews out" less-viable options to the way that a cyclone swoops ups objects, swirls them around, and discharges them

Cyclonic Thinking Time an Enterprise Thinking term referring to the duration one spends engaged in Cyclonic Thinking, suggesting that all leaders need this time to consider ideas and weigh options to make improved decisions

Daily Planning Cycle an Enterprise Thinking diagram that shows a way of planning out a day's activities in order to get the most effective results

Deployment from the military, an activity referring to the movement of assets into a ready position as logistical support before initiating any launch such as a combat engagement

Deployment Gate in Activity III (Development) of the ET Development Funnel the final go/kill checkpoint at which gatekeepers verify that all cross-functional teams and any supporting parties have completed their work and that the new-product development project is in its final ready position before Launch

Deployment Phase in Activity III (Development) of the ET Development Funnel, point at which sub-cross-development groups complete pre-work necessary to place a new-product development project into the ready position prior to a product/service/improvement launch

Detailed Evaluation in Activity II (Elimination) of the ET Development Funnel, point at which NPSD group(s) perform in-depth research of the surviving ideas and recommend a single best "diamond" idea to screeners for final evaluation

Detailed Evaluation Screen in Activity II (Elimination) of the ET Development Funnel, third and final point in the idea-screening process where Screeners objectively determine whether the NPSD group have filtered out all but the single best "diamond" idea for development into a product/service/improvement

Development Activity III of the ET Development Funnel during which a single best "diamond" idea is transformed into a final product/service/improvement and launched

Differentiating Projects from Their Imposters an Enterprise Thinking tool used as a preliminary step before selecting projects to develop in order to first differentiate projects from tasks

Discontinuous innovation (revolutionary innovation) an innovation that may take years for the market to adopt because it requires people to undergo significant behavior changes to use it

Disruptive innovation an innovation that produces rapid and significant changes within a marketplace and creates new value networks, often displacing competing products/services/improvements

Doing more with less   concept describing an inevitable trend faced by organizations to yield higher output utilizing fewer resources; within the context of Enterprise Thinking, a continuous opportunity for leaders to improve their organizations through better decision making and greater efficiencies

Dynamically continuous innovation   an innovation that represents a significant change to a product, service, or improvement while requiring users to make only minimal changes in the way they consume or utilize the product, service, or improvement

Early Finish/Late Finish (EF/LF)   the earliest and latest times that one can finish an activity within a Critical Path Method chart (CPM)

Early Start/Late Start (ES/LS)   the earliest and latest times that one can start an activity within a Critical Path Method chart (CPM)

Economics of Thinking   an Enterprise Thinking tool used to inform and remind leaders that thinking before taking action is beneficial to organizations; the better able a leader is to think through an idea before committing to action, the greater the chances an organization has to achieve higher returns all while mitigating risk, expense, and consequences

Elimination   Activity II of the ET Development Funnel during which a large collection of ideas are evaluated in three phases and filtered through three screens until a single best "diamond" idea has been selected for development into a product/service/idea; consists of Ideation Screen, Expansion and Surface Evaluation, Surface Evaluation Screen, Detailed Evaluation, and Detailed Evaluation Screen

Enterprise Thinking (ET)   an approach to leadership developed by David Goldsmith that displays and explains the twelve essential activities of leadership grouped into four categories, along with accompanying thinking tools to enable anyone in a leadership or management position to improve their abilities to think, solve challenges, create opportunities, make stronger and more future-focused decisions, and achieve desired outcomes faster and more effectively and comprehensively than typical methods of leadership education have provided in the past

Escalator Theory   concept describing how people, when they get closer to achieving desired outcomes, will naturally self-motivate and put forth an extra burst of effort to complete projects and tasks

ET Competitive Intelligence Process (ET CI Process)   six-step Enterprise Thinking tool used to increase knowledge of competitors to inform decision making and gain greater competitive advantages; steps are strategize, collect data, assemble information, create knowledge, review, and make decisions

ET Development Funnel Enterprise Thinking Phase-Gate Process tool for selecting and developing superior products/services/improvements by aligning the end "product" with Desired Outcomes and structuring the creative and subjective aspects of the process into a series of three activities: Ideation, Elimination, and Development; tool used for performing the ET activity of creating new products and services that can be adapted for use in establishing alliances and leveraging technology

ET Empowering Process five-step Enterprise Thinking tool enabling leaders to improve outcomes that the people they empower achieve by ensuring that leaders appropriately equip others and have a plan for guiding them before transferring authority and responsibilities; steps are Strategize, Build the Package, Select People and Transfer Power, Monitor Progress, and Adjust the Process

ET Global Nesting diagram Enterprise Thinking tool consisting of concentric circles illustrating how global awareness can be increased and options for improved decision making expanded through the interconnectivity of individuals, groups, organizations, communities, territories, countries, regions, and the world at large

ET *Guanxi* Mapping Tool an Enterprise Thinking tool that provides leaders with a stepped process for either accessing or building deep and long-lasting relationships for the purpose of accelerating individual, group, or organizational achievement of desired outcomes

ET Leadership Sales Methodology an Enterprise Thinking tool for increasing the success rate of selling one's ideas, credibility, or products and services for the purpose of achieving Desired Outcomes by (1) linking selling continuously to the CST Model, (2) breaking down the sales process so its individual components can be addressed more strategically by organizing the "seller's" approach to gaining yeses from "buyers," eventually leading to a purchase or the approval and cooperation of others

ET Leading Process an Enterprise Thinking process tool that highlights a leader's strengths and weaknesses and improves his or her ability to integrate personal aspirations with organizational Desired Outcomes, thereby resulting in higher returns from leading the charge; used when leader functions solo and works with others

ET Learning Triangles an ET tool that helps leaders to transform ideas to realities by improving their ability to discern differences between gaining awareness and acquiring knowledge according to five criteria: time spent, effort needed, number of individuals, integration needed, and usable information

ET NPSD Ideation Survival Rate an Enterprise Thinking concept curve that shows survival rate (%) in relation to cumulative time in the new product and service development process (%)

Execute   to carry out or perform the activities outlined by Tactics

Execution of Strategizing   When a leader performs the first four steps of the CST Model; Desired Outcome, Strategy, Macro Tactics, and Tactics.

Expansion and Surface Evaluation   an elimination phase in Activity II (Elimination) of the ET Development Funnel during which the NPSD group examines the remaining seven ideas in an attempt to "explode" any of them into better spin-off ideas that still fall within the parameters of the screening criteria. Then, the NPSD group performs a gentle scan and conducts additional research to uncover potential reasons to eliminate more ideas so that they can present the best three ideas of this group of seven to the screeners

Extrapolation Formula   an Enterprise Thinking forecasting tool; Current Conditions + Cycles, Trends, and Patterns + Technology = Future

Falling in love with your own ideas   an Enterprise Thinking concept that reminds leaders to safeguard against decision making that may be too subjective to be in the best interests of their organizations by using ET tools that better inform and take the bias out of decision making

Falling-short forecast   an Enterprise Thinking concept—the most conservative of the three what-if scenarios during forecasting—in which a minimum outcome or worst-case scenario is projected, challenging leaders to incorporate ways of creating more realistic and workable plans into strategizing

Five Reasons Why   an ET rethinking exercise performed for the purpose of gaining competitive advantages by identifying five Order Winner reasons why buyers would select one organization over another within an industry or sector

Forecasted Talent Requirements   the projection of human resource skills and abilities that one expects to need in the future

Forecasted Winners   an Enterprise Thinking tool used by leaders to project future Order Winners that one anticipates will edge out competitors

Forecasting Horizon Markers   an Enterprise Thinking tool used during the activity of forecasting that better enables leaders to make proactive, structured, and specific plans by identifying specific points or dates in the future, forcing them to generate alternative forecasts that align with Strategies and Desired Outcomes

Forecasting Orientation diagram   visual representation of three broad types of ET leadership thinking—Retro, Current, and Forward—that correspond to a leader's focus on the past, present, and future respectively

Forecasting Triggers   an Enterprise Thinking tool that lists factors that could impact an organization's future, intended to be used while forecasting as a means of directing thoughts and discussion into new areas for the purpose of waking up one's mind and forcing one to think beyond typical thoughts about the future and to extrapolate into new frontiers

Forward-oriented forecasters   an Enterprise Thinking term defined as leaders who live mentally in the future

Full Capacity with No Shared Projects   an Enterprise Thinking tool within the activity of developing plans explaining how to calculate the maximum number of projects that a group of leaders can manage at one time in instances when all leaders in a group adhere to the Two-Project Rule, meaning each leader works on only two projects at once, and none of the projects are shared with other leadership

Full Capacity with Outsourcing   an Enterprise Thinking tool within the activity of developing plans explaining how to calculate the appropriate number of projects an organization can successfully manage at any time when all leaders within a group adhering to the Two-Project Rule have reached their maximum capacity and additional projects need completion, requiring more leadership to come in from outside the group to manage these extra projects; leadership may be contracted or outsourced within region or country, to a nearby country (nearshoring) or distant country (offshoring)

Full Capacity with Shared Projects   an Enterprise Thinking tool within the activity of developing plans explaining how to calculate the number of projects an organization can manage at a single time when all of its leaders adhere to the Two-Project Rule but some of the leaders share the management responsibilities of one or more of the organization's active projects

Gatekeepers   in Activity III (Development) of the ET Development Funnel, an impartial group of people who make sure that all requirements have been met before one's product/service/improvement is allowed to progress to the next phase of development

Global Guidance & Travel Checklist   an Enterprise Thinking tool that leaders use to assist members of their staff with their travel planning for the purpose of better preparing staffers to reach desired outcomes once they reach their (global) travel destinations; helps leaders and staff members to potentially become more globally aware . Global organization an organization with a representation of staff around the world to allow for different types of distribution, ranging from local to multinational distributions

Goldsmith Productivity Principle (GPP)   an Enterprise Thinking tool (based on a principle by Vilfredo Pareto) stating that 80% of an organization's ability to compete and perform is driven by its systems and structures and only 20% is by its people (including leadership, which is a subset of the 20%); the tool's purpose is to direct leadership to solve challenges and empower their people effectively

***Guanxi* (pronounced gwan-*chee*)**   concept of deep relationships connecting family and friends that go back several years or even generations, based on personalized networks of influence

Hollywood Model   an Enterprise Thinking comparison tool used to describe a type of alliance called a Project Joint Venture in which individuals and organizations join forces to create something (like a movie) and then disband and reconnect in another group to form something else (like another movie) repeatedly over time as their standard means of completing projects

Horizon Markers   an Enterprise Thinking tool used by leaders during forecasting and planning activities to establish assessment points in time (six months, one year, three years, five years, ten years, and so on) at which individuals make projections about the future

Human-Generated Forecasting   level 1 of the ET Social Forecasting tool; forecasting executed through pure speculation and observation without the use of tools or technologies

Human Genome Project (HGP)   project intended to identify all human DNA genes and to sequence their 3 billion chemical base pairs; within the context of Enterprise Thinking, an example illustrating how one's forecasts must take into consideration that you can't solve tomorrow's challenges with yesterday's thinking

Idea Bank   an idea-gathering mechanism used by leaders and organizational stakeholders to constantly be storing ideas for later retrieval; can be an electronic file or folder stored on an intranet or extranet, a paper file, a suggestion box, or a grouping of index cards or sticky notes: also found in Ideation phase of ET Development Funnel

Ideation   Activity I of the ET Development Funnel; term used to describe the generation and gathering of ideas

Ideation Screen   in Activity II (Elimination) of the ET Development Funnel, the checkpoint within the elimination process where Screeners evaluate ideas against preset broad criteria and eliminate all but the best-matched ideas that fall through to the next level

Indicators of ET Proficiency   an Enterprise Thinking tool listing positive and negative conditions that leaders can use as a reference guide to gauge their progression toward becoming a successful Enterprise Thinker

Individualist   a person or a type of cultural behavior in which the individual is the dominant catalyst for making decisions

Innovation "S" Curve   means of diagramming the progress of any innovative idea from its inception and development within an organization and through its life cycle in its marketplace

Innovation commitment an Enterprise Thinking concept explaining commitment to innovation in terms of three levels—low, medium, and high—measured by capital and human resources relative to time

InterConnectivity of ET Concept visual representation of the interconnectivity between enhancing global awareness and the other eleven activities of Enterprise Thinking, used to highlight the beneficial impacts of global awareness on leadership and vice versa

International organization an organization that works or sells outside its home country

Joint Venture (JV) one of the six forms of alliance; an alliance where two or more parties share resources and risks and invest some form of equity during a longer-term alliance than they would in a Project Joint Venture

Jumpers an Enterprise Thinking term describing leaders who break the Two-Project Rule by repeating the cycle of selecting and assigning projects to people who already have two projects; leaders who are guilty of Jumping the Tracks

Jumping the Tracks an Enterprise Thinking term referring to misuse of the Parallel Project Tracks (used to ensure that people adhere to the Two-Project Rule) by assigning new projects before existing projects are completed; Fatal Mistake #2 in ET project planning

Launch Activity III (Development) of the ET Development Funnel; phase in the product/service/improvement development process in which products are finally created, services are ready for delivery, and improvements (such as new computer networking systems) are installed and in the early stages of operations

Leading the charge process undertaken by a leader that figuratively or literally advances a group or an organization; an activity of Enterprise Thinking that results in leaders reconciling their personal aspirations with organizational Desired Outcomes and simultaneously leading their groups or organizations toward Desired Outcomes

Leadership Execution the carrying out of thinking-related activities by leaders such as (1) completing the first 4 steps of the CST Model, (2) performing the 12 activities of ET, and (3) engaging in the ET Leading Process

Leadership Tactics activities that leadership must perform in doing their jobs, just as frontline individuals must follow Tactics in the Execution phase

Macro Reality of Innovation an Enterprise Thinking diagram illustrating how life cycles of various innovations get shorter as the number of innovations multiply; used for the purpose of reminding leaders that they have less time to react to competing innovations, especially as global factors increasingly expand the number of competing innovations flooding markets over time

Macro Tactics   Step 3 of the CST Model; overarching Tactics without details that support both the selected Strategy and Desired Outcome

Manual technologies   level of automation requiring a significant amount of human participation; the work is basically done manually

Manually automated   level of automation where manual activities are performed with some automated assistance

Maps versus Words   an Enterprise Thinking analysis tool by which individuals identify their preferences for learning by graphing their preference of how they'd like to receive information—in written word format or pictorially—on a continuum; used by leaders to conceptualize ways in which they can deliver information to others that appeals to people with different learning preferences as well as to identify how the leader prefers to receive information.

Market Intelligence (MI)   data that has been accumulated and processed by watching specific markets used by leaders for decision making

Merger   one of the six forms of alliances in which two or more groups unite into a single legal entity, where the parties share ownership, leadership, and management structure, and they join their assets and resources

Metcalfe's Law   a principle that states how the value of a network is equal to the square of its sum of users; the more people within the network, the greater the value of the network to individual members or users

Me-too product   the development and launch of a product or service that closely resembles or is an exact copy of an existing competitors' product/service/improvement

Mind Map   an activity performed individually or collectively to generate and visually connect thoughts and ideas in diagram form for building awareness and enhancing decision making

Modeling   method of testing tactical options; can be done manually or by using a software program to determine expected outcomes and assess a tactic for viability

Modified ET Development Funnel   an adapted version of the ET Development Funnel for use as an instrument to establish alliances and select technologies used to increase odds that an alliance will be more successful or that a technology will deliver a high enough return to be a true benefit to an organization by considering a greater number of ideas than usual up front and screening the ideas against preset criteria

Moore's Law   a concept stating that the processing power of transistors and resistors on a computer chip doubles every eighteen months, which has become an accepted trend in computing hardware; on a greater scale, this means that advancements in technology increase exponentially

Multi-Dimensional Buyer (MDB)   buyer with the ability and preference to purchase through a myriad of options, from in person, to cell phone, to online, and who expects sellers to be proficient at providing ease and convenience in all parts of the sale experience to capture and maintain his or her patronage

Multi-Dimensional Vendor (MDV)   vendor that understands the need to provide a myriad of purchasing options to its buyers in order to stay competitive within its industry or sector

Multinational organization   an organization that has representation in many nations

My ET Toolkit   the collection of all Enterprise Thinking tools for leadership and management, for performing the twelve ET activities

Natural Progression of Innovation   concept explaining a product's innovation status (the lower of the two S curves) in relation to that of a competitor's (indicated by the higher of the two S curves); based on Clayton Christensen's work and illustrated by a diagram in *Paid to Think* by David Goldsmith

New Product and Service Development (NPSD)   the Enterprise Thinking enhancement to the marketing concept of new product development that involves the act of planning, leading, and implementing the development of products, services, and improvements

New Product and Service Development Group (NPSD group)   in the ET Development Funnel, a group of people from multiple disciplines and functional areas to help plan, direct, and implement the development process from the commencement of Ideation to the completion of Development

On-the-Job Training (OJT)   term broadly applied to method(s) of teaching occupations and functions in the workplace

Open Innovation   type of innovation wherein people who are external to an organization are allowed to participate in the organization's innovative improvements; based on the premise that everyone gains cumulative value when they're able to tap into intellectual property, trade secrets, share proprietary technology, research findings, and more

Optimum Forward Orientation   an Enterprise Thinking tool used while forecasting that widens a forecaster's scope of vision and extends it further into the future, enabling the forecaster to uncover and make more opportunities and sustainable decisions possible

Order Qualifiers   concept developed by Terry Hill referring to the basic characteristics that an organization, product, or service needs referring to in order to compete

Order Winners   concept developed by Terry Hill referring to the unique and distinguishing attributes that give an organization, product, or service an edge over their competitors

Outside-In, Inside-Out, Above, and Below innovation-triggering technique used to generate or identify several different perspectives on the same topic

Overcrowding the Canaries the threat to organizational assets and success resulting from breaking the Two-Project Rule based on John Bennion's "canary-cage approach," comparing the effects of too many projects on organizations to overcrowding a canary cage with too many canaries and threatening the well-being of all other canaries in the cage; considered Fatal Mistake #1 in ET project planning

Package an Enterprise Thinking term applied to the collection of systems and structures and other resources that leadership must build to empower people to carry out their responsibilities once their power is transferred to the individual performing the act; *see also* Build the Package

Parallel Project Tracks an Enterprise Thinking tool that keeps everyone focused on his or her projects until completion; ensures that no one takes on additional projects until they have completed the two prioritized projects on their plate

Pathways within Leadership Sales an Enterprise Thinking tool outlining the numerous options available to a leader to sell oneself, and his or her group, organization, and ideas

Patterns repetitive activities, characteristics, or occurrences, a factor to consider for making more accurate predictions about the future

Pentality of Forecasting an Enterprise Thinking tool consisting of five categories: you/your group/your organization, customer/client(s) (members, patrons, sponsors, etc.), supplier/vendor(s), competition, world/universe; used to direct and focus forecasting thoughts in order to cover all areas of thinking so that one's total projections about the future increase in accuracy

Perfectly successful forecast an Enterprise Thinking concept in which the best end result is projected, where everything from Strategy to Execution plays out perfectly, and Desired Outcomes are reached; one of three what-if scenarios

Phase-Gate Process a framework for the incremental development of an idea, product, service, or improvement using both phases and gates to ensure that proper actions are taken

Point of sale (POS) (also referred to as point of purchase, or POP) the location in which a transaction occurs, also referred to as checkout, often integrated into a POS system that tracks transactions (using barcode scanners, credit-card processing systems, signature capture, cash drawers) and connects all data to accounting, inventory, purchasing, and other parts of an organization

Point to You First (P2UF)   an Enterprise Thinking concept suggesting that when things don't go as anticipated, the leader should first look at his or her own behaviors and actions rather than blaming others in order to identify and effect new opportunities for development and growth

Points of Light   visual and mental Enterprise Thinking tool utilizing imagery- or simulation-based programming to assess relationships and activities transpiring inside and outside of an organization, to give clarity and focus to an existing condition or forecasted outcome

Positive Opposite Ultimate End (+OUE)   wordsmithing exercise to identify and then generate an optimum condition and/or situation within the Redefining tool; utilized when converting a Challenge Statement into a Should Statement through examining opposing conditions (for example, converting "the output *is* low" to "the output *should be* high")

Post-Launch Review   phase in Activity III (Development) of the ET Development Funnel in which a Launch's effectiveness and/or success is assessed

Post-Launch Review Gate   phase in Activity III (Development) of the ET Development Funnel in which Gatekeepers are either joined or replaced by members of management who use the data and lessons from the Post-Launch Review to determine how the organization will move forward

Pre-Development Funnel   an Enterprise Thinking tool used only occasionally in instances where one must select the type or structure of a new product, service, improvement, alliance, or technology prior to using the ET Development Funnel for the selection and development of the actual and final new product, service, improvement, alliance, or technology

Process testing   form of testing whereby testers run an end-to-end test of a process to ensure it works

Product Matrix Chart   an Enterprise Thinking methodology tool used for vetting the most viable ideas from the rest by listing ideas on one axis and criteria on the other, then assigning points or a "score" to each idea for each criterion

Project   a complete set of activities that modifies an individual, group, or organization in such a manner that it is improved or altered; within the context of ET, a building block of an organization that must be carefully selected and managed due to its potentially heavy impact on an organization's future.

Project Assignment Worksheet   a graphic listing of an organization's current projects for the purpose of assigning appropriate talent to each project from a big-picture perspective; allows for cross-functional utilization of talents beyond silos of titles and departments

Project Evaluation Chart   an Enterprise Thinking tool used for assessing and selecting the best and most positively transformative projects at a given time based on a rating of project options against specific and relative criteria

Project joint venture (PJV)   one of the six forms of alliances; alliance formed between two or more parties for the duration of a specific project

Reasonably successful forecast   an Enterprise Thinking concept in which average end results are projected, challenging leaders to come up with strategies to compensate for shortfalls and consider whether skills and tools need improving; one of three what-if scenarios

Redefining   a tool developed by David Goldsmith used to always find a better way to discover new competitive mega-advantages by identifying true challenges, problems, and opportunities, because one is asking the right questions

Retro-oriented forecasters   an Enterprise Thinking term referring to leaders who spend more mental time in the past than in the present or future

Return on Bother (ROB)   adaptation of the ROI concept by author Jim Gilmore (*The Experience Economy*) that sizes up situations and opportunities by asking whether they are worth the bother

Return on Investment (ROI)   a measure of performance used to evaluate an investment's gains or losses; a ratio or percentage derived from dividing the gain from investment minus the cost of investment by the cost of the investment

Roadmap to Global Awareness   an Enterprise Thinking tool that outlines for leaders four topics of interest they need to learn about in order to increase their global awareness: humans and living creatures, physical environments, governances, and technologies

Screeners   in Activities I and II of the ET Development Funnel, people who objectively check ideas against criteria to determine which ideas will pass through each of the three elimination screens

Selling across   from the ET tool Pathways within Leadership Sales; the act of selling to colleagues, peers, and other decision makers who are considered to be of equal rank or position to oneself

Selling down   from the ET tool Pathways within Leadership Sales; when one sells ideas to the people who report or buy from him or her, or someone who needs his or her approval, when one must gain buy-in and cooperation from them

Selling for others   from the ET tool Pathways within Leadership Sales; when one steps in to assist another person or group to sell their ideas. Selling groups from the ET tool Pathways within Leadership Sales; presenting ideas to a collection of individuals, groups, or organizations to get buy-in

Selling into other organizations from the ET tool Pathways within Leadership Sales; when one sells into other organizations to gain influence of some sort within it

Selling outside of your organization from the ET tool Pathways within Leadership Sales; selling to individuals, vendors, governments, other countries, etc., who don't reside within one's organization or group

Selling through others from the ET tool Pathways within Leadership Sales; using a go-between source to deliver a message, as a way of persuading others to help one achieve a desired outcome

Selling to reports from the ET tool Pathways within Leadership Sales; when one sells down to a group of people whose rank on the organizational chart falls below his or her own

Selling up from the ET tool Pathways within Leadership Sales; selling ideas to authority-figure decision makers such as the board of directors, supervisors, investors, and councils in order to gain their approval and/or support in one way or another

Selling via social environments from the ET tool Pathways within Leadership Sales; selling ideas in open forums, to media, to masses of people, or when one works a social environment (in a room at a company get-together)

Selling with others from the ET tool Pathways within Leadership Sales; type of concerted group selling process

Selling Your Ideas with Stories Enterprise Thinking tool providing a structured formula to selling that combines storytelling (personal stories, organization/group stories, or outside stories) with reasons and a lesson as a way to connect listeners to a message being delivered, with the ultimate end being buy-in

Semi-Automated Forecasting level 3 of the ET Social Forecasting tool; calculated predictions made by assessing data gathered through a combination of human effort and automated systems

Should Statement (SS) the second step in Redefining in which a descriptive sentence of a situation has been scrubbed using the six Redefining criteria and has been wordsmithed to generate a Should statement; a way of moving beyond the challenge (initial Challenge Statement) and toward an ideal solution

Six Scrubbing Criteria and Diverters for Redefining within the process tool Redefining; meant to reformulate a leader's initial Challenge Statement into a final and accurate What Would it Take . . . question

Silos from farming, individual building-sized canisters used to store separate foods like grain or corn; within Enterprise Thinking, metaphoric reference to single individuals, departments, business units, etc., used to show too much inward focus and/or lack of harmony or synchronization within an organization or entity

Six forms of alliances   a listing of the types of alliances that can be established to achieve a Desired Outcome—ad hoc, consortium, project joint venture, joint venture, merger, and acquisitions

Social Forecasting   utilizing a network of forecasts (from individuals, customers, vendors, staff members, systems, etc.) to gain a comprehensive collective forecast and thereby increase the probability of accuracy

Speaking international   an Enterprise Thinking technique used to improve communications between two or more people or parties who don't share the same first language where one slows the rate of speech, eliminates idiomatic expressions, avoids cultural references unless defined, and repeats the same message multiple times with different dialog so that the receiving party can better understand the speaker

Squirrel Effect   an Enterprise Thinking term used to describe unfocused leadership activity; term is derived from a story of how a squirrel did not achieve his desired outcome because he spread his focus and efforts too widely

Stuck Snowball Theory   an Enterprise Thinking term referring to the stopping of momentum and the necessary force needed to get motion started again

Surface Evaluation Screen   phase in Activity II (Elimination) of the ET Development Funnel where screeners evaluate the work of the NPSD group and scrub the three remaining ideas against the specific criteria of the Surface Evaluation Screen to make sure the remaining ideas are indeed the right ideas to survive and pass through to the next phase

Tactics   tools that are passed on to others to execute, including plans, CPM charts, lists, blueprints, video instructions, etc.; must enable people to accomplish what has been defined in planning, appropriately matched to the experience levels of the people who will execute them; within Enterprise Thinking, the fourth step in the CST Model

Take-a-Fork, Give-a-Spoon Approach   an Enterprise Thinking technique suggesting to leaders that when the occasion arises where undesirable, perhaps dangerous behavior must be halted immediately—referred to as "the fork"—it is effective to replace it with a better and more productive alternative—"a spoon"—so that one is still positively moving the organization and/or people in the direction of desired outcomes.

Technology-Supported Forecasting   level 2 of the ET Social Forecasting tool; forecasting executed by individuals using manual systems to collect data from internal and external sources

Technology Implementation Process   an Enterprise Thinking methodology to help implement technology, following the five steps of the CST Model: Desired Outcome, Strategy, Macro Tactics, Tactics, and Execution

Testing   phase in Activity III (Development) of the ET Development Funnel where ideas, products, services, processes, methodologies, etc., are put under scrutiny to determine that what has been built, proposed, or conceived, will work as planned

Testing Gate   point in Activity III (Development) of the ET Development Funnel where Gatekeepers verify that testers performed the testing properly using accurate testing methodologies, essentially "testing the testing"; all testing should fulfill the pre-established criteria

Theoretical jumps   mental leaps by one person who has already learned about certain topics; within Enterprise Thinking, a cautionary term reminding leaders that in order to ensure that they're being understood, they should not assume that others are making these types of mental connections and should be aware that more explanation may be needed

Transfer the Power   Step 3 of the ET Empowerment Process, where individuals are plugged into the tactical plans built by leadership: right people, right systems and structures

Transparent Career Ladder   a clearly defined set of steps necessary for individuals to follow to advance their career; influenced by the escalator theory

Trend   a tendency in a particular direction; a factor to consider during forecasting to better anticipate future occurrences and events

Triggers of innovation   an Enterprise Thinking tool used for the purpose of initiating ideation within the ET activity of innovating everywhere to advance an organization's competitive advantages

Two-Project Rule   states that two projects are the optimum number of projects that one person can work on effectively at a single time; *see* Project

Ultimate End   a term used in the Redefining tool to engage users in thinking about the best possible condition and/or situation (ultimate customer, ultimate power consumption, ultimate duration)

Wall of life   suggestion to assign a wall in one's home or workplace as a location to post photos of life-enriching experiences to remind a person to "live more"

What-if scenarios   an Enterprise Thinking tool consisting of three groups of potential future conditions that forecasters consider to prepare for alternative futures

What Would It Take . . . (WWIT)   the final future-oriented question one derives during Redefining that prepares one's mind to find solutions; its purpose is to move focus from rear-view thinking to a road of possible solutions and opportunities

White Horse Leader a metaphorical Enterprise Thinking concept touting the benefits of a past leadership style in which leaders once rode into battle alongside their troops; a way of reminding modern-day leaders how being in touch with their people and actively guiding staffers is an effective means of leading people and organizations to desired outcomes

Wildly Successful Project (WSP) an Enterprise Thinking tool referring to the type of completed project that is initially considered undesirable or challenging to pull off that ultimately demonstrates a manager's ability to deliver results that extend beyond normal expectations, causes others to take notice, and furthers a cause, project, or initiative, faster than anticipated; type of project that can be used to gain buy-in and cooperation from others on future projects

Win by a nose (WBAN) term derived from horseracing describing races in which one horse wins by the narrow margin of inching his nose over the finish line before the second-place horse; an Enterprise Thinking tool used to remind leaders that very small factors and advantages can result in "wins"

Wizard of Oz Sydrome an ET concept tool based on the famed 1939 movie *The Wizard of Oz* where the images that leaders and organizations project—skilled, capable, high functioning, etc.—are not in sync with reality—disorganized, low functioning, even disastrous—just as the movie's character—a man hiding behind a curtain—dishonestly projected his image as that of a mighty and powerful wizard

Wordsmithing the act of using different words than those you originally begin with to create a more powerful statement, sentence, value proposition, question, etc., in order to reach a desired outcome faster

Work in Progress (WIP) any work that is not yet finished, but is still in the process of completion

INDEX

MORE RESOURCES

YOUR JOURNEY AS AN ENTERPRISE THINKER has just begun. I'm inviting you to stay in touch and connect with other people who are paid to think through the many venues I've created to help you continue to grow and develop:

- **www.davidgoldsmith.com**—Improve your ability to perform even more and gain a deeper understanding of some of the ET concepts with the many resources on this core website, such as the Goldsmith Institute, where you can engage with video, audio, and other tools. Also available on the site are full courses and products to further your learning process. In addition, if you would like to bring your *Paid to Think* experiences to your organization, there is information about how to contact me for consulting, advising, and speaking.
- **www.paidtothink.com**—Visit this site to download graphics and charts from *Paid to Think* and to add the most up-to-date thinking tools to your ET toolkit. You can ask questions about *Paid to Think* and get answers, watch videos, and discuss with like-minded people how they are using Enterprise Thinking to make a difference in their lives.

"For six months I fought with the publisher... then finally I was able to purchase one chapter."

That's a real quote from an executive named Elizabeth who wanted only multiple copies of a single chapter of a certain book to lead her staff members to desired outcomes, but she wasted valuable time and effort appealing to the book's publisher for the tools she needed. Maybe you've had the same wishes as Elizabeth; perhaps you supervise, oversee, or manage a group of people, and you've wanted similar tools to maximize potential and drive performance but found that chapter singles were inaccessible or unaffordable. Well, put all that behind you, because I've made Paid to Think chapter singles easily and quickly available.

So while I'm sure you're perfectly willing to purchase the entire book of *Paid to Think* for yourself or for a leadership team, I also understand that there may be times when it's more efficient or cost effective to buy single chapters given certain circumstances.

In these types of situations, some of which are included here, single chapters can be a quick and easy solution, such as:

✓ When you work with a large team and you want them to understand a single topic without breaking your budget. Say that you're working on developing new products within a department consisting of 47 staff members and seven leaders. In an instance like this, exposing all 54 participants to Chapter 4, Developing New Products and Services, would put everyone on the same page and ready them to proceed on the project at hand.

✓ When you're about to undertake an endeavor and reading the entire book at that time is not feasible, you can address a particular topic area quickly. Let's assume you about to enter into negotiations with a prospective ally, and you'd like both your team and the other party to build a successful union based on PTT's proven Alliance Pillars. Distribute copies of Chapter 5, Establishing Alliances, and you'll not only fend off the needless challenges that often plague alliances, but build the kinds of alliances that help your organization achieve desired outcomes now and in years to come.

And there may be other occasions:

✓ When you're searching for the type of gift to give that provides real value at any time.

✓ When you want to do a monthly program covering the topics of *Paid to Think* in your own order preference.

Unlike past experiences that you or your colleagues may have had in obtaining individual chapters, *Paid to Think* singles offer you the flexibility to order when you want, how you want, and how much you want, because it's the firstbook that's ever been released in print, as an e-book, and in the form of convenient single chapters! In addition, *Paid to Think*—the book and single chapters—is available in audio format, too. So visit your e-store or paidtothinksingles.com, choose the format and method of delivery that best suit your busy lifestyle, and start to achieve more, earn more, and live more . . . even if it's one chapter at a time!

Kindle | iBooks | Sony Reader | Nook

ACKNOWLEDGMENTS

WHEN I CONSIDER THE PEOPLE who have had some role in the creation of this book, my list goes beyond the realm of business contacts and people in publishing to the vast number of people who have in some way or another helped me to share *Paid to Think* and Enterprise Thinking ET with you.

First and foremost, I thank my family. My wife and business partner, Lorrie, has not only made *Paid to Think* her primary project over the past three years and helped me to transfer Enterprise Thinking from my head to the pages of *Paid to Think,* but she has been working by my side for twenty-six years no matter what the job has entailed, and she's been a trouper. Our sons, Adam and Jake, have been sources of joy to us, and they have challenged me to rethink concepts I may have otherwise accepted without question. I also want to express my appreciation to my parents, sister, and brother-in-law for their support over the years.

To my agent, Scott Hoffman, I say thank you for providing the channel of distribution for *Paid to Think* and for taking on the challenges that come with bringing a larger-than-typical-sized business or leadership book to market.

I would like my NYU students—some of the first Enterprise Thinkers—to know how much I have enjoyed working with them, gaining enhanced global insight from their diverse perspectives, and learning from them how to make the activities and tools easier to understand, perform, and apply. Not only has their class participation helped to refine ET, but their ongoing feedback about sample chapters in this book and online comments as active participants in the David's Forums community (www.davidsforums.com) have created synergistic value to other leaders seeking to improve their performance. I hope to continue to remain in contact and to meet up with many of you in my worldwide travels.

There are several people I want to offer special thanks to for reading sample chapters and offering their feedback: Beha Springer, Faye Matriano, Janine McBee, Steve Rubin, Peter Gerardo, Kevin Brennan, Jake Goldsmith, Adam Goldsmith, Sharon Goldstein, Heath Waldorf, Sheila Francis Jeyathurai,

Kevin Brass, and Rahul Bhandari, along with the many individuals who've read a chapter at a time giving me feedback while in class, on the road, or consulting. And I would especially like to acknowledge Javier Suarez and Jay Abraham for their additional efforts, feedback, support, and friendship.

To the thousands of decision makers who have graciously given their time to the interviews I mentioned at the beginning of this book, to the consulting clients who have shared their inner workings of their organizations, their personal thoughts, opportunities and challenges, and to the countless audience members who have come up to me after speaking presentations to communicate their challenges and experiences, I appreciate your courage, openness, and spirit to want to grow and develop as leaders. Without your engaged participation, Enterprise Thinking would not be what it is today.

I've met numerous people on planes, trains, and boats, and in taxis, offices, warehouses, manufacturing facilities, executive offices, and everywhere else you can imagine around the world who have inspired me and, without knowing it, and helped me to make ET even more universal. I'm glad that our paths have crossed, because ET is an amalgamation of thoughts and interactions that I needed to make sense of and to clarify the needs of leadership and management.

ABOUT THE AUTHORS

DAVID GOLDSMITH, president of the Goldsmith Organization LLC, is an international consultant and advisor, speaker, telecast host, author, and business owner. He has served on the New York University faculty for twelve years and was awarded the SCPS Teacher Excellence Award. David holds an MBA from Syracuse University.

LORRIE GOLDSMITH is co-founder of the Goldsmith Organization LLC, a leadership development organization offering consulting, advising, speaking, and educational resources to decision makers globally.

DAVID AND LORRIE are based in New York State. *Paid to Think* is their first book.